C000184660

STREET ATLAS

East Yorkshire
Northern Lincolnshire

www.philips-maps.co.uk

First published in 2002 by

Philip's, a division of
Octopus Publishing Group Ltd
www.octopusbooks.co.uk
2-4 Heron Quays, London E14 4JP
An Hachette Livre UK Company

Second edition 2005
Second impression with revisions 2007
EYLBB

ISBN-10   0-540-08762-9 (spiral)
ISBN-13   978-0-540-08762-4 (spiral)

© Philip's 2007

Ordnance Survey®

This product includes mapping data licensed
from Ordnance Survey® with the permission of
the Controller of Her Majesty's Stationery Office.
© Crown copyright 2007. All rights reserved.
Licence number 100011710.

To the best of the Publishers' knowledge, the
information in this atlas was correct at the time
of going to press. No responsibility can be
accepted for any errors or their consequences.

The representation in this atlas of a road, track
or path is no evidence of the existence of a right
of way.

Ordnance Survey and the OS Symbol are
registered trademarks of Ordnance Survey, the
national mapping agency of Great Britain.

Post Office is a trade mark of Post Office Ltd
in the UK and other countries.

Printed by Toppan, China

Contents

III	**Key to map symbols**
IV	**Key to map pages**
VI	**Route planning**
X	**Administrative and Postcode boundaries**

1	**Street maps** at 1¾ inches to 1 mile
122	**Street maps** at 3½ inches to 1 mile
154	**Street maps of centres of Beverley, Kingston-upon-Hull and York** at 7 inches to 1 mile

| 157 | **Index** of towns and villages |
| 159 | **Index** of streets, hospitals, industrial estates, railway stations, schools, shopping centres, universities and places of interest |

Digital Data

The exceptionally high-quality mapping found in this atlas is available as digital data in TIFF format, which is easily convertible to other bitmapped (raster) image formats.

The index is also available in digital form as a standard database table. It contains all the details found in the printed index together with the National Grid reference for the map square in which each entry is named.

For further information and to discuss your requirements, please contact james.mann@philips-maps.co.uk

(22a)	**Motorway** with junction number
	Primary route – dual/single carriageway
	A road – dual/single carriageway
	B road – dual/single carriageway
	Minor road – dual/single carriageway
	Other minor road – dual/single carriageway
	Road under construction
	Tunnel, covered road
	Rural track, private road or narrow road in urban area
	Gate or obstruction to traffic (restrictions may not apply at all times or to all vehicles)
	Path, bridleway, byway open to all traffic, road used as a public path
	Pedestrianised area
DY7	**Postcode boundaries**
	County and unitary authority boundaries
	Railway, tunnel, railway under construction
	Tramway, tramway under construction
	Miniature railway
Walsall	**Railway station**
	Private railway station
South Shields	**Metro station**
	Tram stop, tram stop under construction
	Bus, coach station

◆	**Ambulance station**
◆	**Coastguard station**
◆	**Fire station**
◆	**Police station**
✚	**Accident and Emergency entrance to hospital**
H	**Hospital**
+	**Place of worship**
i	**Information Centre** (open all year)
🛒	**Shopping Centre**
P P&R	**Parking, Park and Ride**
PO	**Post Office**
⅄ 🚐	**Camping site, caravan site**
▶	**Golf course**
⋈	**Picnic site**
Prim Sch	**Important buildings, schools, colleges, universities and hospitals**
	Built up area
	Woods
River Ouse	**Tidal water, water name**
	Non-tidal water – lake, river, canal or stream
⟨ ▭◁	**Lock, weir, tunnel**
Church	**Non-Roman antiquity**
ROMAN FORT	**Roman antiquity**
87	**Adjoining page indicators and overlap bands** The colour of the arrow and the band indicates the scale of the adjoining or overlapping page (see scales below)
246	

Enlarged mapping only

	Railway or bus station building
	Place of interest
	Parkland

Acad	**Academy**	Inst	**Institute**
Allot Gdns	**Allotments**	Ct	**Law Court**
Cemy	**Cemetery**	L Ctr	**Leisure Centre**
C Ctr	**Civic Centre**	LC	**Level Crossing**
CH	**Club House**	Liby	**Library**
Coll	**College**	Mkt	**Market**
Crem	**Crematorium**	Meml	**Memorial**
Ent	**Enterprise**	Mon	**Monument**
Ex H	**Exhibition Hall**	Mus	**Museum**
Ind Est	**Industrial Estate**	Obsy	**Observatory**
IRB Sta	**Inshore Rescue Boat Station**	Pal	**Royal Palace**
		PH	**Public House**

Recn Gd	**Recreation Ground**
Resr	**Reservoir**
Ret Pk	**Retail Park**
Sch	**School**
Sh Ctr	**Shopping Centre**
TH	**Town Hall/House**
Trad Est	**Trading Estate**
Univ	**University**
W Twr	**Water Tower**
Wks	**Works**
YH	**Youth Hostel**

■ The small numbers around the edges of the maps identify the 1 kilometre National Grid lines

■ The dark grey border on the inside edge of some pages indicates that the mapping does not continue onto the adjacent page

The scale of the maps on the pages numbered in blue is 5.52 cm to 1 km • 3½ inches to 1 mile • 1: 18103

0 ¼ ½ ¾ 1 mile
0 250m 500m 750m 1 kilometre

The scale of the maps on pages numbered in green is 2.76 cm to 1 km • 1¾ inches to 1 mile • 1: 36206

0 ¼ ½ ¾ 1 mile
0 250m 500m 750m 1 kilometre

The scale of the maps on pages numbered in red is 11.04 cm to 1 km • 7 inches to 1 mile • 1: 9051

0 220 yards 440 yards 660 yards ½ mile
0 125m 250m 375m ½ kilometre

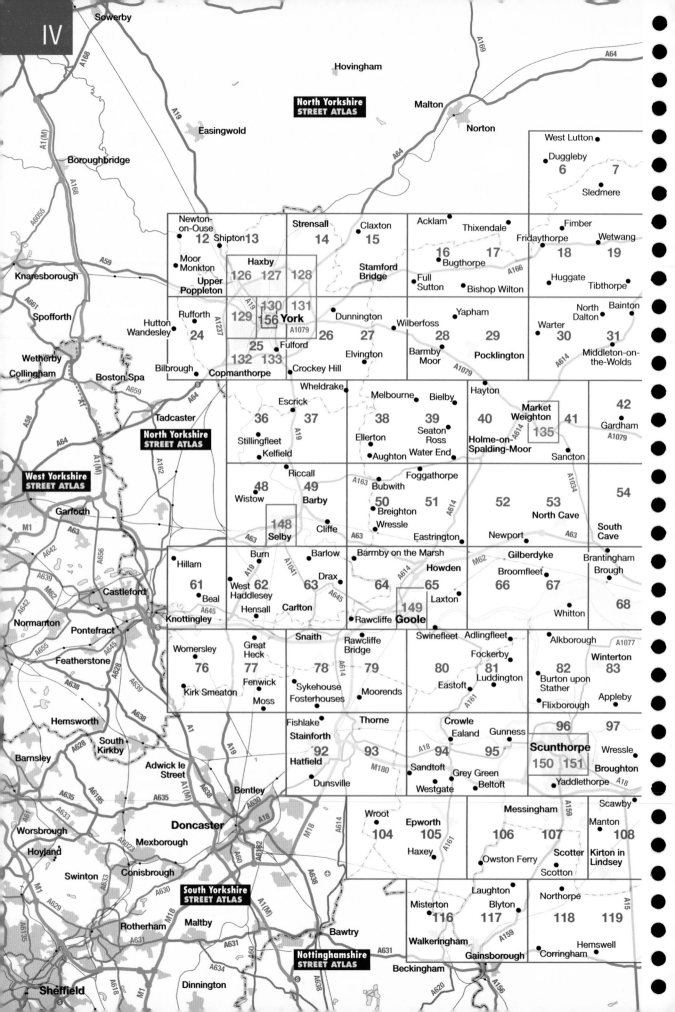

Key to map pages

156	Map pages at 7 inches to 1 mile
141	Map pages at 3½ inches to 1 mile
113	Map pages at 1¾ inches to 1 mile

Scale

0 5 10 15 20 km
0 5 10 miles

A1039

Filey

Hunmanby

Fordon **2** Reighton **3**

1 **4** **5**

A165

Foxholes

Butterwick Grindale Bempton

Flamborough

Langtoft Rudston Boynton **Bridlington**

8 **9** **122** **123**

10 **11**

Kilham A614

Burton Agnes

20 **21** Gransmoor Fraisthorpe

Driffield Nafferton **22** **23**

124 **125** Great Kelk

Skipsea

Kirkburn Skerne

Church End Dunnington

A164 Hutton Cranswick **34** **35**

32 **33** A165 Bewholme

Beswick Brandesburton **134**

Hornsea

Etton **43** Leven Rolston

44 **45**

Leconfield Tickton Rise **46** **47**

Bishop Burton **Beverley** A165 Withernwick

136 137 Aldbrough

154 Skirlaugh

Walkington Swine Flinton

55 A164 **56** **57** Sproatley Garton

Dunswell **58** **59** **60**

Little Weighton Cottingham Owstwick Hilston

138 **139** **140** **141** **142** Preston Burton Pidsea Tunstall

Kingston upon Hull Roos

Kirk Ella A1105 **155** Hedon Burstwick

143 **144** **145** **146** **147** Rimswell **Withernsea**

North Ferriby Hessle **72** **73** **74** **75**

69 **70** **71** Paull Hollym

A1033 Holmpton

Keyingham **Patrington**

New Holland

Barton-upon-Humber Barrow upon Humber Goxhill Patrington Haven Easington

Kingsforth **85** **86** **87** Skeffling

84 **88** **89**

Saxby All Saints Wootton A160 **90** **91**

Bonby A15 Ulceby Kilnsea

A1077 **Immingham**

Worlaby Croxton Habrough A180 **102** **103**

Elsham Kirmington Stallingborough **152** **153**

98 **99** **100** **101** **Grimsby**

Barnetby le Wold A18 Keelby Healing **Cleethorpes**

M180 Bigby Great Limber Laceby A46 A16 A1098

Brigg Humberston

Grasby Irby upon Humber New Waltham

A1084 A1173 Swallow Waltham **114** **115**

Hibaldstow North Kelsey **110** **111** A46 **112** **113** Holton le Clay North Cotes

109 Caistor Croxby A1031

Redbourne South Kelsey Rothwell Ashby cum Fenby North Thoresby

A18 North Somercotes

Fulstow A1031

Lincolnshire STREET ATLAS Ludborough

A46 Binbrook **120** **121**

Utterby

A631 A1103 Fotherby

A631 Market Rasen A16

A631 A157 **Louth**

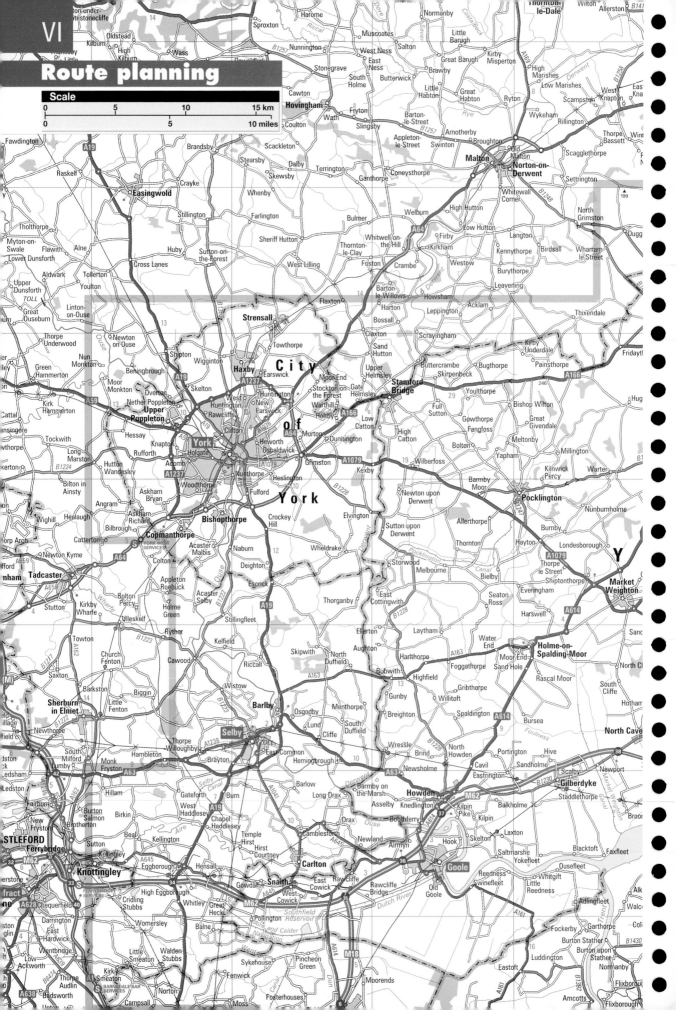

Scale

| 0 | 5 | 10 | 15 km |
| 0 | | 5 | 10 miles |

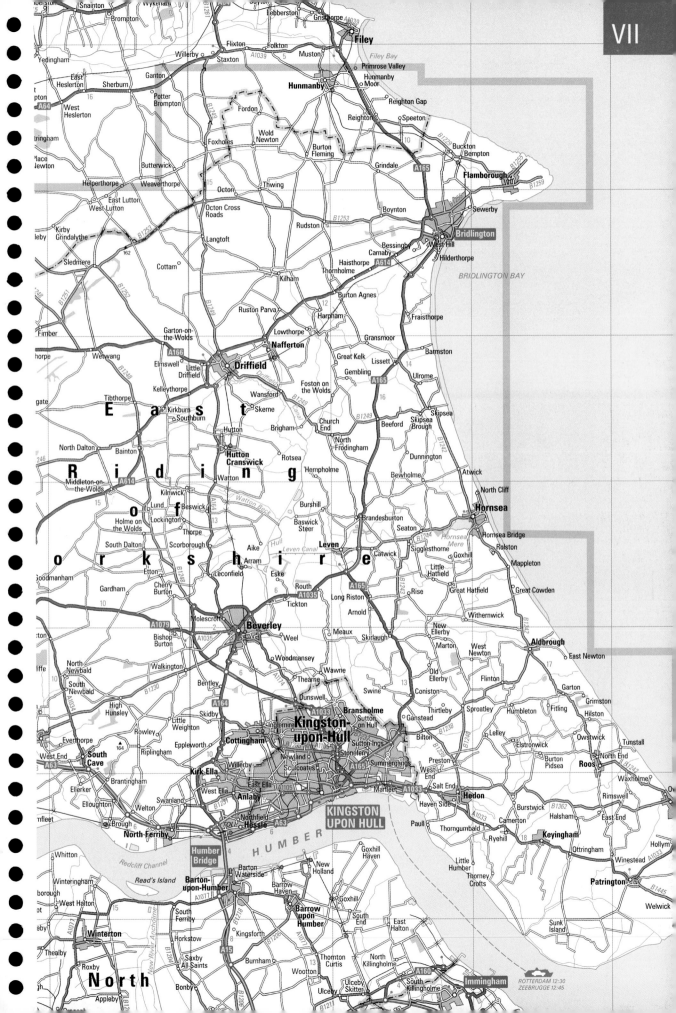

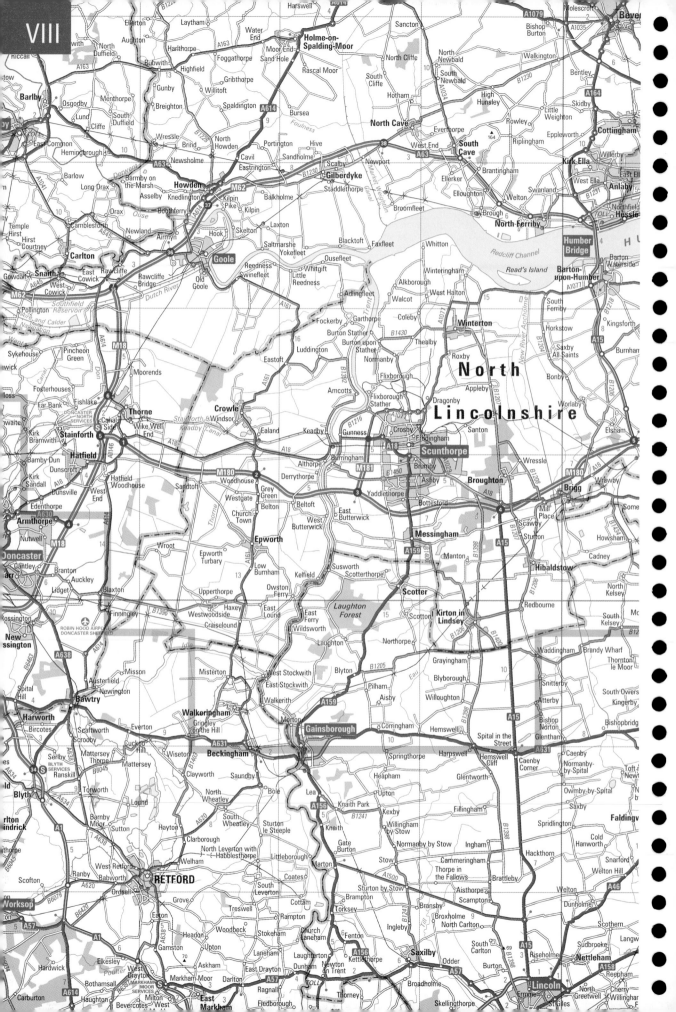

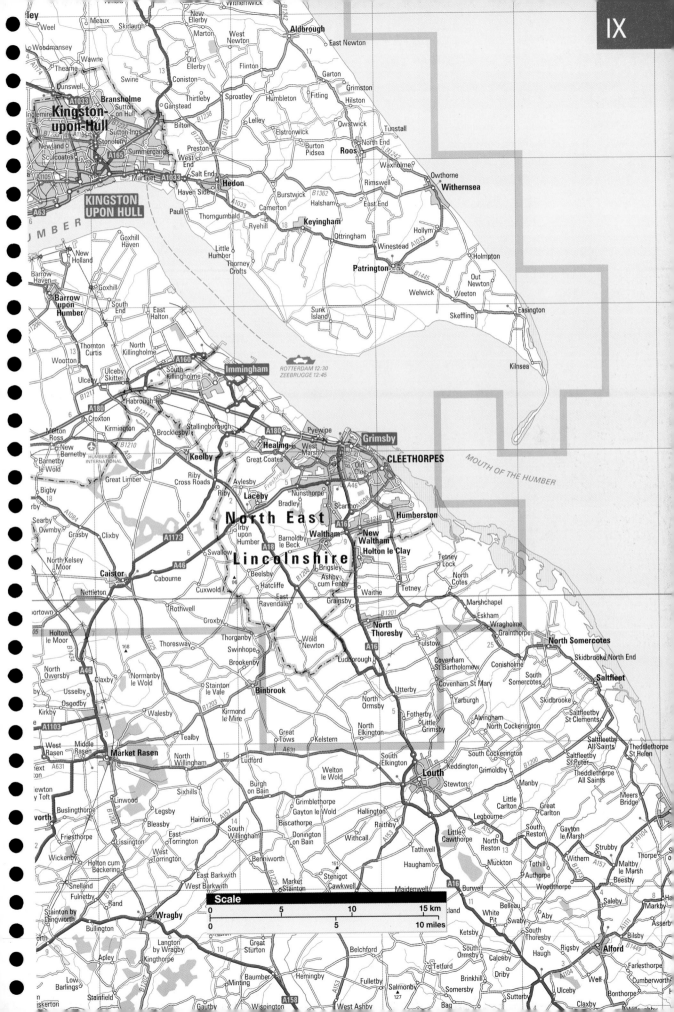

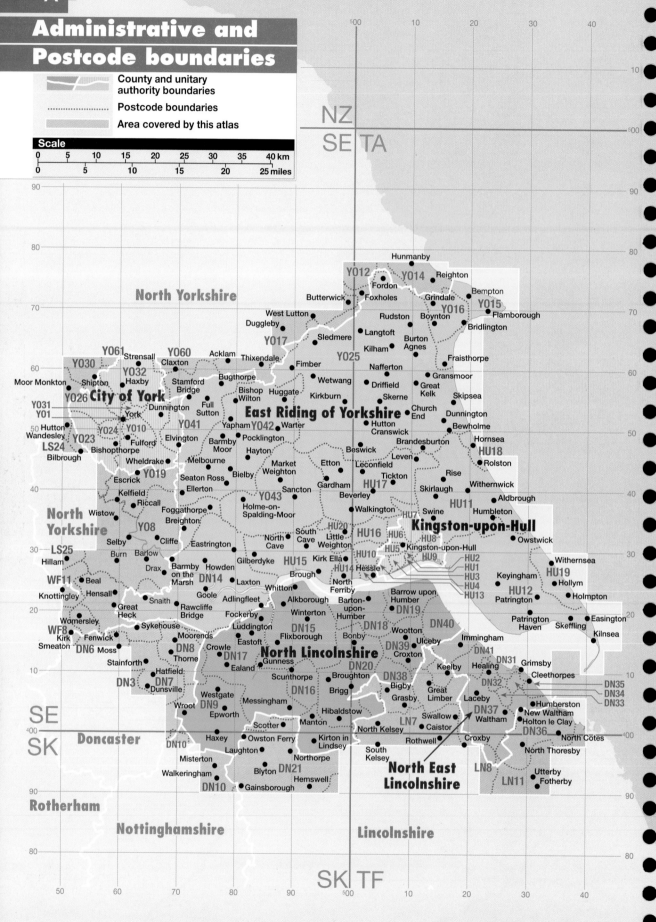

Administrative and Postcode boundaries

County and unitary authority boundaries

Postcode boundaries

Area covered by this atlas

Scale

0   5   10   15   20   25   30   35   40 km

0   5   10   15   20   25 miles

NZ

SE | TA

North Yorkshire

Hunmanby

Y012   Y014   Reighton

Fordon   Bempton

Butterwick   Foxholes   Grindale   Y015

West Lutton   Rudston   Boynton   Y016   Bempton

Duggleby   Sledmere   Langtoft   Flamborough

Y017   Fimber   Kilham   Burton   Bridlington

Acklam   Thixendale   Nafferton   Agnes   Fraisthorpe

Y061   Strensall   Y060   Fimber   Y025   Gransmoor

Y030   Claxton   Wetwang   Driffield   Great   Skipsea

Moor Monkton   Shipton   Y032   Haxby   Stamford   Bishop   Huggate   Kirkburn   Skerne   Kelk

Y026   City of York   Bridge   Wilton   Church   Dunnington

Y031   Dunnington   Full   Warter   Y042   End   Bewholme

Y01   York   Sutton   Yapham   Hutton   Hornsea

Hutton   Y024   Y010   Y041   Pocklington   Cranswick   HU18

Wandesley   Fulford   Elvington   Barmby   Hayton   Beswick   Rolston

LS24   Bishopthorpe   Moor   Melbourne   Etton   Leven   Rise

Bilbrough   Wheldake   Bielby   Market   Leconfield   Tickton   Withernwick

Escrick   Y019   Seaton Ross   Weighton   Gardham   HU17   Skirlaugh   Aldbrough

Kelfield   Ellerton   Sancton   Beverley   Swine   HU11   Humbleton

North   Riccall   Y043   Holme-on-   Walkington   HU7   Kingston-upon-Hull

Yorkshire   Wistow   Foggathorpe   Spalding-Moor   South   HU20   Owstwick

LS25   Breighton   Cliffe   North   Cave   HU16   HU6

Hillam   Selby   Burn   Barlow   Eastrington   Cave   Little   HU5   Kingston-upon-Hull

WF11   Beal   Drax   Gilberdyke   Weighton   HU10   HU8   Withernsea

Knottingley   Hensall   Barmby   Howden   HU15   Kirk Ella   HU9   HU2   Keyingham   HU19

Great   on the   DN14   Laxton   Brough   HU14   Hessle   HU1   Hollym

Womersley   Heck   Snaith   Marsh   Whitton   North   HU3   HU12

WF8   Fenwick   Rawcliffe   Goole   Adlingfleet   Ferriby   HU4   Patrington   Holmpton

Kirk   Sykehouse   Bridge   Fockerby   Alkborough   Barton-   HU13   Patrington   Easington

Smeaton   DN6   Moss   Moorends   Winterton   upon-   DN19   Haven   Skeffling   Kilnsea

Stainforth   Luddington   DN15   Humber   DN18   DN40

DN8   Crowle   Flixborough   Bonby   Wootton   Immingham

DN3   DN7   Thorne   Ealand   North Lincolnshire   DN39   Ulceby   DN41

Dunsville   Gunness   Broughton   DN20   Keelby   Healing   DN31   Grimsby

DN16   Scunthorpe   DN38   Croxton   DN32   Cleetorpes

Westgate   Messingham   Brigg   Bigby   Great   Laceby   DN35

Wroot   DN9   Hibaldstow   Grasby   Limber   DN37   Humberston   DN34

Epworth   Scotter   Manton   LN7   Swallow   Waltham   New Waltham   DN33

SE   Haxey   Owston Ferry   Kirton in   North Kelsey   Caistor   DN36   Holton le Clay

SK   Doncaster   DN10   Laughton   Lindsey   Rothwell   Croxby   North Cotes

Misterton   Northorpe   South   North Thoresby

Walkeringham   Blyton   Hemswell   Kelsey   North East   LN8   Utterby

DN10   Gainsborough   DN21   Lincolnshire   LN11   Fotherby

Rotherham

Nottinghamshire   Lincolnshire

SK | TF

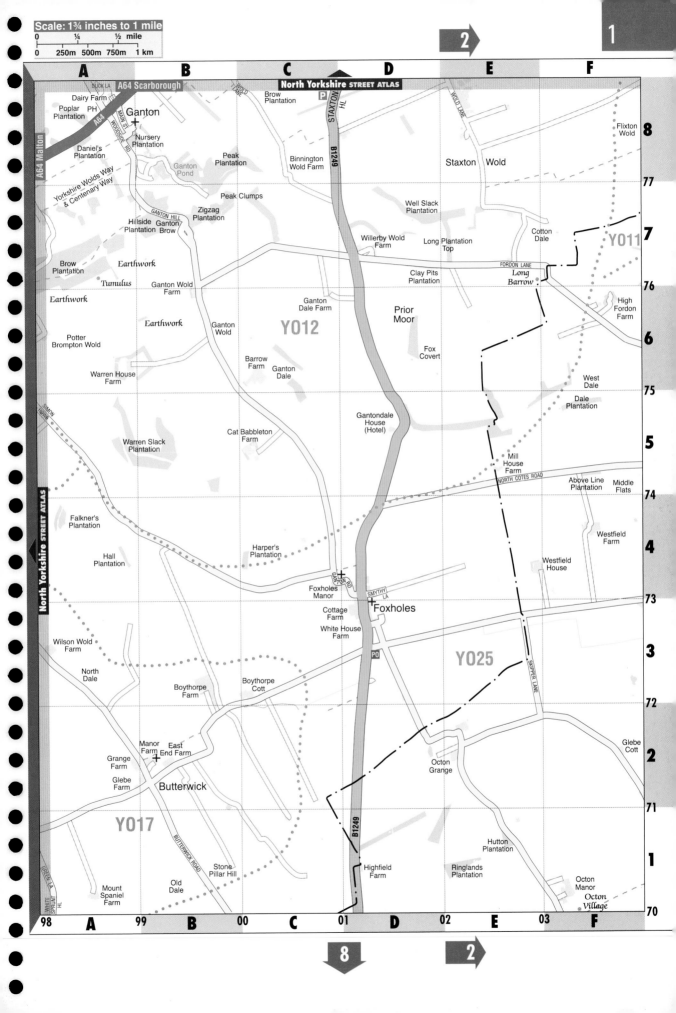

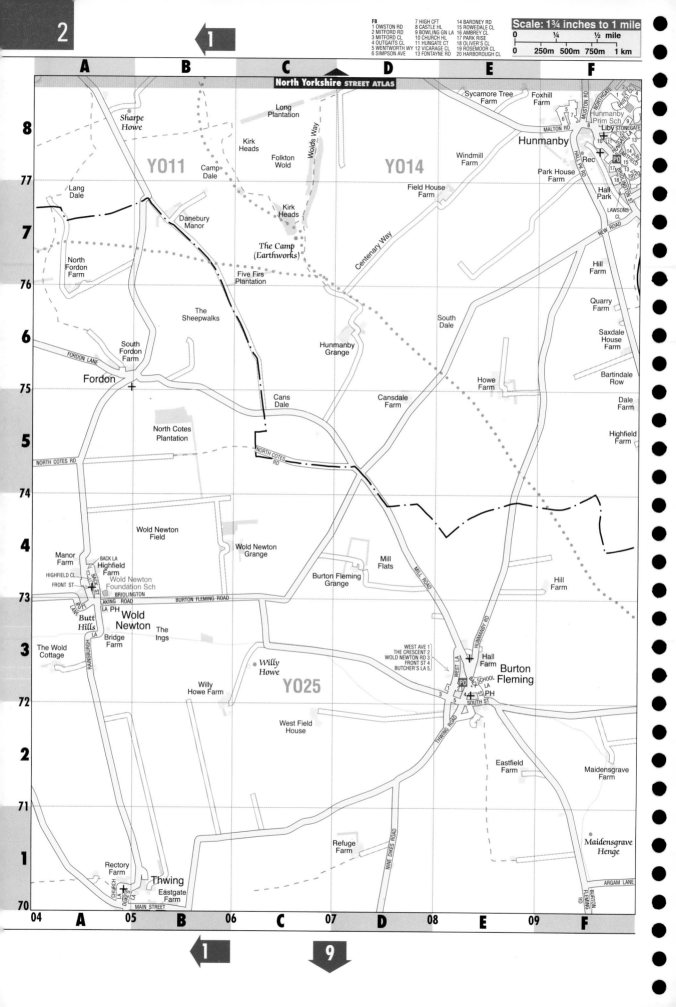

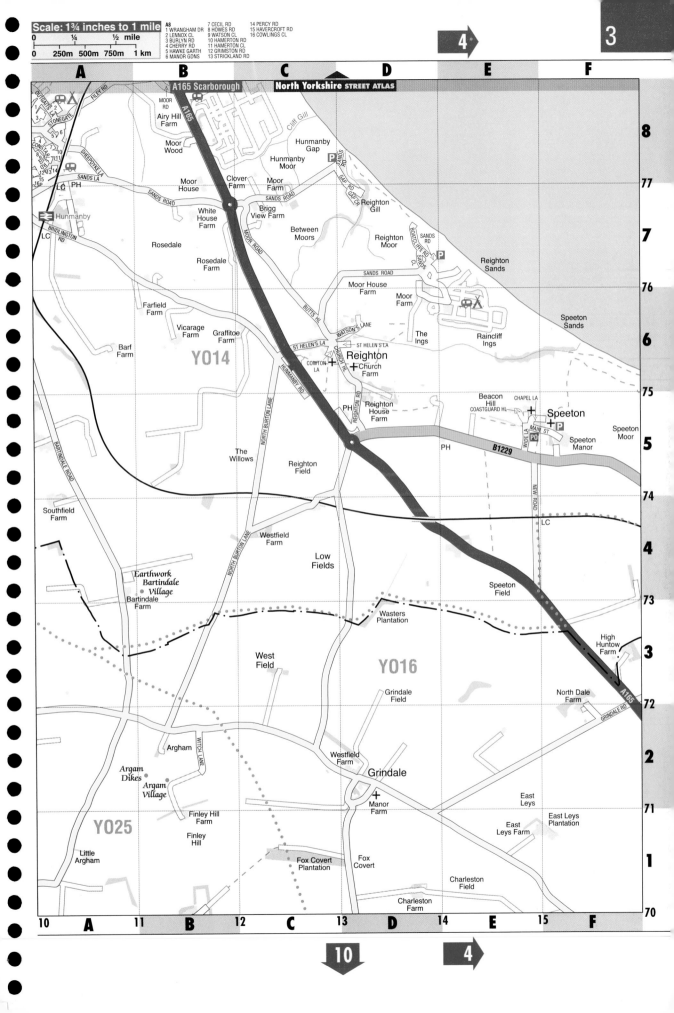

Scale: 1¾ inches to 1 mile

0   ¼   ½   mile
0   250m 500m 750m 1 km

A8
1 WRANGHAM DR
2 LENNOX CL
3 BURLYN RD
4 CHERRY RD
5 HAWKE GARTH
6 MANOR GDNS
7 CECIL RD
8 HOWES RD
9 WATSON CL
10 HAMERTON RD
11 HAMERTON CL
12 GRIMSTON RD
13 STRICKLAND RD
14 PERCY RD
15 HAVERCROFT RD
16 COWLINGS CL

North Yorkshire STREET ATLAS

A165 Scarborough

MOOR RD
Airy Hill Farm
Moor Wood
Cliff Gill
Hunmanby Gap
Hunmanby Moor
Clover Farm
Moor House
Moor Farm
Reighton Gill
Brigg View Farm
SANDS ROAD
Between Moors
Reighton Moor
BOATCLIFFE RD
SANDS RD
Reighton Sands
Hunmanby
Rosedale
White House Farm
Sands Road
Moor House Farm
Moor Farm
Raincliff Ings
Speeton Sands
Farfield Farm
Vicarage Farm
Graffitoe Farm
YO14
St Helen's La
Watson's Lane
The Ings
Barf Farm
Reighton
Church Farm
Cowton La
Beacon Hill
COASTGUARD HL
CHAPEL LA
Speeton
Reighton House Farm
Speeton Manor
Speeton Moor
The Willows
Reighton Field
B1229
NEW ROAD
LC
Southfield Farm
Westfield Farm
Low Fields
Speeton Field
Earthwork Bartindale Village
Bartindale Farm
Wasters Plantation
High Huntow Farm
West Field
YO16
Grindale Field
North Dale Farm
GRINDALE RD
A165
Argham
WITCH LANE
Westfield Farm
Grindale
East Leys
Argam Dikes
Argam Village
Manor Farm
East Leys Plantation
Finley Hill Farm
East Leys Farm
YO25
Finley Hill
Little Argham
Fox Covert Plantation
Fox Covert
Charleston Field
Charleston Farm

Scale: 1¾ inches to 1 mile

0   ¼   ½ mile
0   250m   500m   750m   1 km

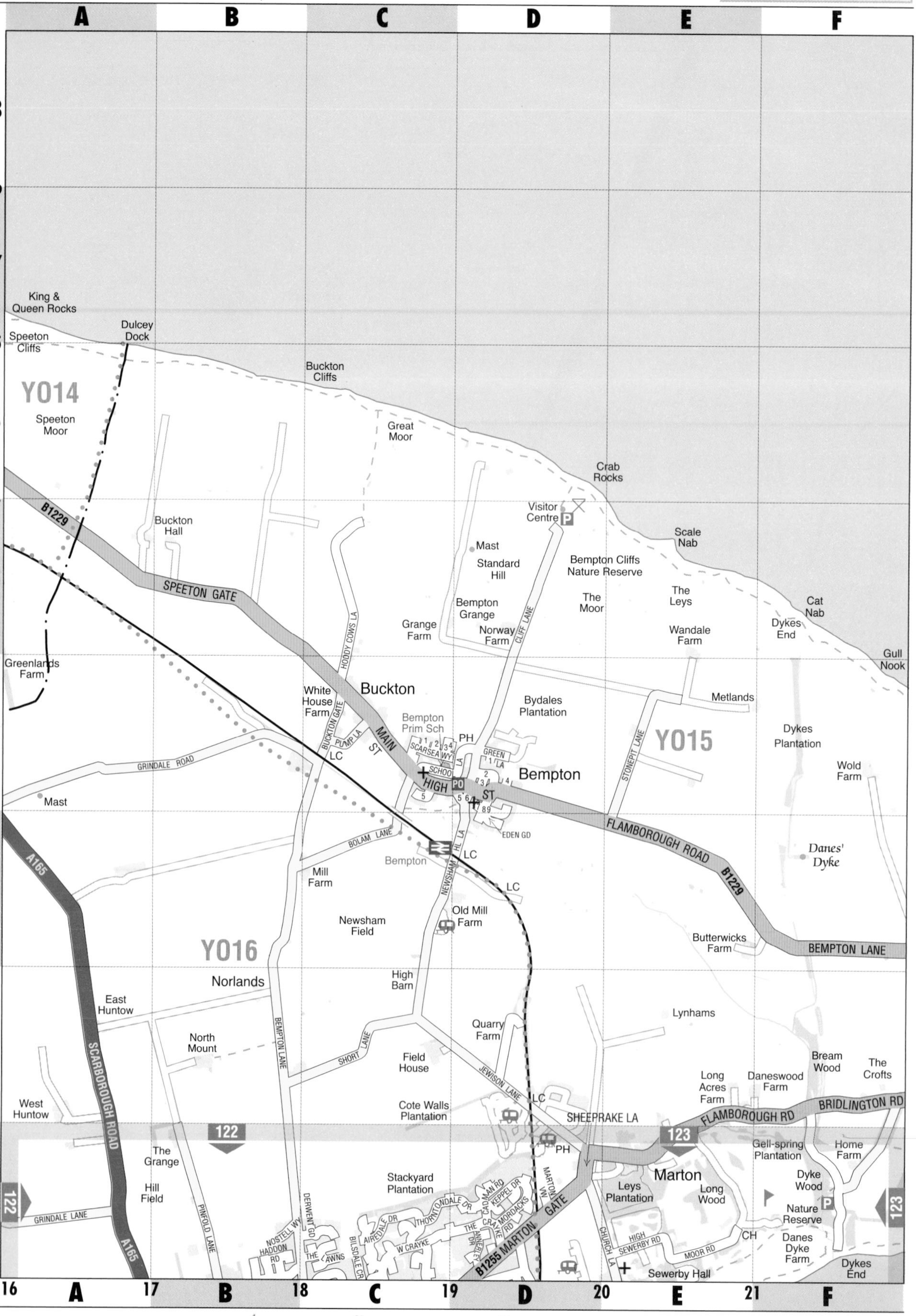

A B C D E F

8
76
7
75

King & Queen Rocks
Speeton Cliffs
Dulcey Dock
Buckton Cliffs

YO14

6
Speeton Moor
Great Moor
Crab Rocks

74
B1229
Buckton Hall
Visitor Centre
P
Scale Nab

SPEETON GATE

5
Mast
Standard Hill
Bempton Cliffs Nature Reserve
The Leys
Cat Nab
Dykes End
Gull Nook

73
Greenlands Farm
HODDY COWS LA
Grange Farm
Bempton Grange
Norway Farm
CLIFF LANE
The Moor
Wandale Farm
Metlands

4
White House Farm
BUCKTON GATE
Buckton
Bempton Prim Sch
1 2 3 4
SCARSEA WY
PH
GREEN LA
1
Bydales Plantation
STONEPIT LANE
YO15
Dykes Plantation
Wold Farm

MAIN ST
PUMP LA
LC
SCHOOL
5
HIGH ST
2 3
5 6
7
8 9
Bempton
EDEN GD

72
Mast
GRINDALE ROAD
BOLAM LANE
Bempton
NEWSHAM LA
LC
FLAMBOROUGH ROAD
B1229
Danes' Dyke

3
A165
Mill Farm
LC
Old Mill Farm
Butterwicks Farm
BEMPTON LANE

YO16
Newsham Field

71
Norlands
High Barn
Lynhams
Bream Wood
The Crofts

2
East Huntow
BEMPTON LANE
North Mount
SHORT LANE
Field House
Quarry Farm
JEWISON LANE
Long Acres Farm
Daneswood Farm

70
West Huntow
SCARBOROUGH ROAD
Cote Walls Plantation
LC
SHEEPRAKE LA
FLAMBOROUGH RD
BRIDLINGTON RD
Gell-spring Plantation
Home Farm

122
The Grange
PH
123
Dyke Wood

1
122
Hill Field
PINFOLD LANE
Stackyard Plantation
DERWENT RD
THORNTONDALE DR
CADMAN RD
TEPPE DR
MORDACS RD
MARTON VW
MARTON GATE
Marton
Leys Plantation
Long Wood
Nature Reserve
P
Danes Dyke Farm
123

GRINDALE LANE
A165
NOSTELL WY
HADDON RD
THE LAWNS
AIREDALE DR
BILSDALE CR
W CRAYKE
THE TINKERS
B1255 MARTON GATE
CHURCH LA
HIGH SEWERBY RD
MOOR RD
CH
Dykes End

69
16 A 17 B 18 C 19 D 20 E 21 F

C4
1 WALMSLEY CL
2 GRANGE CL
3 COLLINGWOOD RD
4 THE MEADOWS
5 RINGLEY MDWS

D4
1 THE PADDOCK
2 SPRING LA
3 ST MICHAEL'S WK
4 BYEDALES
5 GILLUS LA
6 CHURCH LA
7 ACREDYKES
8 VICARAGE LA
9 CLARK CR

For full street detail of the highlighted area see pages 122 and 123.

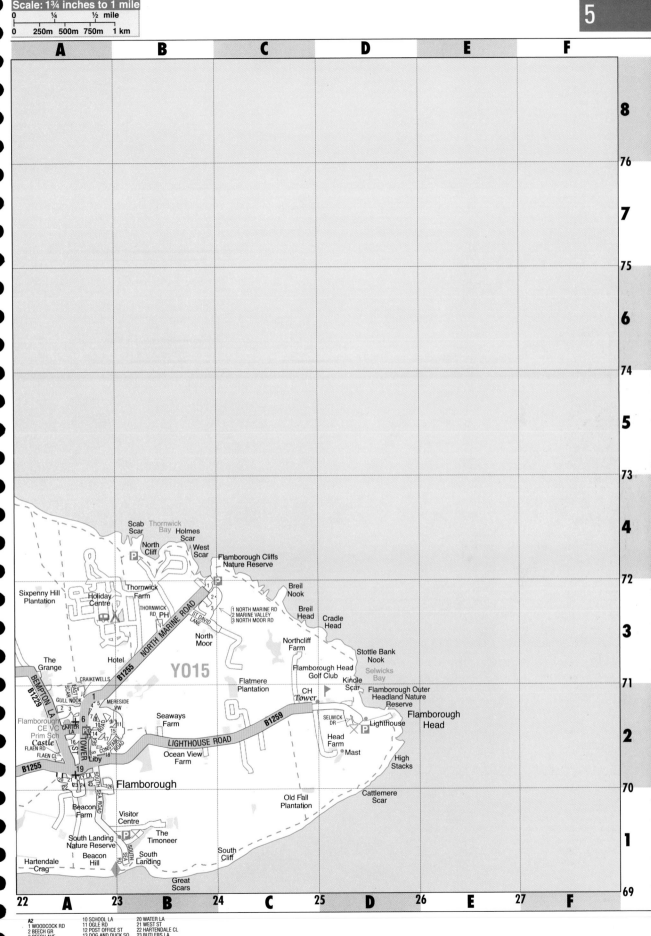

A   B   C   D   E   F

8
76
7
75
6
74
5
73
4

Scab Scar
Thornwick Bay
Holmes Scar
North Cliff
West Scar
Flamborough Cliffs Nature Reserve

72

Sixpenny Hill Plantation
Holiday Centre
Thornwick Farm
Breil Nook
Breil Head
THORNWICK RD PH
ST DAVID LANE
1 NORTH MARINE RD
2 MARINE VALLEY
3 NORTH MOOR RD
Cradle Head

3

The Grange
Hotel
NORTH MARINE ROAD
North Moor
Northcliff Farm
Stottle Bank Nook
Flamborough Head Golf Club
Selwicks Bay

YO15

CRAIKEWELLS
B1255
Flatmere Plantation
Kindle Scar
Flamborough Outer Headland Nature Reserve

71

BEMPTON LA
B1229
MERESIDE VW
Seaways Farm
CH Tower
SELWICK DR
Flamborough Head

Flamborough CE VC Prim Sch
Castle
FLAEN RD
FLAEN CL
TOWER ST
CONSTABLE ROAD
Liby
LIGHTHOUSE ROAD
B1259
Ocean View Farm
Head Farm
Lighthouse
Mast

2

B1255
Flamborough
High Stacks

70

Beacon Farm
Visitor Centre
Cattlemere Scar

South Landing Nature Reserve
SOUTH SEA ROAD
The Timoneer
Old Fall Plantation

1

Hartendale Crag
Beacon Hill
South Landing
South Cliff

Great Scars

69

22 A 23 B 24 C 25 D 26 E 27 F

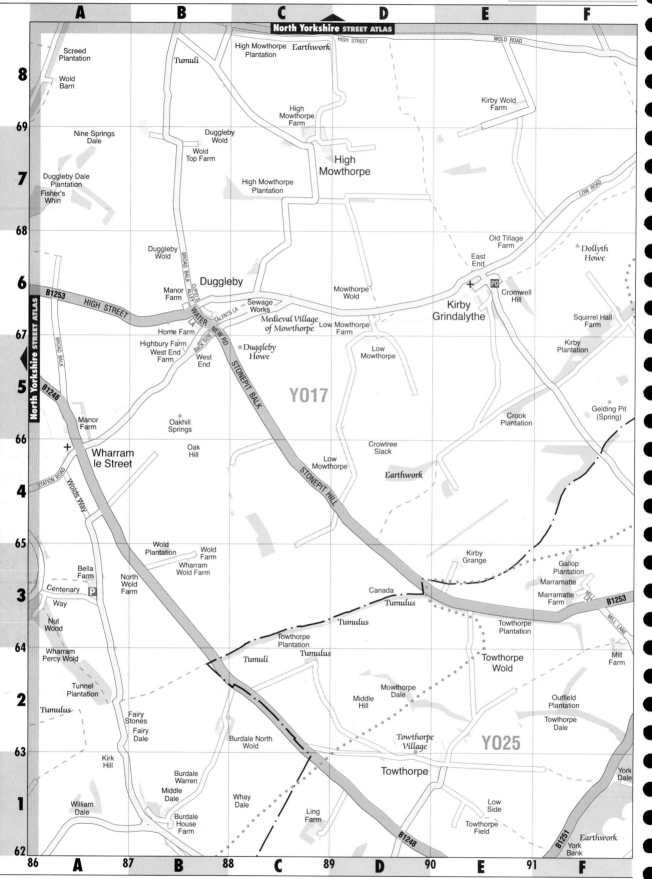

Scale: 1¾ inches to 1 mile

0   ¼   ½ mile
0 250m 500m 750m 1 km

North Yorkshire STREET ATLAS

North Yorkshire STREET ATLAS

Screed Plantation
Wold Barn
Nine Springs Dale
Duggleby Dale Plantation
Fisher's Whin
Tumuli
Duggleby Wold
Wold Top Farm
High Mowthorpe Plantation
Earthwork
High Mowthorpe Farm
High Mowthorpe Plantation
HIGH STREET
High Mowthorpe
WOLD ROAD
Kirby Wold Farm
LOW ROAD

Duggleby Wold
Old Tillage Farm
Dollyth Howe
East End
Cromwell Hill
B1253
HIGH STREET
BROAD BALK
Manor Farm
Duggleby
BROAD BALK ALLEY
CUPID'S ALLEY
WATER LA
SALENTS LA
Sewage Works
NEW RD
Mowthorpe Wold
Kirby Grindalythe
PO
Squirrel Hill Farm
Kirby Plantation

Home Farm
BACK SIDE
Medieval Village of Mowthorpe
Low Mowthorpe Farm
Highbury Farm
West End Farm
West End
Duggleby Howe
Low Mowthorpe

B1248
Manor Farm
Oakhill Springs
STONEPIT BALK
YO17
Crook Plantation
Gelding Pit (Spring)

Wharram le Street
Oak Hill
Crowtree Slack
Low Mowthorpe

STATION ROAD
Wolds Way
Wold Plantation
Low Mowthorpe
Earthwork

Bella Farm
Centenary Way
North Wold Farm
Wold Plantation
Wold Farm
Wharram Wold Farm
STONEPIT HILL
Kirby Grange
Gallop Plantation
Marramatte
Marramatte Farm
B1253
MILL LANE

Nut Wood
Canada
Tumulus
Towthorpe Plantation
Towthorpe Wold
Mill Farm

Wharram Percy Wold
Towthorpe Plantation
Tumulus
Tumulus
Tumuli
Tumulus
Towthorpe Wold
Outfield Plantation
Towthorpe Dale

Tunnel Plantation
Tumulus
Fairy Stones
Fairy Dale
Burdale North Wold
Mowthorpe Dale
Middle Hill
Towthorpe Village
YO25

Kirk Hill
Middle Dale
Towthorpe
York Dale

William Dale
Burdale Warren
Whay Dale
Ling Farm
Low Side
Towthorpe Field
B1248
B1251
Earthwork
York Bank
Burdale House Farm

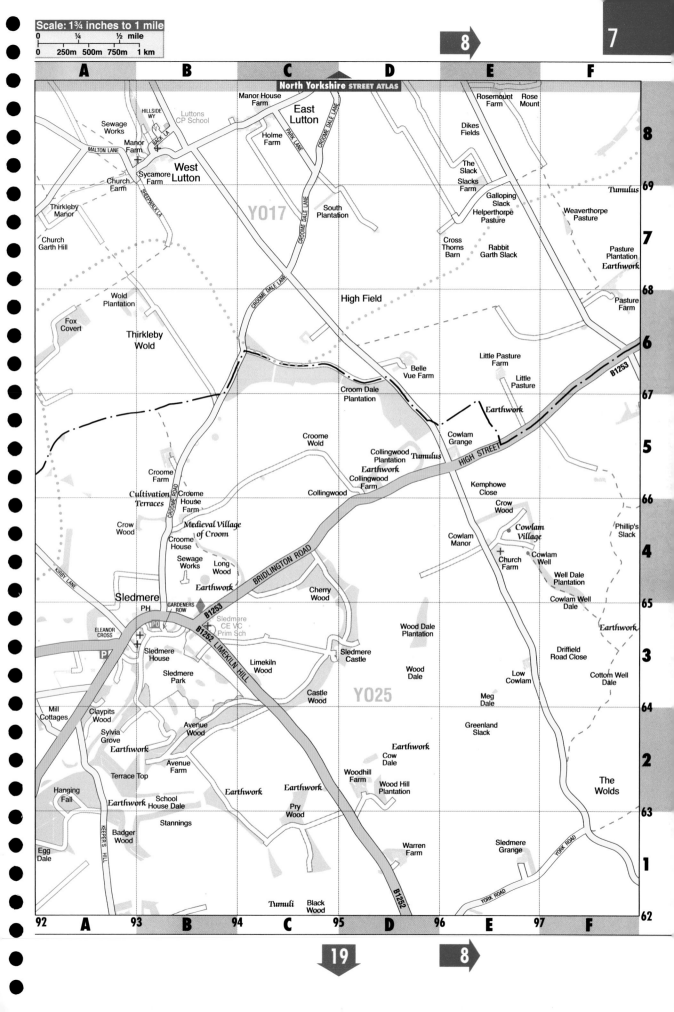

North Yorkshire STREET ATLAS

A   B   C   D   E   F

Rosemount Farm   Rose Mount

Manor House Farm

East Lutton

HILLSIDE WY

Luttons CP School

Sewage Works

Manor Farm

BACK LA

Holme Farm

PARK LANE

CROOME DALE LANE

Dikes Fields

8

MALTON LANE

West Lutton

Sycamore Farm

YO17

CROOME DALE LANE

The Slack

Slacks Farm

69   Tumulus

Church Farm

SHEEPWALK LA

South Plantation

Galloping Slack

Helperthorpe Pasture

Weaverthorpe Pasture

Thirkleby Manor

Cross Thorns Barn

Rabbit Garth Slack

7   Pasture Plantation   Earthwork

Church Garth Hill

68

Wold Plantation

CROOME DALE LANE

High Field

Pasture Farm

Fox Covert

Thirkleby Wold

6

B1253

Belle Vue Farm

Little Pasture Farm

67

Croom Dale Plantation

Little Pasture

Croome Wold

Earthwork

Cowlam Grange

5

Croome Farm

CROOME ROAD

Collingwood Plantation   Tumulus

Collingwood Farm

HIGH STREET

Cultivation Terraces

Croome House Farm

Earthwork

Kemphowe Close

66

Crow Wood

Medieval Village of Croom

Collingwood

Crow Wood

Phillip's Slack

Croome House

Cowlam Village

4

Sewage Works

Long Wood

Cowlam Manor

Church Farm

Cowlam Well

Well Dale Plantation

Earthwork

Cherry Wood

Cowlam Well Dale

65

Sledmere

PH

GARDENERS ROW

B1253

Sledmere CE VC Prim Sch

Earthwork

BRIDLINGTON ROAD

ELEANOR CROSS

B1252   LIMEKILN HILL

Wood Dale Plantation

Driffield Road Close

Cottom Well Dale

3

Sledmere House

Limekiln Wood

Sledmere Castle

Wood Dale

Low Cowlam

YO25

Sledmere Park

Castle Wood

Meg Dale

64

Mill Cottages

Claypits Wood

Avenue Wood

Greenland Slack

2

Sylvia Grove

Earthwork

Avenue Farm

Earthwork   Cow Dale

The Wolds

Terrace Top

Woodhill Farm

Wood Hill Plantation

Hanging Fall

Earthwork

School House Dale

Earthwork   Earthwork

Pry Wood

63

KEEPERS HILL

Stannings

Badger Wood

Warren Farm

Sledmere Grange

YORK ROAD

1

Egg Dale

YORK ROAD

Tumuli   Black Wood

B1252

62

92   A   93   B   94   C   95   D   96   E   97   F

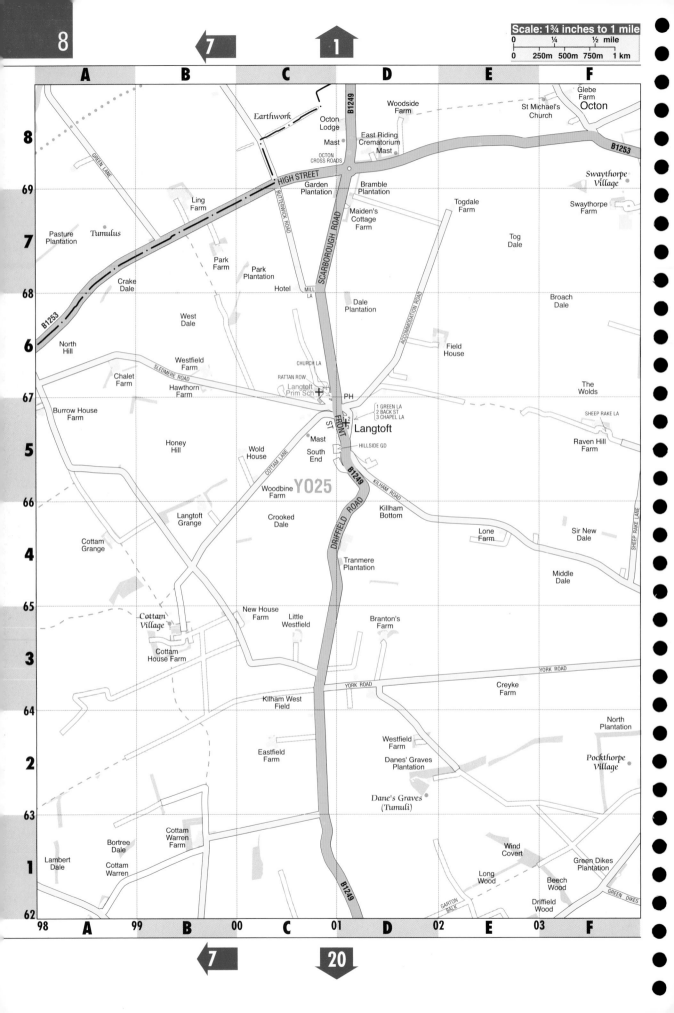

Scale: 1¾ inches to 1 mile

| 0 | ¼ | ½ | mile |
| 0 | 250m | 500m | 750m | 1 km |

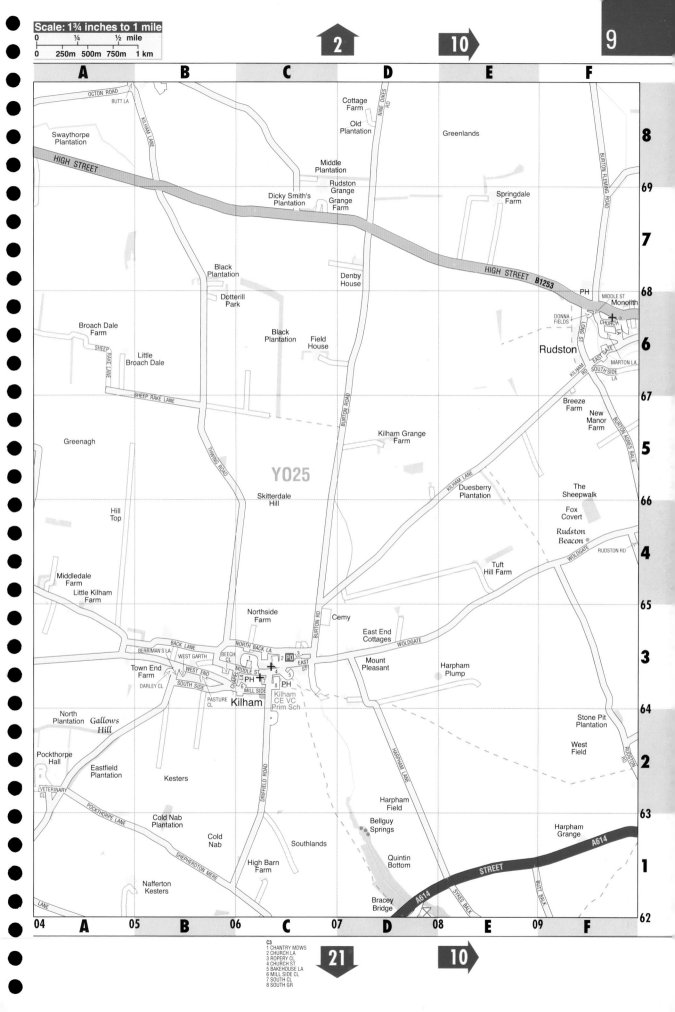

A B C D E F

8
69
7
68
6
67
5
66
4
65
3
64
2
63
1
62

OCTON ROAD
BUTT LA
KILLEY LANE

Swaythorpe
Plantation

HIGH STREET

Cottage
Farm

Old
Plantation

NINE DIKES RD

Greenlands

BURTON FLEMING ROAD

Middle
Plantation

Rudston
Grange

Dicky Smith's
Plantation

Grange
Farm

Springdale
Farm

Black
Plantation

Denby
House

HIGH STREET B1253

PH
MIDDLE ST
Monolith

Dotterill
Park

Black
Plantation

Field
House

DONNA
FIELDS
CHURCH

Rudston

EAST GATE
MARTON LA
SOUTH SIDE
LA

Broach Dale
Farm

SHEEP RAKE LANE

Little
Broach Dale

Breeze
Farm

New
Manor
Farm

BURTON AGNES BALK

LONG ST
KILHAM RD

SHEEP RAKE LANE

Greenagh

Kilham Grange
Farm

THWING ROAD

YO25

KILHAM LANE

Duesberry
Plantation

The
Sheepwalk

Fox
Covert

Skitterdale
Hill

*Rudston
Beacon*

RUDSTON RD

Hill
Top

WOLDGATE

Tuft
Hill Farm

Middledale
Farm

Little Kilham
Farm

Northside
Farm

BURTON RD

Cemy

East End
Cottages

WOLDGATE

BACK LANE
NORTH BACK LA
BERRIMAN'S LA
WEST GARTH
BEECH CL

Town End
Farm

WEST END
DARLEY CL
SOUTH SIDE

PH
CHAPEL LA
MIDDLE ST

PO
EAST ST

Mount
Pleasant

Harpham
Plump

Stone Pit
Plantation

RUDSTON RD

PH
Kilham
CE VC
Prim Sch

MILL SIDE

Kilham

PASTURE
CL

North
Plantation

*Gallows
Hill*

West
Field

Pockthorpe
Hall

VETERINARY
CL

Eastfield
Plantation

Kesters

HARPHAM LANE

Harpham
Field

POCKTHORPE LANE

Cold Nab
Plantation

Cold
Nab

Southlands

Bellguy
Springs

Harpham
Grange

A614

SHEPHERDTON MERE

High Barn
Farm

Quintin
Bottom

STREET
A614
SYKES BALK
BUTT BALK

Nafferton
Kesters

LANE

Bracey
Bridge

04 **A** 05 **B** 06 **C** 07 **D** 08 **E** 09 **F** 62

C3
1 CHANTRY MDWS
2 CHURCH LA
3 ROPERY CL
4 CHURCH ST
5 BAKEHOUSE LA
6 MILL SIDE CL
7 SOUTH CL
8 SOUTH GR

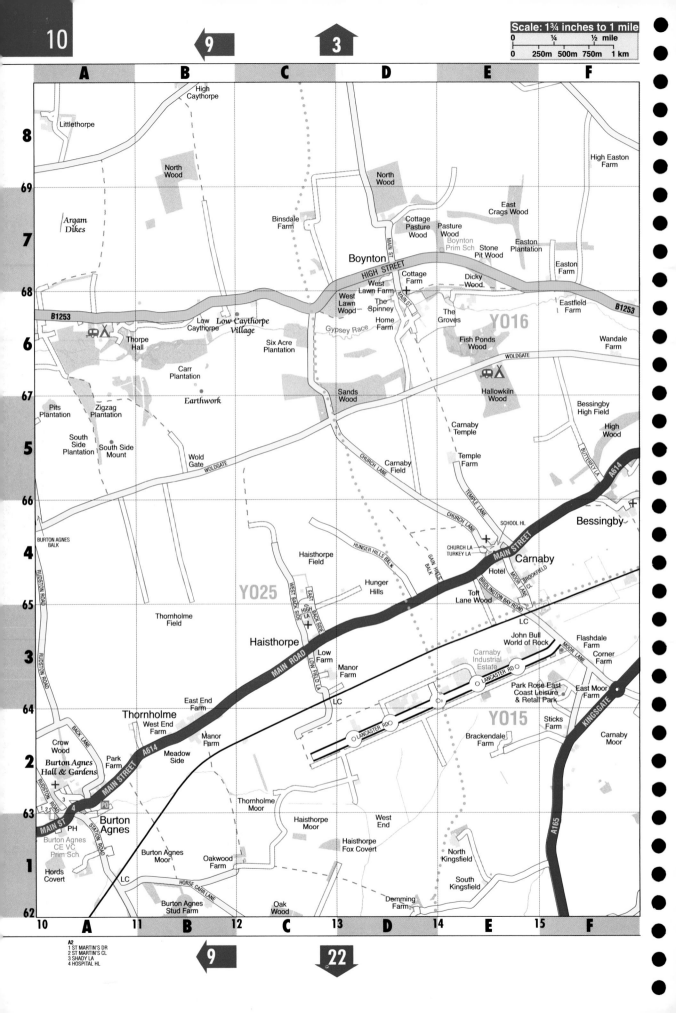

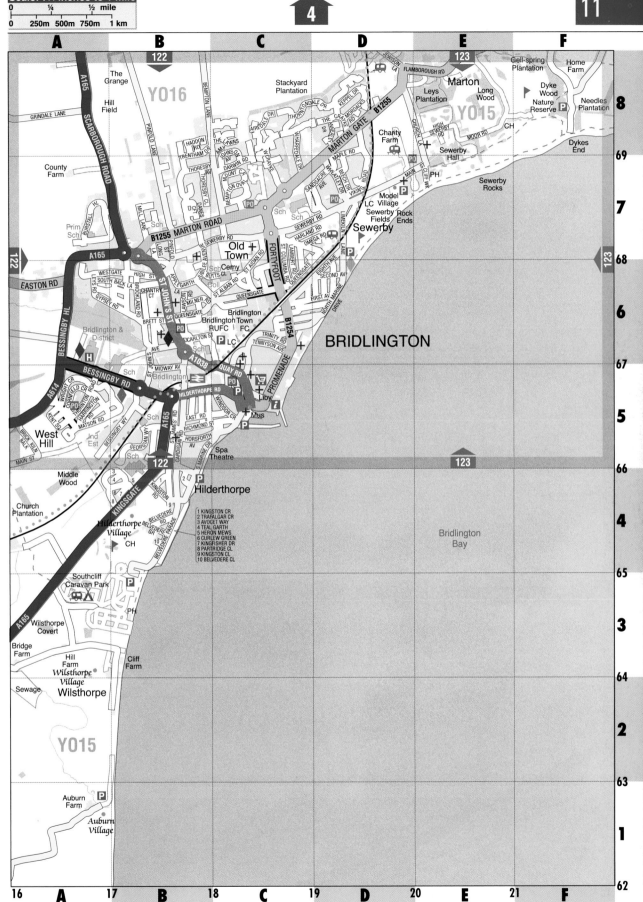

Scale: 1¾ inches to 1 mile

0   ¼   ½   mile
0   250m 500m 750m 1 km

For full street detail of the highlighted area see pages 122 and 123.

23

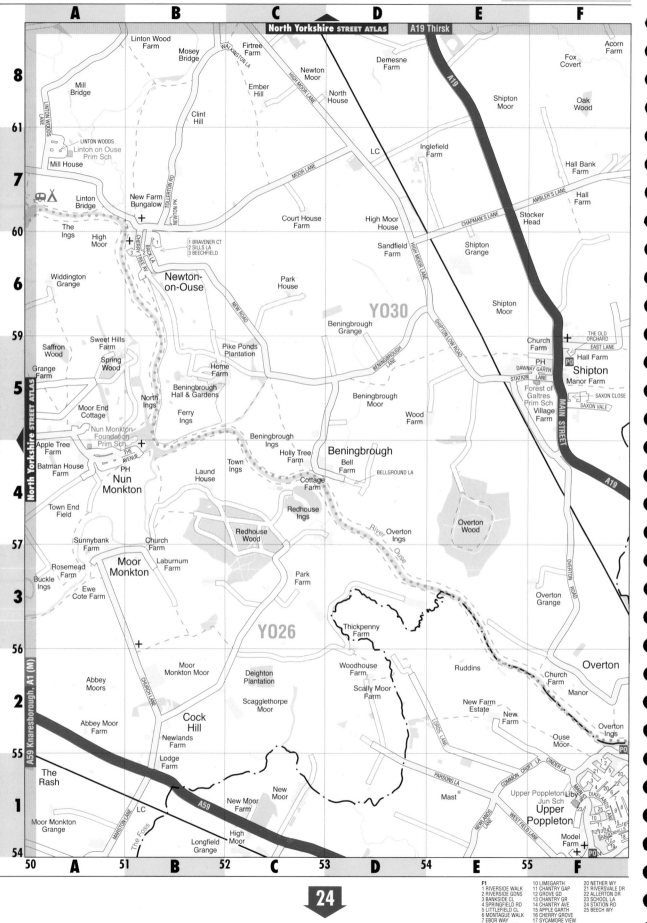
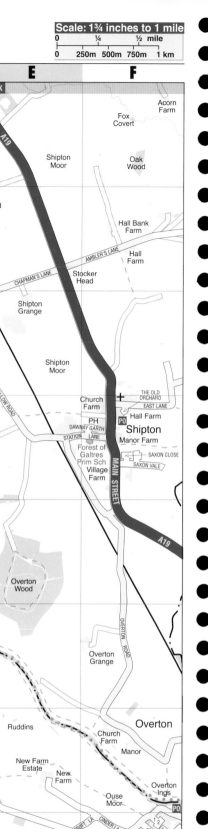

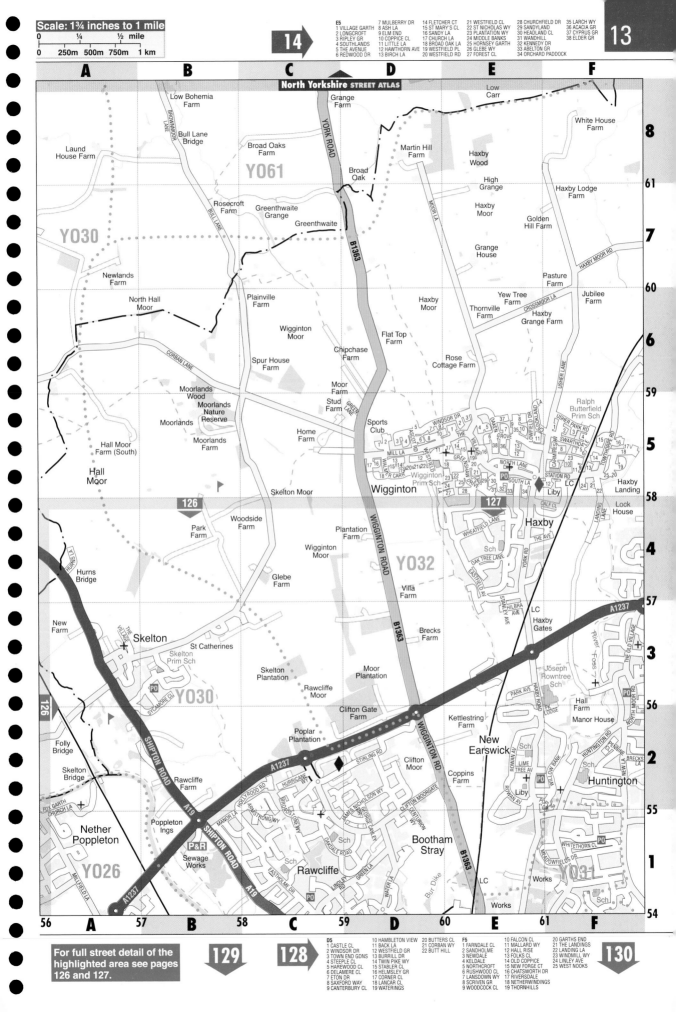

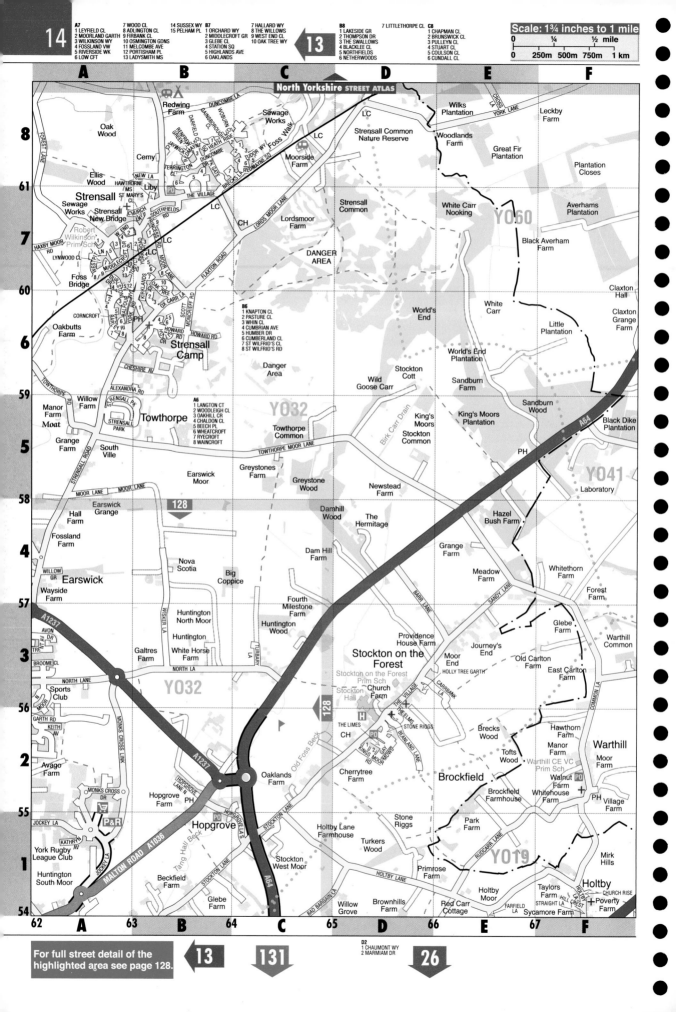

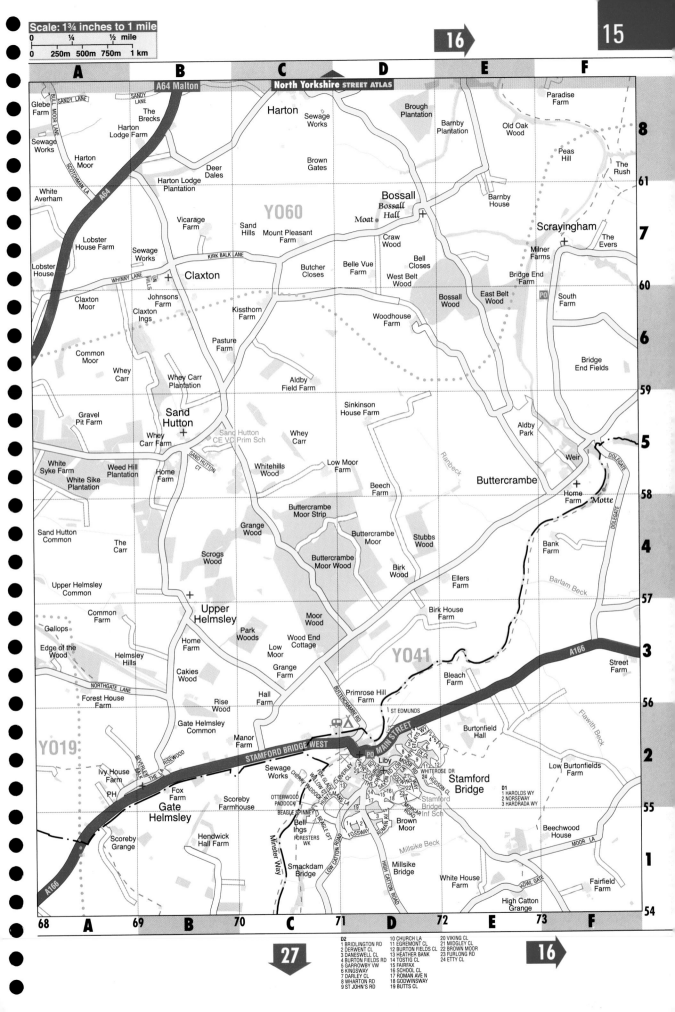

A   B   C   D   E   F

8
61
7
60
6
59
5
58
4
57
3
56
2
55
1
54

A64 Malton

Glebe Farm
SANDY LANE
Harton Moor
White Averham
Lobster House Farm
Lobster House
Claxton Moor
Common Moor
Whey Carr
Gravel Pit Farm
White Syke Farm
White Sike Plantation
Sand Hutton Common
The Carr
Upper Helmsley Common
Common Farm
Gallops
Edge of the Wood
Forest House Farm
Ivy House Farm
PH
Fox Farm
Scoreby Grange

SANDY LANE
The Brecks
Harton Lodge Farm
Deer Dales
Harton Lodge Plantation
Vicarage Farm
Sewage Works
Claxton
KIRK BALK LANE
Johnsons Farm
Claxton Ings
Pasture Farm
Whey Carr Plantation
Sand Hutton
Whey Carr Farm
Home Farm
Weed Hill Plantation
Scrogs Wood
Grange Wood
Upper Helmsley
Home Farm
Helmsley Hills
Cakies Wood
NORTHGATE LANE
Rise Wood
Gate Helmsley Common
Manor Farm
Sewage Works
Gate Helmsley
Scoreby Farmhouse
Hendwick Hall Farm

Harton
Sewage Works
Brown Gates
Sand Hills
Mount Pleasant Farm
Butcher Closes
Kissthorn Farm
Aldby Field Farm
Whey Carr
Whitehills Wood
Buttercrambe Moor Strip
Buttercrambe Moor Wood
Park Woods
Low Moor
Moor Wood
Wood End Cottage
Grange Farm
Hall Farm
Otterwood Paddock
Beagle Spinney
Bell Ings
FORESTERS WK
Minster Way
Smackdam Bridge

YO60

Brough Plantation
Moat
Bossall
Bossall Hall
Craw Wood
Belle Vue Farm
Bell Closes
West Belt Wood
Bossall Wood
Woodhouse Farm
Sinkinson House Farm
Beech Farm
Buttercrambe Moor
Stubbs Wood
Birk Wood
Ellers Farm
Birk House Farm
Primrose Hill Farm
Bleach Farm
ST EDMUNDS
Liby
Stamford Bridge
Stamford Bridge Inf Sch
Brown Moor
Millsike Bridge
White House Farm
High Catton Grange

YO41
STAMFORD BRIDGE WEST
MAIN STREET
PO

Barnby Plantation
Old Oak Wood
Barnby House
East Belt Wood
Aldby Park
Buttercrambe
Home Farm
Bank Farm
Street Farm
A166
Burtonfield Hall
Low Burtonfields Farm
Beechwood House
MOOR LA
Fairfield Farm

Paradise Farm
Peas Hill
The Rush
Scrayingham
The Evers
Milner Farms
Bridge End Farm
South Farm
Bridge End Fields
Weir
Motte
DOLEGATE
Barlam Beck
Flawith Beck
HOWL GATE

Ranbeck

YO19

BRIDLINGTON RD

D2
1 BRIDLINGTON RD
2 DERWENT CL
3 DANESWELL CL
4 BURTON FIELDS RD
5 GARROWBY VW
6 KINGSWAY
7 DARLEY CL
8 WHARTON RD
9 ST JOHN'S RD
10 CHURCH LA
11 EGREMONT CL
12 BURTON FIELDS CL
13 HEATHER BANK
14 TOSTIG CL
15 FAIRFAX
16 SCHOOL CL
17 ROMAN AVE N
18 GODWINSWAY
19 BUTTS CL
20 VIKING CL
21 MIDGLEY CL
22 BROWN MOOR
23 FURLONG RD
24 ETTY CL

D1
1 HAROLDS WY
2 NORSEWAY
3 HARDRADA WY

68   69   70   71   72   73

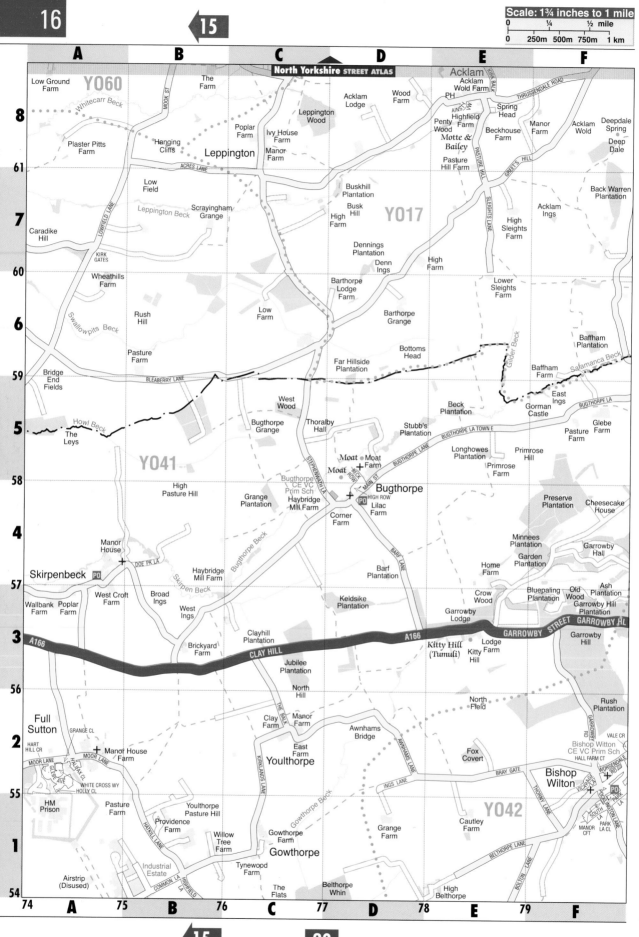

Scale: 1¾ inches to 1 mile

0   ¼   ½ mile
0   250m   500m   750m   1 km

North Yorkshire STREET ATLAS

YO60

Low Ground Farm
Whitecarr Beck
Plaster Pitts Farm
Hanging Cliffs
The Farm
Poplar Farm
Ivy House Farm
Leppington Wood
Acklam Lodge
Wood Farm
Acklam Wold Farm
Acklam
PH
AINSTY VW
Highfield Farm
Penty Wood
Motte & Bailey
Spring Head
Beckhouse Farm
Manor Farm
Acklam Wold
Deepdale Spring
Deep Dale
THRUSSENDALE ROAD
GREET'S HILL
PASTURE HILL

Leppington
ACRES LANE
Manor Farm
Low Field
Leppington Beck
Scrayingham Grange
Buskhill Plantation
Busk Hill
High Farm
YO17
High Farm
Pasture Hill Farm
SLEIGHTS LANE
High Sleights Farm
Acklam Ings
Back Warren Plantation

Caradike Hill
KIRK GATES
Wheathills Farm
LOWFIELD LANE
Rush Hill
Dennings Plantation
Denn Ings
Barthorpe Lodge Farm
Barthorpe Grange
Lower Sleights Farm

Swallowpits Beck
Pasture Farm
Low Farm
Far Hillside Plantation
Bottoms Head
Glider Beck
Baffham Plantation
Baffham Farm
Salamanca Beck

Bridge End Fields
BLEABERRY LANE
West Wood
Thoralby Hall
Beck Plantation
Stubb's Plantation
Gorman Castle
East Ings
BUGTHORPE LA

Howl Beck
The Leys
Bugthorpe Grange
STEPHENWATH LA
Moat Farm
Moat
BECK ROW
Longhowes Plantation
Primrose Hill
BUGTHORPE LA TOWN E
Pasture Farm
Glebe Farm

YO41
High Pasture Hill
Grange Plantation
Bugthorpe CE VC Prim Sch
Haybridge Mill Farm
HIGH ROW
PO
Bugthorpe
MAIN ST
Lilac Farm
Primrose Farm
Preserve Plantation
Cheesecake House

Manor House
DOE PK LA
Haybridge Mill Farm
Bugthorpe Beck
Corner Farm
Barf Lane
Minnees Plantation
Garden Plantation
Garrowby Hall

Skirpenbeck
PO
West Croft Farm
Broad Ings
Skirpen Beck
Barf Plantation
Home Farm
Bluepaling Plantation
Old Wood
Garrowby Hill Plantation
Ash Plantation

Wallbank Farm
Poplar Farm
West Ings
Keldsike Plantation
Crow Wood
Garrowby Lodge
Garrowby Hill

A166
Brickyard Farm
Clayhill Plantation
CLAY HILL
A166
GARROWBY STREET
GARROWBY HL
Garrowby Hill

Jubilee Plantation
North Hill
Kitty Hill (Tumuli)
Kitty Hill
Lodge Farm
GARROWBY RD

Full Sutton
GRANGE CL
THE BECK
Clay Farm
Manor Farm
East Farm
Awnhams Bridge
North Field
Fox Covert
Rush Plantation
VALE CR
Bishop Witton CE VC Prim Sch
HALL FARM CT

HART HILL CR
Manor House Farm
MOOR LANE
HALIFAX LA
AWNHAMS LANE
KIRLANDS LANE
Youlthorpe
INGS LANE
BRAY GATE
THORNY LANE
Bishop Wilton
VICARAGE
PO
WORSENDALE RD

GLEBE AVE
WHITE CROSS WY
HOLLY CL
HM Prison
Pasture Farm
Providence Farm
Youlthorpe Pasture Hill
Willow Tree Farm
Gowthorpe Farm
Gowthorpe Beck
Grange Farm
Cautley Farm
YO42
BELTHORPE LANE
SOUTH LA
PARK LA CL
MANOR CFT

HARNILL LANE
HIGHFIELD LA
COMMON LA
Industrial Estate
Tynewood Farm
Gowthorpe
The Flats
Belthorpe Whin
High Belthorpe
BOLTON LANE

Airstrip (Disused)

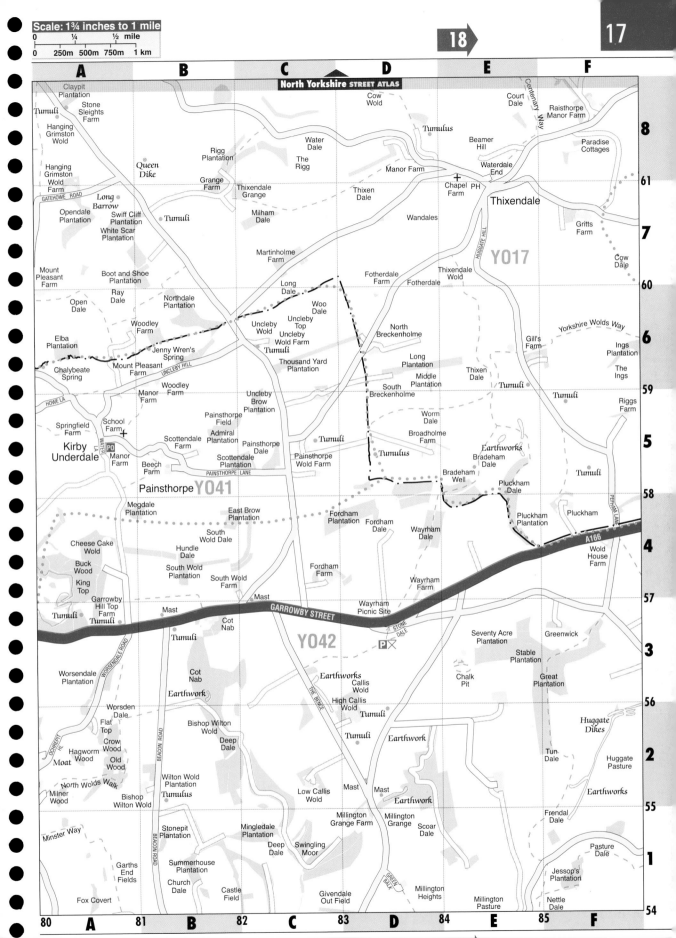

Scale: 1¾ inches to 1 mile

0   ¼   ½ mile
0 250m 500m 750m 1 km

North Yorkshire STREET ATLAS

A   B   C   D   E   F

Claypit
Plantation
Tumuli
Stone
Sleights
Farm
Hanging
Grimston
Wold
Hanging
Grimston
Wold
Farm
GATEHOWE ROAD
Opendale
Plantation
Long
Barrow
Swiff Cliff
Plantation
White Scar
Plantation
Queen
Dike
Rigg
Plantation
Grange
Farm
Thixendale
Grange
Milham
Dale
Tumuli

Cow
Wold
Water
Dale
The
Rigg
Manor Farm
Tumulus
Beamer
Hill
Waterdale
End
Chapel
Farm PH
Thixendale
Court
Dale
Raisthorpe
Manor Farm
Centenary Way
Paradise
Cottages

Mount
Pleasant
Farm
Boot and Shoe
Plantation
Ray
Dale
Northdale
Plantation
Open
Dale
Woodley
Farm
Elba
Plantation
Chalybeate
Spring
Jenny Wren's
Spring
Mount Pleasant
Farm
UNCLEBY HILL
Woodley
Farm

Thixen
Dale
Wandales
Martinholme
Farm
Long
Dale
Woo
Dale
Uncleby
Wold
Uncleby
Top
Uncleby
Wold Farm
Tumuli
Thousand Yard
Plantation
Fotherdale
Farm
Fotherdale
Thixendale
Wold
Fotherdale
North
Breckenholme
South
Breckenholme
Long
Plantation
Middle
Plantation
Thixen
Dale
Tumuli
Tumuli
Gill's
Farm
Yorkshire Wolds Way
Ings
Plantation
The
Ings
Riggs
Farm

HUGGATE HILL
YO17

Thixendale
Gritts
Farm
Cow
Dale

HOWE LA
Manor
Farm
Springfield
Farm
School
Farm
Kirby
Underdale
WATER LA
Manor
Farm
Painsthorpe
Field
Admiral
Plantation
Scottendale
Farm
Beech
Farm
Scottendale
Plantation
Uncleby
Brow
Plantation
Painsthorpe
Dale
PAINSTHORPE LANE
Painsthorpe
Wold Farm
Tumuli
Painsthorpe
Plantation
Tumulus
Worm
Dale
Broadholme
Farm
Earthworks
Bradeham
Dale
Bradeham
Well
Pluckham
Dale
Pluckham
Plantation
Tumuli
Pluckham
PERFIAN LANE

Painsthorpe YO41
Megdale
Plantation
East Brow
Plantation
Fordham
Plantation
Fordham
Dale
Wayrham
Dale
A166
Wold
House
Farm

Cheese Cake
Wold
South
Wold Dale
Hundle
Dale
Buck
Wood
King
Top
South Wold
Plantation
South Wold
Farm
Fordham
Farm
Wayrham
Farm

Garrowby
Hill Top
Farm
Tumuli
Mast
Mast
Cot Nab
Mast
GARROWBY STREET
Wayrham
Picnic Site
Wayrham
Picnic Site
STONE DALE
P
YO42
Seventy Acre
Plantation
Stable
Plantation
Greenwick
Great
Plantation

Tumuli
Worsendale
Plantation
WORSENDALE ROAD
Cot
Nab
Earthwork
Worsden
Dale
Flat
Top
Crow
Wood
Hagworm
Wood
Old
Wood
Moat
DOBREPIT HILL
Milner
Wood
North Wolds Walk
Bishop
Wilton Wold
Tumulus
BEACON ROAD
Bishop Wilton
Wold
Deep
Dale
Wilton Wold
Plantation
Earthworks
Callis
Wold
High Callis
Wold
Tumuli
Tumuli
THE BENGE
Earthwork
Mast
Mast
Earthwork
Low Callis
Wold
Chalk
Pit
Tun
Dale
Huggate
Dikes
Huggate
Pasture
Earthworks
Frendal
Dale

Minster Way
Garths
End
Fields
Fox Covert
BEACON ROAD
Stonepit
Plantation
Summerhouse
Plantation
Church
Dale
Castle
Field
Mingledale
Plantation
Deep
Dale
Swingling
Moor
Millington
Grange Farm
Millington
Grange
Scoar
Dale
GREEN BALK
Givendale
Out Field
Millington
Heights
Millington
Pasture
Pasture
Dale
Jessop's
Plantation
Nettle
Dale

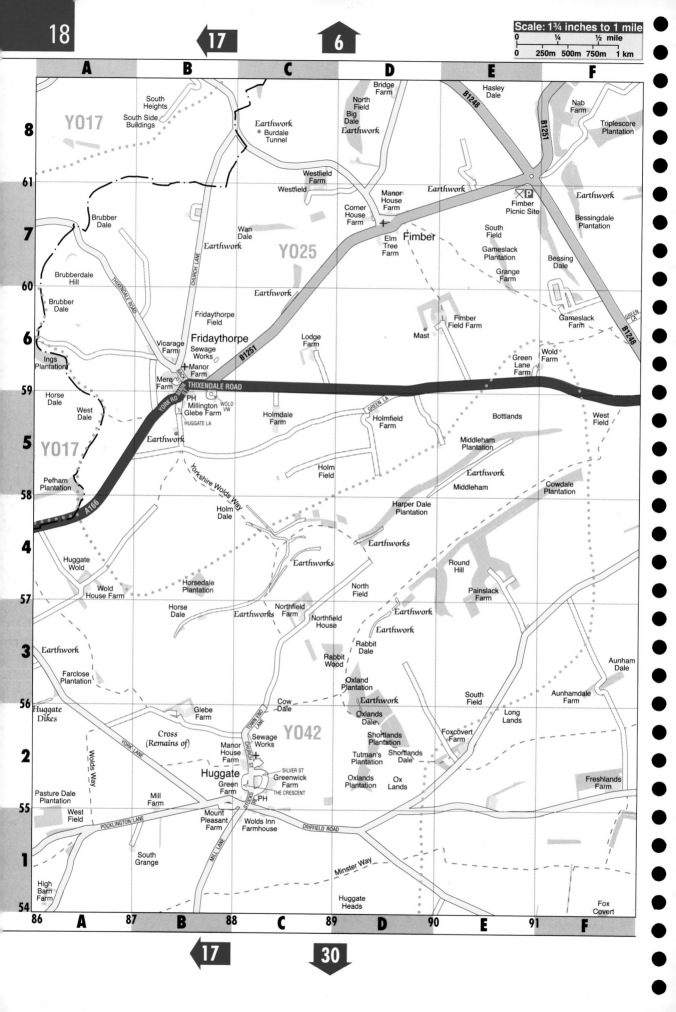

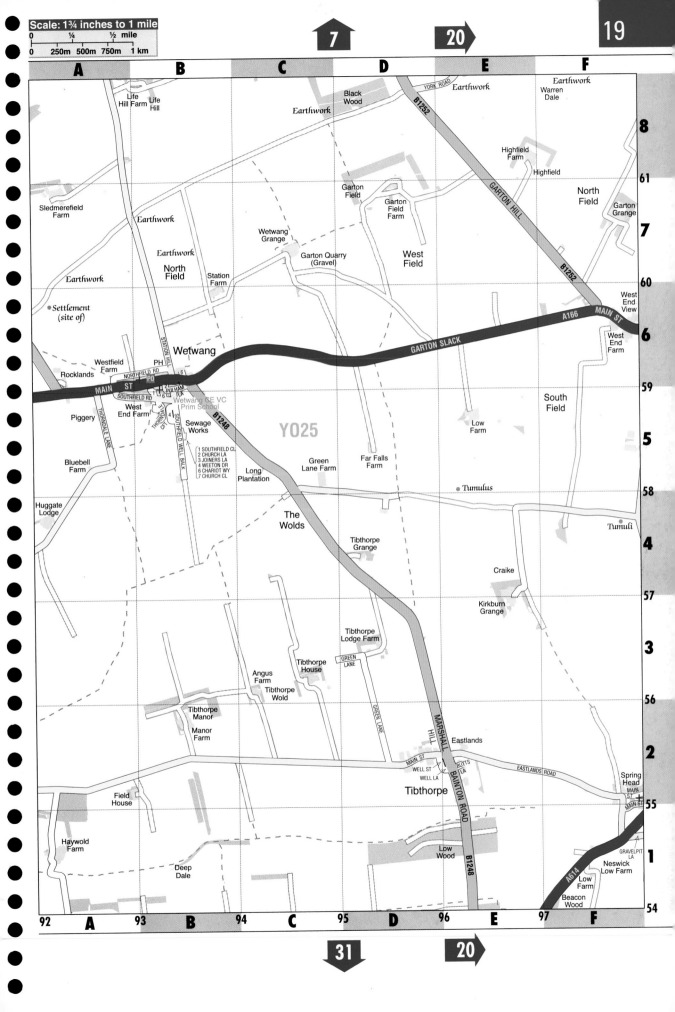

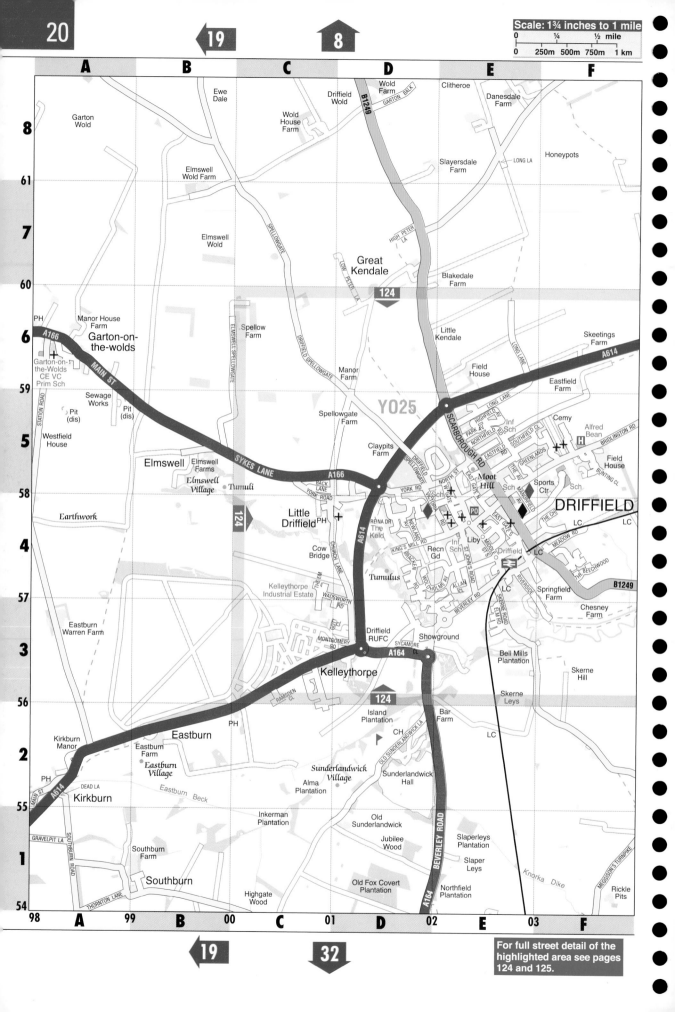

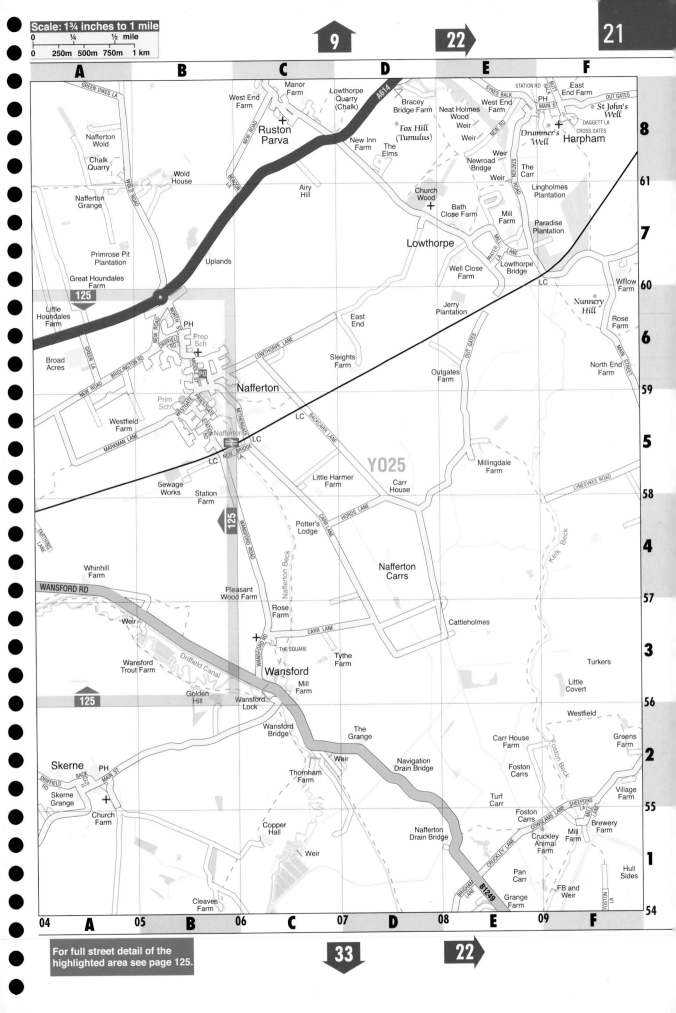

Scale: 1¾ inches to 1 mile

0   ¼   ½ mile
0 250m 500m 750m 1 km

A **B** **C** **D** **E** **F**

GREEN DIKES LA

Nafferton Wold

Chalk Quarry

West End Farm

Manor Farm

Lowthorpe Quarry (Chalk)

A614

Bracey Bridge Farm

STATION RD

BUTT BALK

SYKES BALK

East End Farm

OUT GATES

Ruston Parva

West End Farm

Neat Holmes Wood

PH
MAIN ST

St John's Well

Wold House

NEW ROAD

BEACON LA

Fox Hill (Tumulus)

Weir

Weir

NEW RD

Drummer's Well

DAGGETT LA

CROSS GATES

Harpham

Nafferton Grange

Airy Hill

New Inn Farm

The Elms

Newroad Bridge

Weir

Weir

The Carr

Lingholmes Plantation

8

61

Primrose Pit Plantation

Uplands

Church Wood

Bath Close Farm

Mill Farm

MILL LANE

Paradise Plantation

7

Great Houndales Farm

125

Lowthorpe

WATER LANE

Lowthorpe Bridge

LC

Willow Farm

60

Little Houndales Farm

NORTH ST

PH

Well Close Farm

Nunnery Hill

Rose Farm

Broad Acres

GREEN LA

NEW ROAD

DRIFFIELD RD

Prep Sch

MIDDLE ST

East End

Jerry Plantation

OUT GATES

North End Farm

MAIN STREET

6

NEW ROAD

BRIDLINGTON RD

PO

Sleights Farm

Outgates Farm

59

Nafferton

Westfield Farm

Prim Sch

WESTGATE

PRIESTGATE

STATION RD

NETHERGATE

LC

BACKCARR LANE

LC

YO25

Millingdale Farm

LYNESYKES ROAD

5

MARKMAN LANE

Nafferton

LC

New Bridge

LC

Little Harmer Farm

Carr House

58

Sewage Works

Station Farm

WANSFORD ROAD

Nafferton Beck

Potter's Lodge

CARR LANE

HORDS LANE

Kelk Beck

4

FARTHING LANE

125

Whinhill Farm

Nafferton Carrs

57

WANSFORD RD

Pleasant Wood Farm

Rose Farm

CARR LANE

Cattleholmes

Turkers

3

Wansford Trout Farm

Driffield Canal

Weir

WANSFORD RD

THE SQUARE

Tythe Farm

Little Covert

Westfield

Golden Hill

Wansford Lock

Wansford

Mill Farm

Carr House Farm

Foston Beck

Greens Farm

2

125

56

Skerne

PH

Wansford Bridge

The Grange

Weir

Navigation Drain Bridge

Foston Carrs

Turf Carr

SHEEPDIKE LA

Village Farm

55

DRIFFIELD RD

BACK ST

MAIN ST

Skerne Grange

Thornham Farm

Foston Carrs

COWSLAMS LANE

MILL LANE

CRUCKLEY LANE

Mill Farm

Brewery Farm

Church Farm

Copper Hall

Weir

Nafferton Drain Bridge

Cruckley Animal Farm

1

Cleaves Farm

BRIGHAM LANE

B1249

Pan Carr

Grange Farm

FB and Weir

FOSTON LA

Hull Sides

54

A 04 **B** 05 **C** 06 07 **D** 07 **E** 08 09 **F**

For full street detail of the highlighted area see page 125.

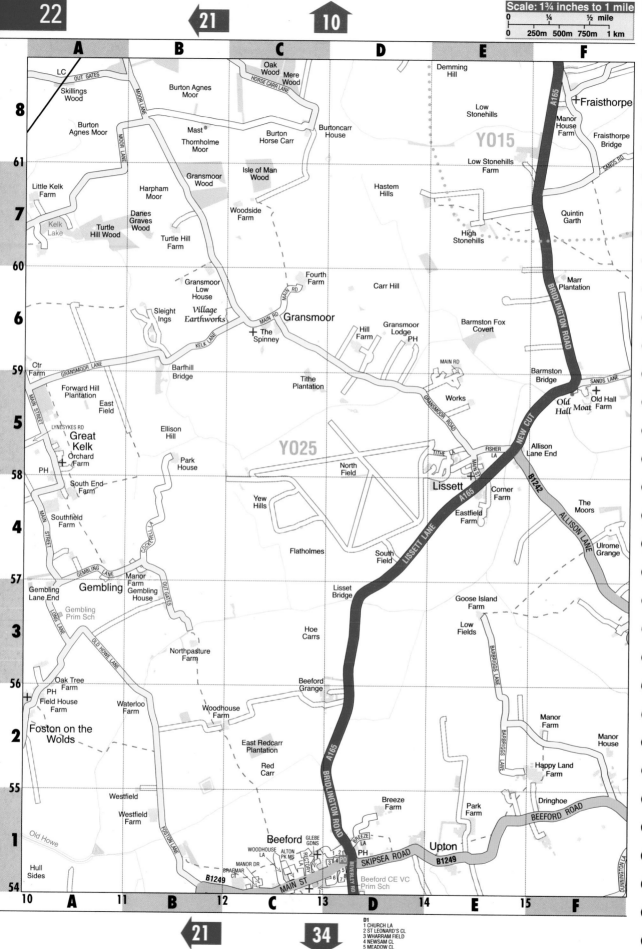

A   B   C   D   E   F

8

LC   OUT GATES
Skillings Wood
Burton Agnes Moor
Oak Wood
Mere Wood
HORSE CARR LANE
Demming Hill
A165
Fraisthorpe
Manor House Farm
Fraisthorpe Bridge

Burton Agnes Moor
MOOR LANE
Mast
Thornholme Moor
Burton Horse Carr
Burtoncarr House
Low Stonehills
YO15
SANDS RD

61

Gransmoor Wood
Isle of Man Wood
Low Stonehills Farm

Little Kelk Farm
Harpham Moor
Quintin Garth

7

Kelk Lake
Turtle Hill Wood
Danes Graves Wood
Turtle Hill Farm
Woodside Farm
Hastem Hills
High Stonehills

60

Gransmoor Low House
Fourth Farm
Carr Hill
Marr Plantation
BRIDLINGTON ROAD

6

Sleight Ings
Village Earthworks
MAIN RD
Gransmoor
The Spinney
Hill Farm
Gransmoor Lodge PH
Barmston Fox Covert

KELK LANE

MAIN RD
Barmston Bridge
SANDS LANE

59

Ctr Farm
GRANSMOOR LANE
Barfhill Bridge
Tithe Plantation
Works
Old Hall
Old Hall Moat
Old Hall Farm

Forward Hill Plantation
East Field
GRANSMOOR ROAD

5

MAIN STREET
LYNESYKES RD
Great Kelk
Ellison Hill
YO25
TITHE LA
FISHER LA
MAIN ST
NEW CUT
Allison Lane End
B1242

Orchard Farm
Park House
North Field
Lissett

58

PH
South End Farm
Corner Farm
The Moors
ALLISON LANE

4

MAIN STREET
Southfield Farm
COOKHILL LA
Yew Hills
A165
Eastfield Farm
Ulrome Grange

LISSETT LANE
Flatholmes
South Field

57

GEMBLING LANE
Gembling Lane End
Manor Farm
Gembling House
Gembling
OUT GATES
Lisset Bridge
Goose Island Farm

3

Gembling Prim Sch
LONG LANE
OLD HOWE LANE
Northpasture Farm
Hoe Carrs
Low Fields
BARBRIGGS LANE

56

Oak Tree Farm
PH
Field House Farm
Waterloo Farm
Woodhouse Farm
Beeford Grange

2

Foston on the Wolds
East Redcarr Plantation
Red Carr
BRIDLINGTON ROAD
A165
Breeze Farm
Manor Farm
Manor House

Happy Land Farm

55

Old Howe
Westfield
Breeze Farm
Park Farm
Dringhoe
BEEFORD ROAD

1

Hull Sides
Westfield Farm
FOSTON LANE
Beeford
GLEBE GDNS
BREEZE LA
PH
Upton
BARBRIGGS LANE
DUNNINGTON LA

WOODHOUSE LA
ALTON PK MS
PO
SKIPSEA ROAD
B1249
Beeford CE VC Prim Sch

54
B1249
MANOR DR
BRAEMAR CT
MAIN ST
BEVERLEY RD

10   A   11   B   12   C   13   D   14   E   15   F

D1
1 CHURCH LA
2 ST LEONARD'S CL
3 WHARRAM FIELD
4 NEWSAM CL
5 MEADOW CL
6 ASHLEIGH DR
7 BARONWOOD CR
8 WELBURN CT

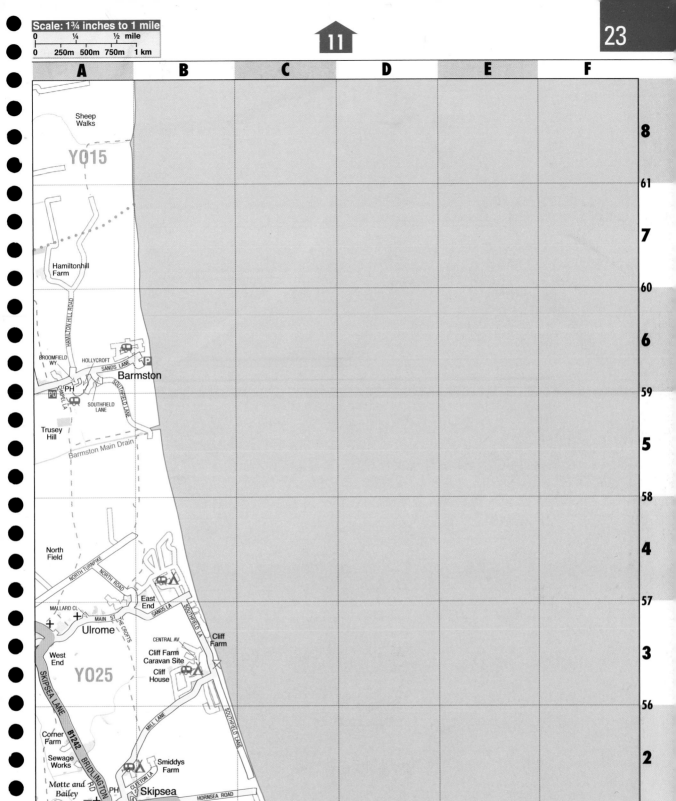

A | **B** | **C** | **D** | **E** | **F**

Sheep
Walks

YO15

8

61

7

Hamiltonhill
Farm

60

6

BROOMFIELD
WY   HOLLYCROFT   SANDS LANE   P
Barmston

59

PO PH CHAPEL LA
SOUTHFIELD
LANE   SOUTHFIELD LANE

Trusey
Hill

Barmston Main Drain

5

58

North
Field

4

57

NORTH TURNPIKE   NORTH ROAD
MALLARD CL   East
End   SANDS LA
MAIN ST   THE CROFTS   SOUTHFIELD LA
Ulrome   Cliff
Farm
CENTRAL AV

West
End   Cliff Farm
Caravan Site   YO25
Cliff
House   MILL LANE   SOUTHFIELD LANE

3

56

Corner
Farm   B1242   BRIDLINGTON RD
Sewage
Works   Smiddys
Farm
CLEETON LA

2

Motte and
Bailey   PH
Skipsea   HORNSEA ROAD

55

PO
Skipsea
Castle   MAIN ST
B1249   Great
Carr   5   Skipsea
Prim Sch
6 7   LEYS LANE

1 MANOR CL
2 BACK ST
3 CROSS ST
4 TOWN FARM CL
5 LEYS LA
6 CASTLE VW
7 CHAPEL GARTH   Southfield
Farm

B1242   HORNSEA ROAD

1

Brough
Carr   BEWHOLME LANE   Stream Dyke

54

16   **A**   17   **B**   18   **C**   19   **D**   20   **E**   21   **F**

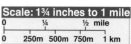

Scale: 1¾ inches to 1 mile

0   ¼   ½ mile
0   250m 500m 750m 1 km

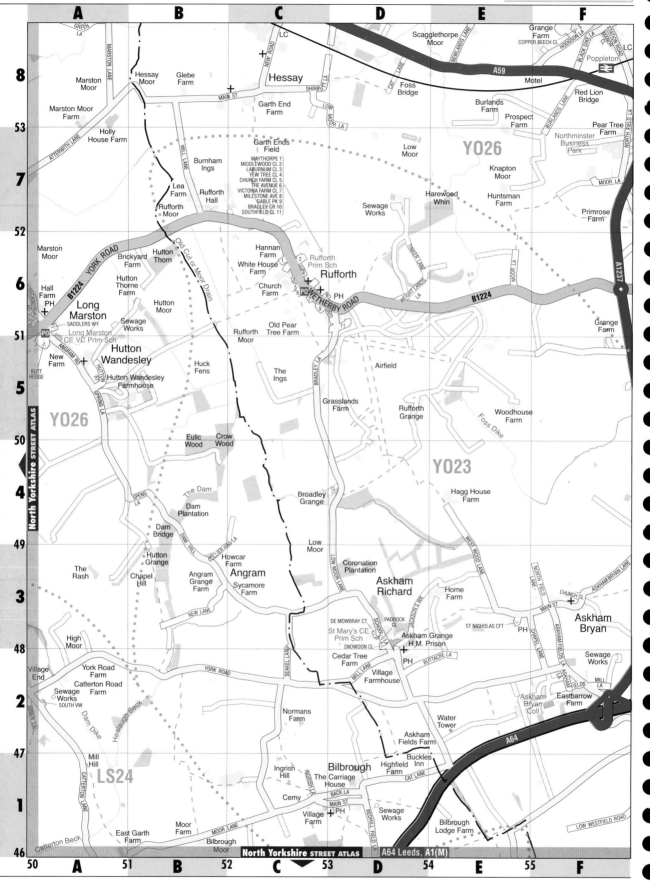

A   B   C   D   E   F

8

Marston Moor

Marston Moor Farm

Hessay Moor

Glebe Farm

New Road

Main St

Hessay

Shirbutt La

Garth End Farm

Low Moor La

Scagglethorpe Moor

Cat Lane

Newlands Lane

Copper Beech Cl

Grange Farm

A59

Black Dike La

Hodgson La

Station Road

Moor End La

LC

Poppleton

Motel

Red Lion Bridge

53

Atterwith Lane

Holly House Farm

Burnham Ings

Mill Lane

Garth Ends Field

MAYTHORPE 1
MIDDLEWOOD CL 2
LABURNUM CL 3
YEW TREE CL 4
CHURCH FARM CL 5
THE AVENUE 6
VICTORIA FARM CL 7
MILESTONE AVE 8
GABLE PK 9
BRADLEY CR 10
SOUTHFIELD CL 11

Low Moor

Foss Bridge

Burlands Farm

Prospect Farm

Burlands Lane

North Field La

Sewage Works

Harewood Whin

Knapton Moor

Northminster Business Park

Pear Tree Farm

YO26

Moor La

7

Lea Farm

Rufforth Hall

Rufforth Moor

Huntsman Farm

Primrose Farm

52

Marston Moor

York Road

B1224

Brickyard Farm

Hutton Thorn

Hutton Thorne Farm

Old Cut or Moor Drain

Mill Lane

Hannan Farm

White House Farm

Church Farm

Rufforth Prim Sch

Rufforth

Tinker Lane

Height Lands La

Moor La

B1224

Grange Farm

A1237

6

Hall Farm PH

Foxcroft Rd

Long Marston

Saddlers Wy

York Road

Hutton Moor

Wetherby Road

PH

PH

51

PO

Long Marston CE VC Prim Sch

Sewage Works

Rufforth Moor

Old Pear Tree Farm

Bradley La

Angram Rd

Hutton Wandesley

New Farm

BUTT HEDGE

Hutton La

Spring La

Huck Fens

The Ings

Airfield

Rufforth Grange

Woodhouse Farm

Foss Dike

YO26

5

Hutton Wandesley Farmhouse

Grasslands Farm

50

Eulic Wood

Crow Wood

YO23

4

Speng La

The Dam

Dam Plantation

Broadley Grange

Hagg House Farm

West Wood Lane

49

Dam Bridge

Dam Hill

Collier Hag La

Howcar Farm

Low Moor

Coronation Plantation

Low Moor Lane

North Field Lane

Ashham Bryan Lane

Church Cl

3

The Rash

Hutton Grange

Chapel Hill

Angram Grange Farm

Angram

Sycamore Farm

Askham Richard

Home Farm

Main St

St Nicholas Cft

PH

Chapel Lane

Askham Bryan

48

High Moor

New Lane

DE MOWBRAY CT

St Mary's CE Prim Sch

Snowdon Cl

Paddock Cl

Jackson's Wk

School La

Askham Grange H.M. Prison

PH

Buttacre La

Askham Fields La

Sewage Works

Mill La

2

Village End

York Road Farm

Catterton Road Farm

Sewage Works

South Vw

York Road

Seakel Lane

Cedar Tree Farm

Village Farmhouse

Mill Lane

Water Tower

Askham Bryan Coll

Eastbarrow Farm

A64

47

Abber La

Dam Dike

Healaugh Beck

Normans Farm

Catterton Lane

Ingrish Hill

Bilbrough

The Carriage House

Askham Fields Farm

Highfield Farm

Buckles Inn

Cat Lane

1

Mill Hill

LS24

Cemy

Back La

Ingbrister La

Redhill Field La

Sewage Works

Bilbrough Lodge Farm

Low Westfield Road

East Garth Farm

Moor Farm

Moor Lane

Village Farm

Main St

PH

Bilbrough Moor

Catterton Beck

46

A64 Leeds, A1(M)

50   A   51   B   52   C   53   D   54   E   55   F

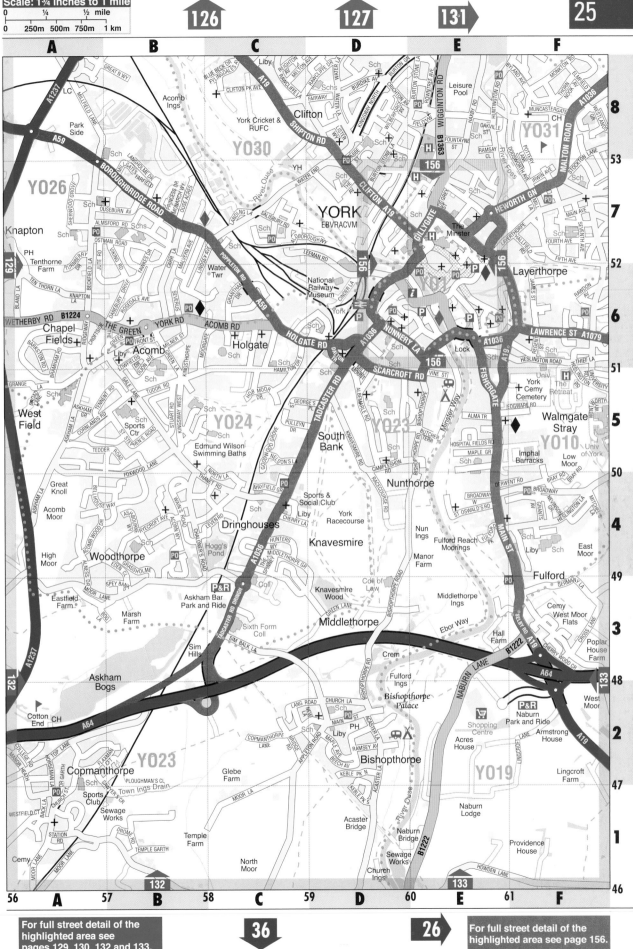

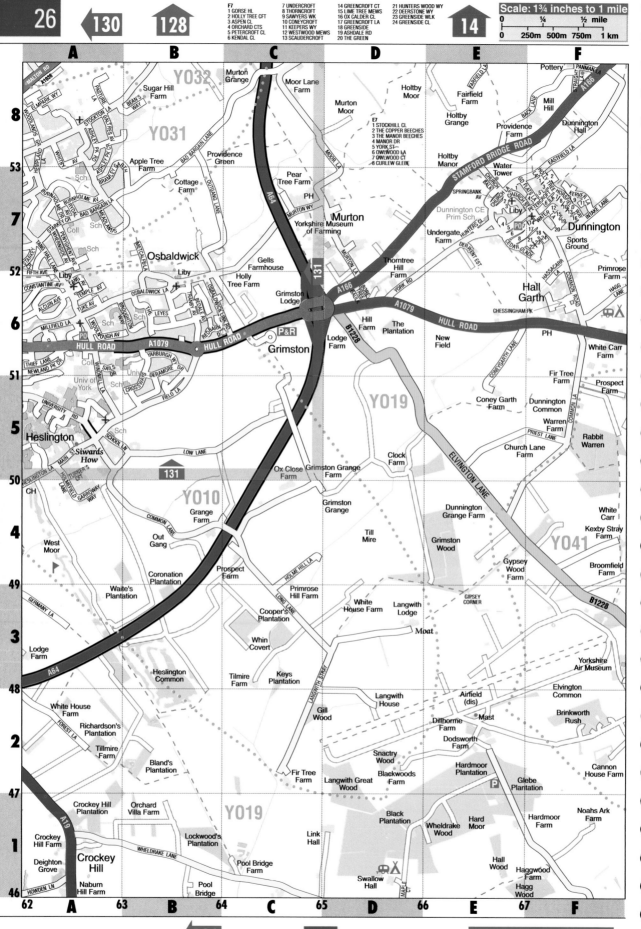

F7
1 GORSE HL
2 HOLLY TREE CFT
3 ASPEN CL
4 ORCHARD CTS
5 PETERCROFT CL
6 KENDAL CL
7 UNDERCROFT
8 THORNCROFT
9 SAWYERS WK
10 CONEYCROFT
11 KEEPERS WY
12 WESTWOOD MEWS
13 SCAUDERCROFT
14 GREENCROFT CT
15 LIME TREE MEWS
16 OX CALDER CL
17 GREENCROFT LA
18 GREENSIDE
19 ASHDALE RD
20 THE GREEN
21 HUNTERS WOOD WY
22 GREENSTONE WY
23 DEERSTONE WY
24 GREENSIDE WLK

For full street detail of the highlighted area see page 131.

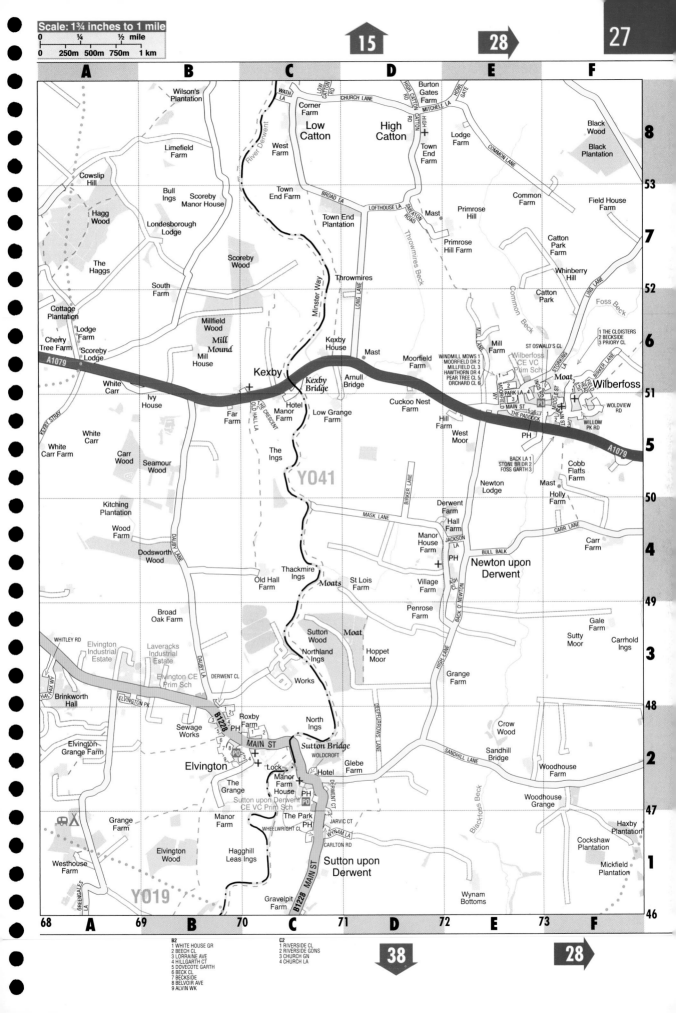

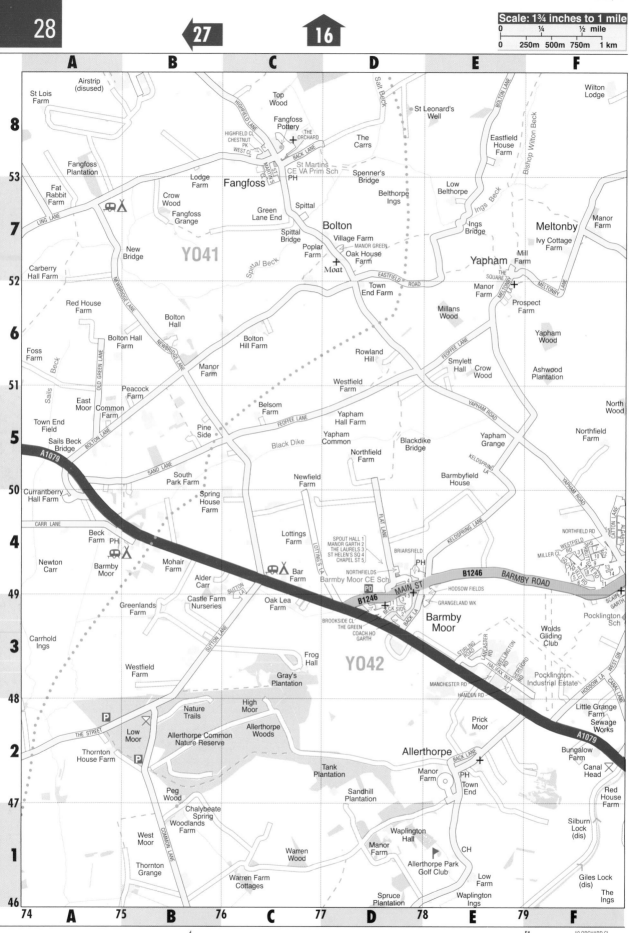

Scale: 1¾ inches to 1 mile

0   ¼   ½   mile
0   250m   500m   750m   1 km

A **B** **C** **D** **E** **F**

St Lois Farm
Airstrip (disused)
Top Wood
Wilton Lodge

8

Fangfoss Pottery
THE ORCHARD
St Leonard's Well
Bolton Lane
Bishop Wilton Beck

HIGHFIELD CL
CHESTNUT PK
WEST CL
HIGHFIELD LANE
The Carrs
Eastfield House Farm

53
Fangfoss Plantation
BACK LANE
St Martins CE VA Prim Sch
PH
Spenner's Bridge
Low Belthorpe

Fat Rabbit Farm
Lodge Farm
ST MARTINS CL
Fangfoss
Belthorpe Ings
Manor Farm

7
Crow Wood
Fangfoss Grange
Green Lane End
Spittal
Bolton
Ings Bridge
Meltonby
Ivy Cottage Farm

LING LANE
New Bridge
Spittal Bridge
Poplar Farm
Village Farm
MANOR GREEN
Ings Farm
Yapham
Mill Farm

52
Carberry Hall Farm
Spittal Beck
Oak House Farm
Moat
EASTFIELD ROAD
Manor Farm
THE SQUARE
Prospect Farm
MELTONBY LANE
Manor Farm

NEWBRIDGE LANE
Town End Farm
Millans Wood
Yapham Wood

6
Foss Farm
Red House Farm
Bolton Hall
Bolton Hill Farm
Rowland Hill
Smylett Hall
Crow Wood
Ashwood Plantation

Sails Beck
OLD GREEN LANE
Manor Farm
Westfield Farm
FEOFFEE LANE
YAPHAM ROAD

51
East Moor
Peacock Farm
Belsom Farm
Yapham Hall Farm
North Wood

Sails
BOLTON LANE
Common Farm
Pine Side
FEOFFEE LANE
Yapham Common
KELDSPRING LA
Yapham Grange
Northfield Farm

5
Town End Field
Sails Beck Bridge
Black Dike
Northfield Farm
Blackdike Bridge
YAPHAM ROAD

A1079
SAND LANE
South Park Farm
Newfield Farm
Barmbyfield House

50
Currantberry Hall Farm
Spring House Farm
FLAT LANE

CARR LANE
Beck Farm
PH
Lottings Farm
SPOUT HALL 1
MANOR GARTH 2
THE LAURELS 3
ST HELEN'S SQ 4
CHAPEL ST 5
Briarsfield
PH
NORTHFIELD RD
WESTFIELD RD
MILLER CL
CATTON LANE

4
Newton Carr
Barmby Moor
Mohair Farm
Bar Farm
NORTHFIELDS
Barmby Moor CE Sch
B1246
BARMBY ROAD

49
Greenlands Farm
Alder Carr
Castle Farm Nurseries
Oak Lea Farm
PO
B1246
MAIN ST
BACK SIDE
BACK LA
HODSOW FIELDS
GRANGELAND WK
SCAIFE GARTH
Pocklington Sch

SUTTON LA
BROOKSIDE CL
THE GREEN
COACH HO GARTH
Barmby Moor
Wolds Gliding Club

3
Carrhold Ings
Westfield Farm
Frog Hall
Gray's Plantation
YO42
STIRLING ROAD
LANCASTER RD
WELLINGTON RD
HEREFORD
HALIFAX WAY
Pocklington Industrial Estate
HODSOW LA
CANAL LANE
WEST GN

48
SUTTON LA
MANCHESTER RD
HAMDEN RD

THE STREET
Nature Trails
High Moor
Allerthorpe Woods
Prick Moor
Little Grange Farm
Sewage Works

2
P
Low Moor
Allerthorpe Common Nature Reserve
Manor Farm
Allerthorpe
PH
Town End
BACK LANE
A1079
Bungalow Farm
Canal Head

Thornton House Farm
P
Peg Wood
Tank Plantation
Sandhill Plantation
Red House Farm

47
Chalybeate Spring Woodlands Farm
Silburn Lock (dis)

West Moor
COMMON LANE
Warren Wood
Manor Farm
Waplington Hall
CH
Giles Lock (dis)

1
Thornton Grange
Warren Farm Cottages
Allerthorpe Park Golf Club
Low Farm
The Ings

46
Spruce Plantation
Waplington Ings

74 **A** **75** **B** **76** **C** **77** **D** **78** **E** **79** **F**

F4
1 DALMAIS CL
2 BURNS CL
3 WESTFIELD CL
4 ORCHARD GD
5 WELLINGTON CL
6 MEADOWFIELD CL
7 NORTHFIELD RISE
8 HALIFAX CL
9 ORCHARD WY
10 ORCHARD CL
11 ST JOHN'S CL
12 NORTHFIELD CL
13 SHERBUTTGATE DR
14 SHERBUTTGATE RD
15 ANDREW'S CT

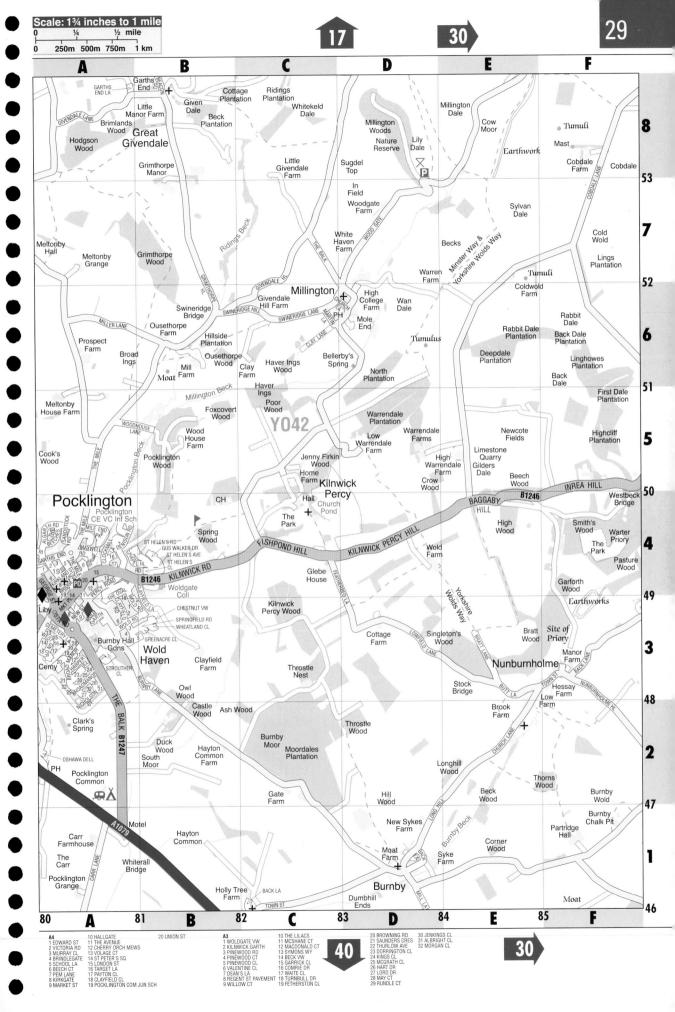

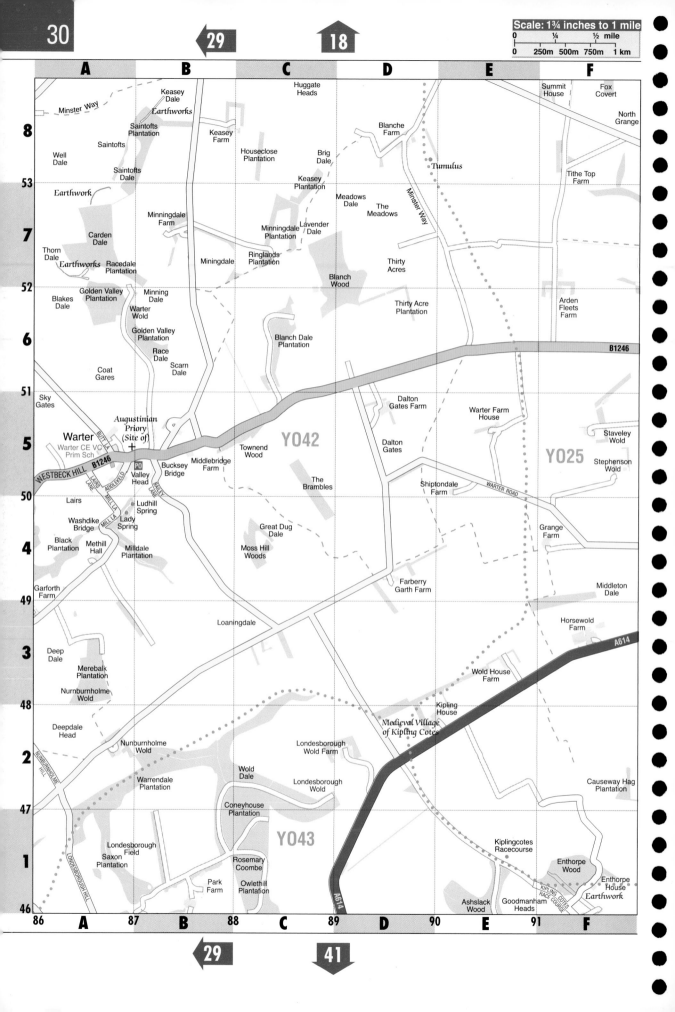

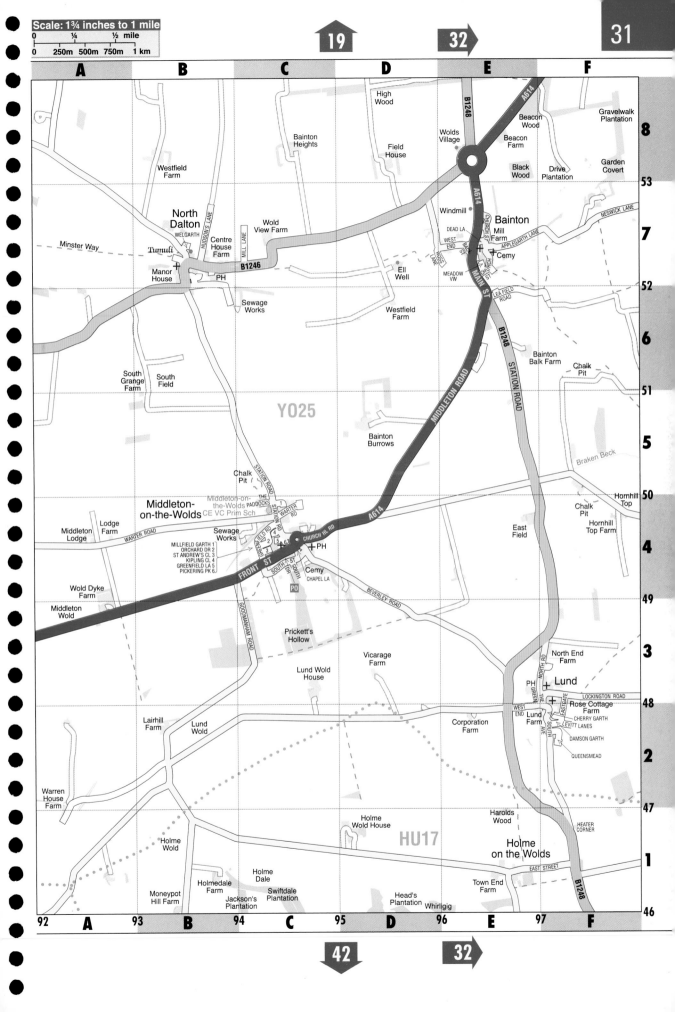

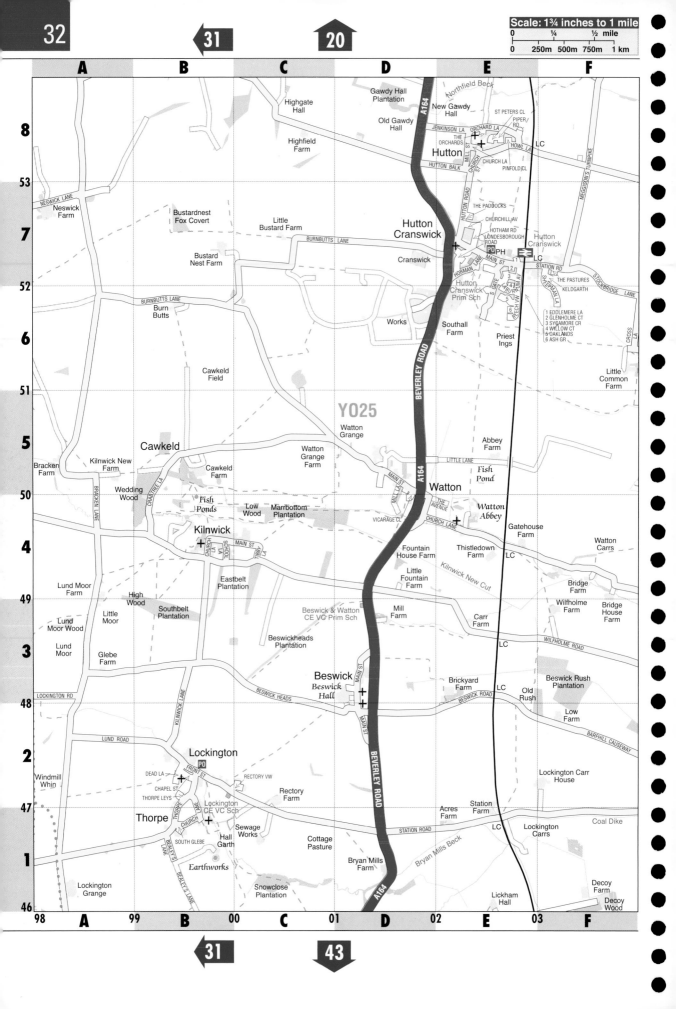

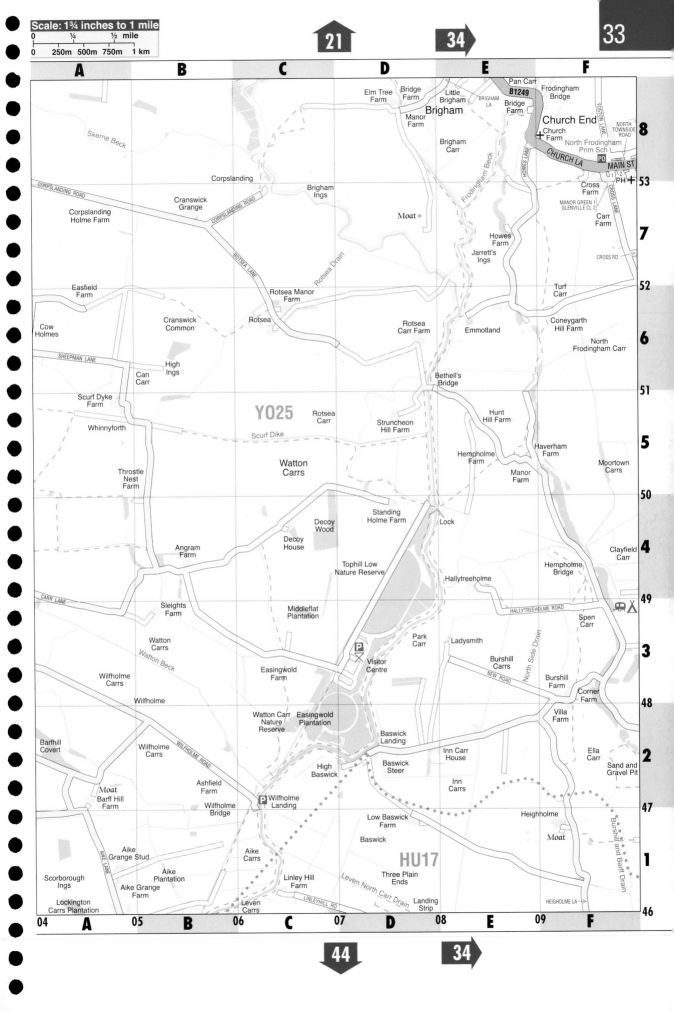

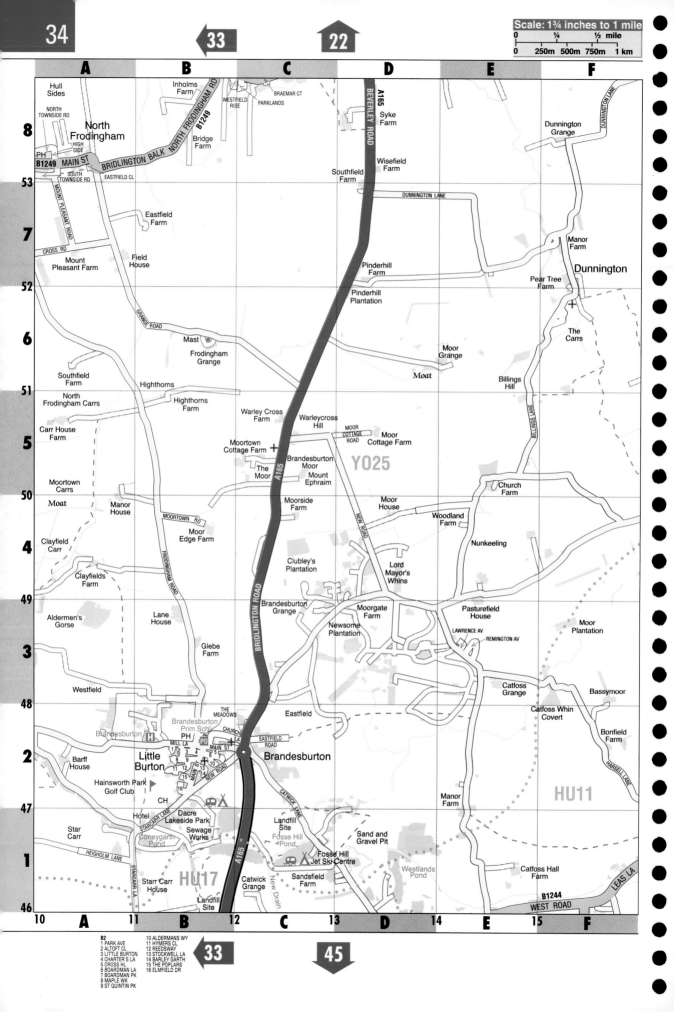

A **B** **C** **D** **E** **F**

Skipsea Grange
B1242 HORNSEA ROAD
CH
Far Grange Leisure Park
Far Grange Country Park
Visitor Centre
Rec
Low Bonwick
Low Skirlington Farm
High Skirlington
High Bonwick
High Grounds
YO25
SKIPSEA ROAD
North Field
LONG LANE
Works
North End Farm
GARDHAM LANE
Cliff Farm
CLIFF RD
North End
NORTH RD
CALAM VILLAS
CHURCH LA
CANHAM LA
STON RD
Hill Top Farm
Field House Farm
NORTH RD
Hall
PH
Atwick
HORNSEA ROAD
Laburnum Farm
FAR LA
WATER LA
Bewholme Prim Sch
Bewholme
ATWICK RD
Model Farm
CATFOSS RD
SEATON RD
Double Gates
Little Atwick
Bewholme Lane
Little Arram
B1242
134
Eastfield Farm
CLIFF RD
WESTHOLME AV
ALMANAV
CLIFF ROAD
North Cliff
Arram Hall
Northfield House
ATWICK ROAD
Birk Crag
BELVEDERE PK
Northfield Farm
Springfield Farm
HU18
P
NORTHGATE
ASHBOURN DR
DRAYCOTT AV
CARLTON AV
NICHOLAS DR
CLIFTON ST
Hotel
Seaton Hold
BEWHOLME LANE
HU11
Honeysuckle Farm
Westfield Farm
134
Sports Ground
WESTWOOD AV
Sch
EASTGATE
H
MARINE DR
ESPL
134
Liby
P
PO
NEW ROAD
SANDS LA
Leisure Centre
HORNSEA
Poplar Farm
MILL LANE
Coll
PH
NEWBEGIN
SOUTH PROM
MARTEGARTH LANE
Seaton Grange
Brockholme
SEATON RD
Swan I
B1244
P
PH
Council Offices
SOUTHGATE
Cemy
HORNSEA BURTON RD
BREAMER LANE
Common Farm
Seaton
Buttercup Farm
Lady I
Hornsea Mere Nature Reserve
HULL ROAD
Beverley Farm
South Cliff
MAIN ST
PO
B1244
HORNSEA ROAD
WASSAND ROAD
Low Wood
Hornsea Rail Trail
MARLBOROUGH
EDENFIELD AV
TRINITY
PO
PICKERING RD
Hornsea Burton
MANOR PARK
BUTCHERS ROW
GRUNDILL
Wassand Hall & Gardens
Decoy Plantation
Southorpe Village
Southorpe Farm
SOUTHORPE RD
POTTERS WAY
ROLSTON RD
B1242
134

8 53 7 52 6 51 5 50 4 49 3 48 2 47 1 46

16 **A** 17 **B** 18 **C** 19 **D** 20 **E** 21 **F** 46

For full street detail of the highlighted area see page 134.

A1
1 COMMON LA
2 NICHOLSON LA
3 BACK LA
4 WITTYS PADDOCK
5 MIDDLE LA

132 **133**

48

D8
1 MAIN ST
2 FERRY FARM CL
3 MAYPOLE GR
4 ST MATTHEW'S CL

F1
1 COPPERGATE
2 ELMS CL
3 NORTHFIELD LA

1 NABURN PK MEWS
2 PALMES CL

North Yorkshire Street Atlas

Moor Farm
Copmanthorpe Lodge
Copmanthorpe Wood
Greenland Wood
Copmanthorpe Grange
Brocket Wood
Woolas Hall Farm
Moat
Old Appleton Farm
Batrudding Farm
Kennel Wood
Hell Hole Wood
Home Farm
Walnut Grove
East Ings
Sicklebit Wood
Ryther Ings
Button Hill Farm
Bracken Hill Hall Farm
Cawood Park

Homestead Farm
Springfield Farm
Park Farm
Woodside Farm
Beechlands Farm
Roebuck Farm
Stonebridge Farm
Whitemoor Farm
Acaster Malbis Moor
Whinny Hills
Mount Pleasant Farm
Nova Scotia Farm
Whin Covert
Stub Wood
Airfield (dis)
Hales Hill Farm
Haverland Farm
College Farm
Ferry Farm
Acaster Selby
Priory Farm
Manor Farm
River Farm
Stillingfleet Ings
Stillingfleet House
Hill Top Farm
Avenue Farm
Lord's Ings
The Marshes
Wharfe Ings
Wharfe's Mouth
Kelfield Ings
The Marshes
Cawood Ings

Foss Farm
Moor End
Acaster Malbis
Cowper La
Moor End
North End Farm
Naburn CE Prim Sch
Naburn
Naburn House Farm
Highfield Farmhouse
Yew Tree Cl
Holly Cl
Tyn Garth
River Ouse
Naburn Ings
Naburn Moor
Gillrudding Grange
Manor Farm
Weir
Lock
Naburn Grange
Bell Hall
Wood End Farm
Naburn Wood
Common Plantation
Park's Farm
Park Farmhouse
South Ings
Moreby Hall
Woodlands Farm
Birkhill Farm
Moreby Wood
Moreby Park
Moreby Farr Wood
Parson Wood
Home Farm
Moreby Ings
Moreby Grange Farm
Stillingfleet Beck
Beck Farm
Wood House Farm
Five Acre Plantation
Hill Farm
Escrick Grange Farm
Orchard Farm
Mast
Stillingfleet Grange
Heron Wood
Laburnum Gr
Stillingfleet Wood
Stillingfleet
Stillingfleet Moor
Stillingfleet Mine
Mount Farm
Hill Top Farm
Stillingfleet Moor
Kelfield Moor
Kelfield Grange
Kelfield Wood
Mount Pleasant Farm
Kelfield Ridge Farm
Moor Farm
Dunn's Plantation
Storkneys Hill
Moor End
Kelfield Lodge
Kelfield
Manor Farm
Village Farm
Claret House Farm
Pear Tree Farm
Wheel Hall
Riccall CP School

YO23
YO8
YO19

B1222 B1223
York Rd
Moor La
Trans Pennine Trail
Cawood Rd
Church
York Road
Riccall Lane
Main St
Broad Lane
Green La
Back Lane
Daw Lane
Acaster Lane
Acaster Avenue
Wood Lane
River Wharfe
River Ouse

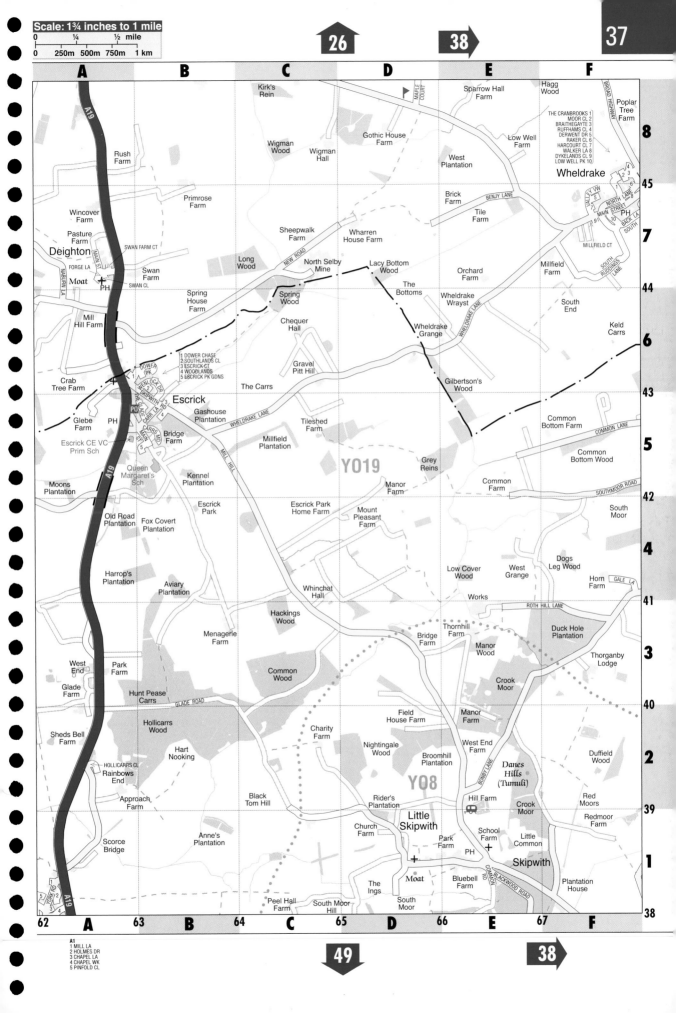

A B C D E F

8

45

7

44

6

43

5

42

4

41

3

2

39

1

38

68 A 69 B 70 C 71 D 72 E 73 F

Wheldrake

Wheldrake CE Prim Sch
BROADLANDS
GREENGALES CT
BLUE SLATES CL
COURTNEYS
GREENGALES LANE
DERWENT PK
CHURCH LANE
MAIN ST
BACK SOUTH
FORGE CL
PO

1 DALTON HL
2 KITTY GARTH
3 ST HELEN'S RISE
4 CHURCH CL

Mount Pleasant
Cheesecake Farm
Gravelpit Plantation
SOUTH RD
B1228 COMMON LANE
Mayfield Grange Farm
Four Beck Ends
Sutton Rush
Eller Carr
The Carr
Town's Ings

The Carr
South Wood
River Derwent
Sutton Farm
Broomhill Plantation
Hagg Bridge
Hagg Bridge Farm
Storwood Carr
Rossmoor Grange
Rossmoor Farm
The Grange
Frogs Nest Farm
Westfield Farm

HAGG LANE
NARROW LA
BALLHALL LANE
GATEHEAD LANE
Storwood Grange
Storwood
Rossmoor Lodge
Oakland Farm
Park Wood
Grove Farm
Farm Wood

INGS LANE
Old Course of the River Derwent
Wheldrake Ings Nature Reserve
White House Farm
GENERAL LANE
Eastroad Plantation
Stackyard Plantation

Suss Carrs
Moat
Quakers' Wood
West Farm
Park House Farm
Woodside Lodge Farm
The Rush
South Wood
Ross Moor

Mattie Brown Wood
Thicket Priory
Home Farm
Storwood Ings
North Hills
Ball Hall Farm
The Whin
Boundary Farm

Crinklety Wood
Whincover Wood
YO19
Langrickgate Field
Forest Farm
Acre Farm

North Moor
COMMON LANE
FERRY LANE
Cottingwith Lock
PH
Cemy
Langrickgate LA
North Moor
Willow Tree Farm
South Acre Farm

Thornums Wood
CANAL RD
CHURCH LA
ST MARYS CL
East Cottingwith
REDCAP LANE
Grange Farm
East Cottingwith Common
B1228

East End PH
INGS LA
GREEN LA
MAIN ST
HAG LANE

South Moor
SOUTHMOOR ROAD
WESTFIELD LA
Glebe Farm
Thorganby Ings
Red Cap Farm
North Ross Farm
South Ross Farm
New Moor

Thorganby Hall Wood
Thorganby
River Derwent
East Cottingwith Ings
Mill House
FOG LANE
Spring House
BRIDGES LANE
Pond Farm

Ings View Farm
INGS RD
Yew Tree Farm
Whitegate Bridge
LONG RAMPART

Gale Farm
WOODHOUSE LA
YO42
Fox Covert

Woodfield Farm
East Lodge
Sike Bridge
Ellerton Common
New Lands
Blue Slates Farm
Ruddings Wood

Scruton Wood
COW PASTURE LA
Priory Farm
Lofty Farm
South View Farm
North Grange
BOWLAND LANE
RUDDINGS LA

East Grange Farm
MAIN ST
BACK LA
Priory Farm
Ellerton
PH
COTTAM LANE
SHORTACRE LANE
Short Acre Farm
Aughton Ruddings

Far Woods
Ellerton Ings
Hall Farm
South Grange

Lawns House Farm
YO8
North Duffield Lodge
Lodge Farm
Aughton Stud Farm
Wentsford House Farm
B1228
BIRK LA
HANKINS LA
Aughton Ruddings Grange
LONG LANE
Glebe Farm

Red Moors
HIGHFIELD LA
Great Wood
MAIN ST
BACK LA
Aughton
PASTURE LANE
BACK LANE
TOWNEND RD
Aughton Plantation
Longlane Plantation

Park Farm
North Duffield Carrs
Aughton Ings
York House Farm
Aughton Common
CH
Autherthaws Farm
Common End Plantation

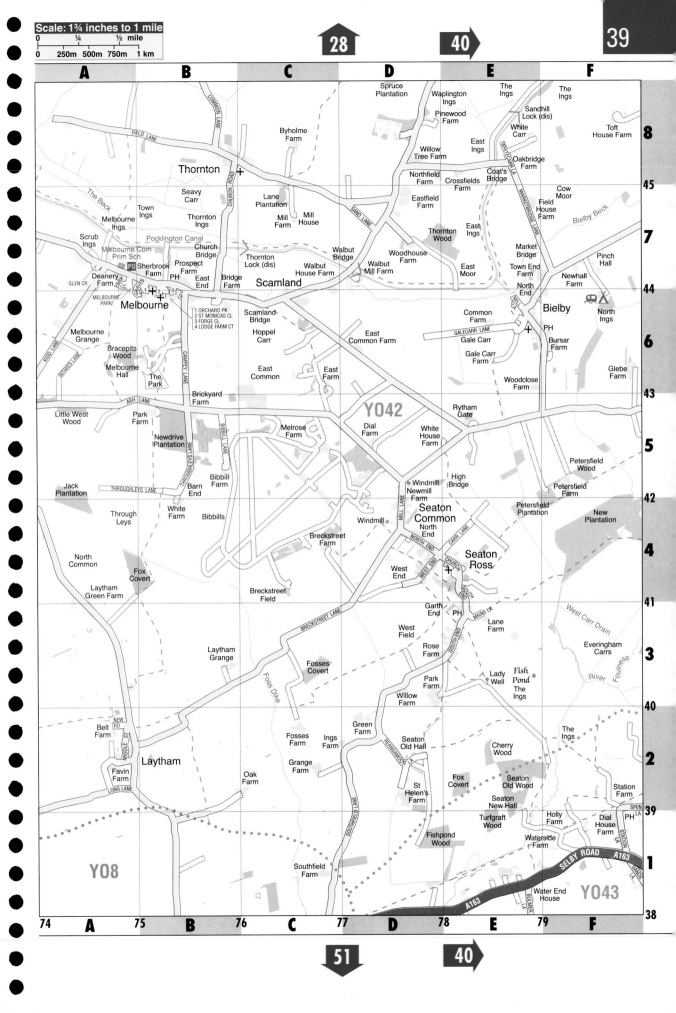

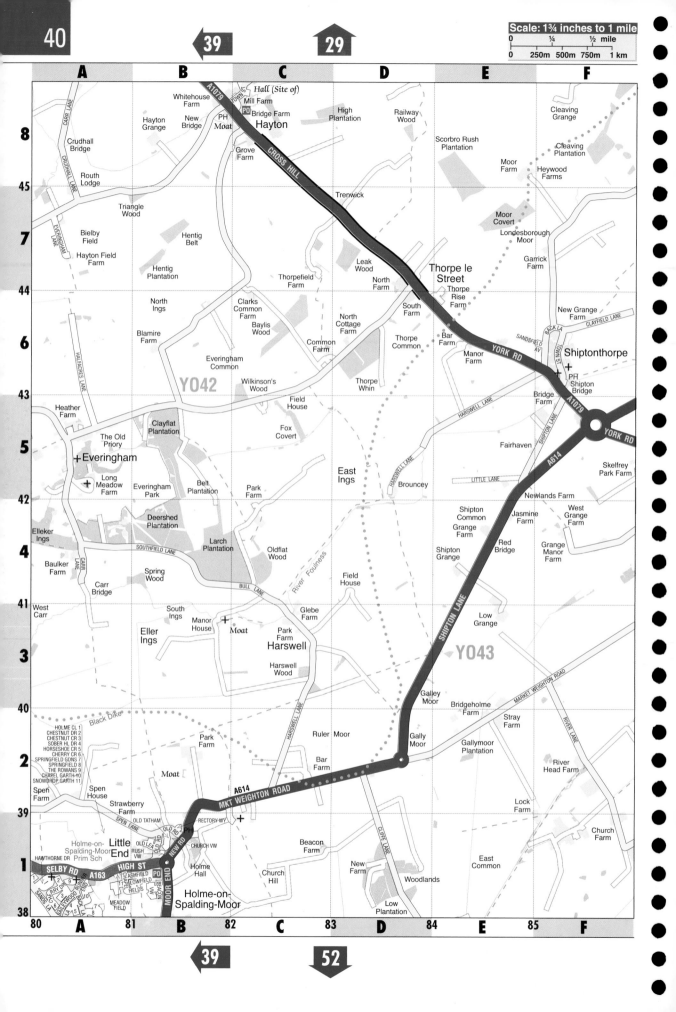

Scale: 1¾ inches to 1 mile

0   ¼   ½ mile
0   250m   500m   750m   1 km

A   B   C   D   E   F

8

Hall (Site of)

CARR LANE

Whitehouse Farm

Mill Farm

High Plantation

Railway Wood

Cleaving Grange

New Bridge

PH Moat

Hayton

Cleaving Plantation

Hayton Grange

Bridge Farm

Scorbro Rush Plantation

Moor Farm

Heywood Farms

Crudhall Bridge

Grove Farm

CROSS HILL

45

Routh Lodge

Trenwick

Moor Covert

CRUDHALL LANE

Londesborough Moor

Triangle Wood

7

EVERINGHAM LANE

Bielby Field

Hentig Belt

Leak Wood

Garrick Farm

Hayton Field Farm

Hentig Plantation

Thorpefield Farm

North Farm

Thorpe le Street

44

Clarks Common Farm

North Farm

Thorpe Rise Farm

New Grange Farm

CLAYFIELD LANE

North Ings

South Farm

SANDSFIELD

BACK LA

HALFACRES LANE

Baylis Wood

YO42

Common Farm

North Cottage Farm

Thorpe Common

Bar Farm

YORK RD

Shiptonthorpe

6

Blamire Farm

Everingham Common

Manor Farm

BACK LA

PH

Shipton Bridge

43

Heather Farm

Wilkinson's Wood

Field House

Thorpe Whin

HARSWELL LANE

Bridge Farm

A1079

YORK RD

Clayflat Plantation

Fox Covert

HARSWELL LANE

SHIPTON LANE

Fairhaven

5

The Old Priory

East Ings

Brouncey

A614

Skelfrey Park Farm

✝ Everingham

LITTLE LANE

Long Meadow Farm

Everingham Park

Belt Plantation

Park Farm

Newlands Farm

42

CARR LANE

Deershed Plantation

Shipton Common Grange Farm

Jasmine Farm

West Grange Farm

Elleker Ings

SOUTHFIELD LANE

Larch Plantation

Oldflat Wood

River Foulness

Shipton Grange

Red Bridge

Grange Manor Farm

4

Baulker Farm

Spring Wood

Carr Bridge

BULL LANE

Field House

SHIPTON LANE

41

West Carr

South Ings

Manor House

✝ Moat

Glebe Farm

YO43

Low Grange

Eller Ings

Park Farm

MARKET WEIGHTON ROAD

RIVER LANE

3

HARSWELL LANE

Harswell

Harswell Wood

Galley Moor

Bridgeholme Farm

Stray Farm

40

Black Dike

Park Farm

Gally Moor

Gallymoor Plantation

River Head Farm

HOLME CL 1
CHESTNUT DR 2
CHESTNUT CR 3
SOBER HL DR 4
HORSESHOE CR 5
CHERRY CR 6
SPRINGFIELD GDNS 7
SPRINGFIELD 8
THE ROWANS 9
CHAPEL GARTH 10
SNOWDROP GARTH 11

2

Moat

Ruler Moor

Bar Farm

A614

Lock Farm

Spen Farm

Spen House

MKT WEIGHTON ROAD

CLIFFE LANE

Church Farm

Strawberry Farm

SPEN LANE

OLD TATHAM

RECTORY WY

✝

39

OLD LEA

OLD RD

NEW RD

PH

East Common

Little End

RUSH VW

CHURCH VW

Beacon Farm

Holme-on-Spalding-Moor Prim Sch

HAWTHORNE DR

OLD RD

Holme Hall

New Farm

1

SELBY RD

A163

HIGH ST

MOOR END

BEACON

Church Hill

Woodlands

PO

Holme-on-Spalding-Moor

Low Plantation

38

80   A   81   B   82   C   83   D   84   E   85   F

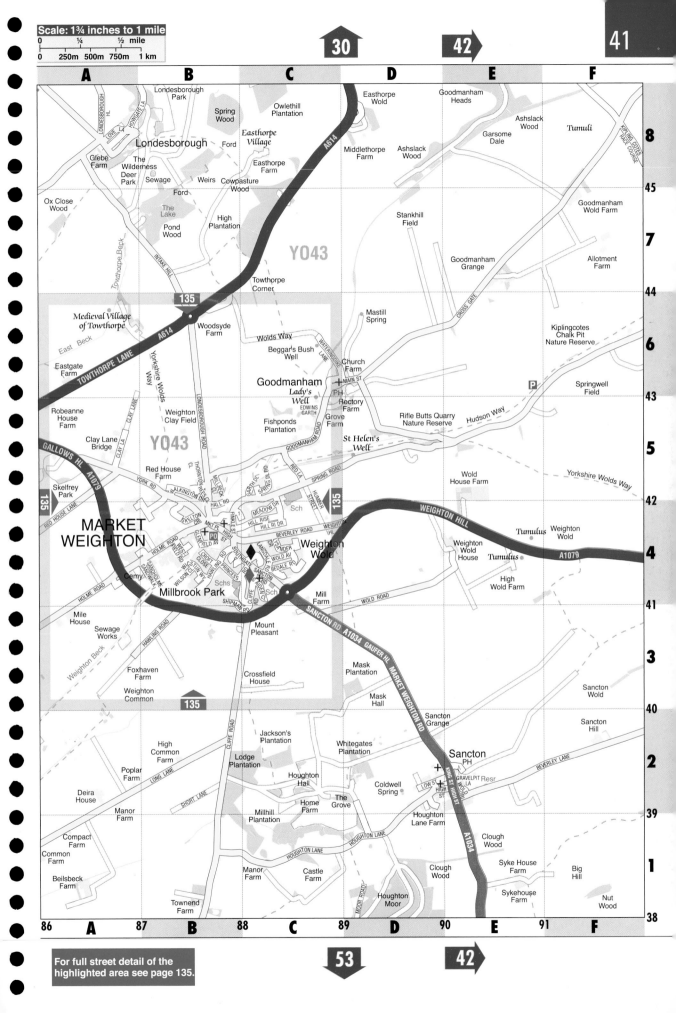

Scale: 1¾ inches to 1 mile

0   ¼   ½   mile
0   250m 500m 750m 1 km

30   42

A   B   C   D   E   F

Londesborough Park
Owlethill Plantation
Spring Wood
Easthorpe Wold
Goodmanham Heads
Ashslack Wood
Tumuli
Kiplingcotes Race Course
8

Londesborough
Glebe Farm
The Wilderness Deer Park
Sewage
Weirs
Ford
Ford
Cowpasture Wood
Easthorpe Village
Eastthorpe Farm
Middlethorpe Farm
Ashslack Wood
Garsome Dale

45

Ox Close Wood
The Lake
Pond Wood
High Plantation
YO43
Stankhill Field
Goodmanham Wold Farm
7

Towthorpe Beck
Intake Hill
Towthorpe Corner
Goodmanham Grange
Cross Gate
Allotment Farm

44

135
Medieval Village of Towthorpe
A614
Woodsyde Farm
Wolds Way
Beggar's Bush Well
Mastill Spring
Kiplingcotes Chalk Pit Nature Reserve
6

East Beck
Eastgate Farm
TOWTHORPE LANE
Yorkshire Wolds Way
Weighton Clay Field
Waterhouse Lane
Church Farm
Main St
PH
Springwell Field

43

Robeanne House Farm
Clay Lane
Clay Lane Bridge
Londesborough Road
YO43
Red House Farm
Fishponds Plantation
Goodmanham
Lady's Well
Edwins Garth
Rectory Farm
Grove Farm
Rifle Butts Quarry Nature Reserve
Hudson Way
5

Gallows Hl
A1079
Skelfrey Park
135
Red House Lane
York Rd
Thornton Rd
Walkington Dr
Millbeck
Hall Rd
Garth Dr
Spring Dr
Red La
Spring Road
Humber Street
St Helen's Well
Yorkshire Wolds Way
42

MARKET WEIGHTON
Holme Road
Cemy
Sandwell
Sancton Dr
Meadow Dr
Hill Rise
Hill Ri Dr
Beverley Road
Weighton Hl
Wold Av
Bedale Rd
Weighton Wold
Wold House Farm
Sch
WEIGHTON HILL
Weighton Wold House
Tumulus
Tumulus
Weighton Wold
A1079
4

Millbrook Park
Holme Road
Hawling Road
Shipman Rd
Cliffe Rd
Sch
Mill Farm
Wold Road
High Wold Farm
41

Mile House
Sewage Works
Weighton Beck
Foxhaven Farm
Mount Pleasant
SANCTON RD A1034
GAUFER HL
MARKET WEIGHTON RD
Mask Plantation
3

Weighton Common
135
Crossfield House
Cliffe Road
Jackson's Plantation
Mask Hall
Sancton Grange
Sancton Wold
40

High Common Farm
Long Lane
Lodge Plantation
Whitegates Plantation
Sancton
PH
Sancton Hill
2

Poplar Farm
Short Lane
Houghton Hall
Coldwell Spring
King St
Low St
High St
Gravelpit Resr
Beverley Lane

Deira House
Manor Farm
Millhill Plantation
Home Farm
The Grove
Houghton Lane Farm
Clough Wood
39

Compact Farm
Common Farm
Beilsbeck Farm
Townend Farm
Manor Farm
Castle Farm
Houghton Lane
Moor Road
Houghton Moor
Clough Wood
A1034
Syke House Farm
Sykehouse Farm
Big Hill
Nut Wood
1

38

86   A   87   B   88   C   89   D   90   E   91   F

For full street detail of the highlighted area see page 135.

53   42

41
31

Scale: 1¾ inches to 1 mile

0   ¼   ½ mile
0   250m   500m   750m   1 km

A **B** **C** **D** **E** **F**

Kiplingcotes
Money Hill
(Tumulus)
High Wold
Fall

Raikeshill
Plantation

Reservoir
Clump

Bryans
Plantation

South
Dalton

Tom Fisher
Plantation

B1248

Admirals
Long
Dale

Short
Dale

Nut
Balks

PH
WEST END
MAIN ST
The
Mere

Dunkeld
End

Holme
Farm

Kiplingcotes
Farm

PARK ROAD

Dalton
Wood

Dalton
Hall

Dalton
Park

Sewage
Works

Dunkeld
Bridge

MERE LANE

Cow
Bridge

8

45

Kipling Cotes Race Course

South
Dalton Wold

Heads
Plantation

Sewage
Works

Walk House
Farm

Old Dale
Plantation

Gabbetis's
Plantation

Holme
Farm

7

Southwold
Farm

Earthwork
Tumulus

Sir John's
Plantation

Sir Charles's
Clump

WARTER ROAD

Manor
Farm

44

P
Hudson Way

Etton
Wold

Westwood
Farm

Etton

6

Earthwork
Goodmanham
Lodge

Chalk
Bridge

Westwood
House

Etton West
Wood

MAIN ST

ELLERINGTON LA
PH

Bank
House
Farm

High
Farm

43

KIPLINGCOTES LANE

Wallis
Grange

Michael's
Bridge

GARDHAM ROAD

Hudson Way

5

YO43

Wold
Farm

Low
Gardham
Farm

Etton Fields
Farm

42

Yorkshire
Wolds Way

Gardham

Grange
Farm

Dunkenhill
Farm

Arras

4

A1079

Cherry
Burton Wold

DUNKEN HL
HIGHGATE

HIGHGATE

41

HESSLESKEW LANE

Furrows
Farm

P

A1079

YORK ROAD

Arras
Wold

3

Hessleskew

The
Farm

Wold
Plantation

Lings
Farm

Deepdale
Plantation

LINGS RD

Hessleskew
Well

High
Gardham

Furrows
Farm

Brogdale
Plantation

40

BEVERLEY LANE

Newbald
Lodge

Lings
Plantation

Gallops
Plantation

The
Spectacles

Lings
Farm

Courtgarth
Rush

2

Tumuli

Wellfield
Plantation

LOW BALK ROAD

Harrison's
Plantation

HU17

RAKES ROAD

Rush Wold
Plantation

Johnie
Wold

39

Hessleskew
Gare

Tumuli

Mast
Burton
Rakes

Bishop
Burton Wold

1

Flower
Hill

Blythe Barn
Plantation

Cold Harbour
Farmhouse

Newbald
Plantation

Cold
Harbour

38

Sober
Hill

Pit
(dis)

Red House
Farm

Tumuli

COW WOLD ROAD

92 **A** **93** **B** **94** **C** **95** **D** **96** **E** **97** **F**

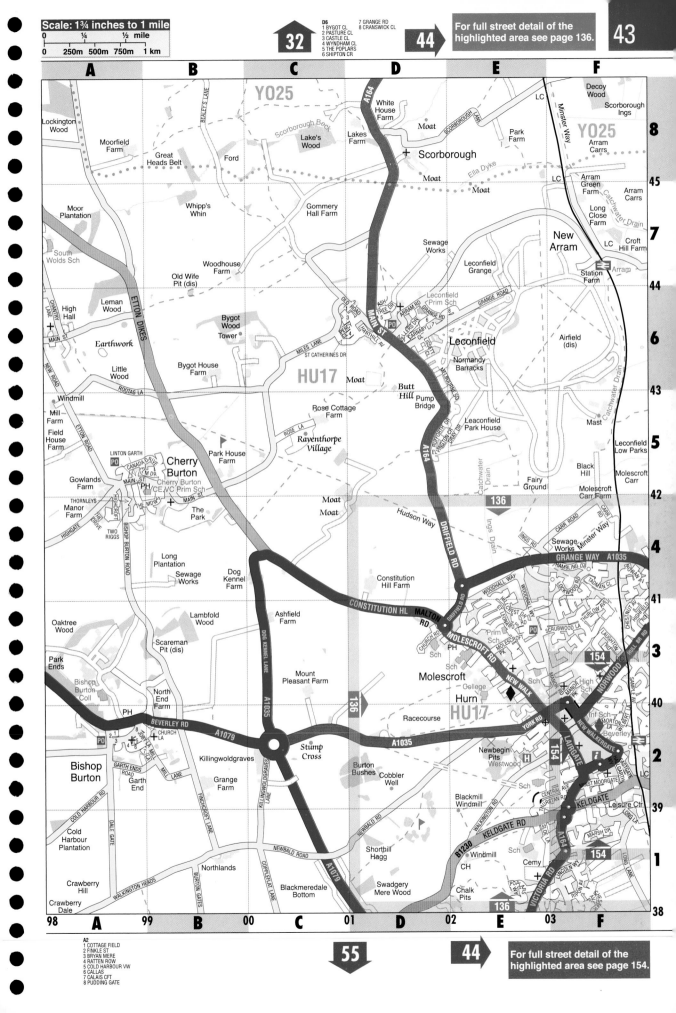

Scale: 1¾ inches to 1 mile

0   ¼   ½ mile
0 250m 500m 750m 1 km

D6
1 BYGOT CL   7 GRANGE RD
2 PASTURE CL   8 CRANSWICK CL
3 CASTLE CL
4 WYNDHAM CL
5 THE POPLARS
6 SHIPTON CR

32

44

For full street detail of the
highlighted area see page 136.

43

A B C D E F

YO25

Lockington Wood

Moorfield Farm

Great Heads Belt

Ford

Scorborough Beck

Lake's Wood

Lakes Farm

White House Farm

Moat

Scorborough

Moat

Moat

Decoy Wood

Scorborough Ings

YO25

Arram Carrs

LC

LC

Arram Green Farm

Arram Carrs

8

45

Moor Plantation

Whipp's Whin

Gommery Hall Farm

Sewage Works

Leconfield Grange

New Arram

Long Close Farm

Croft Hill Farm

Minster Way

Catchwater Drain

7

44

South Wolds Sch

Woodhouse Farm

Old Wife Pit (dis)

Leconfield Prim Sch

Station Farm

Arram

LC

High Hall

Leman Wood

Bygot Wood Tower

Old Road

Ash Tree Dr

Arram Rd

Grange Rd

Leconfield

Airfield (dis)

6

Earthwork

Little Wood

Bygot House Farm

Miles Lane

St Catherines Dr

Carnaby

Normandy Barracks

43

Windmill

Mill Farm

Field House Farm

Rootas La

Rose Cottage Farm

Rose La

Raventhorpe Village

HU17

Moat

Butt Hill

Pump Bridge

Melbourne Rd

Leaconfield Park House

Mast

5

Leconfield Low Parks

Linton Garth

Canada Drive

Cherry Burton

Park House Farm

Moat

Moat

Hudson Way

Ings Drain

Ings Rd

Sewage Works

Fairy Ground

Black Hill

Molescroft Carr

Molescroft Carr Farm

136

42

Gowlands Farm

Cherry Burton CE/VC Prim Sch

The Park

Driffield Rd

Catchwater Drain

Minster Way

Carr Road

Grange Way A1035

4

Thornleys

Manor Farm

Highgate

Two Riggs

The Drive

Long Plantation

Sewage Works

Dog Kennel Farm

Constitution Hill Farm

Constitution Hl

Malton Rd

Hambling Dr

Woodhall Way

Woodhall Way

154

41

Oaktree Wood

Lambfold Wood

Ashfield Farm

Dog Kennel Lane

Church Rd

Molescroft Rd

New Walk

3

Park Ends

Scareman Pit (dis)

Mount Pleasant Farm

A1035

136

Molescroft

Hurn

HU17

College

Racecourse

Norwood

40

Bishop Burton Coll

North End Farm

PH

Beverley Rd A1079

Stump Cross

York Rd A1035

Newbegin Pits Westwood

New Walkergate

Lairgate

Beverley

2

Bishop Burton

Garth Ends Road

Garth End

Killingwoldgraves

Burton Bushes

Cobbler Well

Blackmill Windmill

Keldgate

Leisure Ctr

LC

39

Cold Harbour Plantation

Grange Farm

Northlands

Newbald Road

Shorthill Hagg

Swadgery Mere Wood

Blackmill Windmill

Keldgate Rd

B1230

Windmill

Cemy

A164

Victoria Rd

154

1

Crawberry Hill

Crawberry Dale

Blackmeredale Bottom

Chalk Pits

136

Lincoln Wy

38

98 A 99 B 00 C 01 D 02 E 03 F

A2
1 COTTAGE FIELD
2 FINKLE ST
3 BRYAN MERE
4 RATTEN ROW
5 COLD HARBOUR VW
6 CALLAS
7 CALAIS CFT
8 PUDDING GATE

55

44

For full street detail of the
highlighted area see page 154.

Scale: 1¾ inches to 1 mile

0 | ¼ | ½ mile
0 | 250m | 500m | 750m | 1 km

A B C D E F

8 | 7 | 6 | 5 | 4 | 3 | 2 | 1

45 44 43 42 41 40 39 38

YO25

High Grange Farm
New Farm
Aike
Laurel Farm
Scorborough Ings
Aike Carrs

Linleyhill Road
Landing Strip
Carr Lane
Heighholme Lane
West Street
Sandholme La

Leven South Carr Drain
Leven Carrs
Hall Garth

Far Fox Aqueduct
Leven Canal
Sandholme Cross
Sandholme Farm

Arram Carrs
Eske Boundary Plantation
Waterloo Farm
Eske Boundary Plantation
Glebe Farm

Arram
Eastfield Farm
Beckend Farm
Eske Carrs Drain
Eske Wood
Cross Drain
Routh Carrs

Lodge Farm
Pulfin Bog Nature Reserve
Eske Plantation
Eske Carrs
Eske Carrs Drain
High Farm
Quarry (Sand & Gravel)

Arram Beck
High Eske Farm
Eske Wood
Eske Carrs Drain

Moor Drain
Arram Grange
Eske Village
Eske
Eske Plantation
Crowshore Plantation
High Farm

North Bullock Dike
Eske Lane
Eske Lane
PH
Cottage Farm
Park Farm
Butt Hills
Routh Carrs

HU17

Pumping Station
Crookled Hill
Tickton Hall
Tickton Grange (Hotel)
Tickton Bridge
Hall Farm
A1035
Church Farm
Manor House Farm
Routh

Molescroft Carr
Eske Cl
Scotts Garth Dr
Scotts Garth Cl
The Orchard
Main St
Haver Fields
Manor Farm

South Bullock Dike
137
Hull Bridge
PO
Butt La Green
PH
Tickton Carrs
Tickton Bridge Plantations
Fieldhouse Farm

Stork Hill Farm
Weel Rd
Churchfields
Carr Lane
Tickton
Sewage Works
Tickton Carr Drain
Routh Carrs

Little Storkhill Farm
A1035
Hull Bridge Road
Turf Gutter Bridge
Tickton Carr Drain

A1035
Grange Lane
Grange Way
Hull Br Rd
Turf Gutter & Eske River Side

Sigston Road
A1174
Swinemoor Bank
New Holland Drain
Fosters Bridge
North Carrs
Sandhill Bottoms
Brigham Closes
Meaux Lane

Swine Moor
Dumble Pits Bridge
Long Plantation
Sand Hill
Meaux Abbey Farm
Moat

154
BEVERLEY
North Carr
Holderness Drain
Meaux Decoy
Little Decoy
Fewsome Hill
Cote Bridge
North Grange

Schs
Arden Rd
Queens Rd
Abel Prin Rd
Barnston Cl
HU17
Corporation Farm
Old Main Drain
The Decoy
Peartree Hill Plantation

Thompson Av
Nicholls Cl
Watton Ave
Riverview Rd
Weel Road
Causeway Dale Drain
Carr House Farm
137
Selley Carr
Tippet Lane
Moat
Stud Farm

PO
Holme Church La
Grovehill
Grovehill Rd
Hoggard House Farm
North Carr La
Crown Farm
Site of Meaux Abbey
Bridge Farm

Beaver Rd
Bielby
Annie Reed Rd
Chapel Farm
Weel Carr
Carr La
Weel Carr
Park Lane
Meaux
Meaux Bridge

St Nicholas Rd
Sch
Beckside N
Waterside Rd
Weel Town's Drain
Weel
Halfpenny Hill
Meaux Road

B1230
Spark Mill Lane
Hull Rd
Beverley Beck
Sewage Works
Figham
Springdale Farm
Park Hill

154
Tokenspire Park
Beverley & Skidby Drain
Weel Stone Carr
Selley Carr
Ash Dike Bank
Wawne Grange

Beverley Parklands
The Lummins
Beverley & Skidby Drain
Figham Clough Bridge
Black Bank
Morris Carr
Stone Carr
Ash Dike Plantation
North Wray Closes

Figham Drain
Figham Bridge
Carr Plantation
HU7
Carr House
Drove Lane
East Field

04 A 05 B 06 C 07 D 08 E 09 F

For full street detail of the highlighted area see page 154.

136 **56**

For full street detail of the highlighted area see page 137.

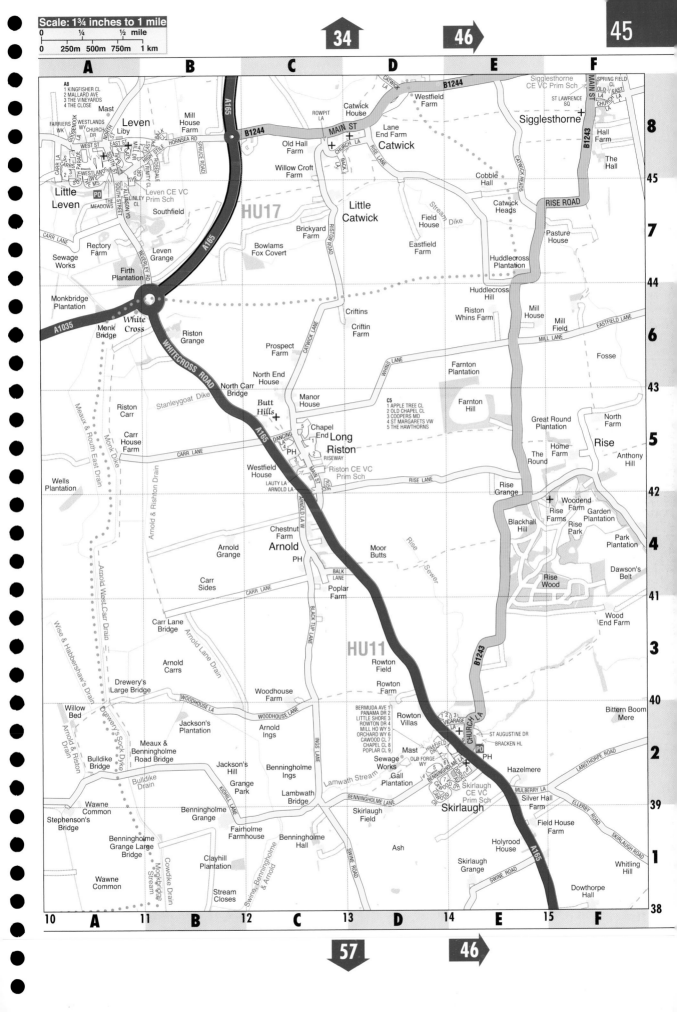

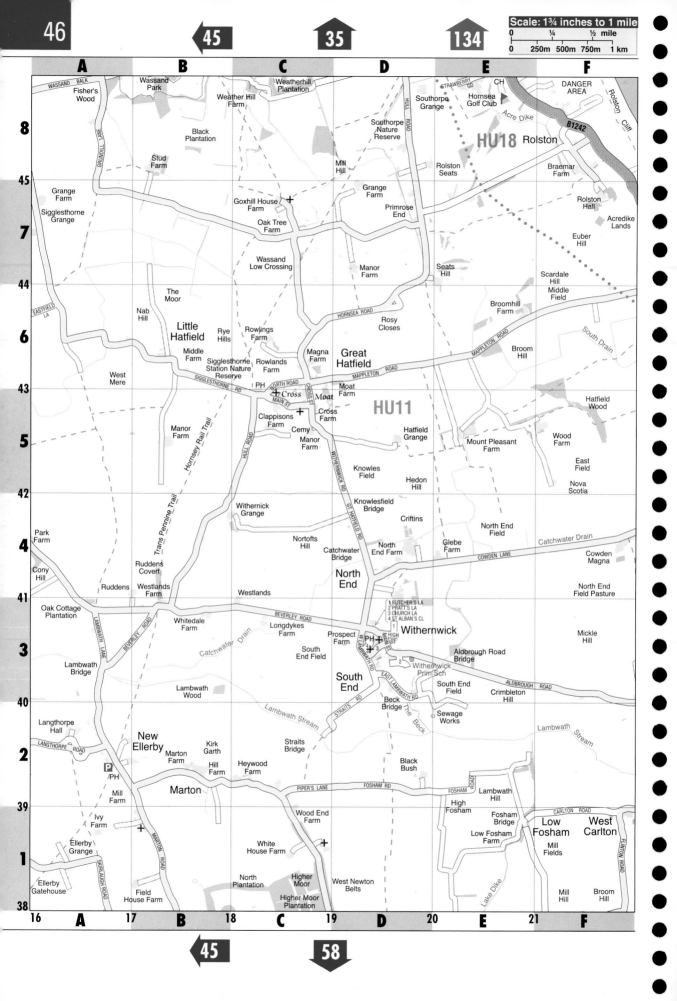

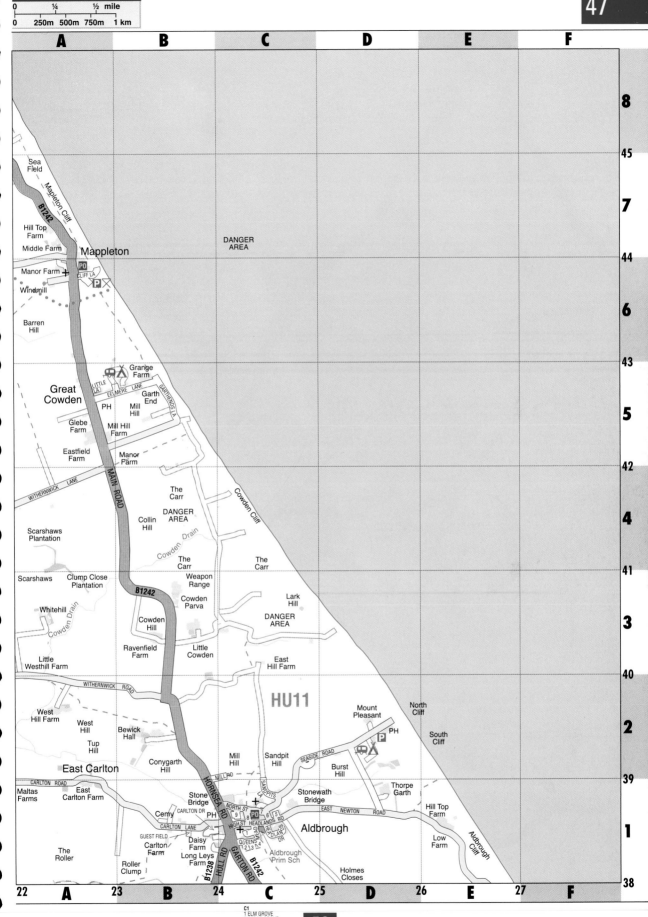

Scale: 1¾ inches to 1 mile

0   ¼   ½ mile

0 250m 500m 750m 1 km

8

45

7

Sea Field

Mappleton Cliff

B1242

Hill Top Farm

Middle Farm

Mappleton

44

PO

Manor Farm

CLIFF LA

P ✕

Windmill

6

Barren Hill

DANGER AREA

43

Grange Farm

LITTLE LA

EELMERE LANE

GARTHENDS LA

Great Cowden

Garth End

PH

Mill Hill

5

Glebe Farm

Mill Hill Farm

Eastfield Farm

Manor Farm

42

WITHERNWICK LANE

MAIN ROAD

The Carr

Scarshaws Plantation

Cowden Cliff

DANGER AREA

Collin Hill

4

Cowden Drain

The Carr

The Carr

41

Scarshaws

Clump Close Plantation

B1242

Weapon Range

Lark Hill

3

Whitehill

Cowden Drain

Cowden Parva

DANGER AREA

Cowden Hill

Ravenfield Farm

Little Cowden

East Hill Farm

Little Westhill Farm

40

WITHERNWICK ROAD

HU11

Mount Pleasant

North Cliff

2

West Hill Farm

West Hill

Bewick Hall

PH

P

South Cliff

Tup Hill

Conygarth Hill

Mill Hill

Sandpit Hill

SEASIDE ROAD

Burst Hill

East Carlton

39

CARLTON ROAD

Maltas Farms

East Carlton Farm

HORNSEA RD

MILL RD

SANDPITS LA

Stone Bridge

Stonewath Bridge

Thorpe Garth

Cemy

PH

CARLTON DR

NORTH ST

PO

EAST NEWTON ROAD

Hill Top Farm

CARLTON LANE

9
8

HIGH ST

HEADLANDS RD

Aldbrough

1

GUEST FIELD

Daisy Farm

QUEENS

Low Farm

The Roller

Carlton Farm

Long Leys Farm

HULL RD

GARTON RD

B1238

B1242

4
2 1 3

Aldbrough Prim Sch

Aldbrough Cliff

Roller Clump

Holmes Closes

38

22 **A** 23 **B** 24 **C** 25 **D** 26 **E** 27 **F**

C1
1 ELM GROVE
2 CEDAR GROVE
3 WILLOW GROVE
4 ASH GROVE
5 WENTWORTH GROVE
6 NOTTINGHAM RD
7 CHURCH ST
8 CROSS ST
9 CASTLE PARK

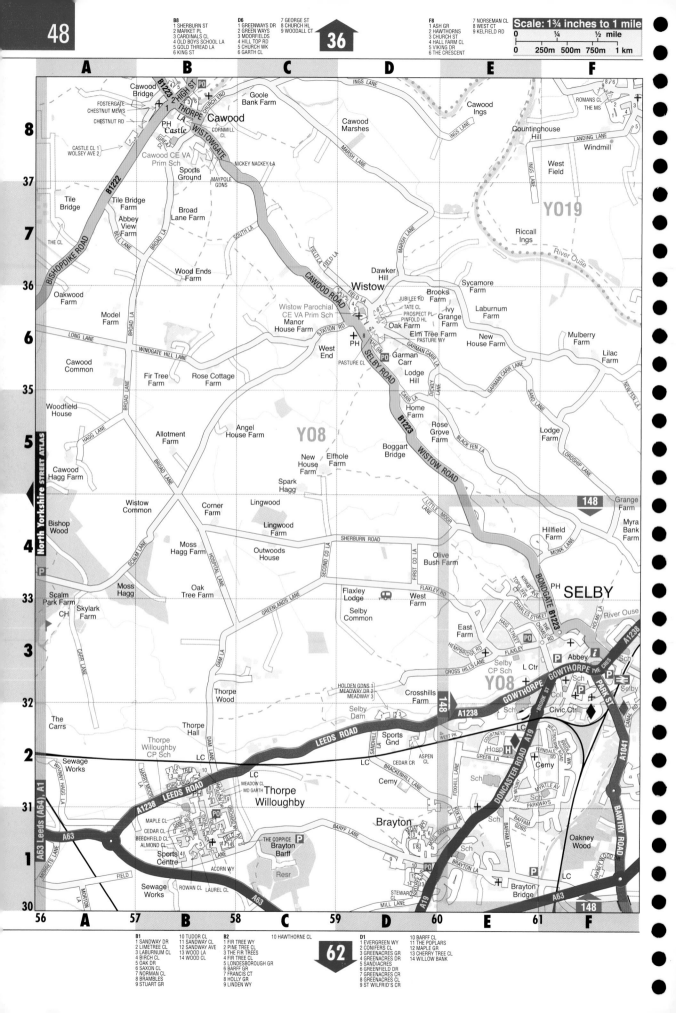

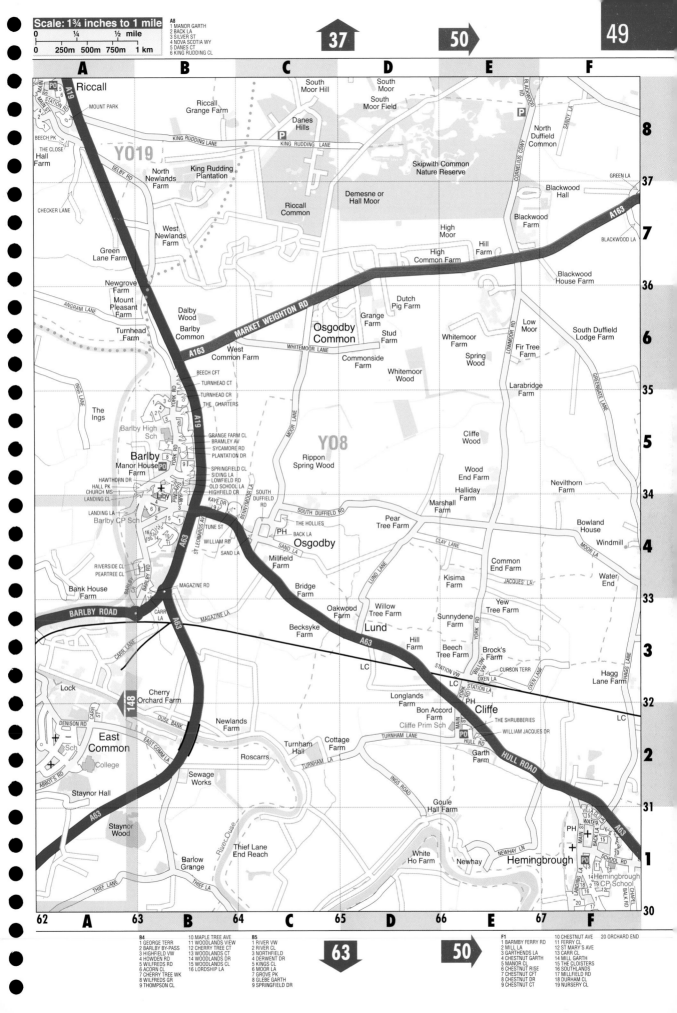

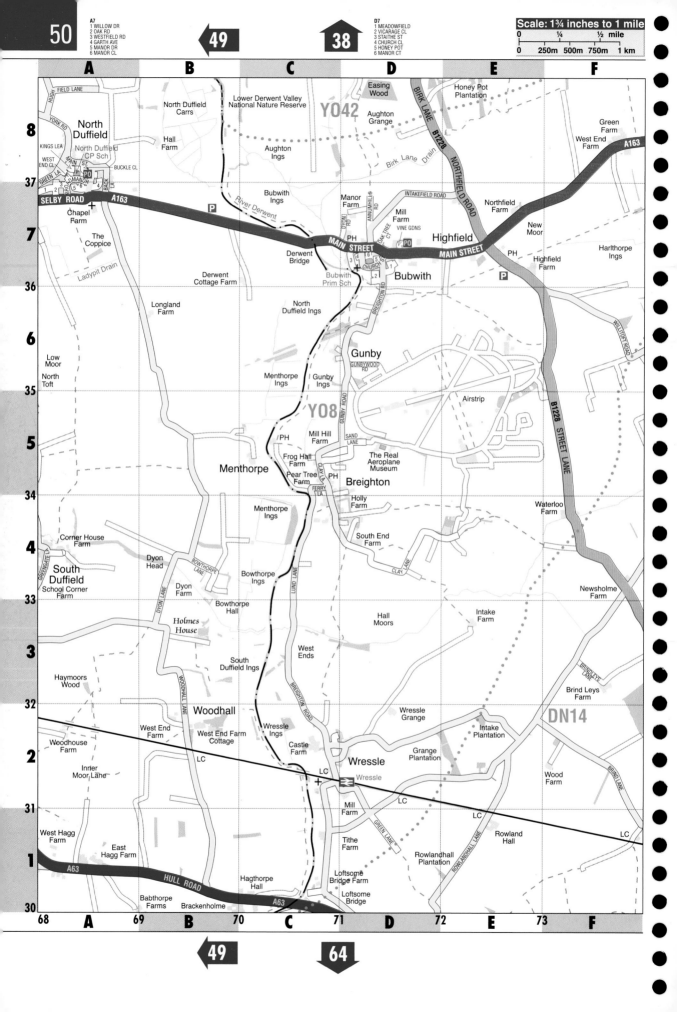

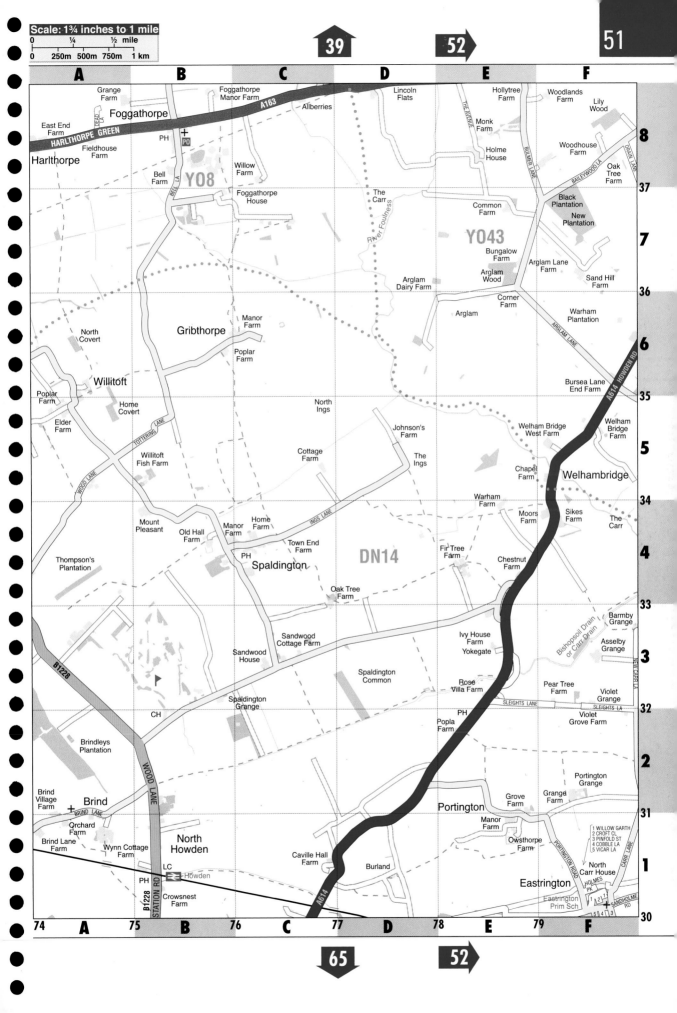

Scale: 1¾ inches to 1 mile
0   ¼   ½ mile
0 250m 500m 750m 1 km

A · B · C · D · E · F

8

Barleywood La · Back Lane · Little End · Moor End · PH · Moor End · Duck Nest · Cliffe Lane
Sober Hill · Prospect Farm · Poplar Farm · New Farm · Avenue Farm
Sober Hill Farm · Lock Lane · Sand Lane

Sand Hole

37

Meadow Farm · Grange Farm · Highgate · High Garth · Carr Farm
Prospect House · Workhouse Farm · Holly Farm · Duck Farm · North Cliffe Carr
A614 · Lock Lane

7

Drain Lane · Rascal Moor · Boundary Wood
Lodge Farm · Holme Common · Forest Farm · Skiff Farm · Ladies Parlour · Land of Nod
Howden Road

36

Woldgate Farm · Skiff Lane · Tollingham Farm · Tollingham · Bunny Hill · Bunnyhill Plantation
Pond Farm · New Bursea Farm · Skiff Lane Industrial Estate · Holme Industrial Estate · South Cliffe Carr

6

Sotheron's Plantation · YO43 · Carr Farm

35

Bursea Lane · Bursea Lane Farm · Grange Farm · Drain Lane · Throlam · Wholsea Grange · Duck Nest Plantation
Bursea Lodge · Bursea Grange · Hasholme Heavy Horses

5

Bursea · Bursea Lane · Hasholme Carr Farm · Wholsea Farm
Bursea Farm · Bursea House · New Lane · Fox Covert Plantation · Hasholme Carr · Long Plantation

4

The Carr · East Bursea Farm · Hotham Carrs
Hasholme Hall · Market Weighton Canal

33

Bloomhill Farm · Barmby La · The Carr · Bishopsoil Drain or Oarr Drain · Hasholme Grange · Hasholme Garth · The Carr
New Carr Lane · River Foulness · Sand Hill Farm · Lorne Farm · Hancock Lane

3

Barmby Lane · The Carr · North America
HU15

32

Sleights Lane · Sleights Lane · Greaves End · Yokefleet Lodge · Sandholme Lodge · Carrhill Farm · Canal Side E · Seavy Carr Lane · Hopwood La · Sandholme Landing
Campbell's Wood · Freeschool La · Metham Grange · Canal Side West

2

Sleights Lane · Common Wood · Ing Nook Plantation · Blacktoft Grange · Canal Side Farm · Thimblehall La
Sleights Lane · Ing Nook Rd · Clubhill Farm
Beech Farm · White House Farm · Drain Lane · Canal Lane · Poplar Farm

31

DN14 · Manor Farm · Owsthorpe · Hive · Hive Farm · Chapel Farm · Townend Farm · Cow Bridge · Mill Lane Farm · Grebe Rd · Hopwood La
Owsthorpe Lane · Hive Lane · Old Trough Lane · Sandholme · Poplar House Farm · Landing Lane · Mill · Landing Lane · Canal Side East · Canal Side West · Southfields · PO

1

Mill Farm · Farms La · The Ings · New Farm · Ings Wood · M62 · Sandholme Rd · Mill Lane · Thornton Dam · Sandholme Grange · Leatheroyd Lane · Thimblehall Lane · B1230 · Newport Prim Sch
Sandholme Rd

30

80 · A · 81 · B · 82 · C · 83 · D · 84 · E · 85 · F

F1
1 TEAL RD
2 GADWALL CL
3 POCHARD CL
4 BRIAR CL
5 HAWTHORN CL
6 THE SPINNEY
7 OCEAN DR
8 BLACKTHORN CL
9 MEADOW LA
10 TURKS HEAD GDNS
11 VILLAGE FARM CL
12 NETTLE HILL

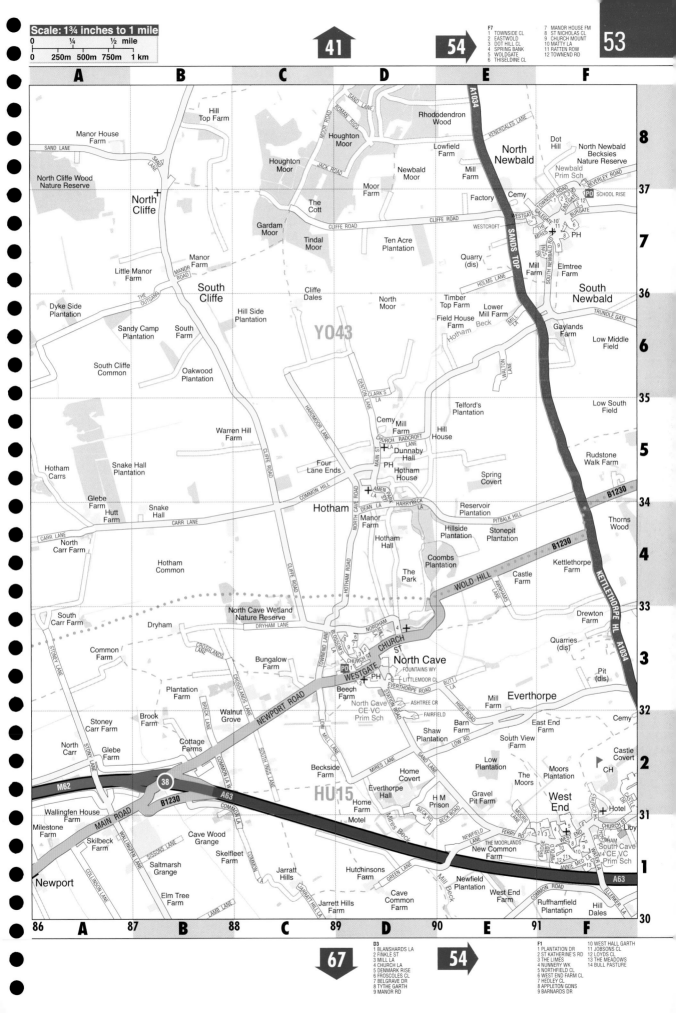

A   B   C   D   E   F

8
Newbald
Wold
Bushey
Hill Farm
Tumuli
Flowery
Dale
STONEACNOWLE HILL
WRANGHAM DR
BEVERLEY ROAD
WOODGATE ROAD
Bullen's
Hill Farm
Tumulus
Little
Wood
WALKINGTON HEADS
Ox
Dale
Remembrance
Wood
WOLD ROAD

37
Resr
Woodgate
Hill
High Hunsley Circuit &
Yorkshire Wolds Way
Swin
Dale
Rigg
Plantation
Littlewood
Lodge
Ella
Hill
Littlewood
Farm
Wold
Farm
Walkington
Wold

7
Nut
Wood
Deep
Dale
Whin
Hill
Y043
Monckton
Walk
HU17
LITTLEWOOD RD
Grange
Farm

36
Dale
Cott
Bungalow
Farm
Dale
Plantation
Howe Hill
Field
East
Plantation
B1230
Samples
Farm

6
Drakes
Hole
Smallwold
Farm
Hunsley
House
The
Rookery
Hunsley
Dike
Lion's
Den

TRUNDLE GATE
Wold House
Farm
THE AVENUE
Little
Hunsley
Farm

35
South
Wold
Bunkers
Hill
WHIN LANE
Mast
High
Hunsley
BRICK DIKE LANE
WHITE GAP LANE
COMMON ROAD

5
Rudstone Walk
Plantation
St Austin's
Stone
Rasp
Clump
Little Weighton
Common

B1230
Factory
Austin
Dale
Riplingham
Common
Double
Dike

34
East
Dale
Hunsley
Dale
Low Hunsley
Farm
HU20
WHITE GAP ROAD
Bungalow
Farm

4
Jackdaw
Plantation
Drewton
Dale
Low Hunsley
Plantation
West
Hill
Hillside
Plantation
Riplingham
Grange
York
Plantation
SHEEPWAL TH LA

DREWTON LA
West Hill
Plantation
Ash
Plantation
Holme
Farm

Drewton
Manor
DREWTON LA
Weedly
Dale
Rowley Manor
(Hotel)
ROWLEY RD

33
Foxhouse
Farm
Comber
Dale
The
Warrens
Weedley
Plantation
Socken
Wood

3
Egg
Plantation
COMBERDALE HILL
SWINESCAIF ROAD
Beverley
Clump
Mast
Weedley
Farm
Manor
Farm
High Hunsley Circuit

SWINESCAIF HILL
SWINESCAIF RD
Quarry
Sweattyhill
Plantation
Riplingham
Village
WEST OBY LA

SWINESCAIF ROAD
Trancledales
Little Wold
Plantation
Great Wold
Plantation
Sweatty
Hill
Great
Wold

32
Cemy
LITTLEWOLD LA
Little
Wold Side
Great
Wold Side
Cave
Wold
Riplingham

THE LEA
Resr
Great Wold
Plantation
Fox Covert
Farm
Field
House
Farm
HU16

STATION RD
THE STRAY
BEVERLEY ROAD
STEEP HL
HU15
LAMBWELL HILLS

2
South
Cave
PLUM TREE WK
Mount
Airy
Far
Wold
Riplingham
Clump
York
Grounds
Farm

MARKET PL
BROUGH RD
CLEAVES AVE
MIDDLE
GARTH DR
HIGHFIELDS
Woodale
Plantation
DALE ROAD

1
PH
FIRST LA
CHURCH ST
RAWDALE CL
Mount
Airey Farm
Woo
Dale
The
Warren
Ellerker
North Wold
Long
Wold
Top
Plantation
Brafrords
Farm

BACCHUS LA
Ryeland
Hill
Cliffs
Plantation
Woodale
Plantation
Brantingham
Wold
Turtle
Hill
Brafrords
Clump

STONEPIT RD
A1034
A63
Woodale
Farm
ELLERKER WOLD LANE
Waltham's Wold
Plantation
Brantingham
Dale Plantation
Long
Plantation
Fox
Covert
Wauldby
Green

30
STONEPIT RD
Hunsdale
Farm
Bilkshill
Plantation
Bilks
Hill
Wandhills
Plantation
Wold View
Farm

92   A   93   B   94   C   95   D   96   E   97   F

A2
1 CASTLE RISE
2 THE PARKLANDS
3 WOLD VW
4 SOUTHCOTE CL

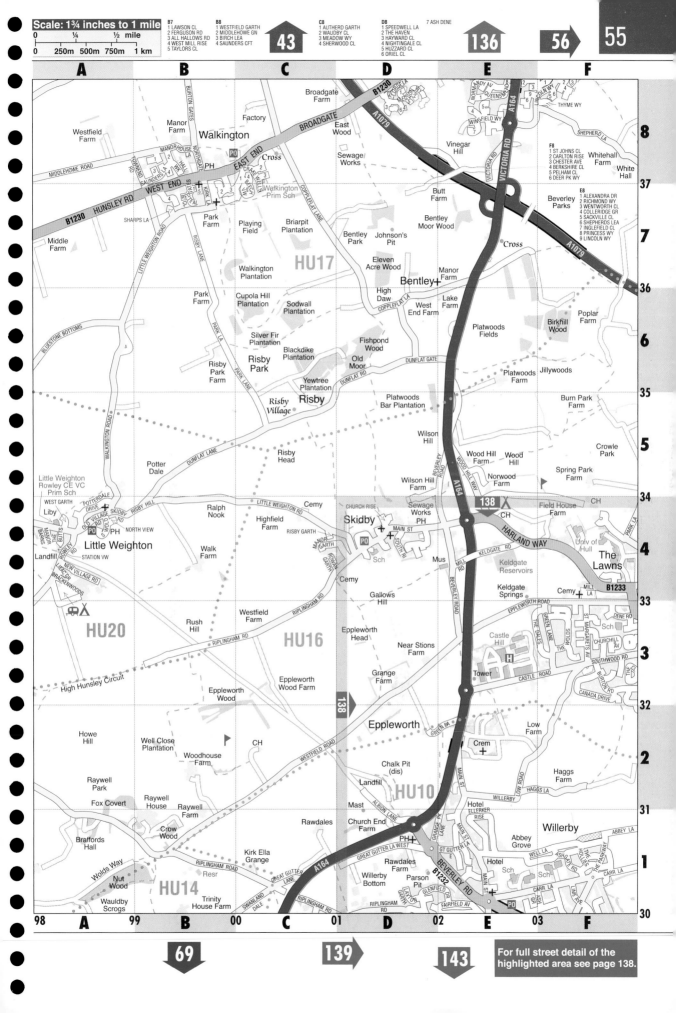

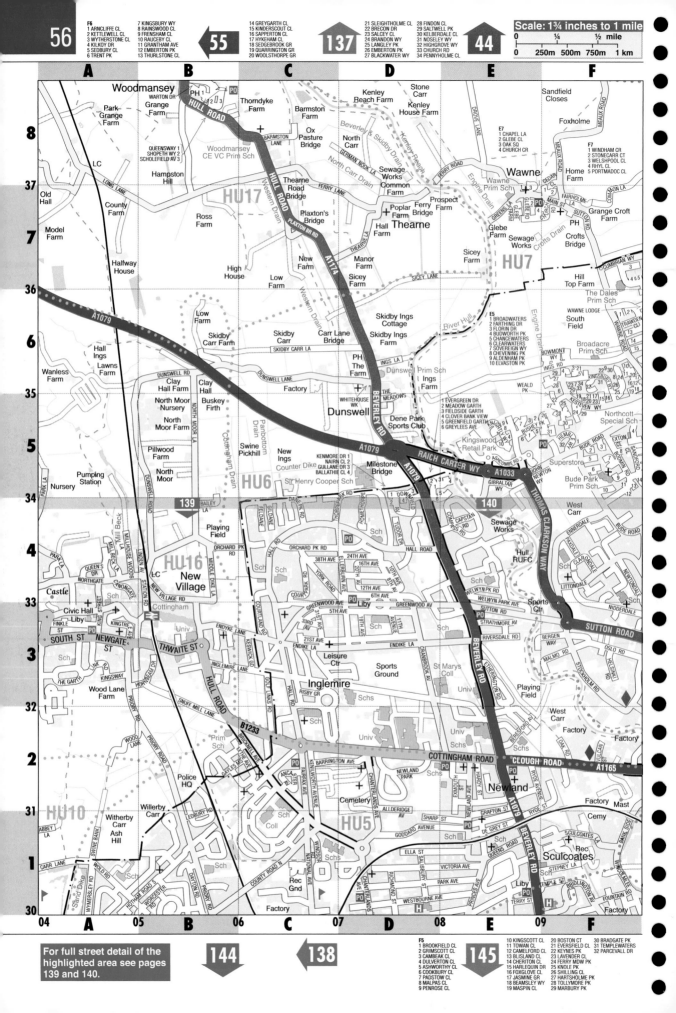

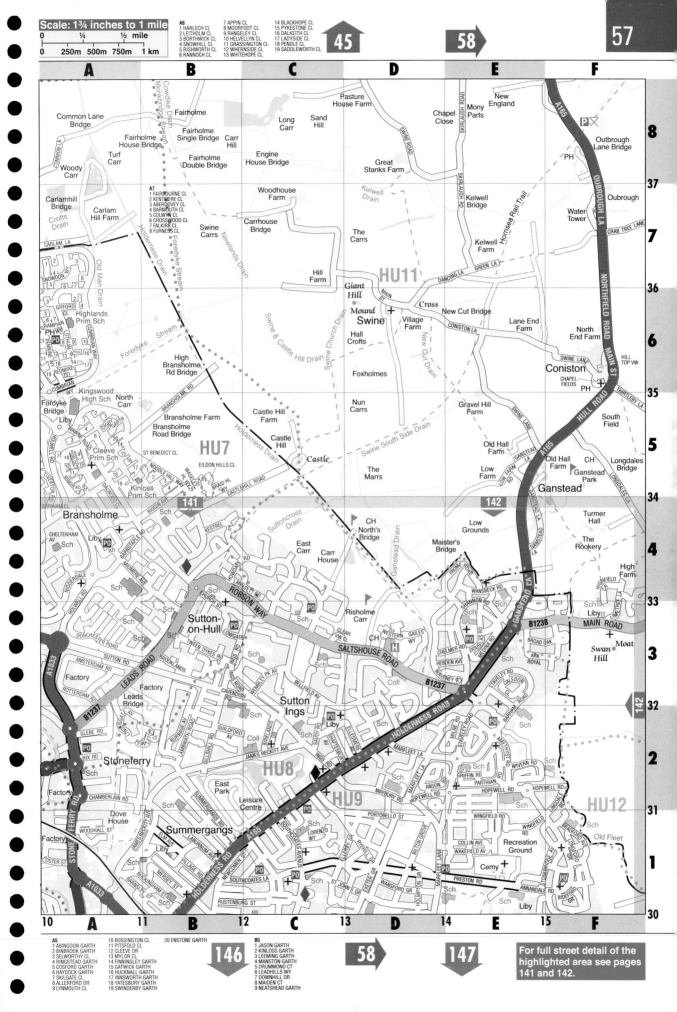

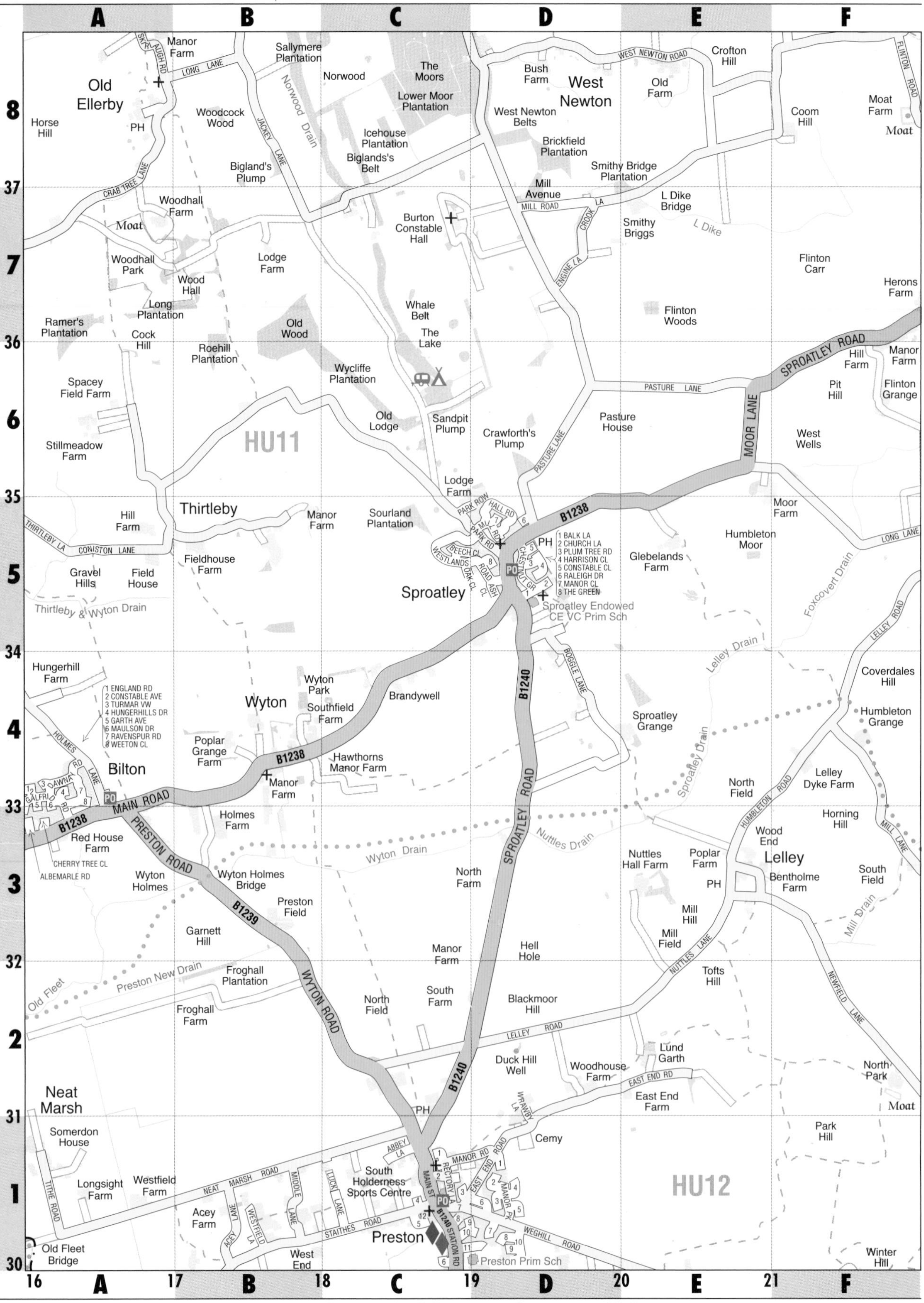

Scale: 1¾ inches to 1 mile

0 ¼ ½ mile
0 250m 500m 750m 1 km

Grid columns: A B C D E F

Grid rows (left): 8 37 7 36 6 35 5 34 4 33 3 32 2 31 1 30

Grid columns (bottom): A 16 17 B 18 C 19 D 20 E 21 F

Old Ellerby
Manor Farm
Sallymere Plantation
Norwood
The Moors
Bush Farm
West Newton
Old Farm
Crofton Hill
West Newton Road
Moat Farm
Horse Hill
PH
Woodcock Wood
Lower Moor Plantation
West Newton Belts
Coom Hill
Moat
Woodhall Farm
Icehouse Plantation
Bigland's Belt
Brickfield Plantation
Smithy Bridge Plantation
Moat
Bigland's Plump
Mill Avenue
L Dike Bridge
Woodhall Park
Burton Constable Hall
Mill Road
Smithy Briggs
L Dike
Flinton Carr
Herons Farm
Lodge Farm
Wood Hall
Whale Belt
The Lake
Flinton Woods
Ramer's Plantation
Long Plantation
Cock Hill
Roehill Plantation
Old Wood
Wycliffe Plantation
The Lake
Pasture Lane
Pasture House
Sproatley Road
Hill Farm
Manor Farm
Flinton Grange
Pit Hill
Spacey Field Farm
Old Lodge
Sandpit Plump
Crawforth's Plump
West Wells
Stillmeadow Farm
HU11
Lodge Farm
Moor Lane
Moor Farm
Hill Farm
Thirtleby
Manor Farm
Sourland Plantation
Park Row
Hall Rd
B1238
Humbleton Moor
Long Lane
Thirtleby La
Coniston Lane
Fieldhouse Farm
Beech Cl
Westlands
Oak Cl
Park Rd
Chestnut Cl
PH
PO
Sproatley
1 BALK LA
2 CHURCH LA
3 PLUM TREE RD
4 HARRISON CL
5 CONSTABLE CL
6 RALEIGH DR
7 MANOR CL
8 THE GREEN
Glebelands Farm
Foxcovert Drain
Gravel Hills
Field House
Thirtleby & Wyton Drain
Sproatley Endowed CE VC Prim Sch
Lelley Drain
Lelley Road
Hungerhill Farm
1 ENGLAND RD
2 CONSTABLE AVE
3 TURMAR VW
4 HUNGERHILLS DR
5 GARTH AVE
6 MAULSON DR
7 RAVENSPUR RD
8 WEETON CL
Wyton Park
Southfield Farm
Brandywell
Poggle Lane
B1240
Sproatley Grange
Coverdales Hill
Humbleton Grange
Wyton
Poplar Grange Farm
B1238
Hawthorns Manor Farm
North Field
Lelley Dyke Farm
Bilton
Holmes La
PO
Main Road
Manor Farm
Holmes Farm
Sproatley Road
Nuttles Drain
Wood End
Horning Hill
B1238
Red House Farm
Preston Road
Wyton Drain
Nuttles Hall Farm
Poplar Farm
PH
Lelley
Bentholme Farm
South Field
Cherry Tree Cl
Albemarle Rd
Wyton Holmes
Wyton Holmes Bridge
Preston Field
North Farm
Mill Hill
Humbleton Rd
Mill Lane
Garnett Hill
B1239
Mill Field
Froghall Plantation
Wyton Road
Manor Farm
Hell Hole
Nuttles Lane
Tofts Hill
Newfield Lane
Old Fleet
Preston New Drain
Froghall Farm
North Field
South Farm
Blackmoor Hill
Lelley Road
Lund Garth
North Park
Neat Marsh
Duck Hill Well
Woodhouse Farm
East End Farm
Moat
Somerdon House
PH
B1240
East End Rd
Wrangy La
Park Hill
Longsight Farm
Westfield Farm
Neat Marsh Road
Abbey La
Manor Rd
Cemy
HU12
Tithe Road
Acey Farm
Middle Lane
Luddy Lane
Westfield Road
Rectory Cl
Main St
East End
Manor Pk
Weghill Road
Old Fleet Bridge
West End
Staithes Road
Preston
PO
Preston Prim Sch
Winter Hill
South Holderness Sports Centre
B1240 Station Rd

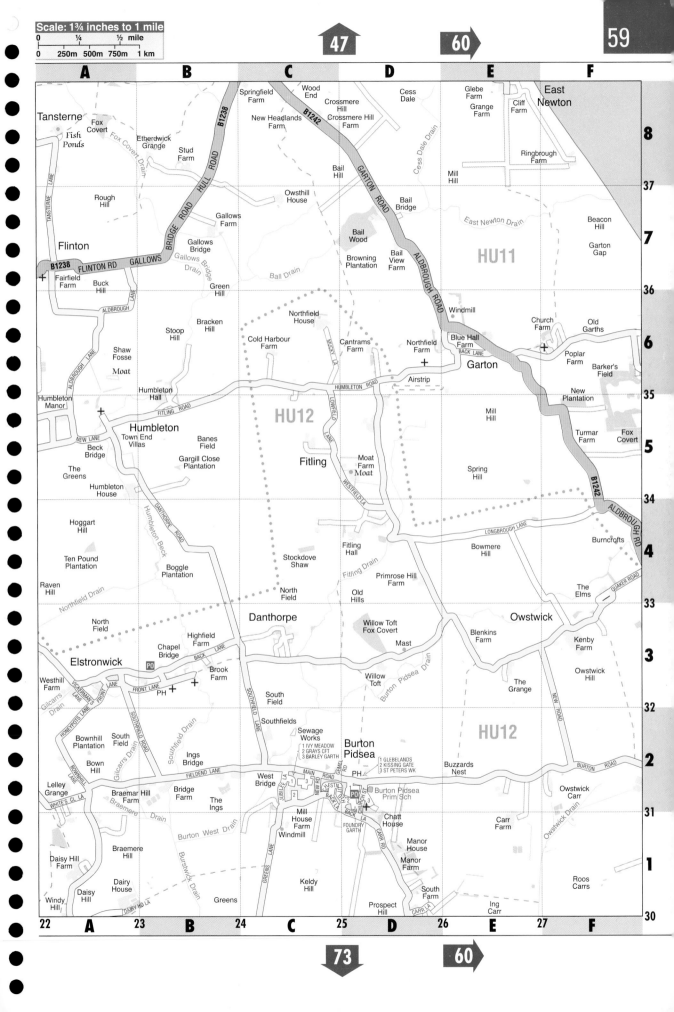

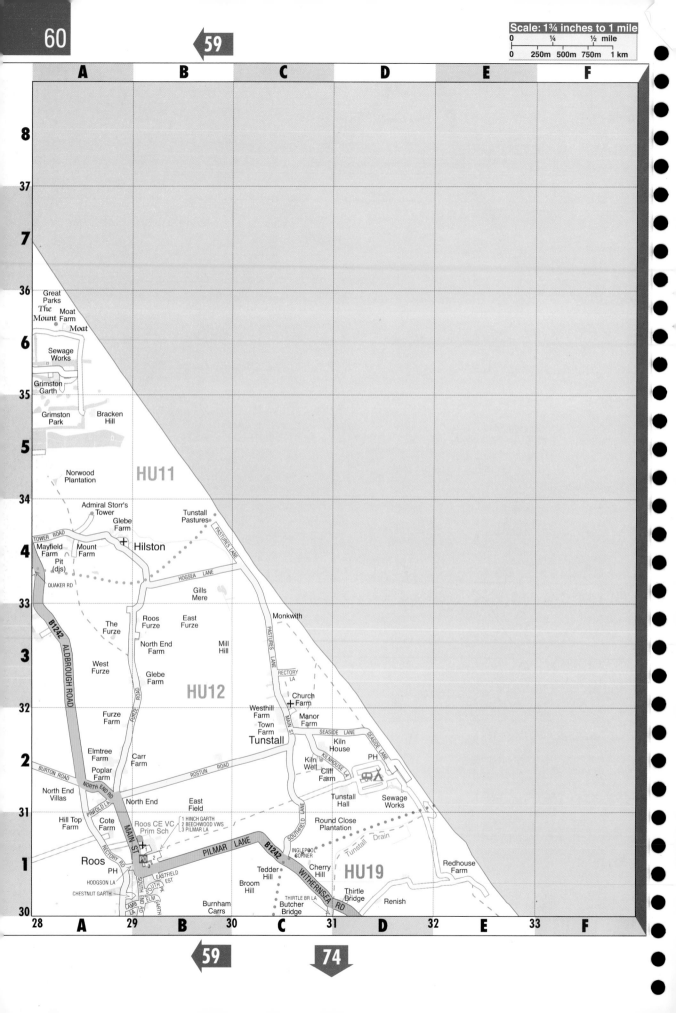

A   B   C   D   E   F

8

37

7

36

Great Parks
The
Moat   Moat Farm
Mount   Moat

6

Sewage Works

Grimston Garth

35

Grimston Park   Bracken Hill

5

Norwood Plantation

HU11

34

Admiral Storr's Tower
Glebe Farm
Tunstall Pastures

TOWER ROAD
Mayfield Farm
Mount Farm   Hilston
Pit (dis)

PASTURES LANE

QUAKER RD

HOGSEA LANE

Gills Mere

33

The Furze
Roos Furze   East Furze
Monkwith

B1242

North End Farm   Mill Hill

West Furze

PASTURES LANE

3

ALDBROUGH ROAD

FURZE ROAD

Glebe Farm

RECTORY LA

HU12

Church Farm

32

Furze Farm

Westhill Farm
Town Farm
Tunstall

Manor Farm

SEASIDE LANE

Kiln House

SEASIDE LANE

2

Elmtree Farm

Carr Farm

BURTON ROAD

Poplar Farm

ROSTUN ROAD

Kiln Well
Cliff Farm

KILNHOUSE LA

PH

NORTH END RD

North End Villas

North End

East Field

Tunstall Hall

Sewage Works

PINFOLD LA

31

Hill Top Farm
Cote Farm

Roos CE VC Prim Sch
1 HINCH GARTH
2 BEECHWOOD VWS
3 PILMAR LA

SOUTHFIELD LANE

Round Close Plantation

Drain

Tunstall

MAIN ST

RECTORY RD

PILMAR LANE

B1242

INGLEPOOL CORNER

1

Roos

PO

PH

EASTFIELD EST

SOUTH END RD

ELM GARTH

Tedder Hill

Cherry Hill

WITHERNSEA RD

HU19

Redhouse Farm

HODGSON LA

Broom Hill

Thirtle Bridge

CHESTNUT GARTH

LAMB LA

Burnham Carrs

THIRTLE BR LA

Butcher Bridge

Renish

30

28   A   29   B   30   C   31   D   32   E   33   F

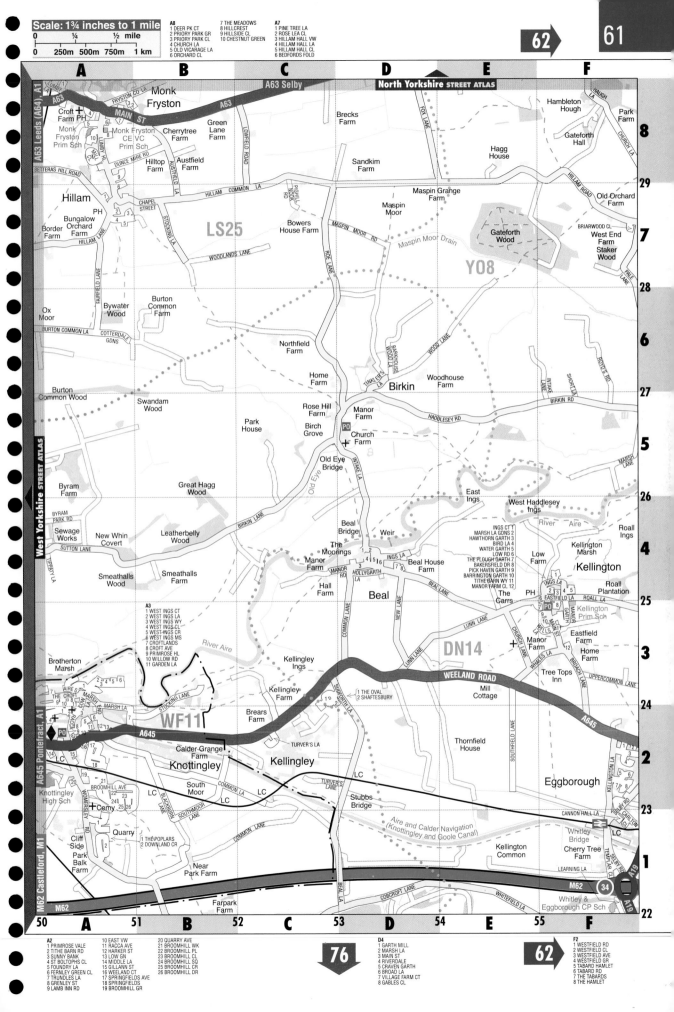

A8
1 DEER PK CT
2 PRIORY PARK GR
3 PRIORY PARK CL
4 CHURCH LA
5 OLD VICARAGE LA
6 ORCHARD CL

7 THE MEADOWS
8 HILLCREST
9 HILLSIDE CL
10 CHESTNUT GREEN

A7
1 PINE TREE LA
2 ROSE LEA CL
3 HILLAM HALL VW
4 HILLAM HALL LA
5 HILLAM HALL CL
6 BEDFORDS FOLD

Monk
Fryston

A63 Selby

A63 Leeds (A64), A1

Croft
Farm PH
Monk
Fryston
Prim Sch

Monk Fryston
CE VC
Prim Sch

Cherrytree
Farm

Green
Lane
Farm

Brecks
Farm

Hambleton
Hough

Park
Farm

Gateforth
Hall

Hillam

Hilltop
Farm

Austfield
Farm

Sandkim
Farm

Hagg
House

Maspin Grange
Farm

Old Orchard
Farm

Border
Farm

Bungalow
Orchard
Farm

PH

LS25

Bowers
House Farm

Maspin
Moor

Maspin Moor Drain

Gateforth
Wood

YO8

West End
Farm
Staker
Wood

Ox
Moor

Bywater
Wood

Burton
Common
Farm

Northfield
Farm

Birkin

Woodhouse
Farm

Burton
Common Wood

Swandam
Wood

Home
Farm

Rose Hill
Farm

Manor
Farm

Birch
Grove

Church
Farm

HADDLESEY RD

BIRKIN RD

Byram
Farm

Park
House

Great Hagg
Wood

Old Eye
Bridge

Old Eye

East
Ings

West Haddlesey
Ings

River Aire

Roall
Ings

Sewage
Works

New Whin
Covert

Leatherbelly
Wood

Beal
Bridge

Weir

INGS CT 1
MARSH LA GDNS 2
HAWTHORN GARTH 3
BIRD LA 4
WATER GARTH 5
LOW RD 6
THE PLOUGH GARTH 7
BAKERSFIELD DR 8
PICK HAVEN GARTH 9
BARRINGTON GARTH 10
TITHE BARN WY 11
MANOR FARM CL 12

Low
Farm

Kellington
Marsh

Kellington

Smeathalls
Wood

Smeathalls
Farm

The
Moorings

Manor
Farm

Beal House
Farm

The
Carrs

PH

Roall
Plantation

A3
1 WEST INGS CT
2 WEST INGS LA
3 WEST INGS WY
4 WEST INGS CL
5 WEST INGS CR
6 WEST INGS MS
7 CROFTLANDS
8 CROFT AVE
9 PRIMROSE HL
10 WILLOW RD
11 GARDEN LA

Hall
Farm

Beal

DN14

Eastfield
Farm

Home
Farm

Brotherton
Marsh

River Aire

Kellingley
Ings

Manor
Farm

Tree Tops
Inn

WF11

Kellingley
Farm

WEELAND ROAD

Mill
Cottage

A645

Calder Grange
Farm

Knottingley

Kellingley

1 THE OVAL
2 SHAFTESBURY

Thornfield
House

Eggborough

Brears
Farm

TURVER'S LA

Knottingley
High Sch

Cemy

South
Moor

Stubbs
Bridge

Whitley
Bridge

Cherry Tree
Farm

Cliff
Side
Park
Balk
Farm

Quarry

1 THE POPLARS
2 DOWNLAND CR

Aire and Calder Navigation
(Knottingley and Goole Canal)

Kellington
Common

Near
Park Farm

Whitley &
Eggborough CP Sch

M62 Castleford, M1

M62

Farpark
Farm

M62

34

A2
1 PRIMROSE VALE
2 TITHE BARN RD
3 SUNNY BANK
4 ST BOLTOPHS CL
5 FOUNDRY LA
6 FERNLEY GREEN CL
7 TRUNDLES LA
8 GRENLEY ST
9 LAMB INN RD

10 EAST VW
11 RACCA AVE
12 HARKER ST
13 LOW GN
14 MIDDLE LA
15 GILLANN ST
16 WEELAND CT
17 SPRINGFIELDS AVE
18 SPRINGFIELDS
19 BROOMHILL GR

20 QUARRY AVE
21 BROOMHILL WK
22 BROOMHILL PL
23 BROOMHILL CL
24 BROOMHILL SQ
25 BROOMHILL CR
26 BROOMHILL DR

D4
1 GARTH MILL
2 MARSH LA
3 MAIN ST
4 RIVERDALE
5 CRAVEN GARTH
6 BROAD LA
7 VILLAGE FARM CT
8 GABLES CL

F2
1 WESTFIELD RD
2 WESTFIELD CL
3 WESTFIELD AVE
4 WESTFIELD GR
5 TABARD HAMLET
6 TABARD RD
7 THE TABARDS
8 THE HAMLET

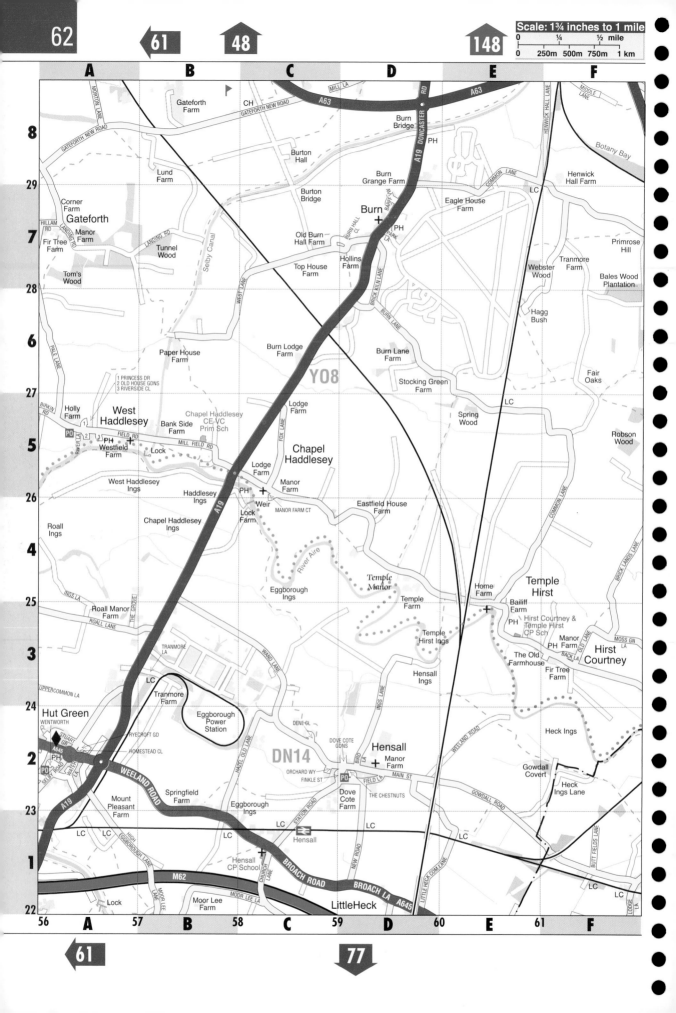

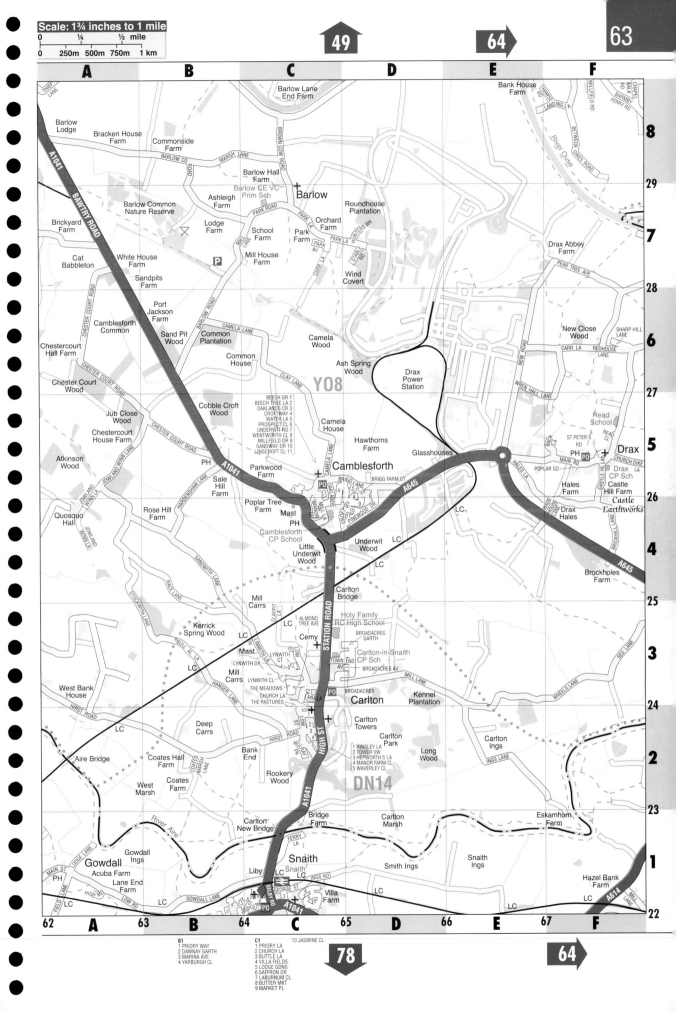

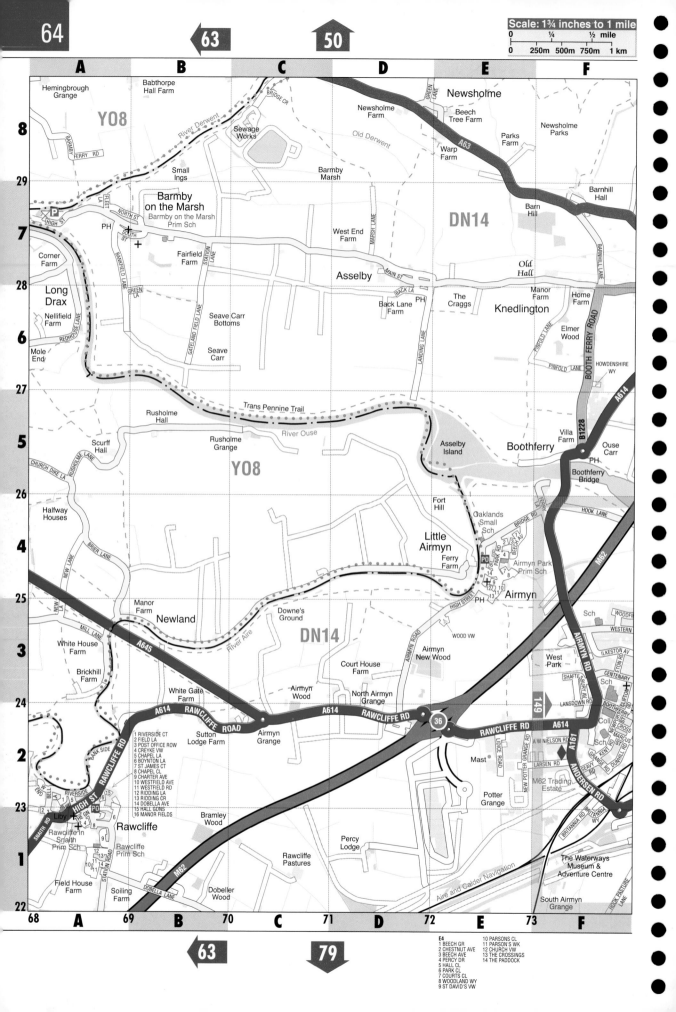

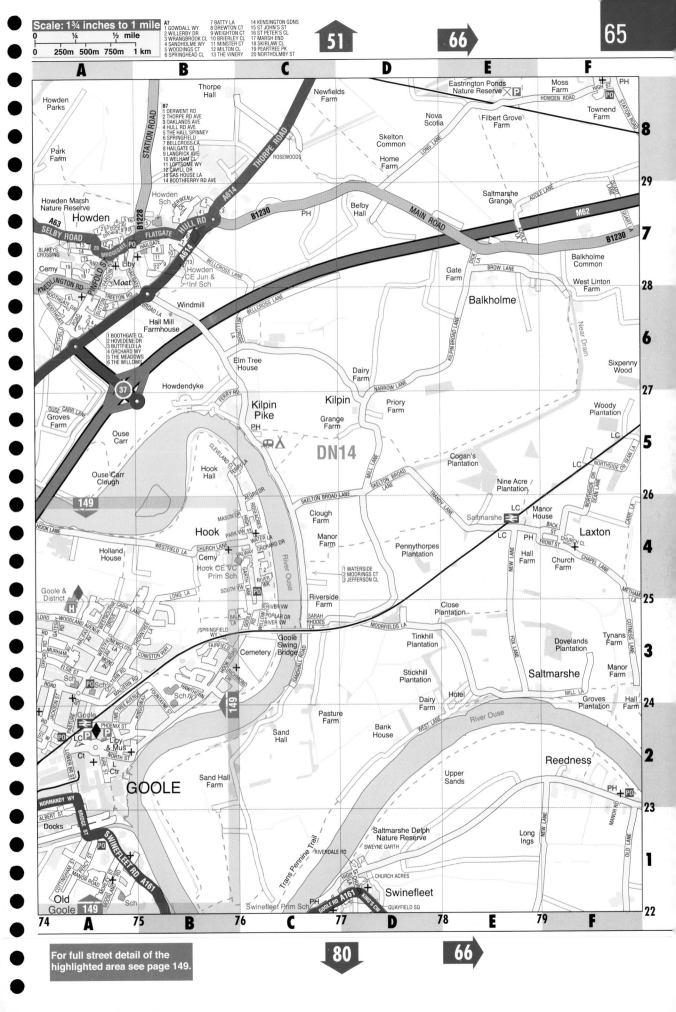

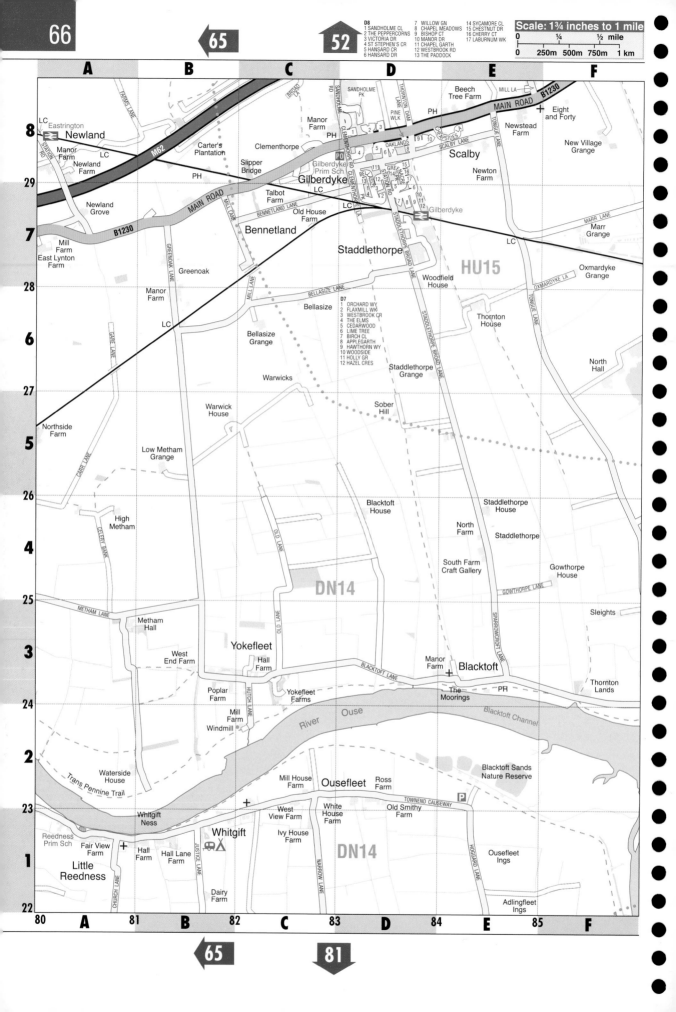

65

52

D8
1 SANDHOLME CL
2 THE PEPPERCORNS
3 VICTORIA DR
4 ST STEPHEN'S CR
5 HANSARD CR
6 HANSARD DR

7 WILLOW GN
8 CHAPEL MEADOWS
9 BISHOP CT
10 MANOR DR
11 CHAPEL GARTH
12 WESTBROOK RD
13 THE PADDOCK

14 SYCAMORE CL
15 CHESTNUT DR
16 CHERRY CT
17 LABURNUM WK

Scale: 1¾ inches to 1 mile
0   ¼   ½   mile
0   250m   500m   750m   1 km

A   B   C   D   E   F

8 LC Eastrington
Newland
Manor Farm
Newland Farm
LC

29 M62
Carter's Plantation
Slipper Bridge
PH
Clementhorpe
Manor Farm
PH
Gilberdyke Prim Sch
PO
Gilberdyke
LC

Beech Tree Farm
MILL LA
MAIN ROAD
B1230
Eight and Forty
Newstead Farm
New Village Grange
Scalby
Newton Farm

Newland Grove
B1230
Talbot Farm
Bennetland Lane
Old House Farm
LC

7 Mill Farm
East Lynton Farm
Greenoak
Bennetland
Staddlethorpe
LC
Gilberdyke
MARR LANE
Marr Grange

28 Manor Farm
Greenoak
Bellasize Lane
Bellasize
Woodfield House
HU15
Oxmardyke Grange

D7
1 ORCHARD WY
2 FLAXMILL WK
3 WESTBROOK CR
4 THE ELMS
5 CEDARWOOD
6 LIME TREE
7 BIRCH CL
8 APPLEGARTH
9 HAWTHORN WY
10 WOODSIDE
11 HOLLY GR
12 HAZEL CRES

6 LC
Bellasize Grange
Thornton House
North Hall

27 Warwicks
Warwick House
Staddlethorpe Grange
Sober Hill

5 Northside Farm
Low Metham Grange

26 High Metham
Blacktoft House
Staddlethorpe House
Sleights

4 DELERY BANK
West End Farm
Metham Hall
DN14
North Farm
Staddlethorpe
Gowthorpe House
GOWTHORPE LANE

25 METHAM LANE

3 West End Farm
Yokefleet
Hall Farm
Blacktoft Lane
Manor Farm
Blacktoft
SPARROWCROFT LANE
South Farm Craft Gallery
Thornton Lands

24 Poplar Farm
Yokefleet Farms
Mill Farm
Windmill
The Moorings
PH
Blacktoft Channel

2 River Ouse
Waterside House
Trans Pennine Trail
Mill House Farm
Ousefleet
Ross Farm
Blacktoft Sands Nature Reserve

23 Whitgift Ness
West View Farm
White House Farm
Old Smithy Farm
Townend Causeway
P

1 Reedness Prim Sch
Fair View Farm
Hall Farm
Hall Lane Farm
Whitgift
Ivy House Farm
DN14
Ousefleet Ings
Little Reedness

22 Dairy Farm
Adlingfleet Ings

65

81

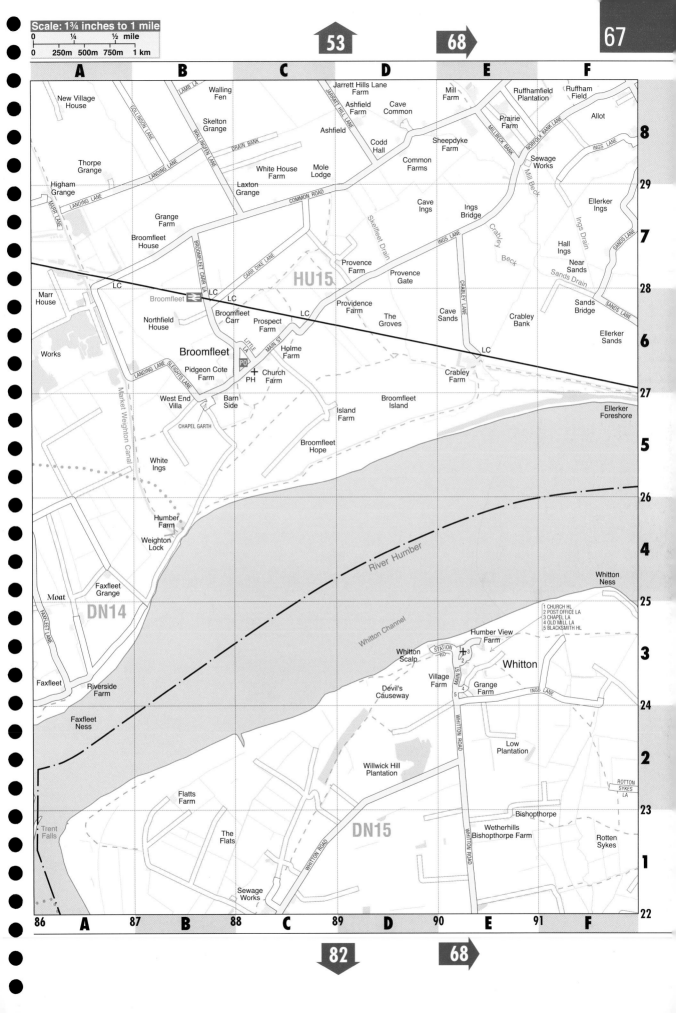

A   B   C   D   E   F

New Village House
Walling Fen
Jarrett Hills Lane Farm
Mill Farm
Ruffhamfield Plantation
Ruffham Field

Skelton Grange
Ashfield Farm
Cave Common
Prairie Farm
Allot

8

Thorpe Grange
White House Farm
Ashfield
Mole Lodge
Common Farms
Sheepdyke Farm
Sewage Works

Higham Grange
Laxton Grange
Codd Hall
Ellerker Ings

29

LANDING LANE
COMMON ROAD
Cave Ings
Ings Bridge

Grange Farm
Broomfleet House
Provence Farm
Provence Gate

MARR LANE
LANDING LANE
Hall Ings
Near Sands

Skelfleet Drain
Crabley Beck
Sands Drain

7

HU15

Marr House
LC
Broomfleet
LC
LC
Providence Farm
The Groves
Cave Sands
Crabley Bank
Sands Bridge

28

Northfield House
Broomfleet Carr
Prospect Farm
LC
Crabley LANE
LC

Works
Broomfleet
Holme Farm
Crabley Farm
Ellerker Sands

6

Pidgeon Cote Farm
PO
PH
Church Farm

Market Weighton Canal
West End Villa
Barn Side
Island Farm
Broomfleet Island
Ellerker Foreshore

CHAPEL GARTH

White Ings
Broomfleet Hope

5

Humber Farm

26

Weighton Lock

River Humber

4

Faxfleet Grange
Whitton Ness

Moat
25

DN14

Whitton Channel
1 CHURCH HL
2 POST OFFICE LA
3 CHAPEL LA
4 OLD MILL LA
5 BLACKSMITH HL

3

Faxfleet
Whitton Scalp
STATION RD
Humber View Farm
Whitton

Riverside Farm
Village Farm
Grange Farm
INGS LANE

FAXFLEET LANE
Devil's Causeway

Faxfleet Ness
24

Low Plantation

2

Willwick Hill Plantation
WHITTON ROAD
ROTTON SYKES LA

Flatts Farm
Bishopthorpe

23

DN15
Wetherhills Bishopthorpe Farm
Rotten Sykes

The Flats
WHITTON ROAD
WHITTON ROAD

Trent Falls
1

Sewage Works

22

86   A   87   B   88   C   89   D   90   E   91   F

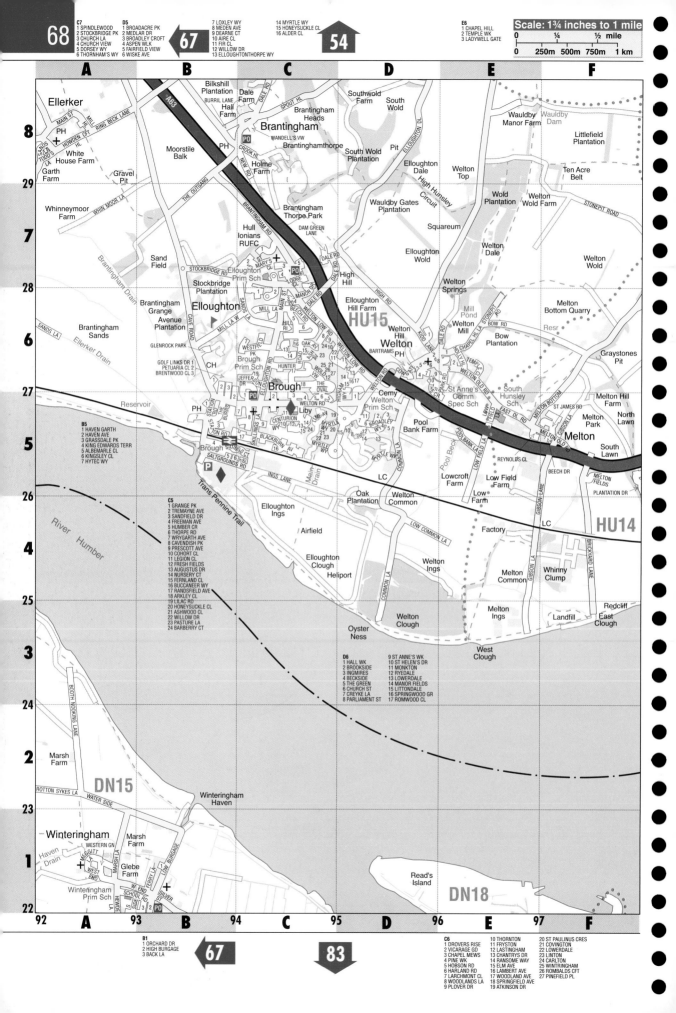

68

C7
1 SPINDLEWOOD
2 STOCKBRIDGE PK
3 CHURCH LA
4 CHURCH VIEW
5 DORSEY WY
6 THORNHAM'S WY

D5
1 BROADACRE PK
2 MEDLAR DR
3 BROADLEY CROFT
4 ASPEN WLK
5 FAIRFIELD VIEW
6 WISKE AVE

7 LOXLEY WY
8 MEDEN AVE
9 DEARNE CT
10 AIRE CL
11 FIR CL
12 WILLOW DR
13 ELLOUGHTONTHORPE WY

14 MYRTLE WY
15 HONEYSUCKLE CL
16 ALDER CL

67

54

E6
1 CHAPEL HILL
2 TEMPLE WK
3 LADYWELL GATE

Scale: 1¾ inches to 1 mile

0   ¼   ½   mile
0   250m 500m 750m 1 km

Ellerker

Brantingham

Bilkshill Plantation

Southwold Farm

South Wold

Wauldby Manor Farm

Wauldby Dam

Littlefield Plantation

White House Farm

Garth Farm

Gravel Pit

Moorstile Balk

Holme Farm

Brantingham Heads

Brantinghamthorpe

South Wold Plantation

Pit

Elloughton Dale

Welton Top

Wold Plantation

Welton Wold Farm

Ten Acre Belt

STONEPIT ROAD

Whinneymoor Farm

Brantingham Thorpe Park

Wauldby Gates Plantation

High Hunsley Circuit

Welton Dale

Welton Wold

Sand Field

Hull Ionians RUFC

Stockbridge Plantation

Elloughton Prim Sch

Elloughton Wold

Welton Springs

Mill Pond

Melton Bottom Quarry

Brantingham Grange Avenue Plantation

Brantingham Sands

Ellerker Drain

Glenrock Park

HU15

High Hill

Elloughton Hill Farm

Welton Hill

Welton Mill

Bow Plantation

Resr

Graystones Pit

Elloughton

CH

Brough Prim Sch

Petuaria Cl 2
Golf Links Dr 1
Brentwood Cl 3

Welton

Bartrams

PH

St Anne's Comm Spec Sch

South Hunsley Sch

Melton Hill Farm

North Lawn

B5
1 HAVEN GARTH
2 HAVEN AVE
3 GRASSDALE PK
4 KING EDWARDS TERR
5 ALBEMARLE CL
6 KINGSLEY CL
7 HYTEC WY

Reservoir

Brough

Liby

Cemy

Welton Prim Sch

Melton Park

Melton

South Lawn

River Humber

Trans Pennine Trail

C5
1 GRANGE PK
2 TREMAYNE AVE
3 SANDFIELD DR
4 FREEMAN AVE
5 HUMBER CR
6 THORPE RD
7 WRYGARTH AVE
8 CAVENDISH PK
9 PRESCOTT AVE
10 COHORT CL
11 LEGION CL
12 FRESH FIELDS
13 AUGUSTUS DR
14 NURSERY CT
15 FERNLAND CL
16 BUCCANEER WY
17 RANDSFIELD AVE
18 ARKLEY CL
19 LILAC RD
20 HONEYSUCKLE CL
21 ASHWOOD CL
22 WILLOW DR
23 PASTURE LA
24 BARBERRY CT

Elloughton Ings

Airfield

Elloughton Clough

Heliport

Oak Plantation

Welton Common

Welton Ings

Lowcroft Farm

Low Field Farm

Pool Bank Farm

Factory

HU14

REYNOLDS CL

BEECH DR

MELTON FIELDS

PLANTATION DR

Low Farm

Melton Common

Whinny Clump

BRICKYARD LANE

Oyster Ness

Welton Clough

Melton Ings

Landfill

Redcliff East Clough

West Clough

D6
1 HALL WK
2 BROOKSIDE
3 INGMIRES
4 BECKSIDE
5 THE GREEN
6 CHURCH ST
7 CREYKE LA
8 PARLIAMENT ST

9 ST ANNE'S WK
10 ST HELEN'S DR
11 MONKTON
12 RYEDALE
13 LOWERDALE
14 MANOR FIELDS
15 LITTONDALE
16 SPRINGWOOD GR
17 ROMWOOD CL

DN15

Marsh Farm

ROTTON SYKES LA

WATER SIDE

Winteringham Haven

Winteringham

Marsh Farm

Glebe Farm

Winteringham Prim Sch

Haven Drain

Read's Island

DN18

67

83

B1
1 ORCHARD DR
2 HIGH BURGAGE
3 BACK LA

C6
1 DROVERS RISE
2 VICARAGE GD
3 CHAPEL MEWS
4 PINE WK
5 HOBSON RD
6 HARLAND RD
7 LARCHMONT CL
8 WOODLANDS LA
9 PLOVER DR

10 THORNTON
11 FRYSTON
12 LASTINGHAM
13 CHANTRYS DR
14 RANSOME WAY
15 ELM AVE
16 LAMBERT AVE
17 WOODLAND AVE
18 SPRINGFIELD AVE
19 ATKINSON DR

20 ST PAULINUS CRES
21 COVINGTON
22 LOWERDALE
23 LINTON
24 CARLTON
25 WINTRINGHAM
26 ROMBALDS CFT
27 PINEFIELD PL

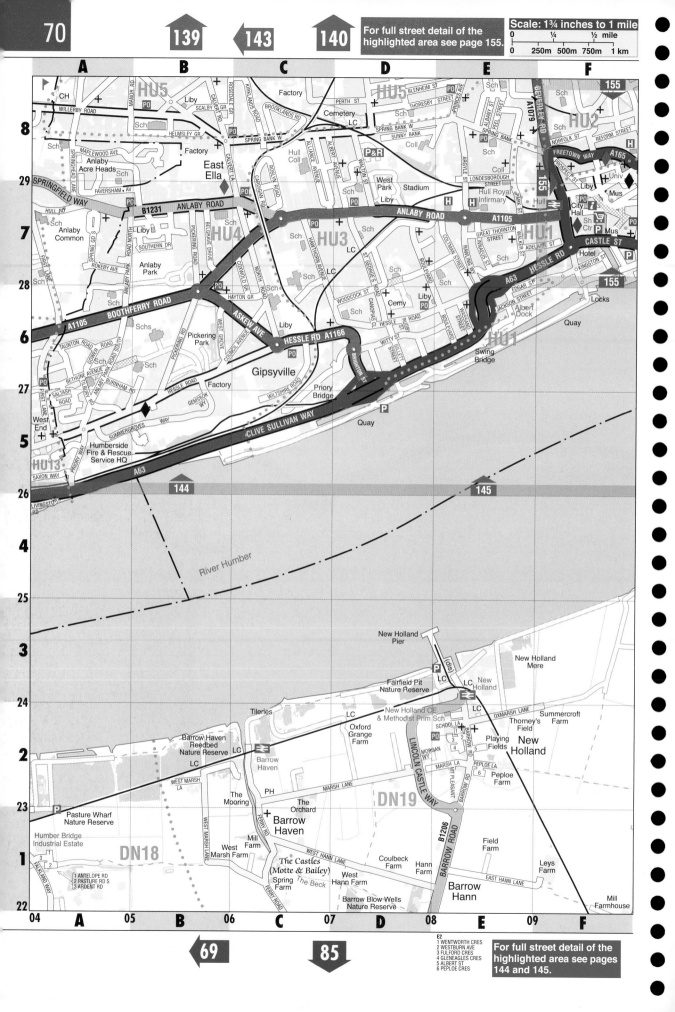

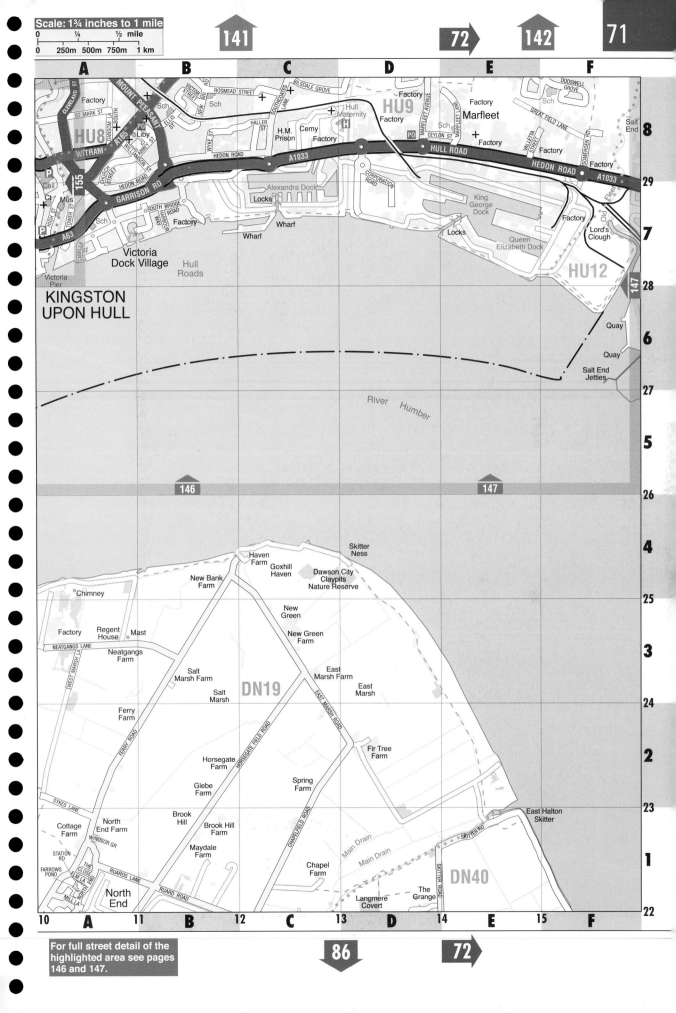

A   B   C   D   E   F

Factory
ST MARK ST
CLEVELAND ST
MOUNT PLEASANT
Sch
VICTOR STREET
NEW BRI
RD
ROSMEAD STREET
BILSDALE GROVE
Sch
SOUTHCOATES LANE
Factory
HU9
Factory
MARFLEET AVENUE
Factory
Marfleet
DODSWELL GROVE
Sch
GREAT FIELD LANE
Salt End
HU8
WITHAM
DANSOM LA SOUTH
ELLIS ST
ABBEY ST
PO
Liby
WYKE ST
HALLER ST
H.M. Prison
Hull Maternity
H
Cemy
Factory
PO
CEYLON ST
MARFLEET LANE
Sch
Factory
VALETTA STREET
Factory
SOMERDEN RD
Factory
8
CHURCH STREET
WILLIAMSON ST
HEDON ROAD
A1033
Hull Road
HEDON ROAD
A1033
Fleet
29
T55
Coll
Mus
Ct
GARRISON RD
CORPORATION ROAD
King George Dock
Factory
Old
Lord's Clough
7
HIGH ST
TOWER ST
P
A63
CAMILLA CL
SOUTH BRIDGE WAY
HARBOUR WAY
Sch
Factory
Alexandra Dock
Locks
Wharf
Wharf
Wharf
Locks
Queen Elizabeth Dock
HU12
147
Victoria Dock Village
Hull Roads
28
Victoria Pier
KINGSTON UPON HULL
Quay
6
Quay
Salt End Jetties
27
River   Humber
5

146   147

26
Skitter Ness
4
Haven Farm
Goxhill Haven
Dawson City Claypits Nature Reserve
25
Chimney
New Bank Farm
New Green
Factory
Regent House
Mast
New Green Farm
3
NEATGANGS LANE
Neatgangs Farm
WEST MARSH LA
Salt Marsh Farm
EAST MARSH ROAD
East Marsh Farm
East Marsh
DN19
Salt Marsh
24
Ferry Farm
FERRY ROAD
HORSEGATE FIELD ROAD
Fir Tree Farm
2
Horsegate Farm
Glebe Farm
Spring Farm
CHAPELFIELD ROAD
East Halton Skitter
23
SYKES LANE
Brook Hill
Brook Hill Farm
Cottage Farm
North End Farm
WINDSOR GR
Maydale Farm
Chapel Farm
Main Drain
Main Drain
SKITTER RD
SKITTER ROAD
DN40
1
STATION RD
THE CLOSE
ELM LA ELM LA RD
FARROWS POND
RUAROS LANE
RUARD ROAD
North End
MILL LA
NORTH END
Langmere Covert
The Grange
22

10   A   11   B   12   C   13   D   14   E   15   F

86   72

For full street detail of the highlighted area see pages 146 and 147.

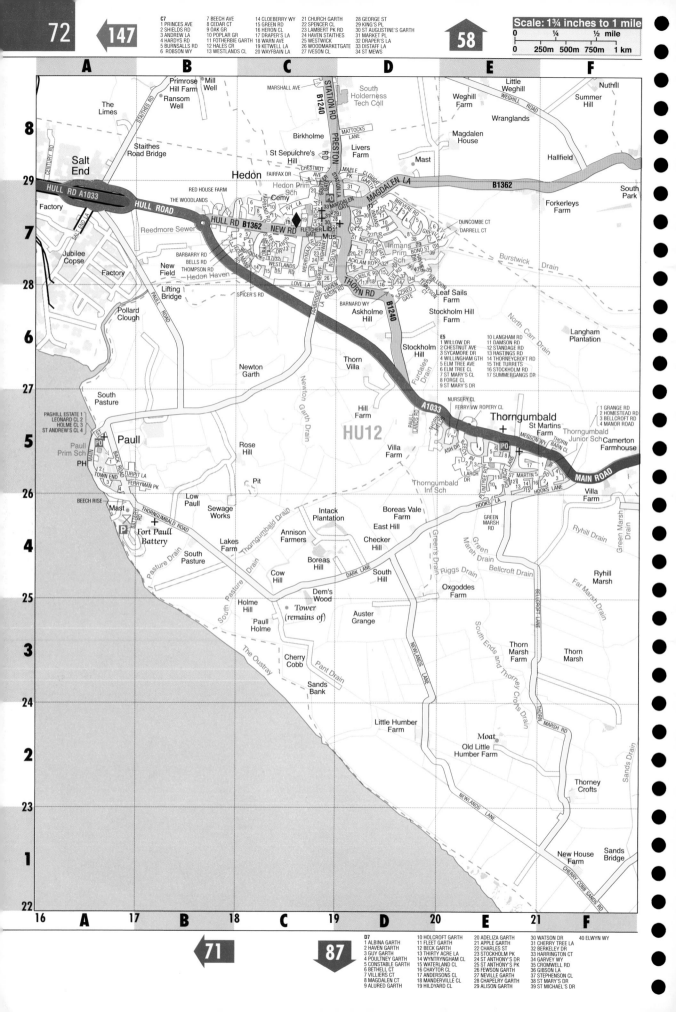

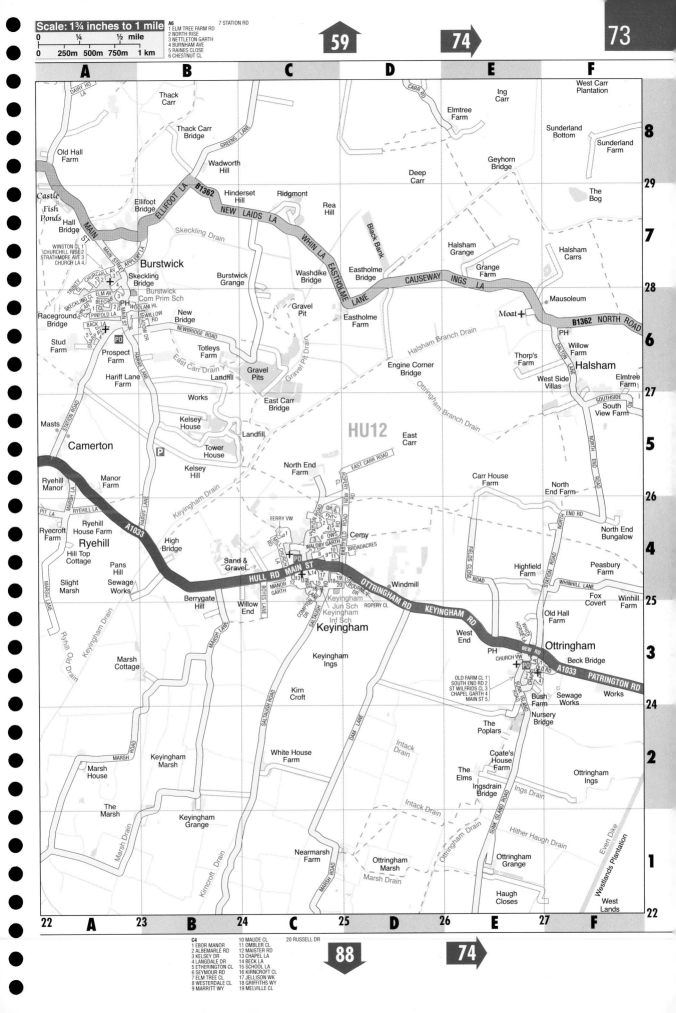

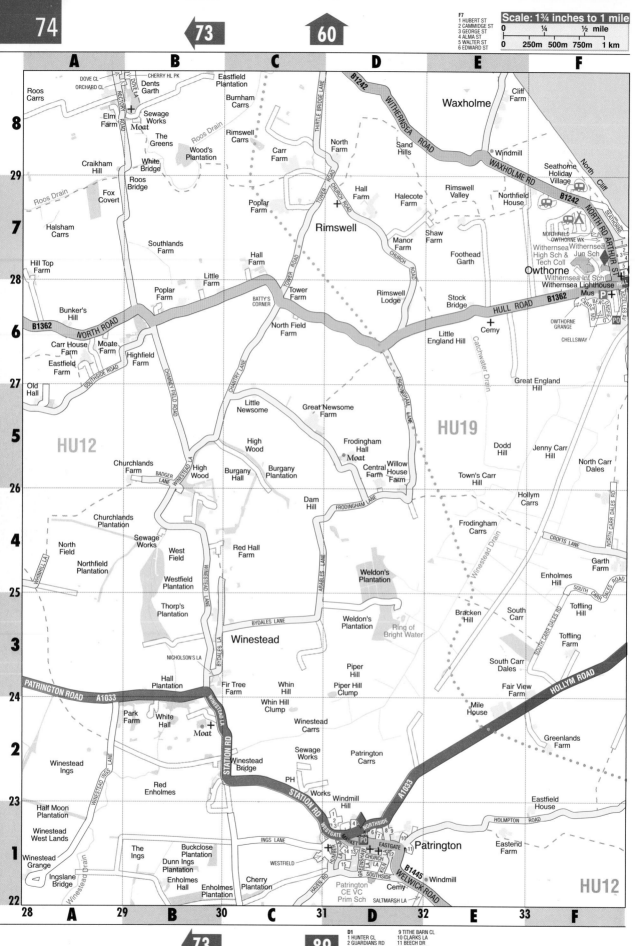

73 60

F7
1 HUBERT ST
2 CAMMIDGE ST
3 GEORGE ST
4 ALMA ST
5 WALTER ST
6 EDWARD ST

Scale: 1¾ inches to 1 mile
0   ¼   ½   mile
0   250m 500m 750m 1 km

73 89

D1
1 HUNTER CL
2 GUARDIANS RD
3 FRANCIS WY
4 WESTGATE MANOR
5 PUMP ROW
6 NORTHSIDE CT
7 CHURCH VW
8 TITHE BARN LA
9 TITHE BARN CL
10 CLARKS LA
11 BEECH DR
12 THE CLOSE
13 THE CRESCENT
14 ST PATRICK'S GN
15 SAFFRON GARTH

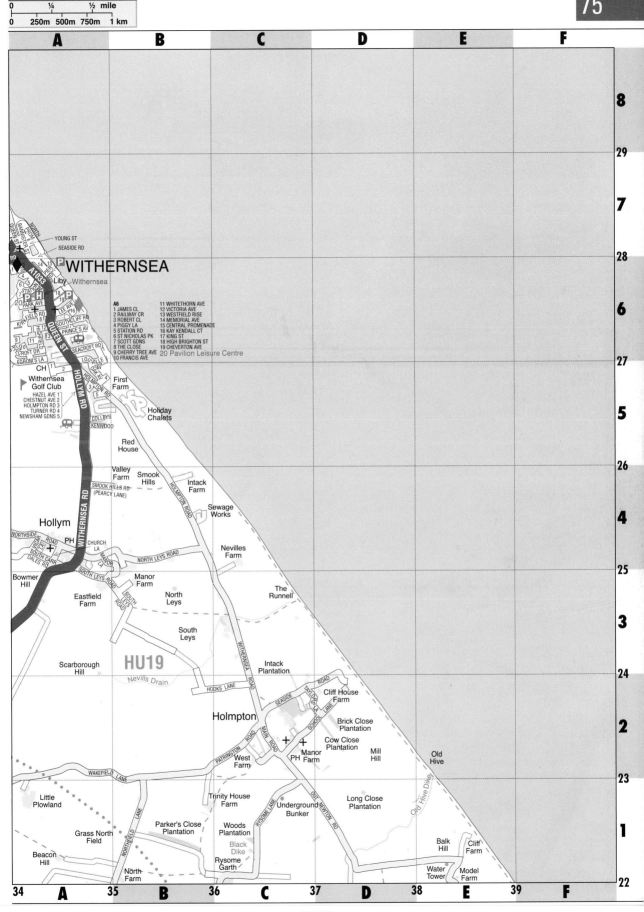

Scale: 1¾ inches to 1 mile

0   ¼   ½   mile
0   250m 500m 750m 1 km

A   B   C   D   E   F

WITHERNSEA
Liby Withernsea

A6
1 JAMES CL
2 RAILWAY CR
3 ROBERT CL
4 PIGGY LA
5 STATION RD
6 ST NICHOLAS PK
7 SCOTT GDNS
8 THE CLOSE
9 CHERRY TREE AVE
10 FRANCIS AVE
11 WHITETHORN AVE
12 VICTORIA AVE
13 WESTFIELD RISE
14 MEMORIAL AVE
15 CENTRAL PROMENADE
16 KAY KENDALL CT
17 KING ST
18 HIGH BRIGHTON ST
19 CHEVERTON AVE
20 Pavilion Leisure Centre

YOUNG ST
SEASIDE RD

First Farm

Holiday Chalets

Red House

Withernsea Golf Club
HAZEL AVE 1
CHESTNUT AVE 2
HOLMPTON RD 3
TURNER RD 4
NEWSHAM GDNS 5

COLLBYS KENWOOD

Valley Farm
Smook Hills
Intack Farm

Hollym

Sewage Works

Nevilles Farm

North Leys Road

Manor Farm

North Leys

The Runnell

Bowmer Hill

Eastfield Farm

South Leys

Scarborough Hill

HU19

Nevills Drain

HODKS LANE

Intack Plantation

Cliff House Farm

Holmpton

Brick Close Plantation

Cow Close Plantation

Mill Hill

Old Hive

West Farm

Manor Farm
PH

Wakefield Lane

Little Plowland

Trinity House Farm

Underground Bunker

Long Close Plantation

Grass North Field

Parker's Close Plantation

Woods Plantation

Black Dike

Rysome Garth

Balk Hill

Cliff Farm

Beacon Hill

North Farm

Water Tower

Model Farm

34   35   36   37   38   39

8 29 7 28 6 27 5 26 4 25 3 24 2 23 1 22

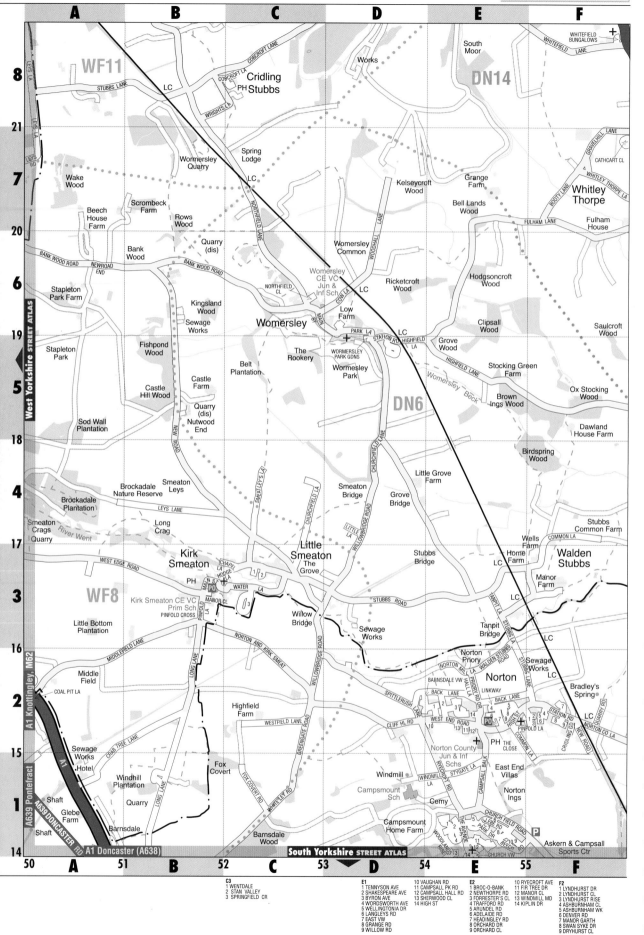

Scale: 1¾ inches to 1 mile

0 ¼ ½ mile
0 250m 500m 750m 1 km

C3
1 WENTDALE
2 STAN VALLEY
3 SPRINGFIELD CR

E1
1 TENNYSON AVE
2 SHAKESPEARE AVE
3 BYRON AVE
4 WORDSWORTH AVE
5 WELLINGTONIA DR
6 LANGLEYS RD
7 EAST VW
8 GRANGE RD
9 WILLOW RD
10 VAUGHAN RD
11 CAMPSALL PK RD
12 CAMPSALL HALL RD
13 SHERWOOD CL
14 HIGH ST

E2
1 BROC-O-BANK
2 NEWTHORPE RD
3 FORRESTER'S CL
4 TRAFFORD RD
5 ARUNDEL RD
6 ADELAIDE RD
7 HEADINGLEY RD
8 ORCHARD DR
9 ORCHARD CL
10 RYECROFT AVE
11 FIR TREE DR
12 MANOR CL
13 WINDMILL MD
14 KIPLIN DR

F2
1 LYNDHURST DR
2 LYNDHURST CL
3 LYNDHURST RISE
4 ASHBURNHAM CL
5 ASHBURNHAM WK
6 DENVER RD
7 MANOR GARTH
8 SWAN SYKE DR
9 DRYHURST CL

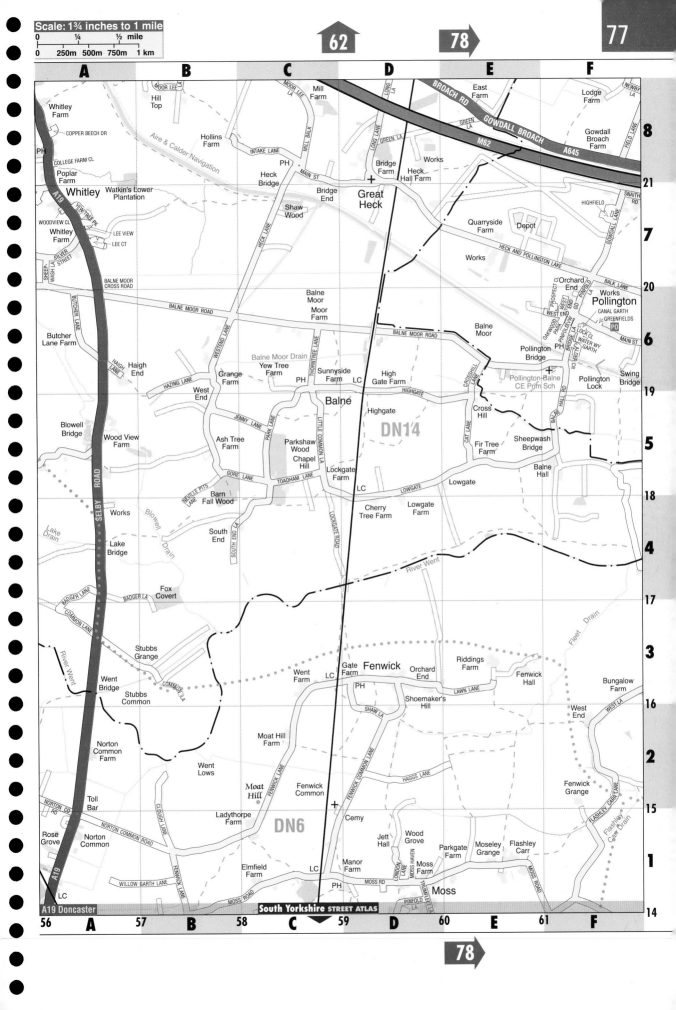

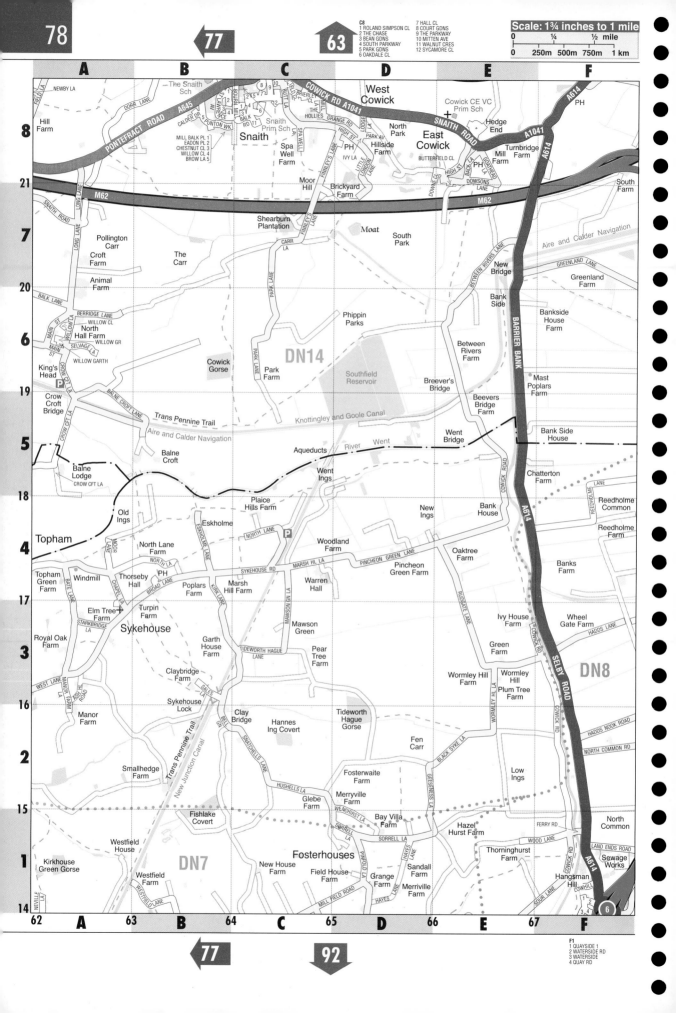

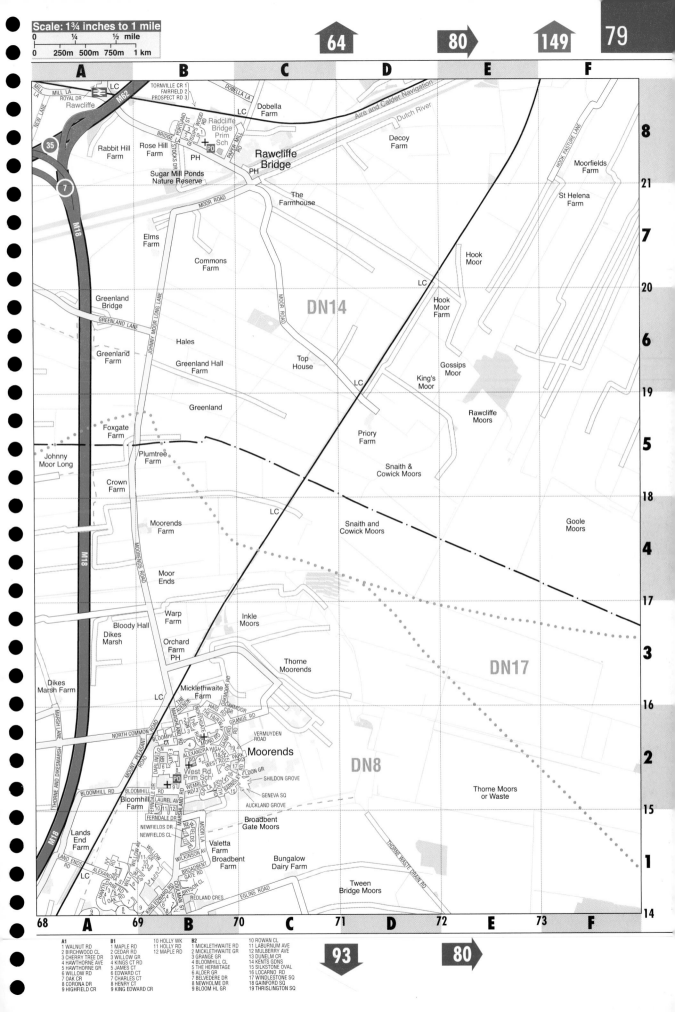

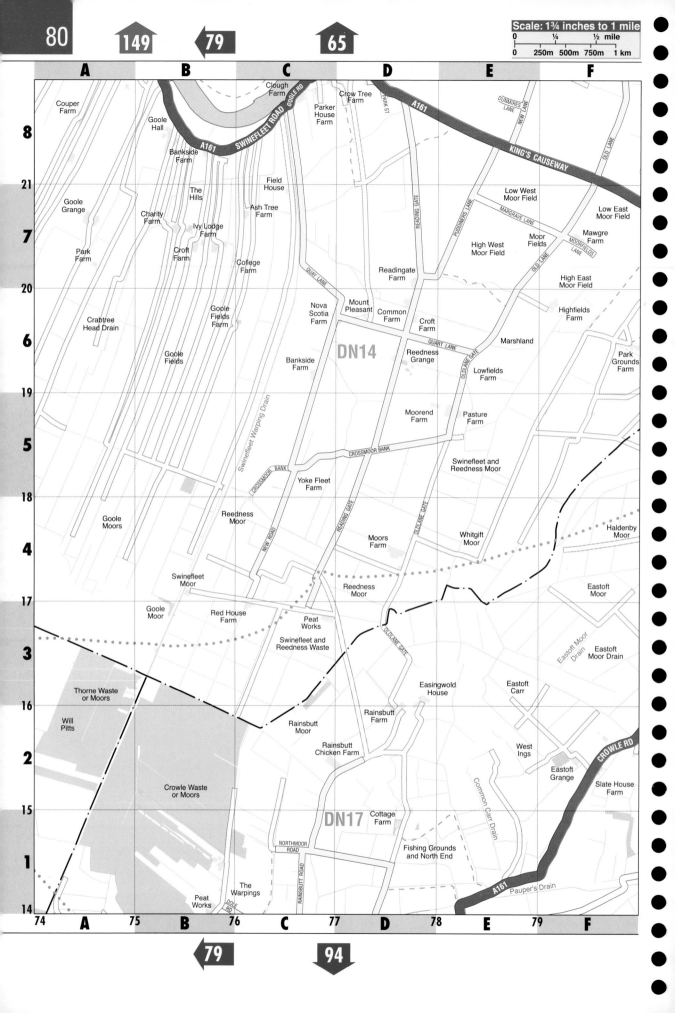

A   B   C   D   E   F

Couper
Farm

Goole
Hall

Clough
Farm

GOOLE RD

Parker
House
Farm

Crow Tree
Farm

Park St

A161

SWINEFLEET ROAD

A161

KING'S CAUSEWAY

DUNMIRES
LANE

NEW
LANE

OLD
LANE

8

Bankside
Farm

Field
House

Low West
Moor Field

Low East
Moor Field

21

Goole
Grange

The
Hills

Ash Tree
Farm

PUDDINERS
LANE

MARGRAVE LANE

Mawgre
Farm

7

Charity
Farm

Ivy Lodge
Farm

High West
Moor Field

Moor
Fields

OLD LANE

MOORFIELDS
LANE

Park
Farm

Croft
Farm

College
Farm

QUAY LANE

READING GATE

Readingate
Farm

High East
Moor Field

20

Nova
Scotia
Farm

Mount
Pleasant

Common
Farm

Croft
Farm

Highfields
Farm

6

Crabtree
Head Drain

Goole
Fields
Farm

DN14

QUART LANE

Marshland

Park
Grounds
Farm

Goole
Fields

Bankside
Farm

Reedness
Grange

OLDLANE GATE

Lowfields
Farm

19

Swinefleet Warping Drain

Moorend
Farm

Pasture
Farm

5

Goole
Moors

CROSSMOOR BANK

CROSSMOOR BANK

Yoke Fleet
Farm

CROSSMOOR BANK

Swinefleet and
Reedness Moor

18

Reedness
Moor

NEW ROAD

READING GATE

Moors
Farm

OLDLANE GATE

Whitgift
Moor

Haldenby
Moor

4

Swinefleet
Moor

Reedness
Moor

Eastoft
Moor

17

Goole
Moor

Red House
Farm

Peat
Works

Swinefleet and
Reedness Waste

OLDLANE GATE

Eastoft Moor Drain

Eastoft
Moor Drain

3

Thorne Waste
or Moors

Easingwold
House

Eastoft
Carr

Will
Pitts

Rainsbutt
Moor

Rainsbutt
Farm

16

CROWLE RD

2

Crowle Waste
or Moors

Rainsbutt
Chicken Farm

Common Carr Drain

West
Ings

Eastoft
Grange

Slate House
Farm

15

DN17

Cottage
Farm

NORTHMOOR ROAD

RAINSBUTT ROAD

Fishing Grounds
and North End

1

Peat
Works

The
Warpings

DOLE RD

A161

Pauper's Drain

14

74   A   75   B   76   C   77   D   78   E   79   F

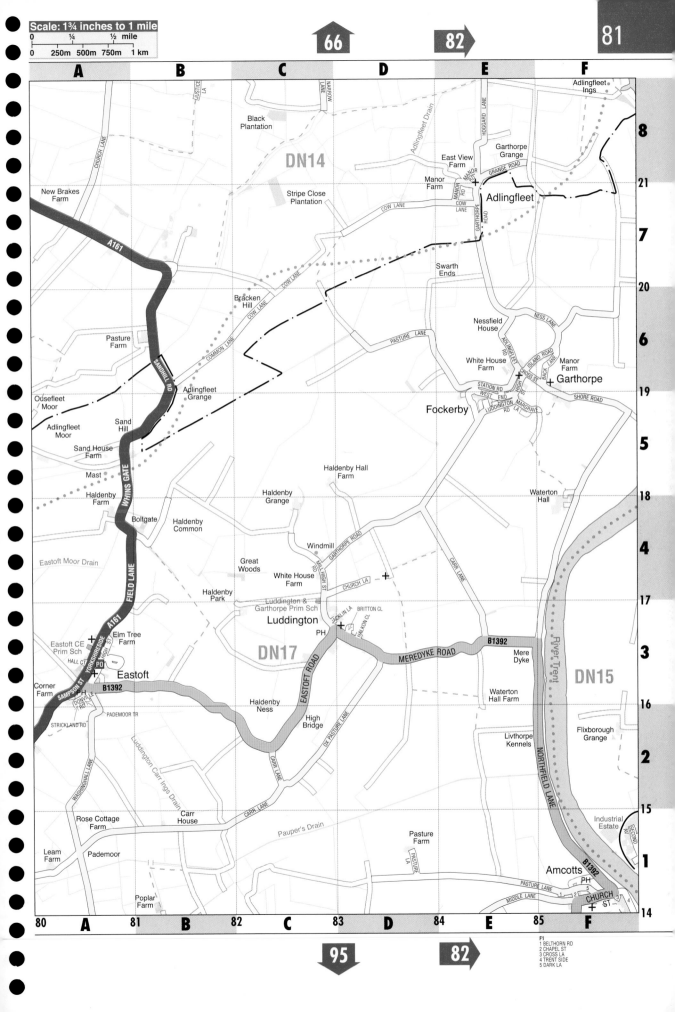

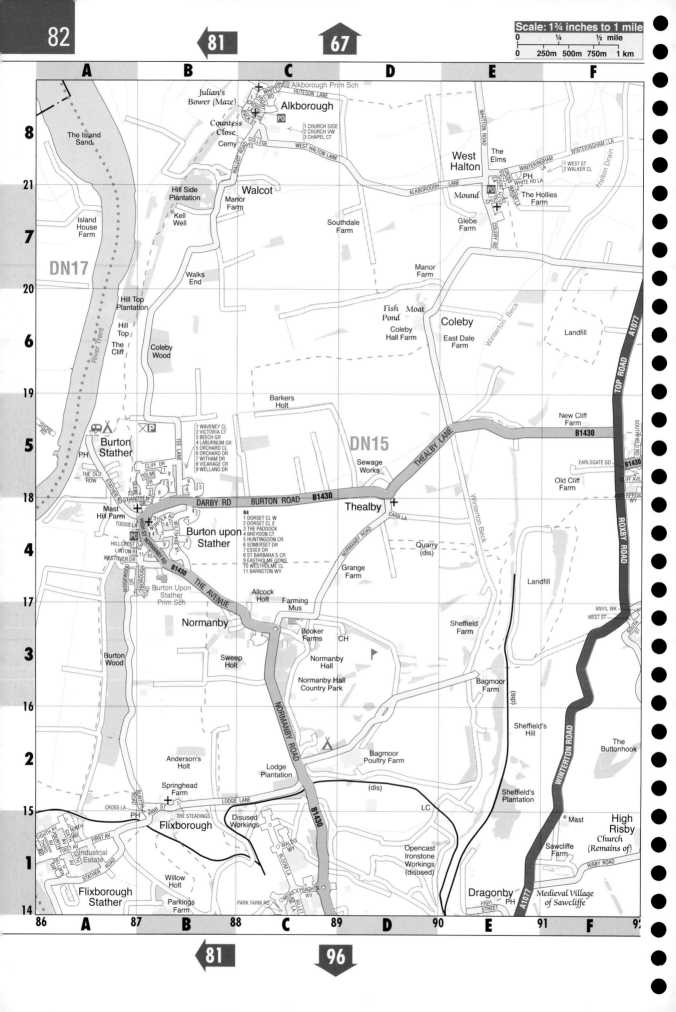

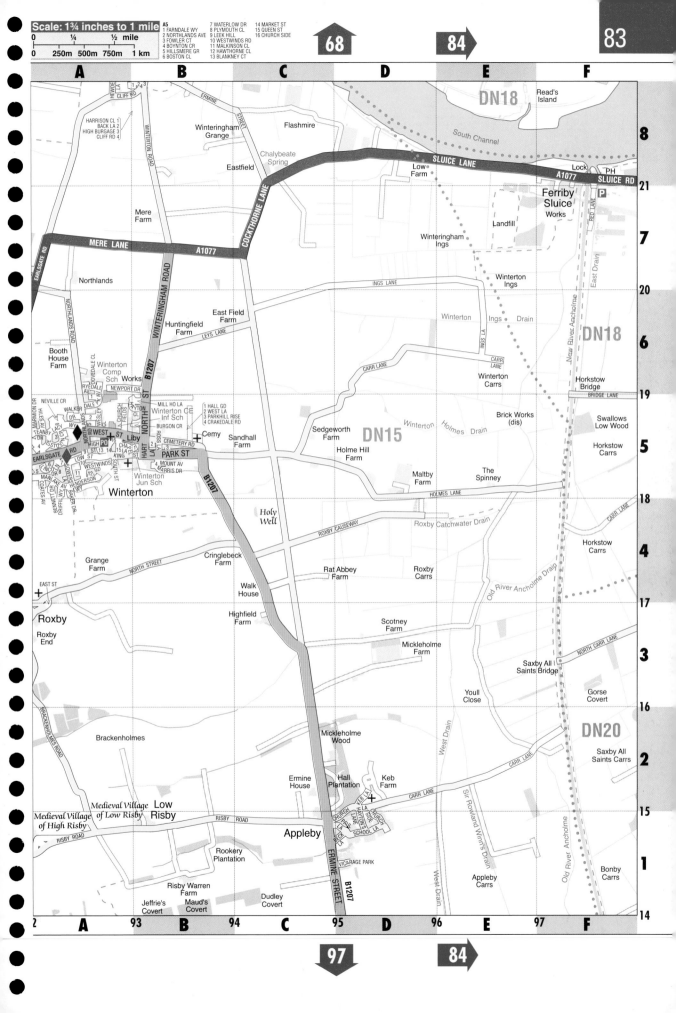

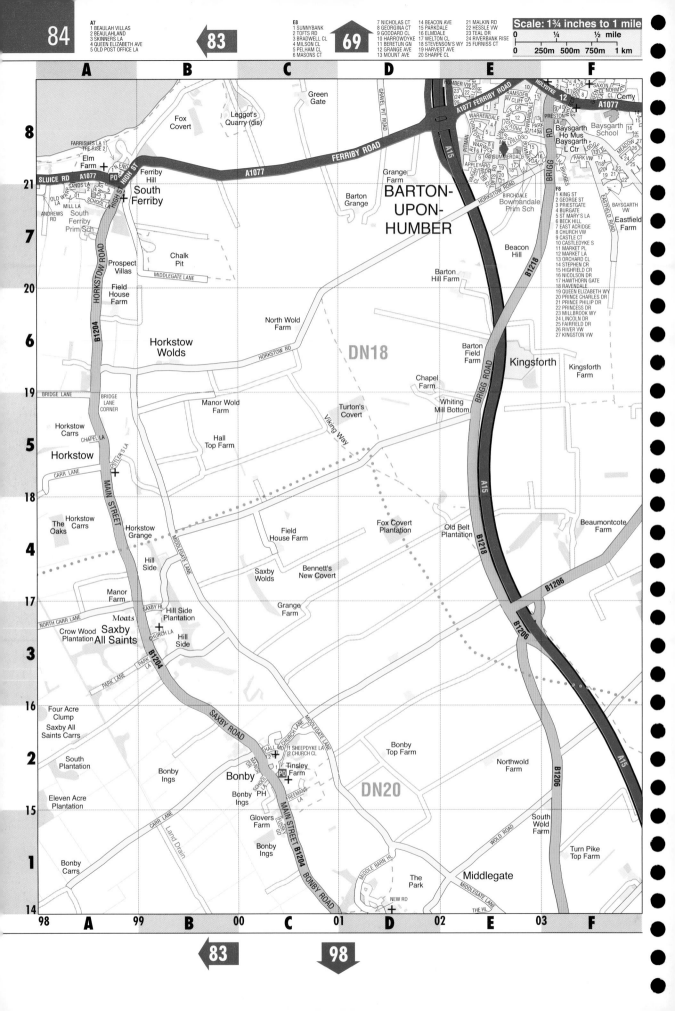

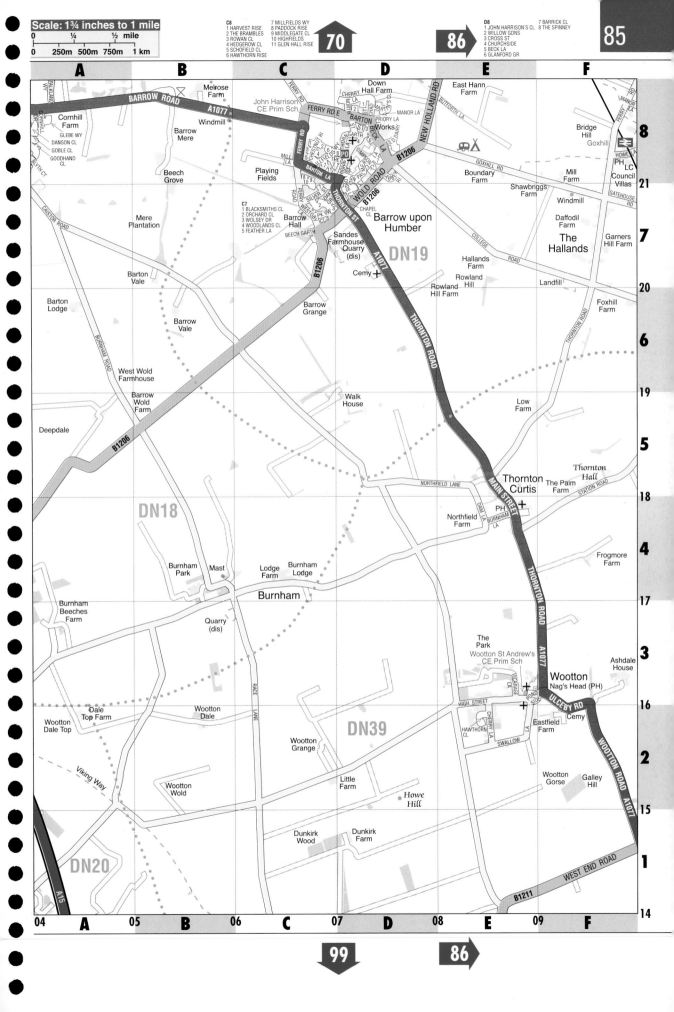

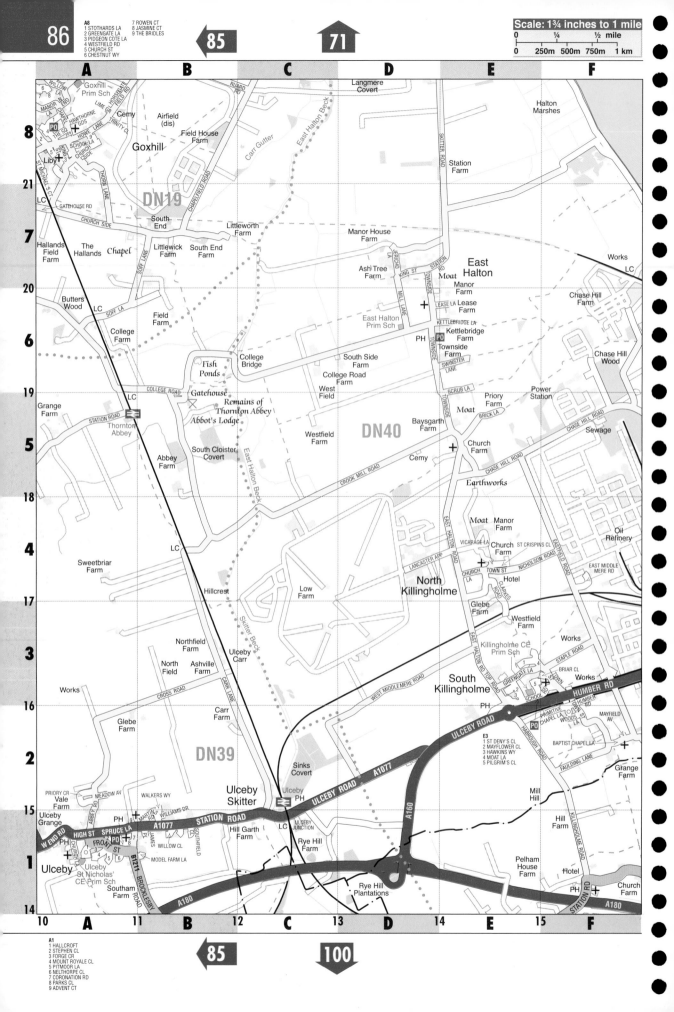

A B C D E F

8
21
7
20
6
19
5
18
4
17
3
16
2
15
1
14

HU12

Cherry Cobb Sands Bank
Cherry Cobb Sands Road

Jetty
North Killingholme Haven

LC
Killingholme Haven Pits Nature Reserve

HAVEN ROAD

ROSPER ROAD

Mast
Burkinshaw's Covert
Sewage

Killingholme Marshes

STATION ROAD

Killingholme North Low Lighthouse

Jetty

LC
Killingholme High Lighthouse

River Humber

EAST MIDDLE MERE ROAD

ROSPER ROAD

MARSH LANE

LC

LC

Humber International Terminal

South Killingholme Haven

Henderson Quay

LC

Ore Terminal

HUMBER ROAD

West Gate

Oil Refinery

WEST RIVERSIDE
WEST HAVEN WY

LOCKSIDE RD

Immingham Dock

Lock Inn (PH)

ALEXANDRA RD

EAST RIVERSIDE

A160 HUMBER ROAD

A1173

HUMBER ROAD
WEST HAVEN WY

SOUTHERN WY

WESTERN ACCESS ROAD

MINERAL QUAY RD

SEVEN QUAY RD

ALEXANDRA RD S

ROBINSON ROAD

EAST DOCK ROAD

DN40

Works

Houlton's Covert

MANBY ROAD

B2
1 STANDISH LA
2 HINKLEY DR
3 WESTON GR
4 ATWOOD CL
5 ST ANDREWS LA

East End Farm

IMMINGHAM
Medieval Village of Immingham (site of)

Homestead Park

Pelham Ind Est

Works

MANBY ROAD

A1173

MIDDLE PLAT RD

GRESLEY WAY

East Gate

LAPORTE ROAD

CH
Cemy

PENNINE CL

MILL LANE

CHURCH LANE

WINSLOW DR

WOODLANDS

KINGS ROAD

QUEENS ROAD

A1173

DN41

Works

PILGRIMS WY

Recreation Ground

Luxmore Farm

Coomb Briggs Prim Sch

STALLINGBOROUGH RD

Sports Ctr
Liby

Pool

PO

Eastfield Inf & Jun Sch

Landfill Site

North Beck Drain
NETHERLANDS WY

SCANDINAVIA WY

EUROPA WY

Kiln Lane Trading Estate

KILN LANE

LC
WORLDWIDE WY

HOBSON WAY

B1210

HABROUGH ROAD

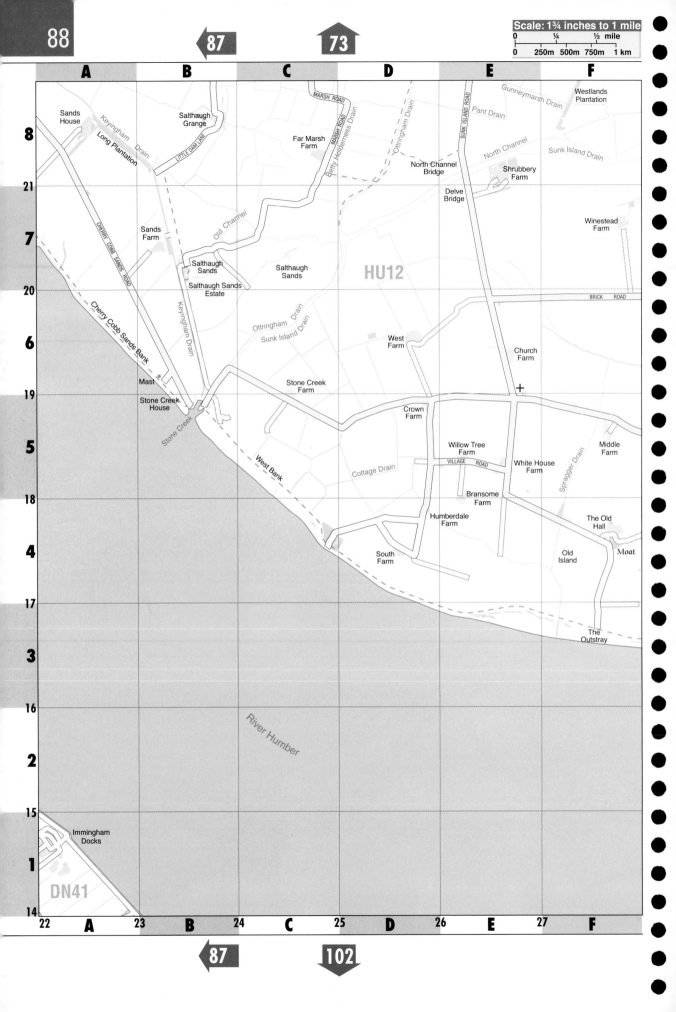

Scale: 1¾ inches to 1 mile

0   ¼   ½   mile
0   250m 500m 750m 1 km

A   B   C   D   E   F

Sands House
Long Plantation
Keyingham Drain
Salthaugh Grange
LITTLE DAM LANE
MARSH ROAD
Far Marsh Farm
Betty Holderness Drain
Ottringham Drain
Gunneymarsh Drain
Pant Drain
SUNK ISLAND ROAD
Westlands Plantation
North Channel Bridge
North Channel
Sunk Island Drain
Shrubbery Farm
Delve Bridge

CHERRY COBB SANDS ROAD
Sands Farm
Old Channel
Salthaugh Sands
Salthaugh Sands
Salthaugh Sands Estate
HU12
Winestead Farm

Cherry Cobb Sands Bank
Ottringham Drain
Sunk Island Drain
West Farm
BRICK ROAD
Church Farm

Mast
Stone Creek House
Stone Creek
Stone Creek Farm
Crown Farm
Willow Tree Farm
VILLAGE ROAD
White House Farm
Spragger Drain
Middle Farm

West Bank
Cottage Drain
Bransome Farm
Humberdale Farm
The Old Hall

South Farm
Old Island
Moat

The Outstray

River Humber

Immingham Docks

DN41

22   A   23   B   24   C   25   D   26   E   27   F

8
21
7
20
6
19
5
18
4
17
3
16
2
15
1
14

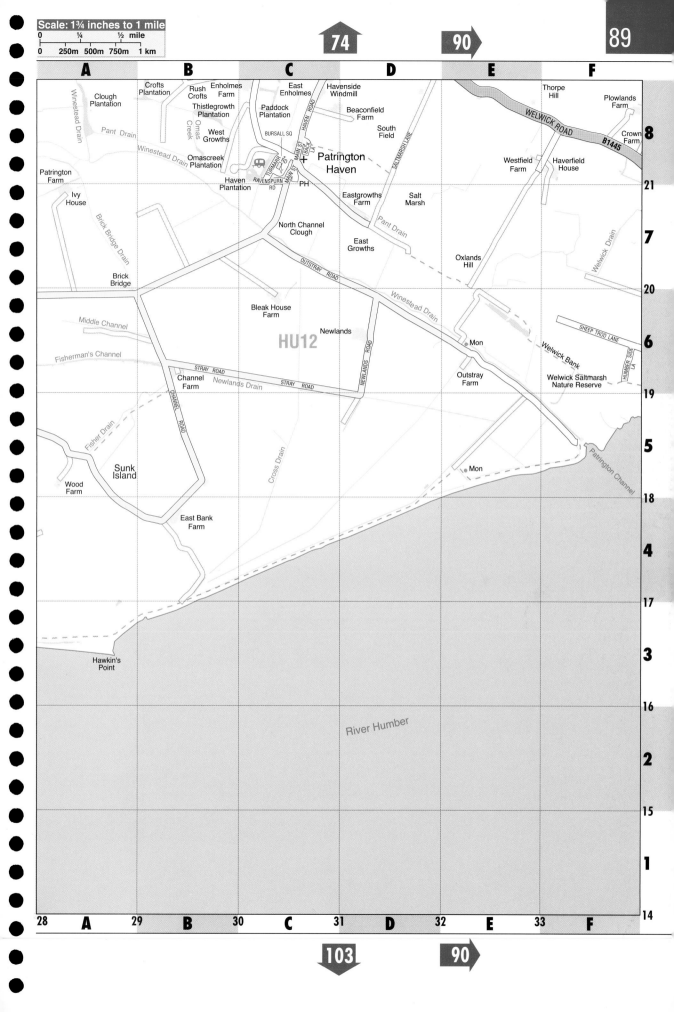

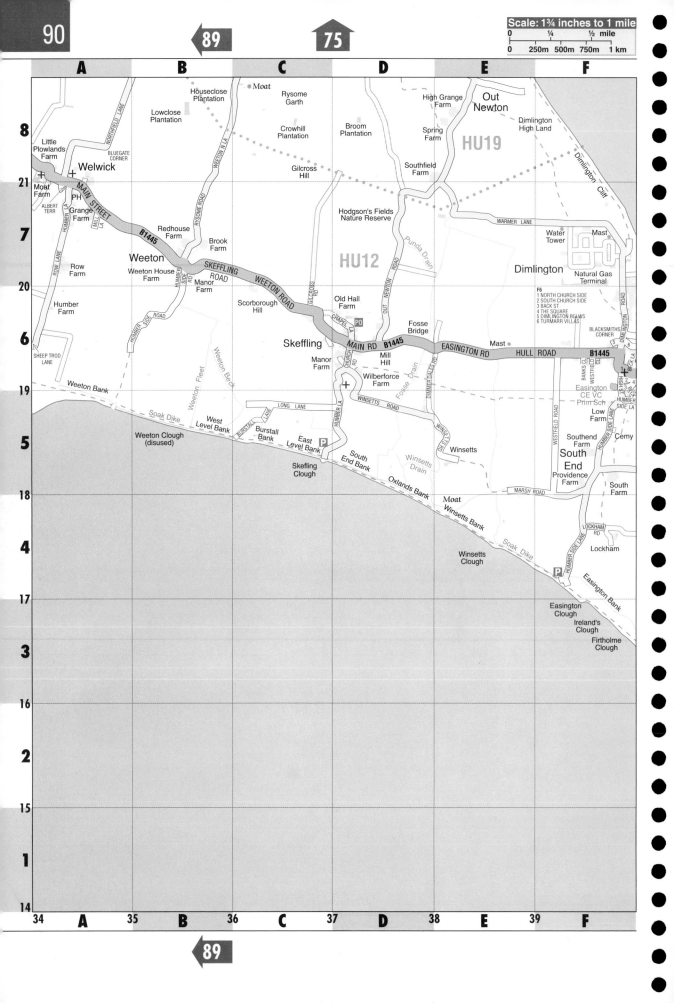

Scale: 1¾ inches to 1 mile

0   ¼   ½ mile

0   250m 500m 750m 1 km

A   B   C   D   E   F

8

Houseclose Plantation

Moat

Rysome Garth

High Grange Farm

Out Newton

Lowclose Plantation

Crowhill Plantation

Broom Plantation

Spring Farm

Dimlington High Land

HU19

Little Plowlands Farm

Welwick

Gilcross Hill

Southfield Farm

Dimlington Cliff

21

Moat Farm

BLUEGATE CORNER

WEETON N LA

Hodgson's Fields Nature Reserve

WARMER LANE

Water Tower

Mast

ALBERT TERR

7

Grange Farm

Redhouse Farm

RYSOME ROAD

HU12

Punda Drain

Dimlington

Weeton

Brook Farm

OUT NEWTON ROAD

Natural Gas Terminal

Row Farm

Weeton House Farm

SKEFFLING ROAD

Manor Farm

WEETON ROAD

GILCROSS RD

Old Hall Farm

F6
1 NORTH CHURCH SIDE
2 SOUTH CHURCH SIDE
3 BACK ST
4 THE SQUARE
5 DIMLINGTON BGLWS
6 TURMARR VILLAS

20

Scorborough Hill

PO

Fosse Bridge

BLACKSMITHS CORNER

Humber Farm

HUMBER SIDE RD

CHAPEL LA

Skeffling

MAIN RD   B1445

EASINGTON RD   HULL ROAD   B1445

Mast

6

SHEEP TROD LANE

Weeton Fleet

Weeton Beck

Manor Farm

CHURCH RD

Mill Hill

Fosse Drain

DIMMER DALES RD

BANKS CL

WESTFIELD

HIGH ST

Easington CE VC Prim Sch

19

Weeton Bank

Soak Dike

West Level Bank

LONG LANE

Wilberforce Farm

HUMBER LA

WINSETTS ROAD

WINSETTS CL

WESTFIELD ROAD

Low Farm

HUMBER SIDE LA

Cemy

Weeton Clough (disused)

BURSTALL LANE

Burstall Bank

East Level Bank

P

South End Bank

Winsetts Drain

Winsetts

Southend Farm

South End

South Farm

5

Skefling Clough

Oxlands Bank

Providence Farm

18

Moat Winsetts Bank

MARSH ROAD

Soak Dike

LOCKHAM RD

4

Winsetts Clough

Lockham

P

Easington Bank

17

Easington Clough

Ireland's Clough

3

Firtholme Clough

16

2

15

1

14

34   A   35   B   36   C   37   D   38   E   39   F

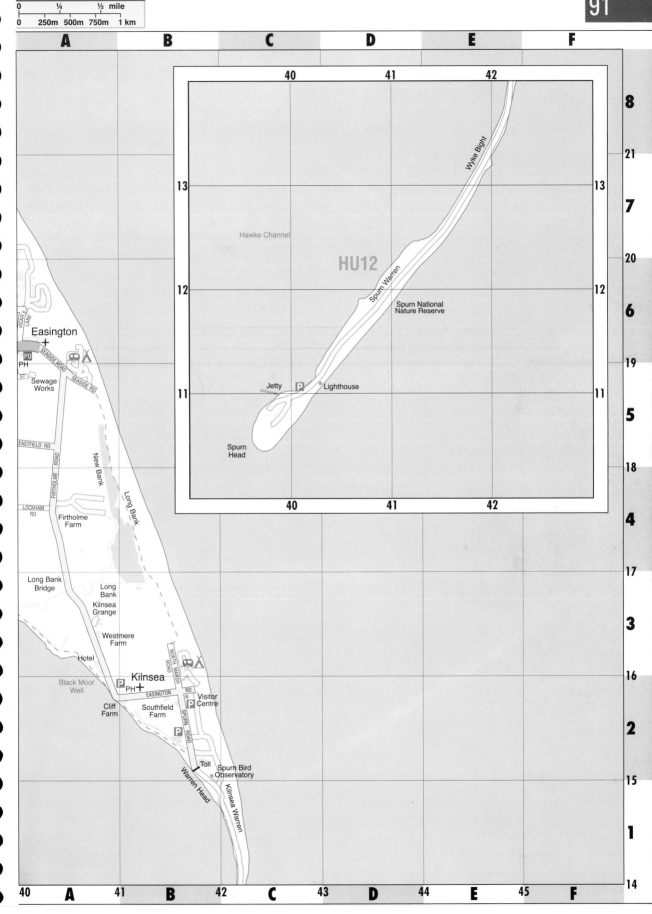

Scale: 1¾ inches to 1 mile

0   ¼   ½   mile
0   250m 500m 750m 1 km

91

A   B   C   D   E   F

40   41   42

8

21

13   13

Hawke Channel

HU12

12   12

Spurn Warren

Spurn National
Nature Reserve

Wyke Bight

7

20

6

11   11
Jetty P • Lighthouse

Spurn
Head

5

18

40   41   42

4

VICARS LANE
Easington
+
P.O.
PH
ST
Sewage
Works

SEASIDE ROAD
SEASIDE RD

EASTFIELD RD

New Bank

FIRTHOLME ROAD

LOCKHAM
RD

Firtholme
Farm

Long Bank

19

Long Bank
Bridge

Long
Bank

Kilnsea
Grange

Westmere
Farm

Hotel

Black Moor
Well

Cliff
Farm

NORTH MARSH
ROAD

P
Kilnsea
PH +
EASINGTON   RD
Visitor
P Centre
Southfield
Farm

SPURN ROAD

P

Toll
Warren Head

Spurn Bird
• Observatory

Kilnsea Warren

17

16

3

2

15

1

14

40   41   42   43   44   45

A   B   C   D   E   F

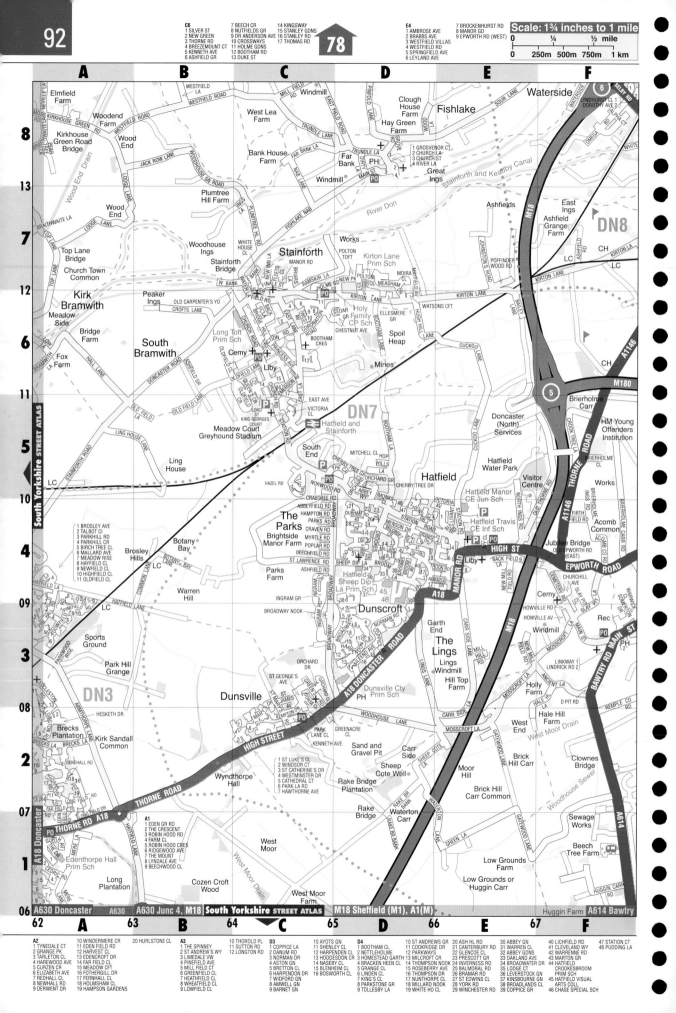

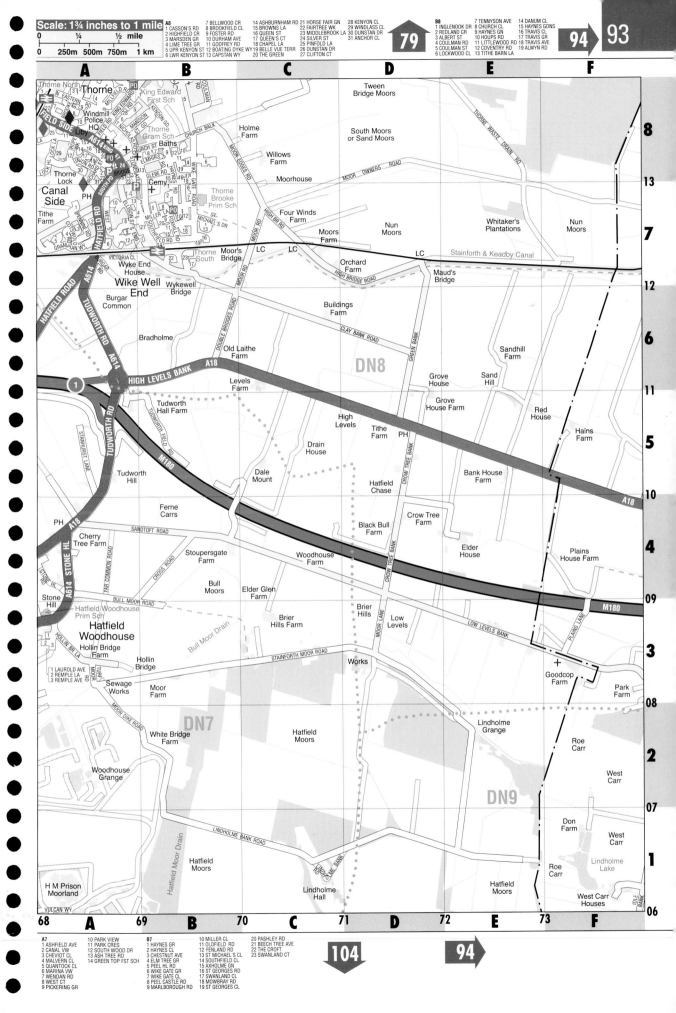

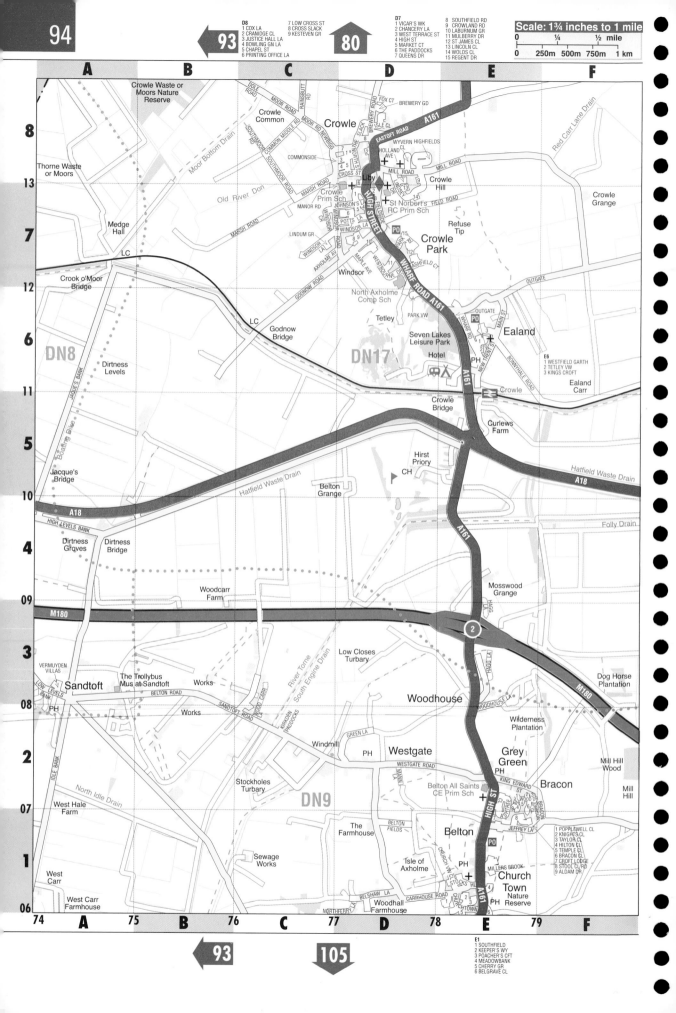

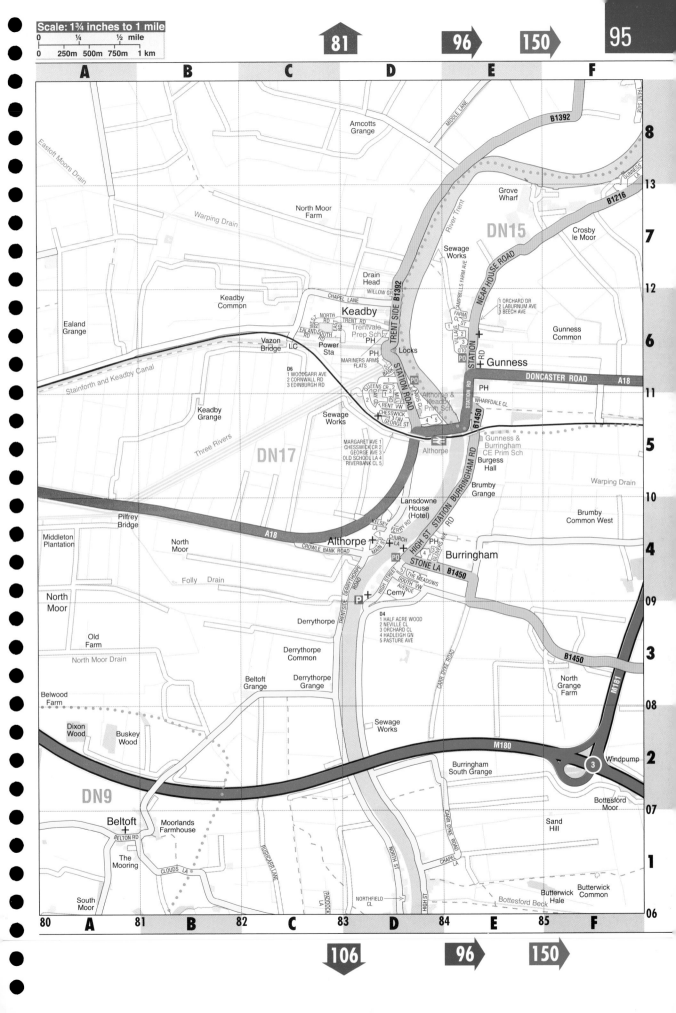

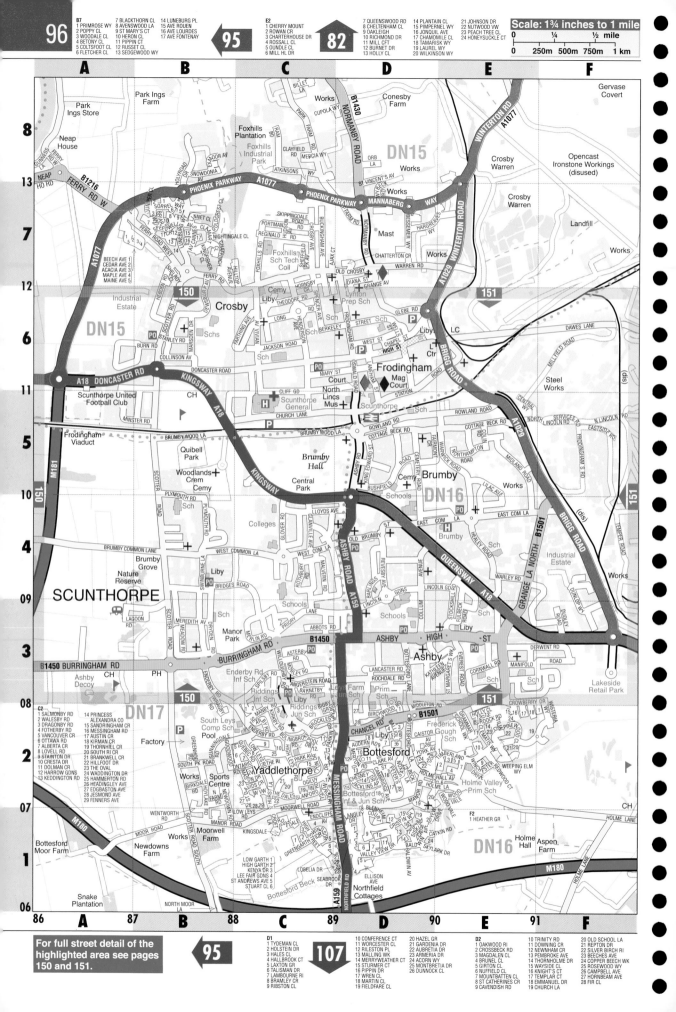

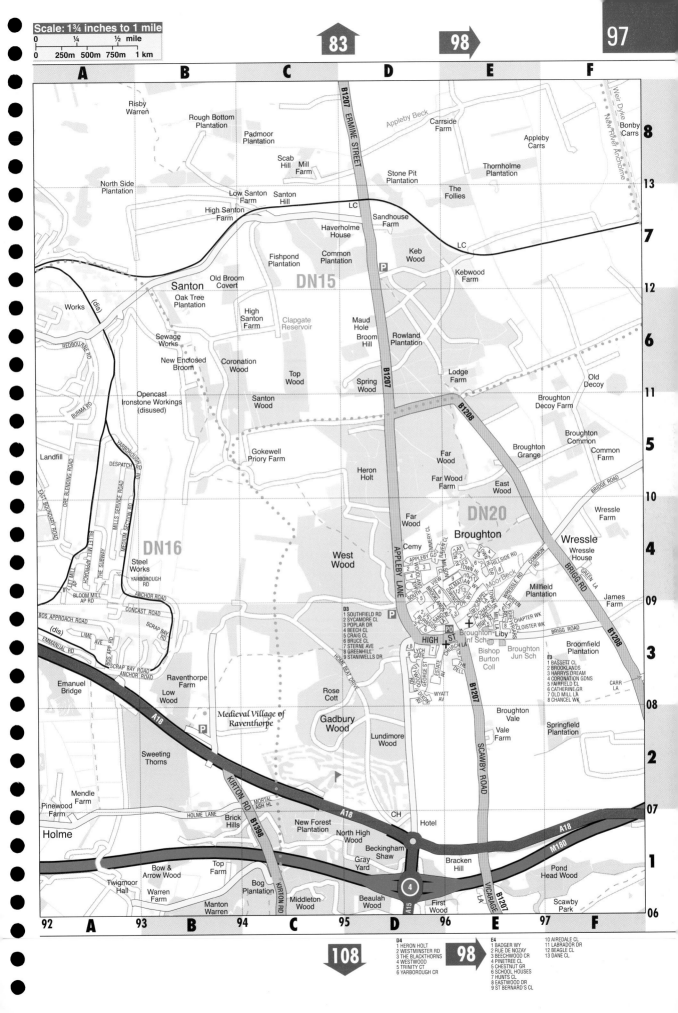

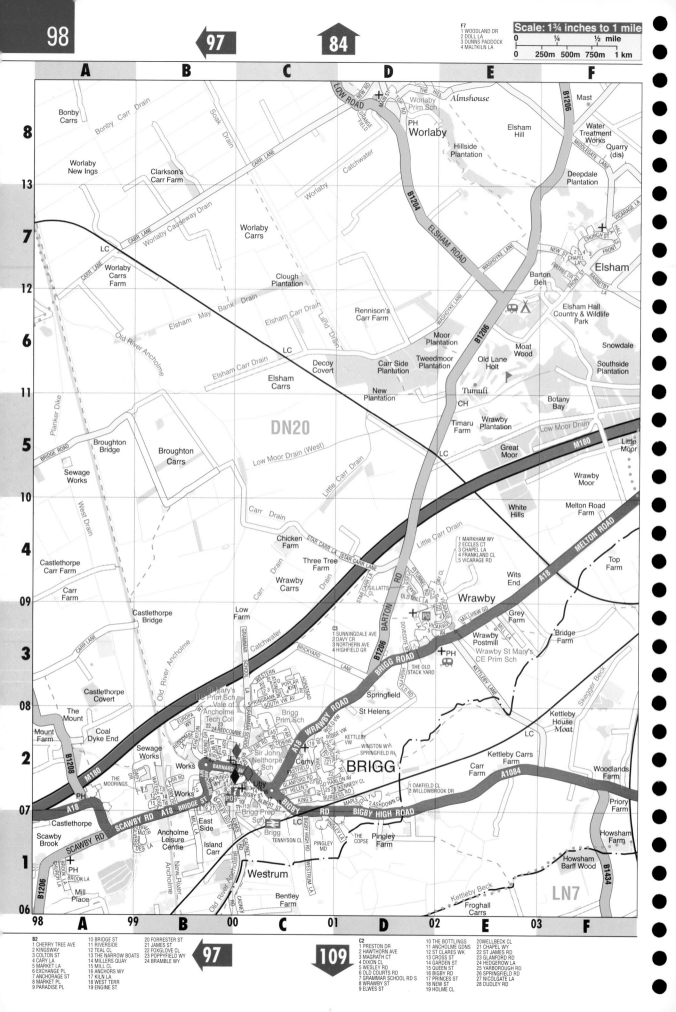

F7
1 WOODLAND DR
2 DOLL LA
3 DUNNS PADDOCK
4 MALTKILN LA

Scale: 1¾ inches to 1 mile
0 ¼ ½ mile
0 250m 500m 750m 1 km

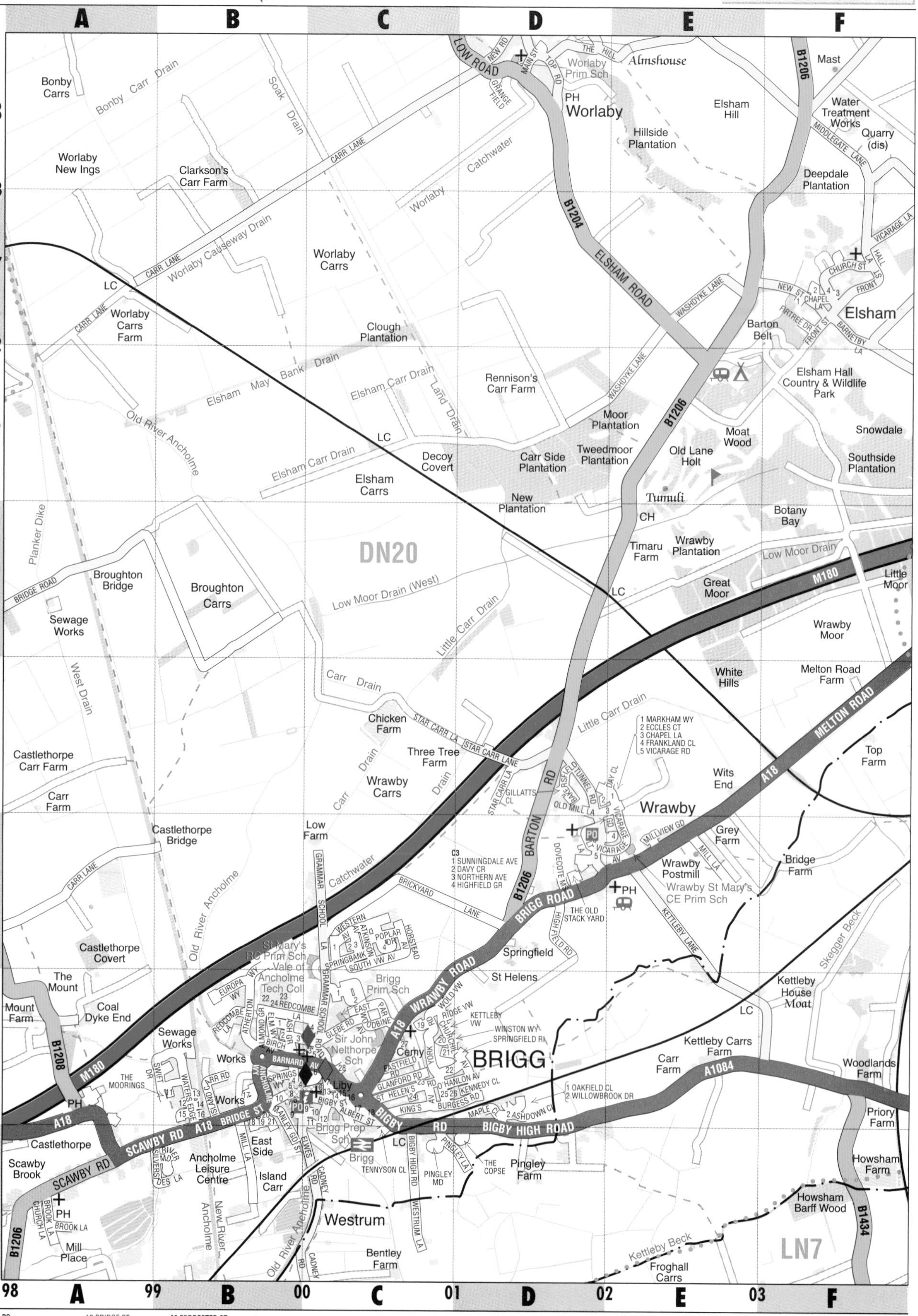
A
B
C
D
E
F
8
13
7
12
6
11
5
10
4
09
3
08
2
07
1
06
98
99
00
01
02
03
Bonby Carrs
Bonby Carr Drain
Soak Drain
LOW ROAD
NEW RD
MAIN ST
THE HILL
TOP RD
GRANGE FIELD
Worlaby Prim Sch
Almshouse
PH
Worlaby
B1206
Mast
Elsham Hill
Water Treatment Works
Quarry (dis)
MIDDLEGATE LANE
Hillside Plantation
Deepdale Plantation
Worlaby New Ings
Clarkson's Carr Farm
CARR LANE
Catchwater
Worlaby
B1204
VICARAGE LA
HALL LA
Worlaby Carrs
Worlaby Causeway Drain
CARR LANE
LC
ELSHAM ROAD
CHURCH ST
WASHDYKE LANE
NEW ST
CHAPEL LA
FRONT ST
FIRTREE DR
Elsham
Barton Belt
BARNETBY LA
Worlaby Carrs Farm
CARR LANE
Clough Plantation
Elsham May Bank Drain
Elsham Carr Drain
Land Drain
Rennison's Carr Farm
WASHDYKE LANE
Elsham Hall Country & Wildlife Park
Old River Ancholme
Moor Plantation
Moat Wood
Snowdale
LC
Elsham Carr Drain
Decoy Covert
Carr Side Plantation
Tweedmoor Plantation
Old Lane Holt
Southside Plantation
Elsham Carrs
New Plantation
Tumuli
CH
Botany Bay
Planker Dike
DN20
Timaru Farm
Wrawby Plantation
Low Moor Drain
BRIDGE ROAD
Broughton Bridge
Broughton Carrs
Low Moor Drain (West)
LC
Great Moor
M180
Little Moor
Sewage Works
Little Carr Drain
Wrawby Moor
West Drain
Carr Drain
White Hills
Melton Road Farm
Chicken Farm
STAR CARR LA
STAR CARR LANE
Little Carr Drain
MELTON ROAD
Castlethorpe Carr Farm
Three Tree Farm
1 MARKHAM WY
2 ECCLES CT
3 CHAPEL LA
4 FRANKLAND CL
5 VICARAGE RD
Top Farm
Carr Drain
Wrawby Carrs
Drain
Wits End
Carr Farm
STAR CARR LA
GILLATTS CL
BARTON RD
TUNNEL RD
OLD MILL LA
Wrawby
A18
Castlethorpe Bridge
Low Farm
PO
VICARAGE AV
MILLVIEW GD
Grey Farm
MILL LA
CARR LANE
Catchwater
C3
1 SUNNINGDALE AVE
2 DAVY CR
3 NORTHERN AVE
4 HIGHFIELD GR
DOVECOTE MS
Wrawby Postmill
Bridge Farm
Old River Ancholme
GRAMMAR SCHOOL LA
BRICKYARD LANE
B1206
BRIGG ROAD
PH
Wrawby St Mary's CE Prim Sch
THE OLD STACK YARD
KETTLEBY LANE
Skegger Beck
Castlethorpe Covert
St Mary's RC Prim Sch
WESTERN AV
ATKINSON AV
POPLAR AV
HORSTEAD AV
SPRINGBANK
SOUTH VW AV
HIGH FIELD RD
Springfield
Vale of Ancholme Tech Coll
WRAWBY ROAD
The Mount
St Helens
Kettleby House
Moat
Mount Farm
Coal Dyke End
EUROPA WY
Brigg Prim Sch
REDCOMBE LA
GLEBE RD
ATHERTON WY
WOLD VW
RIDGE VW
KETTLEBY VW
WINSTON WY
SPRINGFIELD RI
LC
Sewage Works
Sir John Nelthorpe Sch
YORK RD
CHURCHILL AV
Kettleby Carrs Farm
B1208
M180
THE MOORINGS
Works
BARNARD AV
Cemy
BRIGG
Carr Farm
A1084
Woodlands Farm
Liby
EASTFIELD RD
GLANFORD RD
HANLON AV
KENNEDY CL
1 OAKFIELD CL
2 WILLOWBROOK DR
PH
Works
BRIDGE ST
ST HELEN'S RD
KING'S AV
BURGESS RD
MAPLE
2 ASHDOWN CL
Priory Farm
A18
PO
ALBERT ST
BIGBY ST
BIGBY RD
BIGBY HIGH ROAD
Castlethorpe
SCAWBY RD
A18
MILL LA
East Side
Brigg Prep Sch
Brigg
LC
Howsham Farm
Scawby Brook
SCAWBY RD
Ancholme Leisure Centre
Island Carr
ELWES ST
TENNYSON CL
BIGBY HIGH RD
PINGLEY LA
THE COPSE
Pingley Farm
PINGLEY MD
PH
CADNEY RD
Howsham Barff Wood
BROOK LA
CHURCH LA
B1206
Westrum
WESTRUM LA
New River Ancholme
B1434
Mill Place
Old River Ancholme
Bentley Farm
Kettleby Beck
LN7
Froghall Carrs

B2
1 CHERRY TREE AVE
2 KINGSWAY
3 COLTON ST
4 CARY LA
5 MARKET LA
6 EXCHANGE PL
7 ANCHORAGE ST
8 MARKET PL
9 PARADISE PL
10 BRIDGE ST
11 RIVERSIDE
12 TEAL CL
13 THE NARROW BOATS
14 MILLERS QUAY
15 MILL CL
16 ANCHORS WY
17 KILN LA
18 WEST TERR
19 ENGINE ST
20 FORRESTER ST
21 JAMES ST
22 FOXGLOVE CL
23 POPPYFIELD WY
24 BRAMBLE WY

C2
1 PRESTON DR
2 HAWTHORN AVE
3 MAGRATH CT
4 DIXON CL
5 WESLEY RD
6 OLD COURTS RD
7 GRAMMAR SCHOOL RD S
8 WRAWBY ST
9 ELWES ST
10 THE BOTTLINGS
11 ANCHOLME GDNS
12 ST CLARES WK
13 CROSS ST
14 GARDEN ST
15 QUEEN ST
16 BIGBY RD
17 PRINCES ST
18 NEW ST
19 HOLME CL
20WELLBECK CL
21 CHAPEL WY
22 ST JAMES RD
23 GLANFORD RD
24 HEDGEROW LA
25 YARBOROUGH RD
26 SPRINGFIELD RD
27 NICOLGATE LA
28 DUDLEY RD

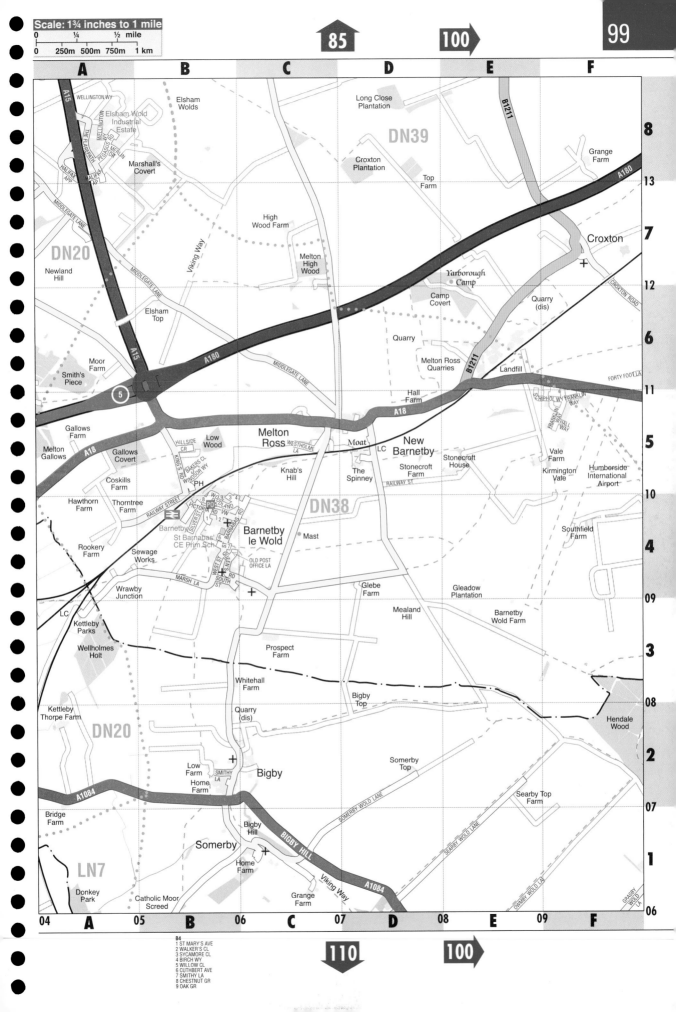

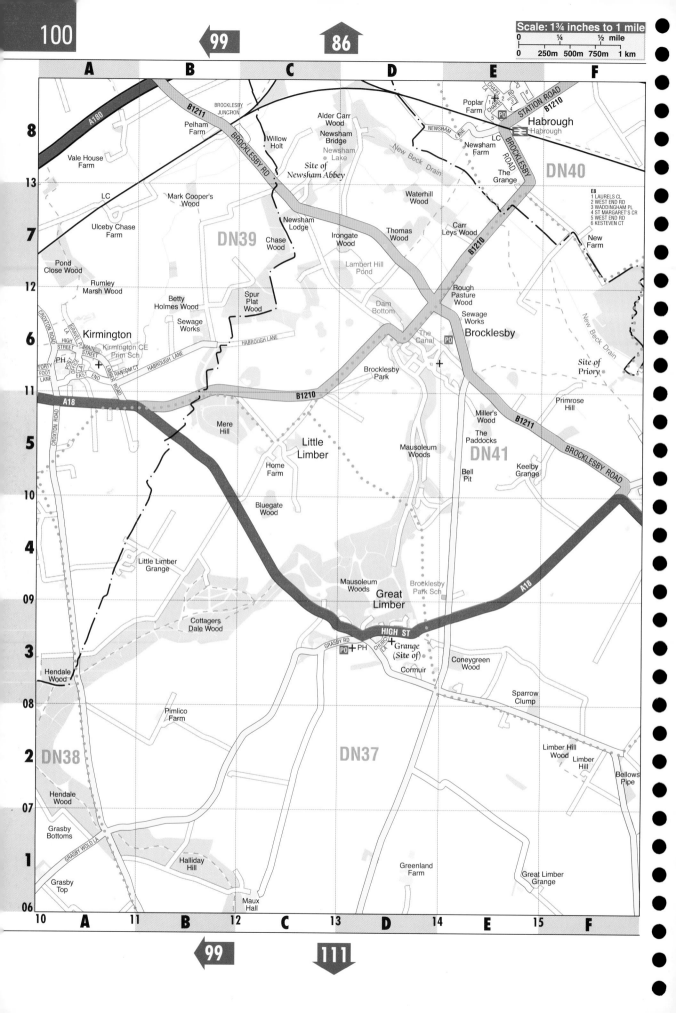

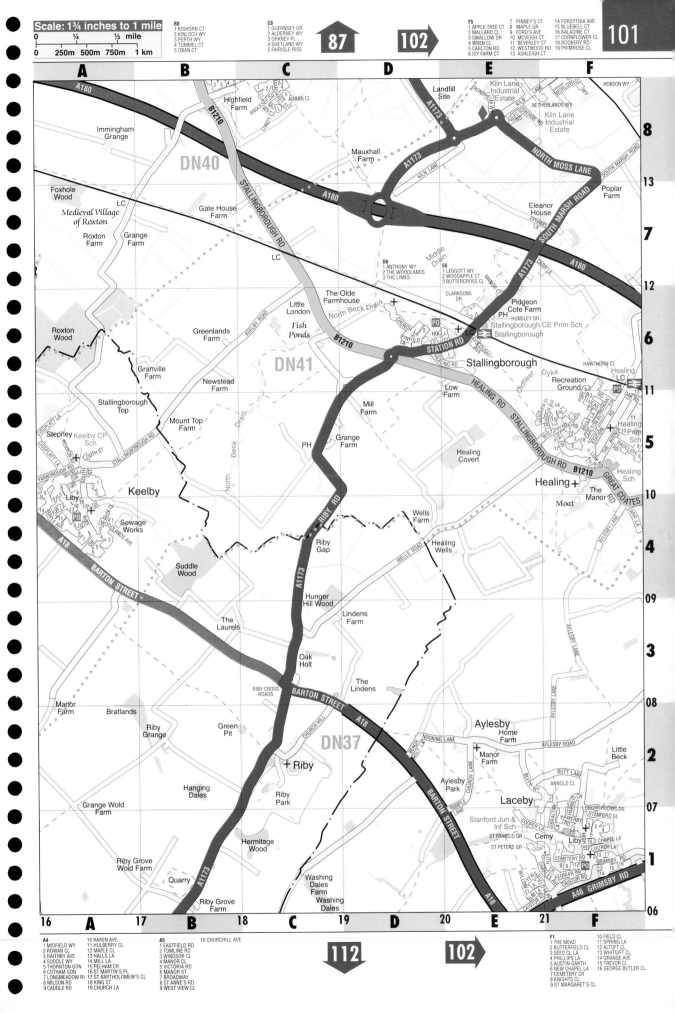

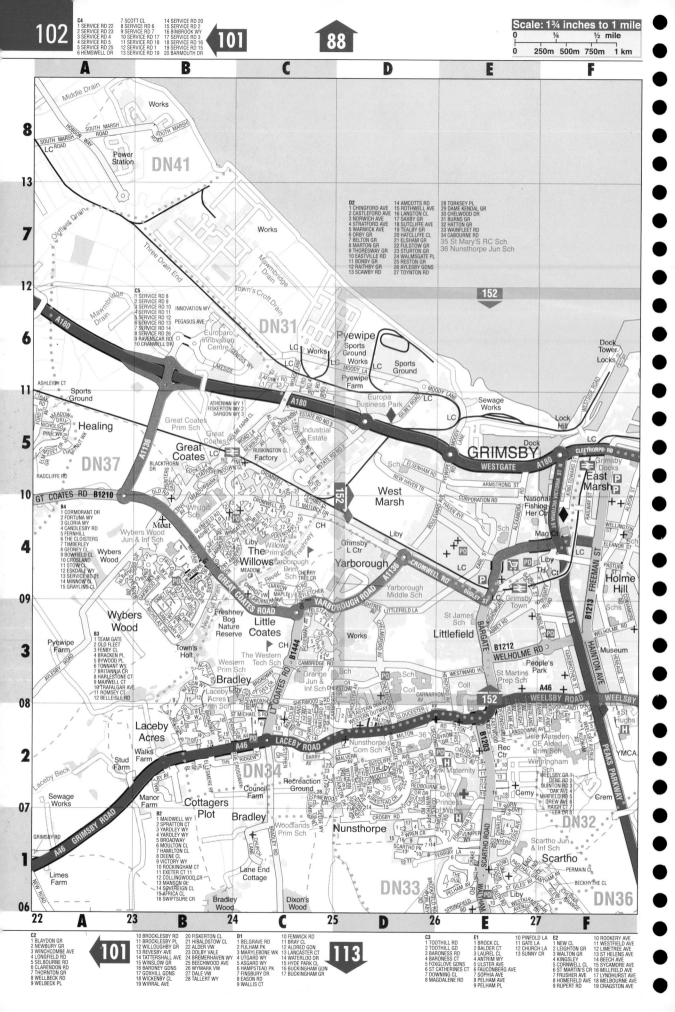

C4
1 SERVICE RD 22
2 SERVICE RD 23
3 SERVICE RD 4
4 SERVICE RD 5
5 SERVICE RD 25
6 HEMSWELL RD

7 SCOTT CL
8 SERVICE RD 6
9 SERVICE RD 7
10 SERVICE RD 17
11 SERVICE RD 18
12 SERVICE RD 11
13 SERVICE RD 19

14 SERVICE RD 20
15 SERVICE RD 2
16 BINBROOK WY
17 SERVICE RD 3
18 SERVICE RD 16
19 SERVICE RD 15
20 BARMOUTH DR

D2
1 CHINGFORD AVE
2 CASTLEFORD AVE
3 NORWICH AVE
4 STRATFORD AVE
5 WARWICK AVE
6 ORBY GR
7 BELTON GR
8 MARTON GR
9 THORESWAY GR
10 EASTVILLE RD
11 BONBY GR
12 RAITHBY GR
13 SCAWBY RD

14 AMCOTTS RD
15 ROTHWELL AVE
16 LANGTON CL
17 SAXBY GR
18 SUTCLIFFE AVE
19 TEALBY GR
20 HATCLLFFE CL
21 ELSHAM GR
22 FULSTOW GR
23 STURTON GR
24 WALMSGATE PL
25 RESTON GR
26 AYLESBY GDNS
27 TOYNTON GR

28 TORKSEY PL
29 DAME KENDAL GR
30 CHELWOOD DR
31 BURNS GR
32 HATTON GR
33 WAINFLEET GR
34 CABOURNE RD

35 St Mary'S RC Sch
36 Nunsthorpe Jun Sch

C5
1 SERVICE RD 8
2 SERVICE RD 9
3 SERVICE RD 10
4 SERVICE RD 11
5 SERVICE RD 12
6 SERVICE RD 13
7 SERVICE RD 14
8 SERVICE RD 26
9 RAVENSCAR RD
10 CRANWELL DR

B4
1 CORMORANT DR
2 FORTUNA WY
3 GLORIA WY
4 CANDLESBY RD
5 FERNHILL
6 THE CLOISTERS
7 TIMBERLEY
8 GEDNEY CL
9 BOWFIELD CL
10 CROSLAND
11 STOW CL
12 ESKDALE WY
13 SERVICE RD 21
14 MINNOW CL
15 GRAYLING CL

B3
1 TEAM GATE
2 OLD FLEET
3 FENBY CL
4 BRACKEN PL
5 BYWOOD PL
6 TONNANT WY
7 BRITANNIA CR
8 HARLESTONE CT
9 MAXWELL CT
10 TRAFALGAR AVE
11 ROMSEY CT
12 BELLEISLE RD

B2
1 MAIDWELL CL
2 SPRATTON CT
3 YARDLEY WY
4 YARDLEY WY
5 BROADWAY
6 MOULTON CL
7 HAMILTON CL
8 DEENE CL
9 VICTORY WY
10 ROCKINGHAM CT
11 EXETER CT 11
12 COLLINGWOOD CR
13 MANSON Gt
14 SOVEREIGN CL
15 AFRICA CL
16 SWIFTSURE CR

C2
1 BLAYDON GR
2 NEWBURY GR
3 WINCHCOMBE AVE
4 LONGFIELD RD
5 SELBOURNE RD
6 CLARENDON RD
7 THORNTON GR
8 WELLBECK RD
9 WELBECK PL

10 BROCKLESBY RD
11 BROCKLESBY PL
12 WILLOUGHBY GR
13 REVESBY AVE
14 TATTERSHALL AVE
15 WINSLOW GR
16 BARDNEY GDNS
17 GOXHILL GDNS
18 WICKENBY CT
19 WIRRAL AVE

20 FISKERTON CL
21 HIBALDSTOW CL
22 ALDER WY
23 DOLBY VALE
24 BREMERHAVEN WY
25 BEECHWOOD AVE
26 WYMARK VW
27 DALE VW
28 TALLERT WY

D1
1 BELGRAVE RD
2 FULHAM PK
3 MARYLEBONE WK
4 UTGARD WY
5 ASGARD WY
6 HAMPSTEAD PK
7 FINSBURY DR
8 EASON RD
9 WALLIS CT

10 FENWICK RD
11 BRAY CL
12 ALDRED GDN
13 LANCASTER CT
14 WATERLOO PL
15 HYDE PARK CL
16 BUCKINGHAM GDN
17 BUCKINGHAM GR

C3
1 TOOTHILL RD
2 TOOTHILL GD
3 BARONESS RD
4 BARONESS CT
5 FOXGLOVE GDNS
6 ST CATHERINES CT
7 DOWNING CL
8 MAGDALENE RD

E1
1 BROCK CL
2 BALDER CT
3 LAUREL CL
4 ANTRIM WY
5 ULSTER AVE
6 FAUCONBERG AVE
7 SOPHIA AVE
8 PELHAM AVE
9 PELHAM PL

10 PINFOLD LA
11 GATE LA
12 CHURCH LA
13 SUNNY CR

E2
1 NEW CL
2 LEIGHTON GR
3 WALTON GR
4 KINGSLEY
5 CORNWELL CL
6 ST MARTIN'S CR
7 FRUSHER AVE
8 HOMEFIELD AVE
9 RUPERT RD

10 ROOKERY AVE
11 WESTFIELD AVE
12 LIMETREE AVE
13 ST HELENS AVE
14 BEECH AVE
15 SYCAMORE AVE
16 MILLFIELD AVE
17 LYNDHURST AVE
18 MELBOURNE AVE
19 CRAGSTON AVE

Scale: 1¾ inches to 1 mile

0   ¼   ½   mile
0   250m 500m 750m 1 km

89

For full street detail of the highlighted area see pages 152 and 153.

103

A   B   C   D   E   F

8
13
7
12
6
11
5
10
09
3
08
2
07
1
06

Grimsby Roads

153

Piers
Locks
Fish Docks
NORTH QUAY
DN31
New Clee
RIBY ST
Thorold
CLEETHORPE ROAD
DN35
HARRINGTON ST
GRIMSBY ROAD
Blundell Park
Sch
Liby
VICTOR ST
OXFORD ST
Sch
PO
Grant Thorold
PARK ST
BRERETON AVE
TIVERTON RD
A180
Jun Sch
Inf School
Sidney Park
ELLISTON ST
Schs
Queen Mary Ave
BRERETON AV
Wonderland
P
Cleethorpes
153
The Pier
CLEETHORPES
DURBAN RD
PO
COLUMBIA ROAD
RUNSWICK RD
CARR LA
DN32
Sch
Old Clee
Rec
LADYSMITH RD
Sch
Weelsby
Moat
Clee Hall Farm
CLEE CR
CLEE ROAD A46
St PETER'S AV
Liby
PO
St PETER'S AV
Civic Offices
KINGSWAY
Cerny Tumulus
BEACON ST
TRINITY RD
HIGHGATE
MILL ROAD
OXFORD RD
Sch
RD
153
HERON ST
A1051 HUMBERSTON ROAD
THIRKLEY PL
Queen's RD
Cleethorpes Leisure Centre
Kingsway
P
Matthew Humberstone CE Sch
WARWICK RD
SANDRINGHAM RD
DUDLEY
THORNTON
BRAMELEY
CROMWELL RD
Discovery Centre
Cleethorpes Coast Light Railway
St Joseph's RC Prim Sch
BRIAN AVENUE
LADY DRG
MIDDLE THORPE
ALDRICH RD
PEARSON RD
Signhills Jun & Inf Sch
KINGS RD
Meridian Pl Ret Pk
P
The Jungle
Weelsby Woods
Middlethorpe Prim Sch
HUMBERSTON ROAD
TAYLOR'S AVENUE
CHESTER RD
LINKS RD
P
Lakeside
Old Hall Farm
Hall Farm
BEVOIR RD
HEYTHROP RD
COTTESMORE
The Lindsey Sch & Corn Arts Coll
DN35
Pleasure Island Theme Park
P
B1
HEWITT'S CIRCUS
Cleethorpes Country Park
Visitor Centre
Humberston
CH
Fairway Ct
Kings Ms
DN36
HEWITT'S AVENUE
Superstore
HONEYSUCKLE CT
BLAKENEY LEA
HILTON RD
Thorpe Park Holiday Centre
Peaks Covert Farm
WILTON RD
GRIMSBY ROAD A1098
JACKSON'S PL
CHELTENHAM WY
WALDORF RD
WESTBURY RD
NORTH SEA LA
SEAFORD RD
North Sea La
ANTHONY'S BANK RD
P
A16
HUMBERSTON RD
LIDGARD RD
FOREST
BROOKLYN
DN36

114

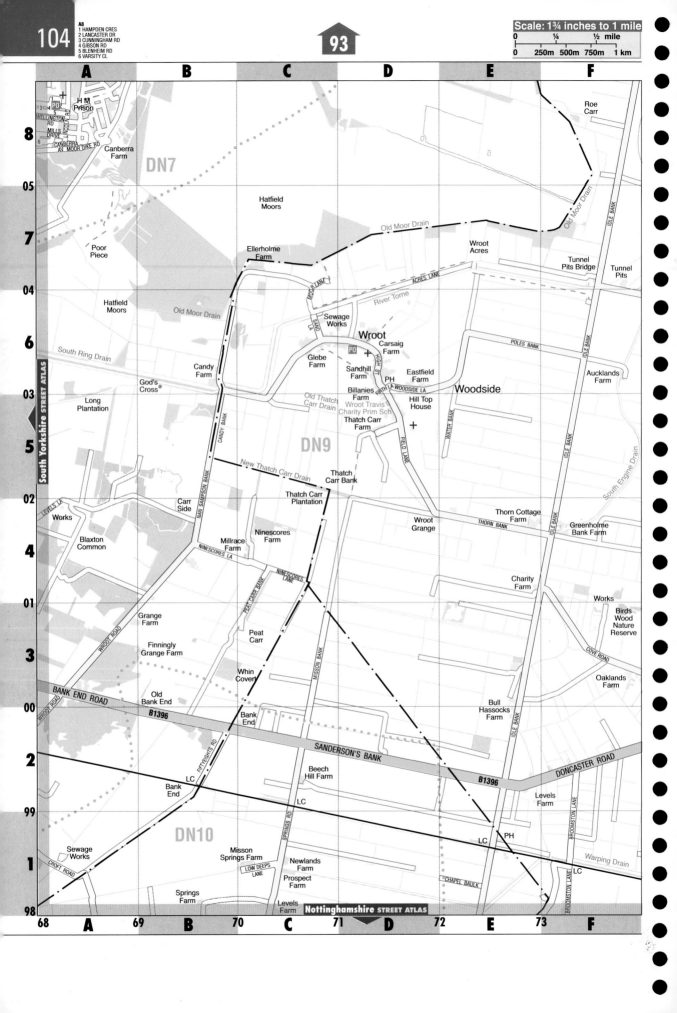

A8
1 HAMPDEN CRES
2 LANCASTER DR
3 CUNNINGHAM RD
4 GIBSON RD
5 BLENHEIM RD
6 VARSITY CL

93

A   B   C   D   E   F

South Yorkshire STREET ATLAS

HM Prison
Canberra Farm
WELLINGTON RD
LINCOLN RD
MILLS DRIVE
CANBERRA AV
MOOR DIKE RD

DN7

Poor Piece

Hatfield Moors

Old Moor Drain

Roe Carr

IDLE BANK

Old Moor Drain

Ellerholme Farm

Wroot Acres

Tunnel Pits Bridge

Tunnel Pits

Hatfield Moors

Old Moor Drain

MOOR LANE

River Torne

ACRES LANE

Sewage Works

Candy Farm

Glebe Farm

HIGH ST
SAND LA

Wroot

PO

Carsaig Farm

Sandhill Farm

FIRTH LA

PH

WOODSIDE LA

Eastfield Farm

POLES BANK

Aucklands Farm

God's Cross

Long Plantation

CANDY BANK

Old Thatch Carr Drain

Wroot Travis Charity Prim Sch

Billanies Farm

Thatch Carr Farm

Hill Top House

Woodside

WATER BANK

DN9

New Thatch Carr Drain

Thatch Carr Bank

FIELD LANE

South Engine Drain

NAB SAMPSON BANK

Carr Side

Thatch Carr Plantation

Wroot Grange

Thorn Cottage Farm

THORN BANK

IDLE BANK

Greenholme Bank Farm

LEVELS LA

Works

Blaxton Common

Millrace Farm

Ninescores Farm

NINESCORES LA

Ninescores Lane

Charity Farm

Works

Birds Wood Nature Reserve

PEAT CARR BANK

Grange Farm

Peat Carr

MISSON BANK

COVE ROAD

Oaklands Farm

WROOT ROAD

Finninngly Grange Farm

Whin Covert

Bull Hassocks Farm

BANK END ROAD

Old Bank End

WROOT ROAD

B1396

Bank End

SANDERSON'S BANK

IDLE BANK

DONCASTER ROAD

B1396

FIFTEIGHTS RD

LC

Bank End

Beech Hill Farm

LC

Levels Farm

BROOMSTON LANE

DN10

Sewage Works

CROFT ROAD

Misson Springs Farm

LOW DEEPS LANE

SPRINGS RD

LC

Newlands Farm

Prospect Farm

LC

PH

Warping Drain

BROOMSTON LANE

LC

Springs Farm

Levels Farm

CHAPEL BAULK

Nottinghamshire STREET ATLAS

68   A   69   B   70   C   71   D   72   E   73   F

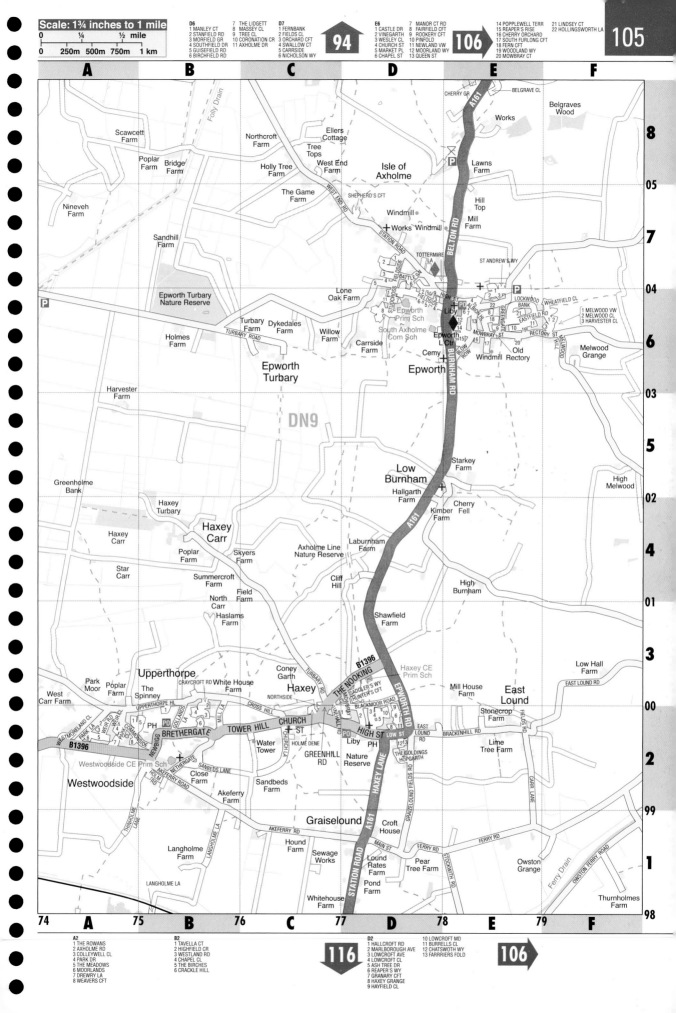

D6
1 MANLEY CT
2 STANFIELD RD
3 MORFIELD GR
4 SOUTHFIELD DR
5 GUISEFIELD RD
6 BIRCHFIELD RD

7 THE LIDGETT
8 MASSEY CL
9 TREE CL
10 CORONATION CR
11 AXHOLME DR

D7
1 FERNBANK
2 FIELDS CL
3 ORCHARD CFT
4 SWALLOW CL
5 CARRSIDE
6 NICHOLSON WY

94

E6
1 CASTLE DR
2 VINEGARTH
3 WESLEY CL
4 CHURCH ST
5 MARKET PL
6 CHAPEL ST

7 MANOR CT RD
8 FAIRFIELD CFT
9 ROOKERY CFT
10 PINFOLD
11 NEWLAND WY
12 MOORLAND WY
13 QUEEN ST

106

14 POPPLEWELL TERR
15 REAPER'S RISE
16 CHERRY ORCHARD
17 SOUTH FURLONG CFT
18 FERN CFT
19 WOODLAND WY
20 MOWBRAY CT

21 LINDSEY CT
22 HOLLINGSWORTH LA

105

A2
1 THE ROWANS
2 AXHOLME RD
3 COLLEYWELL CL
4 PARK DR
5 THE MEADOWS
6 MOORLANDS
7 DREWRY LA
8 WEAVERS CFT

B2
1 TAVELLA CT
2 HIGHFIELD CR
3 WESTLAND RD
4 CHAPEL CL
5 THE BIRCHES
6 CRACKLE HILL

116

D2
1 HALLCROFT RD
2 MARLBOROUGH AVE
3 LOWCROFT AVE
4 LOWCROFT CL
5 ASH TREE DR
6 REAPER'S WY
7 GRANARY CFT
8 HAXEY GRANGE
9 HAYFIELD CL

10 LOWCROFT MD
11 BURRELLS CL
12 CHATSWORTH WY
13 FARRIERS FOLD

106

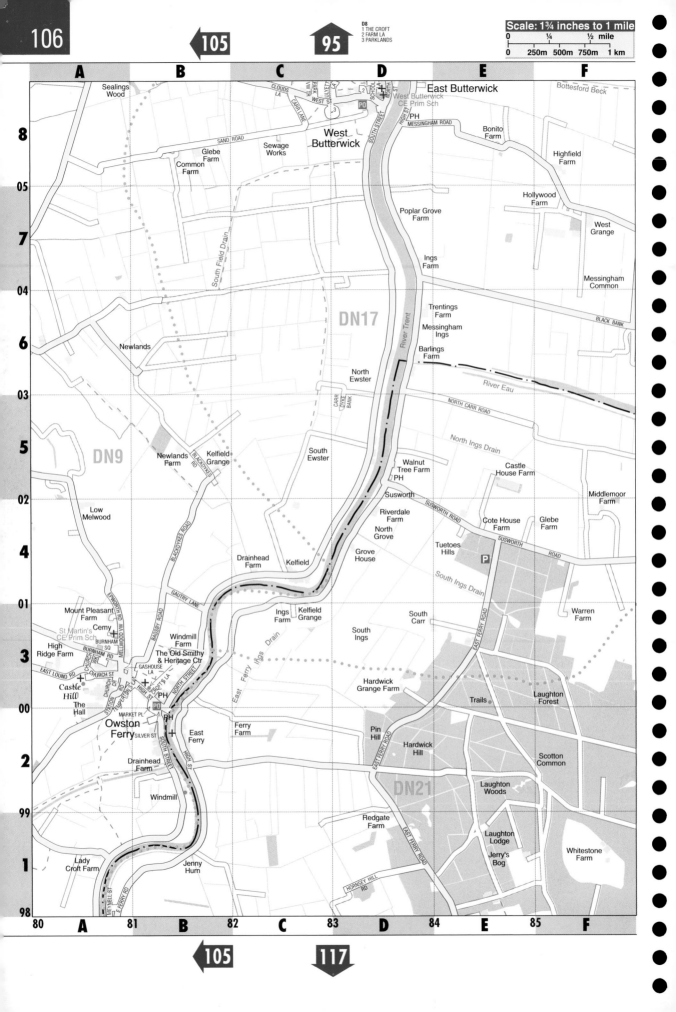

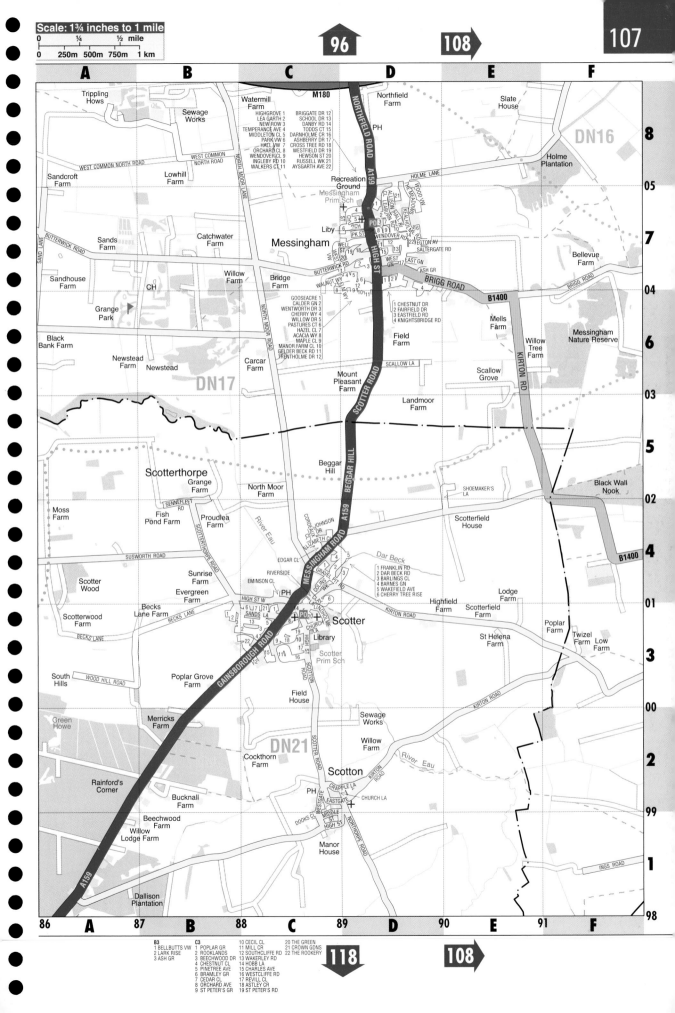

A   B   C   D   E   F

8
05
7
04
6
03
5
02
4
01
3
00
2
99
1
98

DN16

Trippling Hows
Sewage Works
Watermill Farm
M180
Northfield Farm
Slate House
Holme Plantation

HIGHGROVE 1
LEA GARTH 2
NEW ROW 3
TEMPERANCE AVE 4
MIDDLETON CL 5
PARK VW 6
HAEL VW 7
ORCHARD CL 8
WENDOVER CL 9
INGLEBY RD 10
WALKERS CT 11

BRIGGATE DR 12
SCHOOL DR 13
DANBY RD 14
TODDS CT 15
DARNHOLME CR 16
ASHBERRY DR 17
CROSS TREE RD 18
WESTFIELD DR 19
HEWSON ST 20
RUSSELL WK 21
AYSGARTH AVE 22

West Common North Road
NORTH MOOR LANE
WEST COMMON NORTH ROAD
Sandcroft Farm
Lowhill Farm
Recreation Ground
Messingham Prim Sch
NORTHFIELD ROAD
A159
HOLME LANE
WOOD VW
THE MEADOWS

Sands Farm
Catchwater Farm
Messingham
Liby
WELL ST
A159
HIGH ST
EGTON AV
SALTERGATE RD
Bellevue Farm

BUTTERWICK ROAD
Sandhouse Farm
Willow Farm
PK ST
PO
WENDOVER
WEST GN
EAST GN
ASH GR
BRIGG ROAD
BRIGG ROAD

Butterwick Road
CH
Bridge Farm
WALNUT VW
B1400

Grange Park
GOOSEACRE 1
CALDER GN 2
WENTWORTH DR 3
CHERRY WY 4
WILLOW DR 5
PASTURES CT 6
HAZEL CL 7
ACACIA WY 8
MAPLE CL 9
MANOR FARM CL 10
GELDER BECK RD 11
TRENTHOLME DR 12
1 CHESTNUT DR
2 FAIRFIELD DR
3 EASTFIELD RD
4 KNIGHTSBRIDGE RD
Field Farm
Mells Farm

Black Bank Farm
Newstead Farm
Newstead
Carcar Farm
DN17
Mount Pleasant Farm
SCALLOW LA
Landmoor Farm
Scallow Grove
KIRTON RD
Willow Tree Farm
Messingham Nature Reserve

SCOTTER ROAD
Beggar Hill
BEGGAR HILL
A159
SHOEMAKER'S LA
Black Wall Nook

Scotterthorpe
Grange Farm
North Moor Farm
Scotterfield House
B1400

Moss Farm
SENNEFLEET RD
Fish Pond Farm
Proudlea Farm
River Eau
JOHNSON DR
ELIZABETH DR
CORBEAUX DR
MESSINGHAM ROAD
GRAVEL PIT RD
COLLINS WK
1 FRANKLIN RD
2 DAR BECK RD
3 BARLINGS CL
4 BARNES GN
5 WAKEFIELD AVE
6 CHERRY TREE RISE
Dar Beck
Scotterfield Farm
Lodge Farm
Poplar Farm

SUSWORTH ROAD
EDGAR CL
RIVERSIDE
EMINSON CL
CLAY
Highfield Farm
KIRTON ROAD
Twizel Farm
Low Farm

Scotter Wood
Sunrise Farm
Evergreen Farm
HIGH ST W
PH
SANDS LA
PO
CHURCH LA
Scotter
Library
Scotter Prim Sch

Scotterwood Farm
Becks Lane Farm
BECKS LANE
BECKS LANE
HIGH ST
SCOTTON RD
SCOTTER RD
St Helena Farm
KIRTON ROAD

South Hills
WOOD HILL ROAD
Poplar Grove Farm
GAINSBOROUGH ROAD
Field House
Sewage Works

Green Howe
Merricks Farm
DN21
Cockthorn Farm
Willow Farm
River Eau

Rainford's Corner
A159
Bucknall Farm
Scotton
GRAPPLE LA
KIRTON ROAD

Beechwood Farm
Willow Lodge Farm
PH
EASTGATE
WESTGATE
DOOKS CL
MIDDLE ST
HIGH ST
NORTHORPE RD
CHURCH LA
INGS ROAD

Dallison Plantation
Manor House

86   87   88   89   90   91   98

A   B   C   D   E   F

B3
1 BELLBUTTS VW
2 LARK RISE
3 ASH GR

C3
1 POPLAR GR
2 ROOKLANDS
3 BEECHWOOD DR
4 CHESTNUT CL
5 PINETREE AVE
6 BRAMLEY GR
7 CEDAR CL
8 ORCHARD AVE
9 ST PETER'S GR
10 CECIL CL
11 MILL CR
12 SOUTHCLIFFE RD
13 WAKERLEY RD
14 HOBB LA
15 CHARLES AVE
16 WESTCLIFFE RD
17 REVILL CL
18 ASTLEY CR
19 ST PETER'S RD
20 THE GREEN
21 CROWN GDNS
22 THE ROOKERY

118   108

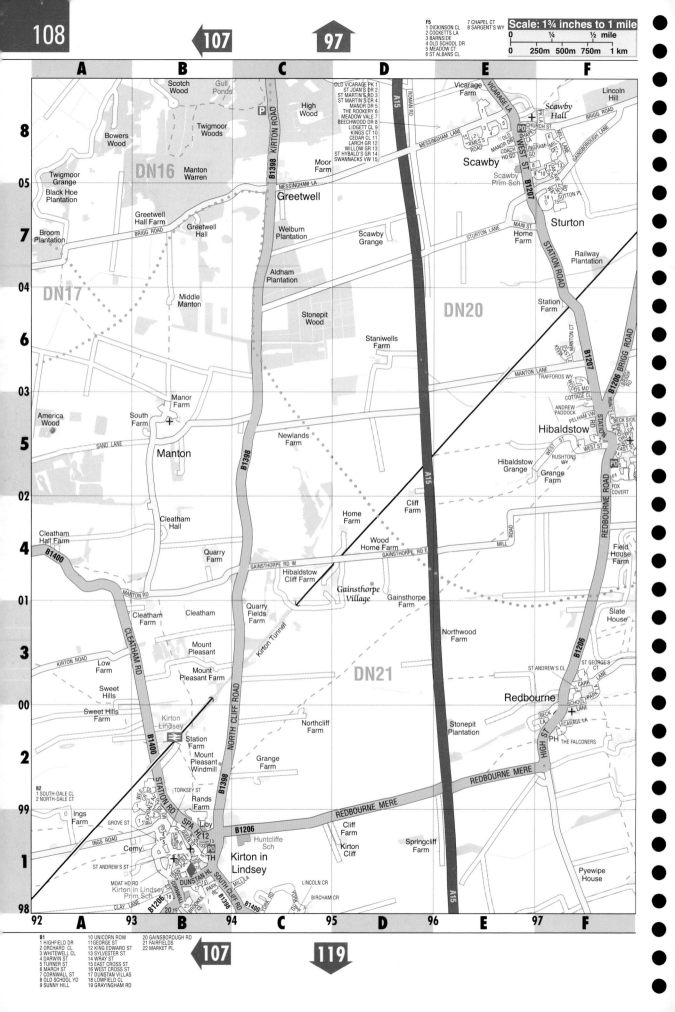

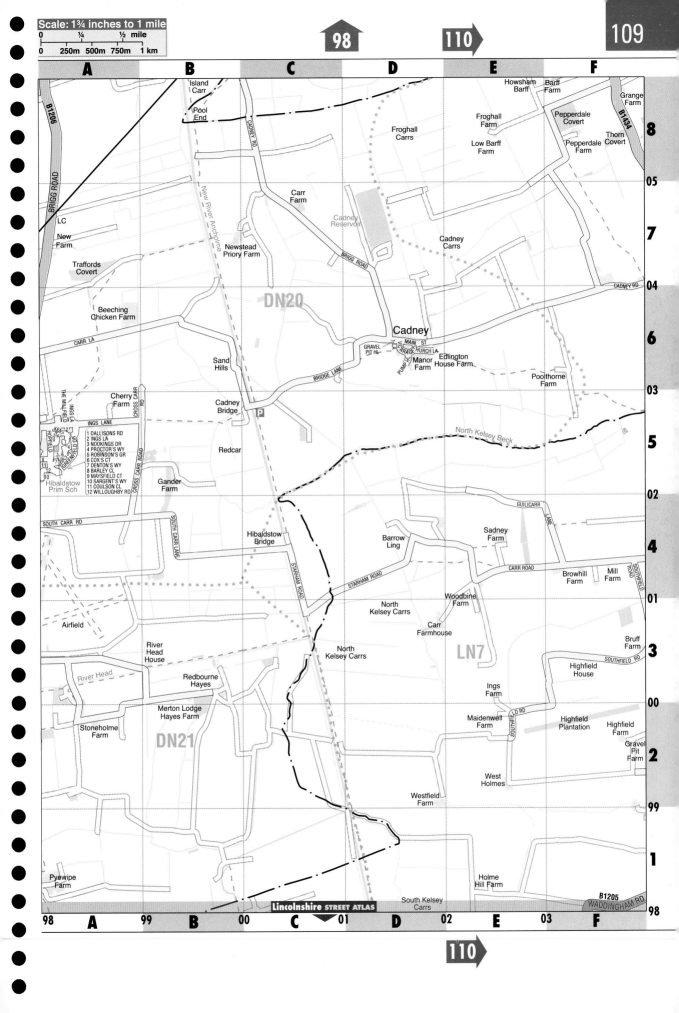

A   B   C   D   E   F

8
05
7
04
6
03
5
02
4
01
3
00
2
99
1
98

B1206

BRIGG ROAD

LC

New Farm

Traffords Covert

CARR LA

Beeching Chicken Farm

Island Carr

Pool End

CADNEY RD

New River Ancholme

Newstead Priory Farm

Carr Farm

Sand Hills

Cherry Farm

CROSS CARR RD

THE MILLFIELD
INGS LA
INGS LANE

1 DALLISONS RD
2 INGS LA
3 NOOKINGS DR
4 PROCTOR'S WY
5 ROBINSON'S GR
6 COX'S CT
7 DENTON'S WY
8 BARLEY CL
9 MAYSFIELD CT
10 SARGENT'S WY
11 COULSON CL
12 WILLOUGHBY RD

HOPFIELD
GREENFIELD DR

Hibaldstow Prim Sch

Cadney Bridge

P

Redcar

Gander Farm

SOUTH CARR RD

SOUTH CARR LANE

Hibaldstow Bridge

STARHAM ROAD

Airfield

River Head House

River Head

Redbourne Hayes

Stoneholme Farm

Merton Lodge Hayes Farm

DN21

Pyewipe Farm

DN20

BRIGG ROAD

BRIDGE LANE

Cadney Reservoir

Froghall Carrs

Cadney Carrs

Cadney

GRAVEL PIT HL

MAIN ST
COTTAGE LA
CHURCH LA
PUMP HL

Manor Farm

Edlington House Farm

North Kelsey Beck

Barrow Ling

STARHAM ROAD

North Kelsey Carrs

North Kelsey Carrs

Sadney Farm

GUILICARR LANE

CARR ROAD

Woodbine Farm

Carr Farmhouse

LN7

Westfield Farm

West Holmes

Maidenwell Farm

SOUTHFIELD RD

Ings Farm

Howsham Barff

Barff Farm

Froghall Farm

Low Barff Farm

Pepperdale Covert

Pepperdale Farm

Grange Farm

B1434

Thorn Covert

CADNEY RD

Poolthorne Farm

Browhill Farm

Mill Farm

SOUTHFIELD ROAD

Bruff Farm

SOUTHFIELD RD

Highfield House

Highfield Plantation

Highfield Farm

Gravel Pit Farm

Holme Hill Farm

South Kelsey Carrs

B1205

WADDINGHAM RD

98   99   00   01   02   03   98

A   B   C   D   E   F

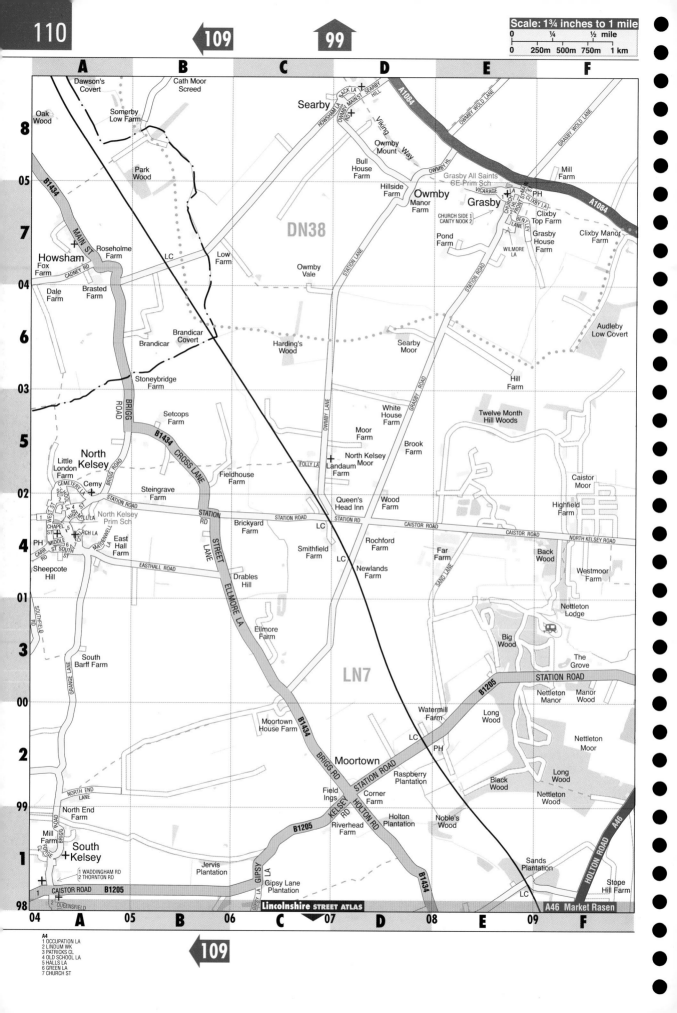

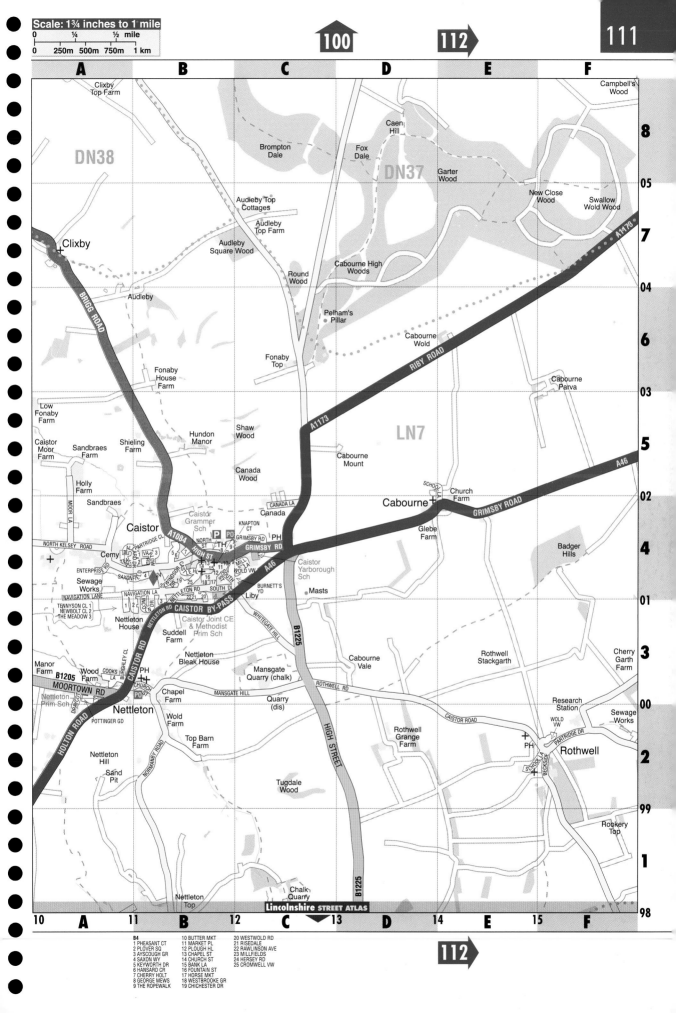

A   B   C   D   E   F

8
05
7
04
6
03
5
02
4
01
3
00
2
99
1
98

DN38

Clixby Top Farm

Campbell's Wood

Brompton Dale

Caen Hill

Fox Dale

DN37

Garter Wood

New Close Wood

Swallow Wold Wood

Audleby Top Cottages

Audleby Top Farm

Clixby

Audleby Square Wood

Round Wood

Cabourne High Woods

A1173

BRIGG ROAD

Audleby

Pelham's Pillar

Cabourne Wold

RIBY ROAD

Cabourne Parva

Low Fonaby Farm

Fonaby House Farm

Fonaby Top

A1173

LN7

Cabourne Mount

Cabourne Parva

Caistor Moor Farm

Sandbraes Farm

Shieling Farm

Hundon Manor

Shaw Wood

Holly Farm

Canada Wood

A46

Cabourne

Church Farm

SCHOOL

Sandbraes

CANADA LA

Canada

Glebe Farm

GRIMSBY ROAD

Badger Hills

Caistor

Caistor Grammer Sch

KNAPTON CT

GRIMSBY RD

PH

MOOR LA

NORTH KELSEY ROAD

A1084

NORTH ST

TH

GRIMSBY RD

Cemy

HIGH ST

Caistor Yarborough Sch

Masts

Cherry Garth Farm

ENTERPRISE RD

SAXON FLD

A46

SOUTH DL

BURNETT'S YD

Sewage Works

NAVIGATION LANE

NETTLETON RD

Liby

WHITEGATE HILL

Cabourne Vale

Rothwell Stackgarth

TENNYSON CL 1
NEWBOLT CL 2
THE MEADOW 3

NAVIGATION LA

CAISTOR BY-PASS

Caistor Joint CE & Methodist Prim Sch

B1225

Nettleton House

Suddell Farm

Nettleton Bleak House

Mansgate Quarry (chalk)

ROTHWELL RD

Rothwell Grange Farm

Research Station

Manor Farm

CAISTOR RD

Wood Farm

COOKS LA

BURGHLEY CL

PH

CHURCH ST

Chapel Farm

MANSGATE HILL

Quarry (dis)

CAISTOR ROAD

WOLD VW

Sewage Works

B1205

MOORTOWN RD

Nettleton Prim Sch

PO

DRAYCOTT

Nettleton

POTTINGER GD

NORMANBY ROAD

Wold Farm

HIGH STREET

Rothwell Grange Farm

PH

SCHOOL LA

BECKSIDE

PARTRIDGE DR

Rothwell

HOLTON ROAD

Nettleton Hill

Sand Pit

Top Barn Farm

Tugdale Wood

Rookery Top

Nettleton Top

Chalk Quarry

B1225

Lincolnshire STREET ATLAS

112

10   A   11   B   12   C   13   D   14   E   15   F

B4
1 PHEASANT CT
2 PLOVER SQ
3 AYSCOUGH GR
4 SAXON WY
5 KEYWORTH DR
6 HANSARD CR
7 CHERRY HOLT
8 GEORGE MEWS
9 THE ROPEWALK
10 BUTTER MKT
11 MARKET PL
12 PLOUGH HL
13 CHAPEL ST
14 CHURCH ST
15 BANK LA
16 FOUNTAIN ST
17 HORSE MKT
18 WESTBROOKE GR
19 CHICHESTER DR
20 WESTWOLD RD
21 RISEDALE
22 RAWLINSON AVE
23 MILLFIELDS
24 HERSEY RD
25 CROMWELL VW

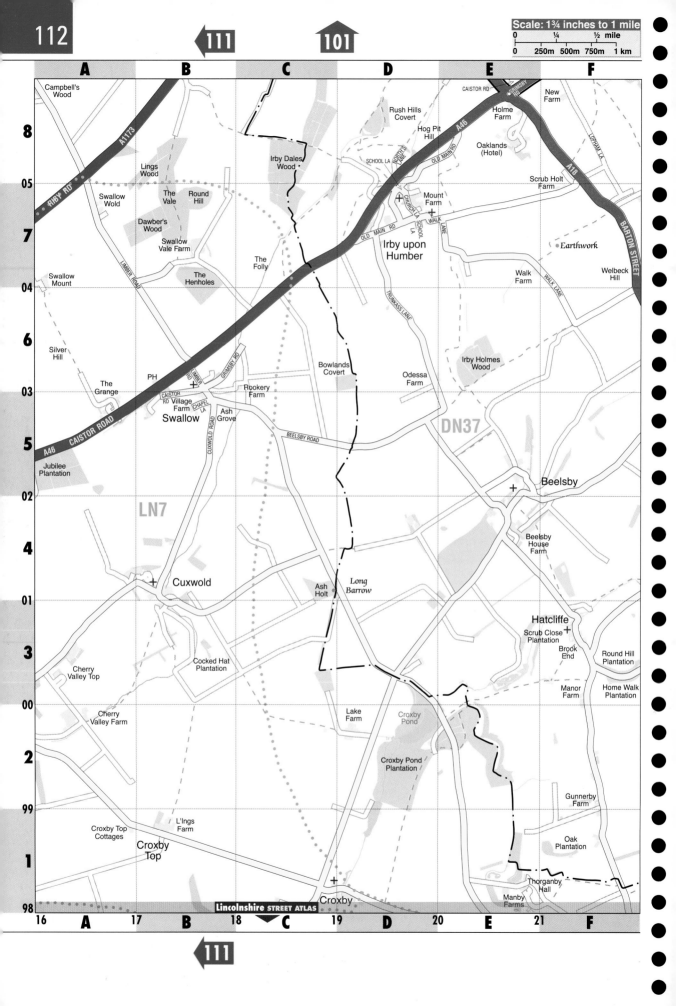

Scale: 1¾ inches to 1 mile

Campbell's Wood

New Farm

CAISTOR RD

Holme Farm

Rush Hills Covert

Hog Pit Hill

Oaklands (Hotel)

Lings Wood

Irby Dales Wood

SCHOOL LA

NORTH'S LANE

OLD MAIN RD

Scrub Holt Farm

Swallow Wold

The Vale

Round Hill

Mount Farm

LOPHAM LA

Dawber's Wood

CHURCH LA

SCHOOL LA

WALK

Irby upon Humber

Earthwork

Welbeck Hill

Swallow Vale Farm

The Folly

OLD MAIN RD

WALK LANE

Walk Farm

Swallow Mount

The Henholes

WALK LANE

BARTON STREET

A18

Silver Hill

TRUNKASS LANE

Bowlands Covert

Irby Holmes Wood

The Grange

PH

Rookery Farm

Odessa Farm

LIMBER ROAD

GRIMSBY RD

CAISTOR RD

Village Farm

CHAPEL LA

Ash Grove

DN37

A46 CAISTOR ROAD

Swallow

CUXWOLD ROAD

BEELSBY ROAD

Beelsby

Jubilee Plantation

LN7

Beelsby House Farm

Cuxwold

Ash Holt

Long Barrow

Hatcliffe

Scrub Close Plantation

Brook End

Round Hill Plantation

Cherry Valley Top

Cocked Hat Plantation

Manor Farm

Home Walk Plantation

Cherry Valley Farm

Lake Farm

Croxby Pond

Croxby Pond Plantation

Gunnerby Farm

Croxby Top Cottages

L'Ings Farm

Oak Plantation

Croxby Top

Thorganby Hall

Manby Farms

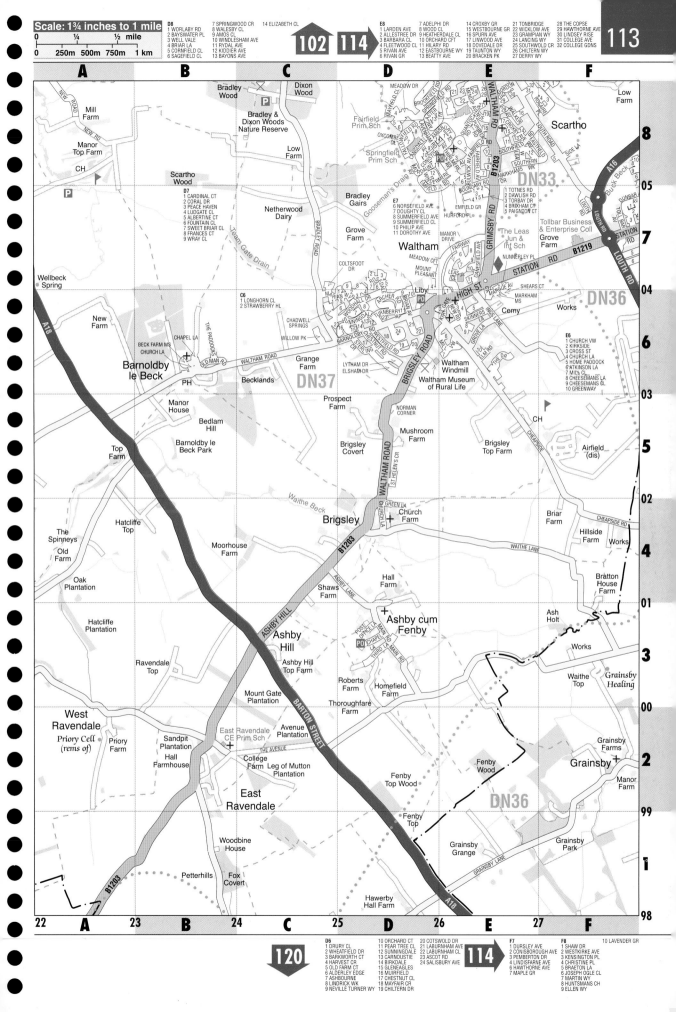

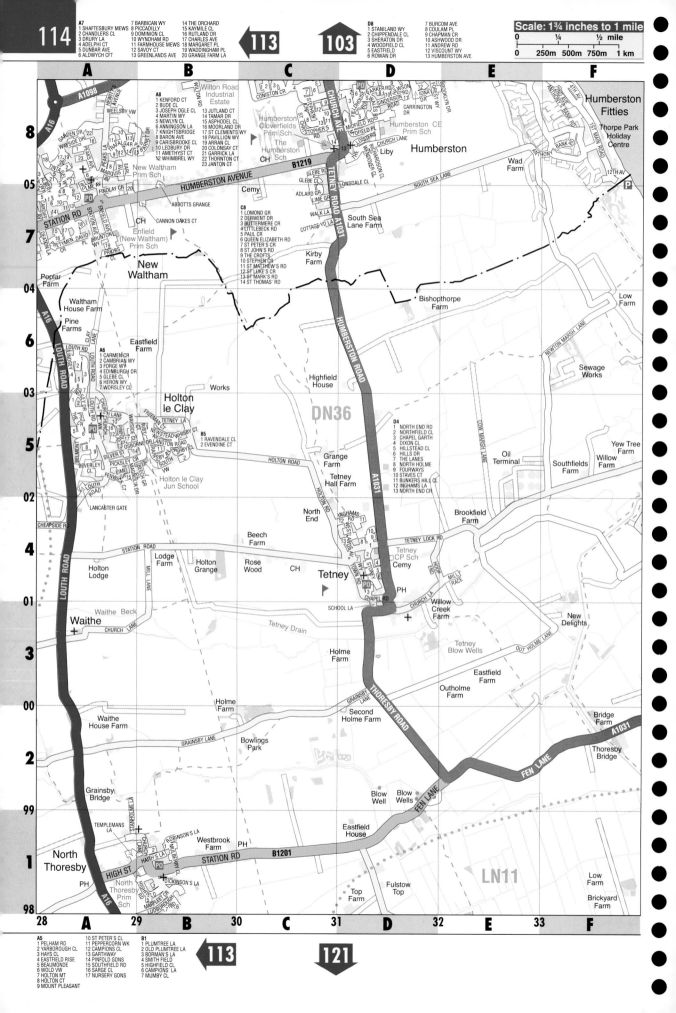

◀ 113   103

A7
1 SHAFTESBURY MEWS
2 CHANDLERS CL
3 DRURY LA
4 ADELPHI CT
5 DUNBAR AVE
6 ALDWYCH CFT

7 BARBICAN WY
8 PICCADILLY
9 DOMINION CL
10 WYNDHAM RD
11 FARMHOUSE MEWS
12 SAVOY CT
13 GREENLANDS AVE

14 THE ORCHARD
15 KAYMILE CL
16 RUTLAND DR
17 CHARLES AVE
18 MARGARET PL
19 WADDINGHAM PL
20 GRANGE FARM LA

D8
1 STANILAND WY
2 CHIPPENDALE CL
3 SHERATON DR
4 WOODFIELD CL
5 EASTFIELD
6 ROWAN DR

7 BURCOM AVE
8 COULAM PL
9 CHAPMAN CR
10 ASHWOOD DR
11 ANDREW RD
12 VISCOUNT WY
13 HUMBERSTON AVE

Scale: 1¾ inches to 1 mile
0   ¼   ½   mile
0   250m 500m 750m   1 km

A8
1 KENFORD CT
2 BUDE CL
3 JOSEPH OGLE CL
4 MARTIN WY
5 NEWLYN CL
6 ANNINGSON LA
7 KNIGHTSBRIDGE
8 BARON AVE
9 CARISBROOKE CL
10 LEDBURY DR
11 AMETHYST CT
12 WHIMBREL WY

13 JUTLAND CT
14 TAMAR DR
15 ASPHODEL CL
16 MOORLAND DR
17 ST CLEMENTS WY
18 PAVILLION WY
19 ARRAN CL
20 COLONSAY CT
21 GARRICK LA
22 THORNTON CT
23 JANTON CT

C8
1 LOMOND GR
2 DERWENT DR
3 BUTTERMERE CR
4 LITTLEBECK RD
5 PAUL CR
6 QUEEN ELIZABETH RD
7 ST PETER'S CR
8 ST JOHN'S RD
9 THE CROFTS
10 STEPHEN CR
11 ST MATTHEW'S RD
12 ST LUKE'S CR
13 ST MARK'S RD
14 ST THOMAS' RD

A6
1 CARMEN CR
2 CAMBRIAN WY
3 FORGE WY
4 EDINBURGH DR
5 GLEBE CL
6 HERON WY
7 WORSLEY CL

B5
1 RAVENDALE CL
2 EVENDINE CT

D4
1 NORTH END RD
2 NORTHFIELD CL
3 CHAPEL GARTH
4 DIXON CL
5 HILLSTEAD CR
6 HILLS DR
7 THE LANES
8 NORTH HOLME
9 FOURWAYS
10 STAVES CT
11 BUNKERS HILL CL
12 INGHAMS LA
13 NORTH END CR

◀ 113   121

A5
1 PELHAM RD
2 YARBOROUGH CL
3 HAYS CL
4 EASTFIELD RISE
5 BEAUMONDE
6 WOLD VW
7 HOLTON MT
8 HOLTON CT
9 MOUNT PLEASANT

10 ST PETER'S CL
11 PEPPERCORN WK
12 CAMPIONS CL
13 GARTHWAY
14 PINFOLD GDNS
15 SOUTHFIELD RD
16 SARGE CL
17 NURSERY GDNS

B1
1 PLUMTREE LA
2 OLD PLUMTREE LA
3 BORMAN'S LA
4 SMITH FIELD
5 HIGHFIELD CL
6 CAMPIONS' LA
7 MUMBY CL

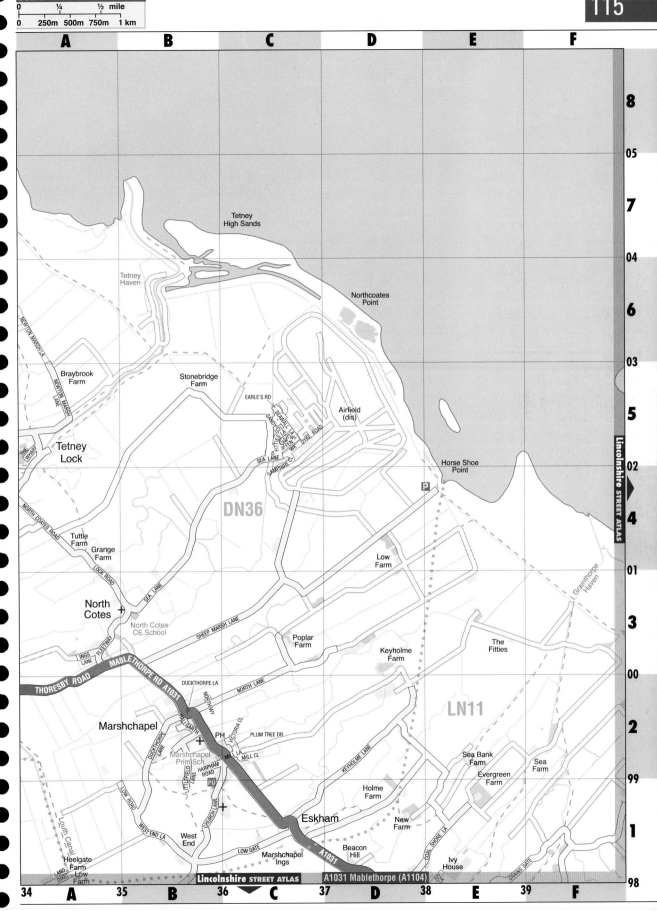

Scale: 1¾ inches to 1 mile

0   ¼   ½ mile
0 250m 500m 750m 1 km

Tetney
High Sands

Tetney
Haven

Braybrook
Farm

Stonebridge
Farm

Northcoates
Point

EARLE'S RD

Airfield
(dis)

SCAWELL LA
SAND-CEL LA
FITTIES LA
GLEN
WK
DYKE ROAD

SEA LANE

SAMPHIRE CL

Tetney
Lock

THE WHARF

NEWTON MARSH LA
NEWTON MARSH LA

DN36

Horse Shoe
Point

P

NORTH COTES ROAD

Tuttle
Farm

Grange
Farm

LOCK ROAD

SEA LANE

Low
Farm

North
Cotes

North Cotes
CE School

SHEEP MARSH LANE

Poplar
Farm

Keyholme
Farm

The
Fitties

Grainthorpe
Haven

INGS
LANE
FLEETWAY

THORESBY ROAD

MABLETHORPE RD A1031

DUCKTHORPE LA

NORTH LANE

00

LN11

NORTHWY

Marshchapel

HALL GARTH

PH

VICTORIA CL

PLUM TREE DR

KEYHOLME LANE

Sea Bank
Farm

Sea
Farm

DUCKTHORPE LANE

Marshchapel
Prim Sch

HARPHAM ROAD

LITTLEFIELD LANE

MILL LA
MILL CL

Evergreen
Farm

PO

Holme
Farm

LOW ROAD

WEST END LA

CHURCH LANE

Eskham

New
Farm

COAL SHORE LA

Louth Canal

Heelgate
Farm

Low
Farm

LAND DIKE

West
End

LOW GATE

Marshchapel
Ings

A1031

Beacon
Hill

Ivy
House

BRAINS GATE

Lincolnshire STREET ATLAS

A1031 Mablethorpe (A1104)

Lincolnshire STREET ATLAS

8
05
7
04
6
03
5
02
4
01
3
00
2
99
1
98

A   34   B   35   C   36   37   D   38   E   39   F
A   B   C   D   E   F

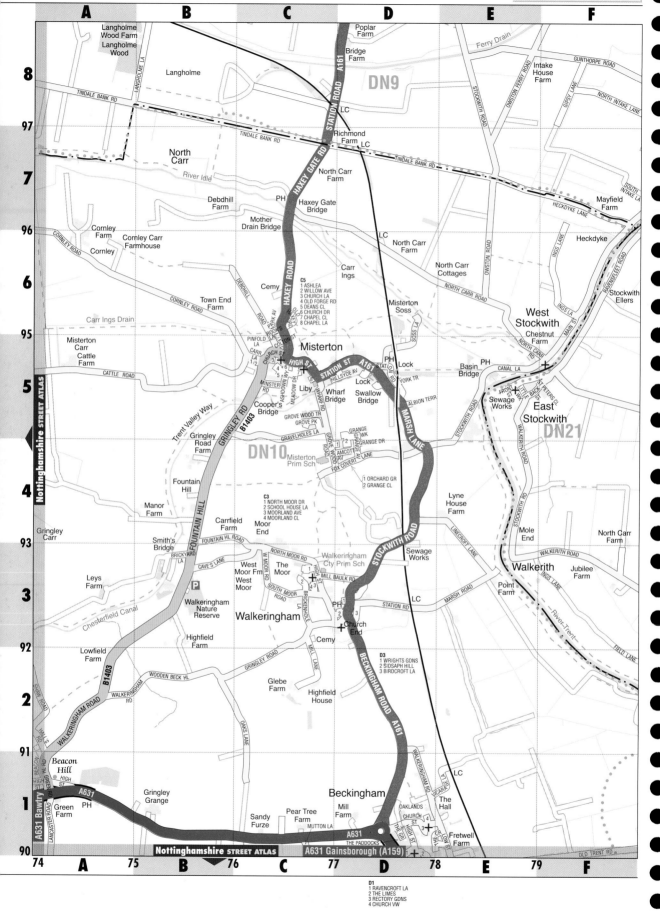

C5
1 ASHLEA
2 WILLOW AVE
3 CHURCH LA
4 OLD FORGE RD
5 DEANS CL
6 CHURCH DR
7 CHAPEL CL
8 CHAPEL LA

C3
1 NORTH MOOR DR
2 SCHOOL HOUSE LA
3 MOORLAND AVE
4 MOORLAND CL

D3
1 WRIGHTS GDNS
2 SIDSAPH HILL
3 BIRDCROFT LA

1 ORCHARD GR
2 GRANGE CL

D1
1 RAVENCROFT LA
2 THE LIMES
3 RECTORY GDNS
4 CHURCH VW

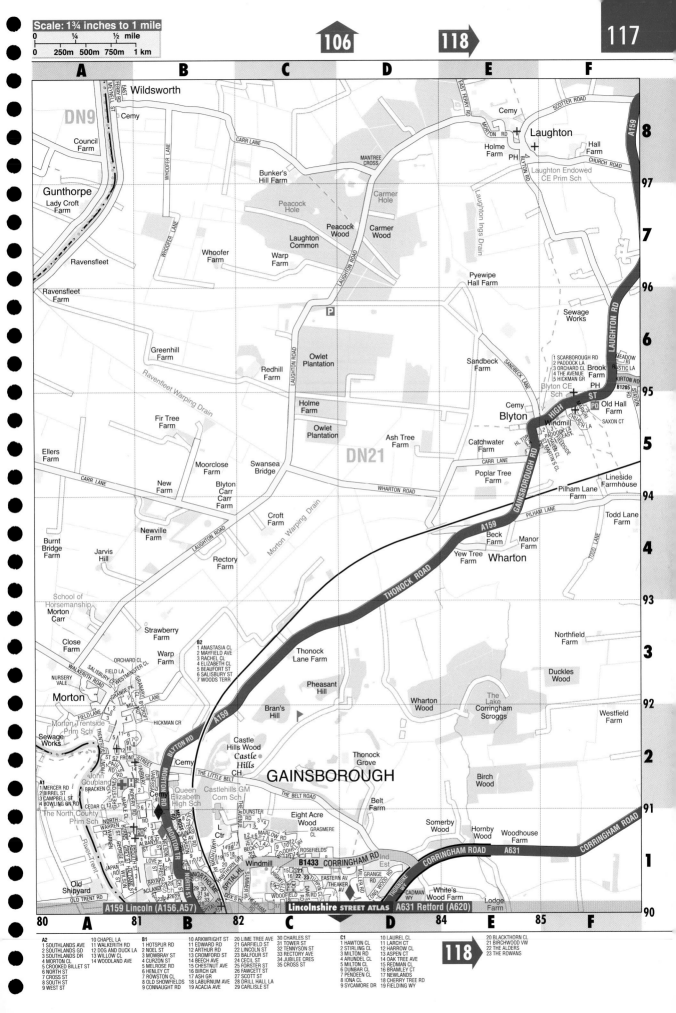

Scale: 1¾ inches to 1 mile

0   ¼   ½ mile
0   250m 500m 750m 1 km

A   B   C   D   E   F

8
97
7
96
6
95
5
94
4
93
3
92
2
91
1
90

Wildsworth
DN9
Cemy
Council Farm
Gunthorpe
Lady Croft Farm
Ravensfleet
Ravensfleet Farm
Ellers Farm
Burnt Bridge Farm
School of Horsemanship
Morton Carr
Close Farm
Morton
Sewage Works
The North County Phm Sch
John Couplands
Old Shipyard
River Trent

Whoofer Lane
Carr Lane
Bunker's Hill Farm
Peacock Hole
Laughton Common
Whoofer Farm
Warp Farm
Peacock Wood
Carmer Wood
Greenhill Farm
Redhill Farm
Fir Tree Farm
Owlet Plantation
Holme Farm
Owlet Plantation
Moorclose Farm
Swansea Bridge
New Farm
Blyton Carr Carr Farm
Croft Farm
Morton Warping Drain
Newville Farm
Rectory Farm
Strawberry Farm
Warp Farm
Laughton Road

MANTREE CROSS
Carmer Hole
DN21
Ash Tree Farm
Wharton Road

Laughton
Cemy
Holme Farm
PH
Laughton Endowed CE Prim Sch
Laughton Ings Drain
Pyewipe Hall Farm
Sandbeck Farm
Sewage Works
1 SCARBOROUGH RD
2 PADDOCK LA
3 ORCHARD CL
4 THE AVENUE
5 HICKMAN GR
Brook Farm
PH
Blyton CE Sch
Blyton
Cemy
Windmill
Poplar Tree Farm
Beck Farm
Yew Tree Farm
Manor Farm
Wharton
Thonock Road
Gainsborough Rd

SCOTTER ROAD
EAST FERRY RD
A159
Hall Farm
CHURCH ROAD
MEADOW
KIRTON RD
B1205
STATION RD
Old Hall Farm
SAXON CT
Catchwater Farm
Carr Lane
Pilham Lane Farm
Lineside Farmhouse
A159
Pilham Lane
Todd Lane Farm
Northfield Farm
Duckles Wood
Westfield Farm
Corringham Scroggs
The Lake
Wharton Wood
Birch Wood
Somerby Wood
Hornby Wood
Woodhouse Farm
Corringham Road
A631

Thonock Lane Farm
Bran's Hill
Pheasant Hill
Castle Hills Wood
Castle Hills CH
GAINSBOROUGH
Queen Elizabeth High Sch
Eight Acre Wood
Belt Farm
Thonock Grove
The Belt Road
Corringham Rd
A631
Ind Est
Lodge Farm
White's Wood Farm
Grange

B2
1 ANASTASIA CL
2 MAYFIELD AVE
3 RACHEL CL
4 ELIZABETH CL
5 BEAUFORT ST
6 SALISBURY ST
7 WOODS TERR

A1
1 MERCER RD
2 BIRREL ST
3 CAMPBELL ST
4 BOWLING GN RD

Windmill
B1433
CORRINGHAM RD
EASTERN AV THEAKER AV

A2
1 SOUTHLANDS AVE
2 SOUTHLANDS GD
3 SOUTHLANDS DR
4 MORTON CL
5 CROOKED BILLET ST
6 NORTH ST
7 CROSS ST
8 SOUTH ST
9 WEST ST
10 CHAPEL LA
11 WALKERITH RD
12 DOG AND DUCK LA
13 WILLOW CL
14 WOODLAND AVE

B1
1 HOTSPUR RD
2 NOEL ST
3 MOWBRAY ST
4 CURZON ST
5 MELROSE RD
6 HENLEY CT
7 ROWSTON CL
8 OLD SHOWFIELDS
9 CONNAUGHT RD
10 ARKWRIGHT ST
11 EDWARD RD
12 ARTHUR RD
13 CROMFORD ST
14 BEECH AVE
15 CHESTNUT AVE
16 BIRCH GR
17 ASH GR
18 LABURNUM AVE
19 ACACIA AVE
20 LIME TREE AVE
21 GARFIELD ST
22 LINCOLN ST
23 BALFOUR ST
24 CECIL ST
25 FORSTER ST
26 FAWCETT ST
27 SCOTT ST
28 DRILL HALL LA
29 CARLISLE ST
30 CHARLES ST
31 TOWER ST
32 TENNYSON ST
33 RECTORY AVE
34 JUBILEE CRES
35 CROSS ST

C1
1 HAWTON CL
2 STIRLING CL
3 MILTON RD
4 ARUNDEL CL
5 MILTON CL
6 DUNBAR CL
7 PENDEEN CL
8 IONA CL
9 SYCAMORE DR
10 LAUREL CL
11 LARCH CT
12 HARROW CL
13 ASPEN CT
14 OAK TREE AVE
15 REDMAN CL
16 BRAMLEY CT
17 NEWLANDS
18 CHERRY TREE RD
19 FIELDING WY
20 BLACKTHORN CL
21 BIRCHWOOD VW
22 THE ALDERS
23 THE ROWANS

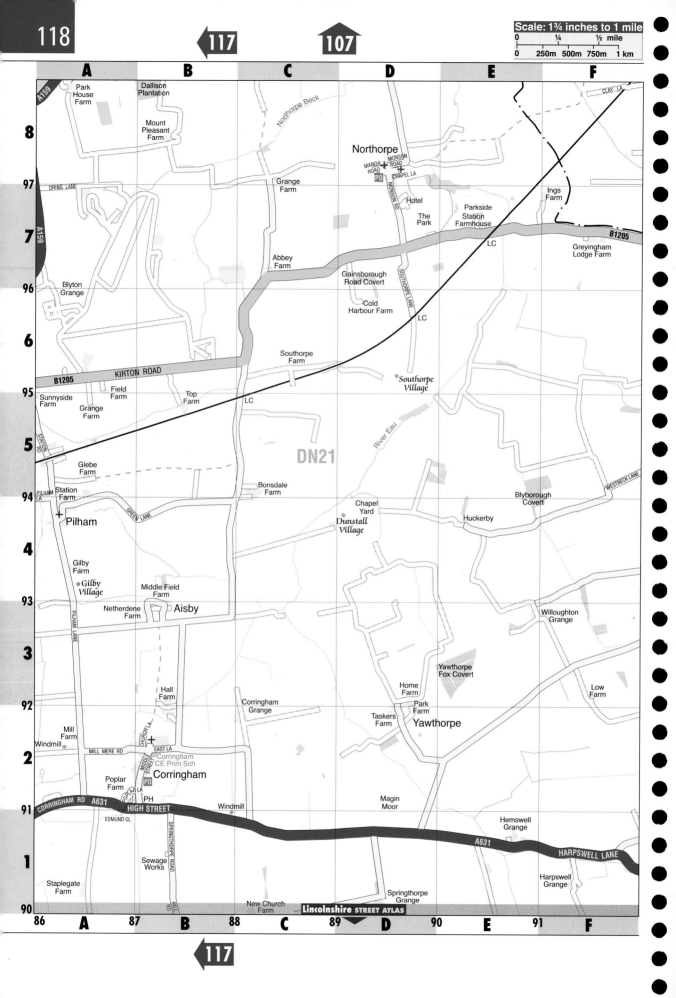

118

117

107

Scale: 1¾ inches to 1 mile

0   ¼   ½ mile
0 250m 500m 750m 1 km

A   B   C   D   E   F

A159
Park House Farm
Dallison Plantation
Mount Pleasant Farm
Northorpe Beck
8

Northorpe
MANOR ROAD   MONSON ROAD
PO   CHAPEL LA
Grange Farm
97
DRING LANE
MONSON RD
Hotel
The Park
Parkside Station Farmhouse
Ings Farm

A159
7
Abbey Farm
LC
B1205
Greyingham Lodge Farm

SOUTHORPE LANE
Gainsborough Road Covert
96
Blyton Grange
Cold Harbour Farm
LC

6
Southorpe Farm
Southorpe Village

B1205
KIRTON ROAD
95
Sunnyside Farm
Field Farm
Top Farm
LC
River Eau
WESTBECK LANE

STATION RD
Grange Farm
DN21
Blyborough Covert

5
Glebe Farm
Bonsdale Farm
Chapel Yard
Huckerby

PILHAM LA
Station Farm
94
Pilham
Dunstall Village

GREEN LANE
PILHAM LANE
Gilby Farm
Willoughton Grange

4
Gilby Village
Middle Field Farm
93
Netherdene Farm
Aisby

3
Hall Farm
Yawthorpe Fox Covert
Low Farm

CHURCH LA
Corringham Grange
Home Farm
Park Farm
92
Mill Farm
Windmill
MILL MERE RD
EAST LA
Taskers Farm
Yawthorpe

MIDDLE STREET
Corringham CE Prim Sch
PO
Corringham
2
Poplar Farm
POPLAR LA
PH
Magin Moor

CORRINGHAM RD   A631
HIGH STREET
Windmill
Hemswell Grange
91
EDMUND CL
SPRINGTHORPE ROAD
A631
HARPSWELL LANE

1
Sewage Works
Springthorpe Grange
Harpswell Grange

Staplegate Farm
HILL RD
New Church Farm
90

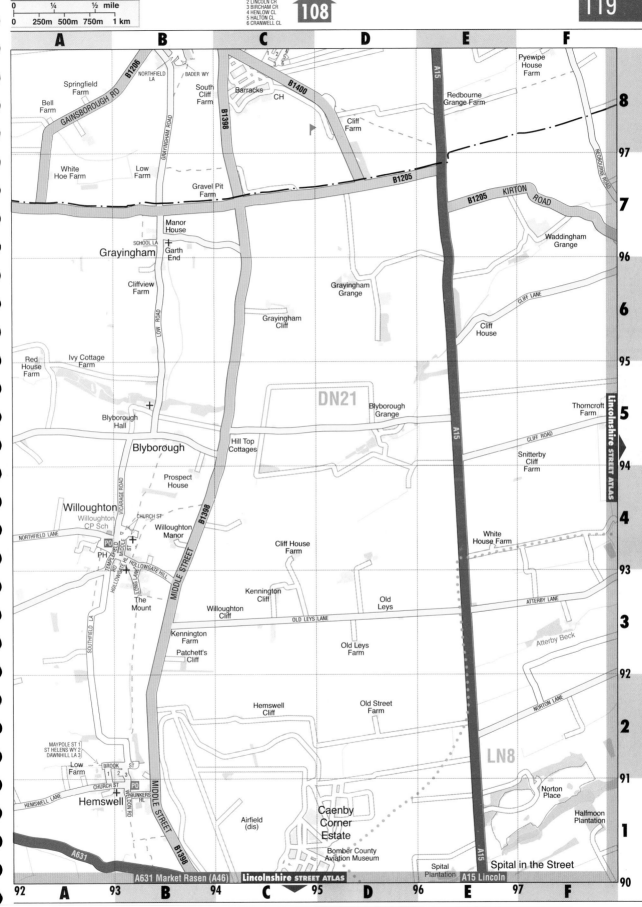

C8
1 YORK RD
2 LINCOLN CR
3 BIRCHAM CR
4 HENLOW CL
5 HALTON CL
6 CRANWELL CL

B1206
NORTHFIELD LA
BADER WY
Springfield Farm
South Cliff Farm
Bell Farm
GAINSBOROUGH RD
Barracks
CH
B1400
Pyewipe House Farm
Redbourne Grange Farm

White Hoe Farm
Low Farm
GRAYINGHAM ROAD
Cliff Farm
B1398
Gravel Pit Farm
B1205
B1205 KIRTON ROAD
REDBOURNE ROAD

Manor House
SCHOOL LA
Grayingham
Garth End
Waddingham Grange

Cliffview Farm
LOW ROAD
Grayingham Grange
Cliff House
CLIFF LANE

Grayingham Cliff

Red House Farm
Ivy Cottage Farm
A15
CLIFF ROAD
Thorncroft Farm

DN21
Blyborough Grange
Snitterby Cliff Farm
Lincolnshire STREET ATLAS

Blyborough Hall
Hill Top Cottages
CLIFF ROAD

Blyborough

Prospect House
VICARAGE ROAD
B1398
White House Farm

Willoughton
Willoughton CP Sch
CHURCH ST
Cliff House Farm
NORTHFIELD LANE
PO
Willoughton Manor
ST
PH
TEMPLEFIELD RD MIDDLE
HOLLOWGATE HILL
HOLLOWGATE HL
LONG LANE
Kennington Cliff
Old Leys
ATTERBY LANE

The Mount
MIDDLE STREET
Willoughton Cliff
OLD LEYS LANE
Old Leys Farm
Atterby Beck

SOUTHFIELD LA
Kennington Farm
Patchett's Cliff
Old Leys Farm
NORTON LANE

Hemswell Cliff
Old Street Farm

LN8

MAYPOLE ST 1
ST HELENS WY 2
DAWNHILL LA 3
BROOK ST
Norton Place

Low Farm
CHURCH ST
PO
MIDDLE STREET
Halfmoon Plantation

HEMSWELL LANE
WELDON RD
BUNKERS HL
Hemswell

Airfield (dis)
Caenby Corner Estate
A15

A631
B1398
Bomber County Aviation Museum
Spital Plantation
Spital in the Street

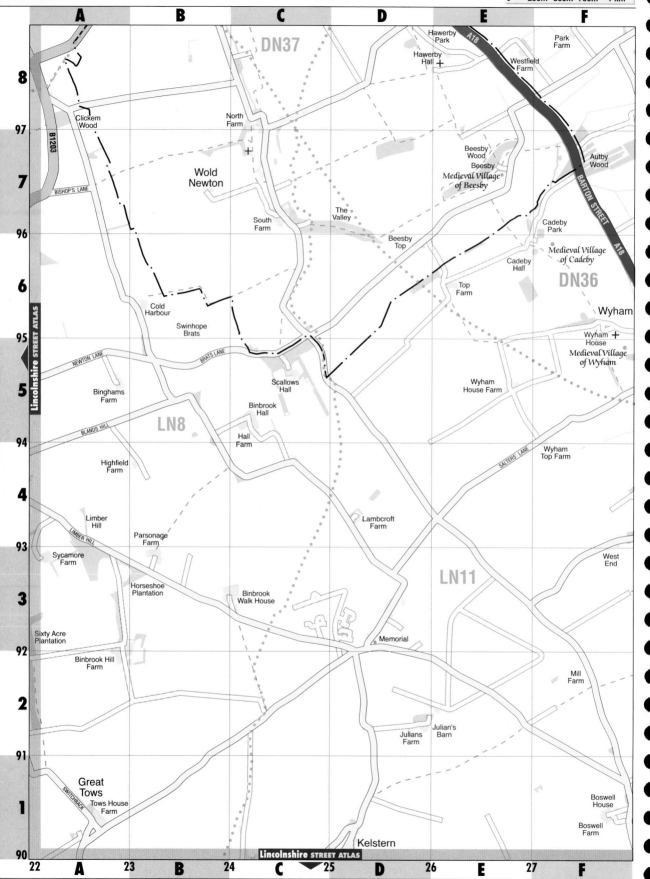

Scale: 1¾ inches to 1 mile
0   ¼   ½ mile
0   250m 500m 750m 1 km

A   B   C   D   E   F

DN37

8

97

Clickem Wood

B1203

BISHOP'S LANE

Hawerby Park
A18
Hawerby Hall
Westfield Farm
Park Farm

North Farm

7

Wold Newton

Beesby Wood
Beesby
Medieval Village of Beesby

BARTON STREET

Autby Wood

96

South Farm

The Valley

Beesby Top

Cadeby Park

A18

Medieval Village of Cadeby

6

Cold Harbour

Swinhope Brats

Top Farm

Cadeby Hall

DN36

Wyham

NEWTON LANE

BRATS LANE

Wyham House
Medieval Village of Wyham

95

Binghams Farm

Scallows Hall

Wyham House Farm

Lincolnshire STREET ATLAS

5

BLANDS HILL

LN8

Binbrook Hall

Hall Farm

SALTERS LANE

Wyham Top Farm

94

Highfield Farm

4

Limber Hill

Parsonage Farm

Lambcroft Farm

LN11

West End

LIMBER HILL

93

Sycamore Farm

Horseshoe Plantation

Binbrook Walk House

3

Sixty Acre Plantation

Memorial

Mill Farm

92

Binbrook Hill Farm

2

Julians Farm

Julian's Barn

91

Great Tows

SWITCHBACK

Boswell House

1

Tows House Farm

Boswell Farm

90

Kelstern

22   A   23   B   24   C   25   D   26   E   27   F

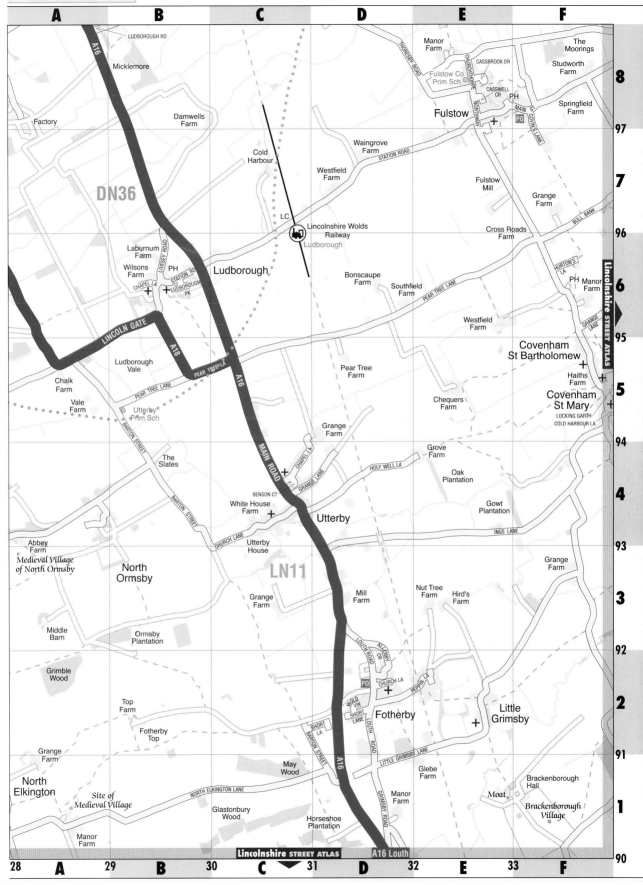

Scale: 1¾ inches to 1 mile
0   ¼   ½   mile
0   250m 500m 750m 1 km

A B C D E F

8
97
7
96
6
95
5
94
4
93
3
92
2
91
1
90

LUDBOROUGH RD
Micklemore
Factory
Damwells Farm
Cold Harbour
DN36
Laburnum Farm
Wilsons Farm
PH
CHAPEL LA
STATION RD
LUDBOROUGH PK
Ludborough
LIVESEY ROAD
A18
LINCOLN GATE
Ludborough Vale
Chalk Farm
Vale Farm
PEAR TREE LANE
Utterby Prim Sch
BARTON STREET
The Slates
PEAR TREE LA
A16
MAIN ROAD
Abbey Farm
Medieval Village of North Ormsby
North Ormsby
BARTON STREET
CHURCH LANE
Grange Farm
White House Farm
BENSON CT
CHAPEL LA
GRANGE LANE
Utterby
Utterby House
LN11
Middle Barn
Ormsby Plantation
Grimble Wood
Top Farm
Fotherby Top
Grange Farm
North Elkington
Site of Medieval Village
NORTH ELKINGTON LANE
Glastonbury Wood
Manor Farm
May Wood
SHORT LA
BARTON STREET
A16
Horseshoe Plantation
GRIMSBY ROAD
A16 Louth

THORESBY ROAD
Manor Farm
Fulstow Co Prim Sch
CHURCHTHORPE
CASSBROOK DR
CASSWELL CR
NORTHWAY
PH
MAIN RD
PO
Fulstow
Waingrove Farm
STATION ROAD
Westfield Farm
Lincolnshire Wolds Railway Ludborough
LC
Bonscaupe Farm
Southfield Farm
PEAR TREE LANE
Pear Tree Farm
Grange Farm
HOLY WELL LA
Grove Farm
Oak Plantation
Gowt Plantation
INGS LANE
Mill Farm
Nut Tree Farm
Hird's Farm
LOUTH ROAD
ALLENBY CR
PO
NEW VW
SHORT LANE
CHURCH LA
PEPPER LA
Fotherby
LOUTH ROAD
LITTLE GRIMSBY LANE
Little Grimsby LANE
Glebe Farm
Manor Farm

The Moorings
Studworth Farm
Springfield Farm
Fulstow Mill
Grange Farm
BULL BANK
Cross Roads Farm
HURTON'S LA
PH
Manor Farm
GRANGE LANE
Westfield Farm
Covenham St Bartholomew
Haiths Farm
Covenham St Mary
LOCKING GARTH
COLD HARBOUR LA
Chequers Farm
Grange Farm
Brackenborough Hall
Moat
Brackenborough Village

Lincolnshire STREET ATLAS

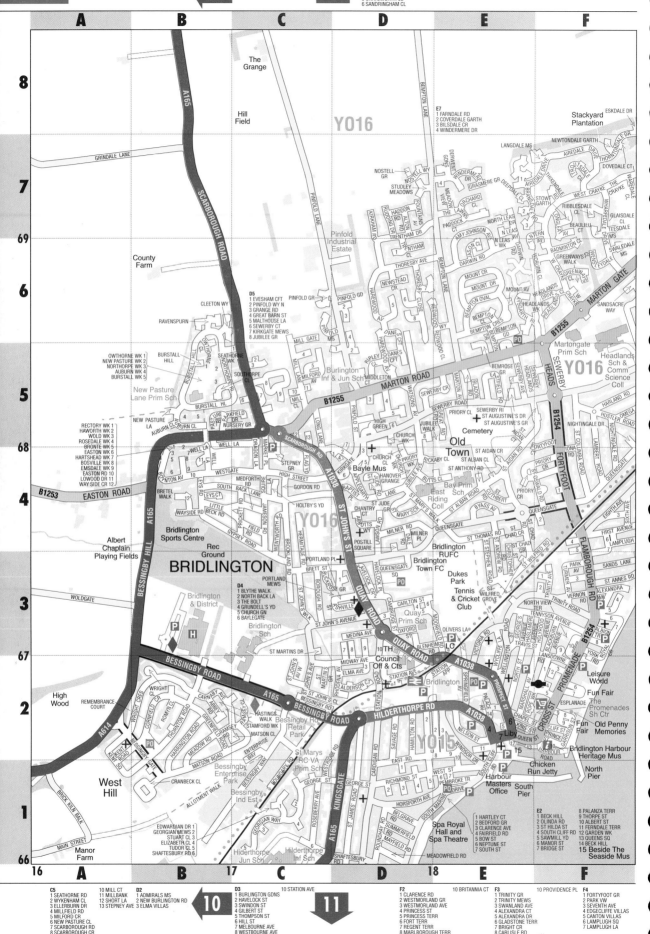

A   B   C   D   E   F

8

7

69

6

5

68

4

3

67

2

1

66

19   A   **B**   20   **C**   **D**   21   **E**   **F**

Martonia
Caravan Park
PH

Marton
FLAMBOROUGH ROAD B1255
JEWISON LANE
SHEEPRAKE LA

Home Farm
Plantation
Gell-spring
Plantation
Home
Farm
Maidlands
Plantation

West
Wood
Marton
Hall
Marton Valley
Caravan Park

YO16

PLANTATION VW
Crow
Plantation
GEORGE RD

Leys
Plantation

YO15

Bridlington Links
& Heritage Park
Dyke
Wood

Long
Wood

Danes Dyke
Nature Reserve

Needles
Plantation

WILLOWDALE CL

West
Wood

Danes
Dyke Farm

CH

Dykes
End

KESTREL DR

THE GLIMPSE
THE CRAYKE

WOODLANDS CL

CHESTNUT CL

MARTONGATE

Sewerby
Park

Crow
Wood

MOOR ROAD

Pheasant
Plantation

HIGH SEWERBY ROAD

CHURCH LANE

Pigeoncote
Plantation

POPLAR DR
MAPLE ROAD

Charity Farm
Caravan Park
VIKING RD

SEWERBY
PK CL

Sewerby Hall
& Gardens

Home
Farm

3 ROSEWOOD
WALK

VIKING ROAD

Westfield
Plantation
SEWERBY
ROAD

PO

SEAGATE

Liby
SANDGATE
RD

BEACON RD

WILLOW DR

YO15

Sewerby Village
PH

Sewerby
Rocks

SANDSACRE AVE
CALLINGS RD

BAXLEY

MAIN ST
CLIFF ROAD
RIVIERA DR

OAKWELL
AV

PO

LC

Bondville
Model Village

SEAGATE VIEW

HORSESHOE DR

SANDSACRE ROAD

Sewerby
Fields

CLOVERLEY RD

A6
1 SANDSACRE DR
2 MAPEL CL
3 ROSEWOOD CL
4 LABURNUM CT
5 BIRCH CL
6 CLOVERLEY RD

Rock
Ends

SEWERBY ROAD

Sewerby

LIMEKILN LANE
GREAME ROAD

Headland Way

OMEGA CL

ROAD

P

EIGHTH AVENUE
LIMEKILN LA
NORTH MARINE RD

North
Sands

SECOND AVE
THIRD AVE
FOURTH AVE
FIFTH AVE

P
ROAD

ALEXANDRA PR

20 20

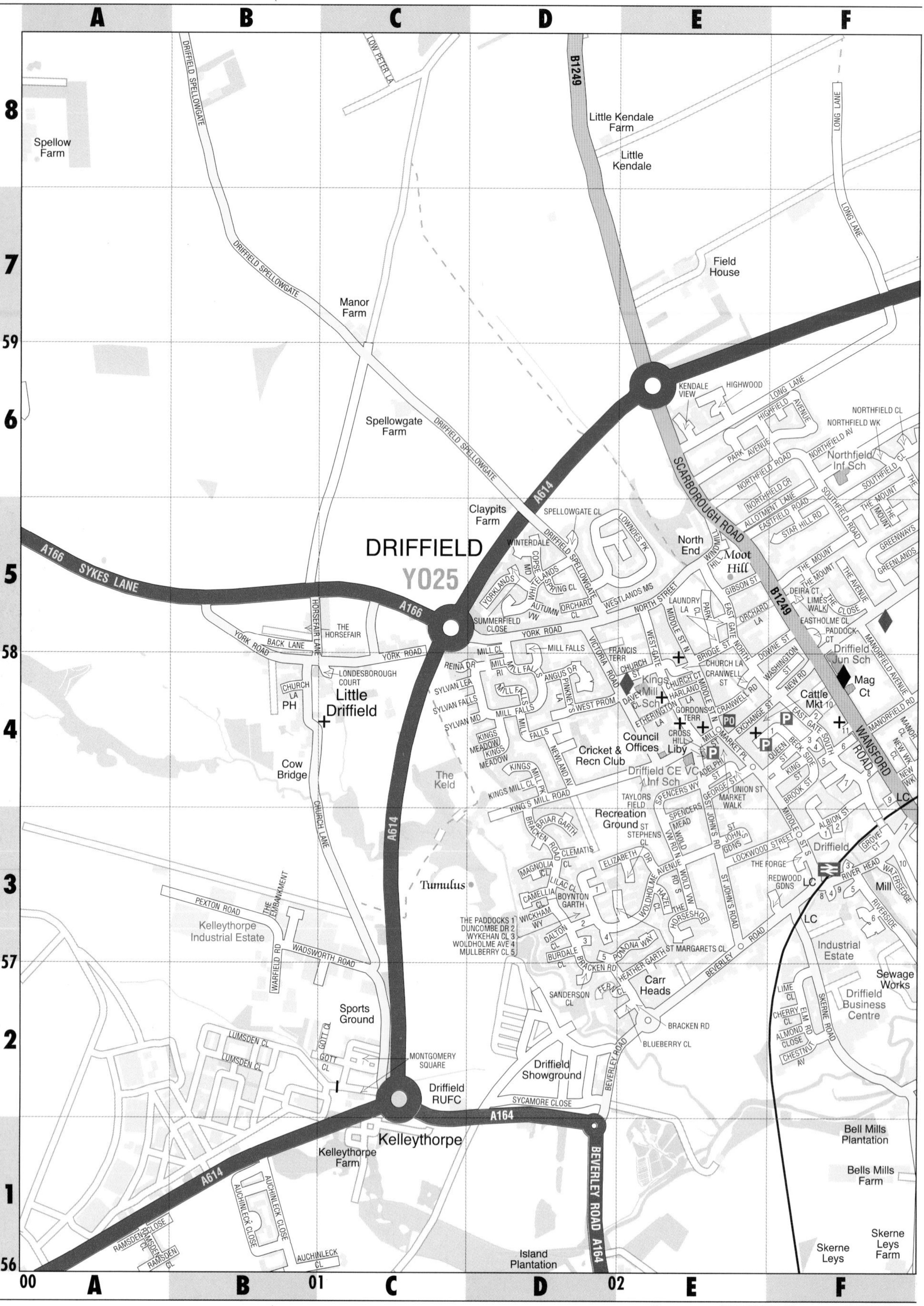
A B C D E F
8 7 59 6 5 58 4 3 57 2 1 56
00 01 02
DRIFFIELD
YO25
Spellow Farm
Driffield Spellowgate
Low Peter La
B1249
Little Kendale Farm
Little Kendale
Long Lane
Field House
Manor Farm
Spellowgate Farm
Claypits Farm
A614
A166
Sykes Lane
North End
Moot Hill
Scarborough Road
Wansford Road
Northfield Inf Sch
Driffield Jun Sch
Mag Ct
Cattle Mkt
Kings Mill Sch
Council Offices
Cricket & Recn Club
Driffield CE VC Inf Sch
Cross Hill
Liby
The Keld
Little Driffield
PH
Cow Bridge
Church Lane
York Road
The Horsefair
Londesborough Court
Recreation Ground
Tumulus
Kelleythorpe Industrial Estate
Pexton Road
Wadsworth Road
Sports Ground
Montgomery Square
Driffield RUFC
Kelleythorpe
Kelleythorpe Farm
A164
Beverley Road
Sycamore Close
Driffield Showground
Carr Heads
Island Plantation
Driffield
LC
Mill
Industrial Estate
Sewage Works
Driffield Business Centre
Bell Mills Plantation
Bells Mills Farm
Skerne Leys
Skerne Leys Farm
Auchinleck Close
Lumsden Cl
Ramsden Close
The Paddocks 1
Duncombe Dr 2
Wykehan Cl 3
Woldholme Ave 4
Mullberry Cl 5

20 20

F3
1 ST JOHN'S WK
2 ST JOHN'S PL
3 RIVER HEAD DR
4 GEORGIAN MEWS
5 RIVERSIDE MEWS
6 RIVERSIDE CL
7 ANDERSON ST
8 WOODLANDS
9 BEECHLANDS
10 BEECHWOOD LA

F4
1 PROVIDENCE PL
2 JEVANS CT
3 GALLOWAY LA
4 GALLOWAY CT
5 BRIDGE LA
6 DUNN'S LA
7 NAYFIELD CL
8 HARPER ST
9 FAWCETT GDNS
10 EASTERFIELD CT
11 LANGLEY GARTH

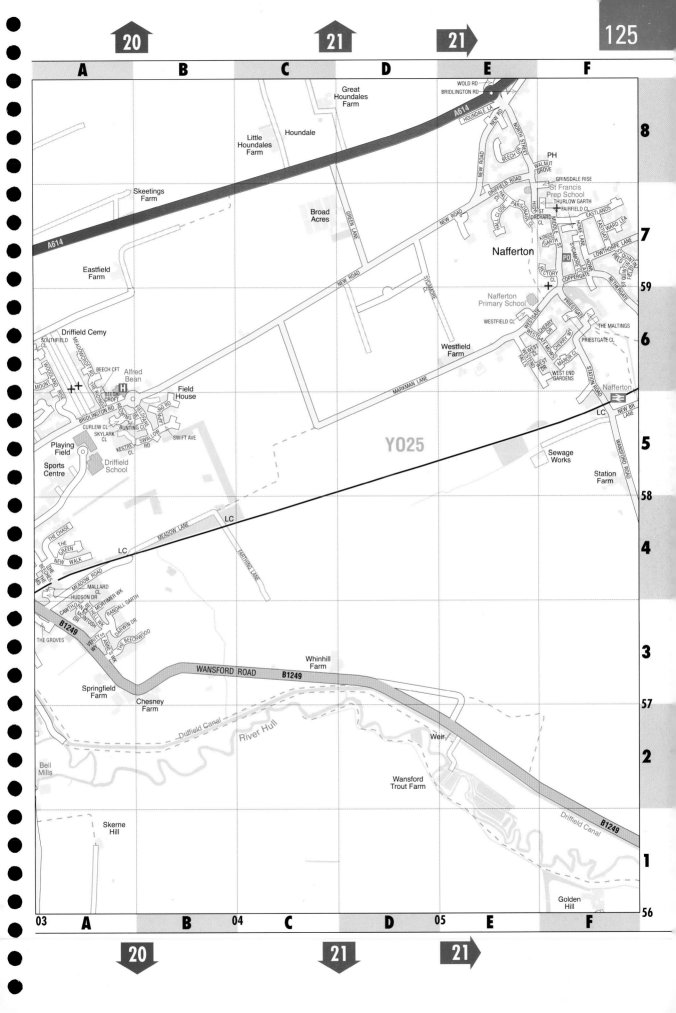

A   B   C   D   E   F

Great
Houndales
Farm

WOLD RD
BRIDLINGTON RD

8

A614   HOUNDALE LA

NORTH STREET

NEW RD

Little
Houndales
Farm

Houndale

NEW ROAD

BEECH CL

PH

WALNUT
GROVE

Skeetings
Farm

Broad
Acres

GREEN LANE

NEW ROAD

DRIFFIELD ROAD

GRINSDALE RISE

St Francis
Prep School

THURLOW GARTH

FAIRFIELD CL

EASTLANDS

WARD LEA

7

A614

NEW ROAD

HALL CLOSE CL

PARSONAGE CL

ORCHARD CL

HOWE LANE

EASTGATE

LOWTHORPE LANE

ST QUINTIN FIELD

ST QUINTIN CL

Nafferton

Eastfield
Farm

KINGS
GARTH

HOWE LANE

SYCAMORE CL

SYCAMORE CL

RECTORY CL

COPPERGATE

PO

59

NETHERGATE

Driffield Cemy

SOUTHFIELD
CL

MEADOWCROFT RD

BEECH CFT

Nafferton
Primary School

PRIESTGATE

WESTFIELD CL

WESTGATE

CHERRY DR

CHERRY WAY

THE MALTINGS

PRIESTGATE CL

6

THE AVENUE

BEECH
CROFT

Alfred
Bean

H

WOODLAND RISE

MOUNT

Westfield
Farm

WESTGATE MEWS

WEST CL

WEST
DR

MANOR CL

WEST END
GARDENS

STATION ROAD

Nafferton

BRIDLINGTON RD

Field
House

REDWING DR

KESTREL DR

BUNTING CL

SWALLOW RD

SWIFT AVE

CURLEW CL

SKYLARK
CL

MARKMAN LANE

YO25

Sewage
Works

NEW BR
LANE

LC

Playing
Field

Sports
Centre

Driffield
School

58

LC

MEADOW LANE

LC

WANSFORD ROAD

Station
Farm

5

THE CHASE

THE
GREEN

NEW WALK

FARTHING LANE

4

THE BEECHES

MEADOW ROAD

MALLARD
CL

HUDSON DR

CAWTHORN DR

BETHELL WK

HILL WK

MORTIMER WK

RANDALL GARTH

MCINTOSH DR

DARWIN DR

B1249

VERITY WY

ST ANNE'S WK

THE BEECHWOOD

THE GROVES

Whinhill
Farm

3

WANSFORD ROAD   B1249

Springfield
Farm

Chesney
Farm

57

Driffield Canal

River Hull

Weir

2

Bell
Mills

Wansford
Trout Farm

Driffield Canal

B1249

Skerne
Hill

1

Golden
Hill

56

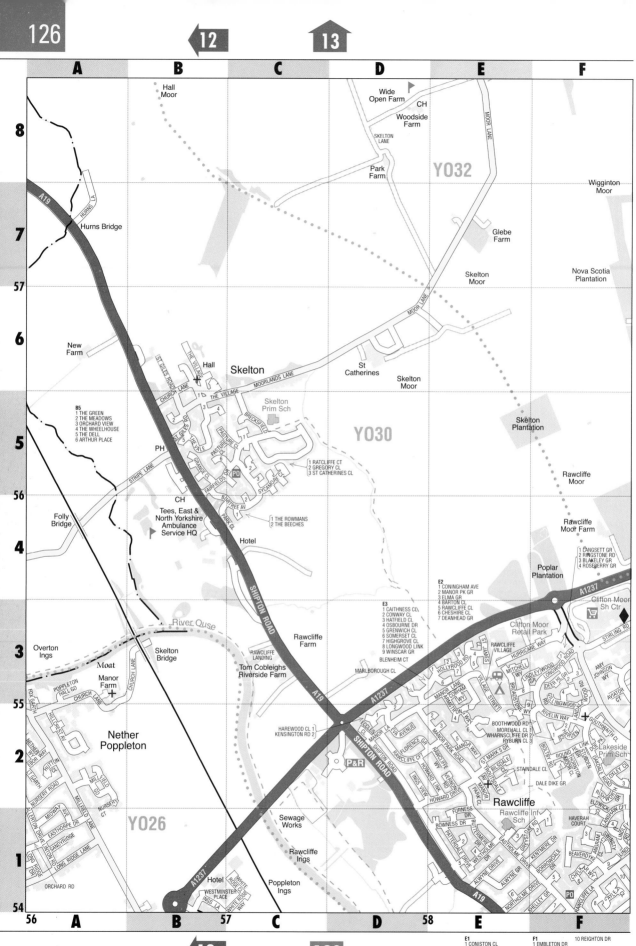

	A	B	C	D	E	F

8

Hall Moor

Wide Open Farm

CH

Woodside Farm

SKELTON LANE

Park Farm

YO32

Wigginton Moor

MOOR LANE

7

Hurns Bridge

HURNS LA

A19

Glebe Farm

Skelton Moor

Nova Scotia Plantation

57

MOOR LANE

6

New Farm

ST GILES ROAD LANE

Hall

THE VILLAGE

Skelton

CHURCH LANE

MOORLANDS LANE

St Catherines

Skelton Moor

Skelton Plantation

Skelton Prim Sch

B5
1 THE GREEN
2 THE MEADOWS
3 ORCHARD VIEW
4 THE WHEELHOUSE
5 THE DELL
6 ARTHUR PLACE

THE VILLAGE

BRECKSFIELD

YO30

5

STRIPE LANE

PH

ST GILES

TRI VALE

GRANGE LANE

PASTURE CL

FAIRFIELDS DR

SYCAMORE CL

PO

1 RATCLIFFE CT
2 GREGORY CL
3 ST CATHERINES CL

Rawcliffe Moor

56

Folly Bridge

CH

Tees, East & North Yorkshire Ambulance Service HQ

PARK CL

BURTREE AV

1 THE ROWMANS
2 THE BEECHES

Rawcliffe Moor Farm

Hotel

4

SHIPTON ROAD

Poplar Plantation

1 LANGSETT GR
2 RINGSTONE RD
3 BLAKELEY GR
4 ROSEBERRY GR

A1237

Clifton Moor Sh Ctr

STIRLING RD

E2
1 CONINGHAM AVE
2 MANOR PK GR
3 ELMA GR
4 BARTON CL
5 RAWCLIFFE CL
6 CHESHIRE CL
7 DEANHEAD CL

Clifton Moor Retail Park

3

Overton Ings

River Ouse

Skelton Bridge

Rawcliffe Farm

E3
1 CAITHNESS CL
2 CONWAY CL
3 HATFIELD CL
4 OSBOURNE DR
5 GRENWICH CL
6 SOMERSET CL
7 HIGHGROVE CL
8 LONGWOOD LINK
9 WINSCAR GR

BLENHEIM CT

Clifton Moor Village

Rawcliffe Village

HURRICANE WAY

AMY JOHNSON CT

AVIATOR CT

Moat

CHURCH LANE

Manor Farm

POPPLETON HALL GD

CHURCH LANE

RAWCLIFFE LANDING

Tom Cobleighs Riverside Farm

MARLBOROUGH CL

HOLLYROOD RD

ST JAMES

MANOR LANE

COBHAM WY

INDLEYWOOD

DEER HL GR

CRINGLEWOOD

LANGWOOD

GOUTHWAITE CL

SOUTHWAITE CL

2

FOX GARTH

HILLCREST AV

NETHER WY

TABOR GARTH

HUTTON

MILL FIELD RD

NURSERY ROAD

Nether Poppleton

HAREWOOD CL 1
KENSINGTON RD 2

SHIPTON ROAD

P&R

MANOR LA

FLORENCE GR

RAWCLIFFE CFT

MANOR PARK RD

ST MARK'S GR

ST BILSDALE

BROADSTONE WY

RIVELIN WY

MITCHELL

ROUND HL LINK

DEE PK

STAINDALE CL

BOOTHWOOD RD
MOREHALL CL
WHARNSCLIFFE DR 2
RYBURN CL 3

Lakeside Prim Sch

LOXLEY CL

DALE DIKE GR

ELDWICK

55

MIDWAY

MILLFIELD LANE

EASTHORPE DR

SANDYRIDGE

NURSERY ROAD

MANOR WAY

AVENUE

HOWARD LINK

INGS VIEW

HOWARD DRIVE

Rawcliffe

Rawcliffe Inf Sch

MANOR PK CL

KENTMERE DR

BORROWDALE DR

GRASSHAW CFT

RUSKIN CL

ELDWICK CL

GRNSTY

1

YO26

ALLERTON DRIVE

LONG RIDGE

LONG RIDGE LANE

Sewage Works

Rawcliffe Ings

FURNESS DR

BOWNESS DR

BUTTERMERE DR

PATTERDALE DRIVE

WESTHOLME

GREYSTOKE RD

EASTHOLME DR

ALWYNE DR

ALWYNE GR

BEAVERDYKE

HAVERAH COURT

LANGSHAW CFT

CAYTON

ORCHARD RD

A1237

Hotel

WHITE ROSE CL

WHITE ROSE WAY

WESTMINSTER PLACE

INGS LA

Poppleton Ings

NORTHOLME DR

SHELLEY GR

RAWCLIFFE LA

A19

PO

54

E1
1 CONISTON CL
2 WASDALE CL
3 GARBURN GR
4 SCAFELL CL
5 LOWESWATER RD
6 FYLINGDALES AVE

F1
1 EMBLETON DR
2 COLEDALE CL
3 LEIGHTON CFT
4 BARMBY CL
5 GRASMERE GR
6 BARDEN CT
7 SOUTHOLME DR
8 MILTON CARR
9 FEWSTON DR

10 REIGHTON DR

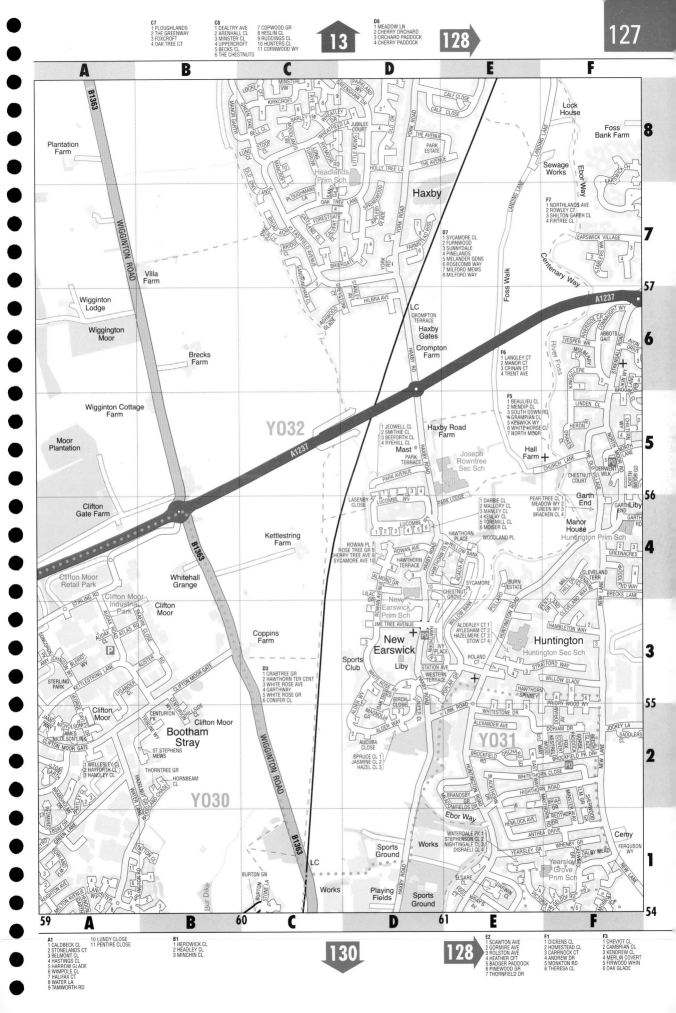

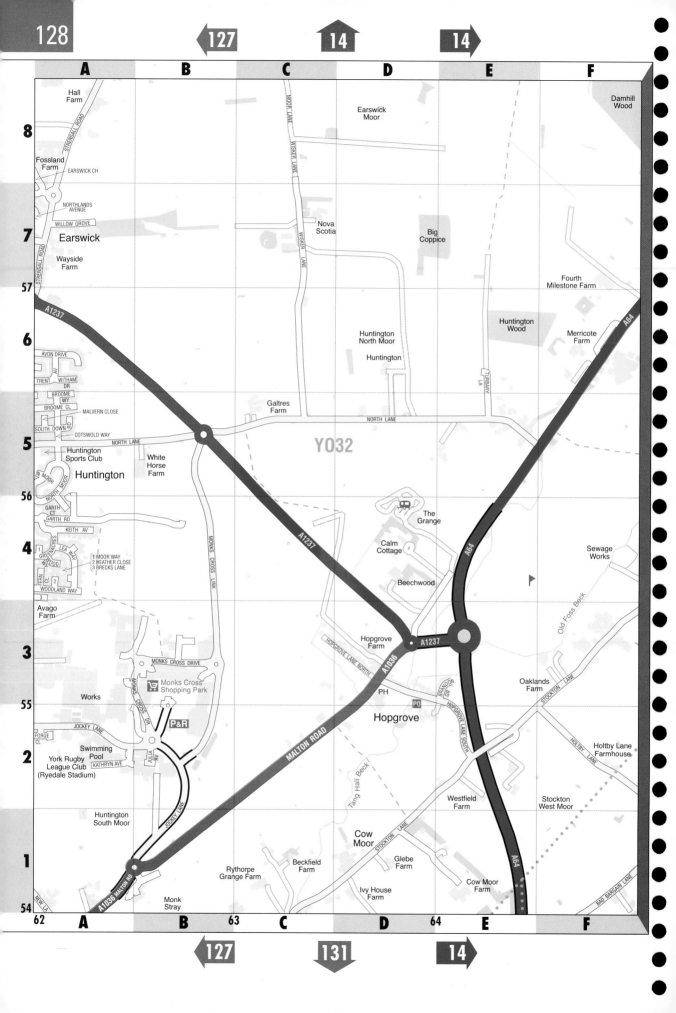

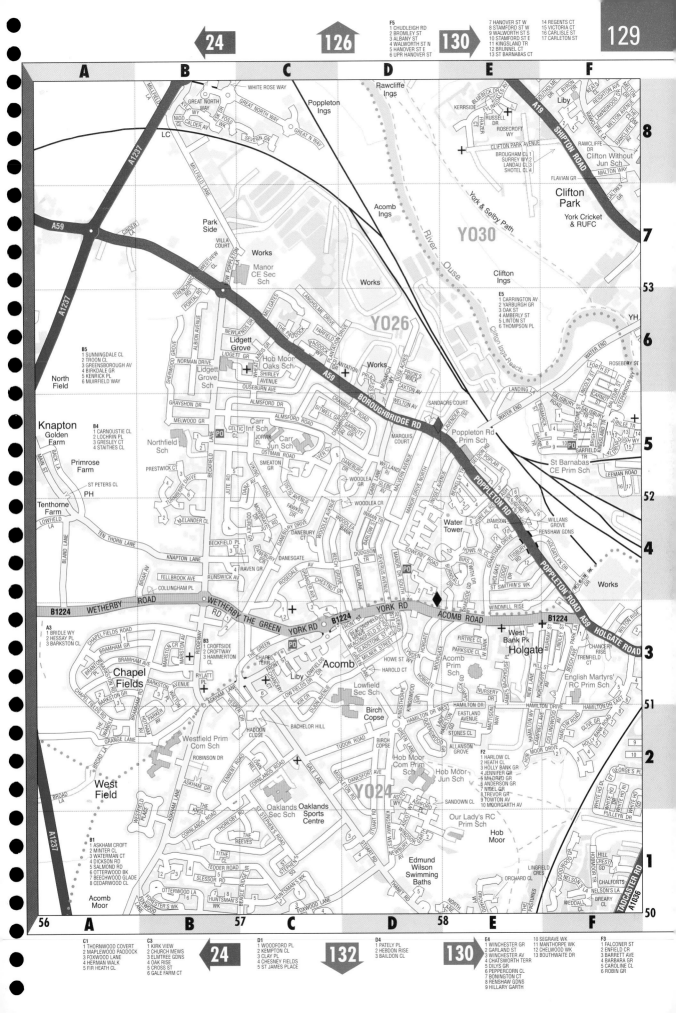

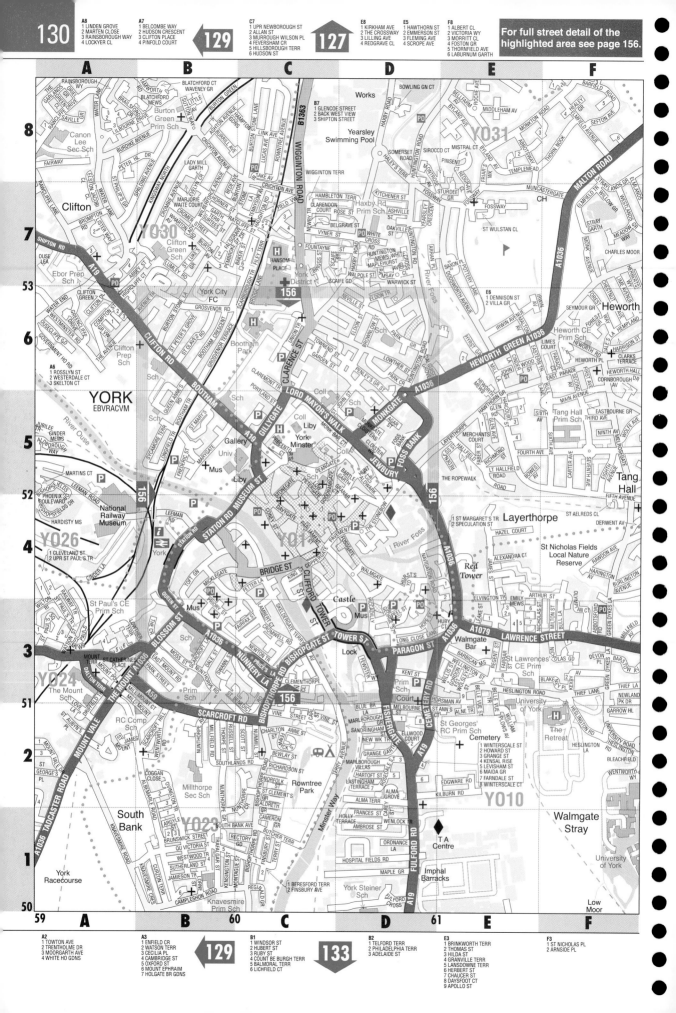

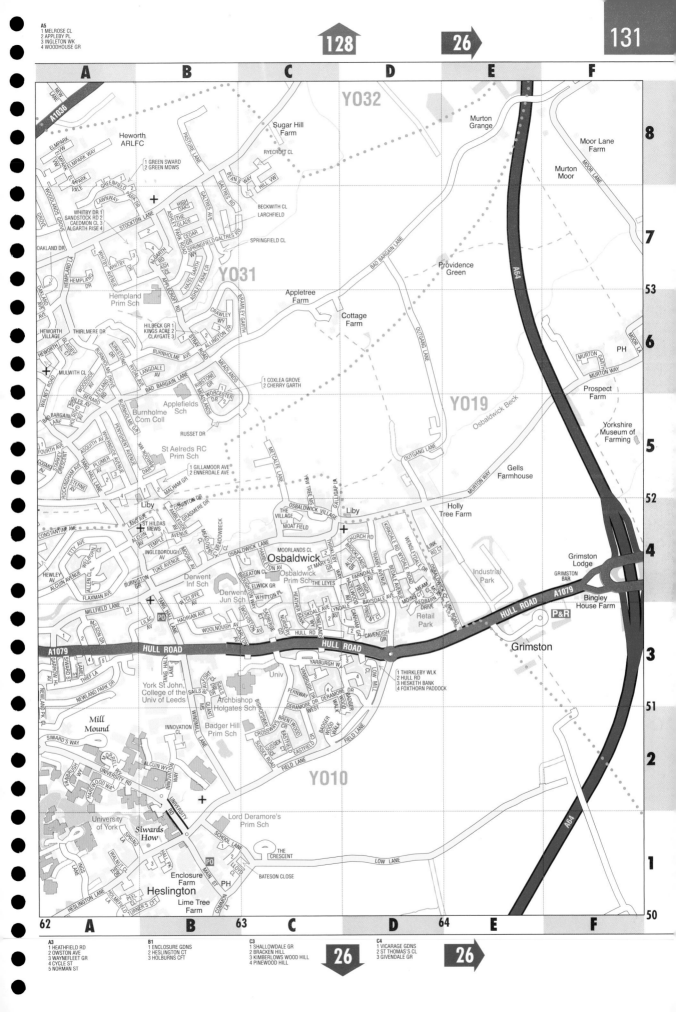

128
26

A5
1 MELROSE CL
2 APPLEBY PL
3 INGLETON WK
4 WOODHOUSE GR

A B C D E F

8
7
53
6
5
52
4
3
51
2
1
50

YO32

Sugar Hill
Farm

RYECROFT CL

Murton
Grange

Moor Lane
Farm

Heworth
ARLFC

ELMPARK
WY

1 GREEN SWARD
2 GREEN MDWS

HILL VW

BECKWITH CL
LARCHFIELD

Murton
Moor

ELMPARK WAY

PASTURE LANE

BEAN'S WY

GALTRES RD

MOOR LANE

MPARK
VALE

GREENFIELD

PARK DR

GALTRES AVE

SPRINGFIELD CL

LAWNWAY

HIGH
OAKS

WOODLANDS GROVE

WHITBY DR 1
SANDSTOCK RD 2
CAEDMON CL 3
ALGARTH RISE 4

STOCKTON LANE

ASHLEY PARK ROAD

THE
GLADE

CEDAR
WY

ALLINGTON DR

BRAMLEY GARTH

Bad Bargain Lane

Providence
Green

A64

YO31

OAKLAND DR

WHITBY AVENUE

WHITBY

ALGARTH
RD

ASH

HAZEL GARTH

SPRINGFIELD GALTRES RD

STRAY ROAD

Appletree
Farm

Cottage
Farm

MOOR LA

Murton
GARTH RD

PH

HEMPLAND LA

HEMPLAND
DR

Hempland
Prim Sch

APPLECROFT RD

CRAWLEY
WY

OUTGANG LANE

MURTON WAY

Prospect
Farm

OAKLAND
AVE

HEWORTH
VILLAGE

THIRLMERE DR

GLASSY

HEWORTH

BURNHOLME AVE

HILBECK GR 1
KINGS ACRE 2
CLAYGATE 3

MEADLANDS

YO19

Osbaldwick Beck

Yorkshire
Museum of
Farming

MULWITH CL

WOODSIDE
AVE

RYDAL AVE

LANGDALE
AV

Bad Bargain Lane

RIBSTONE
DR

WORCESTER
DR

1 COXLEA GROVE
2 CHERRY GARTH

GELLS
Farmhouse

GILES
AVE

BELFORD
RD

BURNHOLME DR

Applefields
Sch

RUSSET DR

MURTON WAY

Holly
Tree Farm

BAD BARGAIN
LANE

Burnholme
Com Coll

FOURTH AVE

ASQUITH
AVE

WENLOCK TER

PENYGHENT AVENUE

PLUMER
AV

St Aelreds RC
Prim Sch

METCALFE LANE

COSMO
AV

ROCKINGHAM AVE

STERNE
AV

MALHAM GR

1 GILLAMOOR AVE
2 ENNERDALE AVE

YEW TREE MS

GALLIGAP LA

Liby

Holly
Tree Farm

Liby

CONSTANTINE AVE

LANGWAY

CONISTON DR

GRASMERE DR

St HILDAS
MEWS

MEADOWBECK

OSBALDWICK VILLAGE

THE
VILLAGE

MOAT FIELD

Liby

Grimston
Lodge

ETTY AVE

ALCUIN
AVE

TEMPLE
AVENUE

AVENUE

MOORE
AV

OSBALDWICK LANE

MOORLANDS CL

ST MARY'S
WY

CHURCH RD

KIRKDALE GR

BROCKLANDS

WENSLEYDALE DR

OSBALDWICK LINK ROAD

Industrial
Park

GRIMSTON
BAR

HEWLEY
AV

ALCUIN AVENUE

WELBORN
CL

INGLEBOROUGH
AV

TUKE AVENUE

Osbaldwick
Prim Sch

Osbaldwick

BEECKTON CT

ELWICK GR

WHITTON PL

THE LEYES

FARNDALE
AVE

TRANBY
AVENUE

HIGH
FIELD

BEDALE AVENUE

MEAM
MOOR

LINK
RD CT

Grimston

Bingley
House Farm

ALLEN CR

FLAXMAN AVE

BURNISTON
GR

DERWENT
GR

Derwent Inf Sch

NYCLIFFE
PL

Derwent
Jun Sch

BEESTON CT

WOLISTON
AV

HEATHER AVE

CARR LA

BEESKDALE AVE

LYNDALE

HAZELWOOD

REDBARN
DRIVE

CAVENDISH
GR

HULL ROAD

A1079

P&R

MILLFIELD LANE

LILAC
AV

TANG HALL LANE

HADRIAN AVE

NURSERY
GDNS

WOOLNOUGH AV

HULL RD

Retail
Park

HULL ROAD

A1079

HULL ROAD

MAJSON GR

GARROW HL

SIWARD ST

THIEF LA

LAMEL ST

LONG HALL
LANE

YARBURGH WY

1 THIRKLEBY WLK
2 HULL RD
3 HESKETH BANK
4 FOXTHORN PADDOCK

NEWLAND PARK DR

York St John,
College of the
Univ of Leeds

Univ

FERNWAY

VANBRUGH DR
DERAMORE DR
BADGER
WOOD
WALK

DERAMORE
DR

LOW
MILL

NEWLAND PK CL

Archbishop
Holgates Sch

WINDMILL LANE

BISHOPSMA

CROSSWAYS

BRENTWOOD

DERAMORE
WEST

EASTFIELD
CT

FIELD LANE

Mill
Mound

SIWARD'S WAY

INNOVATION
CL

Badger Hill
Prim Sch

SUSSEX
CR

SUSSEX
CL

SUSSEX ROAD

EASTFIELD

BADGER
WOOD
WALK

FIELD LANE

YO10

YARBOROUGH
WY

HAZELWOOD WA

University of York

University
RD

ALCUIN
WAY

INNOVATION
WAY

Lord Deramore's
Prim Sch

SCHOOL
LANE

Siwards
How

UNIVERSITY
RD

SPRING
LA

THE
CRESCENT

LOW LANE

A64

WALNUT CT

INGS
LANE

HESLINGTON LANE

HOLMEFIELD LA

HALL FIELD

PO

Enclosure
Farm

MAIN ST

LLOYD
LLOYD

PH

BATESON CLOSE

Heslington

Lime Tree
Farm

PEEL
CL

TURNER'S CT

COMMON LA

62 A 63 B C 64 D E F

A3
1 HEATHFIELD RD
2 OWSTON AVE
3 WAYNEFLEET GR
4 CYCLE ST
5 NORMAN ST

B1
1 ENCLOSURE GDNS
2 HESLINGTON CT
3 HOLBURNS CFT

C3
1 SHALLOWDALE GR
2 BRACKEN HILL
3 KIMBERLOWS WOOD HILL
4 PINEWOOD HILL

C4
1 VICARAGE GDNS
2 ST THOMAS'S CL
3 GIVENDALE GR

26
26

← 24

129 →

Column headers: **A B C D E F**

Row numbers (left): **8 7 49 6 5 48 4 3 47 2 1 46**

Bottom column headers: **A B C D E F**
Bottom coordinates: **56 57 58**

Map labels

Great Knoll

Acomb Moor
High Moor Close
Mast
Eastfield Farm
Woodthorpe Prim Sch
Woodthorpe
Acomb Wood Close
Marsh Farm
Bog Lane
Askham Bryan Lane
Askham Lane

Dringhouses Prim Sch
Dringhouses
Sports & Social Club
Libry
St Edward's CL
YO24
The Covert
Hunters Way
The Spinney
Bracken Road
Middlethorpe Grove
Hogg's Pond
Glaisdale Dene
Windermere
Bramble Dene
1 CHALONER'S CR
2 WAIN'S GR
3 SILVERDALE CT
Askham Bar Park and Ride
P&R
P+R
Superstore
York College
Whin Garth
Sim Hills
Sim Balk Lane

Askham Bogs
Askham Bog Nature Reserve
Bond Hill Ash Farm
A64
Middlethorpe Grange Farm

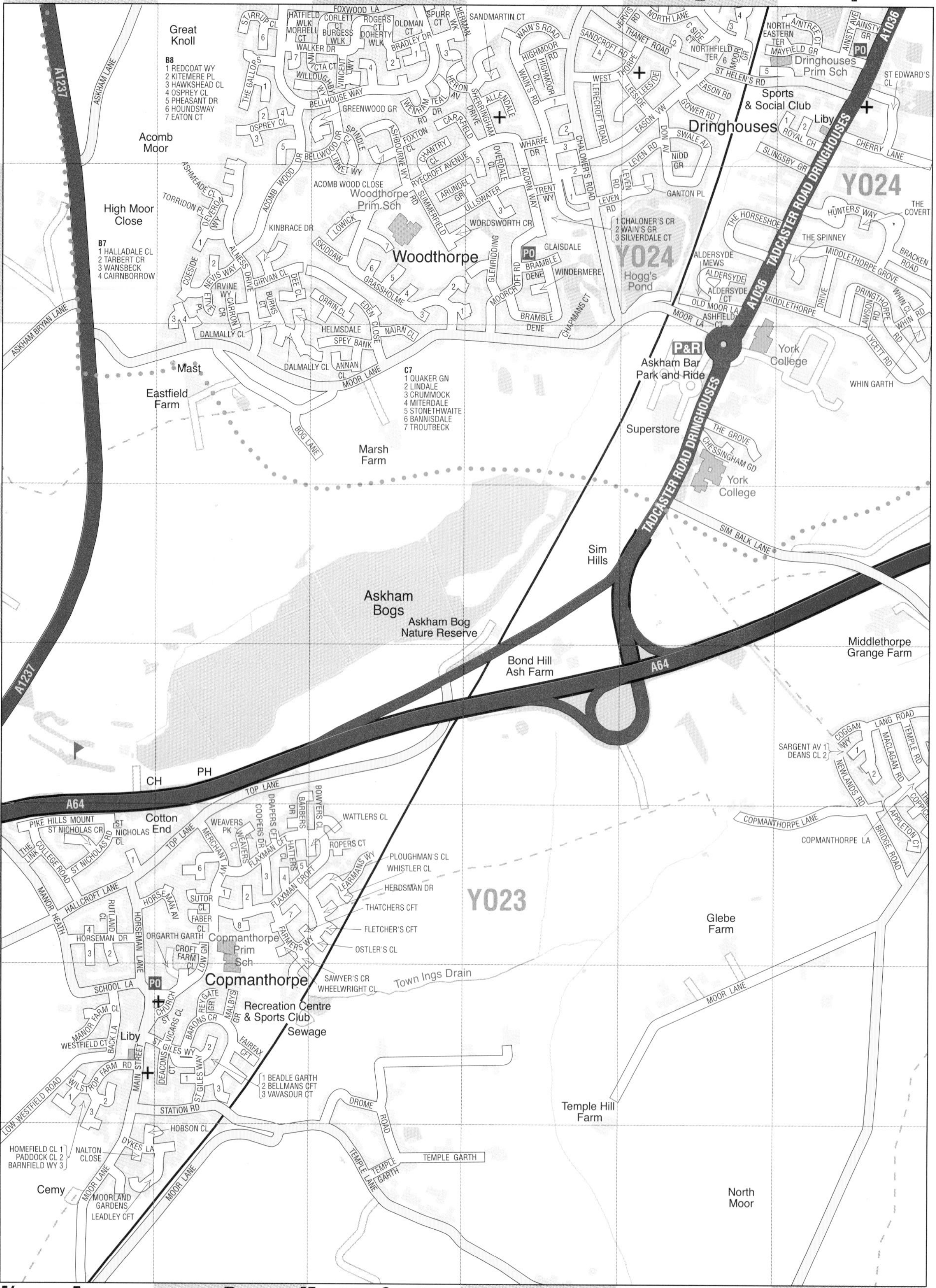

Cotton End
Pike Hills Mount
St Nicholas Cr
College Road
Copmanthorpe
Copmanthorpe Prim Sch
Copmanthorpe Lane
YO23
Glebe Farm
Moor Lane
Recreation Centre & Sports Club
Sewage
1 BEADLE GARTH
2 BELLMANS CFT
3 VAVASOUR CT
Temple Hill Farm
Temple Garth
North Moor
Cemy
MOORLAND GARDENS
LEADLEY CFT
HOMEFIELD CL 1
PADDOCK CL 2
BARNFIELD WY 3
Station Rd

← 24

36

130
D8
1 STOCKHOLM CL
2 DANES CFT

26
E8
1 ENDFIELDS RD
2 CROSSLANDS RD
3 BROADWAY GR

F8
1 WILSTHORPE GR
2 TILMIRE CL
3 LOW MOOR AV

133

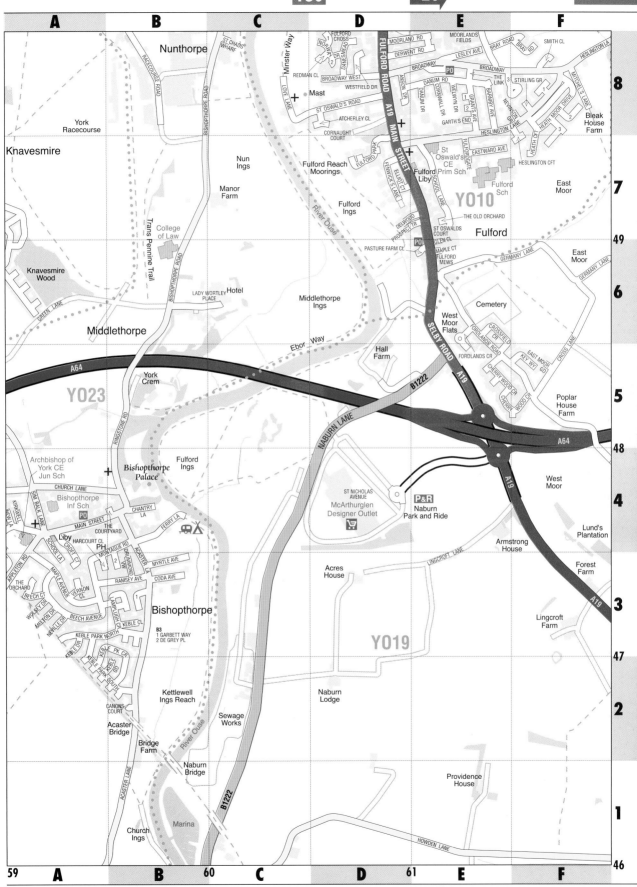

35 35

A B C D E F

8

HORNSEA ROAD

Eastfield Farm

7

Northfield House

B1242

ATWICK ROAD

Hornsea Caravan Park

CLIFF ROAD

WESTHOLME AVE

NUTANA AVE

Barcourt Estate

North Cliff

49

Golden Imp Holiday Bungalow Park

Birk Crag

CLIFF ROAD

BAY VW

AV

ELDEVERE PK

Lowcroft Leisure Park

1 ROSE CARR WK
2 DARNELEY CT

6

Springfield Farm

VICTORIA GD

HOLTBY GD

LOTEN DRI

LOTEN GDR

ACKLAM DR

SANDPIPER CT

NORTHGATE

CARRINGTON AVENUE

CARLTON AVE

MORROW AVE

P

HU18

SAWLEY CL

SHARDLOW AV

DRANCOTT AVENUE

ST NICHOLAS CL

CLIFFORD ST

CLIFTON STREET

Floral Hall

HEADLAND VW

Hotel

5

NORTHUMBERLAND AVENUE

COLLEGE GDS

ASHCOURT DR

AMBASTON RD

ASHCOURT DR

DERWENT CL

SHAFTESBURY AV

BELGRAVE DR

HARTLEY HALL RD

Hornsea & District War Memorial

H

CHRYSTALS WK

CHRYSTALS RD

ESPLANADE

MARINE AVE

CONSTABLE ST

VICTORIA AVE

Elm Lodge Gdns

EASTGATE CT

HORNSEA

48

CHEYNE GARTH

CHEYNE GARTH

CHEYNE WK

WESTWOOD AVE

THE LEYS

B1242

Hornsea Sch & Language Coll

EASTGATE

CLIFF ROAD

WESTBOURNE RD

NEW PARK

BROADWAY

1 GROSVENOR RD
2 PARVA RD
3 STATION MEWS
4 SHUTTLEWORTH CT
5 WILTON TERR

Hollis Sports Ground

Hall Garth Park

Liby

Meml Gdns

CINEMA ST

P

PARK ROW

Leisure Centre

4

CHEYNE WALK

SPRINGBANK AV

MILL LA

Holderness Community Coll

Moat

P P

PO

THE LEVELS

Folk Mus

NEWBEGIN

ALEXANDRA RD

NEW PARK

WESTBOURNE RD

STATION CT

SANDS LANE

PASTURE RD

Market

SOUTH PROMENADE

B1244

SEATON ROAD

WESTGATE MARKET PL

FAIR

PH

P

WILLOWS LANE

Hornsea Prim Sch

CLIFF ROAD

BURTON RD

WILTON RD

GRAINGERS RD

EASTBOURNE

Boat Yard

MOUNT PLEASANT 1
HARTS CL 2
EASTGATE VW 3
EASTGATE 4
BACK WESTGATE 5
MERESIDE TERR 6
SCALBY PL 7
HILLERBY LA 8
MERE GARTH 9

QUEENS GARDENS

SOUTHGATE

Cemy

BECKSIDE

FOOTBALL GREEN

MASCOTTE GDS

TRANMERE PK

Promenade Caravan Park

3

Swan I

Hornsea Mere Nature Reserve

P

KING ST 1
SOUTHGATE GDNS 2
WALLER LA 3
BACK SOUTHGATE 4
THE WILLOWS 5

B1242

HORNSEA BURTON ROAD

Longbeach Caravan Park

47

HU11

BANK TERR 1
WELLINGTON AVE 2
TRINITY ROAD 3
LEYBURN AVE 4
BEAUFORT AVE 5
THE GREENWAY 6
SALISBURY AVE 7
BROOKE DR 8
EDENFIELD AVE 9

OLD BRIDGE RD

BURTON LANE

TRINITY RD

THE CRESCENT

Hornsea Burton Prim Sch

BERESFORD AVE

Beverley Farm

2

Hornsea Bridge Ind Est

HULL ROAD

MARLBOROUGH AVENUE

STANLEY AVE

WHIMBREL AVE

PO

RANBY DR

RANBY CR

EGAR AVENUE

PICKERING AVENUE

1 ROWAN WK
2 THE HOLLIES
3 OAKLANDS

THE BIRCHES

South Cliff

MERE VIEW AV

LINDALE AVE

ROLSTON ROAD

GREENACRE PK

BEECHWOOD AVE

TANSLEY LANE

Hornsea Burton

Southorpe Village

Hornsea Rail Trail

1

Freeport Hornsea Outlet Village

POTTERS WAY

1 CEDAR CL
2 CHERRY CL

Southorpe Farm

SOUTHORPE ROAD

HULL RD

B1242

STRAWBERRY GDNS

CH

46

19 A B 20 C D 21 E F

C4
1 CHAMBERS LA
2 QUALES MEWS
3 BANK ST
4 DESMOND AVE
5 THE WILLOWS
6 MERE WK
7 WITTY'S PASS
8 GRANGER'S YD

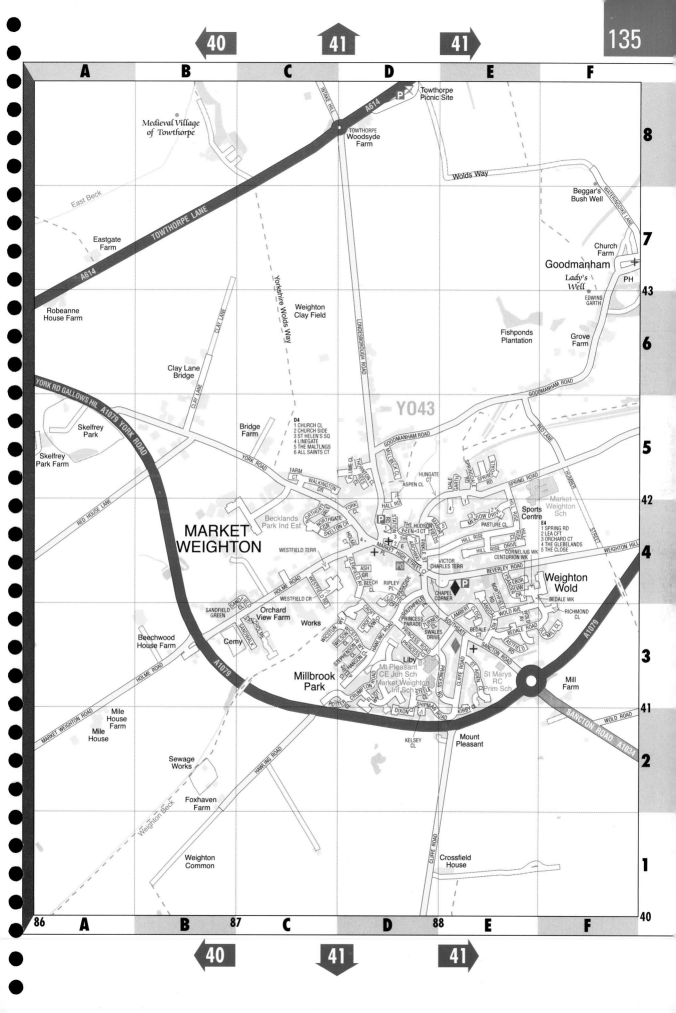

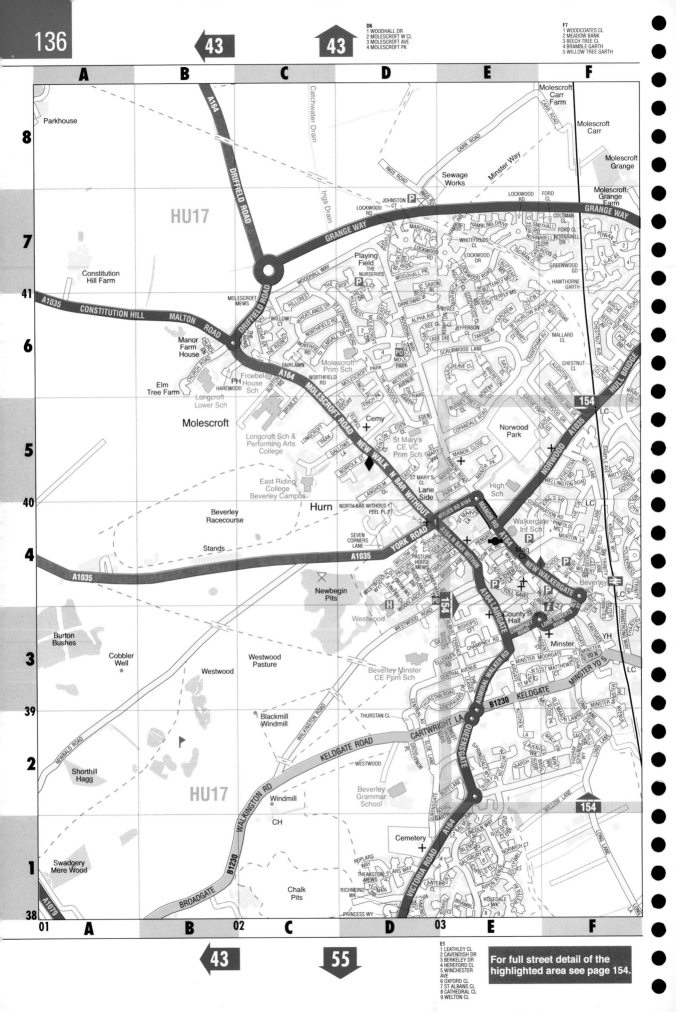

← 43
↑ 43

← 43
55

For full street detail of the highlighted area see page 154.

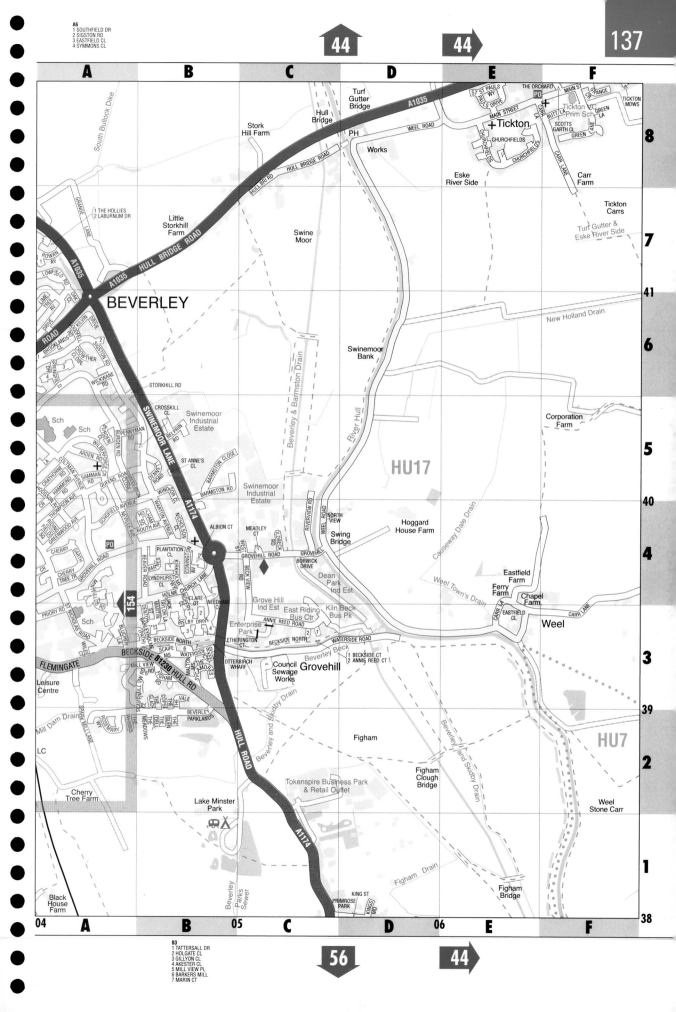

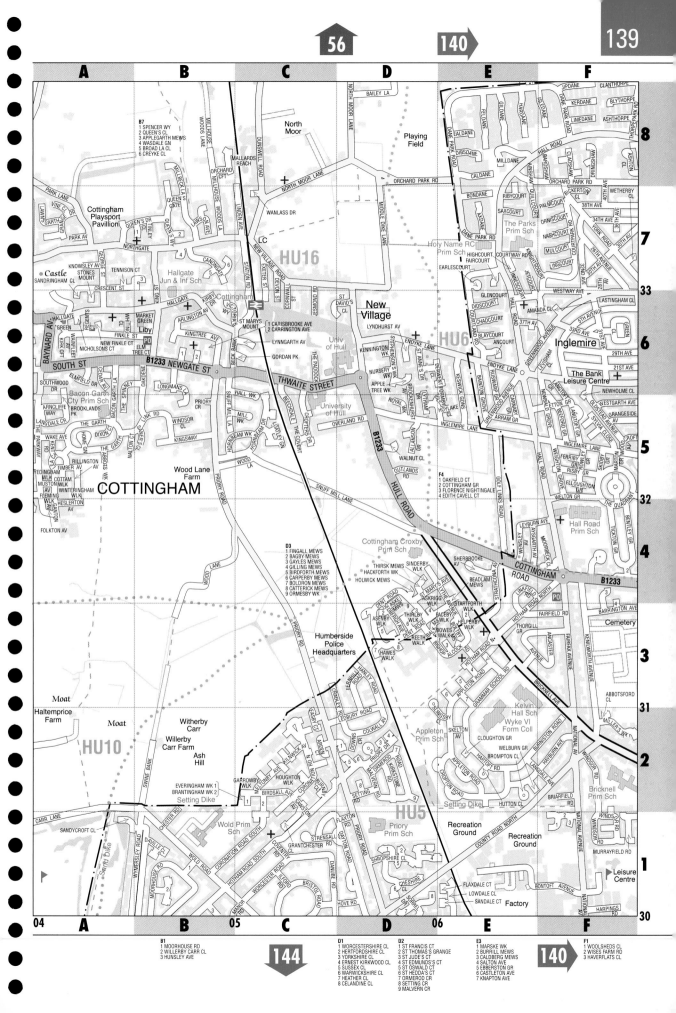

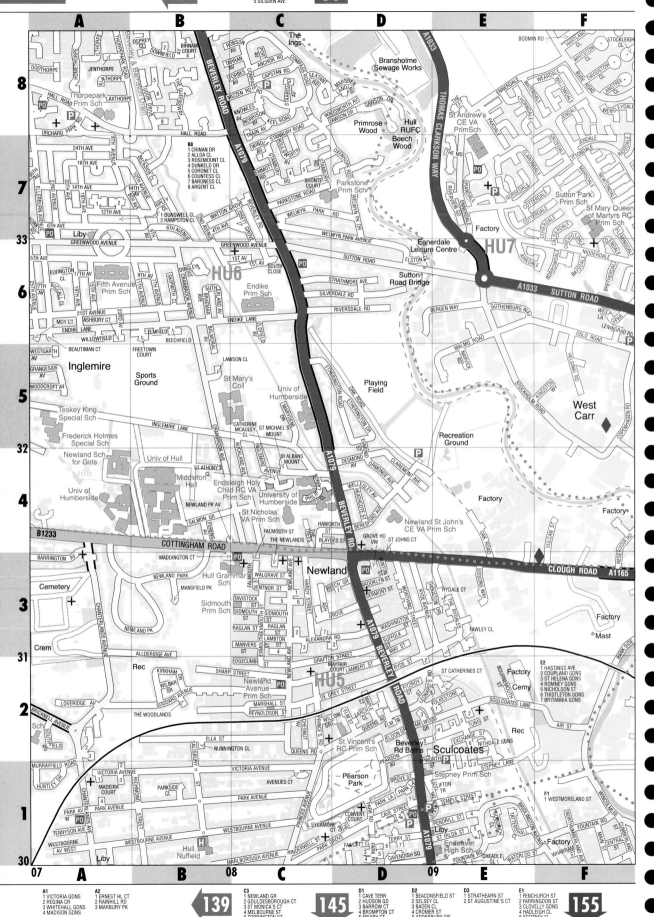

139

C8
1 FLAG WK
2 LARARD AVE

C7
1 BEECHCLIFFE AVE
2 CULLINGWORTH AVE
3 DENHOLME AVE
4 STEETON AVE
5 SILSDEN AVE

56

A1
1 VICTORIA GDNS
2 REGINA CR
3 WHITEHALL GDNS
4 MADISON GDNS

A2
1 ERNEST HL CT
2 RAINHILL RD
3 MARBURY PK

139

C3
1 NEWLAND GR
2 GOULDESBOROUGH CT
3 ST MONICA'S CT
4 MELBOURNE ST
5 TORRINGTON ST
6 WALTER'S TERR
7 THEARNE CL

145

D1
1 CAVE TERR
2 HUDSON GD
3 BARROW CT
4 BROMPTON CT
5 FRIARY CT
6 HAMPSTEAD CT
7 KNIGHTSBRIDGE CT

D2
1 BEACONSFIELD ST
2 SELSEY CL
3 BADEN CL
4 CROMER ST
5 ADDERBURY GR

D3
1 STRATHEARN ST
2 ST AUGUSTINE'S CT

E1
1 FENCHURCH ST
2 FARRINGDON ST
3 CLOVELLY GDNS
4 HADLEIGH CL
5 SCOTNEY CL
6 STAFFORD ST

155

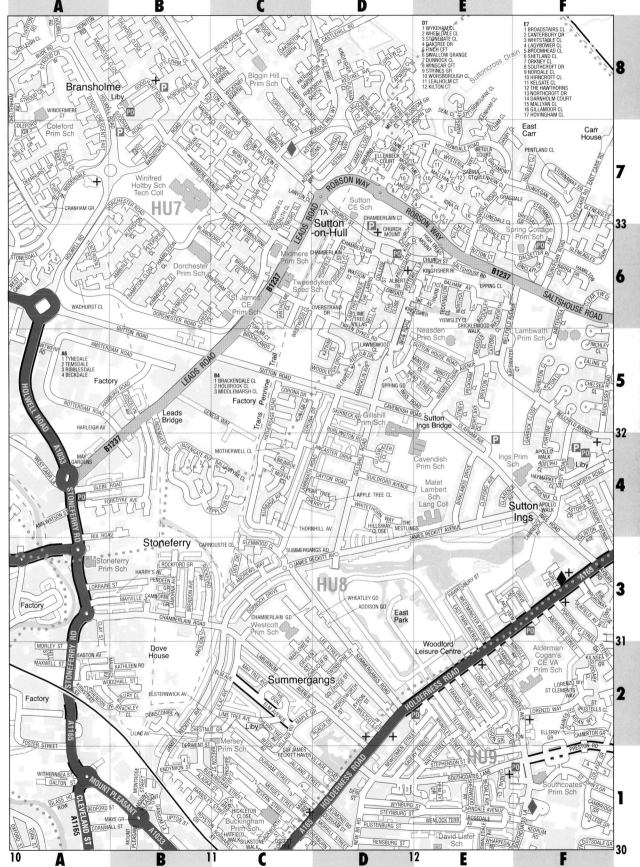

B7
1 PEVENSEY CL
2 PEACEHAVEN CL

D8
1 GOLDCREST CL
2 CORMORANT CL
3 LOWLAND CL
4 HOUSEMARTIN DR

F5
1 HAMMERSMITH RD
2 SHOREDITCH CL
3 TOTTENHAM CL
4 WILLESDEN CL

D7
1 WYKEHAM CL
2 WHEELDALE CL
3 STONEGATE CL
4 OAKTREE CT
5 FINCH CFT
6 SWALLOW GRANGE
7 DUNNOCK CL
8 WINSCAR CFT
9 STRINES GR
10 WORSBOROUGH CL
11 LEALHOLM CL
12 KILTON CT

E7
1 BROADSTAIRS CL
2 CANTERBURY CL
3 WHITSTABLE CL
4 LADYBOWER CL
5 BROOMHEAD CL
6 SHETLAND CL
7 ORKNEY CL
8 SOUTHCROFT DR
9 NORDALE CL
10 HIRNCROFT CL
11 KELGATE CL
12 THE HAWTHORNS
13 NORTHCROFT DR
14 DARNHOLM COURT
15 MALLYAN CL
16 GILLAMOOR CL
17 HOVINGHAM CL

A6
1 TYNEDALE
2 TEMSDALE
3 RIBBLESDALE
4 BECKDALE

B4
1 BRACKENDALE CL
2 HOLBROOK CL
3 MIDDLEMARSH CL

B1
1 CUDWORTH GR
2 OAKWELL GR
3 WOMBWELL GR
4 ALSTON AVE

C1
1 DEARNE GR
2 AVON ST
3 DUNELM CL
4 BRANDON CT
5 BUCKINGHAM ST

D1
1 JAMES NIVEN CT
2 FERENS CT

E1
1 ROTHESAY CL
2 ESKDALE AVE

F1
1 EDGEWARE AVE
2 NORTH COUNTRY CT
3 TRINITY GR
4 WADHAM GR
5 MERTON GR

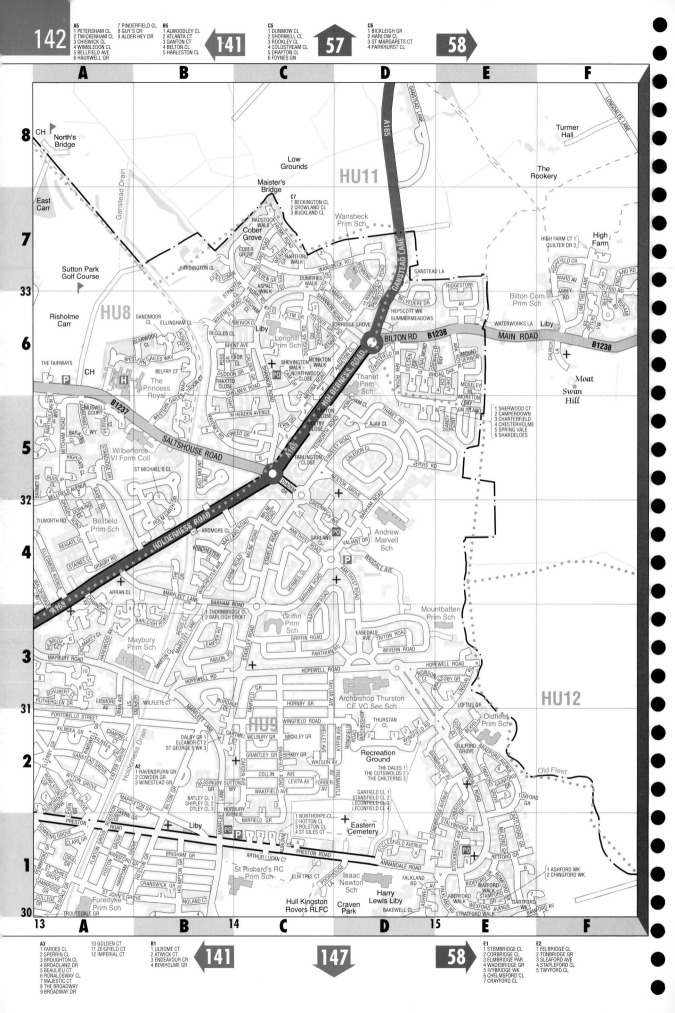

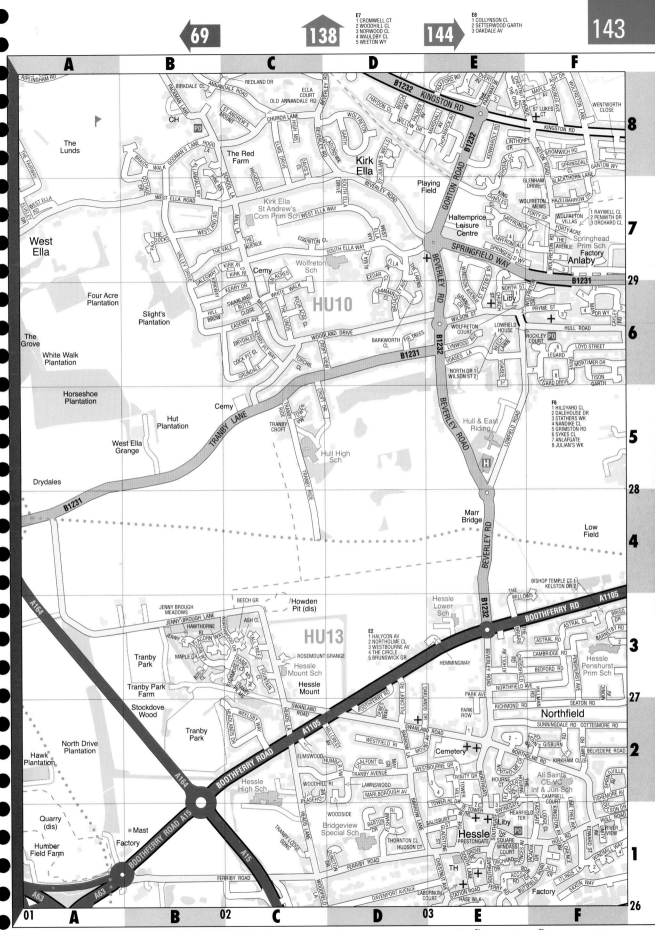

E7
1 CROMWELL CT
2 WOODHILL CL
3 NORWOOD CL
4 WAULDBY CL
5 WEETON WY

E8
1 COLLYNSON CL
2 SETTERWOOD GARTH
3 OAKDALE AV

F6
1 HILDYARD CL
2 DALEHOUSE DR
3 STATHERS WK
4 NANDIKE CL
5 GRIMSTON RD
6 SYKES CL
7 ANLAGATE
8 JULIAN'S WK

1 RAYWELL CL
2 PENWITH DR
3 ORCHARD CL

E2
1 HALYCON AV
2 NORTHOLME CL
3 WESTBOURNE AV
4 THE CIRCLE
5 BRUNSWICK GR

E1
1 SPIRE VW
2 TOWER HILL MEWS
3 VICARAGE LA
4 CLOWES CT
5 FISHWICK AV

F1
1 MARGARET GR
2 BISHOP BLUNT CL
3 BISHOP KEMPTHORNE CL
4 BISHOP GURDON CL

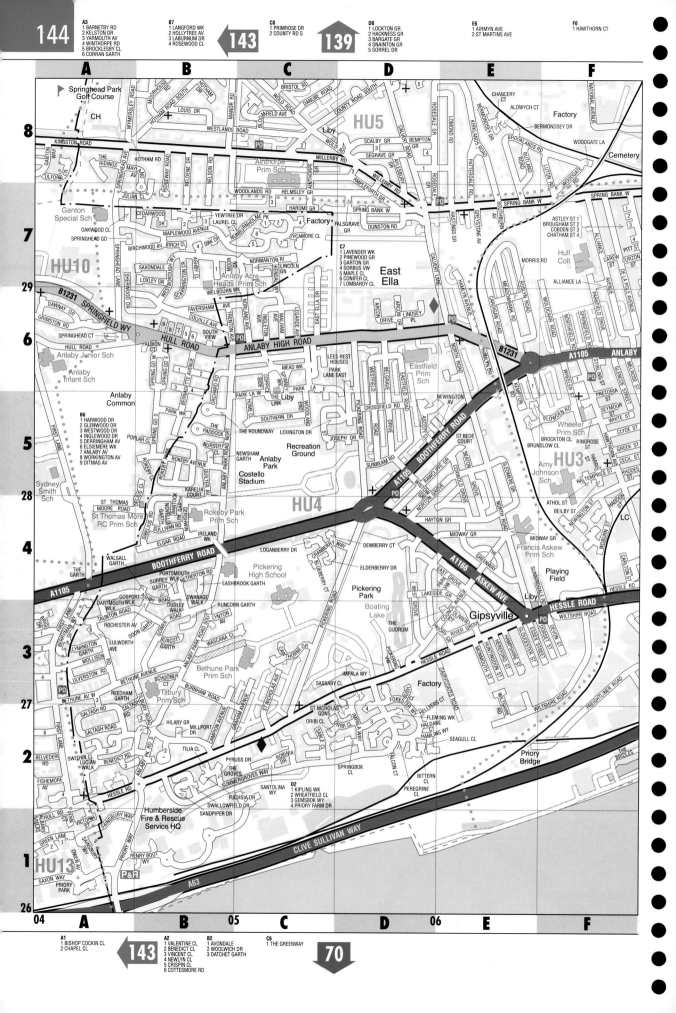

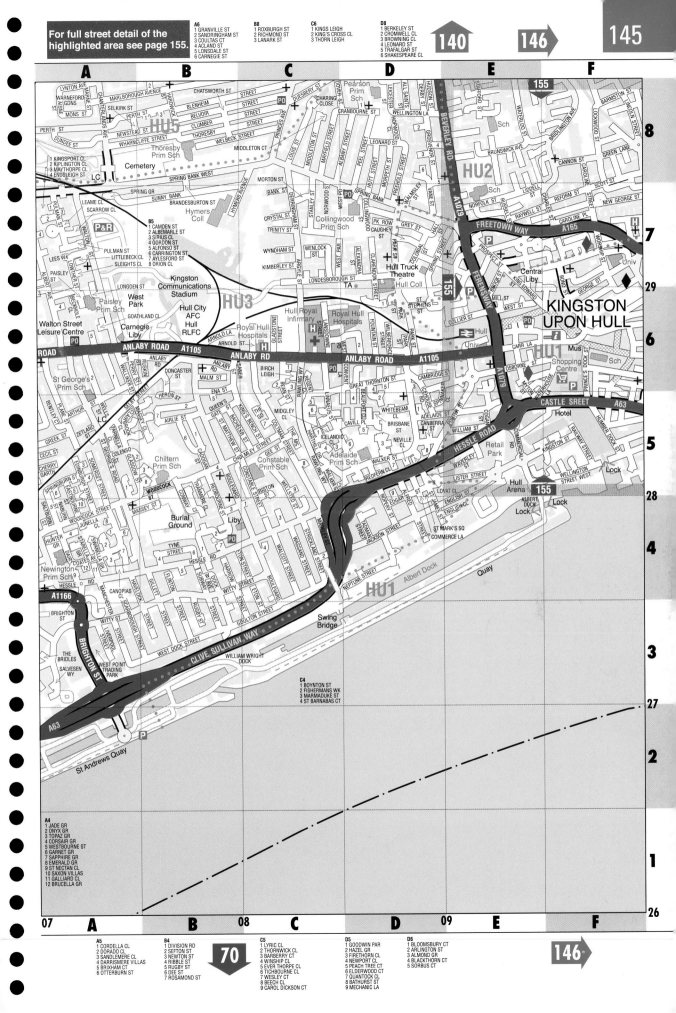

← 155

141 ↑

A B C D E F

155

HU8

CHAPMAN ST
DENABY COURT
A1165 CLEVELAND STREET
NEW CLEVELAND STREET
CUMBERLAND
OXFORD ST
MINCOLMLEE
CHEAPSIDE
SITWELL ST
CHURCH ROW
Factory
DANSOM LA S
A1033
CORRING STREET
BURLEIGH ST
HOLDERNESS ROAD A165
ROLAND STREET
SHERBURN STREET
MIDDLEBURG STREET
Estcourt Prim Sch
ROSMEAD STREET
TEESDALE AVE
BILSDALE GROVE
GLAISDALE GR
BILSDALE GROVE

8
LIME STREET
ST MARK ST
WHITBY ST
James Reckitt Liby
Hull Coll
VICTOR STREET
NEW BRI RD
Craven Prim Sch
ESTCOURT STREET
WESTCLIFFE
SOUTHCOATES LANE
1 BRANSDALE GR
2 TROUTSDALE GR

JENNING STREET
MULGRAVE ST
EGTON ST
STUDLEY
ABBEY STREET
WALLER ST
ARUNDEL
BELMONT ST
SWEET DEWS GR
SAXTON CT
BELMONT
East Lodge Cemetery

HODGSON ST
LIME STREET
MINCOLME LEE
HODGSON ST
SPYVEE ST
PENNINGTON ST
HOLBORN
WILTON ST
FRANKLIN ST
BRAZIL STREET
MOUNT PLEASANT
FIELD ST
ELLIS ST
RIPON ST
KENT ST
HARCOURT DR
BIRKDALE
RAVEN ST
GRINDELL ST
CHURCHILL
HALLER ST
HM Prison Hull
West Lodge Cemy
Factory

7
GEORGE ST
A165 WITHAM
GREAT UNION ST
A165 CLARENCE ST
THOMAS ST
SHAW'S
STRAWBERRY ST
WILLIAMSON ST
BANNISTER DR
WYKE ST
CROWLE ST
HOTHAM ST
FERRIES ST
LEE SMITH STREET
NEWTOWN
HEDON ROAD
A63
NEWTOWN
A1033

COELUS ST
HYPERION ST
BLENKIN ST
CHURCH STREET
MARVEL ST
WARWICK STREET
MERRICK
HEDON ROAD
BELLAMY ST
WOODHOUSE ST
CRIVEN
WAVERLEY ST
Coll
N WALL'S
Univ

29
A1165
PROSPECT PL
POPPLE ST
DRYPOOL WAY
GARRISON ROAD
MASK DR
HU9
Alexandra Dock

City Council Cts
SALTHOUSE LA
THE HAVEN
CHANDLERS COURT
NAVIGATION
MAST DR
MAST DR
EARLES ROAD
RALEIGH DR
Locks

6
CHAPEL LA
BISHOP
Mus
SCALE LA
LIBERTY LA
TOWER STREET
CITADEL WAY
Mus
LOCK KEEPERS CT
SOUTH BRIDGE RD
BRIDGEGATE DR
HALES ENTRY
HARBOUR WY
SAILORS WHARF
CORINTHIAN WAY
BRIDGE CL
SPINNAKER CL
Factory
Wharf

PO
HIGH STREET
BLACKFRIAR GA
HUMBER STREET
QUEEN ST
NELSON ST
SOUTH BR RD
PILOTS WY
OCEAN BVD
PLIMSOLL WAY
HA PEN LA
CALEDONIA
CAMILLA CL
CONSORT CT
CRANE RD
MALDON DR
CHARLESTOWN WY
AXHOLME COURT
SEQUANA COURT
Locks
Victoria Dock Prim Sch
Wharf

5
Victoria Pier
The Deep (Aquarium & Marine Research Centre)
Victoria Dock Village
1 HARTLEY BRIDGE
2 MARINERS CL
3 GALLEY CT
4 APPLEDORE CL
5 LANCELOT CT
6 GALLEON CT

28

4

3
River Humber

27

2

1

26
10 A 11 B C D 12 E F

← 145

71 ↑

A   B   C   D   E   F

Holderness Drain
Bewholme Gr
Factory
Burma Drive
Marfleet La
Great Field La
Factory
Factory
Marfleet Avenue
Marfleet Lane
Marfleet
Hull Maternity
H
Cyprus St
Delhi St
Frodsham St
Egypt St
Ceylon St
Marfleet Prim Sch
Church Lane
A1033
Bywell Wlk
Hemswell
Bothwell Grove
Ashwell Av
Stockwell Prim Sch
Stockwell Gr
Dodswell Grove
Falkland Road
1 SOUTHWELL AVE
2 BAMFORD AVE
3 SALTFORD AVE
4 HALLIWELL CL

8

Littlefair Road
Northern Gateway
Factory
Elba St
Factory
Valletta Street
Great Field Lane
Factory
Somerden Road
Factory

7

Corporation Road
King George Dock
A1033   HEDON ROAD   A1033
A1033
Old Fleet
HULL RD
Tower Ho La

29

HU9
Factory

Corporation Rd
King George Dock
Lord's Clough

6

Lock
Lock
Lock
Queen Elizabeth Dock
Factory
HU12
Salt End

5

28

Quay

4

River Humber
Quay
Salt End

3

Salt End Jetties No 1

27

Salt End Jetties No 3

2

1

26

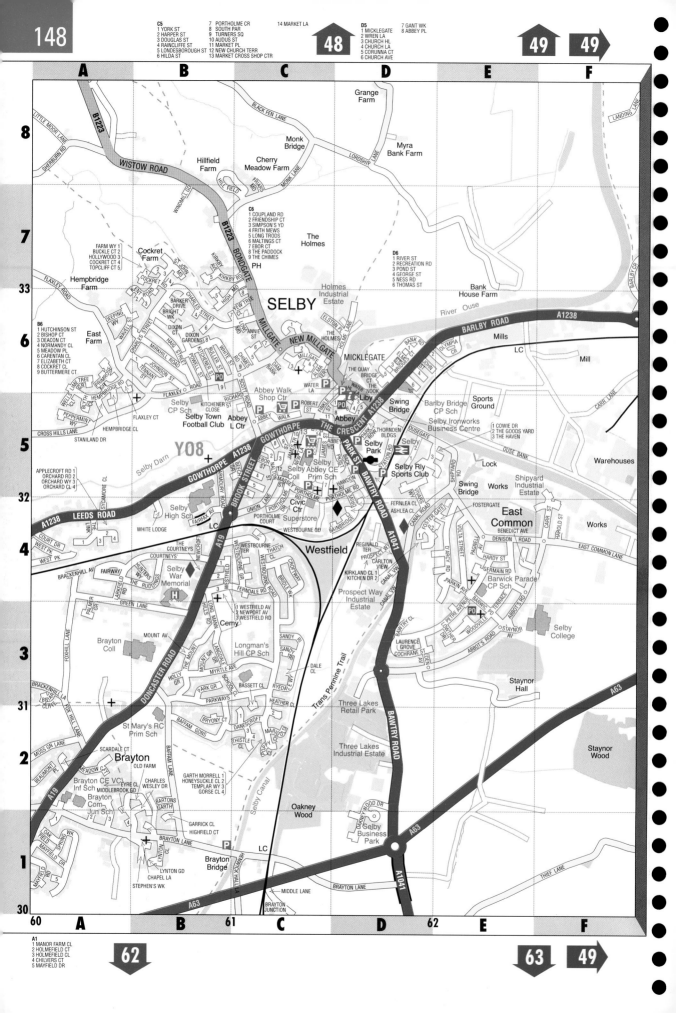

C5
1 YORK ST
2 HARPER ST
3 DOUGLAS ST
4 RAINCLIFFE ST
5 LONDESBOROUGH ST
6 HILDA ST
7 PORTHOLME CR
8 SOUTH PAR
9 TURNERS SQ
10 AUDUS ST
11 MARKET PL
12 NEW CHURCH TERR
13 MARKET CROSS SHOP CTR
14 MARKET LA

48

D5
1 MICKLEGATE
2 WREN LA
3 CHURCH HL
4 CHURCH LA
5 CORUNNA CT
6 CHURCH AVE
7 GANT WK
8 ABBEY PL

49   49

C6
1 COUPLAND RD
2 FRIENDSHIP CT
3 SIMPSON'S YD
4 FRITH MEWS
5 LONG TRODS
6 MALTINGS CT
7 EBOR CT
8 THE PADDOCK
9 THE CHIMES

D6
1 RIVER ST
2 RECREATION RD
3 POND ST
4 GEORGE ST
5 NESS RD
6 THOMAS ST

B6
1 HUTCHINSON ST
2 BISHOP CT
3 DEACON CT
4 NORMANDY CL
5 MEADOW PL
6 CARENTAN CL
7 ELIZABETH CT
8 COCKRET CT
9 BUTTERMERE CT

A1
1 MANOR FARM CL
2 HOLMEFIELD CT
3 HOLMEFIELD CL
4 CHILVERS CT
5 MAYFIELD DR

62   63   49

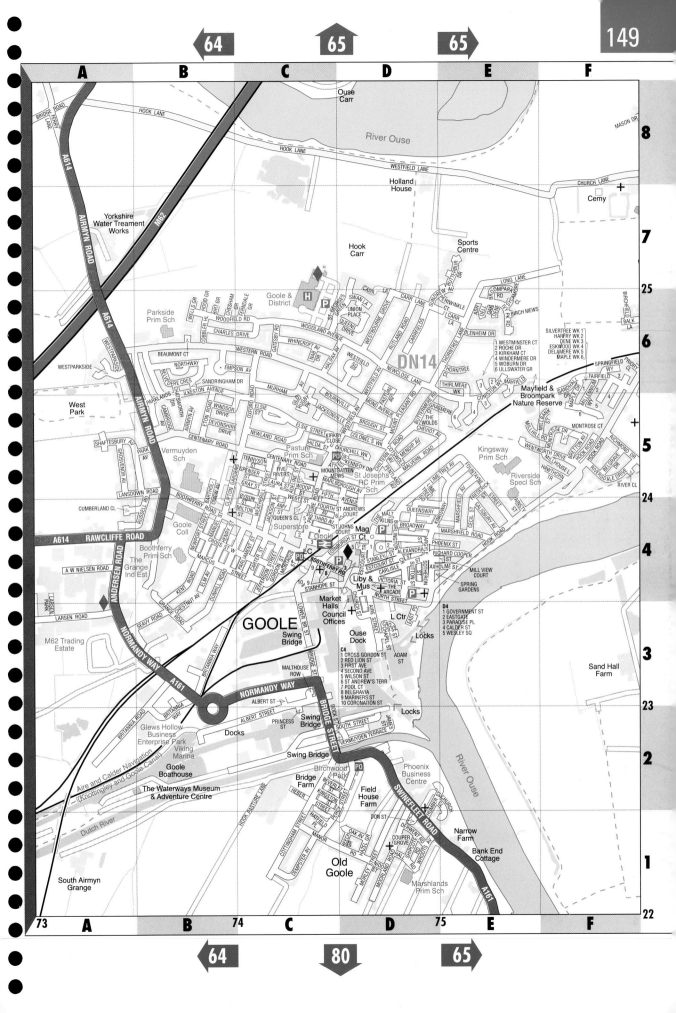

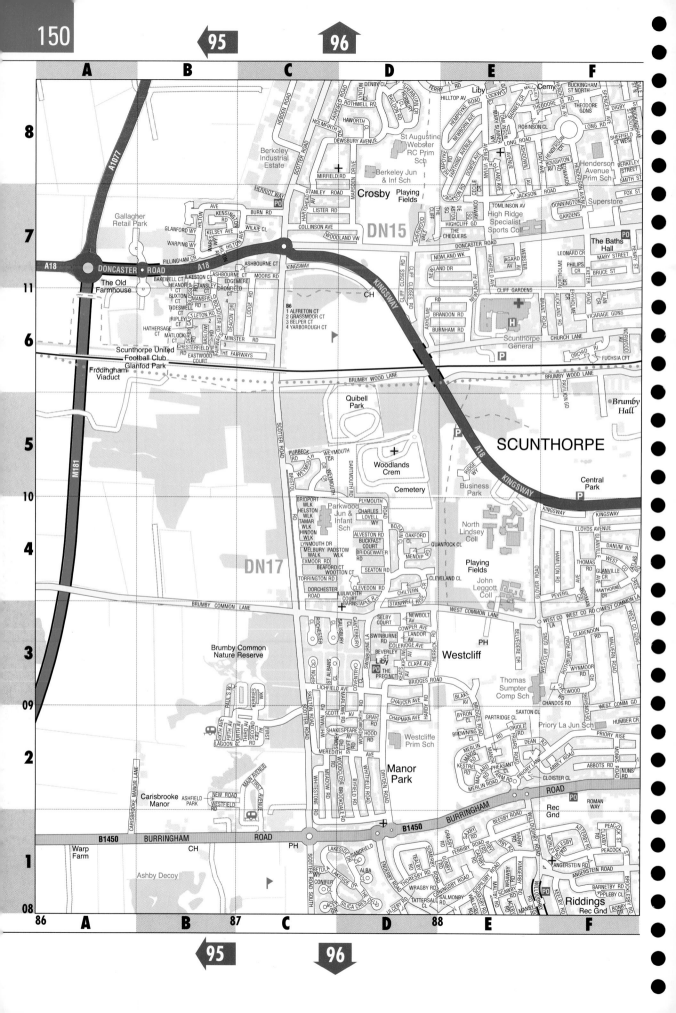

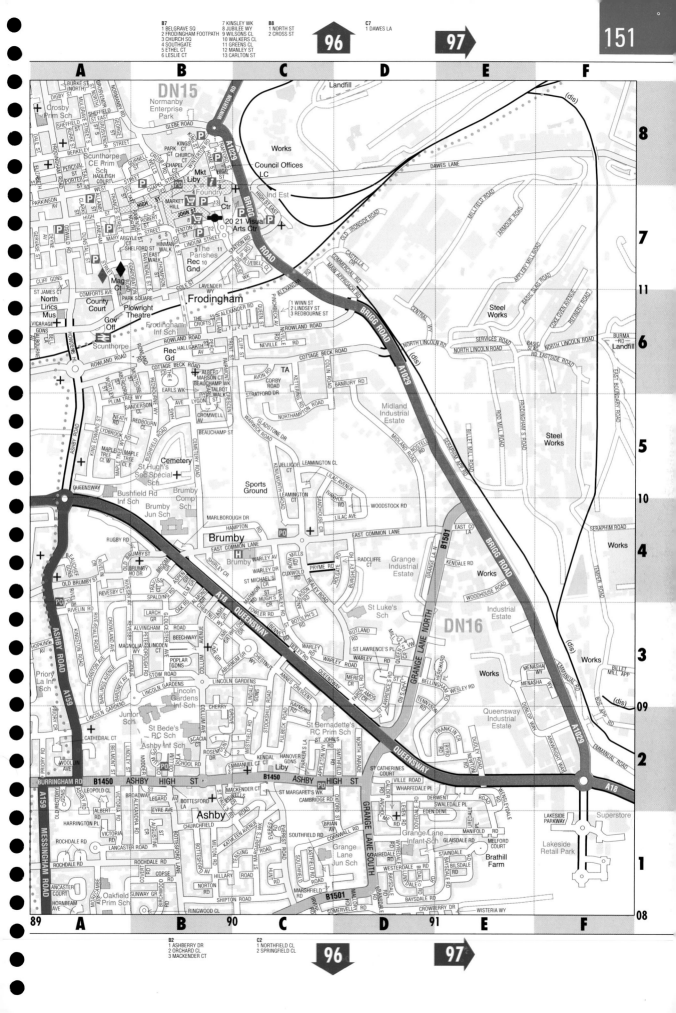

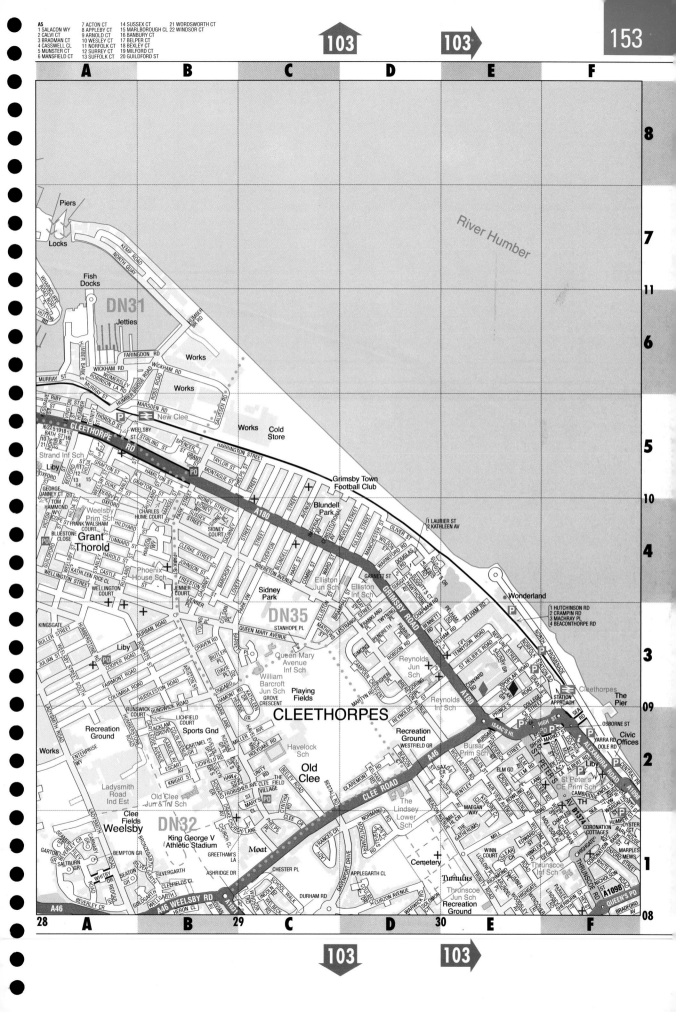

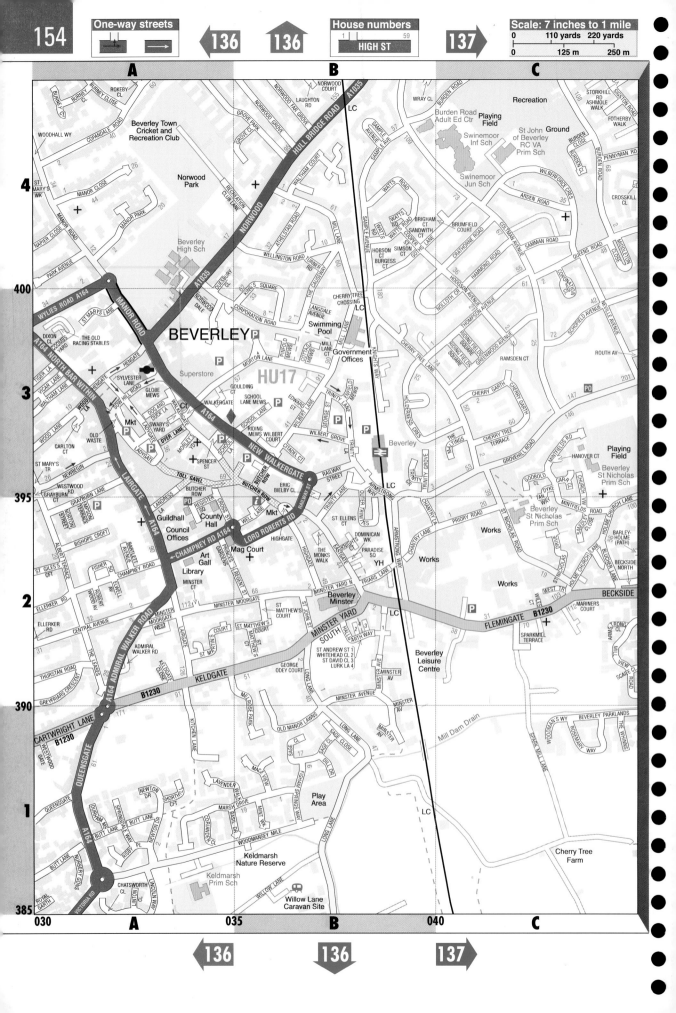

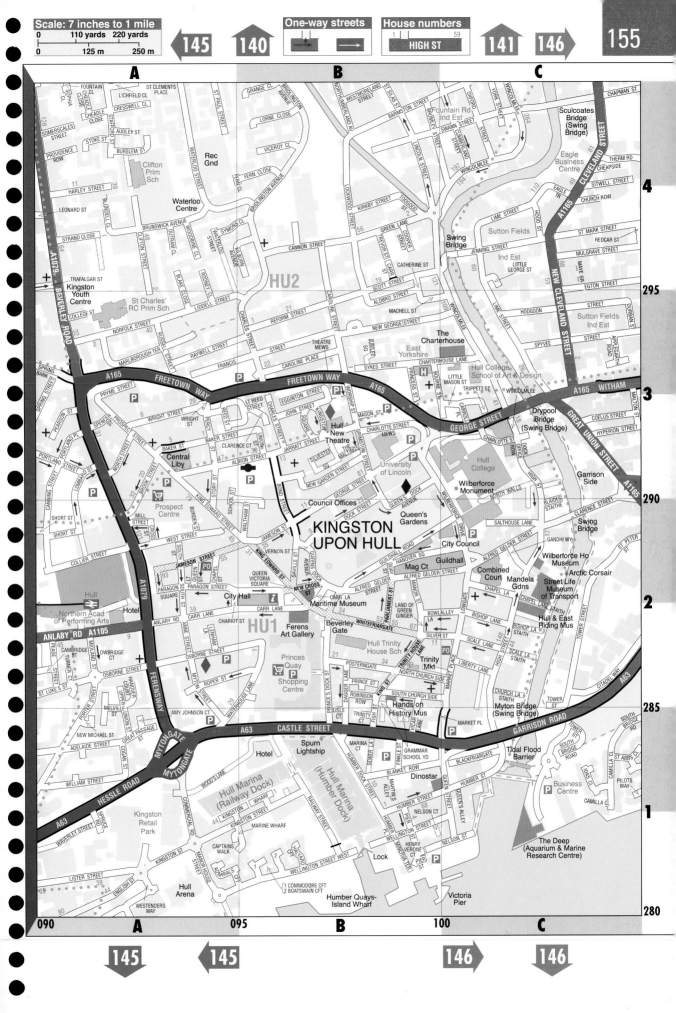

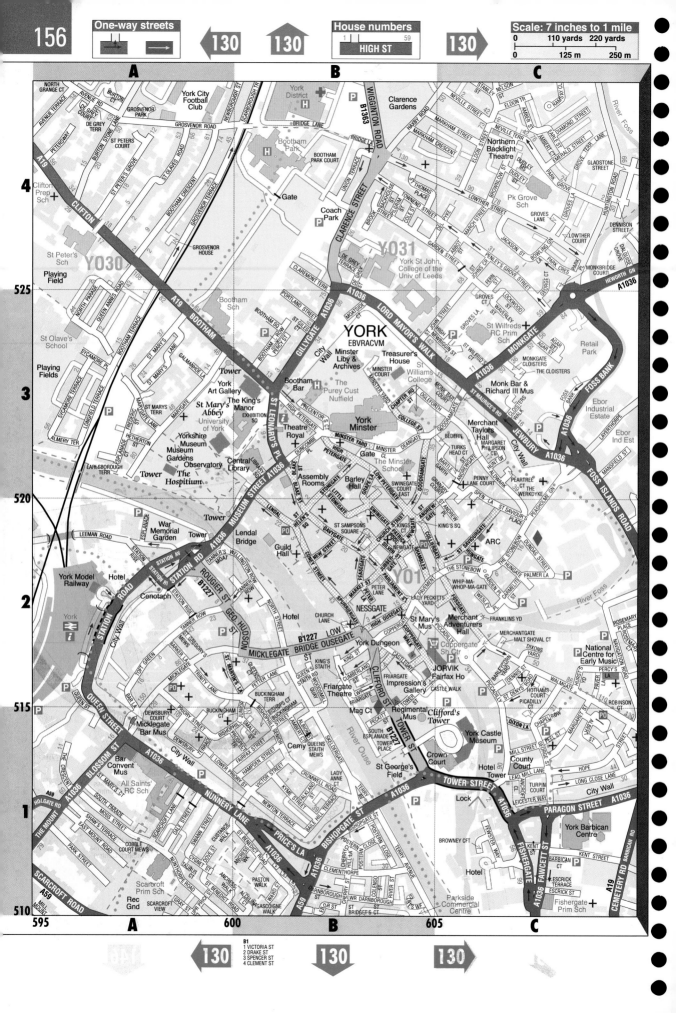

Index

Church Rd 6 Beckenham BR2..........**53** C6

Place name	Location number	Locality, town or village	Postcode district	Page and grid square
May be abbreviated on the map	Present when a number indicates the place's position in a crowded area of mapping	Shown when more than one place has the same name	District for the indexed place	Page number and grid reference for the standard mapping

Public and commercial buildings are highlighted in magenta   **Places of interest** are highlighted in blue with a star ★

Abbreviations used in the index

Acad	**Academy**	Comm	**Common**	Gd	**Ground**	L	**Leisure**	Prom	**Promenade**
App	**Approach**	Cott	**Cottage**	Gdn	**Garden**	La	**Lane**	Rd	**Road**
Arc	**Arcade**	Cres	**Crescent**	Gn	**Green**	Liby	**Library**	Recn	**Recreation**
Ave	**Avenue**	Cswy	**Causeway**	Gr	**Grove**	Mdw	**Meadow**	Ret	**Retail**
Bglw	**Bungalow**	Ct	**Court**	H	**Hall**	Meml	**Memorial**	Sh	**Shopping**
Bldg	**Building**	Ctr	**Centre**	Ho	**House**	Mkt	**Market**	Sq	**Square**
Bsns, Bus	**Business**	Ctry	**Country**	Hospl	**Hospital**	Mus	**Museum**	St	**Street**
Bvd	**Boulevard**	Cty	**County**	HQ	**Headquarters**	Orch	**Orchard**	Sta	**Station**
Cath	**Cathedral**	Dr	**Drive**	Hts	**Heights**	Pal	**Palace**	Terr	**Terrace**
Cir	**Circus**	Dro	**Drove**	Ind	**Industrial**	Par	**Parade**	TH	**Town Hall**
Cl	**Close**	Ed	**Education**	Inst	**Institute**	Pas	**Passage**	Univ	**University**
Cnr	**Corner**	Emb	**Embankment**	Int	**International**	Pk	**Park**	Wk, Wlk	**Walk**
Coll	**College**	Est	**Estate**	Intc	**Interchange**	Pl	**Place**	Wr	**Water**
Com	**Community**	Ex	**Exhibition**	Junc	**Junction**	Prec	**Precinct**	Yd	**Yard**

Index of localities, towns and villages

A

Acaster Malbis 36 D8
Acaster Selby 36 B4
Acklam 16 E8
Acomb 129 C3
Adlingfleet 81 E7
Aike 44 A8
Airmyn 64 E4
Aisby 118 B3
Aldbrough 47 C1
Alkborough 82 C8
Allerthorpe 28 E2
Althorpe 95 D4
Amcotts 81 F1
Angram 24 C3
Anlaby 143 F7
Appleby 83 C1
Arnold 45 C4
Arram 44 A7
Ashby 151 B1
Ashby cum Fenby 113 D3
Ashby Hill 113 C3
Askham Bryan 24 F3
Askham Richard 24 D3
Asselby 64 D7
Atwick 35 C5
Aughton 38 C1
Aylesby 101 E2

B

Bainton 31 E7
Balkholme 65 E6
Balne 77 C5
Barlby 49 B5
Barlow 63 C7
Barmby Moor 28 E3
Barmby on the Marsh ..64 B7
Barmston 23 A6
Barnetby le Wold 99 C4
Barnoldby le Beck ...113 B6
Barrow Hann 70 E1
Barrow Haven 70 C1
Barrow upon Humber ...85 D7
Barton-upon-Humber ..84 D7
Barton Waterside 69 F2
Beal 61 D4
Beckingham 116 D1
Beeford 22 C1
Beelsby 112 F5

Beltoft 95 A1
Belton 94 E1
Bempton 4 D4
Beningbrough 12 D4
Bennetland 66 C7
Bentley 55 D7
Bessingby 10 F4
Beswick 32 D3
Beverley 154 A3
Bewholme 35 A5
Bielby 39 F6
Bigby 99 C2
Bilbrough 24 D1
Bilton 58 A4
Birkin 61 D6
Bishop Burton 43 A2
Bishopthorpe 133 B3
Bishop Wilton 16 F2
Blacktoft 66 E3
Blyborough 119 B5
Blyton 117 E5
Bolton 28 D7
Bonby 84 C2
Bootham Stray 127 B2
Boothferry 64 E5
Bossall 15 D7
Bottesford 96 D2
Boynton 10 D7
Bracon 94 F2
Bradley 102 B3
Bradley 102 C1
Brandesburton 34 C2
Bransholme 141 A8
Brantingham 68 C8
Brayton 148 A2
Breighton 50 D5
Bridlington 122 B3
Brigg 98 D2
Brigham 33 E8
Brigsley 113 D4
Brind 51 A2
Brockfield 14 E2
Brocklesby 100 E6
Broomfleet 67 B6
Brough 68 C5
Broughton 97 E4
Brumby 151 B4
Bubwith 50 D7
Buckton 4 C4
Bugthorpe 16 D4
Burn 62 D7
Burnby 29 D1
Burnham 85 C3
Burringham 95 E4

Bursea 52 A4
Burstwick 73 B7
Burton Agnes 10 A1
Burton Fleming 2 E3
Burton Pidsea 59 D2
Burton Stather 82 A5
Burton upon Stather ..82 B4
Buttercrambe 15 E5
Butterwick 1 B2

C

Cabourne 111 D4
Cadney 109 D6
Caenby Corner Estate .119 D1
Caistor 111 B4
Camblesforth 63 D5
Camerton 73 A5
Canal Side 93 A7
Carlton 63 D3
Carnaby 10 E4
Catwick 45 D8
Cawkeld 32 B5
Cawood 48 B8
Chapel Fields 129 B3
Chapel Haddlesey 62 C5
Cherry Burton 43 B5
Church End 33 F8
Church Town 94 E1
Claxton 15 B7
Cleethorpes 153 C2
Cliffe 49 E2
Clifton 130 A7
Clifton Park 129 F7
Clixby 111 A7
Cock Hill 12 B2
Coleby 82 E6
Coniston 57 F6
Copmanthorpe 132 B2
Corringham 118 B2
Cottagers Plot 102 B2
Cottingham 139 A5
Covenham St
  Bartholomew 121 F5
Covenham St Mary ...121 F5
Cridling Stubbs 76 C3
Crockey Hill 26 A1
Crosby 150 D7
Crowle 94 D8
Crowle Park 94 D7
Croxby 112 C1
Croxby Top 112 B1

Croxton 99 F7
Cuxwold 112 B4

D

Danthorpe 59 C3
Deighton 37 A7
Dimlington 90 F7
Dragonby 82 E1
Drax 63 F5
Driffield 124 C5
Dringhouses 132 E8
Duggleby 6 B6
Dunnington 26 F7
Dunnington 34 F7
Dunscroft 92 D3
Dunsville 92 B3
Dunswell 56 D5

E

Ealand 94 E6
Earswick 128 A2
Easington 91 A6
Eastburn 20 B2
East Butterwick 106 E8
East Carlton 47 A2
East Common 148 E4
East Cottingwith 38 C5
East Cowick 78 B3
East Ella 144 D7
East Halton 86 E7
East Lound 105 E3
East Lutton 7 C8
East Marsh 152 F5
East Newton 59 F8
Eastoft 81 A3
East Ravendale 113 C2
Eastrington 51 F1
East Stockwith 116 F5
Eggborough 61 F2
Ellerker 68 A8
Ellerton 38 C2
Elloughton 68 C7
Elmswell 20 B5
Elsham 98 F7
Elstronwick 59 A3
Elvington 27 B2
Eppleworth 138 A4
Epworth 105 D6

Epworth Turbary 105 C6
Escrick 37 B5
Eskham 115 C1
Etton 42 F6
Everingham 40 A5
Everthorpe 53 E3

F

Fangfoss 28 C7
Fenwick 77 D3
Ferriby Sluice 83 F7
Fimber 18 D7
Fishlake 92 E8
Fitling 59 C5
Flamborough 5 B2
Flinton 59 A7
Flixborough 82 B1
Flixborough Stather ..82 A1
Fockerby 81 E5
Foggathorpe 51 B8
Fordon 2 A6
Fosterhouses 78 C1
Foston on the Wolds ..22 A2
Fotherby 121 C2
Foxholes 1 D3
Fraisthorpe 22 F8
Fridaythorpe 18 B6
Frodingham 151 B6
Fulford 133 E7
Full Sutton 16 A2
Fulstow 121 E8

G

Gainsborough 117 C2
Ganstead 57 F7
Ganton 1 A8
Gardham 42 D5
Garthorpe 81 F6
Garton 59 E6
Garton-on-the-Wolds ..20 A6
Gateforth 62 A7
Gate Helmsley 15 B2
Gembling 22 A3
Gilberdyke 66 C8
Gipsyville 144 E3
Goodmanham 135 F7
Goole 149 C3
Gowdall 63 A1

Gowthorpe 16 C1
Goxhill 86 B8
Grainsby 113 F2
Graiselound 105 C1
Grange 152 A1
Gransmoor 22 C6
Grant Thorold 153 A4
Grasby 110 E7
Grayingham 119 B3
Great Coates 102 B5
Great Cowden 47 A5
Great Givendale 29 B8
Great Hatfield 46 D6
Great Heck 77 D7
Great Kelk 22 A5
Great Kendale 20 D7
Great Limber 100 D3
Great Tows 120 A1
Greetwell 108 C7
Grey Green 94 E2
Gribthorpe 51 B6
Grimsby 152 E2
Grimston 131 E3
Grindale 3 D2
Grovehill 137 C3
Gunby 50 D6
Gunness 95 E6
Gunthorpe 117 A7

H

Habrough 100 E8
Haisthorpe 10 C3
Hall Garth 26 F6
Halsham 73 F6
Harlthorpe 51 A8
Harpham 21 F8
Harswell 40 C3
Harton 15 C8
Hatcliffe 112 F3
Hatfield 92 D5
Hatfield Woodhouse ...93 A3
Haxby 127 D7
Haxey 105 C3
Haxey Carr 105 B4
Hayton 40 C8
Healing 102 A5
Hedon 72 C8
Hemingbrough 49 F1
Hemswell 119 A1
Hensall 62 D2
Heslington 131 B1
Hessay 24 C8
Hessle 143 E1
Heworth 130 F6
Hibaldstow 108 F5
High Catton 27 D8
Highfield 50 E7
High Hunsley 54 D6
High Mowthorpe 6 D7
High Risby 82 F1
Hilderthorpe 11 B4
Hillam 61 A7
Hilston 60 B4
Hirst Courtney 62 F3
Hive 52 C2
Holgate 129 F3
Hollym 75 A4
Holme 97 A1
Holme Hill 152 F3
Holme-on-Spalding
  -Moor 40 B1
Holme on the Wolds ...31 E1
Holmpton 75 C2
Holtby 14 F1
Holton le Clay 114 B5
Hopgrove 128 D2
Horkstow 84 A5
Horkstow Wolds 84 B6
Hornsea 134 D5
Hornsea Burton 134 D2
Hotham 53 D4
Howden 65 A7
Howsham 110 A7
Huggate 18 B2
Humberston 114 E8
Humberston Fitties ...114 F8
Humbleton 59 B5
Hunmanby 2 F8
Huntington 127 E3
Hurn 136 C4
Hut Green 62 A2
Hutton 32 E8
Hutton Cranswick 32 D7
Hutton Wandesley 24 A5

I

Immingham 87 B2
Inglemire 139 F6
Irby upon Humber 112 D7

K

Keadby 95 D6
Keelby 101 B5
Kelfield 36 D1
Kelleythorpe 124 C1
Kellingley 61 C2
Kellington 61 F4
Kelstern 120 D1

Kexby 27 C6
Keyingham 73 D3
Kilham 9 C3
Kilnsea 91 B2
Kilnwick 32 B4
Kilnwick Percy 29 C5
Kilpin 65 D5
Kilpin Pike 65 C5
Kingsforth 84 E6
Kingston upon Hull ...155 B2
Kirby Grindalythe 6 B6
Kirby Underdale 17 A5
Kirk Bramwith 92 A4
Kirk Ella 143 D8
Kirk Smeaton 76 B3
Kirkburn 20 A2
Kirmington 100 A6
Kirton in Lindsey 108 B1
Knapton 129 A5
Knavesmire 133 A7
Knedlington 64 E6
Knottingley 61 B2

L

Laceby 101 E2
Laceby Acres 102 B2
Langtoft 8 D5
Laughton 117 F8
Laxton 65 F4
Layerthorpe 130 E4
Laytham 39 B2
Leconfield 43 D6
Lelley 58 F3
Leppington 16 C8
Leven 45 A8
Lissett 22 E4
Little Airmyn 64 E4
Little Burton 34 B2
Little Catwick 45 D7
Little Coates 102 C3
Little Driffield 124 C4
Little End 40 A1
Littlethorpe 152 C2
Little Grimsby 121 E2
Little Hatfield 46 B6
Little Heck 62 D1
Little Leven 45 A7
Little Limber 100 C5
Little Reedness 66 A1
Little Skipwith 37 D1
Little Smeaton 76 C3
Little Weighton 55 A4
Lockington 32 B2
Londesborough 41 B8
Long Drax 64 A6
Long Marston 24 A6
Long Riston 45 C5
Low Burnham 105 D5
Low Catton 27 C8
Low Fosham 46 F1
Low Risby 83 B1
Lowthorpe 21 E7
Ludborough 121 C6
Luddington 81 C3
Lund
  Beverley 31 F3
  Selby 49 D3

M

Manor Park 150 D2
Manton 108 B5
Mappleton 47 A7
Marfleet 147 C8
Market Weighton 135 B4
Marshchapel 115 B2
Marton 123 D8
Marton 46 B2
Meaux 44 F2
Melbourne 39 B6
Melton 68 F5
Meltonby 28 F7
Melton Ross 99 C5
Menthorpe 50 C5
Messingham 107 C7
Middlegate 84 E1
Middlethorpe 133 B6
Middleton-on-the
  -Wolds 31 B4
Millbrook Park 135 C3
Millington 29 C6
Misterton 116 C5
Molescroft 136 B5
Monk Fryston 61 B8
Moor End 52 B8
Moorends 79 C2
Moor Monkton 12 A3
Moortown 110 D2
Morton 117 A3
Moss 77 D1
Murton 26 D7

N

Naburn 36 D8
Nafferton 125 E7
Neat Marsh 58 A2
Nether Poppleton 126 A2
Nettleton 111 A2
New Arram 43 F7

New Barnetby 99 D5
New Earswick 127 D3
New Ellerby 46 A2
New Holland 70 E2
Newland
  Goole 64 B3
  Howden 66 A8
  Hull 140 C3
Newport 53 A1
Newsholme 64 E8
Newton-on-Ouse 12 B6
Newton upon Derwent ..27 E4
New Village 139 D6
New Waltham 114 A7
Normanby 82 B3
North Cave 53 D3
North Cliffe 53 B8
North Cotes 115 A3
North Dalton 31 B7
North Duffield 50 A8
North Elkington 121 A1
North End
  Goxhill 71 A3
  Withernwick 46 D4
North Ferriby 69 B4
Northfield 143 F2
North Frodingham 34 A8
North Howden 51 B1
North Kelsey 110 A5
North Killingholme ...86 D4
North Newbald 53 E8
North Ormsby 121 B3
Northorpe 118 D6
North Thoresby 114 A1
Norton 76 E2
Nunburnholme 29 E3
Nun Monkton 12 A4
Nunsthorpe 102 D1
Nunthorpe 133 C8

O

Octon 8 F8
Old Clee 153 C2
Old Ellerby 58 A8
Old Goole 149 C1
Old Town 122 E5
Osbaldwick 131 C4
Osgodby 49 C4
Osgodby Common 49 C6
Ottringham 73 F3
Ousefleet 66 D2
Out Newton 90 E8
Overton 12 F2
Owmby 110 D7
Owston Ferry 106 A2
Owstwick 59 E3
Owthorne 74 F7

P

Painsthorpe 17 B5
Patrington 74 E1
Patrington Haven 89 C8
Paull 72 A5
Pilham 118 A4
Pocklington 29 A4
Pollington 77 F6
Portington 51 E2
Preston 58 C1
Pyewipe 152 A8

R

Rascal Moor 52 B7
Rawcliffe
  Goole 64 A1
  York 126 C6
Rawcliffe Bridge 79 C8
Redbourne 108 F3
Reedness 65 F2
Reighton 3 D6
Riby 101 C2
Riccall 49 A8
Riddings 150 F1
Rimswell 74 D7
Riplingham 54 E2
Rise 45 F5
Rolston 46 E8
Roos 60 A1
Rothwell 111 F2
Routh 44 F5
Roxby 83 A3
Rudston 9 F6
Rufforth 24 C6
Ruston Parva 21 C8
Ryehill 73 A4

S

Salt End 72 A8
Saltmarshe 65 F3
Sancton 41 A8
Sand Hole 52 B8
Sandholme 52 C1
Sand Hutton 15 B5
Sandtoft 94 A3
Santon 97 B7

Saxby All Saints 84 A3
Scalby 66 E8
Scamland 39 C7
Scartho 102 F1
Scawby 108 E8
Scorborough 43 D8
Scotter 107 D3
Scotterthorpe 107 B5
Scotton 107 D2
Scrayingham 15 F7
Sculcoates 140 E2
Scunthorpe 150 F5
Searby 110 C8
Seaton 35 A1
Seaton Common 39 D4
Seaton Ross 39 E4
Selby 148 C6
Sewerby 123 A5
Sewerby Village 123 C6
Shipton 12 F5
Shiptonthorpe 40 F6
Sigglesthorne 45 F8
Skeffling 90 C6
Skelton
  Goole 65 C4
  York 126 C6
Skerne 21 A2
Skidby 138 B8
Skipsea 23 B2
Skipwith 37 E1
Skirlaugh 45 E2
Skirpenbeck 16 A4
Sledmere 7 B4
Snaith 63 C1
Somerby 99 B1
South Bank 130 A1
South Bramwith 92 B6
Southburn 20 B1
South Cave 54 A2
South Cliffe 53 B7
South Dalton 42 E8
South Duffield 50 A4
South End 46 D3
South End 90 F5
South Ferriby 84 B7
South Field 69 E4
South Kelsey 110 A1
South Killingholme ...86 E3
South Newbald 53 F6
Spaldington 51 C4
Speeton 3 F5
Spital in the Street .119 E1
Sproatley 58 C5
Staddlethorpe 66 D7
Stainforth 92 C7
Stallingborough 101 E6
Stamford Bridge 15 E2
Stillingfleet 36 C3
Stockton on the Forest .14 D3
Stoneferry 141 B3
Strensall 14 A7
Strensall Camp 14 B6
Sturton 108 F7
Summergangs 141 C2
Sutton Ings 141 F4
Sutton-on-Hull 141 D6
Sutton upon Derwent ..27 C1
Swallow 112 B5
Swanland 69 B6
Swine 57 D6
Swinefleet 65 D1
Sykehouse 78 B3

T

Tang Hall 130 F5
Tansterne 59 A8
Temple Hirst 62 E4
Tetney 114 D4
Tetney Lock 115 A5
Thealby 82 D4
Thearne 56 D7
The Hallands 85 F7
The Lawns 138 F7
The Lings 92 D3
The Parks 92 C4
The Willows 102 C4
Thirtleby 58 B5
Thixendale 17 E7
Thorganby 38 B4
Thorne 93 A8
Thorngumbald 72 E5
Thornholme 10 B2
Thornton 39 B8
Thornton Curtis 85 E5
Thorpe 32 B1
Thorpe le Street 40 D7
Thorpe Willoughby 48 C2
Thwing 2 B1
Tibthorpe 19 D2
Tickton 137 E8
Topham 78 A4
Towthorpe 14 B5
Towthorpe 6 D1
Tunstall 60 C2

U

Ulceby 86 A1
Ulceby Skitter 86 C2
Ulrome 23 A3
Upper Helmsley 15 B3
Upper Poppleton 12 F1

Upperthorpe 105 B3
Upton 22 E1
Utterby 121 D4

V

Victoria Dock Village ...146 B5

W

Waithe 114 A3
Walcot 82 C7
Walden Stubbs 76 F3
Walkeringham 116 C3
Walkerith 116 E3
Walkington 55 B8
Walmgate Stray 130 F1
Waltham 113 D7
Wansford 21 C3
Warter 30 A5
Warthill 14 F2
Waterside 92 F8
Watton 32 D5
Wawne 56 E8
Waxholme 74 E8
Weel 137 F3
Weelsby 153 A1
Weeton 90 B7
Weighton Wold 135 F4
Welhambridge 51 F5
Wellow 152 D1
Welton 68 D6
Welwick 90 A8
West Butterwick 106 D8
West Carlton 46 F1
West Carr 140 F5
Westcliff 150 E3
West Cowick 78 D8
West Ella 143 A7
West End 53 F2
Westfield 148 C4
West Field 129 A2
Westgate 94 D2
West Haddlesey 62 A5
West Halton 82 E8
West Hill 122 A1
West Lutton 7 B8
West Marsh 152 B5
West Newton 58 D8
West Ravendale 113 A2
Westrum 98 C1
West Stockwith 116 F6
Westwoodside 105 A2
Wetwang 19 B6
Wharram le Street 6 A4
Wharton 117 E4
Wheldrake 38 A7
Whitgift 66 B1
Whitley 77 A7
Whitley Thorpe 76 F7
Whitton 67 E3
Wigginton 13 D5
Wike Well End 93 B7
Wilberfoss 27 F5
Wildsworth 117 A8
Willerby 138 C1
Willitoft 51 A6
Willoughton 119 A4
Wilsthorpe 11 A2
Winestead 74 C3
Winteringham 68 A1
Winterton 83 A5
Wistow 48 D6
Withernsea 75 A6
Withernwick 46 D3
Wold Haven 29 B3
Wold Newton
  Binbrook 120 B7
  Hunmanby 2 A3
Womersley 76 C6
Woodhall 50 B2
Woodhouse 94 E3
Woodmansey 56 B8
Woodside 104 E6
Woodthorpe 132 C7
Wootton 85 F3
Worlaby 98 D8
Wrawby 98 E4
Wressle
  Broughton 97 F4
  Howden 50 D2
Wroot 104 D6
Wybers Wood 102 A3
Wyham 120 F6
Wyton 58 B4

Y

Yaddlethorpe 96 C2
Yapham 28 E7
Yarborough 152 A3
Yawthorpe 118 D2
Yokefleet 66 C3
York 156 B3
Youlthorpe 16 C2

1

1st Ave HU6 ....140 C6
1st Main Rd DN36 ......114 F8
10th Ave HU6 ....140 B7
11th Ave HU6 ....140 B6
12th Ave
  Humberston DN36 ......114 F8
  Kingston upon Hull HU6 ..140 A7
14th Ave HU6 ....140 A6
15th Ave HU6 ....140 A6
16th Ave HU6 ....140 A6
17th Ave HU6 ....140 A6
18th Ave HU6 ....140 A6
19th Ave HU6 ....140 A6

2

2nd Ave
  Humberston DN36 ......114 F8
  Kingston upon Hull HU6 ..140 B7
20 21 Visual Arts Ctr
  DN15 ....151 C7
20th Ave HU6 ....140 A7
21st Ave HU6 ....139 F6
22nd Ave HU6 ....140 A7
23rd Ave HU6 ....140 A6
24th Ave HU6 ....140 A6
25th Ave HU6 ....140 A6
26th Ave HU6 ....139 F7
27th Ave HU6 ....140 A6
28th Ave HU6 ....139 F7
29th Ave HU6 ....139 F6

3

30th Ave HU6 ....139 F7
31st Ave HU6 ....139 F7
32nd Ave HU6 ....139 F7
33rd Ave HU6 ....139 F7
34th Ave HU6 ....139 F7
36th Ave HU6 ....139 F7
37th Ave HU6 ....139 E6
38th Ave HU6 ....139 F7

4

4th Ave
  Humberston DN36 ......114 F8
  Kingston upon Hull HU6 ..140 B7
40th Ave HU6 ....139 F7

5

5th Ave HU6 ....139 F6

6

6th Ave HU6 ....140 A7

7

7th Ave HU6 ....140 B6

8

8th Ave HU6 ....140 A7

9

9th Ave HU6 ....140 B6

A

A W Nielsen Rd DN14 ..149 A4
Abber La LS24 ....24 A2
Abbey Dr E DN32 ......152 D2
Abbey Dr W DN32 ......152 D2
Abbey Gdns 32 DN7 ....92 D4
Abbey Gn 30 DN7 ......92 D4
Abbey La
  Kingston upon Hull
    HU10 ....138 E2
  Preston HU12 ....58 C1
Abbey Leisure Ctr
  YO8 ....148 C5
Abbey Pk Mews DN32 ..152 D2
Abbey Pk Rd DN32 ......152 D2
Abbey Pl 9 YO8 ....148 D5
Abbey Rd
  Bridlington YO16 ......122 B2
  Grimsby DN32 ....152 D2
  Hatfield DN7 ....92 D4
  Kingston upon Hull
    HU11 ....142 F6
  Scunthorpe DN17 ......150 F2
  Ulceby DN39 ....86 A1
Abbey Rise DN19 ......85 D8
Abbey St
  Kingston upon Hull HU9 ..146 C7
  York YO30 ....130 A7
Abbey Way DN7 ....92 D5
Abbey Wlk
  Grimsby DN32 ....152 D3
  Selby YO8 ....148 C5
Abbey Wlk Sh Ctr
  YO8 ....148 C6
Abbey Yd YO8 ....148 C5

Abbeyfield Rd DN7 ......92 C4
Abbeygate 12 DN31 ....152 D3
Abbot St YO31 ....156 C4
Abbot's Rd YO8 ....148 E3
Abbots Cl HU8 ....141 E6
Abbots Gait YO32 ......127 F6
Abbots Rd DN17 ......150 F2
Abbots Wlk HU16 ......139 A5
Abbotsford Cl HU5 ....139 F3
Abbotsford Rd YO10 ....130 F3
Abbotsway
  Grimsby DN32 ....152 D2
  York YO31 ....130 E8
Abbotts Grange DN36 ..114 B7
Abbotts Way YO16 ....122 C4
Abelton Gr 33 YO32 ....13 C5
Abercorn St DN16 ......151 A6
Aberdeen St HU5 ......141 F3
Aberdovey Cl 3 HU7 ....57 A7
Aberford Wlk HU9 ......142 E1
Abingdon Garth 1 HU7 ..57 A5
Acacia Ave
  Flixborough DN15 ......96 B7
  19 Gainsborough DN21 ..117 B3
  York YO32 ....127 E4
Acacia Ct DN16 ......151 D5
Acacia Dr HU8 ....141 D2
Acacia Way DN17 ......107 C6
Acadia Gr HU13 ......143 F1
Acaster Ave YO23 ......132 F8
Acaster La
  Acaster Malbis YO23 ..133 B1
  Acaster Selby YO23 ....36 A4
Accommodation Rd
  YO25 ....8 D6
Acer Gr DN17 ....150 C1
Acey La HU11 ....58 B1
Achille Rd DN34 ......102 B3
Acklam Dr HU18 ......134 D6
Acklam Gr DN32 ......153 B2
Acklam Rd HU12 ......72 D7
Ackworth St HU8 ......141 C1
Acland St
  Gainsborough DN21 ....117 B1
  4 Kingston upon Hull
    HU3 ....145 A6
Acomb Comm Rd DN7 ..92 F4
Acomb Prim Sch
  YO24 ....129 E3
Acomb Rd YO24 ......129 D3
Acomb Wood Cl YO24 ..132 C7
Acomb Wood Dr YO24 ..132 B7
Acorn Cl 6 Barlby YO8 ..49 B4
  Bridlington YO16 ......123 B7
Acorn Gr HU8 ....141 E7
Acorn Way
  24 Bottesford DN16 ......96 D1
  Gateforth YO8 ....48 B1
  Hessle HU13 ....143 B3
  York YO24 ....132 D7
Acredykes 7 YO15 ......4 D3
Acres La
  Scrayingham YO41 ......16 B8
  Wroot DN9 ....104 D7
Acton Cl HU8 ....141 F5
Acton Ct 7 DN32 ......153 A5
Adam Smith St DN31 ..152 C5
Adam St DN14 ....149 D3
Adderbury Gr 5 HU5 ..140 D2
Addison Gdns HU8 ....141 D3
Addison Rd 10 HU12 ....58 D1
Addle La DN14 ....65 E7
Addlekeld YO42 ......30 A5
Adelaide Prim Sch
  HU3 ....145 D5
Adelaide Rd 6 DN6 ....76 E2
Adelaide St
  Kingston upon Hull HU1 ..155 A1
  3 York YO23 ....130 B2
Adeline St DN14 ......149 C5
Adeliza Garth 29 HU12 ..72 D7
Adelphi Cl HU8 ....141 F4
Adelphi Cl 4 DN36 ....114 A7
Adelphi Dr 7 DN33 ....113 E8
Adelphi St YO25 ......124 E4
Adlard Gr DN36 ......114 C7
Adlingfleet Rd DN17 ..81 C6
Adlington Cl 8 YO32 ..14 A7
Admiral Walker Rd
  HU17 ....154 A2
Admirals Croft HU1 ....155 A1
Admirals Mews 1
  YO15 ....122 D2
Advent Ct 9 DN39 ......86 A1
Aegre Dr DN14 ....65 C4
Africa Cl 15 DN34 ....102 B2
Agar St YO31 ....156 C3
Agard Ave DN15 ......150 E7
Aike La YO25 ....33 A1
Ainshaw HU8 ....139 E8
Ainslie Rd HU12 ......72 D7
Ainslie St DN32 ......152 E2
Ainsty Ave YO24 ......132 F8
Ainsty Gr YO24 ......132 F8
Ainsty St DN14 ......149 E4
Ainsty View YO17 ......16 E8
Ainsworth Rd 16 DN40 ..87 B1
Ainthorpe Gr HU5 ....144 C7
Ainthorpe Prim Sch
  HU5 ....144 C8
Aintree Cl HU17 ......136 E6
Aintree Ct YO24 ......132 F6
Air St HU5 ....140 F2
Aire Cl 10 Brough HU15 ..68 D5
  36 Immingham DN40 ....87 B1
Aire St Goole DN14 ....149 D3
  Knottingley WF11 ......61 A3

Airedale HU7 ....140 E6
Airedale Cl 10 DN20 ....97 E4
Airedale Dr HU16 ......122 F7
Airedale Rd DN16 ......151 D1
Airedale Way DN31 ....152 D4
Airlie St HU3 ....145 B5
Airmyn Ave
  Goole DN14 ....149 B5
  1 Kingston upon Hull
    HU3 ....144 E6
Airmyn Pk Prim Sch
  DN14 ....64 E4
Airmyn Rd Airmyn DN14 ..64 D3
  Goole DN14 ....149 B5
Aisne St HU5 ....145 A8
Ajax Cl Grimsby DN34 ..102 B2
  Kingston upon Hull HU9 ..142 D5
Ajax Ct DN15 ....96 C7
Akeferry Rd
  Haxey DN9 ....105 C1
  Westwoodside DN9 ......105 B2
Akester Cl 4 HU17 ....137 B3
Alan Cres DN15 ......150 F6
Alaska St HU8 ....141 B1
Alba Cl DN17 ....150 D1
Albany St
  Gainsborough DN21 ....117 B3
  Kingston upon Hull HU3 ..145 D8
  3 York YO24 ....129 F5
Albany Villas HU13 ....144 A1
Albatross Dr DN37 ....102 A4
Albemarle Cl 5 HU15 ..68 B5
Albemarle Rd
  Bilton HU11 ....58 A3
  2 Keyingham HU12 ......73 C4
  York YO23 ....130 B2
Albemarle St 2 HU3 ..145 B5
Albert Aur Pools HU3 ..145 A7
Albert Ave HU3 ......145 A4
Albert Cl
  4 Grimsby DN32 ......152 F5
  1 York YO32 ....130 F8
Albert Dock HU1 ......145 E4
Albert Marson Ct
  DN16 ....151 B6
Albert Pl 3 DN32 ......152 F5
Albert Rd
  Cleethorpes DN35 ......153 F2
  Scunthorpe DN16 ......151 A1
Albert St
  10 Bridlington YO15 ....122 E2
  Brigg DN20 ....98 C2
  Goole DN14 ....149 C2
  3 New Holland DN19 ....70 E2
  3 Thorne/Moorends DN8 ..93 B8
  York YO10 ....156 C1
Albert St E DN32 ......152 F5
Albert St W DN32 ......152 F5
Albert Terr
  Beverley HU17 ....154 A2
  Kingston upon Hull HU7 ..141 D6
  Welwick HU12 ....90 A7
Alberta Cres 7 DN17 ....96 C2
Albertine St 5 DN37 ..113 D7
Albery Way DN36 ......114 A8
Albina Garth 1 HU12 ..72 D7
Albion Ave YO26 ......129 B6
Albion Ct
  Beverley HU17 ....137 B4
  Kingston upon Hull HU4 ..144 B6
Albion Hill DN9 ......105 E6
Albion La HU10 ......138 A3
Albion St
  Great Driffield YO25 ..124 F3
  Grimsby DN32 ....152 F4
  Kingston upon Hull HU1 ..155 A3
  York YO1 ....156 B1
Albion Terr
  Bridlington YO15 ......122 F3
  Misterton DN10 ......116 D5
Albourne Ave DN15 ....151 A6
Albright Cl 31 YO42 ....29 A3
Alcelina Ct YO23 ......156 B1
Alcuin Ave YO10 ......131 A4
Alcuin Way YO10 ......131 B2
Aldam Dr DN9 ....94 F1
Aldborough Gr HU9 ..142 A2
Aldborough Way YO26 ..129 F5
Aldbro' St HU2 ......155 B3
Aldbrough La HU11 ....59 A6
Aldbrough Prim Sch
  HU11 ....47 C1
Aldbrough Rd
  East Garton HU11 ......59 D7
  Withernwick HU11 ......46 E3
Alden Ct DN40 ......87 C1
Aldenham Pk HU7 ......56 E5
Alder Cl 16 HU15 ......68 D5
Alder Gr 6 DN8 ......79 B2
Alder Hey Dr 9 HU9 ..142 A4
Alder View 22 DN33 ..102 C2
Alder Way YO32 ......127 D2
Alderley Edge 6 DN37 ..113 D6
Alderman Cogans CE Prim
  Sch HU9 ....141 F2
Aldermans Way 10 YO25 ..34 B2
Alderney Way 2 DN40 ..101 C8
Alders The 22 DN21 ..117 C1
Alderson Ct YO15 ......122 D2
Alderson Mews 5 HU9 ..146 C7
Aldersyde YO24 ......132 E2
Aldersyde Ct YO24 ......132 E4
Aldersyde Mews YO24 ..132 E4
Aldfield YO24 ....132 C6

Aldwych Ct HU5 ......144 E8
Alexander Ave YO31 ..127 E2
Alexander Rd DN16 ..151 B6
Alexandra Ct
  4 Bridlington YO15 ....122 F3
  York YO10 ....130 E4
Alexandra Dock DN31 ..152 D6
Alexandra Dock N
  DN31 ....152 C6
Alexandra Dr
  1 Beverley HU17 ......55 E8
  5 Bridlington YO15 ....122 F3
Alexandra Prom YO15 ..123 A3
Alexandra Rd
  Cleethorpes DN35 ......153 F2
  Grimsby DN31 ....152 D4
  Hornsea HU18 ....134 D4
  Kingston upon Hull HU5 ..140 C3
  Scunthorpe DN16 ......151 B2
  Strensall YO32 ....14 A6
  Thorne/Moorends DN8 ..79 B2
Alexandra Rd S DN40 ..87 D2
Alexandra Ret Pk
  DN31 ....152 D5
Alexandra St
  Goole DN14 ....149 D4
  Kingston upon Hull HU3 ..145 D7
  Thorne DN8 ....79 A1
Alexandra Wlk YO15 ..122 F3
Alfonso St 3 HU3 ......145 B5
Alfred Bean Hospl
  YO25 ....124 F2
Alfred Gelder St HU1 ..155 B2
Alfred St
  Gainsborough DN21 ....117 B1
  Grimsby DN31 ....152 D4
  Kingston upon Hull HU3 ..145 D5
Alfreton Ct 1 DN15 ....150 B6
Alfriston Cl HU7 ......141 B6
Algarth Rd
  Pocklington YO42 ......29 A4
  York YO31 ....131 B7
Algarth Rise
  Pocklington YO42 ......28 F4
  York YO31 ....131 B7
Algernon St DN32 ......152 F1
Alison Garth 29 HU12 ..72 D7
Alkborough La DN15 ..82 D7
Alkborough Prim Sch
  DN15 ....82 C8
All Hallows Rd 3 HU17 ..55 B7
All Saints CE VC Inf Sch
  HU13 ....143 F2
All Saints Cl 4 HU13 ..69 F4
All Saints Ct 6 YO43 ..135 D4
All Saints' RC Sch
  YO24 ....156 A1
All Saints' St HU3 ....145 D8
All Saints VE VC Jun Sch
  HU13 ....143 F2
Allan St 2 YO30 ......130 C7
Allanby St DN15 ......151 A7
Allanhall Way HU16 ..143 B8
Allanson Dr HU16 ......139 D5
Allanson Gr YO24 ......129 E2
Allen Cl YO24 ....131 A4
Allenby Ave DN34 ......152 A2
Allenby Cres LN11 ....121 D3
Allendale YO24 ......132 D8
Allerford Dr 8 HU7 ....57 A5
Allerthorpe Comm Nature
  Reserve* YO42 ....28 B2
Allerton Dr
  1 Immingham DN40 ....87 C1
  22 Poppleton YO26 ......12 F1
Allerton Prim Sch
  DN40 ....87 B1
Allestree Dr 2 DN33 ..113 E8
Alliance Ave HU3 ......144 F7
Alliance La HU3 ......144 F7
Allington Dr
  Great Coates DN31 ....102 C5
  York YO31 ....131 B6
Allinson Yd HU17 ......45 A7
Allison Cl DN17 ......107 D7
Allison La
  14 Flamborough YO15 ....5 A3
  Ulrome YO25 ....22 F4
Alloa Cl 2 HU6 ......140 B8
Allotment La DN25 ....124 E5
Allotment Wlk YO16 ..122 B1
Alma Cl HU10 ....143 D7
Alma Gr YO10 ....130 D2
Alma St
  6 Kingston upon Hull
    HU9 ....146 B7
  4 Withernsea HU19 ....74 F7
Alma Terr Selby YO8 ..148 C6
  York YO10 ....130 D2
Almery Terr YO30 ......156 A3
Almond Cl
  Great Driffield YO25 ..124 F2
  Hambleton YO8 ....48 B1
Almond Gr Brigg DN20 ..98 B2
  3 Kingston upon Hull
    HU9 ....145 D6
  Scunthorpe DN16 ......151 B4
  York YO32 ....127 D3
Almond Tree Ave DN14 ..63 C3
Almsford Dr YO26 ......129 C5
Almsford Rd YO26 ......129 C5
Alne Terr YO10 ......130 E2
Alness Dr YO24 ......132 B7
Alpha Ave HU17 ......136 D6
Alpha Ct DN8 ....92 F8
Alsenham Pk 9 HU7 ..56 E5

1st - Ann 159

Alston Ave 4 HU8 ......141 B1
Althorpe & Keadby Prim Sch
  DN17 ....95 C5
Althorpe Sta DN17 ....95 D5
Altoft Cl
  2 Brandesburton YO25 ..34 B2
  12 Laceby DN37 ....101 F2
Alton Pk Mews YO25 ..22 C1
Alton Rd YO16 ....122 D7
Altyre Way DN36 ......103 B1
Alured Garth 9 HU12 ..72 D7
Alveston Rd DN17 ......150 D4
Alvin Wlk 9 YO41 ......27 B2
Alvingham Ave 25 DN36 ..103 C2
Alvingham Rd DN16 ....151 B3
Alvis Gr YO10 ....131 D4
Alwoodley Cl 1 HU8 ..142 B5
Alwyn Rd 19 DN8 ......93 B8
Alwyne Dr YO30 ......126 E1
Alwyne Gr YO30 ......126 E1
Amanda Cl HU6 ......139 E6
Amanda Dr DN7 ......92 C3
Ambaston Rd HU18 ....134 C5
Amber Ct YO31 ......156 C4
Amber St YO31 ......156 C4
Amberley Cl HU7 ......141 B6
Amberly St 4 YO26 ..129 E5
Ambler's La YO30 ......12 F7
Ambleside Ave YO10 ..131 B4
Ambrey Cl 16 YO14 ......2 E8
Ambrose Ave 1 DN7 ..92 E4
Ambrose St YO10 ......130 D1
Amcott Ave DN10 ......116 C4
Amcotts Rd 14 DN33 ..102 D1
Amen La YO43 ....53 D5
Amesbury Ave DN33 ..113 D8
Amethyst Ct 11 DN36 ..114 A8
Amethyst Rd HU9 ......142 A4
Amos Cl 9 DN33 ......113 D8
Amos Cres DN16 ......151 D3
Ampleforth Gr HU5 ....144 D8
Amsterdam Rd HU7 ....141 A5
Amwell Gn 8 DN7 ......92 D5
Amy Johnson Ave
  YO16 ....122 E6
Amy Johnson Ct HU1 ..155 A1
Amy Johnson Sch
  HU3 ....144 F5
Amy Johnson Way
  YO30 ....127 A3
Amy St DN14 ....149 C4
Anastasia Cl 1 DN21 ..117 B2
Ancaster Ave
  Grimsby DN33 ....113 D8
  Kingston upon Hull HU5 ..139 F3
Ancaster Ct DN34 ......151 A1
Anchholme Ave 10 DN40 ..87 B1
Ancholme Gdns 11 DN20 ..98 C2
Ancholme Rd DN16 ....151 D2
Ancholme Way DN20 ..98 B2
Anchor Cl 31 DN8 ......93 B8
Anchor Rd
  Kingston upon Hull HU6 ..140 C8
  Scunthorpe DN16 ......97 A3
Anchorage St 7 DN20 ..98 B2
Anchors Way 16 DN20 ..98 B2
Ancient La DN7 ......139 E6
Ancourt 1 HU7 ......56 E5
Ancress Wlk YO23 ......156 A1
Ancroft Cl YO1 ....156 C1
Anderby Dr DN37 ......102 B4
Anderson Gr 6 YO24 ..129 C2
Anderson Rd
  Goole DN14 ....149 A4
  Scunthorpe DN16 ......151 C3
Anderson St
  7 Great Driffield YO25 ..124 F3
  Grimsby DN31 ....152 D3
Andersons Cl 17 HU12 ..72 D7
Andrew Dr 4 YO32 ....127 F1
Andrew La 3 HU12 ......72 C7
Andrew Marvell Sch
  HU9 ....142 D4
Andrew Paddock
  DN20 ....108 F5
Andrew Rd 11 DN36 ..114 D8
Andrew's Ct 15 YO42 ..28 F4
Andrews Rd DN18 ......84 A7
Andrews Way 8 DN40 ..87 B1
Angerstein Rd DN17 ..150 F1
Anglesey Dr DN40 ......101 C8
Angram Dr YO30 ......126 E5
Angram La YO19 ......49 A6
Angram Rd YO26 ......24 A5
Angus Dr YO25 ......124 D4
Anlaby Acre Head Prim Sch
  HU4 ....144 B7
Anlaby Ave 7 HU4 ....144 B6
Anlaby High Rd HU4 ..144 A6
Anlaby Inf Sch HU10 ..144 A6
Anlaby Jun Sch HU10 ..144 A6
Anlaby Pk Rd N HU4 ..144 B5
Anlaby Pk Rd S HU4 ..144 B2
Anlaby Rd HU1 ......155 A2
Anlafgate 7 HU10 ......143 F6
Anlary Rd HU1 ......155 A2
Ann Gr DN35 ....103 B2
Ann Watson St HU7 ..141 A4
Annan Cl YO24 ......132 C6
Annandale Rd
  Kingston upon Hull HU9 ..142 E1
  Willerby HU10 ....138 B1
Anne St
  Kingston upon Hull HU1 ..155 A2
  York YO23 ....130 C2

Annerley Dr YO16 ... 123 A7
Annes Cres DN16 ... 151 C3
Annesley St DN31 ... 152 D5
Annie Med La HU15 ... 53 F1
Annie Rd Ct HU17 ... 137 C3
Annie Reed Rd HU17 ... 137 C3
Annie St YO8 ... 148 C6
Anningson La 6 DN36 ... 114 A8
Annumhills Rd YO8 ... 50 D7
Anserdam La HU15 ... 52 C2
Anson Dr YO10 ... 133 D8
Anson Rd HU9 ... 142 B3
Antelope Rd DN18 ... 70 A1
Anthea Dr YO31 ... 127 E1
Antholme Cl HU7 ... 141 C6
Anthony Way 1 DN41 ... 101 D6
Anthony's Bank Rd
DN36 ... 103 E1
Antrim Way 4 DN33 ... 102 E1
Antwerp Rd HU7 ... 141 A5
Anvil Wlk DN15 ... 82 F3
Apollo St 9 YO10 ... 130 E3
Apollo Wlk HU8 ... 141 F4
Appian Way DN31 ... 152 A6
Appin Cl 7 HU7 ... 57 A6
Apple Croft HU16 ... 138 B8
Apple Garth
21 Hedon HU12 ... 72 D7
15 Poppleton YO26 ... 12 F1
Apple Tree Cl
Kingston upon Hull HU8 ... 141 D4
1 Long Riston/Arnold
HU11 ... 45 C5
Apple Tree Ct 1 DN41 ... 101 F5
Apple Tree Wlk HU16 ... 139 D6
Appleby Cl DN17 ... 150 F1
Appleby Ct 8 DN32 ... 153 A5
Appleby Gdns DN20 ... 97 D4
Appleby Glade YO32 ... 127 D7
Appleby La
Broughton DN20 ... 97 D4
Burstwick HU12 ... 73 A7
Appleby Mill Rd DN16 ... 151 E7
Appleby Pl 2 YO31 ... 131 A5
Applecroft Rd
Selby YO8 ... 148 A4
York YO31 ... 131 B7
Appledore Cl HU9 ... 146 C6
Applefields Sch YO31 ... 131 B5
Applegarth 8 HU15 ... 66 D7
Applegarth Cl DN35 ... 153 D1
Applegarth La
Bainton YO25 ... 31 E7
Bridlington YO16 ... 122 D4
Applegarth Mews 3
HU16 ... 139 B7
Applegarth Rd HU8 ... 155 C3
Appleton Ct YO23 ... 132 F3
Appleton Gdns 8 HU15 ... 53 F1
Appleton Prim Sch
HU5 ... 139 E2
Appleton Rd
Bishopthorpe YO23 ... 133 A3
Kingston upon Hull HU5 ... 139 E3
Appleton Way DN16 ... 151 C2
Appleyard Dr DN18 ... 84 E8
Arables La HU12 ... 74 C4
ARC★ YO1 ... 156 C2
Arcade The DN14 ... 149 D4
Archbishop Cl HU9 ... 142 D2
Archbishop Holgate's Sch
YO10 ... 131 B3
Archbishop of York CE Jun
Sch YO23 ... 133 A4
Archbishop Thurston CE VC
Sec Sch HU9 ... 142 D3
Archer Rd DN37 ... 113 D6
Archway The YO43 ... 135 D4
Arcon Dr HU4 ... 144 D6
Arctic Corsair★ HU1 ... 155 C2
Arden Ct HU5 ... 139 C2
Arden Rd HU17 ... 154 C4
Arden Village 21 DN35 ... 103 C1
Ardent Rd DN18 ... 70 A1
Ardmore Cl HU9 ... 142 B4
Arenhall Cl 2 YO32 ... 127 C8
Argam Dikes★
Grindale YO25 ... 3 B2
Rudston YO25 ... 10 A7
Argam La YO25 ... 2 F1
Argent Cl 8 HU6 ... 140 B8
Arglam La YO43 ... 51 F6
Argyle Ct DN15 ... 151 A7
Argyle St Goole DN14 ... 149 D4
Kingston upon Hull HU3 ... 145 C7
York YO23 ... 130 B1
Ariston St DN32 ... 153 B3
Ark Royal HU11 ... 142 E6
Arkley Cl 18 HU15 ... 68 C5
Arkwright St 10 DN21 ... 117 B1
Arkwright Way DN16 ... 151 F2
Arlington Ave HU16 ... 139 B6
Arlington Rd YO30 ... 127 A1
Arlington St 2 HU3 ... 145 D6
Armeria Dr 23 DN17 ... 96 D1
Armour Rd DN16 ... 151 E7
Armoury Rd YO8 ... 148 B5
Armstrong Cl HU17 ... 154 C2
Armstrong Pl E DN31 ... 152 C5
Armstrong Pl W DN31 ... 152 C5
Armstrong St DN31 ... 152 C5
Armstrong Way
Beverley HU17 ... 154 B2
Rawcliffe YO32 ... 128 E3
Armthorpe La DN3 ... 92 A3
Arncliffe Cl 1 HU7 ... 56 F6
Arncliffe Way HU16 ... 139 A5
Arnold Cl DN37 ... 101 F2
Arnold Ct 9 DN32 ... 153 A5
Arnold La
Kingston upon Hull HU3 ... 145 B6
Riston HU11 ... 45 C5
Arnold La W HU11 ... 45 C4
Arnold St HU3 ... 145 B6
Arnside Pl 2 YO10 ... 130 F3
Arram Gr HU6 ... 139 E5
Arram Rd HU17 ... 43 D6
Arram Sta HU17 ... 43 F7
Arran Cl
Immingham DN40 ... 101 C8
Kingston upon Hull HU9 ... 142 A4
19 New Waltham DN36 ... 114 A8
Arran Pl YO31 ... 130 D7
Arras Dr HU16 ... 138 E6
Arreton Cl HU8 ... 142 D6
Art Coll Mews DN32 ... 152 F4
Arthur Lucan Ct HU9 ... 142 C1
Arthur Pl 6 YO30 ... 126 B5
Arthur Rd 12 DN21 ... 117 B1
Arthur St
Grimsby DN31 ... 152 C4
Kingston upon Hull HU3 ... 145 A5
Withernsea HU19 ... 74 F7
York YO10 ... 130 E4
Arundel Cl
4 Gainsborough DN21 ... 117 C1
Kingston upon Hull HU9 ... 146 C8
Arundel Gr YO24 ... 132 C7
Arundel Pl DN35 ... 153 E1
Arundel Rd 5 DN6 ... 76 E2
Arundel St 4 HU9 ... 146 C8
Arundel Wlk DN34 ... 152 A3
Ascot Rd 23 DN37 ... 113 D6
Ascot Way YO24 ... 129 D1
Ascott Cl
Beverley HU17 ... 136 E7
Kingston upon Hull HU4 ... 144 D5
Asenby Wlk HU5 ... 139 D3
Asgard Way 5 DN33 ... 102 D1
Ash Ave HU15 ... 68 C6
Ash Cl Hessle HU13 ... 143 C3
Newton on Derwent YO41 ... 27 E4
Sproatley HU11 ... 58 D5
York YO31 ... 131 B7
Ash Ct 18 DN35 ... 103 B1
Ash Dell DN14 ... 149 E6
Ash Dene 7 HU17 ... 55 D8
Ash Dr
Kingston upon Hull
HU10 ... 143 F8
Thorngumbald HU12 ... 72 E5
Ash Gr 4 Aldbrough HU11 ... 47 C1
Brigg DN20 ... 98 B2
17 Gainsborough DN21 ... 117 B1
Hutton Cranswick YO25 ... 32 E6
Market Weighton YO43 ... 135 D4
Messingham DN17 ... 107 D7
Newland HU5 ... 140 C3
1 Riccall YO19 ... 48 F8
3 Scotter DN21 ... 107 B3
Scunthorpe DN16 ... 151 B3
Willerby HU10 ... 138 D1
Ash Hill Cres DN7 ... 92 D4
Ash Hill Mid Sch DN7 ... 92 D4
Ash Hill Rd
20 Hatfield DN7 ... 92 D4
Sykehouse DN14 ... 78 A3
Ash La 8 Haxby YO32 ... 13 E5
Melbourne YO42 ... 39 A5
Ash St YO26 ... 129 E4
Ash Tree Cl 5 DN40 ... 87 C2
Ash Tree Dr
5 Haxey DN9 ... 105 D2
Leconfield HU17 ... 43 D6
Ash Tree Rd 13 DN8 ... 93 A7
Ashberry Dr
Messingham DN17 ... 107 D7
1 Scunthorpe DN16 ... 151 B2
Ashbourne 7 DN37 ... 113 D6
Ashbourne Ct DN15 ... 150 B7
Ashbourne Way YO24 ... 132 C8
Ashburnham Cl 4 DN6 ... 76 F2
Ashburnham Rd 14 DN8 ... 93 A8
Ashburnham Wlk 5 DN6 ... 76 F2
Ashbury Ct HU6 ... 140 A6
Ashby Cl Grimsby DN37 ... 102 B4
Holton le Clay DN36 ... 114 B5
Kingston upon Hull HU4 ... 144 B7
Ashby High St DN16 ... 151 A2
Ashby Hill DN37 ... 113 C3
Ashby Inf Sch DN16 ... 151 B2
Ashby La DN37 ... 113 C4
Ashby Rd
Cleethorpes DN35 ... 103 B2
Kingston upon Hull HU4 ... 144 B4
Scunthorpe DN16 ... 151 A2
Ashcombe Rd HU7 ... 56 E5
Ashcourt Cl HU18 ... 134 C5
Ashcourt Dr HU18 ... 134 B5
Ashdale Pk 14 HU14 ... 69 A5
Ashdale Rd 19 YO19 ... 26 F7
Ashdene Cl HU10 ... 143 E7
Ashdown Ave DN15 ... 150 E8
Ashdown Cl DN20 ... 98 D2
Ashdown Way DN10 ... 116 C5
Ashendon Dr HU8 ... 141 A2
Ashfield YO43 ... 40 A1
Ashfield Ave 1 DN8 ... 93 A7
Ashfield Ct Crowle DN17 ... 94 D7
York YO24 ... 132 E7
Ashfield Gr 6 DN7 ... 92 C6
Ashfield Pk DN17 ... 150 B2
Ashfield Rd Hatfield DN7 ... 92 C4
Ashfield Rd *continued*
Thorne DN8 ... 92 F7
Ashford Pl YO24 ... 129 D2
Ashford Wlk HU9 ... 142 E1
Ashgate Rd HU10 ... 138 E2
Ashlea 1 DN10 ... 116 C5
Ashlea Cl YO8 ... 148 D4
Ashleigh Ct 18 DN41 ... 101 F5
Ashleigh Dr 6 YO25 ... 22 D1
Ashley Pk Cres YO31 ... 131 B6
Ashley Pk Rd YO31 ... 131 B7
Ashmeade Cl YO24 ... 132 B8
Ashmole Wlk HU17 ... 154 C4
Ashridge Dr DN32 ... 153 B1
Ashthorpe HU6 ... 139 F8
Ashton Ave YO30 ... 130 B8
Ashton Cl HU6 ... 139 F8
Ashtree Ave DN34 ... 152 A2
Ashtree Cl DN9 ... 94 E1
Ashtree Cres HU15 ... 53 D3
Ashtree Dr YO8 ... 48 D1
Ashville St
Bridlington YO16 ... 122 D3
York YO31 ... 130 D7
Ashwell Ave HU9 ... 142 D1
Ashwood Cl 21 HU15 ... 68 C5
Ashwood Dr 17 DN36 ... 103 D1
Ashwood Glade YO32 ... 127 C6
Ashworthy Cl 5 HU7 ... 56 F5
Aske Mews HU5 ... 139 D3
Askern & Campsall Sports Ctr
DN6 ... 76 F1
Askew Ave HU4 ... 144 E4
Askham Bog Nature
Reserve★ YO23 ... 132 C5
Askham Bryan Coll
YO23 ... 24 F2
Askham Bryan La
YO23 ... 132 A6
Askham Croft 1 YO24 ... 129 B1
Askham Fields La YO23 ... 24 F2
Askham Gr YO24 ... 129 B2
Askham La
Askham Bryan YO24 ... 132 A8
York YO24 ... 129 B1
Askrigg Wlk HU5 ... 139 D4
Aspall Wlk HU8 ... 142 C7
Aspen Cl
3 Dunnington YO19 ... 26 F7
Market Weighton YO43 ... 135 D5
Selby YO8 ... 48 D2
Aspen Ct
15 Cleethorpes DN35 ... 103 B1
13 Gainsborough DN21 ... 117 C1
Aspen Gr DN16 ... 151 B4
Aspen Wlk 4 HU15 ... 68 D5
Asphodel Cl 15 DN36 ... 114 B8
Asquith Ave YO31 ... 131 A5
Asquith St DN21 ... 117 A1
Asterby Rd DN17 ... 150 F1
Astley Cres 18 DN21 ... 107 C3
Astley St HU3 ... 144 F7
Aston Gn 4 DN7 ... 92 D3
Aston Hall Dr 11 HU14 ... 69 A5
Aston Rd HU10 ... 143 F8
Astoria Cres HU8 ... 141 F4
Astral Cl
Northfield HU13 ... 143 F3
Sutton-on-Hull HU7 ... 141 D7
Astral Gdns HU7 ... 141 C7
Astral Rd HU13 ... 143 F3
Astral Way HU7 ... 141 C7
Atcherley Cl YO10 ... 133 D8
Athelstan Rd HU17 ... 154 B4
Athena Dr DN31 ... 152 A6
Athenian Way DN37 ... 102 C6
Atherton Way DN20 ... 98 B2
Athol St HU3 ... 144 F4
Atholl Ave HU13 ... 143 E3
Atkinson Ave DN20 ... 98 C3
Atkinson Dr 19 HU15 ... 68 C6
Atkinson La 6 DN37 ... 113 E6
Atkinsons Way DN15 ... 96 C8
Atlanta Ct 2 HU8 ... 142 B5
Atlas Rd
Scunthorpe DN17 ... 150 F4
York YO30 ... 127 A3
Atterby La LN8 ... 119 F3
Atterwith La YO26 ... 24 A7
Attlee Dr DN14 ... 149 C5
Atwick Ct 2 HU9 ... 142 B1
Atwick Rd
Bewholme YO25 ... 35 A4
Hornsea HU18 ... 134 B6
Atwood Cl 4 DN40 ... 87 B2
Aubretia Dr 22 DN17 ... 96 D1
Auburn Cl
Bridlington YO16 ... 122 B5
Kingston upon Hull HU9 ... 142 C1
Auburn Wlk YO16 ... 122 B5
Auchinleck Cl YO25 ... 124 B1
Auckland Ave HU6 ... 140 C5
Auckland Gr DN8 ... 79 C2
Auckland Rd
Grimsby DN31 ... 152 F6
Scunthorpe DN15 ... 150 F6
Aucuba Cl YO32 ... 127 D2
Audax Cl YO30 ... 127 A3
Audax Rd YO30 ... 127 A3
Audern Rd DN16 ... 96 D2
Audley St HU2 ... 155 A4
Audus St 10 YO8 ... 148 C5
Augusta Cl
Grimsby DN34 ... 152 C2
Kingston upon Hull HU8 ... 142 B6
Augusta Oaks DN34 ... 152 C2
Augusta St DN34 ... 152 B2
Augustinian Priory (site of)★
YO42 ... 30 B5
Augustus Dr 13 HU15 ... 68 C5
Auster Rd YO30 ... 127 B3
Austfield La LS25 ... 61 B8
Austin Cres 17 DN17 ... 96 C2
Austin Garth 5 DN37 ... 101 F1
Autherd Garth 1 HU17 ... 55 C8
Autumn View YO25 ... 124 D5
Avenswood La 8 DN15 ... 96 B7
Avenue Cannes DN15 ... 96 B7
Avenue Clamart DN15 ... 96 B7
Avenue Fontenay 17
DN15 ... 96 B7
Avenue Lourdes 16 DN15 ... 96 B7
Avenue Nozay DN20 ... 97 E4
Avenue Rd YO30 ... 156 A4
Avenue Rouen 15 DN15 ... 96 B7
Avenue Terr YO30 ... 156 A4
Avenue The
Blyton DN21 ... 117 E5
Burton upon Stather
DN15 ... 82 B4
Campsall DN6 ... 76 E1
East Ravendale DN37 ... 113 C2
19 Gainsborough DN21 ... 117 B1
Great Driffield YO25 ... 124 F5
Grimsby DN37 ... 102 B4
5 Haxby YO32 ... 13 E5
Healing DN41 ... 101 F5
Holme-on-Spalding-Moor
YO43 ... 51 E8
Kirk Ella HU10 ... 143 C7
Nun Monkton YO26 ... 12 A4
11 Pocklington YO42 ... 29 A4
Rowley HU20 ... 54 D6
Rufforth YO23 ... 24 C6
Sutton-on-Hull HU7 ... 141 E6
Thorne/Moorends DN8 ... 79 B3
Watton YO25 ... 32 D4
York YO30 ... 130 A6
Avenue Vivian DN15 ... 150 E8
Avenues Ct HU5 ... 140 C1
Aviator Ct YO30 ... 126 F3
Avocet Way YO15 ... 11 B4
Avon Dr YO32 ... 127 F6
Avon Rd DN16 ... 151 C6
Avon St 2 HU8 ... 141 C1
Avondale 1 HU4 ... 144 B2
Awmand Gn HU16 ... 138 F5
Awnhams La
Bishop Wilton YO42 ... 16 D2
North Cave HU15 ... 53 E4
Axdane HU6 ... 139 E7
Axholme Ave DN17 ... 94 C7
Axholme Ct HU9 ... 146 B5
Axholme Dr 11 DN9 ... 105 D6
Axholme Gn 15 DN8 ... 93 B7
Axholme Line Nature
Reserve★ DN9 ... 105 C4
Axholme Rd
Scunthorpe DN15 ... 150 D6
2 Westwoodside DN9 ... 105 A2
Axholme St DN14 ... 149 E4
Axminster Cl HU7 ... 141 A8
Aylesbury Gr HU5 ... 144 D8
Aylesby Gdns 26 DN33 ... 102 D2
Aylesby La DN37 ... 101 F2
Aylesby Rd
Aylesby DN37 ... 101 E2
Scunthorpe DN17 ... 150 F1
Aylesford St 7 HU3 ... 145 B5
Aylesham Ct YO32 ... 127 E3
Ayots Gn 10 DN7 ... 92 D3
Ayscough Ave DN41 ... 101 E6
Ayscough Gr 3 LN7 ... 111 B4
Ayscough St DN31 ... 152 C4
Aysgarth Ave
Kingston upon Hull HU6 ... 139 E4
Messingham DN17 ... 107 D7
Aysgarth Rise YO16 ... 122 E6

B

Babington Row HU9 ... 146 C8
Bacchus La HU15 ... 54 A1
Bacheler St HU3 ... 145 B5
Bachelor Hill YO24 ... 129 C2
Back Field La DN7 ... 92 E4
Back La
Acaster Selby YO23 ... 36 B3
Allerthorpe YO42 ... 28 E2
Appleton Roebuck YO23 ... 36 A5
Asselby DN14 ... 64 D6
Barlby with Osgodby YO8 ... 49 C4
Bilbrough YO23 ... 24 D1
Burstwick HU12 ... 73 A6
Burton Agnes YO25 ... 10 A2
Burton Pidsea HU12 ... 59 C2
Catwick HU17 ... 45 C8
Copmanthorpe YO23 ... 132 A2
Cottingwith YO42 ... 38 C5
Drax YO8 ... 63 F5
Driffield YO25 ... 124 B5
East Garton HU11 ... 59 E6
Ellerton YO42 ... 38 C1
Elstronwick HU12 ... 59 B3
Fangfoss YO41 ... 28 C8
Garthorpe & Fockerby
DN17 ... 81 F6
11 Haxby YO32 ... 13 D5
Hayton YO42 ... 29 C1
Hemingbrough YO8 ... 49 F1
Hirst Courtney YO8 ... 62 F3
Holme-on-Spalding-Moor
YO43 ... 40 A1
Holtby YO19 ... 26 E8
Back La *continued*
Kilham YO25 ... 9 B3
Luttons YO17 ... 7 B8
Newton-on-Ouse YO30 ... 12 B6
North Duffield YO8 ... 50 A7
Norton DN6 ... 76 E2
Nunburnholme YO42 ... 29 F3
Patrington Haven HU12 ... 89 C8
2 Riccall YO19 ... 49 A8
Searby cum Owmby
DN38 ... 110 D8
3 Seaton HU11 ... 35 A1
Shiptonthorpe YO43 ... 40 F6
Snaith & Cowick DN14 ... 78 E8
Stainforth DN7 ... 92 C6
Wilberfoss YO41 ... 27 F5
3 Winteringham DN15 ... 68 B1
Wold Newton YO25 ... 2 A4
York YO26 ... 129 A5
Back La S YO19 ... 37 F7
Back O' Newton YO41 ... 27 E3
Back Pk St YO8 ... 148 D5
Back Rd HU12 ... 72 A5
Back Side YO17 ... 6 B5
Back Southgate HU18 ... 134 C3
Back St Alkborough DN15 ... 82 C8
Bainton YO25 ... 31 E7
Burton Fleming YO25 ... 2 E3
3 Easington HU12 ... 90 F6
East/West Stockwith
DN21 ... 116 E5
Fridaythorpe YO25 ... 18 B6
Langtoft YO25 ... 8 D5
Laxton DN14 ... 65 F4
Skerne & Wansford YO25 ... 21 A2
Skipsea YO25 ... 23 A2
Wold Newton YO25 ... 2 A4
Back W View 2 YO30 ... 130 B7
Back Westgate HU18 ... 134 B4
Backcarr La YO25 ... 21 C5
Backhouse St YO31 ... 156 B4
Bacon Garth La HU16 ... 139 A5
Bad Bargain La YO31 ... 131 A5
Baden Cl 3 HU5 ... 140 D2
Bader Way DN21 ... 119 B8
Badger Hill Prim Sch
YO10 ... 131 B2
Badger La
Halsham HU12 ... 74 B5
Walden Stubbs DN6 ... 77 A3
Badger Paddock 5
YO31 ... 127 E2
Badger Way 1 DN20 ... 97 E4
Badger Wood Wlk
YO10 ... 131 D3
Badgers Wood HU16 ... 138 F8
Badminton Cl YO16 ... 122 F6
Baffam Gdns YO8 ... 148 B2
Baffam La YO8 ... 148 B2
Bagby Mews 2 HU5 ... 139 D3
Baggaby Hill YO42 ... 29 E4
Bagsby Rd DN9 ... 106 B3
Baildon Cl 3 YO26 ... 129 D4
Baildon Rd DN15 ... 150 D8
Baile Hill Terr YO1 ... 156 B1
Bailey La Hatfield DN7 ... 92 E6
Kingston upon Hull
HU16 ... 139 D8
Warter YO42 ... 30 B5
Baileywood La YO43 ... 51 F8
Bainbridge Ave HU9 ... 142 D2
Bainbridge Dr YO8 ... 148 C4
Bainton Cl HU17 ... 136 D5
Bainton Gr HU6 ... 139 E6
Bainton Rd YO25 ... 19 E2
Bakehouse La 5 YO25 ... 9 C3
Baker Dr DN15 ... 83 A5
Baker St
Kingston upon Hull HU2 ... 155 A3
York YO30 ... 130 C7
Bakers Cl DN38 ... 99 B5
Bakersfield DN20 ... 98 D4
Bakersfield Dr DN14 ... 61 F3
Bakewell Cl HU9 ... 142 D1
Bakewell Ct DN15 ... 150 B7
Balder Ct 2 DN33 ... 102 E1
Baldwin Ave DN16 ... 96 D1
Balfour Pl 14 DN40 ... 87 B1
Balfour St
23 Gainsborough DN21 ... 117 B1
3 Kingston upon Hull
HU9 ... 146 C8
York YO26 ... 129 F5
Balfour Way YO32 ... 14 A6
Balham Ave HU8 ... 141 E6
Balk Cl HU17 ... 45 B8
Balk La Hook DN14 ... 149 F6
Pollington DN14 ... 77 F7
Riston HU11 ... 45 C4
Sproatley HU11 ... 58 D5
Balk Mews HU5 ... 139 D3
Balk The
Bishop Wilton YO41 ... 16 C2
Millington YO42 ... 29 C7
Pocklington YO42 ... 29 A3
Ballantyne Cl HU7 ... 141 C4
Balldon Ct HU12 ... 72 D7
Ballhall La YO42 ... 38 E6
Balliol Dr DN16 ... 96 D2
Balmoral Ave
Grimsby DN34 ... 152 A3
Kingston upon Hull HU6 ... 140 B6
Balmoral Cl 8 YO16 ... 122 D6
Balmoral Dr HU17 ... 136 E1
Balmoral Rd
2 Cleethorpes DN35 ... 103 B2
25 Hatfield DN7 ... 92 D4
Balmoral Terr 5 YO23 ... 130 B1

Balne Croft La DN14 ....78 A6
Balne Hall Rd DN14 ....77 F5
Balne Moor Rd DN14 ...77 F8
Bamford Ave HU9 .....142 E1
Banbury Ct 16 DN32 ...153 A5
Banbury Rd DN16 .....151 D6
Bank End Rd DN9 .....104 A3
Bank L Ctr The HU6 ...139 F6
Bank La 15 LN7 ....111 B4
Bank Rd YO8 ....148 D6
Bank Side
  Kingston upon Hull HU5 .140 F2
  Rawcliffe DN14 ....64 A2
Bank St
  3 Hornsea HU18 ......134 C4
  Kingston upon Hull HU3 .145 C7
Bank Terr HU18 ....134 C4
Bankfield La DN14 .....64 A7
Banks Cl HU12 ....90 F6
Bankside Cl 3 YO26 ....12 F1
Bannisdale 6 YO24 ...132 C2
Bannister Dr HU9 .....146 C7
Bannister St HU19 .....75 A7
Bantock Garth HU4 ...144 B4
Baptist Chapel La DN40 .86 F2
Baptist Pl YO16 ......122 D4
Bar Convent Mus★
  YO24 ....156 A1
Bar La YO1 ....156 A2
Barbara Cl 3 DN33 ...113 E8
Barbara Gr 4 YO24 ...129 F3
Barbarry Rd HU12 .....72 B7
Barberry Ct
  24 Brough HU15 ....68 C5
  3 Kingston upon Hull
    HU3 ....145 C5
Barbers Dr YO23 .....132 B4
Barbican Cl YO10 ....156 C1
Barbican Mews YO10 .130 E3
Barbican Rd YO10 ....156 C1
Barbican Way 7 DN36 .114 A7
Barbriggs La YO25 .....22 E2
Barcroft St DN35 .....153 B4
Barden Ct 6 YO30 ....126 F1
Bardney Ave HU16 ....151 A3
Bardney Gdns 16 DN34 .102 C2
Bardney Rd 14 YO14 ....2 F8
Bardshaw HU6 ....139 F8
Barf La YO41 ....16 D4
Barff Cl 10 YO8 ....48 D1
Barff Gr 6 YO8 ....48 B2
Barff La YO8 ....48 C1
Barff View YO8 ....62 D7
Barfhill Cswy YO25 ....32 F2
Barfield Rd YO31 ....130 F8
Bargate DN34 ....152 C2
Bargate Ave DN32 ....152 D1
Bargate Gr 3 HU5 ...144 D8
Barham Rd HU4 ......142 B4
Bark House La DN35 ..153 F1
Bark St DN35 ....153 F1
Barker Dr YO8 ....148 B6
Barker St YO1 ....156 A2
Barkers Mill 6 YO17 ..137 B3
Barkhouse La DN35 ..153 F1
Barkhouse Wood La
  WF11 ....61 D6
Barking Cl HU8 ......142 A5
Barkston Ave YO26 ..129 B3
Barkston Cl 3 YO26 ..129 A3
Barkston Gr YO26 ...129 A3
Barkston Rd YO26 ...129 A3
Barkworth Cl HU10 ..143 D6
Barkworth Ct 3 DN37 .113 D6
Barlby Bridge CP Sch
  YO8 ....148 D5
Barlby By-pass 2 YO8 .49 B4
Barlby CP Sch YO8 ...49 B4
Barlby Cres YO8 ....148 F7
Barlby High Sch YO8 .49 B5
Barlby Rd YO8 ......148 E6
Barleigh Croft HU9 ..142 B3
Barleigh Rd HU9 ....142 B3
Barley Cl DN20 ......109 A5
Barley Garth
  14 Brandesburton YO25 .34 B2
  Burton Pidsea HU12 ..59 C2
Barley Gate HU17 .....45 A8
Barley Hall★ YO1 ...156 B3
Barley Rise
  Bridlington YO16 .....123 A6
  Strensall YO32 ....14 A6
Barley View YO32 ...127 C8
Barleycorn Yd YO1 ..156 C2
Barleyholme HU17 ...154 C2
Barlings Ave DN16 ...151 A3
Barlings Cl DN21 ....107 D4
Barlow CE VC Prim Sch
  YO8 ....63 C7
Barlow Comm Nature
  Reserve★ YO8 ....63 B7
Barlow Comm Rd YO8 .63 B8
Barlow Rd YO8 ....63 B6
Barlow St 7 DN14 ...129 D4
Barmby Ave YO10 ...133 E8
Barmby Cl 4 YO8 ....49 B4
Barmby Ferry Rd 1 YO8 .49 F1
Barmby La 2 YO8 ....52 A3
Barmby Moor CE Prim Sch
  YO42 ....28 D4
Barmby on the Marsh Prim
  Sch DN14 ....64 B7
Barmby Rd YO42 .....28 D4
Barmouth Cl 4 HU7 ..57 A7
Barmouth Dr 20 DN37 .102 C4
Barmston Cl HU17 ...137 B5

Barmston La HU17 .....56 C8
Barmston Rd HU17 ...137 B5
Barmston St HU2 ....155 B4
Barnard Ave DN20 ....98 B3
Barnard Way HU12 ....72 C6
Barnards Dr 9 HU15 ..53 F1
Barnet Cl HU13 ......142 A5
Barnet Dr DN36 ......114 B8
Barnet Gn 9 DN7 .....92 D3
Barnetby La DN20 .....98 F7
Barnetby Rd
  1 Kingston upon Hull
    HU13 ....144 A3
  Scunthorpe DN17 ....150 F1
Barnetby Sta DN38 ...99 B4
Barnett Pl DN35 .....153 B3
Barnfield Way YO23 .132 A3
Barnhill La DN14 .....64 F7
Barnoldby Rd DN37 ..113 D6
Barnside DN20 ....108 F5
Barnsley Rd DN8 .....79 B2
Barnsley St HU8 .....141 B1
Barnstaple Rd
  Kingston upon Hull HU7 .141 B7
  Scunthorpe DN17 ....150 D3
Barnston Way 11 DN15 .82 B4
Baron Ave 8 DN6 ....114 A8
Baroness Cl 7 HU6 ..140 B8
Baroness Ct 4 DN34 .102 C3
Baroness Rd DN34 ...152 A3
Barons Cres YO23 ...132 B2
Baronwood Cres 7
  YO25 ....22 D1
Barr La YO32 ....14 D4
Barra Cl HU8 ....141 F6
Barraclough's La DN18 .69 E2
Barrett Ave 3 YO24 ..129 F3
Barrick Cl 7 DN19 ...85 D8
Barrier Bank DN14 ...78 E6
Barrington Ave HU5 .139 F3
Barrington Garth DN14 .61 F3
Barrow Blow Wells Nature
  Reserve★ DN19 ...70 D1
Barrow Ct 3 HU3 ...140 D1
Barrow Haven Reedbed
  Nature Reserve★
  DN18 ....70 B2
Barrow Haven Sta
  DN19 ....70 C2
Barrow La HU13 .....143 D2
Barrow Rd
  Barrow upon Humber
    DN19 ....70 E1
  Barton-upon-Humber
    DN18 ....85 A8
  New Holland DN19 ...70 D2
Barry Ave DN18 .....102 C2
Barstow Ave YO10 ..130 F3
Bartholomew Ave
  DN14 ....149 B5
Bartindale Rd YO14 ...3 A3
Bartle Garth YO1 ....156 C3
Bartlett Ave HU17 ...154 A2
Bartlett Cl 9 HU12 ..58 D1
Barton Cl 4 YO31 ...127 E3
Barton Dr HU13 ......143 D1
Barton La DN19 ......85 C8
Barton Rd DN20 ......98 D3
Barton St
  Barrow upon Humber
    DN19 ....85 D8
  Irby DN37 ....112 F7
  Keelby DN41 ....101 A4
  Wyham cum Cadeby
    DN36 ....120 F7
Barton St Peter's CE Prim
  Sch DN18 ....69 F1
Bartons Garth YO8 ..148 B2
Bartrams 1 YO8 .....68 D6
Barwic Par YO8 .....148 E4
Barwick Par CP Sch
  YO8 ....148 E4
Basic Slag Rd DN16 .151 E6
Basil Dr HU17 ....154 A1
Baslow Rd DN15 ....150 B6
Bassett Cl
  1 Broughton DN20 ...97 B3
  Selby YO8 ....148 C3
Bassett Rd 2 DN35 ..103 D2
Bate La DN14 ....78 A4
Bateson Cl YO10 ....131 C1
Bath St DN32 ....153 A5
Baths Hall The DN15 .150 F7
Bathurst St 8 HU3 ...145 D5
Batley Cl HU9 ....142 C2
Battersea Cl HU8 ...141 F5
Battery Rd HU12 .....72 A4
Battery St DN40 ......87 C1
Battle Gn DN9 ....105 D4
Battleflats Way YO41 .15 D2
Batty La DN14 ....65 A4
Bawtry Cl YO8 ......148 D3
Bawtry Rd Hatfield DN7 .92 F3
  Selby YO8 ....148 D3
Baxter Gate HU12 ....72 D7
Bay Prim Sch YO16 .122 E4
Bay View Ave HU18 .134 C6
Bayard St DN21 .....117 B1
Bayle Mus★ YO16 ..122 D4
Baygate 6 YO16 ....122 D4
Baynard Ave HU16 ..139 A6
Bayons Ave 13 DN33 .113 D8

Baysdale HU7 ....140 F6
Baysdale Ave YO10 ..131 D3
Baysdale Rd DN16 ...151 D1
Baysgarth House Mus★
  DN18 ....84 F8
Baysgarth L Ctr DN18 .84 F8
Baysgarth Sch DN18 ..84 F8
Baysgarth View DN18 .84 F7
Bayswater Ct HU8 ..141 E5
Bayswater Pl 2 DN33 .113 E8
Baytree Ave DN34 ...152 A2
Beach Holt La DN37 ..101 D2
Beacon Ave
  14 Barton-upon-Humber
    DN18 ....84 E8
  Cleethorpes DN35 ..153 D2
Beacon Ct 5 DN35 ...153 D2
Beacon Hill★ DN10 ..116 A1
Beacon La YO25 ......21 B8
Beacon Rd
  Bridlington YO16 ....123 A6
  Millington YO42 .....17 B1
Beacon View YO43 ...40 B1
Beaconsfield HU12 ...74 F6
Beaconsfield Mews
  YO24 ....129 D3
Beaconsfield St
  1 Kingston upon Hull
    HU5 ....140 D2
  York YO24 ....129 D3
Beaconthorpe Rd
  DN35 ....153 E3
Beadlam Mews HU5 .139 E4
Beadle Garth 7 YO23 132 B2
Beaford Ct DN17 ....150 C4
Beagle Cl 12 DN20 ...97 D8
Beagle Croft YO41 ...15 C1
Beagle Ridge Dr 9 YO41 129 C1
Beagle Spinney YO41 .15 C1
Beal La Beal DN14 ...61 D4
  Cridling Stubbs WF11 .61 C5
Bealey's La YO25 ....32 B1
Beamsley Way 18 HU7 .56 F5
Bean Gdns 3 DN14 ..78 C8
Bean St HU3 ....145 C6
Beanland La YO32 ...14 C2
Bean's Way YO31 ...131 B8
Beatty Ave 13 DN33 .113 E8
Beauchamp Wlk DN16 151 B5
Beauchief Gdns DN16 151 A4
Beaufort Ave HU18 ..134 C2
Beaufort Cl
  Kingston upon Hull HU3 145 D6
  York YO10 ....131 B3
Beaufort Cres 5 DN35 103 B1
Beaufort St 5 DN17 .117 B2
Beaulah Villas 1 DN18 .84 A7
Beaulahland 2 DN18 ..84 A7
Beaulieu Cl 1 YO32 ..127 F5
Beaulieu Ct
  Bridlington YO16 ....122 F7
  5 Kingston upon Hull
    HU9 ....142 A3
Beaumonde Ct DN36 114 A5
Beaumont Cl
  Goole DN14 ....149 B6
  3 Kingston upon Hull
    HU9 ....146 D7
Beaumont Pl YO8 ...148 A2
Beautiman Ct HU6 ..140 A5
Beaver Rd HU17 ....137 B4
Beaverdyke YO30 ...126 F1
Beccles Cl HU8 .....142 B6
Beck Bank HU16 ....139 C6
Beck Cl 6 Elvington YO41 .27 B2
  Keelby DN41 ....101 A4
Beck Farm Mews
  DN37 ....113 B6
Beck Garth 12 HU12 ..72 D7
Beck Hill
  6 Barton-upon-Humber
    DN18 ....84 F8
  14 Bridlington YO16 ..122 E2
  1 Bridlington YO15 ..122 E2
Beck La Appleby DN15 .83 D1
  5 Barrow upon Humber
    DN19 ....85 D8
  Broughton DN20 .....97 E3
  Easington HU12 .....90 F6
  Redbourne DN21 ....108 F2
  Scunthorpe DN16 ....96 D2
  Wheldrake YO19 .....38 A8
Beck Rd
  Cottingham HU16 ....138 E6
  North Cave HU15 ....53 D2
  Willerby HU10 ....138 D1
Beck Row YO41 ......16 D5
Beck Side
  Barmby Moor YO42 ...28 D3
  Great Driffield YO25 .124 F4
  Hibaldstow DN20 ...108 F5
  Skelton YO30 ....126 C4
Beck St HU12 ....90 F6
Beck View 14 YO42 ..29 A3
Beck View Rd HU17 ..137 C4
Beck Wlk 7 DN35 ...103 C1
Beckdale 4 HU7 .....141 A6
Beckett Ave DN21 ..117 C1
Beckfield La YO26 ..129 B5
Beckfield Pl YO26 ..129 B5
Beckhole Cl HU3 ....145 A6
Beckington Cl 1 HU8 .142 C7

Becklands Pk Ind Est
  YO43 ....135 C4
Becks Cl 5 YO32 ....127 C8
Becks La DN21 ......107 A3
Beckside
  Beverley HU17 .....154 C2
  4 Brough HU15 .....68 D6
  7 Elvington YO41 ...27 B2
  Hornsea HU18 .....134 C3
  Rothwell LN7 ....111 F2
  Wilberfoss YO41 ....27 F6
Beckside Cl
  4 Humberston DN35 103 C1
  Kingston upon Hull HU6 140 B7
Beckside Ct HU17 ...137 C3
Beckside N HU17 ....154 C2
Beckwith Cl YO43 ...131 C7
Bedale Ave
  Kingston upon Hull HU9 141 E1
  York YO10 ....131 D4
Bedale Ct YO43 .....135 E3
Bedale Rd
  Market Weighton YO43 135 D4
  Scunthorpe DN16 ...151 D1
Bedale Wlk YO43 ...135 E4
Bede Ave YO30 .....130 B7
Bedern YO1 ....156 C3
Bedford Gr YO15 ...122 C1
Bedford Rd
  Humberston DN35 ..103 C1
  Kingston upon Hull
    HU13 ....143 F3
Bedford St
  Grimsby DN32 ......153 A5
  Kingston upon Hull HU8 141 A1
Bedfords Fold 6 LS25 .61 A7
Beech Ave
  3 Airmyn DN14 .....64 E4
  Beverley HU17 .....136 F6
  Bishopthorpe YO23 .133 A3
  3 Flamborough YO15 ..5 A2
  14 Gainsborough DN21 117 B1
  3 Grimsby DN33 ....102 E2
  Gunness DN15 ......95 E6
  Kingston upon Hull HU8 141 C2
  1 Preston HU12 .....74 D1
  York YO24 ....129 F3
Beech Cl
  4 Broughton DN20 ..97 D3
  Burstwick HU12 .....73 A6
  2 Elvington YO41 ...27 B2
  Kilham YO25 ....9 B3
  8 Kingston upon Hull
    HU3 ....145 C5
  Market Weighton YO43 135 D4
  Sproatley HU11 .....58 C5
Beech Cres 7 DN7 ...92 C6
Beech Croft
  Barlby with Osgodby YO8 49 B6
  Driffield YO25 ......125 A5
Beech Ct
  Bishopthorpe YO23 .133 A3
  6 Pocklington YO42 .29 A4
Beech Dr
  Bridlington YO16 ....123 A6
  2 North Ferriby HU14 .69 A4
  11 Patrington HU12 ..74 D1
Beech Garth DN19 ...85 C7
Beech Glade YO31 ..127 F2
Beech Gr 1 Airmyn DN14 64 E4
  Burton upon Stather
    DN15 ....82 B5
  Camblesforth YO8 ..63 C5
  Goole DN14 ....149 D1
  Holton le Clay DN36 114 B5
  Nafferton YO25 .....125 E8
  Newland HU5 ......140 C3
  Northfield HU13 ....143 C3
  Selby YO8 ....148 C5
  1 Swanland HU14 ...69 C7
  York YO26 ....129 C4
Beech Hill Rd HU14 ..69 C7
Beech Lawn HU10 ...143 B6
Beech Pk YO19 .....49 A8
Beech Pl 5 YO32 ....14 A6
Beech Rd Brough HU15 68 C6
  Campsall DN6 ......76 E1
Beech Rise HU12 ....72 A4
Beech Tree Ave 21 DN8 93 B7
Beech Tree Cl 3 DN7 136 F7
Beech Tree La YO8 ..63 C5
Beech View
  Hutton Cranswick YO25 32 E6
  Walkington HU17 ...55 C8
Beech Way
  10 Cleethorpes DN36 103 B1
  28 Upper Poppleton YO26 12 F1
Beechcliffe Ave 1 HU6 140 E4
Beechdale HU16 ....139 C5
Beeches Ave 23 DN16 96 D2
Beeches The
  Great Driffield YO25 125 A4
  Pocklington YO42 ...29 A4
Beechfield
  Kingston upon Hull HU6 140 B6
  Newton-on-Ouse YO30 12 B6
Beechfield Cl YO32 ..127 F5
Beechfield Ct DN34 .152 C1
Beechfield Dr HU10 .138 C2
Beechfield Rd DN7 ...92 C4
Beechlands 9 YO25 .124 F3
Beechway HU17 ....151 B3
Beechwood HU18 ...134 D1
Beechwood Ave
  25 Grimsby DN33 ...102 C2

Beechwood Ave continued
  3 Immingham DN40 ..87 C1
Beechwood Cl 9 DN33 .92 A1
Beechwood Cres 3
  DN20 ....97 E4
Beechwood Dr
  Scawby DN20 ......108 E8
  3 Scotter DN21 ....107 C3
Beechwood Glade 7
  YO24 ....129 B1
Beechwood La 10 YO25 124 F2
Beechwood The YO25 125 A3
Beechwood Views
  HU12 ....60 B1
Beeford CE VC Prim Sch
  YO25 ....22 C1
Beeford Gr HU6 .....139 F5
Beeford Rd YO25 ....22 F1
Beeforth Cl 9 YO32 .127 D5
Beeley Rd DN32 ....153 C2
Beel's Rd DN41 .....101 E8
Beelsby Rd DN37 ...112 C3
Beesby 22 DN35 ....103 C2
Beesby Medieval Village★
  DN36 ....120 E7
Beesby Rd DN17 ....150 E1
Beeson Gr DN31 ....152 C5
Beeson St DN31 ....152 C5
Beggar Hill DN21 ...107 D5
Beilby St HU3 ....144 F4
Belcombe Way 1 YO30 130 A7
Beldevere Pk HU18 .134 C6
Belfry Ct HU8 ....142 B6
Belgrave Cl 6 Belton DN9 94 E1
  Belton DN9 ....105 E8
Belgrave Dr
  Goole DN14 ....149 F5
  Hornsea HU18 .....134 C5
  Kingston upon Hull HU4 144 D5
  7 North Cave HU15 .53 D3
Belgrave Rd
  Bridlington YO16 ...122 D1
  1 Grimsby DN33 ...102 C1
Belgrave Sq 1 DN15 .151 B7
Belgrave St YO31 ...130 C7
Belgravia 8 DN14 ...149 C4
Bell Cl Haxby YO32 ..127 C8
  Kingston upon Hull HU7 141 C5
Bell Hall★ YO19 ....36 E6
Bella La Cawood YO8 .48 A7
  Foggathorpe YO8 ...51 B7
  Rawcliffe DN14 .....64 A2
Bell Mills YO25 .....125 A4
Bellamy Ct HU9 ....146 C7
Bellasize La HU15 ...66 C6
Bellasize Pk HU15 ..66 D8
Bellbutts View 1 DN21 107 B3
Bellcroft La HU12 ...72 E4
Bellcroft Rd HU12 ...72 F5
Bellcross La 7 DN14 .65 D7
Belle Vue St YO10 ..130 E3
Belle Vue Terr
  19 Thorne/Moorends DN8 93 A8
  York YO10 ....130 E3
Belleisle Rd 12 DN34 102 B3
Bellfarm Ave YO31 ..130 E8
Bellfield Ave 5 HU8 .142 A4
Bellfield Dr HU10 ...138 D1
Bellfield Prim Sch
  HU8 ....142 A4
Bellground La YO30 ..12 D4
Bellhouse Way YO24 132 B8
Bellingham Rd DN16 .151 D3
Bellmans Croft YO23 132 B2
Bells Rd HU12 ....72 B7
Bellwin Dr DN15 ....82 A1
Bellwood Cres 7 DN8 .93 A8
Bellwood Dr YO24 ..132 B8
Belmont DN36 ......114 A5
Belmont Cl
  13 Cleethorpes DN35 103 B2
  3 York YO30 ....127 A1
Belmont St
  Kingston upon Hull HU9 146 D8
  Scunthorpe DN16 ...151 A2
Belper Ct
  17 Cleethorpes DN32 153 A5
  3 Scunthorpe DN15 150 B6
Belprin Rd HU17 ....137 B5
Belshaw La DN9 .....94 A1
Belt Rd The DN21 ...117 C2
Beltham Gn HU16 ...138 F4
Belthorn La DN17 ...81 F1
Belthorpe La YO42 ..16 B1
Belton All Saints CE Prim Sch
  DN9 ....94 E2
Belton Cl 4 HU8 ....142 B5
Belton Fields DN9 ...94 D1
Belton Gr 7 DN33 ..102 D2
Belton Rd Belton DN9 .95 A1
  Epworth DN9 ....105 E2
  Sandtoft DN9 ....94 B3
Belvedere Cl YO15 ..11 B4
Belvedere Cres DN14 149 B6
Belvedere Dr
  Kingston upon Hull
    HU11 ....142 D6
  Scunthorpe DN17 ...150 E3
  7 Thorne/Moorends DN8 79 B4
Belvedere Gr YO15 ..11 B4
Belvedere Par YO15 .11 B4
Belvedere Rd
  Bridlington YO15 ....11 B4

Belvedere Rd *continued*
Kingston upon Hull
HU13 .....143 F2
Belvoir Ave 8 YO41 .....27 B2
Belvoir Rd DN35 .....103 B1
Belvoir St HU5 .....145 C8
Belwood Dr DN9 .....94 E2
Bempton Cl YO16 .....122 E6
Bempton Cliffs Nature Reserve* YO15 .....4 D4
Bempton Cres YO16 .....122 E6
Bempton Dr YO16 .....122 E6
Bempton Gdns YO16 .....122 E6
Bempton Gr
Grimsby DN32 .....153 A1
Kingston upon Hull HU5 .....144 D8
Bempton La
Bempton YO16 .....4 B1
Bridlington YO16 .....122 D8
Bempton Oval YO16 .....122 E6
Bempton Prim Sch YO15 .4 C4
Bempton Sta YO16 .....4 C2
Bemrose Gr YO16 .....122 E5
Bemrose Way DN31 .....152 C4
Bence The YO42 .....17 C3
Benedict Ave YO8 .....148 E4
Benedict Cl 2 HU4 .....144 A2
Benedict Rd HU4 .....144 A2
Beningborough Hall & Gdns* YO30 .....12 B5
Beningbrough La YO30 .12 D5
Benjy La YO19 .....37 E7
Bennetland La HU15 .....66 C7
Bennett Dr DN15 .....83 A4
Bennett Rd
Cleethorpes DN35 .....153 D3
Scunthorpe DN16 .....151 C3
Benningholme La
HU11 .....45 D2
Bennymoor La YO8 .....49 C4
Benson Ct LN11 .....121 C4
Bentley Ct HU3 .....145 A5
Bentley Gr HU6 .....139 F4
Bentley La DN38 .....110 E7
Bentley St DN35 .....153 E2
Berea The DN34 .....152 C1
Beresford Ave
Hornsea HU18 .....134 D2
Kingston upon Hull HU6 .....140 D4
Beresford Terr YO23 .....130 C1
Beretun Gn 11 DN18 .....84 E8
Bergen Way HU7 .....140 D6
Berkeley Dr
3 Beverley HU17 .....136 E1
32 Hedon HU12 .....72 D7
Berkeley Ind Est DN15 .150 C8
Berkeley Jun & Inf Sch
DN15 .....150 D8
Berkeley Rd DN35 .....103 D1
Berkeley St
1 Kingston upon Hull
HU3 .....145 D8
Scunthorpe DN15 .....150 F8
Berkeley Terr YO26 .....129 E5
Berkshire Cl 4 HU17 .....55 F8
Berkshire St HU8 .....141 C1
Bermondsey Dr HU5 .....144 E8
Bermuda Ave HU11 .....45 D2
Bernadette Ave HU4 .....144 B5
Berners Rd 15 DN35 .....103 D1
Berridge La DN14 .....78 A6
Berriman's La YO25 .....9 B3
Berryman Way HU13 .....144 A3
Berwick Ct 5 DN40 .....87 C1
Beside the Seaside Mus* YO16 .....122 E2
Bessacarr Ave HU10 .....138 F1
Bessemer Way DN15 .....96 D7
Bessingby Gate YO16 .....122 A2
Bessingby Gr HU9 .....142 B2
Bessingby Hill YO16 .....122 B3
Bessingby Rd YO16 .....122 C2
Bessingby Rd Ret Pk
YO16 .....122 C2
Bessingby Way YO16 .....122 C1
Bestall Rd DN32 .....153 C2
Beswick & Walton CE VC Prim Sch YO25 .....32 D3
Beswick Hall* YO25 .....32 D3
Beswick Heads YO25 .....32 C3
Beswick Rd YO25 .....32 E4
Bethell Ct 6 HU12 .....72 D7
Bethell Wlk YO25 .....125 A3
Bethlehem St DN32 .....152 D3
Bethune Ave HU4 .....144 A3
Bethune Ave W HU13 .....144 A3
Bethune Pk Prim Sch
HU4 .....144 C3
Betony Cl 4 DN15 .....96 B7
Betteras Hill Rd LS25 .....61 A8
Betula Ct HU8 .....141 E7
Betula Way DN17 .....150 C1
Between Dikes Rd YO8 .....63 F8
Between Rivers La
DN14 .....78 E7
Beverley Balk YO41 .....15 B2
Beverley Cl DN36 .....114 A5
Beverley Cres DN32 .....153 A1
Beverley Ct
11 Healing DN41 .....101 F5
Scunthorpe DN17 .....150 D3
Beverley Dr HU17 .....136 D7
Beverley Gram Sch
HU17 .....136 D2
Beverley High Sch
HU17 .....154 A4
Beverley L Ctr HU17 .....154 C2
Beverley La YO43 .....41 E2
Beverley Minst*
HU17 .....154 B2
Beverley Minst CE Prim Sch
HU17 .....136 D3
Beverley Parklands
HU17 .....154 C1
Beverley Racecourse
HU17 .....136 B4
Beverley Rd
Beeford YO25 .....22 D1
Bishop Burton HU17 .....43 B2
Great Driffield YO25 .....124 E2
Hutton Cranswick YO25 .....20 E1
Kingston upon Hull HU3 .....155 A4
Kirkburn YO25 .....124 D1
Leven HU17 .....45 A7
Market Weighton YO43 .....135 E4
Middleton YO25 .....31 D4
Newbald YO43 .....53 F8
Northfield HU13 .....143 E3
Skidby HU16 .....138 C7
South Cave HU15 .....54 A2
Watton YO25 .....32 D5
Withernwick HU11 .....46 A3
Beverley Rd Baths
HU5 .....140 D2
Beverley St DN14 .....149 C2
Beverley St Nicholas Prim Sch HU17 .....154 C2
Beverley Sta HU17 .....154 B3
Beverley Swimming Pool
HU17 .....154 B4
Bewholme Gr
4 Kingston upon Hull
HU9 .....142 B1
Kingston upon Hull HU9 .....147 B8
Bewholme La
Bewholme YO25 .....35 A8
Seaton HU11 .....35 A2
Skipsea YO25 .....23 A1
Bewholme Rd YO25 .....35 C5
Bewlay St YO23 .....130 C2
Bexhill Ave HU9 .....142 E2
Bexley Ct 18 DN32 .....153 A5
Bibbill La YO42 .....39 B5
Bibury Cl HU8 .....141 B2
Bickerton Cl HU6 .....139 F7
Bickleigh Gr 1 HU8 .....142 C6
Bideford Gr HU9 .....142 E1
Bielby Dr HU17 .....137 B3
Bigby Gr DN17 .....96 C2
Bigby High Rd DN20 .....98 C1
Bigby Hill DN38 .....99 C1
Bigby Rd 16 DN20 .....98 C2
Bigby St DN20 .....98 C2
Biggin Ave HU7 .....141 C8
Biggin Hill Prim Sch
HU7 .....141 C8
Billet La DN15 .....96 C8
Billet Mill App DN16 .....151 F3
Billet Mill Rd DN16 .....151 E5
Billinghay Ct 16 DN35 .....103 C2
Billings La YO25 .....34 E5
Bilsdale Cl YO30 .....126 E2
Bilsdale Cres 3 YO16 .....122 E7
Bilsdale Gr HU9 .....146 F8
Bilsdale Rd DN16 .....151 E1
Bilton Com Prim Sch
HU11 .....142 E6
Bilton Gr HU9 .....142 B2
Bilton Rd HU11 .....142 D6
Binbrook Garth 2 HU7 .....57 A5
Binbrook Way 16 DN37 .....102 C4
Birch Ave Brigg DN20 .....98 B2
Grimsby DN34 .....152 A2
Birch Cl Beverley HU17 .....136 F6
5 Bridlington YO16 .....123 A6
East Ella HU4 .....144 B7
7 Gilberdyke HU15 .....66 D7
Northfield HU13 .....143 B3
4 Thorpe Willoughby YO8 .....48 B1
York YO32 .....127 D3
Birch Copse YO24 .....129 D2
Birch Dr HU10 .....138 E1
Birch Gr 16 DN21 .....117 B1
Birch La 18 YO32 .....13 E5
Birch Lea 3 HU17 .....55 B8
Birch Leigh HU3 .....145 C6
Birch Mews DN14 .....149 E6
Birch Tree Cl DN3 .....92 A4
Birch Way 4 DN38 .....99 B4
Bircham Cres 3 DN21 .....119 C8
Birchdale DN18 .....84 E7
Birches The
5 Haxey DN9 .....105 B2
Hornsea HU18 .....134 D2
Birchfield DN14 .....149 F6
Birchfield Rd 6 DN9 .....105 D6
Birchin Way DN31 .....152 B5
Birchin Way Ind Est
DN31 .....152 B5
Birchwood Ave HU4 .....144 A7
Birchwood Cl 2 DN8 .....79 A1
Birchwood Pk DN14 .....149 C2
Birchwood Rd DN16 .....151 B1
Birchwood View 21
DN21 .....117 C1
Bird La Hensall DN14 .....62 D2
Kellington DN14 .....61 F4
Birdcroft La 3 DN10 .....116 D3
Birdforth Mews 5 HU5 .139 D3
Birds Wood Nature Reserve*
DN9 .....104 F3
Birdsall Ave HU5 .....139 C2
Birdsall Cl HU16 .....138 E5
Birk La YO42 .....50 D8
Birkby Gr HU9 .....142 C2
Birkdale 14 DN37 .....113 D6
Birkdale Cl HU10 .....143 B8
Birkdale Dr 8 DN40 .....87 C2
Birkdale Gr 4 YO26 .....129 B5
Birkdale Rd DN17 .....96 B2
Birkdale Way HU9 .....146 D8
Birker La
Newton on Derwent YO41 .....27 D4
Wilberfoss YO41 .....27 F6
Birkin La WF11 .....61 B4
Birkin Rd YO8 .....61 F5
Birklands Dr HU8 .....141 E4
Birnam Ct HU6 .....140 B8
Birrel St 2 DN21 .....117 A1
Birstwith Dr YO26 .....129 E4
Birt Gr DN14 .....149 B6
Bishop Alcock Rd
HU5 .....139 D3
Bishop Blunt Cl 2
HU13 .....143 F1
Bishop Burton Coll
Bishop Burton HU17 .....43 A3
Broughton DN20 .....97 E3
Bishop Burton Rd
HU17 .....43 A4
Bishop Cockin Cl 1
HU4 .....144 A1
Bishop Ct
9 Gilberdyke HU15 .....66 D8
2 Selby YO8 .....148 B6
Bishop Gurdon Cl 4
HU13 .....143 F1
Bishop Kempthorne Clo 3
HU13 .....143 F1
Bishop La HU1 .....155 C2
Bishop La Staith HU1 .....155 C2
Bishop Temple Ct
HU13 .....143 F3
Bishop Wilton CE VC Prim Sch YO42 .....16 F2
Bishop's La LN8 .....120 A7
Bishop's Wlk DN34 .....152 C2
Bishopdike Rd YO8 .....48 A6
Bishopgate St YO23 .....156 B1
Bishophill Jun YO1 .....156 A1
Bishophill Senior YO1 .....156 B1
Bishops Croft HU17 .....154 A2
Bishops Ct YO1 .....156 B1
Bishopsfields Dr YO26 .....130 A5
Bishopsway YO10 .....131 C3
Bishopthorpe Inf Sch
YO23 .....133 A4
Bishopthorpe Pal*
YO23 .....133 B4
Bishopthorpe Rd
Bishopthorpe YO23 .....133 B5
Cleethorpes DN35 .....103 C2
Bisley Gr HU7 .....141 A7
Bismarck St YO26 .....129 E5
Bittern Cl HU4 .....144 D2
Black Bank DN17 .....106 F6
Black Dike La YO26 .....24 F8
Black Fen La YO8 .....148 C8
Black Syke La DN14 .....78 E2
Black Tup La HU11 .....45 C3
Blackburn Ave
Bridlington YO15 .....122 F3
Brough HU15 .....68 C5
Blackburn La WF11 .....61 B2
Blackdykes Rd DN9 .....106 B4
Blackfriargate HU1 .....155 C1
Blackhope Cl 14 HU7 .....57 A6
Blacklee Cl 4 YO32 .....14 B8
Blackmoor Rd DN9 .....105 D2
Blacksmith Hill DN15 .....67 E3
Blacksmiths Cl 1 DN19 .85 C7
Blacksmiths Cnr HU12 .....90 F6
Blackthorn Cl
20 Gainsborough DN21 .....117 C1
8 Newport HU15 .....52 F1
7 Scunthorpe DN15 .....96 B7
Blackthorn Ct 4 HU3 .....145 D6
Blackthorn Dr
Healing DN37 .....102 B5
York YO31 .....127 E2
Blackthorn La HU10 .....143 F7
Blackthorns The 3
DN20 .....97 D4
Blacktoft La DN14 .....66 D3
Blackwater Way 27 HU7 .56 F6
Blackwood La YO8 .....49 F7
Blackwood Rd YO8 .....49 E8
Bladon Rd YO16 .....122 E5
Bladons Wlk HU10 .....143 C8
Blaides Staithe HU1 .....155 C2
Blake Ave DN17 .....150 E3
Blake Cl HU2 .....155 A4
Blake Ct YO19 .....38 A8
Blake St YO1 .....156 B3
Blakeley Gr YO30 .....126 F3
Blakeney Lea DN35 .....103 C1
Blakeney Pl YO10 .....130 F3
Blakeys Crossing DN14 .65 A7
Bland La YO26 .....129 A4
Blandford Cl HU7 .....141 B6
Blands Hill LN8 .....120 A5
Blanket Row HU1 .....155 B1
Blankney Ct 13 DN15 .....83 A5
Blanshards La 1 HU15 .....53 D3
Blatchford YO30 .....130 B8
Blatchford Mews
YO30 .....130 B8
Blaycourt HU6 .....139 E6
Blaydes St HU6 .....140 C4
Blaydon Gr 1 DN34 .....102 C2
Bleaberry La YO41 .....16 B5
Bleachfield YO10 .....130 F2
Blenheim Cl 15 DN7 .....92 D3
Blenheim Ct
Rawcliffe YO30 .....126 D3
Scunthorpe DN16 .....96 D1
Blenheim Dr DN14 .....149 E6
Blenheim Pl 4 DN35 .....103 C2
Blenheim Rd
Beverley HU17 .....136 E1
Bridlington YO16 .....122 E3
5 Moorland Prison DN7 .104 A8
Blenheim St HU5 .....145 C8
Blenkin St HU9 .....146 B7
Bleriot Way YO30 .....127 A3
Blisland Cl 13 HU7 .....56 F5
Bloom Hill Gr 16 DN8 .....79 B2
Bloom La DN15 .....82 C1
Bloom Mill App Rd
DN16 .....97 A4
Bloomfield Ave HU5 .....144 C8
Bloomhill Cl 4 DN8 .....79 B2
Bloomhill Ct DN8 .....79 B2
Bloomhill Rd DN8 .....79 A2
Bloomsbury Ct 1 HU3 .145 D6
Bloomsbury Gdn 16
DN33 .....102 D1
Blossom Gr HU8 .....141 D8
Blossom St YO24 .....156 A1
Blossom Way 21 DN40 .....87 B1
Blossom's La HU15 .....53 C3
Blow Row DN9 .....105 E6
Blucher La HU17 .....154 C2
Blue Bridge La YO10 .....130 D2
Blue Slates Cl YO19 .....38 A8
Bluebeck Dr YO30 .....129 E8
Bluebell Cl DN15 .....151 C7
Bluebell Ct 15 DN41 .....101 F5
Blueberry Cl YO25 .....124 E2
Blueberry Ct HU4 .....144 C4
Bluestone Bottoms
HU17 .....55 A6
Bluestone Cl DN32 .....153 A4
Bluestone La DN40 .....87 B1
Blundell Ave DN35 .....153 C4
Blundell Cl HU2 .....155 A4
Blyth Cl YO8 .....148 A5
Blyth Ct DN18 .....85 A8
Blyth St 2 HU9 .....146 B7
Blyth Way DN37 .....101 E2
Blythe Wlk 1 YO16 .....122 D4
Blythorpe HU6 .....139 F8
Blyton CE Sch DN21 .....117 F6
Blyton Rd
Gainsborough DN21 .....117 B2
Laughton DN21 .....117 E8
Boardman La 6 YO25 .....34 B2
Boardman Pk 7 YO25 .....34 B2
Boatcliffe Rd YO14 .....3 D7
Boating Dyke Way 12
DN8 .....93 A8
Boatswain Croft HU1 .....155 B1
Bodiam Way DN32 .....152 F4
Bodmin Cl DN17 .....150 D4
Bodmin Rd HU7 .....140 E8
Bog La YO24 .....132 B6
Boggle La HU11 .....58 D5
Bolam La YO16 .....4 C2
Boldron Mews 7 HU5 .....139 D3
Bolingbroke Rd
Cleethorpes DN35 .....103 D2
Scunthorpe DN17 .....96 C2
Bolsover Rd DN15 .....150 B6
Bolt The 3 YO16 .....122 D4
Boltby Mews HU5 .....139 E3
Boltby Rd YO30 .....126 F2
Bolton La
Bishop Wilton YO42 .....16 E1
Wilberfoss YO41 .....28 A5
Bomber Cty Aviation Mus*
DN21 .....119 D1
Bon Accord Rd HU13 .....143 E1
Bonby Gr
11 Grimsby DN33 .....102 D2
Scunthorpe DN17 .....150 F1
Bonby La YO8 .....37 E2
Bonby Rd DN20 .....84 C1
Bond St Hedon HU12 .....72 D7
Kingston upon Hull HU1 .....155 B3
Bondane HU6 .....139 E7
Bondgate YO8 .....148 B7
Bondville Model Village*
YO15 .....123 B6
Bondyke Cl HU16 .....138 E6
Bonington Ct 7 YO26 .....129 E4
Bonnyhale Rd DN17 .....94 E6
Bontoft Ave HU5 .....139 E1
Booth Ferry Rd DN14 .....64 F6
Booth Nooking La
DN15 .....68 A3
Bootham YO30 .....156 A3
Bootham Bar* YO31 .....156 B3
Bootham Cl 1 DN7 .....92 D4
Bootham Cres
Stainforth DN7 .....92 C6
York YO30 .....156 A4
Bootham La DN7 .....92 D5
Bootham Pk Ct YO31 .....156 B4
Bootham Pk Hospl
YO31 .....156 B4
Bootham Rd 12 DN7 .....92 C6
Bootham Row YO31 .....156 B3
Bootham Sch YO31 .....156 A3
Bootham Sq YO31 .....156 B3
Bootham Terr YO30 .....156 A3
Boothferry Prim Sch
DN14 .....149 B4
Boothferry Rd HU13 .....143 B2
Boothferry Rd Ave 14
DN14 .....65 B7
Boothgate DN14 .....65 A6
Boothgate Cl DN14 .....65 A6
Boothgate Dr DN14 .....65 A6
Boothwood Rd YO30 .....126 E2
Booty La DN14 .....76 F7
Bore Tree Baulk YO19 .....26 D6
Borman's La 3 DN36 .....114 B1
Borodales HU12 .....72 C7
Borough Rd YO16 .....122 C3
Boroughbridge Rd
YO26 .....129 D5
Borrowdale HU7 .....140 F6
Borrowdale Dr YO30 .....126 F1
Borthwick Cl 3 HU7 .....57 A6
Borwick Dr HU17 .....137 C4
Bos App Rd DN16 .....151 F3
Bossington Cl 10 HU7 .....57 A5
Boston Cl 6 DN15 .....83 A5
Boston Ct 20 HU7 .....56 F5
Bosville Wlk YO16 .....122 B4
Bosworth Cl 16 DN7 .....92 D3
Botany Bay DN3 .....92 B4
Botany Bay La DN3 .....92 B4
Bothwell Gr HU9 .....147 D8
Bottesford Ave DN16 .....151 B1
Bottesford Inf Sch
DN16 .....96 D2
Bottesford Jun Sch
DN16 .....96 D2
Bottesford La DN16 .....151 B1
Bottlings The 10 DN20 .....98 C2
Boughton Ave DN15 .....150 F8
Boulevard HU3 .....145 B5
Boulevard Ave DN31 .....152 B4
Boulevard Gdns DN31 .152 B4
Boulevard Way DN31 .....152 B3
Boulevard Wlk DN31 .....152 B4
Boulsworth Ave HU6 .....140 C7
Boulton Gr HU9 .....141 E2
Boundary Rd
Bridlington YO15 .....122 C1
Grimsby DN33 .....113 E7
Bourn Mill Balk Rd
DN14 .....78 B8
Bourne St HU2 .....155 B3
Bournemouth St HU5 .....140 E2
Bournville DN14 .....149 C5
Bouthwaite Dr 13 YO26 .129 E4
Bovill Cl DN31 .....152 C3
Bow Rd HU15 .....68 E6
Bow St YO15 .....122 D1
Bowers Ave DN34 .....152 B3
Bowes Ave YO31 .....130 E5
Bowes Wlk HU5 .....139 E3
Bowfield Cl 9 DN37 .....102 B4
Bowlalley La HU1 .....155 B2
Bowland La YO42 .....38 E2
Bowland Way YO30 .....127 A1
Bowling Gn Ct YO31 .....130 D8
Bowling Gn La
4 Crowle DN17 .....94 D8
Grimsby DN32 .....152 E3
9 Hunmanby YO14 .....2 F8
York YO31 .....156 C4
Bowling Gn Rd 4 DN21 117 A1
Bowling La DN35 .....153 E2
Bowman Way 26 DN40 .....87 B1
Bowmandale DN18 .....84 E8
Bowmandale Prim Sch
DN18 .....84 E7
Bowmont Way HU17 .....56 F6
Bowness Dr YO30 .....126 E1
Bownhill La HU12 .....59 A2
Bowthorpe La YO8 .....50 B4
Bowyers Cl YO23 .....132 C4
Boyes La HU12 .....73 C4
Boynton Ave YO16 .....122 B4
Boynton Cres 4 DN15 .....83 A5
Boynton Garth YO25 .....124 D3
Boynton La DN14 .....64 A1
Boynton Prim Sch
YO16 .....10 E7
Boynton St 1 HU3 .....145 C4
Brabbs Ave 2 DN7 .....92 E4
Bracken Cl
Gainsborough DN21 .....117 A2
York YO32 .....127 F4
Bracken Heen Cl 4 DN7 .92 D4
Bracken Hill
Skirlaugh HU11 .....45 E2
2 York YO10 .....131 C3
Bracken La YO25 .....32 A5
Bracken Pk 20 DN33 .....113 E8
Bracken Pl 4 DN37 .....102 B3
Bracken Rd
Great Driffield YO25 .....124 D3
York YO24 .....132 F7
Brackendale Cl 1 HU7 .141 B4
Brackenhill Ave YO8 .....148 A4
Brackenhill La YO8 .....148 A3
Brackenhill Rd DN9 .....105 E2
Brackenhills YO26 .....12 F1
Brackenholmes Rd
DN15 .....83 A2
Brackenwoods HU20 .....55 A4
Brackley Cl HU8 .....141 B2
Bracon DN9 .....94 F2
Bracon Cl DN9 .....94 E2
Bradford Ave
Cleethorpes DN35 .....103 C2
Kingston upon Hull HU9 .....142 E2
Bradford Rd 20 DN40 .....87 B1
Bradgate Pk 30 HU7 .....56 F5
Bradley & Dixon Woods Nature Reserve*
DN37 .....113 C8

Bradley Cres YO23 ... 24 D6
Bradley Dr YO24 ... 132 C8
Bradley La YO23 ... 24 C5
Bradley Rd DN37 ... 102 C1
Bradley St DN32 ... 152 E4
Bradman Ct 3 DN32 ... 153 A5
Bradwell Cl 3 DN18 ... 84 E8
Braemar Ave HU6 ... 140 B6
Braemar Ct YO25 ... 34 C8
Braemar Rd DN35 ... 103 C2
Braeside Gdns YO24 ... 129 E3
Braeton La 5 DN33 ... 113 F8
Braid Hill Way HU7 ... 57 B5
Braids Wlk HU10 ... 143 B8
Brailsford Cres YO30 ... 130 A8
Braithegayte YO19 ... 37 F8
Braithwaite La DN7 ... 92 A7
Bramar Rd 26 DN7 ... 92 D4
Bramble Dene YO24 ... 132 D7
Bramble Garth 4 HU17 ... 136 F7
Bramble Hill HU17 ... 136 E1
Bramble Way
24 Brigg DN20 ... 98 B2
15 Humberston DN35 ... 103 C1
Brambles 8 YO8 ... 48 B1
Brambles The 2 DN19 ... 85 C8
Bramhall St DN35 ... 153 C3
Bramham Ave YO26 ... 129 A3
Bramham Gr YO26 ... 129 A3
Bramham Rd YO26 ... 129 A2
Bramley Ave YO8 ... 49 B5
Bramley Cl DN18 ... 69 F1
Bramley Cres 8 DN16 ... 96 D1
Bramley Ct 16 DN21 ... 117 C1
Bramley Garth YO31 ... 131 B6
Bramley Gr 6 DN21 ... 107 C3
Brampton Way DN35 ... 103 B2
Bramwith La DN7 ... 92 A6
Brandesburton Hospl
YO25 ... 34 B2
Brandesburton Prim Sch
YO25 ... 34 B2
Brandesburton St
HU3 ... 145 B7
Brandon Ct 4 HU8 ... 141 C1
Brandon Gr YO32 ... 128 E3
Brandon Rd DN15 ... 150 D6
Brandon Way 24 HU7 ... 56 F6
Brandsby Gr
Kingston upon Hull HU9 ... 142 E3
York YO31 ... 127 E2
Brankwell Cres 21 DN17 ... 96 C2
Bransdale Gr HU9 ... 146 F8
Bransdale Rd
Bridlington YO16 ... 122 E7
Scunthorpe DN16 ... 151 D1
Bransholme Dr YO30 ... 127 A2
Bransholme Rd HU7 ... 57 B5
Brant Rd DN15 ... 150 E6
Brantingham Cl 5
HU16 ... 138 E6
Brantingham Rd HU15 ... 68 C7
Brantingham Wlk
HU5 ... 139 C2
Branton Pl YO26 ... 129 A3
Brats La LN8 ... 120 B5
Bratt La YO42 ... 29 E3
Bravener Ct YO30 ... 12 B6
Bray Cl 11 DN33 ... 102 D1
Bray Gate YO42 ... 16 E2
Bray Rd YO10 ... 133 F8
Brayton CE VC Sch
YO8 ... 148 A2
Brayton Coll YO8 ... 148 A3
Brayton Com Jun Sch
YO8 ... 148 A2
Brayton Junc YO8 ... 148 C1
Brayton La YO8 ... 148 B1
Brazil St HU9 ... 146 C8
Breamer La HU11 ... 35 A2
Breary Cl YO24 ... 129 F1
Breck La HU15 ... 53 B3
Brecks La
Kirk Sandall DN3 ... 92 A2
Strensall YO32 ... 14 B7
York YO32 ... 127 F4
Brecksfield YO30 ... 126 C5
Breckstreet La YO42 ... 39 C3
Brecon Dr 22 HU7 ... 56 F6
Brecon St HU8 ... 141 B1
Breeze La YO25 ... 22 D1
Breezemount Ct 4 DN7 ... 92 C6
Breighton Rd
Bubwith YO8 ... 50 D6
Wressle YO8 ... 50 C3
Bremerhaven Way 24
DN33 ... 102 C2
Brendon Ave HU8 ... 141 B3
Brent Ave HU8 ... 142 B6
Brentwood Cl HU15 ... 68 B6
Brentwood Cres YO10 ... 131 C2
Brereton Ave DN35 ... 153 C4
Brereton Cl HU17 ... 136 E6
Bretel Wlk YO16 ... 122 B4
Bretherdale HU7 ... 140 F6
Brethergate DN9 ... 105 B2
Brett St YO16 ... 122 C3
Bretton Ave DN14 ... 149 F5
Bretton Cl 5 DN7 ... 92 D3
Brevere Rd HU12 ... 72 D7
Brewery Gdns DN17 ... 94 D8
Brewery Rd DN17 ... 94 D8
Brewster Ave 17 DN40 ... 87 C1
Breydon Ct 4 DN15 ... 82 B4
Brian Ave
Cleethorpes DN35 ... 103 B2
Scunthorpe DN16 ... 151 C1
Waltham DN37 ... 113 D6
Briar Ave YO26 ... 129 B4
Briar Cl 4 Newport HU15 ... 52 F1
South Killingholme DN40 ... 86 F3
Briar Cliffe YO8 ... 148 A3
Briar Dr YO31 ... 127 F2
Briar Garth YO25 ... 124 D3
Briar La
4 Grimsby DN33 ... 113 D8
Healing DN41 ... 101 F5
Briar Way DN15 ... 96 B7
Briarfield Rd HU5 ... 139 F2
Briars La DN7 ... 92 C7
Briars The HU13 ... 143 E3
Briarsfield YO42 ... 28 D4
Briarwood Cl YO8 ... 61 F7
Brick Dike La HU20 ... 54 C5
Brick Kiln Balk YO16 ... 122 A1
Brick Kiln La YO8 ... 62 D6
Brick La DN40 ... 86 E5
Brick Lands La YO8 ... 62 F4
Brick Rd HU12 ... 88 F6
Brickenhole La DN10 ... 116 C3
Brickhill La YO8 ... 63 F4
Bricknell Ave HU5 ... 139 E3
Bricknell Prim Sch
HU5 ... 139 F2
Brickyard La
Melton HU14 ... 68 F4
Walkeringham DN10 ... 116 B3
Wrawby DN20 ... 98 C3
Bridge Cl Haxby YO32 ... 127 C7
Kingston upon Hull HU9 ... 146 D6
Bridge Cres DN14 ... 64 C8
Bridge Ct YO8 ... 148 D6
Bridge Gdns DN31 ... 152 A5
Bridge Hill DN7 ... 92 C6
Bridge La Cadney DN20 ... 109 C6
5 Great Driffield YO25 ... 124 F4
Horkstow DN18 ... 83 F5
Pollington DN14 ... 77 F6
Rawcliffe DN14 ... 79 B8
York YO30 ... 156 B4
Bridge Rd Airmyn DN14 ... 149 A8
Bishopthorpe YO23 ... 132 F3
Broughton DN20 ... 97 F5
South Cave HU15 ... 53 F1
Bridge St
7 Bridlington YO15 ... 122 E2
10 Brigg DN20 ... 98 B2
Goole DN14 ... 149 C3
Great Driffield YO25 ... 124 E4
Pocklington YO42 ... 29 A4
Thorne/Moorends DN8 ... 93 A8
York YO1 ... 156 B2
Bridgegate DN14 ... 65 A7
Bridgegate Dr HU9 ... 146 C6
Bridges Ct YO8 ... 148 D6
Bridges La YO42 ... 38 E4
Bridges Rd DN17 ... 150 E3
Bridges The DN18 ... 84 F8
Bridgeview Specl Sch
HU13 ... 143 D1
Bridgewater Rd DN17 ... 150 D4
Bridle Way 1 YO26 ... 129 A3
Bridle Wlk YO8 ... 148 C4
Bridles The
9 Goxhill DN19 ... 86 A8
Kingston upon Hull HU3 ... 144 F2
Bridlington & District Hospl
YO16 ... 122 B3
Bridlington Ave HU2 ... 155 B4
Bridlington Balk YO25 ... 34 A8
Bridlington Bay Rd
YO16 ... 10 E4
Bridlington Harbour Heritage
Mus★ YO15 ... 122 F2
Bridlington Leisure World
YO15 ... 122 F2
Bridlington Rd
Barmston YO25 ... 22 F6
Brandesburton YO25 ... 34 C3
Flamborough YO15 ... 4 F1
Hunmanby YO14 ... 3 A7
Sledmere YO25 ... 7 C4
1 Stamford Bridge YO41 ... 15 D2
Ulrome YO25 ... 23 A2
Wold Newton YO25 ... 2 A4
Bridlington Sch YO16 ... 122 C3
Bridlington Sports Ctr
YO16 ... 122 B4
Bridlington St YO14 ... 2 F8
Bridlington Sta YO15 ... 122 D2
Bridport Cl HU7 ... 141 C7
Bridport Wlk DN17 ... 150 C4
Brier La YO8 ... 64 A4
Briergate YO32 ... 127 C7
Brierholme Carr Rd
DN7 ... 92 F5
Brierholme Cl DN7 ... 92 F5
Brierholme Ings Rd
DN7 ... 92 F5
Brierley Cl
10 Howden DN14 ... 65 A7
Snaith DN14 ... 78 C8
Brigg Dr HU13 ... 143 F3
Brigg Farm Ct YO8 ... 63 D5
Brigg La YO8 ... 63 D5
Brigg Prep Sch DN20 ... 98 C1
Brigg Prim Sch DN20 ... 98 C2
Brigg Rd
Barton-upon-Humber
DN18 ... 84 E5
Broughton DN20 ... 97 F3
Cadney DN20 ... 109 C7
Grasby LN7 ... 111 A6
Hibaldstow DN20 ... 108 F6
Messingham DN17 ... 107 D7
North Kelsey LN7 ... 110 A5
Brigg Rd *continued*
Scunthorpe DN15 ... 151 C7
South Kelsey LN7 ... 110 A1
Wrawby DN20 ... 98 D3
Brigg Sta DN20 ... 98 C1
Briggate Dr DN17 ... 107 D7
Briggs St YO31 ... 130 C7
Brigham Ct HU17 ... 154 B4
Brigham Gr HU9 ... 142 B1
Brigham La
Brigham YO25 ... 33 E8
Foston YO25 ... 21 E1
Brighowgate DN34 ... 152 D2
Bright Cres 7 YO15 ... 122 F3
Bright St
Kingston upon Hull HU8 ... 146 B8
York YO26 ... 129 F5
Bright Wlk YO8 ... 148 B6
Brighton St HU3 ... 145 A3
Brigsley Rd DN37 ... 113 D6
Brimington Rd HU10 ... 138 F2
Brimley HU17 ... 136 C5
Brind La DN14 ... 50 F2
Brindlegate 4 YO42 ... 29 A4
Brindley St HU9 ... 141 E2
Brindleys La DN14 ... 50 F3
Brinkworth Terr 1
YO10 ... 130 E3
Brisbane St HU3 ... 145 D5
Bristol Rd
Kingston upon Hull HU5 ... 144 C8
Scunthorpe DN17 ... 150 C5
Britannia Cres 7 DN34 ... 102 B3
Britannia Ct 10 YO16 ... 122 F2
Britannia Gdns 7 HU5 ... 140 E2
Britannia Rd DN14 ... 149 A2
Britannia Way DN14 ... 149 B3
Britton Cl DN17 ... 81 D3
Brixham Ct
5 Kingston upon Hull
HU3 ... 145 A5
Waltham DN33 ... 113 E7
Brixton Cl HU8 ... 141 E5
Broach La Heck DN14 ... 62 D1
Kellington DN14 ... 61 F3
Broach Rd Heck DN14 ... 77 D8
Hensall DN14 ... 62 C1
Broad Acres YO32 ... 127 C7
Broad Balk YO17 ... 6 A5
Broad Highway YO19 ... 37 F8
Broad La
Appleton Roebuck YO23 ... 36 A6
6 Beal DN14 ... 61 D4
Catton YO41 ... 27 C7
Cawood YO8 ... 48 A6
Gilberdyke HU15 ... 66 C8
Howden DN14 ... 65 B6
Rufforth YO23 ... 129 A2
Sykehouse DN14 ... 78 B4
Wistow YO8 ... 48 A5
Broad La Cl 5 HU16 ... 139 B7
Broad Manor YO42 ... 29 A3
Broad Oak
Kingston upon Hull
HU11 ... 142 D6
Sutton-on-the-Forest
YO61 ... 13 D8
Broad Oak La 18 YO32 ... 13 E5
Broadacre Pk 1 HU15 ... 68 D5
Broadacre Prim Sch
HU7 ... 56 F6
Broadacres
Carlton DN14 ... 63 D3
Keyingham HU12 ... 73 D4
Broadacres Ave DN14 ... 63 D3
Broadacres Garth
DN14 ... 63 D3
Broadbent Gate Rd
DN8 ... 79 B1
Broadgate HU17 ... 136 B1
Broadland Dr 4 HU9 ... 142 A3
Broadlands YO19 ... 38 A8
Broadlands Cl 33 DN7 ... 92 D4
Broadley Ave HU10 ... 143 D6
Broadley Cl 6 HU9 ... 146 C7
Broadley Croft 3 HU15 ... 68 D5
Broadley Way HU15 ... 68 D5
Broadmanor
North Duffield YO8 ... 50 A7
Pocklington YO42 ... 29 A3
Broadstairs Cl 1 HU8 ... 141 E7
Broadstone Cl HU7 ... 141 C6
Broadstone Way YO30 ... 126 E3
Broadwater Dr 34 DN7 ... 92 D4
Broadwaters 1 HU7 ... 56 E5
Broadway Goole DN14 ... 149 D4
5 Grimsby DN34 ... 102 B2
Hatfield DN7 ... 92 C3
Hornsea HU18 ... 134 D4
7 Keelby DN41 ... 101 A5
Scunthorpe DN16 ... 151 A2
York YO10 ... 133 E8
Broadway Dr 9 HU9 ... 142 A3
Broadway Gr 3 YO10 ... 133 E8
Broadway Nook DN7 ... 92 C3
Broadway The 8 HU9 ... 142 A3
Broadway W YO10 ... 133 D8
Brock Cl 1 DN33 ... 102 E1
Brockadale Nature Reserve★
WF8 ... 76 B4
Brockenhurst Ave
HU16 ... 139 D6
Brockenhurst Rd 7 DN7 ... 92 E4
Brockfield Pk Dr YO31 ... 127 F2
Brockfield Rd YO31 ... 127 E2
Brockle Bank Ct 9 HU12 ... 58 C1
Brocklesby Cl 5 HU13 ... 144 A3
Brocklesby Junc
DN39 ... 100 B8
Brocklesby Pk Sch
DN41 ... 100 E4
Brocklesby Pl 11 DN34 ... 102 C2
Brocklesby Rd
10 Grimsby DN34 ... 102 C2
Scunthorpe DN17 ... 150 F1
Ulceby DN39 ... 100 B8
Brockley Cl HU8 ... 141 E6
Brockton Cl HU3 ... 144 F5
Broc-o-bank 1 DN6 ... 76 E2
Bromley St
Kingston upon Hull HU2 ... 155 B4
2 York YO26 ... 129 F5
Brompton Cl HU5 ... 139 E2
Brompton Ct 4 HU3 ... 140 D1
Brompton Rd YO30 ... 130 A7
Bromwich Rd HU10 ... 143 F8
Bronte Ct HU6 ... 140 C7
Bronte Wlk YO16 ... 122 B4
Bronzegarth DN32 ... 153 B1
Brook La DN20 ... 98 A1
Brook St
Great Driffield YO25 ... 124 F4
Hemswell DN21 ... 119 A2
Kingston upon Hull HU2 ... 155 A3
Selby YO8 ... 148 C4
York YO31 ... 156 B4
Brookdale Rd DN17 ... 150 D2
Brooke Dr HU18 ... 134 C2
Brooke St DN8 ... 93 A8
Brookes Cl DN21 ... 108 B1
Brookfield Cl
Carnaby YO16 ... 10 E4
1 Kingston upon Hull HU7 ... 56 F5
8 Thorne/Moorends DN8 ... 93 A8
Brookfield Rd DN33 ... 102 D1
Brookland Rd YO16 ... 122 C4
Brooklands
2 Broughton DN20 ... 97 E3
Kingston upon Hull HU7 ... 141 C5
York YO10 ... 131 D4
Brooklands Ave
Broughton DN20 ... 97 D4
Cleethorpes DN35 ... 103 D3
Brooklands Cl HU17 ... 137 A6
Brooklands Pk HU16 ... 139 A5
Brooklands Rd HU5 ... 144 E8
Brooklyn Dr DN36 ... 114 D8
Brooklyn St HU5 ... 140 D3
Brookside 2 HU15 ... 68 D6
Brookside Cl YO42 ... 28 D3
Broom Gr DN16 ... 151 B4
Broome Cl YO32 ... 127 F5
Broome Way YO32 ... 128 A5
Broomfield Way YO25 ... 23 A6
Broomfleet Carr La
HU15 ... 67 B7
Broomfleet Sta HU15 ... 67 B6
Broomhead Cl 5 HU7 ... 141 E7
Broomhill Cl 23 WF11 ... 61 A2
Broomhill Cres 25 WF11 ... 61 A2
Broomhill Dr 26 WF11 ... 61 A2
Broomhill Gr 19 WF11 ... 61 A2
Broomhill Pl 22 WF11 ... 61 A2
Broomhill Sq 24 WF11 ... 61 A2
Broomhill Wlk 21 WF11 ... 61 A2
Broompark Rd DN14 ... 149 E6
Broomston La DN9 ... 104 F1
Brosley Ave DN3 ... 92 A4
Brough Prim Sch HU15 ... 68 C6
Brough Rd HU15 ... 54 A1
Brough St DN14 ... 149 D5
Brough Sta HU15 ... 68 B5
Brougham Cl YO30 ... 129 F8
Brougham St HU3 ... 144 F7
Broughton Cl 3 HU9 ... 142 A3
Broughton Inf Sch
DN20 ... 97 E3
Broughton Jun Sch
DN20 ... 97 E3
Broughton Way YO10 ... 131 B4
Brow La Kilpin DN14 ... 65 E7
Snaith DN14 ... 78 B8
Brown Cow Rd YO8 ... 63 C8
Brown Moor 22 YO41 ... 15 D2
Brown St DN31 ... 152 F7
Browney Croft YO10 ... 156 C1
Browning Cl
3 Kingston upon Hull
HU3 ... 145 D8
Scunthorpe DN17 ... 150 E2
Browning Rd 20 YO42 ... 29 A3
Brownlow St YO31 ... 156 C4
Brownmoor La YO61 ... 13 B8
Browns La 15 DN8 ... 93 A8
Browns Orch DN32 ... 152 D2
Bruce Cl 6 DN20 ... 97 D3
Bruce St DN15 ... 150 F7
Brucella Gr 12 HU3 ... 145 A4
Brumby Comm La
DN17 ... 150 C3
Brumby Comm Nature
Reserve★ DN17 ... 150 C3
Brumby Comp Sch
DN16 ... 151 B5
Brumby Hall★ DN17 ... 150 F5
Brumby Hospl DN16 ... 151 C4
Brumby House Dr
DN16 ... 151 A4
Brumby Jun Sch
DN16 ... 151 B4
Brumby Wood La
DN15 ... 150 D6
Brumby's Terr 4 HU9 ... 146 D7
Brumfield Ct HU17 ... 154 C4
Brunel Cl
Grimsby DN32 ... 152 F1
4 Scunthorpe DN16 ... 96 D2
Brunel Ct 12 YO26 ... 129 F5
Brunslow Cl HU3 ... 144 E5
Brunswick Ave HU2 ... 155 A4
Brunswick Cl 2 YO32 ... 14 C8
Brunswick Gr 5 HU13 ... 143 E2
Brunswick St YO23 ... 130 B1
Brunton Way DN36 ... 114 A7
Bryan Mere 3 HU17 ... 43 A2
Bryony Ct YO8 ... 148 B2
Bryson Cl DN8 ... 79 B1
Bubwith Prim Sch YO8 ... 50 D7
Buccaneer Way 16 HU15 ... 68 C5
Buck Beck Way 12
DN36 ... 103 B1
Buckfast Ct DN17 ... 150 D4
Buckingham Ave DN15 ... 96 C7
Buckingham Ct YO1 ... 156 A1
Buckingham Gr 17
DN33 ... 102 D1
Buckingham Prim Sch
HU8 ... 141 C1
Buckingham St
5 Kingston upon Hull
HU8 ... 141 C1
York YO1 ... 156 B1
Buckingham St N
DN15 ... 150 F8
Buckingham St S
DN15 ... 150 F8
Buckingham Terr YO1 ... 156 B2
Buckland Cl 3 HU8 ... 142 C7
Buckle Cl YO8 ... 50 A8
Buckle Ct YO8 ... 148 B7
Buckrose Gr YO16 ... 122 C3
Buckton Gate YO15 ... 4 C3
Buddleia Cl DN41 ... 101 F5
Bude Cl 2 DN36 ... 114 A8
Bude Pk Prim Sch HU7 ... 56 F5
Bude Rd HU7 ... 140 F8
Budworth Pk 4 HU7 ... 56 E5
Bugthorpe La YO41 ... 16 D5
Bugthorpe La Town E
YO41 ... 16 E5
Bull Alley La DN14 ... 63 B3
Bull Balk YO41 ... 27 E4
Bull Bank LN11 ... 121 F7
Bull La Everingham YO42 ... 40 C4
Huby YO61 ... 13 B7
York YO10 ... 130 F3
Bull Moor La YO60 ... 15 A8
Bull Moor Rd DN7 ... 93 A4
Bull Pasture 14 HU15 ... 53 F1
Bull Ring La 11 DN31 ... 152 D3
Buller St Grimsby DN32 ... 153 A3
Selby YO8 ... 148 B6
Bullfinch La 5 DN35 ... 103 C1
Bullivant Rd DN7 ... 92 E4
Bulmer La YO43 ... 51 E8
Bulwick Ave DN33 ... 113 E8
Bunkers Hill DN21 ... 119 B1
Bunkers Hill Cl 11 DN36 ... 114 D4
Bunting Cl YO25 ... 125 A5
Burbage Ave HU8 ... 141 C4
Burcom Ave 7 DN36 ... 114 D8
Burcott Garth HU4 ... 144 B3
Burdale Cl
Great Driffield YO25 ... 124 D3
Kingston upon Hull HU9 ... 142 B3
Burden Cl HU17 ... 154 C4
Burden Rd HU17 ... 154 C4
Burden Rd Adult Ed Ctr
HU17 ... 154 B5
Burden St HU1 ... 155 A2
Burdike Ave YO30 ... 130 A8
Burdock Rd DN16 ... 96 E2
Burgar Rd DN8 ... 93 A7
Burgate
4 Barton-upon-Humber
DN18 ... 84 F8
North Newbald YO43 ... 53 F7
Burgess Ct HU17 ... 154 B4
Burgess Rd DN20 ... 98 C2
Burgess Wlk YO24 ... 132 C8
Burghley Cl LN7 ... 111 A3
Burghley Rd DN16 ... 151 D4
Burgon Cres DN15 ... 83 B5
Burke St DN15 ... 151 A8
Burke St N DN15 ... 151 A8
Burlands La YO26 ... 24 F7
Burleigh St HU8 ... 146 C8
Burley Ave 18 DN35 ... 103 C2
Burlington Ave YO10 ... 130 F4
Burlington Cres DN14 ... 149 D4
Burlington Gdns YO16 ... 122 D3
Burlington Inf Sch
YO16 ... 122 D5
Burlington Jun Sch
YO16 ... 122 C5
Burlington Rd HU8 ... 141 D5
Burlyn Rd 3 YO14 ... 3 A8
Burma Dr HU9 ... 147 B8
Burma Rd DN16 ... 151 F6
Burn Est YO32 ... 127 E4
Burn Hall Cl YO8 ... 62 D7
Burn La YO8 ... 62 D6
Burn Rd DN15 ... 150 C7
Burnaby Cl HU17 ... 136 E6
Burnbutts La YO25 ... 32 C7
Burnby Cl HU5 ... 139 C2
Burnby Hall Gdns★
YO42 ... 29 A3
Burnby La YO42 ... 29 A3

Burnet Dr 12 DN16 ....96 E2
Burnett's Yd LN7 ....111 C4
Burney Cl HU17 ....154 A4
Burnham Ave 4 HU12 ..73 A6
Burnham La DN39 .....85 E4
Burnham Rd
  Barton-upon-Humber
  DN18 ....85 A6
  Epworth DN9 ....105 E6
  Kingston upon Hull HU4 ..144 B3
  Owston Ferry DN9 .....106 A3
  Scunthorpe DN15 .....150 D6
Burnham Reach 26
  DN35 ....103 A3
Burnham Sq DN9 .....106 A3
Burnholme Ave YO31 ..131 B6
Burnholme Com Coll
  YO31 ....131 A5
Burnholme Dr YO31 ..131 A5
Burnholme Gr YO31 ..131 A5
Burniston Gr YO10 .....131 A6
Burniston Rd HU5 .....139 E2
Burns Cl 2 YO42 ....28 E4
Burns Ct YO24 ....132 B7
Burns Gr 31 DN33 .....102 D2
Burns St DN21 ....117 A1
Burnsall Dr YO26 .....129 E4
Burnsalls Rd 5 HU12 ..72 C7
Burnside DN20 ....97 D3
Burrells Cl 11 DN9 .....105 D2
Burrill Ave YO30 .....130 B8
Burrill Dr 13 YO32 .....13 D5
Burrill La HU15 ....68 B8
Burrill Mews 2 HU5 ..139 E3
Burringham Rd DN17 ..150 B8
Burrs The HU15 ....68 B5
Bursall Sq HU12 ....89 C8
Bursar Prim Sch
  DN35 ....153 E2
Bursar St DN35 ....153 E2
Bursea La YO43 ....52 A5
Burslem St HU2 ....155 A4
Burstall Hill YO16 .....122 B5
Burstall La HU12 ....90 C5
Burstall Wlk YO16 .....122 B5
Burstwick Com Prim Sch
  HU12 ....73 B6
Burton Agnes Balk YO25 .9 F5
Burton Agnes CE VC Prim
  Sch YO25 ....10 A1
Burton Agnes Hall & Gdns*
  YO25 ....10 A2
Burton Agnes Hall*
  YO25 ....10 A2
Burton Ave YO30 .....130 B7
Burton Comm La LS25 ..61 A6
Burton Constable Hall*
  HU11 ....58 C7
Burton Ct YO30 ....156 A4
Burton Fields Cl 12 YO41 15 D2
Burton Fields Rd 4
  YO41 ....15 D2
Burton Fleming Rd
  Rudston YO25 ....9 F8
  Wold Newton YO25 .....2 B3
Burton Gates HU17 .....55 B8
Burton Gn YO30 ....130 B8
Burton Gn Prim Sch
  YO30 ....130 B8
Burton La HU18 ....134 C2
Burton Pidsea Prim Sch
  HU12 ....59 D2
Burton Rd
  Beverley HU17 ....136 C6
  Flixborough DN15 .....82 B2
  Hornsea HU18 ....134 D4
  Kilham YO25 ....9 C3
  Kingston upon Hull
  HU16 ....138 F5
  Roos HU12 ....59 F2
Burton Stone La YO30 ..156 A4
Burton upon Stather Prim
  Sch DN15 ....82 B4
Burtree Ave YO30 .....126 B4
Burwell Dr DN33 ....102 D2
Bush Cl HU4 ....144 D3
Bushey Pk HU7 ....56 F5
Bushfield Rd DN15 .....151 B5
Bushfield Rd Inf Sch
  DN16 ....151 A5
Butcher La HU11 ....77 A6
Butcher Row HU17 .....154 A3
Butcher Terr YO23 .....130 C1
Butcher's La
  Burton Fleming YO25 ..2 E3
  Withernwick HU11 .....46 D3
Butchers Row HU11 .....35 A1
Butforth La DN19 .....85 E8
Butler Pl DN35 ....153 B3
Butlers La 23 YO15 .....5 A2
Butt Balk YO25 ....9 E1
Butt Fields La DN14 .....62 F1
Butt Hedge YO26 ....24 A5
Butt Hill 22 Haxby YO32 ..13 D5
  Leconfield HU17 ....43 D6
Butt Hills* Riston HU11 ..45 C5
  Routh HU17 ....44 F5
  Wold Newton YO25 .....2 A3
Butt La Beverley HU17 ..154 A1
  Laceby DN37 ....101 F2
  North Cave HU15 .....53 E3
  Nunburnholme YO42 .....29 E3
  Snaith DN14 ....78 C8
  Thwing YO25 ....9 A8
  Tickton HU17 ....137 F8

Butt La continued
  Warter YO42 ....30 A5
  Wold Newton YO25 .....2 A3
Buttacre La YO23 .....24 D2
Butter Mkt
  10 Caistor LN7 ....111 B4
  8 Snaith DN14 ....63 C1
Butterbur Dr DN14 .....149 E7
Buttercrambe Rd YO41 ..15 C3
Buttercross Cl 3 DN41 ..101 E6
Buttercup Cl 1 HU9 ..146 D7
Butterfield Cl
  2 Laceby DN37 ....101 F1
  Snaith DN14 ....78 D8
Butterfly La YO16 .....10 F5
Butterfly Mdws HU17 ..136 E6
Buttermere Cres 3
  DN36 ....114 C8
Buttermere Ct 9 YO8 ..148 B6
Buttermere Dr YO30 ..126 E1
Buttermere Rd DN14 ..149 D5
Buttermere Way DN32 ..152 F4
Butters Cl 20 YO32 .....13 D5
Butterwick Cl 23 DN35 ..103 C2
Butterwick Rd
  Foxholes YO17 ....1 B1
  Langtoft YO25 ....8 C7
  Messingham DN17 .....107 A7
Buttfield La DN14 .....65 A6
Buttfield Rd
  Howden DN14 ....65 A6
  Kingston upon Hull
  HU13 ....143 E1
Buttle La 3 DN14 .....63 C1
Butts Cl
  Bridlington YO16 .....122 D4
  19 Stamford Bridge YO41 ..15 D2
Butts Hill YO14 ....3 C6
Butts La YO25 ....19 E2
Butts Rd DN18 ....69 F1
Butts The HU20 ....55 A4
Buxton Ct DN15 ....150 B6
Byass Ave YO16 ....122 E4
Bycroft Rd DN21 ....117 B3
Bydales La HU12 ....74 B3
Byedales 4 YO15 ....4 D3
Byfield Rd DN17 ....150 D2
Bygot Cl 1 HU17 ....43 D6
Byland Ave YO31 .....130 E8
Byland Ct 4 HU9 .....146 E8
Byram Pk Rd WF11 .....61 A4
Byrd Rd DN6 ....151 E2
Byron Ave 3 DN6 .....76 E1
Byron Cl DN17 ....150 E2
Byron Dr YO30 ....129 F8
Byron Gr DN33 ....102 E2
Byron St Goole DN14 ..149 C5
  Kingston upon Hull HU8 ..141 D2
Bywell HU9 ....147 D8
Bywood Pl 5 DN37 .....102 B3

C

Cabourne Rd 34 DN33 ..102 D2
Caddle Rd 9 DN41 .....101 A4
Cadeby Medieval Village*
  DN36 ....120 F6
Cadeleigh Cl HU7 .....141 A8
Cadman Rd HU7 ....146 C4
Cadney Rd Bigby DN20 ..98 C1
  Cadney DN20 ....109 C8
Cadogan St HU3 ....145 B5
Caedmon Cl HU17 .....131 A7
Caenby Rd
  14 Cleethorpes DN35 ..103 C2
  Scunthorpe DN17 .....150 E1
Cairnborrow 4 YO24 ..132 B7
Cairnsmore Cl HU7 .....141 A8
Caistor Ave DN16 .....96 D2
Caistor By-pass LN7 ..111 B3
Caistor Dr DN33 ....102 D2
Caistor Joint CE & Methodist
  Prim Sch LN7 ....111 B4
Caistor Rd
  Barton-upon-Humber
  DN18 ....85 A7
  Laceby DN37 ....112 E8
  Nettleton LN7 ....111 A3
  North Kelsey LN7 .....110 D4
  Rothwell LN7 ....111 E2
  South Kelsey LN7 .....110 A1
  Swallow LN7 ....112 A5
Caistor Yarborough Sch
  LN7 ....111 C4
Caithness Cl 1 YO30 ..126 E3
Calais Croft 7 HU17 ..43 A2
Calam Villas YO25 .....35 C5
Caldane HU6 ....139 E8
Caldbeck Cl 1 YO30 ..127 A1
Caldberg Mews 3 HU5 ..139 E3
Calder Ave YO26 .....129 B8
Calder Cl 35 DN40 .....87 B1
Calder Cres DN14 .....77 F6
Calder Dr DN14 ....78 B8
Calder Gn DN17 ....107 D7
Calder Gr HU8 ....142 C6
Calder Rd DN16 ....151 D2
Calder St 4 DN14 .....149 D4
Calderdale HU7 ....140 F6
Calderdale Cl 2 YO16 ..123 A7
Caledon HU9 ....142 D5
Caledonia Pk HU9 .....146 B5
Calf Cl YO32 ....127 D8
Callas 6 HU17 ....43 A4
Calver Cres DN37 .....102 B4
Calvert Cl YO32 ....127 C7
Calvert La HU4 ....144 D7
Calvert Rd HU5 ....144 D8

Calvi Ct 2 DN32 ....153 A5
Cam Gr HU8 ....142 C6
Camargue Ave DN37 ..113 E7
Cambeak Cl 3 HU7 .....56 F5
Camberwell Way HU8 ..142 A5
Camblesforth CP Sch
  YO8 ....63 C4
Camborne Gr HU8 .....141 B3
Cambrian Cl 2 YO32 ..127 F1
Cambrian Way 2 DN36 ..114 A6
Cambridge Ave
  Goole DN14 ....149 B5
  Scunthorpe DN16 .....96 D2
Cambridge Gr HU9 .....141 F1
Cambridge Pk Sch
  DN34 ....152 A1
Cambridge Rd
  Grimsby DN34 ....152 A1
  Kingston upon Hull
  HU13 ....143 F3
  Scunthorpe DN16 .....151 C2
Cambridge St
  Bridlington YO16 .....122 D3
  Cleethorpes DN35 .....153 F2
  Kingston upon Hull HU1 ..155 A2
  4 York YO24 ....130 A3
Camden St 1 HU3 .....145 B5
Camela La YO8 ....63 B6
Camelford Cl 12 HU7 ..56 F5
Camellia Cl YO25 .....124 D3
Cameron Gr YO23 .....130 C1
Camerton Gr HU9 .....141 F2
Camilla Cl HU9 ....155 C1
Camm La DN14 ....63 C3
Cammidge St 2 HU19 ..74 F7
Camp The (Earthworks)*
  YO11 ....2 C7
Campbell Ave
  26 Scunthorpe DN16 ..96 D2
  York YO24 ....129 E2
Campbell Ct HU9 .....142 A2
Campbell St 3 DN21 ..117 A1
Campbells Farm Ave
  DN15 ....95 E6
Campden Cres DN35 ..153 D3
Camperdown HU11 .....142 D6
Campey La YO42 ....39 B6
Campion Ave HU4 .....144 B2
Campions Cl 12 DN36 ..114 A5
Campions' La 6 DN36 ..114 B1
Campleshon Rd YO23 ..130 B1
Campsall Balk DN6 .....76 E1
Campsall Hall Rd 12 DN6 76 E1
Campsall Pk Rd 11 DN6 ..76 E1
Campsmount Sch DN6 ..76 D1
Canada Dr
  Cherry Burton HU17 ..43 A5
  Kingston upon Hull
  HU16 ....138 E5
Canada La LN7 ....111 C4
Canal Garth DN14 .....77 F6
Canal La
  Barmby Moor YO42 .....28 F3
  West Stockwith DN10 ..116 E5
Canal Rd
  Cottingwith YO42 .....38 C5
  Selby YO8 ....148 D4
Canal Side E HU15 .....52 E3
Canal Side W HU15 .....52 E2
Canal View Selby YO8 ..148 D3
  2 Thorne/Moorends DN8 ..93 A7
Canberra Ave DN7 .....104 A8
Canberra St HU3 .....145 D5
Candlesby Rd 4 DN37 ..102 B4
Candy Bank DN9 .....104 B5
Canham Gr YO10 .....131 D3
Canham La YO25 ....35 C5
Canning St HU1 ....155 A4
Cannon Hall La DN14 ..61 F1
Cannon Oakes Ct
  DN36 ....114 B7
Cannon St HU2 ....155 B4
Canon Lee Sec Sch
  YO30 ....130 A8
Canon Peter Hall CE Prim
  Sch DN40 ....87 C1
Canongate HU16 ....139 B7
Canons Ct YO23 ....133 B2
Canopias Cl HU3 .....145 A4
Canterbury Cl
  Beverley HU17 ....136 D1
  9 Haxby YO32 ....13 D5
  Scunthorpe DN17 .....150 D3
Canterbury Dr
  Grimsby DN34 ....152 C2
  2 Kingston upon Hull
  HU8 ....141 E7
Canterbury Rd 2 DN7 ..92 D4
Canton Villas 5 YO15 ..122 F4
Canty Nook DN38 .....110 E7
Capstan Rd HU6 ....140 C8
Capstan Way 13 DN8 ..93 A8
Captains Wlk HU1 .....155 A1
Carden Ave HU9 ....142 C2
Cardiff Ave DN36 .....114 A7
Cardigan Rd
  Bridlington YO15 .....122 D1
  Kingston upon Hull HU3 ..144 E6
Cardinal Ct 1 DN37 ..113 D7
Cardinals Cl 3 YO8 .....48 B8
Carentan Cl 6 YO8 .....148 B6
Carew St HU3 ....144 F7
Carey St YO10 ....130 D1
Carisbrooke Ave
  HU16 ....139 B6
Carisbrooke Cl 9 DN36 114 A4
Carisbrooke Manor La
  DN17 ....150 A1

Carl St YO23 ....130 C2
Carlam La HU7 ....57 A7
Carleton St 17 YO8 ..129 E5
Carlisle Rd 8 YO15 ..122 F3
Carlisle St
  29 Gainsborough DN21 ..117 B1
  Goole DN14 ....149 D4
  16 York YO26 ....129 F5
Carlton 24 HU15 ....68 C6
Carlton Ave
  Healing DN41 ....101 F5
  Hornsea HU18 ....134 C5
  York YO10 ....131 B3
Carlton Cl
  Eggborough DN14 .....61 F1
  22 Humberston DN35 ..103 D1
Carlton Ct HU17 .....154 A3
Carlton Dr HU11 ....47 B1
Carlton Rd
  Aldbrough HU11 ....46 F1
  Grimsby DN34 ....152 B2
  5 Healing DN41 .....101 F5
  Sutton upon Derwent
  YO41 ....27 C1
Carlton Rise 2 HU17 ..55 F8
Carlton St
  Bridlington YO16 .....122 D3
  Kingston upon Hull HU3 ..144 F4
  13 Scunthorpe DN15 ..151 B7
Carlton Twrs* DN14 ..63 D2
Carlton View YO8 .....148 D4
Carlton-in-Snaith CP Sch
  DN14 ....63 C3
Carmelite St YO1 .....156 C2
Carmen Cres 1 DN36 ..114 A6
Carmires Ave YO32 ..13 F5
Carnaby Ave YO16 .....122 B2
Carnaby Cl HU17 .....43 D6
Carnaby Gr
  Grimsby DN33 ....153 A1
  Kingston upon Hull HU6 ..139 E5
Carnaby Ind Est YO15 ..10 E3
Carnegie St 6 HU3 ..145 A6
Carnforth Cres DN34 ..152 A1
Carnforth Par DN34 ..152 A1
Carnot St YO26 ....129 F5
Carnoustie 13 DN37 ..113 D6
Carnoustie Cl
  Kingston upon Hull HU8 ..141 C3
  1 York YO26 ....129 B4
Carol Dickson Ct 9
  DN34 ....145 C5
Caroline Cl 5 YO24 ..129 F3
Caroline Pl HU2 ....155 B3
Carolines Pl HU2 ....155 B4
Carolines Pl HU16 .....138 B8
Carperby Mews 6 HU5 139 D3
Carr Cl Beverley HU17 ..154 C3
  13 Hemingbrough YO8 ..49 F1
Carr Dike La HU11 .....67 C7
Carr Dyke Bank DN17 ..106 D5
Carr Dyke Rd DN17 .....95 D3
Carr Inf Sch YO26 .....129 C5
Carr Jun Sch YO26 .....129 C5
Carr La Appleby DN15 ..83 D2
  Barlby with Osgodby
  YO8 ....148 F5
  Barlow YO8 ....63 C7
  Blyton DN21 ....117 A5
  Bonby DN20 ....84 B1
  Bridlington YO16 .....123 A8
  Broughton DN20 .....97 F3
  Burton Pidsea HU12 ..59 D1
  Burton upon Stather
  DN15 ....82 D4
  Eastrington DN14 .....51 F1
  Escrick YO19 ....37 B5
  Everingham YO42 .....40 A4
  Garthorpe & Fockerby
  DN17 ....81 E4
  Goole DN14 ....149 D6
  Grimsby DN32 ....153 B3
  Haxey DN9 ....105 E2
  Healing DN41 ....101 F4
  Hibaldstow DN20 .....109 A6
  Horkstow DN18 ....83 F4
  Hotham YO43 ....53 A4
  Kingston upon Hull HU1 ..155 A2
  Laxton DN14 ....65 F4
  Leven HU17 ....44 E8
  Long Drax YO8 ....63 F6
  Luddington & Haldenby
  DN17 ....81 C1
  Misterton DN10 .....116 C5
  Nafferton YO25 ....21 C4
  Newport HU15 ....52 E2
  Newton on Derwent YO41 ..27 F7
  Pocklington YO42 .....40 A8
  Redbourne DN21 .....108 F3
  Riston HU11 ....45 B5
  Seaton Ross YO42 .....39 E4
  Snaith & Cowick DN14 ..78 C7
  Stallingborough DN41 ..101 E7
  Tickton HU17 ....137 E3
  Ulceby DN39 ....86 B3
  Watton YO25 ....33 A4
  West Butterwick DN17 ..106 C8
  Wildsworth DN21 .....117 C8
  Winterton DN15 ....83 D6
  Wistow YO8 ....48 A3
  Worlaby DN20 ....98 A4
  York YO26 ....129 D5
Carr Rd
  Burton Pidsea HU12 ..59 D1
  Molescroft HU17 .....136 E8
  North Kelsey LN7 .....109 E4
Carr Side La DN7 .....92 E2

Carr St
  Kingston upon Hull HU2 ..155 B4
  Selby YO8 ....148 F4
Carrbank La YO32 .....14 E3
Carrfield YO24 ....132 C8
Carrfields DN14 ....149 D6
Carrhouse Rd DN9 .....94 D1
Carrick Gdns YO24 .....129 E3
Carrington Ave
  Hornsea HU18 ....134 C6
  Kingston upon Hull
  HU16 ....139 B6
  1 York YO26 ....129 E5
Carrington Dr
  20 Humberston DN36 ..103 D1
  Humberston DN36 .....114 D8
Carrington St 6 HU3 ..145 B5
Carrnock Ct 3 YO32 ..127 F1
Carroll Pl HU1 ....155 C3
Carron Cres YO24 .....132 B7
Carroway Cl 4 YO16 ..123 A7
Carrs Mdw Escrick YO19 ..37 B5
  Withernsea HU19 .....74 F6
Carrside 5 DN9 ....105 D7
Carson Ave DN34 .....152 B2
Carson Rd DN21 ....117 B1
Carter Ave YO31 .....130 F5
Carter Dr HU17 ....136 E7
Carter La YO15 ....5 A2
Carter St DN14 ....149 C4
Cartergate DN31 .....152 D3
Cartledge Ave DN32 ..153 B2
Cartmel Ct HU9 ....142 B2
Cartmel Gr DN32 .....153 B2
Cartwright La HU17 ..154 A1
Carver Rd DN40 ....87 C1
Cary La 4 DN20 ....98 B2
Cassbrook Dr LN11 ..121 E8
Casson's Rd 1 DN8 ..93 A8
Casswell Cl 4 DN32 ..153 A5
Casswell Cres LN11 ..121 E8
Castella Dr DN16 .....151 D7
Castle Cl Cawood YO8 ..48 A8
  1 Haxby YO32 ....13 D5
  3 Leconfield HU17 ..43 D6
Castle Cres 16 YO15 ..5 A2
Castle Ct 9 DN18 .....84 F8
Castle Dr
  1 Epworth DN9 ....105 E6
  South Cave HU15 .....53 F2
Castle Earthworks*
  YO8 ....63 F4
Castle Gn HU16 ....138 E6
Castle Hill Caistor LN7 ..111 B4
  8 Hunmanby YO14 .....2 F8
  Owston Ferry DN9 .....106 A3
Castle Hill Hospl
  HU16 ....138 D5
Castle Hill Rd 1 HU5 ..63 F5
Castle Hills* DN21 .....117 C2
Castle Hills GM Com Sch
  DN21 ....117 B1
Castle Keep DN20 .....108 F6
Castle Pk 9 HU11 .....47 C1
Castle Rd HU16 ....138 D5
Castle Rise 1 HU15 .....54 A2
Castle St Grimsby DN32 ..153 A4
  Kingston upon Hull HU1 ..155 A1
Castle View YO25 .....23 A1
Castle Way HU13 ....69 F4
Castle Wlk YO1 ....156 B2
Castledyke Prim Sch
  DN18 ....69 E1
Castledyke S 10 DN18 ..84 F8
Castledyke W 10 DN18 ..69 E1
Castleford Ave 2 DN34 102 D2
Castleford Gr HU9 .....142 E2
Castlegate YO1 ....156 B2
Castlehill Rd HU7 .....141 D8
Castleton Ave 6 HU5 ..139 E3
Castleton Rd DN15 .....150 B6
Cat La Balne DN14 .....77 E5
  Bilbrough YO23 ....24 D1
Catford Cl HU8 ....141 E5
Catfoss Rd YO25 ....35 A4
Cathcart Cl DN14 .....76 F7
Cathedral Cl 8 HU17 ..136 E1
Cathedral Ct
  Hatfield DN7 ....92 C2
  Scunthorpe DN16 .....151 A2
Catherine Gr 8 DN20 ..97 C3
Catherine McAuley Cl
  HU6 ....140 C5
Catherine St
  13 Barton-upon-Humber
  DN18 ....69 F1
  Grimsby DN32 ....152 E3
  Kingston upon Hull HU2 ..155 B4
Catkin Rd DN16 ....96 D1
Catterick Mews 8 HU5 139 D3
Catterton La LS24 .....24 A1
Cattistock Rd 27 DN35 ..103 C2
Cattle Rd DN10 ....116 A5
Catton La YO42 ....28 F4
Catwick Heads HU11 ..45 E4
Catwick La
  Brandesburton YO25 ..34 C2
  Catwick HU17 ....45 D8
Caughey St HU3 .....145 D7
Causeway Ings La
  HU12 ....73 E7
Causeway The HU15 ..154 B3
Cave Cres HU16 ....138 E5
Cave Rd HU15 ....68 B6
Cave St HU5 ....140 D1
Cave Terr 1 HU5 .....140 D1
Cavendish Cl 14 DN35 ..103 D1
Cavendish Dr 2 HU17 ..136 E1

Cavendish Gr YO10 ....131 D3
Cavendish Pk 8 HU15 ...68 C5
Cavendish Prim Sch
HU8 ....141 E4
Cavendish Rd
Kingston upon Hull HU8 ..141 D5
9 Scunthorpe DN16 ......96 D2
Cavendish Sq HU3 ....140 D1
Cavendish Way DN32 ..152 F3
Cave's La DN10 ....116 B3
Cavill Dr 12 DN14 ......65 B7
Cavill Pl HU3 ....145 D5
Cawood CE VA Prim Sch
YO8 ....48 B8
Cawood Cl HU11 ....45 D2
Cawood Cres HU11 .....45 D2
Cawood Dr HU11 ....45 D2
Cawood Rd
Stillingfleet YO19 ....36 D3
Wistow YO8 ....48 C7
Cawthorn Cl YO25 .....125 A3
Cawthorne Dr HU4 ....144 C3
Caxton Ave YO26 ......129 D6
Cayley Cl YO30 ....126 F1
Cayley Rd HU10 ....143 F6
Cayton Rd HU8 ....141 D4
Cecil Cl 10 DN21 ....107 C3
Cecil Rd 7 YO14 ....3 A8
Cecil St
24 Gainsborough DN21 ...117 B1
Goole DN14 ....149 E4
Kingston upon Hull HU3 ..144 F5
Cecile Cres DN15 .....150 E7
Cecilia Pl 3 YO24 .....130 A3
Cedar Ave
Flixborough DN15 ....96 A7
Kingston upon Hull
HU16 ....139 A6
Cedar Cl
11 Cleethorpes DN35 ....103 B1
Gainsborough DN21 .....117 A2
Hambleton YO8 ....48 B1
Hornsea HU18 ....134 D1
Kingston upon Hull
HU10 ....143 D7
Scawby DN20 ....108 F8
7 Scotter DN21 ....107 C3
Wawne HU7 ....56 F8
Cedar Cres YO8 ....48 D2
Cedar Ct
Bridlington YO16 ....123 A8
8 Hedon HU12 ....72 C7
Cedar Dr 2 DN40 ....87 C2
Cedar Glade YO19 ......26 E7
Cedar Gr
2 Aldbrough HU11 ....47 C1
Stainforth DN7 ....92 D6
York YO31 ....131 B7
Cedar Gr The HU17 ....136 C6
Cedar Rd 2 DN8 ....79 B1
Cedarwood 5 HU15 .....66 D7
Cedarwood Cl 8 YO24 .129 B1
Cedarwood Dr HU4 ....144 B7
Cedric Rd DN3 ....92 A1
Celandine Cl 8 HU5 ...139 D1
Celery Bank DN14 ......66 A4
Celtic Cl YO26 ....129 B5
Cemetery Cres 7 DN37 .101 F1
Cemetery La
North Kelsey LN7 ....110 A5
Pocklington YO42 ....29 A3
Cemetery Rd
Hatfield DN7 ....92 F4
Laceby DN37 ....101 F1
Scunthorpe DN16 ....151 B5
Winterton DN15 ....83 B5
York YO10 ....156 C1
Centenary Rd DN14 ...149 B5
Central Ave
Beverley HU17 ....154 A2
Ulrome YO25 ....23 B3
Central Parade DN34 ..152 A3
Central Promenade
DN35 ....153 F2
Central St HU2 ....140 F1
Central Way DN16 .....151 D6
Centurion Pk YO30 ....127 B2
Centurion Way
Brough HU15 ....68 C5
Clifton YO30 ....127 B3
Centurion Wlk YO43 ...135 E4
Century Rd HU12 ....72 A8
Ceylon St HU9 ....147 C7
Chadcourt HU6 ....139 E6
Chadwell Springs
DN37 ....113 C6
Chaffinch Cl DN15 ......96 B7
Chaffinch Dr 14 DN35 ..103 C1
Chaldon Cl 4 YO32 .....14 A6
Chalfont Cl HU13 .....143 D2
Chalfonts YO24 ....129 F1
Chaloner's Cres YO24 .132 D7
Chaloner's Rd YO24 ...132 D8
Chamberlain Cl HU7 ..141 D6
Chamberlain Ct HU7 ..141 D7
Chamberlain Gdns
HU8 ....141 C3
Chamberlain Rd HU8 ..141 B3
Chamberlain St HU7 ..141 D6
Chambers La 1 HU18 ..134 C4
Chamomile Cl 17 DN16 ..96 E2
Champney Rd HU17 ...154 A2
Chancel Rd DN16 ......96 D2
Chancel Wlk 8 DN20 ....97 E3
Chancery Ct
Kingston upon Hull HU5 ..144 E8
York YO24 ....129 C3
Chancery La 2 DN17 ....94 D7
Chancery Rise YO24 ...129 F3
Chancewaters 5 HU7 ...56 E5
Chandlers Cl 2 DN36 ..114 A7
Chandlers Ct HU9 .....146 C6
Chandos Rd DN17 ......150 F3
Channel Rd HU12 ....89 B6
Chanterlands Ave
HU5 ....140 A1
Chantreys Dr 18 HU15 ...68 C6
Chantry Ave 14 YO26 ....12 F1
Chantry Cl
Grimsby DN31 ....152 C3
York YO24 ....132 C8
Chantry Ct YO16 ......122 D4
Chantry Gap 11 YO26 ....12 F1
Chantry Gr 18 YO26 ......12 F1
Chantry La
Beverley HU17 ....154 B2
Bishopthorpe YO23 ......133 B4
Etton HU17 ....43 A6
Grimsby DN31 ....152 C3
Rimswell HU12 ....74 C5
Chantry Mdws 1 YO25 ....9 C3
Chantry Way 18 HU14 ....69 B7
Chantry Way E 9 HU14 ..69 B7
Chapefield Rd DN19 .....86 B7
Chapel Balk Rd YO8 ....49 F1
Chapel Baulk DN9 .....104 E1
Chapel Cl
Barrow upon Humber
DN19 ....85 D7
2 Kingston upon Hull
HU4 ....144 A1
7 Misterton DN10 ......116 C5
12 Preston HU12 ....58 C1
Rawcliffe DN14 ....64 A1
Skidby HU16 ....138 A8
Skirlaugh HU11 ....45 E2
4 Westwoodside DN9 ...105 B2
Chapel Cnr YO43 ......135 D4
Chapel Ct
Alkborough DN15 ....82 C8
7 Hibaldstow DN20 .....108 F5
Scunthorpe DN15 ....151 B8
Chapel Fields
Coniston HU11 ....57 F6
Holme-on-Spalding-Moor
YO43 ....40 A1
Chapel Fields Rd
YO26 ....129 A3
Chapel Garth
Broomfleet HU15 ....67 B5
11 Gilberdyke HU15 ......66 D8
Holme-on-Spalding-Moor
YO42 ....40 A1
Ottringham HU12 ....73 E3
Skipsea YO25 ....23 A1
3 Tetney DN36 ....114 D4
Chapel Haddlesey CE VC
Prim Sch YO8 ....62 B5
Chapel Hill 1 HU15 .....68 E6
Chapel Hill La HU15 ....68 E6
Chapel Hill Rd YO42 ....29 A4
Chapel La
Ashby cum Fenby DN37 ..113 D3
Askham Bryan YO23 ......24 F3
Barmston YO25 ....23 A6
Barnoldby le Beck DN37 ..113 B6
14 Barton-upon-Humber
DN18 ....69 E1
Brayton YO8 ....148 B1
Broughton DN20 ....97 E3
Elsham DN20 ....98 F7
10 Gainsborough DN21 ...117 A2
Habrough DN40 ....100 E8
Horkstow DN18 ....84 A5
Keadby with Althorpe
DN17 ....95 C6
18 Keyingham HU12 ......73 C4
Kilham YO25 ....9 B3
Kingston upon Hull HU1 ..155 C2
Langtoft YO25 ....8 D5
Laxton DN14 ....65 F4
Little Smeaton WF8 ......76 B3
Ludborough DN36 ....121 B6
Middleton YO25 ....31 C4
8 Misterton DN10 ....116 C5
Northorpe DN21 ....118 D8
Ottringham HU12 ....73 E3
Rawcliffe DN14 ....64 A2
Reighton YO14 ....3 E5
3 Riccall YO19 ....37 A1
Scawby DN20 ....108 E8
Skeffling HU12 ....90 C6
Swallow LN7 ....112 B5
Sykehouse DN14 ....78 A4
18 Thorne/Moorends DN8 .93 A8
Utterby LN11 ....121 C4
1 Wawne HU7 ....56 E7
West Ella HU10 ....69 C8
West/East Butterwick
DN17 ....95 D1
Whitton DN15 ....67 E3
Winterton DN15 ....83 A5
Wrawby DN20 ....98 D4
Chapel La Staith HU1 ..155 C2
Chapel Mdws 8 HU15 ...66 D8
Chapel Mews 3 HU15 ...68 C6
Chapel Rd
Broughton DN20 ....97 E3
Habrough DN40 ....100 E8
Tetney DN36 ....114 D4
Chapel Row YO10 .....156 C1
Chapel St
2 Amcotts DN17 ....81 F1
Barmby Moor YO42 ......28 D3
Bridlington YO15 ....122 E2
13 Caistor LN7 ....111 B4
Chapel St *continued*
5 Crowle DN17 ....94 D8
6 Epworth DN9 ....105 E6
6 Flamborough YO15 ....5 A2
Goole DN14 ....149 D3
Goxhill DN19 ....86 A8
Hillam LS25 ....61 B7
Kingston upon Hull HU1 ..155 A2
Lockington YO25 ....32 B2
North Kelsey LN7 ....110 A4
Scunthorpe DN15 ....151 B7
Chapel Terr YO24 .....129 C3
Chapel Way 21 DN20 ....98 C2
Chapel Wlk 4 YO19 .....37 A1
Chapelry Garth 28 HU12 .72 D7
Chapman Ave DN17 ...150 D2
Chapman Cl 1 YO32 .....14 C8
Chapman Ct DN31 .....152 D4
Chapman Gr DN35 ....153 F1
Chapman Rd DN35 ....153 D3
Chapman St HU8 ......155 C4
Chapman's La YO30 .....12 E7
Chapmans Ct YO24 ....132 D6
Chapter House St YO1 .156 B3
Chapter Wk DN20 ....97 E3
Charing Cl HU3 ....145 C8
Chariot St HU1 ....155 A2
Chariot Way 6 YO25 ....19 B6
Charles Ave
Grimsby DN33 ....102 E1
Laceby DN37 ....101 E1
17 New Waltham DN36 ...114 A7
15 Scotter DN21 ....107 C3
Charles Ct 7 DN8 ....79 B1
Charles Dr DN14 ......149 B6
Charles Hume Ct
DN32 ....153 B4
Charles Lovell Way
DN17 ....150 D4
Charles Moor YO31 ....130 F7
Charles St
Cleethorpes DN35 ....153 F1
30 Gainsborough DN21 ...117 B1
22 Hedon HU12 ....72 D7
Kingston upon Hull HU2 ..155 B3
Selby YO8 ....148 B6
Charles Wesley Dr
YO8 ....148 B2
Charlestown Way
HU9 ....146 C6
Charlotte St HU1 ......155 C3
Charlotte St Mews
HU1 ....155 B3
Charlton St
Grimsby DN31 ....152 C4
York YO23 ....130 C2
Charnock Ave HU9 ....142 A4
Charnwood Cl 29 HU7 ...56 F6
Charter Ave DN14 ......64 A1
Charter's La 4 YO25 ....34 B2
Charterfield HU11 .....142 D6
Charterhouse Dr 3
DN16 ....96 E2
Charterhouse La HU2 ..155 B3
Charterhouse The★
HU2 ....155 C3
Charters The YO8 ......49 B5
Chase Hill Rd DN40 .....86 E5
Chase Side Ct YO24 ...132 E8
Chase Specl Sch DN7 ..92 D4
Chase The
Driffield YO25 ....125 A4
2 Snaith DN14 ....78 C8
Chatham St HU3 ......144 F7
Chatsworth Cl
Beverley HU17 ....154 A1
5 Bridlington YO16 .....122 D6
Chatsworth Dr
Goole DN14 ....149 B6
16 Haxby YO32 ....13 F5
Chatsworth Pl 1 DN35 .103 B2
Chatsworth St HU5 ....145 B8
Chatsworth Terr 4
YO26 ....129 E4
Chatsworth Way 12
DN9 ....105 D2
Chatterton Cres DN15 ..96 D7
Chaucer Ave DN17 ....150 D3
Chaucer St
Kingston upon Hull HU8 ..141 C2
7 York YO10 ....130 E3
Chaumont Way 1 YO32 .14 D2
Chaytor Cl 16 HU12 .....72 D6
Cheadle Cl
Kingston upon Hull HU2 ..155 A4
Sculcoates HU2 ....140 E1
Cheapside
Kingston upon Hull HU8 ..155 C4
Waltham DN37 ....113 E5
Cheapside Rd DN37 ...113 F4
Cheapsides La HU15 ....66 D8
Checker La YO19 ....49 A7
Cheesemans Cl 9
DN37 ....113 E6
Cheesemans La 8
DN37 ....113 E6
Chelkar Way YO30 .....126 F1
Chellsway HU19 ....74 F6
Chelmer Rd HU8 ......142 B5
Chelmsford Ave DN34 .152 A1
Chelmsford Cl 6 HU9 ..142 E1
Chelmsford Pl DN34 ...152 B2
Chelsea Cl HU8 ....141 F5
Chelsea Ct 3 HU16 .....138 F5
Chelsea Wlk 1 DN35 ...103 D1
Cheltenham Ave HU7 ..141 A8
Cheltenham Cl 8 DN16 ..96 E2
Cheltenham Way
DN35 ....103 C1
Chelwood Dr 30 DN33 ..102 D2
Chelwood Rd DN17 ....150 F3
Chelwood Wlk 12 YO26 .129 E4
Chepstow Gr DN34 ....152 A1
Chequers The DN15 ...150 E7
Cheriton Cl 14 HU7 .....56 F5
Cherry Burton CE VC Prim
Sch HU17 ....43 B5
Cherry Cl
Great Driffield YO25 .....124 F2
Hornsea HU18 ....134 D1
Cherry Cobb Sands Rd
HU12 ....87 F8
Cherry Cres YO43 .....40 A1
Cherry Ct 16 HU15 ......66 D8
Cherry Dale 11 DN35 ...103 B2
Cherry Dr
Holme-on-Spalding-Moor
YO43 ....40 A1
Nafferton YO25 ....125 F6
Cherry Garth
Beverley HU17 ....154 C3
Kingston upon Hull HU3 ..145 A5
Lund YO25 ....31 F2
York YO31 ....131 B5
Cherry Gr 5 Belton DN9 ..94 E1
Belton DN9 ....105 E8
16 Poppleton YO26 ....12 F1
Scunthorpe DN16 ....151 B2
Cherry Hill La YO23 ....156 B1
Cherry Hill Pk HU12 ....74 B8
Cherry Holt 7 LN7 .....111 B4
Cherry La
Barrow upon Humber
DN19 ....85 D8
Kingston upon Hull HU8 ..141 C4
Wootton DN39 ....85 E2
York YO24 ....132 F8
Cherry Mount 1 DN16 ...96 E2
Cherry Orch
16 Epworth DN9 ....105 E6
2 Haxby YO32 ....127 D8
Cherry Orch Mews 12
YO42 ....29 A4
Cherry Paddock
4 Haxby YO32 ....127 D8
Kexby YO41 ....15 C2
Cherry Rd 4 YO14 ....3 A8
Cherry St YO23 ....156 B1
Cherry Tree Ave
1 Brigg DN20 ....98 B2
Kingston upon Hull HU8 ..141 C2
Newton-on-Ouse YO30 ....12 B6
9 Withernsea HU19 ......75 A6
York YO32 ....127 D4
Cherry Tree Cl
Bilton HU11 ....58 A3
13 Brayton YO8 ....48 D1
Cherry Tree Cres
DN34 ....102 C4
Cherry Tree Crossing
HU17 ....154 B3
Cherry Tree Ct 12 YO8 ...49 B4
Cherry Tree Dr
Hatfield DN7 ....92 D5
3 Thorne/Moorends DN8 .79 A1
Cherry Tree Gr DN7 .....92 C5
Cherry Tree La
Beverley HU17 ....154 B3
31 Hedon HU12 ....72 D7
Cherry Tree Rd 18
DN21 ....117 C1
Cherry Tree Rise
DN21 ....107 D4
Cherry Tree Terr
HU17 ....154 C3
Cherry Tree Wlk 7 YO8 ..49 B4
Cherry Trees HU16 ....138 A7
Cherry Tree's Bsns Pk
DN31 ....152 A6
Cherry Way
Messingham DN17 ......107 D7
Nafferton YO25 ....125 F6
Cherry Wood Cres
YO19 ....133 E5
Chesham Gr DN14 .....149 B6
Cheshire Ave YO32 .....14 A6
Cheshire Cl
Kingston upon Hull HU5 ..139 D1
6 Rawcliffe YO32 ....128 E4
Chesney Dr DN16 ......96 D2
Chesney Fields 4 YO24 129 D1
Chesnut Ave HU5 .....140 C2
Chesnut Way 6 DN19 ....86 A8
Chessingham Gdns
YO24 ....132 E6
Chessingham Pk YO19 ..26 F6
Chesswick Ave DN17 ....95 D5
Chesswick Cres DN17 ..95 D5
Chester Ave HU17 .....136 E1
Chester Ct Rd YO8 ......63 A6
Chester Grange DN33 ..102 F1
Chester Pl DN35 ....153 C1
Chester Rd HU5 ....139 B1
Chester Wlk DN34 .....152 A1
Chesterfield Rd DN15 ..150 B6
Chesterholme HU11 ...142 E6
Chestnut Ave
2 Airmyn DN14 ....64 E4
Beverley HU17 ....136 F6
15 Gainsborough DN21 ...117 B1
Goole DN14 ....149 B3
Great Driffield YO25 .....124 F2
Grimsby DN31 ....152 B3
Hedon HU12 ....72 C8
10 Hemingbrough YO8 .....49 F1
Chestnut Ave *continued*
Hessle HU13 ....143 E1
Immingham DN40 ....87 D2
Kirk Ella HU10 ....143 E8
Stainforth DN7 ....92 D6
3 Thorne/Moorends DN8 .93 B7
2 Thorngumbald HU12 ....72 E5
Withernsea HU19 ....75 A5
York YO31 ....130 F6
Chestnut Cl
Beverley HU17 ....136 F6
Bridlington YO15 ....123 B7
6 Burstwick HU12 ....73 A6
4 Scotter DN21 ....107 C3
Snaith DN14 ....78 B8
17 Waltham DN37 ....113 D6
Chestnut Cres YO43 ....40 A1
Chestnut Croft 7 YO8 ...49 F1
Chestnut Ct
9 Hemingbrough YO8 .....49 F1
York YO32 ....127 F5
Chestnut Dr
15 Gilberdyke HU15 ......66 D8
8 Hemingbrough YO8 .....49 F1
Holme-on-Spalding-Moor
YO43 ....40 A1
Messingham DN17 ......107 D7
Chestnut Garth
Burton Pidsea HU12 ......59 C2
4 Hemingbrough YO8 .....49 F1
Roos HU12 ....60 A1
Chestnut Gn 10 LS25 ....61 A8
Chestnut Gr
Acomb YO26 ....129 C4
8 Barnetby le Beck DN38 .99 B4
5 Broughton DN20 ....97 E4
Huntington YO32 ....127 E4
Kingston upon Hull HU8 ..141 B2
Sproatley HU11 ....58 D5
Chestnut Mews YO8 ....48 A8
Chestnut Pk YO41 ......28 C8
Chestnut Rd
Cawood YO8 ....48 A8
Waltham DN37 ....113 D6
Chestnut Rise
Barrow upon Humber
DN19 ....85 C8
6 Hemingbrough YO8 .....49 F1
Chestnut View YO42 ....29 B3
Chestnut Way DN16 ...151 B3
Chestnut Wlk DN41 ...102 A5
Chestnuts The
6 Haxby YO32 ....127 C8
Hensall DN14 ....62 D2
Chevering Pk 8 HU7 ....56 E5
Cheverton Ave 19 HU19 ..75 A6
Cheviot Ave DN14 .....149 D5
Cheviot Cl
3 Thorne/Moorends DN8 .93 A7
1 York YO32 ....127 F3
Cheviotdale HU7 ......140 F6
Chevy Chase HU11 ....142 E6
Cheyne Garth HU18 ...134 A4
Cheyne Wlk HU18 .....134 A4
Chichester Dr 19 LN7 ...111 B4
Chichester Rd DN35 ...103 C2
Chiltern Cres DN17 ...150 D4
Chiltern Dr 19 DN37 ...113 D6
Chiltern Prim Sch
HU3 ....145 B5
Chiltern Rd DN14 .....149 D5
Chiltern Way
26 Grimsby DN33 ....113 E8
York YO32 ....127 F5
Chilterns The HU9 ....142 D2
Chilton Cl 19 DN40 ......87 B1
Chilton Rise HU10 .....138 B1
Chilvers Ct 4 YO8 .....148 A1
Chimes Rd YO8 ....148 C6
Chimes The 9 YO8 ....148 C6
Chimney Field Rd HU12 .74 B6
Chingford Ave 1 DN34 .102 D2
Chingford Wlk HU9 ....142 E1
Chippendale Cl 2
DN36 ....114 D8
Chiswick Cl 3 HU8 ....142 A5
Cholmley St HU3 ......145 B5
Christine Pl 4 DN33 ...113 F8
Chrystals Rd HU18 ....134 D5
Chrystals Wlk HU18 ...134 D5
Chudleigh Rd 1 YO26 ..129 F5
Church Acres DN14 .....65 D1
Church Ave
Humberston DN36 ......114 C8
6 North Ferriby HU14 ....69 A4
6 Selby YO8 ....148 D5
Church Balk
Dunnington YO19 ....26 E7
Thorne/Moorends DN8 ....93 B8
Church Cl
Askham Bryan YO23 ......24 F3
Bonby DN20 ....84 C2
Bridlington YO16 ....122 D4
4 Bubwith YO8 ....50 D7
25 Flamborough YO15 ......5 A2
Goole DN14 ....149 E2
Grimsby DN32 ....153 B1
Kingston upon Hull HU7 ..141 D6
Laxton DN14 ....65 F4
1 Market Weighton
YO43 ....135 D4
8 Thorne/Moorends DN8 .93 B8
5 Wetwang YO25 ....19 B5
Wheldrake YO19 ....38 A7

Church Cres
Owston Ferry DN9 ......**106** A3
4 Wawne HU7 ....**56** E7
Church Ct
Great Driffield YO25 ...**124** E4
Scunthorpe DN15 ....**151** B8
Church Dike La YO8 ....**63** F5
Church Dr Leven HU17 ...**45** A8
6 Misterton DN10 ......**116** C5
Church End YO8 ....**48** B8
Church Farm Cl YO23 ...**24** C6
Church Field Rd DN6 ....**76** E1
Church Fields DN15 .....**83** A5
Church Gate 21 HU12 ....**72** C7
Church Gn
Beverley HU17 ....**136** B6
5 Bridlington YO16 ...**122** D4
3 Elvington YO41 ......**27** C2
Church Hill
Grasby DN38 ....**110** E7
10 Hunmanby YO14 ....**2** F8
Reighton YO14 ....**3** C6
Riby DN37 ....**101** B2
3 Selby YO8 ....**148** D5
South Cave HU15 ....**53** F2
Stillingfleet YO19 ......**36** D3
Whitton DN15 ....**67** E3
8 Wistow YO8 ....**48** B6
Church Hill Rd YO25 ....**31** C4
Church La Appleby DN15 .**83** C1
Atwick YO25 ....**35** C5
Aylesby DN37 ....**101** E2
Barnetby le Beck DN37 .**113** B6
1 Beeford YO25 ....**22** D1
Beswick YO25 ....**32** B4
Bilton HU11 ....**142** F6
Bishop Burton HU17 .....**43** B2
Bishopthorpe YO23 ....**133** A4
Blyton DN21 ....**117** F5
Bonby DN20 ....**84** C2
Bradley DN37 ....**102** C1
Brandesburton YO25 .....**34** B2
Bridlington YO15 .....**123** B7
Brigsley DN37 ....**113** D4
3 Brough HU15 ....**68** C7
Broughton DN20 ....**97** E3
6 Buckton/Bempton YO15 .**4** D3
Burstwick HU12 ....**73** A7
Cadney DN20 ....**109** D6
Carlton DN14 ....**63** C3
Carnaby YO16 ....**10** D5
Catton YO41 ....**27** D8
Catwick HU17 ....**45** C8
Corringham DN21 .....**118** B2
Driffield YO25 ....**124** B4
Dunnington YO19 ....**26** E7
4 Elvington YO41 ......**27** C2
Fishlake DN7 ....**92** D8
24 Flamborough YO15 .....**5** A2
Fotherby LN11 ....**121** D2
Fridaythorpe YO25 .....**18** B7
Garton YO25 ....**124** B4
Gateforth YO8 ....**61** F8
Great Driffield YO25 ..**124** E4
Great Limber DN37 ....**100** D3
12 Grimsby DN33 ......**102** E1
Grimsby DN32 ....**152** D3
17 Haxby YO32 ....**13** E5
Haxey DN9 ....**105** C2
Hedon HU12 ....**72** C7
Hensall DN14 ....**62** C1
Hollym HU19 ....**75** A4
Holton le Clay DN36 ...**114** A5
Hook DN14 ....**149** F7
Hotham YO43 ....**53** D5
Humberston DN36 .....**114** D8
Hutton Cranswick YO25 .**32** E8
Immingham DN40 ....**86** E4
Irby DN37 ....**112** D7
Keadby with Althorpe
  DN17 ....**95** D4
Kellington DN14 ....**61** E3
Keyingham HU12 ....**73** C4
2 Kilham YO25 ....**9** C3
Kirk Ella HU10 ....**143** C8
Laceby DN37 ....**101** F1
Langtoft YO25 ....**8** C1
Lockington HU17 ....**32** B1
Luddington & Haldenby
  DN17 ....**81** D4
Marfleet HU9 ....**147** C8
Marsh Chapel DN36 ....**115** B1
Millington YO42 ....**29** D6
3 Misterton DN10 .....**116** C5
4 Monk Fryston LS25 ...**61** A8
Moor Monkton YO26 .....**12** B2
Nether Poppleton YO26 .**126** B3
New Earswick YO32 ....**127** F5
4 North Cave HU15 .....**53** D3
North Frodingham YO25 ..**33** F8
North Kelsey LN7 .....**110** A4
North Thoresby DN36 ..**114** B1
Nunburnholme YO42 .....**29** E2
Patrington HU12 ....**74** D1
Poppleton YO26 ....**126** A3
Rudston YO25 ....**9** F6
Saxby All Saints DN20 ..**84** B3
Scawby DN20 ....**98** A1
Scotter DN21 ....**107** C3
19 Scunthorpe DN16 .....**96** D2
Scunthorpe DN15 .....**150** F6
Seaton Ross YO42 ......**39** E4
4 Selby YO8 ....**148** D5
Sigglesthorne HU11 ....**45** F8
Skelton YO30 ....**126** B5

Church La *continued*
Skirlaugh HU11 ....**45** E2
2 Snaith DN14 ....**63** C1
Sproatley HU11 ....**58** D5
Stallingborough DN41 ..**101** D6
10 Stamford Bridge YO41 .**15** D2
Strensall YO32 ....**14** A7
Swinefleet DN14 ....**65** D1
Tetney DN36 ....**114** D3
Thorngumbald HU12 .....**72** E5
Thwing YO25 ....**2** A1
Twin Rivers DN14 ......**81** A8
Ulceby DN39 ....**86** A1
Utterby LN11 ....**121** C3
Waithe DN36 ....**114** A3
Watton YO25 ....**32** D4
Wetwang YO25 ....**19** B6
Wheldrake YO19 ....**38** A7
Withernwick HU11 ......**46** D3
York YO1 ....**156** B2
Church La Staith HU1 .**155** C2
Church Mews
Barlby YO8 ....**49** A5
2 York YO26 ....**129** C3
Church Mount
Kingston upon Hull HU7 .**141** D6
9 North Newbald YO43 ..**53** F7
Church Rd
Beverley HU17 ....**136** B6
33 Dunswell HU7 ....**56** F6
Laughton DN21 ....**117** F8
North Ferriby HU14 ....**69** A4
Rimswell HU19 ....**74** D7
Skeffling HU12 ....**90** D6
Stainforth DN7 ....**92** C6
Stamford Bridge YO41 ..**15** D2
Thornton YO42 ....**39** B7
Wawne HU7 ....**56** E7
York YO10 ....**131** D4
Church Rise Holtby YO19 .**14** F1
Skidby HU16 ....**138** A8
Church Row HU8 ....**155** C4
Church Side
Alkborough DN15 ....**82** C8
Appleby DN15 ....**83** D2
Goxhill DN19 ....**86** A7
Grasby DN38 ....**110** E7
2 Market Weighton
  YO43 ....**135** D4
West Halton DN15 ......**82** E7
16 Winterton DN15 ......**83** A5
Church Sq 3 DN15 ....**151** B7
Church St
7 Aldbrough HU11 ......**47** C1
Amcotts DN17 ....**81** F1
Bainton YO25 ....**31** E7
Beckingham DN10 .....**116** D1
6 Brough HU15 ....**68** D6
Bubwith YO8 ....**50** D7
Burton Pidsea HU12 ....**59** D1
14 Caistor LN7 ....**111** B4
Copmanthorpe YO23 ....**132** B2
Dunnington YO19 ....**26** E7
4 Elvington HU17 .....**105** E6
Fishlake DN7 ....**92** D8
19 Flamborough YO15 .....**5** A2
Gainsborough DN21 ....**117** B1
Goole DN14 ....**149** D4
5 Goxhill DN19 ....**86** A4
Great Driffield YO25 ..**124** D4
Grimsby DN32 ....**152** F5
Haxey DN9 ....**105** C2
Hemswell DN21 ....**119** A1
Hibaldstow DN20 .....**108** F5
Huggate YO42 ....**18** C2
Hutton Cranswick YO25 .**32** E8
4 Kilham YO25 ....**9** C3
Kingston upon Hull HU7 .**141** E6
Anlaby HU10 ....**143** E6
Kirton in Lindsey DN21 .**108** B1
Messingham DN17 .....**107** D7
Misterton DN10 ......**116** C5
Nettleton LN7 ....**111** B3
North Cave HU15 ....**53** D3
North Kelsey LN7 .....**110** A4
Owston Ferry DN9 .....**106** A3
Scawby DN20 ....**108** E8
South Cave HU15 ....**53** F1
Thorne/Moorends DN8 ...**93** A8
Willoughton DN21 .....**119** B4
York YO1 ....**156** B2
Church View
12 Airmyn DN14 ....**64** E4
Alkborough DN15 ......**82** C8
8 Barton-upon-Humber
  DN18 ....**84** F8
4 Beckingham DN10 ....**116** D1
4 Brough HU15 ....**68** C7
Grimsby DN34 ....**102** C4
Norton DN6 ....**76** E1
Ottringham HU12 ......**73** E3
7 Patrington HU12 .....**74** D1
1 Waltham DN37 ....**113** E6
Church View Cl DN9 ...**94** E1
Church Wlk
Bridlington YO16 .....**122** D5
Holton le Clay DN36 ..**114** A5
Owston Ferry DN9 .....**106** A3
5 Wistow YO8 ....**48** D6
Churchfield Dr 28 YO32 .**13** E5
Churchfield La DN6 ....**76** C4
Churchfield Rd DN16 ..**151** B1
Churchfields HU17 ....**137** E8
Churchill Ave
Brigg DN20 ....**98** C2

Churchill Ave *continued*
Burstwick HU12 ....**73** A7
Hatfield DN7 ....**92** F4
Hutton Cranswick YO25 .**32** E7
10 Keelby DN41 ....**101** A5
Kingston upon Hull
  HU16 ....**138** F6
Churchill Rise HU12 ...**73** A7
Churchill St HU9 .....**146** D7
Churchill Way DN32 ...**152** F3
Churchill Wlk DN14 ...**149** C5
Churchside 4 DN19 ....**85** D8
Churchthorpe LN11 ...**121** E8
Churchtown DN9 ....**94** E1
Cinder La
Upper Poppleton YO26 .**129** A7
York YO26 ....**130** A4
Cinder Mews YO26 ...**130** A5
Cinema St HU8 ....**134** C4
Circle The 4 HU13 ...**143** E2
Cissplatt La DN41 ...**101** A5
Citadel Ct HU17 ....**154** B3
Citadel Way HU9 ....**155** C2
Cladshaw HU6 ....**139** F8
Clanthorpe HU6 .....**139** F8
Clapham Ave HU4 ....**141** E5
Clare Ave DN17 .....**150** D3
Clare Ct Beverley HU17 **137** B4
Grimsby DN34 ....**152** A1
Clare Gr HU9 ....**142** A1
Claremont Ave HU6 ..**140** D4
Claremont Rd DN32 ..**153** D2
Claremont Terr YO31 .**156** B4
Clarence Ave
Bridlington YO15 .....**122** D1
Kingston upon Hull HU8 **141** E4
Clarence Cl 25 DN40 ...**87** B1
Clarence Ct HU2 ....**155** A3
Clarence Rd 1 YO15 .**122** F2
Clarence St
Kingston upon Hull HU9 **155** C2
York YO31 ....**156** B4
Clarendon Ct YO30 ..**130** C7
Clarendon Rd
6 Grimsby DN34 ....**102** C2
Scunthorpe DN17 ....**150** F3
Clarendon St HU3 ...**145** D7
Clark Ave DN34 .....**152** A3
Clark's La YO43 .....**53** D6
Clarke Cres 9 YO15 ...**4** D3
Clarke St DN15 .....**151** A7
Clarkes Rd DN40 .....**86** C4
Clarks La 10 HU12 ...**74** D1
Clarks Terr YO31 ...**130** F6
Clarksons Dr DN41 ..**101** E6
Clarondale HU7 .....**140** E7
Clavering St DN31 ..**152** B5
Claxby Rd DN17 .....**150** F1
Clay Bank Rd DN8 ....**93** C6
Clay Hill YO41 ......**16** C3
Clay La Bubwith YO8 ..**50** C5
  Camblesforth YO8 .....**63** C6
  Cliffe YO8 ....**49** D4
  Holton le Clay DN36 .**114** A6
  Kirton in Lindsey DN21 **118** F8
  Market Weighton YO43 **135** B5
  Millington YO42 ......**29** C6
  Scotter DN21 ....**107** C4
Clay Pl 3 YO24 .....**129** D1
Clay St HU8 ....**141** A3
Clayden St DN31 ....**152** B5
Clayfield Cl 18 YO42 .**29** A3
Clayfield La
Pocklington YO42 .....**29** A4
Shipton Thorpe YO43 ..**40** F6
Clayfield Rd
Pocklington YO42 .....**29** A3
Scunthorpe DN15 ......**96** C7
Claygate YO31 .....**131** B6
Claymore Cl DN35 ...**153** E2
Claypit La DN14 .....**63** C2
Clear View Cl HU8 ..**141** F6
Clearwaters 6 HU7 ...**56** E5
Cleatham Rd DN21 ..**108** A3
Cleaves Ave HU15 ....**54** A2
Clee Cres DN32 .....**153** C1
Clee Ness Dr 16 DN36 .**103** D1
Clee Rd DN35 ....**153** D2
Clee Village DN32 ..**153** C2
Cleefields Cl DN32 .**153** B1
Cleethorpe Rd DN32 .**153** A5
Cleethorpes Coast Light Rly*
  DN35 ....**103** E2
Cleethorpes Ctry Pk*
  DN35 ....**103** C1
Cleethorpes Discovery Ctr*
  DN35 ....**103** D2
Cleethorpes L Ctr
  DN35 ....**103** D2
Cleethorpes Sta DN35 .**153** F3
Cleeton La YO25 .....**23** A2
Cleeton Way YO16 ..**122** B6
Cleeve Dr 12 HU7 ....**57** A5
Cleeve Prim Sch HU7 ..**57** A5
Cleeve Rd HU12 ......**72** D6
Clematis Ave DN41 ..**101** F5
Clematis Cl YO25 ...**124** D3
Clematis Way DN16 ...**96** E2
Clement St 4 YO23 .**156** B1
Clementhorpe YO23 .**156** B1
Clementhorpe La HU15 **66** D8
Clementhorpe Rd
  HU15 ....**66** D8
Clerke St DN35 .....**153** B4
Clevedon Rd DN17 ..**150** D4
Cleveland Cl Hook DN14 .**65** B5
4 Immingham DN40 .....**87** B1
Scunthorpe DN17 .....**150** D4

Cleveland Gdns DN31 ..**152** B5
Cleveland St
Grimsby DN31 ....**152** B5
Kingston upon Hull HU8 **155** C4
York YO24 ....**130** A4
Cleveland Terr YO32 .**127** F4
Cleveland Way
41 Hatfield DN7 ....**92** D4
York YO32 ....**127** F3
Cliff Ave DN15 ......**82** F5
Cliff Closes Rd DN15 **150** D6
Cliff Dr
Burton upon Stather
  DN15 ....**82** B5
3 Kingston upon Hull HU13 **69** E4
Cliff Gdns DN15 ....**150** E6
Cliff Gr DN18 ....**84** E8
Cliff Hill Rd DN6 ....**76** D2
Cliff La Bempton YO15 ..**4** D4
  Mappleton HU18 ....**47** A6
  Waddingham DN21 ....**119** F6
Cliff Rd Atwick YO25 ..**35** D5
  Bridlington YO15 ....**123** B6
  Hessle HU13 ....**69** E4
  Hornsea HU18 ....**134** C6
  Snitterby DN21 .....**119** F5
  Winteringham DN15 ....**83** A8
Cliff St Bridlington YO15 **122** F2
  Scunthorpe DN16 ....**151** C6
Cliff The DN15 .....**150** D7
Cliff Top La 2 HU13 ..**69** E4
Cliffe La YO43 ......**52** D8
Cliffe Rd
  Market Weighton YO43 **135** D1
  Newbald YO43 ....**53** C7
Cliffe VC Prim Sch YO8 **49** E2
Clifford Ave HU8 ...**141** E4
Clifford St
Hornsea HU18 ....**134** C5
York YO1 ....**156** B2
Clifford's Twr ★ YO1 .**156** B1
Clifton YO30 ....**156** A4
Clifton Ct 27 DN8 ...**93** A8
Clifton Dale YO30 ..**130** A6
Clifton Gdns DN14 ..**149** B4
Clifton Gn YO30 ....**130** A6
Clifton Gn Jun Sch
  YO30 ....**130** A6
Clifton Gn Sch YO30 .**130** A6
Clifton Moor Gate
  YO30 ....**127** A2
Clifton Moor Ind Pk ★
  YO30 ....**127** A4
Clifton Moor Ret Pk
  YO30 ....**126** E3
Clifton Moor Sh Ctr
  YO30 ....**126** F3
Clifton Moorgate
  YO30 ....**127** B3
Clifton Pk Ave YO30 .**129** E8
Clifton Pl 3 YO30 ..**130** A7
Clifton Prep Sch
  YO30 ....**156** A4
Clifton Prim Sch HU2 **155** A4
Clifton Rd DN34 ....**152** A2
Clifton St
Hornsea HU18 ....**134** C5
Kingston upon Hull HU2 **155** A4
Clifton Terr HU5 ...**140** E1
Clifton Without Jun Sch
  YO30 ....**129** F8
Clive Gr YO24 .....**129** F2
Clive Sullivan Way
  HU4 ....**144** C1
Clixby Cl DN35 ....**103** D2
Clixby La DN38 ....**110** E7
Clockmill La DN20 ..**29** A4
Cloeberry Way 14 HU12 **72** C7
Cloister Cl DN17 ...**150** F2
Cloister Wk DN20 ...**97** E3
Cloisters The
6 Grimsby DN37 ......**102** B4
15 Hemingbrough YO8 ...**49** F1
Humberston DN36 ....**114** D8
Wilberfoss YO41 ......**27** C1
York YO31 ....**156** C3
Cloisters Wlk YO31 .**156** C3
Close The Cawood YO8 ..**48** A7
Goxhill DN19 ....**71** A1
Great Driffield YO25 .**124** F5
Grimsby DN34 ....**152** C2
Kingston upon Hull
  HU10 ....**138** F1
4 Leven HU17 ....**45** A8
5 Market Weighton YO43 **135** E4
Norton DN6 ....**76** E2
12 Patrington HU12 .....**74** D1
Riccall YO19 ....**49** A8
Scunthorpe DN16 ....**151** B6
Sutton-on-Hull HU7 ..**141** D6
8 Withernsea HU19 ....**75** A6
York YO32 ....**129** F8
Clouds La Belton DN9 ..**95** B1
West Butterwick DN17 .**106** C8
Clough Garth HU12 ...**72** D8
Clough La DN6 ....**77** B2
Clough Rd HU5 ......**140** F3
Cloughton Gr HU5 ...**139** E2
Clovelly Gdns 3 HU5 **140** E1
Clover Bank View HU6 .**56** E7
Cloverley Cl YO41 ..**15** C2
Cloverley Rd 6 YO16 **123** A6
Clowes Ct 4 HU13 ..**143** E1
Clumber Pl DN35 ...**153** E1
Clumber St HU5 ....**145** C8
Clyde St Grimsby DN32 **152** F4
Kingston upon Hull HU3 **144** F5
Clyfton Cres DN40 ...**87** B1

Coach House Garth
  YO42 ....**28** D3
Coach House Gdns
  DN20 ....**108** E8
Coachings The 4 HU13 .**69** E4
Coal Pit La WF8 ......**76** A2
Coal Shore La LN11 ..**115** E1
Coastguard Hill YO14 ...**3** E5
Coates Ave DN15 .....**83** A5
Coates Marsh La DN14 .**63** B2
Cobble Ct Mews YO24 .**156** A1
Cobble La HU17 ......**51** F1
Cobbler Hill DN14 ..**149** B6
Cobcroft La WF11 ....**76** B8
Cobdale La YO42 .....**29** F7
Cobden St HU3 ......**144** F7
Cobden St N End
  DN32 ....**152** F4
Cober Gr HU8 ......**142** C7
Cobham Way YO32 ...**128** E3
Cochrane St YO8 ...**148** D3
Cock Pit Cl HU10 ...**143** C6
Cockerell La YO25 ...**22** B4
Cocketts La DN20 ..**108** F5
Cockret Cl 8 YO8 ...**148** B6
Cockret Ct YO8 ....**148** B7
Cockret Rd YO8 ....**148** B7
Cockthorne La DN15 ..**83** C7
Coda Ave YO23 .....**133** B3
Coelus St HU9 .....**155** C3
Coeside YO24 ......**132** B7
Cogan St HU1 ......**155** A1
Coggan Cl YO23 ....**130** B2
Coggan Way YO23 ..**132** F4
Cohort St 10 HU15 ...**68** C5
Coke Oven Ave DN16 .**151** F6
Cold Harbour La LN11 **121** F4
Cold Harbour Rd HU17 .**43** A1
Cold Harbour View 5
  HU17 ....**43** A4
Coldstream Cl 4 HU8 .**142** C5
Cole St
Scunthorpe DN15 ....**151** B6
York YO31 ....**156** B4
Coleby Rd DN15 .....**82** E7
Coledale Cl 2 YO30 .**126** F1
Coleford Gr HU7 ...**141** A7
Coleford Prim Sch
  HU7 ....**141** A4
Colemans Rd HU12 ...**72** C7
Colenso St
Kingston upon Hull HU3 **145** A5
York YO23 ....**156** B1
Coleridge Ave DN17 .**150** D3
Coleridge St HU8 ..**141** D2
Colin Ave DN32 ....**153** B2
Colin Rd DN16 .....**151** C6
Colins Wlk DN21 ...**107** C4
Coll of Ripon & York St John
York YO31 ....**130** E6
York YO31 ....**156** B3
Coll of Ripon YO31 .**130** E5
College Ave 31 DN33 **113** E8
College Cl DN15 .....**82** C8
College Farm Cl DN14 .**77** A8
College Gdns
32 Grimsby DN33 .....**113** E8
Hornsea HU18 ....**134** B5
College Gr HU9 ....**141** F1
College of Law YO23 **133** B7
College Rd
Barrow upon Humber
  DN19 ....**85** E7
Copmanthorpe YO23 ..**132** A3
Thornton Curtis DN39 .**86** B6
College St
Cleethorpes DN35 ...**153** E2
Grimsby DN34 ....**152** C2
Kingston upon Hull HU2 **155** A4
York YO1 ....**156** B3
Colleridge Gr 4 HU17 .**55** E8
Colleys HU19 ....**75** A5
Colleywell Cl 3 DN9 .**105** A2
Collier Cl 10 HU14 ..**69** A4
Collier Hag La YO23 ..**24** B3
Collier Rd 16 DN40 ..**87** C4
Collier St HU1 .....**155** A2
Colliergate YO1 ...**156** B2
Collin Ave HU9 ....**142** C2
Collingwood Ave
  YO24 ....**129** F2
Collingwood Cres 12
  DN34 ....**102** B2
Collingwood Prim Sch
  HU3 ....**145** C7
Collingwood Rd 8 YO15 **.4** C3
Collingwood St HU3 .**145** D7
Collinson Ave DN15 .**150** C7
Collinson La HU15 ...**67** A8
Collum Ave DN16 ...**151** B3
Collum Gdns DN16 ..**151** B2
Collum La DN16 ....**151** B2
Collynson Cl 1 HU10 **143** E8
Colonel St HU2 ....**145** D7
Colonsay Ct 20 DN36 **114** A8
Colson Pl DN35 ....**153** B3
Coltman Ave HU17 ..**154** C4
Coltman Cl HU17 ...**136** F7
Coltman St HU3 ....**145** C5
Colton St 3 Brigg DN20 **98** B2
Misterton DN10 ....**116** C5
Columbia Rd DN32 ..**153** A3
Columbus Way DN33 .**102** C2
Colville Ave HU4 ...**144** B6
Colwall Ave HU5 ...**139** D2

Colwyn Cl **5** HU7 . . . . . .57 A7
Combe St DN35 . . . . . . .153 C4
Comber Pl **5** DN32 . . . .152 F5
Comberdale Hill Swinescaif
Rd HU15 . . . . .54 B3
Comforts Ave DN15 . . . .151 A6
Commerce La HU1 . . . .145 D4
Commercial Rd
 Kingston upon Hull HU1 . .155 A1
 Scunthorpe DN16 . . . . . .151 C7
Commodore Croft
 HU1 . . . . .155 B1
Common Croft La YO26 .12 E1
Common Hill YO43 . . . .53 C5
Common La
 Barnby Dun with Kirk Sandall
  DN3 . . . . .92 B4
 Beal DN14 . . . . .61 D3
 Burn YO8 . . . . .62 E7
 Catton YO41 . . . . .27 E8
 Dunnington YO19 . . . . . .26 F5
 Fangfoss YO41 . . . . .16 B1
 Knottingley WF11 . . . . . . .61 B1
 North Cave HU15 . . . . . . .53 B2
 Norton DN6 . . . . .76 E2
 1 Seaton HU11 . . . . . . .35 A1
 Sutton upon Derwent
  YO41 . . . . .38 C8
 Temple Hirst YO8 . . . . . . .62 F4
 Thorganby YO19 . . . . . . .37 F5
 Thornton YO42 . . . . .39 B8
 Twin Rivers DN17 . . . . . .81 B6
 Walden Stubbs DN6 . . . . .76 F4
 Warthill YO19 . . . . .14 F2
 Wawne HU7 . . . . .56 F7
 Welton HU15 . . . . .68 D4
 York YO10 . . . . .131 B1
Common La W HU15 . . . .53 B2
Common Mid Rd DN17 . .94 C8
Common Rd
 Broughton DN20 . . . . . . .97 E4
 Dunnington YO19 . . . . . .26 F7
 Rowley HU17 . . . . .54 F5
 Skipwith YO8 . . . . .37 E1
 South Cave HU15 . . . . . .67 C7
Commonside
 Crowle DN17 . . . . .94 C8
 Westwoodside DN9 . . . . .105 A2
Compass Rd HU6 . . . . .140 C8
Compton Dr
 Grimsby DN34 . . . . .152 C3
 Keyingham HU12 . . . . . . .73 C3
Compton St **16** YO42 . . . .29 A3
Comrie Dr **16** YO42 . . . .29 A3
Concast Rd DN16 . . . . . .97 A3
Concorde Pk YO30 . . . .127 A3
Coney St YO1 . . . . .156 B2
Coneycroft **10** YO19 . . . . .26 F7
Coneygarth La YO19 . . . .26 F7
Conference Ct **10** DN16 . .96 D1
Conifer Cl
 6 Kingston upon Hull
  HU4 . . . . .144 C7
 Scunthorpe DN17 . . . . . .150 C1
 6 York YO32 . . . . .127 D3
Conifers Cl **2** YO8 . . . . . .48 D1
Coningham Ave **1**
 YO30 . . . . .126 E2
Coningsby Dr DN34 . . . .152 A1
Coningsby Rd DN17 . . . .150 D1
Conington Ave HU17 . . .137 B4
Conisborough Ave **2**
 DN36 . . . . .113 F7
Coniston Ave DN33 . . . .113 D8
Coniston Cl **1** YO30 . . . .126 E1
Coniston Cres **19** DN36 .103 C1
Coniston Dr YO10 . . . . .131 B4
Coniston La
 Coniston HU11 . . . . .58 A5
 Swine HU11 . . . . .57 E6
Coniston Way DN14 . . . .149 E5
Connaught Ave DN32 . . .152 D1
Connaught Rd **9** DN21 . .117 B1
Connaught Way YO32 . . .127 F6
Consort Ct HU9 . . . . . .146 B5
Constable Ave HU11 . . . .58 A4
Constable Cl
 18 Flamborough YO15 . . . .5 A2
 Sproatley HU11 . . . . .58 D5
Constable Garth **5** HU12 72 D7
Constable Prim Sch
 HU3 . . . . .145 C5
Constable Rd
 Flamborough YO15 . . . . . . .5 A2
 Hornsea HU18 . . . . .134 D5
 Hunmanby YO14 . . . . .3 A8
Constable St HU3 . . . . .145 C5
Constantine Ave YO10 . .131 A4
Constitution Hill
 HU17 . . . . .136 A6
Constitutional Ave
 DN35 . . . . .153 C4
Convamore Rd DN32 . . .152 E2
Convent Ct HU5 . . . . . .140 D1
Convent La HU3 . . . . . .145 D6
Conway Ave DN34 . . . .152 A3
Conway Cl
 Kingston upon Hull HU3 . .145 B5
 2 York YO30 . . . . .126 E3
Conway Sq DN15 . . . . .150 E7
Conyard Rd DN35 . . . . .153 C3
Conyers Ave YO23 . . . .102 E1
Cookbury Cl **6** HU7 . . . . .56 F5
Cookridge Dr **1** DN7 . . . .92 D4
Cooks La
 Nettleton LN7 . . . . .111 A3
Coomb Briggs Prim Sch
 DN40 . . . . .87 B1

Coombs Yd HU17 . . . . .154 A3
Cooper La DN37 . . . . . .101 E1
Cooper Rd DN32 . . . . . .153 A3
Cooper St
 Beverley HU17 . . . . .154 B4
 Kingston upon Hull HU2 . .155 B4
Coopers Dr YO23 . . . . .132 B3
Coopers Mdw **3** HU11 . . .45 C5
Copandale Rd HU17 . . . .154 A4
Cope St DN32 . . . . .153 A4
Copenhagen Rd HU7 . . .140 F5
Copmanthorpe La
 YO23 . . . . .132 E3
Copmanthorpe Prim Sch
 YO23 . . . . .132 E3
Copmanthorpe Sports Club
 YO23 . . . . .132 B2
Copper Beech Cl
 6 Swanland HU14 . . . . .69 B6
 Upper Poppleton YO26 . . .24 F8
Copper Beech Dr DN14 . .77 A8
Copper Beech Wlk **24**
 DN16 . . . . .96 D2
Copper Beeches The **2**
 YO19 . . . . .26 E7
Coppergate
 Nafferton YO25 . . . . . . .125 F7
 1 Riccall YO19 . . . . .36 F1
 York YO1 . . . . .156 B2
Coppergate Sh Ctr
 YO1 . . . . .156 B2
Coppergate Wlk YO1 . . .156 B2
Coppice Ave DN7 . . . . . .92 D3
Coppice Cl **10** YO32 . . . .13 E5
Coppice Gr **39** DN7 . . . . .92 D3
Coppice La **1** DN7 . . . . .92 D3
Coppice Side HU4 . . . . .144 C6
Coppice The
 Bishopthorpe YO23 . . . . .132 F4
 Brayton YO8 . . . . .48 C1
Coppleflat La
 Rowley HU17 . . . . .55 D6
 Walkington HU17 . . . . . . .43 C1
Copse Cl **1** DN40 . . . . . .87 C2
Copse Mead YO25 . . . .124 D5
Copse Rd DN16 . . . . . .151 B1
Copse The
 Beverley HU17 . . . . .137 B3
 Bigby DN20 . . . . .98 D1
 28 Grimsby DN33 . . . . . .113 E8
Copwood Gr **7** YO32 . . .127 C8
Coral Dr **2** DN37 . . . . .113 D7
Corban La YO23 . . . . . . .13 B6
Corban Way **21** YO32 . . .13 E5
Corbridge Cl **2** HU9 . . .142 E1
Cordeaux Cl DN21 . . . .107 C4
Cordella Cl **1** HU3 . . . .145 A5
Coriander Cl HU17 . . . .154 A1
Corinthian Ave DN34 . . .152 B2
Corinthian Way HU9 . . .146 D6
Corlett Ct YO24 . . . . . .132 C8
Cormorant Cl **2** HU7 . . .141 D8
Cormorant Dr **1** DN37 . .102 B4
Cornaught Ct YO10 . . . .133 D8
Cornborough Av YO31 . .130 F6
Cornelius Cswy YO8 . . . .49 E8
Cornelius Wlk YO43 . . . .135 E4
Corner Cl **17** YO32 . . . . .13 D5
Cornfield Cl **5** DN36 . . .113 D8
Cornfield Cres YO16 . . .122 B2
Cornflower Cl **17** DN41 .101 F5
Cornhill Dr DN18 . . . . . .85 A4
Cornlands Rd YO24 . . . .129 B1
Cornley Dr DN10 . . . . . .116 A6
Cornmill Cl YO8 . . . . . . .48 B8
Cornwall Dr YO10 . . . . .133 E8
Cornwall Rd
 2 Keadby DN17 . . . . . . .95 D6
 Scunthorpe DN16 . . . . . .151 C1
Cornwall St
 7 Kirton in Lindsey DN21 108 B1
 New Village HU16 . . . . . .139 C6
 Stoneferry HU8 . . . . . . .141 A1
Cornwell Cl **5** DN33 . . .102 E2
Cornwood Way **11** YO32 127 C8
Corona Dr
 Kingston upon Hull HU8 . .141 C4
 8 Thorne/Moorends DN8 . .79 A1
Coronation Cl HU17 . . . .154 C3
Coronation Cotts
 DN35 . . . . .153 F1
Coronation Cres **10**
 DN9 . . . . .105 D6
Coronation Gdns **4**
 DN20 . . . . .97 E3
Coronation Rd
 Cleethorpes DN35 . . . . . .153 F1
 Stainforth DN7 . . . . .92 C6
 7 Ulceby DN39 . . . . .86 A1
Coronation Rd N HU5 . .139 C2
Coronation Rd S HU5 . .139 C2
Coronation St **10** DN14 .149 C4
Coronet Cl **5** HU6 . . . .140 B8
Corporation Rd
 Beverley HU17 . . . . .154 A3
 Grimsby DN31 . . . . .152 C6
 Kingston upon Hull HU9 . .147 A2
 Scunthorpe DN15 . . . . . .151 B8
Corpslanding Rd YO25 . .33 A7
Corran Garth **4** HU4 . . .144 A4
Corringham CE Prim Sch
 DN21 . . . . .118 B2
Corringham Rd DN21 . . .117 D1
Corsair Gr **4** HU3 . . . . .145 A4
Corunna Ct **5** YO8 . . . .148 D5
Cosford Garth **5** HU7 . . .57 A5

Cosgrove St DN35 . . . . .153 F2
Cosmo Ave YO31 . . . . .131 A5
Costello Stadium ★
 HU4 . . . . .144 C5
Cotham Gdns **6** DN41 . .101 A4
Cotness La DN14 . . . . . .65 F3
Cotswold Ave DN14 . . . .149 D5
Cotswold Dr **20** DN37 . .113 D6
Cotswold Rd DN8 . . . . . .93 A7
Cotswold Way YO32 . . . .128 A5
Cotswolds The HU9 . . . .142 D2
Cottage Beck Rd
 DN16 . . . . .151 B6
Cottage Cl DN20 . . . . . .108 F5
Cottage Dr HU10 . . . . . .143 B8
Cottage Field **1** HU17 . . .43 A2
Cottage Mews HU17 . . . .154 B3
Cottage Yd La DN36 . . .114 C7
Cottam La YO25 . . . . .8 C5
Cottam Wlk HU11 . . . . .139 A5
Cotterdale HU7 . . . . . . .140 E7
Cotterdale Gdns LS25 . . .61 A6
Cottesmore Rd
 Cleethorpes DN35 . . . . . .103 C1
 6 Kingston upon Hull
  HU13 . . . . .144 A2
Cottingham Bacon Garth Cty
 Prim Sch HU16 . . . . . .139 A5
Cottingham Croxby Prim Sch
 HU5 . . . . .139 D4
Cottingham High Sch
 HU16 . . . . .138 E8
Cottingham Playsport
 HU16 . . . . .139 A7
Cottingham Gr **2** HU6 . .139 F4
Cottingham Rd HU5 . . . .139 E4
Cottingham St DN14 . . .149 C1
Cottingham Sta HU16 . .139 B6
Cottingham Prim Sch HU9 .146 C8
Cottom La YO42 . . . . . . .38 C2
Coulam Pl **8** DN36 . . . .114 D8
Coulbeck Dr DN35 . . . .153 D1
Coulman Rd **4** DN8 . . . .93 B8
Coulman St **5** DN8 . . . .93 B8
Coulson Cl
 Hibaldstow DN20 . . . . . .109 A5
 5 Strensall YO32 . . . . . .14 C8
Coulson Dr HU13 . . . . . .143 F2
Coultas St **3** HU3 . . . . .145 A6
Council Ave HU4 . . . . . .144 E3
Council Terr **9** DN18 . . .69 E1
Council Villas YO19 . . . .85 F8
Count De Burgh Terr **4**
 YO23 . . . . .130 B1
County Rd N HU5 . . . . .139 E1
County Rd S **2** HU5 . . .144 C8
Couper Gr DN14 . . . . . .149 D1
Coupland Gdns **2** HU5 .140 E2
Coupland Rd **1** YO8 . . .148 C6
Courcey Gr YO26 . . . . .129 C4
Court Dr YO8 . . . . .148 A4
Court Gdns **8** DN14 . . . .78 C8
Courtland Rd HU6 . . . . .139 E6
Courtney St HU8 . . . . . .146 B8
Courtneys Selby YO8 . . .148 B4
Courtneys The YO8 . . . .148 B4
Courtpark Rd HU6 . . . . .139 F7
Courts Cl **7** DN14 . . . . .64 E4
Courtway Rd HU6 . . . . .139 E7
Courtyard The YO23 . . . .133 B4
Cove Rd DN9 . . . . .104 F3
Coventry Ave DN34 . . . .152 A1
Coventry Cl DN17 . . . . .150 D3
Coventry Rd
 Kingston upon Hull HU5 . .139 C1
 12 Thorne/Moorends DN8 . .93 B8
Coverdale HU7 . . . . . . .140 F7
Coverdale Garth **2**
 YO16 . . . . .122 E7
Covert Rd DN16 . . . . . .151 B1
Covert The
 Kingston upon Hull
  HU16 . . . . .139 C5
 York YO24 . . . . .132 F7
Covington **21** HU15 . . . . .68 C6
Covin's La LN11 . . . . . .121 F8
Cow La Knottingley WF11 .61 A2
 Twin Rivers DN17 . . . . . . .81 C6
 Womersley DN6 . . . . .76 D6
Cow Marsh La DN36 . . .114 E5
Cow Pasture La YO42 . . .38 C3
Cow Wold Rd HU17 . . . . .42 E1
Cowden Gr **2** HU9 . . . .142 A2
Cowden La HU11 . . . . . .46 A1
Cowgate HU15 . . . . .68 D6
Cowick CE VC Prim Sch
 DN14 . . . . .78 A8
Cowick Rd Fishlake DN8 .78 F1
 22 Thorne/Moorends DN8 . .93 B7
 1 West/East Butterwick
  DN17 . . . . .106 D7
Cowlings Cl **16** YO14 . . . . .3 D3
Cowper Ave DN17 . . . . .150 D3
Cowper La YO23 . . . . . . .36 C3
Cowslams La YO25 . . . . .21 C5
Cowton La YO14 . . . . .3 C6
Cox La DN17 . . . . .94 D8
Cox's Ch DN20 . . . . . . .109 A5
Cox's Hill DN21 . . . . . . .117 B1
Coxlea Gr YO31 . . . . . .131 B6
Coxwold Gr HU4 . . . . . .144 C4
Crab Tree La
 Coniston HU11 . . . . .57 F7
 Kirk Smeaton WF8 . . . . . .76 A1
Crabley La HU15 . . . . . . .67 E7
Crabtree Gr **1** YO32 . . .127 D3

Crabtree La YO25 . . . . . .32 B4
Crabtree Rd DN7 . . . . . .92 C4
Crackle Hill **6** DN9 . . . .105 B2
Cradley Rd HU5 . . . . . .139 C3
Cragston Ave **13** DN33 . .102 E2
Craig Cl **5** DN20 . . . . . .97 D3
Craik Hill Ave **18** DN40 . .87 C1
Craikewells YO15 . . . . . .5 A3
Craithie Rd **11** DN35 . . .103 C2
Crake Ave DN33 . . . . . .102 E1
Crake Wells HU17 . . . . . .55 C8
Crakedale Rd DN15 . . . . .83 B5
Crampin Rd DN35 . . . . .153 E3
Cranbeck Rd YO16 . . . .122 B1
Cranberry Way HU4 . . . .144 C4
Cranbourne Cl **28** DN35 .103 C1
Cranbourne St HU3 . . . .145 C5
Cranbrook Ave
 Kingston upon Hull HU6 . .140 B6
 York YO26 . . . . .129 C5
Cranbrook Rd YO26 . . . .129 C5
Cranbrooks The YO19 . . .37 F8
Crane Rd HU5 . . . . .146 C6
Cranfield Pl **4** YO24 . . .132 E2
Cranidge Cl **2** DN17 . . . .94 D8
Cranham Gr HU7 . . . . . .141 A7
Cranswick Cl **8** HU17 . . .43 E6
Cranswick Gr HU9 . . . . .142 B1
Cranwell Cl **6** DN21 . . . .119 C8
Cranwell Dr **10** DN37 . . .102 C5
Cranwell Rd YO25 . . . . .124 E4
Cranwell St YO25 . . . . .124 E4
Crapple La DN21 . . . . . .107 C2
Crathorne Rd HU17 . . . .154 C1
Craven Garth **5** DN14 . . .61 D4
Craven Prim Sch HU9 . .146 C8
Craven Rd
 Cleethorpes DN35 . . . . . .153 D3
 Hatfield DN7 . . . . .92 C4
Craven St N HU9 . . . . . .146 C8
Craven St S HU9 . . . . . .146 D7
Crawley Way YO31 . . . .131 B6
Crawshaw Ave YO31 . . .130 F8
Craycroft Rd DN9 . . . . .105 B3
Crayford Cl **7** HU9 . . . .142 E1
Crayke The YO16 . . . . . .122 F7
Crescent Cl
 Grimsby DN31 . . . . .152 C3
 Kingston upon Hull
  HU16 . . . . .139 A6
Crescent The
 Beckingham DN10 . . . . . .116 E1
 9 Bridlington YO15 . . . . .122 F2
 Brough HU15 . . . . .68 D6
 Burton Fleming YO25 . . . . .2 E3
 Hatfield DN7 . . . . .92 C5
 Holton le Clay DN36 . . . .114 A5
 Hornsea HU18 . . . . .134 D3
 Huggate YO42 . . . . .18 C2
 Kelfield YO19 . . . . .36 D1
 Kexby YO41 . . . . .27 C5
 2 Kirk Sandall DN3 . . . . .92 A1
 13 Patrington HU12 . . . . .74 D1
 1 Riccall YO19 . . . . .48 F8
 Stamford Bridge YO41 . . . .15 D2
 York YO10 . . . . .131 C1
 York YO24 . . . . .156 A1
Cressey St DN31 . . . . . .152 E5
Cresswell Cl HU2 . . . . . .155 A4
Cresta Dr **10** DN17 . . . . .96 C2
Cresta The DN34 . . . . . .152 C1
Creyke Cl **6** HU16 . . . . .139 B7
Creyke La **7** HU15 . . . . .68 D6
Creyke View DN14 . . . . .64 A1
Crichton Ave YO30 . . . .130 A7
Cricklewood Wlk HU8 . . .141 E6
Cridling Gdns DN6 . . . . .76 F2
Cridling Pl **5** DN35 . . . .103 B2
Crinan Ct **3** YO32 . . . . .127 F6
Crinan Dr **1** HU6 . . . . .140 B8
Crispin Cl **5** HU4 . . . . .144 A2
Crispin Way DN16 . . . . .96 D1
Croft Ave **8** WF11 . . . . .61 A3
Croft Cl
 Eastrington DN14 . . . . . . .51 F1
 Market Weighton YO43 . . .135 D3
 Swanland HU14 . . . . .69 B7
Croft Ct YO23 . . . . .133 A4
Croft Dr HU10 . . . . .143 C5
Croft Farm Cl YO23 . . . .132 B3
Croft La DN17 . . . . .96 C1
Croft Lodge DN9 . . . . . .94 E1
Croft Pk HU14 . . . . .69 A5
Croft Rd
 Camblesforth YO8 . . . . . .63 D4
 Finningley DN10 . . . . . . .104 A3
Croft The
 Beverley HU17 . . . . .136 C7
 Kingston upon Hull HU7 . .140 E8
 Knottingley WF11 . . . . . . .61 A3
 22 Thorne/Moorends DN8 . .93 B7
Croft View
 Bransholme HU7 . . . . . . .141 C7
 Kirk Ella HU10 . . . . .143 C6
 Market Weighton YO43 . . .135 D3
Croft's La YO25 . . . . . . .21 D6
Crofters Dr HU16 . . . . . .139 C5
Croftlands **7** WF11 . . . . .61 A3
Crofts La Hollym HU19 . . .74 F4
 Stainforth DN7 . . . . .92 B6
Crofts The
 9 Humberston DN36 . . .114 C8
 Scunthorpe DN16 . . . . . .151 B6
 Ulrome YO25 . . . . .23 A3
Croftside **1** YO26 . . . . .129 B3

Croftway
 Camblesforth YO8 . . . . . .63 C5
 Selby YO8 . . . . .148 C4
 2 York YO26 . . . . .129 B3
Cromarty Cl HU9 . . . . . .142 A3
Crombie Ave YO30 . . . .130 B7
Cromer Ave DN34 . . . . .152 A1
Cromer St
 4 Kingston upon Hull
  HU5 . . . . .140 D2
 York YO30 . . . . .130 B7
Cromford St **13** DN21 . . .117 B1
Crompton Terr YO32 . . .127 D6
Cromwell Ave
 Grimsby DN31 . . . . .152 C3
 Scunthorpe DN16 . . . . . .151 B5
Cromwell Cl **2** HU3 . . . .145 D8
Cromwell Ct **1** HU10 . . .143 E7
Cromwell Rd
 Cleethorpes DN35 . . . . . .103 D2
 Grimsby DN31 . . . . .152 A4
 85 Hedon HU12 . . . . . . .72 D7
 York YO1 . . . . .156 B1
Cromwell View **25** LN7 . .111 B4
Crook Hill HU15 . . . . . . .68 C8
Crook La HU11 . . . . .58 D7
Crook Mill Rd DN40 . . . .86 D5
Crook Tree La DN7 . . . . .92 F5
Crooked Billet St **5**
 DN21 . . . . .117 A2
Crookes Broom Ave
 DN7 . . . . .92 D4
Crookes Broom La
 DN7 . . . . .92 D4
Crookland La **3** YO43 . . .13 F5
Croom Medieval Village ★
 YO25 . . . . .7 A4
Croome Dale La YO17 . . .7 C6
Croome Rd YO25 . . . . . . .7 B4
Cropton Rd HU5 . . . . . .139 E2
Crosby Ave DN15 . . . . . .96 C7
Crosby Prim Sch
 DN15 . . . . .151 A8
Crosby Rd
 Grimsby DN33 . . . . .102 D1
 Scunthorpe DN15 . . . . . .151 B8
Crosland Cl DN37 . . . . .102 B4
Cross Carr Rd DN20 . . .109 A5
Cross Coates Rd
 DN34 . . . . .152 A2
Cross Gate YO43 . . . . . .41 E6
Cross Gates YO25 . . . . .21 F8
Cross Gordon St **1**
 DN14 . . . . .149 C4
Cross Hill
 5 Brandesburton YO25 . . .34 B2
 Driffield YO25 . . . . .124 E4
 Haxey DN9 . . . . .105 C3
 Hayton YO42 . . . . .40 C3
Cross Hills La YO8 . . . .148 A5
Cross La
 Alkborough DN15 . . . . . . .82 C8
 3 Amcotts DN17 . . . . . .81 F1
 Flaxton YO60 . . . . .14 E8
 Flixborough DN15 . . . . . .82 A2
 Fulford YO19 . . . . .133 F5
 Hutton Cranswick YO25 . . .32 F6
 Leven HU17 . . . . .44 F7
 North Frodingham YO25 . . .33 F7
 North Kelsey LN7 . . . . . .110 B5
Cross Rd Hatfield DN7 . . .93 B4
 North Frodingham YO25 . . .33 F7
 Ulceby DN39 . . . . .86 B3
Cross Slack **8** DN17 . . . .94 D8
Cross St
 8 Aldbrough HU11 . . . . . .47 C1
 3 Barrow upon Humber
  DN19 . . . . .85 D8
 Beverley HU17 . . . . .154 A2
 Bridlington YO15 . . . . . .122 F2
 13 Brigg DN20 . . . . .98 C2
 Cleethorpes DN35 . . . . . .153 E2
 Crowle DN17 . . . . .94 D8
 85 Gainsborough DN21 . . .117 B1
 Garthorpe & Fockerby
  DN17 . . . . .81 E6
 Goole DN14 . . . . .149 D3
 Grimsby DN31 . . . . .152 F6
 Hatfield DN7 . . . . .46 C6
 Kingston upon Hull HU1 . .155 A2
 2 Scunthorpe DN15 . . . .151 B8
 Skipsea YO25 . . . . .23 A2
 3 Waltham DN37 . . . . . .113 E6
 West Halton DN15 . . . . . .82 E8
 5 York YO24 . . . . .129 C3
Cross St W DN14 . . . . .149 B4
Cross Tree Rd DN17 . . .107 D7
Crossbeck Rd **2** DN16 . .96 D2
Crossfield Cres YO19 . . .133 E6
Crossfield Rd HU13 . . . .143 E3
Crosshill La DN14 . . . . . .77 E6
Crossings The **13** DN14 . .64 E4
Crosskill Cl **1** YO17 . . . .154 C4
Crosslands La HU15 . . . .53 B3
Crosslands Rd **2** YO10 .133 E8
Crossmoor Bank DN14 . .80 C5
Crossmoor La YO32 . . . .13 E6
Crossway The
 Grimsby DN34 . . . . .102 A2
 York YO31 . . . . .130 E8
Crossways
 10 Stainforth DN7 . . . . . .92 C6
 York YO10 . . . . .131 C2
Crosswood Cl **6** HU7 . . . .57 A7
Crow Croft La DN14 . . . .78 A5

Crow Hill Ave DN35 ...153 E2
Crow Tree Bank DN8 ..93 D4
Crowberry Dr DN16 ..151 D1
Crowland Ave
 Grimsby DN34 ....102 C2
 Scunthorpe DN16 ....151 A3
Crowland Cl 2 HU8 ....142 C7
Crowland Rd 9 DN17 ....94 D7
Crowle Bank Rd DN17 ..95 C4
Crowle Dr DN33 ....102 C2
Crowle Prim Sch DN17 ..94 C7
Crowle Rd DN17 ....80 F2
Crowle St HU9 ....146 D2
Crowle Sta DN17 ....94 E6
Crowle Waste or Moors
 Nature Reserve★
 DN17 ....94 B8
Crown Gdns 21 DN21 ...107 C3
Crowther Cl HU17 ......137 A6
Crowther Way 5 HU6 ....69 B7
Croxby Ave DN33 ....113 E8
Croxby Gr 14 DN33 .....113 E8
Croxton Rd
 Croxton DN39 ....99 F7
 Kirmington DN39 ....100 A5
Cruckley Animal Farm★
 YO25 ....21 E1
Cruckley La YO25 ....21 E1
Crudhall La YO42 ....40 A8
Crummock 3 YO24 .....132 C7
Crumpton Rd YO43 .....135 C3
Crystal St HU3 ....145 C7
Cuckoo La DN7 ....92 E6
Cudworth Gr 1 HU8 ....141 B1
Cullen Cl HU8 ....141 C5
Cullingworth Ave 2
 HU6 ....140 C7
Cumberland Ave
 DN32 ....152 D1
Cumberland Cl
 Goole DN14 ....149 A4
 6 Strensall YO32 ....14 B6
Cumberland Rd DN35 ..103 D1
Cumberland St
 Kingston upon Hull HU2 .155 C4
 York YO1 ....156 B2
Cumbrian Ave 4 YO32 ...14 B6
Cumbrian Way HU7 ......56 F7
Cundall Cl
 Kingston upon Hull HU9 ..141 E1
 6 Strensall YO32 ......14 C8
Cunningham Rd 3 DN7 104 A8
Cupid's Alley YO17 ......6 B6
Cupola Way DN15 ....96 C8
Curlew Cl
 Beverley HU17 ....136 E6
 Driffield YO25 ....125 A5
 Kingston upon Hull HU7 .141 D8
Curlew Glebe 8 YO19 ...26 E7
Curlew Gn YO15 ....11 B4
Curry Rd DN34 ....102 C4
Curzen Terr YO8 ....49 E3
Curzen Cres 5 DN3 ......92 A2
Curzon Ave DN35 ....153 D1
Curzon Ct 3 DN35 .....103 D1
Curzon St
 4 Gainsborough DN21 ..117 B1
 Kingston upon Hull HU3 .144 F7
Curzon Terr YO23 ......130 B1
Cushman Cres 10 DN40 ..87 C1
Custance Wlk YO23 ....156 A1
Cuthbert Ave 6 DN38 ...99 B4
Cuxwold Rd
 Scunthorpe DN16 ....151 C4
 Swallow LN7 ....112 B5
Cycle St 4 YO10 ....131 A3
Cygnet St YO23 ....156 A1
Cynthia Rd DN32 ....153 C1
Cyprus St HU9 ....147 B8
Cyrano Way DN37 ......102 B4
Cyril Cooper Ct DN32 ..152 E2

D

Dacre Lakeside Pk★
 YO25 ....34 B1
Dagger La HU1 ....155 B2
Daggett La YO25 ....21 F8
Daggett Rd DN35 ....103 D2
Dairy House La HU12 ....73 A8
Dairycoates Ave HU3 ...145 A4
Dairycoates Rd HU4 ....144 E3
Daisyfield Dr HU9 ......142 D6
Dalby Gr HU9 ....142 B2
Dalby Mead YO32 ......127 F1
Dale Cl Selby YO8 ......148 C3
 8 Swanland HU14 ......69 B7
Dale Dike Gr YO30 .....126 F2
Dale Garth YO43 ....135 E5
Dale Gate HU17 ....43 A1
Dale Pit Rd DN7 ....92 F3
Dale Pk Ave DN15 ......83 A5
Dale Rd
 Brantingham HU15 ....68 C8
 Bridlington YO16 ......122 D4
 Elloughton-cum-Brough
 HU15 ....68 C6
 Swanland HU14 ....69 B7
 Welton HU15 ....68 E6
Dale St
 Scunthorpe DN15 ....151 A8
 York YO23 ....156 A1
Dale St N DN15 ....150 F8
Dale View 27 DN33 .....102 C2

Dale's La YO31 ....130 F6
Dalehouse Dr 2 HU10 ..143 F6
Dales Prim Sch The
 HU7 ....56 F6
Dales The
 Kingston upon Hull HU9 .142 D8
 Scunthorpe DN17 ....96 C2
 Willerby HU10 ....138 D6
Dalesway HU10 ....143 B6
Dalguise Gr YO31 ......156 C4
Dalkeith Cl 16 HU7 ......57 A6
Dallisons Rd DN17 .....109 A5
Dalmais Cl 1 YO42 ......28 F4
Dalmatian Way DN20 ...97 E4
Dalton Cl YO25 ....124 D3
Dalton Hill YO19 ....38 A8
Dalton La HU12 ....73 F6
Dalton St HU8 ....141 A1
Dalwood Cl HU7 ....141 B8
Dam Bank YO8 ....148 C6
Dam Gn La HU15 ....68 C7
Dam Hill YO23 ....24 B4
Dam La Ottringham HU12 .73 D2
 Selby YO8 ....48 B3
 Thornton Curtis DN39 ...85 E4
Dam Rd DN18 ....69 E1
Dame Kendal Gr 29
 DN33 ....102 D2
Damson Cl YO26 ....129 E4
Damson Garth YO25 .....31 F2
Danby Cl YO26 ....141 E7
Danby Rd DN17 ....107 D7
Dancing La Riston HU11 ..45 C5
 Swine HU11 ....57 D7
Dane Ave
 Thorpe Willoughby YO8 ..48 B1
 York YO26 ....129 C5
Dane Cl 13 DN20 ....97 E4
Dane Pk Rd HU6 ....139 E7
Dane's Graves (Tumuli)★
 YO25 ....8 D2
Danebury Cres YO26 ...129 C4
Danebury Ct YO26 .....129 C4
Danebury Dr YO26 .....129 C4
Danes Croft
 Bridlington YO16 ......122 D5
 2 York YO10 ....133 D8
Danes Ct 5 YO19 ....49 A8
Danes Dr 3 YO19 ....69 F4
Danes' Dyke★ YO15 .....4 F2
Danes Dyke Nature Reserve★
 YO15 ....123 E8
Danes Hills (Tumuli)★
 YO8 ....37 E2
Danes Rd DN21 ....117 C1
Danescroft YO8 ....148 C2
Danesfield Ave DN37 ..113 E7
Danesfort Ave YO24 ...129 D2
Danesgate YO26 ....129 C4
Danesmead YO10 ......133 D8
Danesway HU17 ....136 D6
Daneswell Cl 3 YO41 ...15 D2
Dansom La HU8 ....141 B1
Dansom La S HU8 ......146 B8
Danson Cl DN18 ....85 A8
Danthorpe Rd HU11 .....59 B4
Danube Rd HU5 ....144 C8
Danum Cl 14 DN8 ....93 B8
Danum Dr YO10 ....133 E8
Danum Rd
 3 Hatfield DN7 ....92 D3
 Scunthorpe DN17 ......150 F4
 York YO10 ....133 E8
Dar Beck Rd DN21 .....107 C4
Darbie Cl YO32 ....127 D4
Darby Rd DN15 ....82 B4
D'arcy Rd YO8 ....148 E4
Darfield Cl YO32 ....14 B8
Dark La 5 Amcotts DN17 .81 F1
 Paull HU12 ....72 D4
Darley Cl Kilham YO25 ...9 B3
 7 Stamford Bridge YO41 .15 D2
Darling La YO23 ....36 C8
Darlington Gr DN8 ......79 B2
Darnborough St YO23 ..156 B1
Darnbrook Wk YO31 ...131 B5
Darneley Ct HU18 ......134 D6
Darnholme Cres
 DN17 ....107 D7
Darrismere Villas 4
 HU3 ....145 A5
Dart Gr HU8 ....142 B5
Dartford Wlk HU9 ......142 E1
Dartmouth Rd DN17 ...150 D5
Dartmouth Wlk HU4 ...144 A3
Darwin Cl YO31 ....127 E1
Darwin Ct DN34 ....102 C3
Darwin Dr YO25 ....125 A3
Darwin Rd YO16 ....122 E6
Darwin St 4 DN21 .....108 B1
Datchet Garth 3 HU4 ..144 B2
Daubney St DN35 ......153 B4
Dauby La YO41 ....27 B3
Davenport Ave 4 HU13 .143 D1
Davenport Dr DN35 ....153 D1
Davey Cl YO25 ....124 E4
David Lister Sch HU9 ..141 E1
David Pl DN36 ....114 A7
David St DN32 ....152 F1
David's Cl HU16 ....138 B8
Davidstow Cl HU7 .....140 F8
Davie Pl DN35 ....153 B3
Daville Cl HU5 ....139 B1
Davisons Ave DN31 ....152 D4

Davis's Cl HU10 ....143 C8
Davy Ave DN15 ....150 E8
Davy Cres DN20 ....98 C3
Davygate YO1 ....156 B2
Daw La YO23 ....36 A5
Dawes La 1 DN15 .....151 C7
Dawlish Rd DN33 ......113 E7
Dawnay Dr HU10 ......144 A6
Dawnay Garth
 Shipton YO30 ....12 E5
 2 Snaith DN14 ....63 B1
Dawnay Rd HU11 ....58 A4
Dawnhill La DN21 ......119 B2
Daysfoot Ct 3 YO10 ...130 E3
Dayton Rd HU5 ....139 D1
De Aston Sq DN15 .....150 E7
De Grey Cl YO30 ......156 A4
De Grey Pl 2 YO23 ....133 B3
De Grey St
 Kingston upon Hull HU5 .140 C2
 York YO31 ....156 B4
De Grey Terr YO30 ....156 A4
De La Pole Ave HU3 ...144 F7
De Lacy La DN35 ....153 F2
De Lacy Way DN15 .....83 A5
De Mowbray Ct YO23 ..24 D3
Deacon Cl 3 YO8 ......148 B6
Deacon Dr DN15 ......150 B6
Deacons Ct DN32 .....132 B2
Dead La Bainton YO25 ..31 E7
 Foggathorpe YO8 ....51 A8
 Kirkburn YO25 ....20 A4
 Lockington YO25 ....32 B2
Deal Cl HU8 ....141 E8
Dealtry Ave 1 YO32 ...127 C8
Dean La YO43 ....53 D4
Dean Pk Ind Est HU17 .137 C4
Deane Rd 12 DN40 .....87 C1
Deangate YO1 ....156 B3
Deanhead Gr 7 YO30 ..126 E2
Deans Cl
 Bishopthorpe YO23 .....132 F4
 5 Misterton DN10 ......116 C5
Dean's La 7 YO42 ......29 A3
Deansgate DN34 ......152 C2
Deansgrove DN32 .....152 D3
Dearne Ct 9 HU15 ......68 D5
Dearne Gr 1 HU8 ......141 C1
Deaton La DN36 ....114 A7
Debdhill Rd DN10 ......116 C6
Deben Gr HU8 ....142 C7
Dee Cl YO24 ....132 B7
Dee St 8 HU3 ....145 B4
Deene Cl 8 DN34 ......102 B2
Deep The (Aquarium &
 Marine Research Ctr)★
 HU9 ....155 C1
Deepdale 5 YO24 ......132 D8
Deepdale Cl YO16 .....122 E7
Deepdale Gr 2 HU9 ....146 E8
Deepfurrows La YO41 ..27 D3
Deeping Way YO8 ......148 A6
Deer Hill Gr YO30 .....126 F3
Deer Pk Ct 1 LS25 ......61 A8
Deer Pk Way 6 HU17 ...55 F8
Deerhurst Gr HU7 .....141 A7
Deerstone Way 22 YO19 .26 F7
Defender Dr DN17 ......102 A4
Deira Ct YO25 ....124 F5
Del Pyke YO31 ....156 C4
Delamere Cl 6 YO32 ...13 D5
Delamere Ct DN35 .....102 E1
Delamere Wlk DN14 ...149 F5
Delhi St HU9 ....147 B7
Delius Cl HU4 ....144 B4
Dell The Beverley HU17 .137 B2
 1 Broughton DN20 .....97 D3
 Scunthorpe DN17 ......150 D1
 5 Skelton YO30 ....126 B5
Delwood YO10 ....133 D7
Dempster Ave DN14 ...149 C1
Denaby Ct HU8 ....146 B8
Denby Cl DN15 ....150 D8
Denby Dr DN36 ....103 B2
Dene Cl Dunswell HU6 ..56 D5
 Hensall DN14 ....62 C2
Dene Pk Sports Club
 HU6 ....138 F6
Dene Rd Grimsby DN32 .102 F2
 Kingston upon Hull
 HU16 ....138 F6
Dene St HU9 ....141 D1
Dene Wlk DN14 ....149 F6
Denehall Rd DN3 ....92 A2
Denesway HU13 ....143 D2
Denholme Ave 3 HU6 ..140 C7
Denison Rd
 Pocklington YO42 ....29 A4
 Selby YO8 ....148 E4
Denmark St 11 HU8 ....141 A1
Denmark Rise 5 HU15 ..53 D3
Dennett Rd HU17 ......137 B5
Dennis St YO1 ....156 C1
Dennison St YO31 .....156 C4
Dent Rd HU5 ....139 D3
Denton La YO43 ....53 D6
Denton's Way DN20 ...109 A5
Denver Rd 6 DN6 ....76 F2
Deramore Dr YO10 ....131 C3
Deramore Dr W YO10 ..131 C3
Derby Cl DN32 ....153 A5

Derby Rd DN15 ....150 B6
Derby St HU3 ....145 D8
Derringham Ave 5 HU4 144 B6
Derringham St DN15 ...145 C7
Derry Way 27 DN33 ....113 E8
Derrymore Rd HU10 ...138 C2
Derrythorpe Rd DN17 ..95 D4
Derwent Ave
 18 North Ferriby HU14 ..69 A4
 York YO31 ....130 F4
Derwent Cl
 Elvington YO41 ....27 B3
 Kingston upon Hull HU6 .139 D6
 2 Stamford Bridge YO41 ..15 D2
Derwent Cres DN14 .....65 B7
Derwent Ct YO41 ....27 C2
Derwent Dr 4 Barlby YO8 49 B5
 12 Humberston DN36 ...103 C1
 9 Kirk Sandall DN3 .....92 A2
 Wheldrake YO19 ....37 F7
Derwent Est YO19 ......26 E7
Derwent Gdns YO16 ...122 E7
Derwent Inf Sch YO10 .131 B4
Derwent Jun Sch
 YO10 ....131 B4
Derwent Pk YO10 ....38 A8
Derwent Rd
 1 Howden DN14 ....65 B7
 Scunthorpe DN16 ....151 D2
 York YO10 ....133 D8
Derwent St HU8 ....141 B1
Derwent Wlk YO32 ....127 F5
Desmond Ave
 4 Hornsea HU18 ......134 C4
 Kingston upon Hull HU6 .140 D4
Despatch Rd DN16 ......97 A5
Detuyll St W DN15 ......96 C7
Deveron Way YO24 ....132 B7
Devon Pl YO10 ....130 F3
Devon St
 Cottingham HU16 ......139 C7
 Gipsyville HU4 ....144 F3
Devonshire Ave DN32 ..102 E2
Devonshire Dr DN14 ...149 B5
Devonshire Dr DN17 ...150 F2
Dewberry Ct HU4 ......144 D4
Dewsbury Ave DN15 ...150 C8
Dewsbury Ct YO1 .....156 A1
Dewsbury Terr YO1 ...156 A1
Deyne Ave DN15 ....151 A4
Diadem Gr HU9 ....142 C5
Dial Sq DN31 ....152 E3
Diamond St YO31 .....156 C4
Diana Princess of Wales
 Hospl DN33 ....102 E2
Diana St DN15 ....96 D7
Dibsdane HU6 ....139 E8
Dick La DN14 ....65 E7
Dickens Cl 1 YO32 ....127 F1
Dickey La YO8 ....48 D5
Dickinson Cl DN20 ....108 F5
Dickinson's La DN36 ..114 B1
Dickson Rd 4 YO24 ...129 B1
Didscourt HU6 ....139 E6
Digby Garth HU7 ....57 A5
Digby Gdns DN34 .....152 A1
Digby St DN15 ....150 F8
Dijon Ave YO24 ....129 C2
Dike Ray Cl YO32 .....127 C7
Dikelands Cl 19 YO26 ...12 F1
Dikelands La YO26 ......12 F1
Dill Dr HU17 ....154 B1
Dilys Gr 5 YO26 ....129 E4
Dimlington Bglws 5
 HU12 ....90 F6
Dimlington Rd HU12 ....90 F6
Dimmer Dales Rd
 HU12 ....90 D5
Dingley Cl HU6 ....140 B6
Dinostar★ HU1 ....155 B1
Dirty La DN7 ....92 D8
Disraeli Cl YO32 ......127 E1
Distaff La 33 HU12 .....72 C7
Ditmas Ave 9 HU4 ....144 B6
Division Rd 1 HU3 .....145 B4
Dixon Ave
 Broughton DN20 ....97 D3
 Grimsby DN32 ....102 F2
Dixon Cl Beverley HU17 .154 A3
 4 Brigg DN20 ....98 C2
 Market Weighton YO43 .135 D2
 4 Tetney DN36 ....114 D4
Dixon Ct
 Kingston upon Hull
 HU16 ....139 A5
 Selby YO8 ....148 B6
Dixon Gdns YO8 ....148 B6
Dixon La YO1 ....156 C1
Dixons Yd YO1 ....156 C2
Dobella Ave DN14 ......64 A1
Dobella La DN14 ....79 B8
Dock Office Row HU1 ..155 C3
Dock St Goole DN14 ...149 C2
 Kingston upon Hull HU1 .155 B2
Dodgson Terr YO26 ...129 D4
Dodsell Gr HU9 ....147 E8
Dodsworth Ave YO31 .130 E7
Dodthorpe HU6 ....140 A8
Doe Pk YO30 ....126 F2
Doe Pk La YO41 ....16 B4
Dog & Duck La
 Beverley HU17 ....154 A3
 12 Gainsborough DN21 ..117 B1
Dog & Duck Sq 13 YO15 ..5 A2
Dog Kennel La HU17 ...43 C5
Doherty Wlk YO24 ....132 C6
Dolby Vale 23 DN34 ...102 C2

Dole Rd DN17 ....80 B1
Dolegate YO41 ....15 F4
Doll La 2 DN20 ....98 F7
Dollyth Howe★ YO17 ....6 F6
Dolman Cres 11 DN17 ..96 C2
Dolphin St DN35 ......153 F2
Dominican Wlk HU17 ..154 B2
Dominion Cl 9 DN36 ..114 A7
Don Ave YO24 ....132 E8
Don St DN14 ....149 D1
Doncaster Rd
 Brayton YO8 ....148 B3
 Gunness DN15 ....95 E6
 Hatfield DN7 ....92 D3
 Haxey DN9 ....104 F2
 North Elmsall WF8 ......76 A1
 Scunthorpe DN15 ......150 A4
 Stainforth DN7 ....92 B6
Doncaster St HU3 .....145 B6
Donna Fields YO25 .....9 F6
Donnington Gdns
 DN15 ....150 F7
Donnington St DN32 ...152 F3
Donville Rd DN17 ....81 A3
Dooks Cl DN21 ....107 C1
Doon Garth HU4 ......144 A3
Dorado Cl 2 HU3 ......145 A5
Dorchester Prim Sch
 HU7 ....141 B6
Dorchester Rd
 Kingston upon Hull HU7 .141 B7
 Scunthorpe DN17 ......150 C4
Doriam Ave YO31 .....127 F2
Doriam Dr YO31 ......127 F2
Dorking Cl HU8 ....142 A4
Dornoch Dr HU8 ......141 C3
Dorothy Ave
 Thorne/Moorends DN8 ..92 F8
 6 Waltham DN37 .....113 E7
Dorr La DN14 ....78 A8
Dorrington Cl 23 YO42 .29 A3
Dorset Ave HU11 ....45 C1
Dorset Cl E 2 DN15 ....82 B4
Dorset Cl W 1 DN15 ...82 B4
Dorset St HU4 ....144 F3
Dorsey Way 5 HU4 .....68 C2
Dot Hill Cl 3 YO43 .....53 F7
Double Bridges Rd
 DN8 ....93 B6
Double Dike★ HU20 ....54 E5
Doughty Cl 2 DN37 ...113 E7
Doughty Rd DN32 ....152 E3
Douglas Ave DN34 ....152 A4
Douglas Rd
 Cleethorpes DN35 ......153 D4
 Kingston upon Hull HU8 .142 C6
Douglas St 3 YO8 .....148 C5
Dove Cl HU12 ....74 A8
Dove Cote Gdns DN14 .62 D2
Dove La HU12 ....74 B8
Dove St YO23 ....156 A1
Dovecote Garth 5 YO41 .27 B2
Dovecote Mdws DN20 ..98 D3
Dovedale Cl DN15 ......83 A6
Dovedale Ct YO16 ....122 F7
Dovedale Dr 18 DN33 ..113 E8
Dovedale Gr 1 HU9 ...146 E8
Dovedale Rd DN16 ....151 D1
Dover St Grimsby DN31 .152 C4
 Kingston upon Hull HU3 .145 C8
Dower Chase YO19 .....37 A6
Dower Pk YO19 ....37 B6
Dower Rise 11 HU14 ....69 B7
Downe Cl DN14 ....78 D7
Downe St YO25 ....124 E4
Downfield Ave HU6 ...140 B8
Downhill Dr 7 HU7 .....57 B5
Downing Cl 7 DN34 ...102 C3
Downing Cres 11 DN16 .96 C2
Downing Gr HU9 ......142 A1
Downland Cres WF11 ..61 A2
Downs Cres HU5 ......139 D2
Dowse Ave DN15 ......150 E8
Dowsons La DN14 ......78 E8
Dr Anderson Ave 9 DN7 92 C6
Dragon La YO16 ....122 C5
Dragonby Rd 3 DN17 ..96 C2
Drain Bank HU15 ....67 B8
Drain La
 Gilberdyke HU15 ....52 D2
 Holme-on-Spalding-Moor
 YO43 ....51 F8
Drake Ave DN32 ......153 B2
Drake St 2 YO23 ......156 B1
Drakes Cl YO32 ....127 C5
Draper's La 17 HU12 ...72 C7
Drapers Croft YO23 ...132 B4
Drax CP Sch YO8 ....63 F5
Dray Dr HU7 ....43 E5
Draycot LN7 ....111 A2
Draycott Ave HU18 ...134 C5
Drayton Cl 5 HU8 .....142 C5
Dressay Gr HU8 ....141 F7
Drew Ave DN32 ....102 F2
Drewry La 7 DN9 .....105 A2
Drewton Ct 8 DN14 ....65 A7
Drewton La HU15 ......54 A4
Driffield Bsns Ctr
 YO25 ....124 F2
Driffield CE VC Inf Sch
 YO25 ....124 E4
Driffield Cl HU16 ......138 E6
Driffield Jun Sch
 YO25 ....124 F5
Driffield Rd
 Beverley HU17 ....136 C6
 Huggate YO42 ....18 C1
 Kilham YO25 ....9 C2

Driffield Rd *continued*
Langtoft YO25 8 C4
Molescroft HU17 136 B8
Nafferton YO25 125 E7
Skerne & Wansford YO25 21 A2
Driffield Sch YO25 125 A5
Driffield Showground★ YO25 124 D2
Driffield Spellowgate YO25 124 B7
Driffield Sports Ctr YO25 125 A5
Driffield Sta YO25 124 F3
Driffield Terr YO24 130 A2
Driffil Way DN15 83 A4
Drill Hall La 28 DN21 117 B1
Dring La DN21 118 A7
Dringfield Cl 2 YO24 132 D8
Dringhouses Prim Sch YO24 132 F8
Dringhouses Sports Club YO24 132 F8
Dringshaw HU6 139 F8
Dringthorpe Rd YO24 132 F7
Drive The
Cherry Burton HU17 43 A4
Kirk Sandall DN3 92 A1
Waltham DN37 113 E6
Drome Rd YO23 132 C2
Dronfield Ct DN15 150 B7
Drove La HU7 44 E1
Drovers Rise 1 HU15 68 C6
Drummer's Well★ YO25 21 F8
Drummond Ct 5 HU7 57 B5
Drummond View YO23 133 B4
Drury Cl 1 DN37 113 D6
Drury La 3 DN36 114 A7
Drydales HU10 143 C6
Dryden Rd DN17 150 D2
Dryden St HU8 141 C2
Dryham La HU15 53 C3
Dryhurst Cl 9 DN6 76 F2
Drypool Way HU9 146 B6
Duchess St DN32 152 D2
Duck La YO12 1 A8
Duckthorpe La DN36 115 B2
Duddon Gr HU8 142 B6
Dudley Mews YO31 156 C4
Dudley Pl DN35 103 B2
Dudley Rd 28 Brigg DN20 98 C2
Scunthorpe DN16 151 E2
Dudley St
Grimsby DN34 152 C3
York YO31 156 C4
Dudley Wlk HU4 144 B3
Duesbery St HU5 145 C8
Duesbury Cl HU17 154 A3
Dugard Rd DN32 153 B3
Duggleby Howe★ YO17 6 C5
Duke St Grimsby DN32 153 A5
13 Stainforth DN7 92 C6
Duke's La YO25 2 A1
Dukes Wharf YO23 156 B1
Dulverton Cl 4 HU7 56 F5
Dumfries Wlk HU8 142 C7
Dunbar Ave 5 DN36 114 A7
Dunbar Cl 6 DN21 117 C1
Dunce Mire Rd LS25 61 A8
Duncombe Ct HU12 72 E7
Duncombe Dr
Great Driffield YO25 124 D3
Strensall YO32 14 B8
Duncombe Gdns DN32 152 F5
Duncombe La YO32 14 B8
Duncombe Pl YO1 156 B3
Duncombe St DN32 152 F4
Dundas St YO1 156 C2
Dundee St HU5 145 A8
Dunelm Cl 3 HU8 141 C1
Dunelm Cres 15 DN8 79 B2
Dunflat Gate HU17 55 D6
Dunflat La HU20 55 B5
Dunflat Rd HU17 55 D6
Dunhill Rd DN14 149 B4
Dunkeld Dr 4 HU6 140 B8
Dunken Hill Highgate HU17 42 F4
Dunlin Cl HU7 141 D8
Dunlop Way DN16 151 E3
Dunmires La DN14 80 E8
Dunmow Cl 1 HU8 142 C5
Dunmow St DN31 152 B5
Dunnington CE Prim Sch YO19 26 E7
Dunnington La
Beeford YO25 34 D7
Skipsea YO25 22 F1
Dunnock Cl
7 Kingston upon Hull HU8 141 D7
26 Yaddlethorpe DN17 96 D1
Dunn's La 6 YO25 124 F4
Dunns Paddock 3 DN20 98 F7
Dunscombe Pk HU8 141 B2
Dunstall St DN15 151 A7
Dunstan Dr
30 Canal Side DN8 93 A8
26 Thorne/Moorends DN8 93 A8
Dunstan Hill DN21 108 B1
Dunstan Villas 17 DN21 108 B1
Dunster Rd DN21 117 C1
Dunston Dr HU13 143 D1
Dunston Rd HU4 144 D7
Dunsville Cty Prim Sch DN7 92 D3
Dunswell Cl HU6 140 A7
Dunswell La HU6 56 C6
Dunswell Prim Sch HU6 56 D6
Dunswell Rd
Cottingham HU16 56 B6
Kingston upon Hull HU16 139 C8
Dunvegan Rd HU8 141 F6
Durban Rd DN32 153 B3
Durban St HU8 155 C3
Durham Ave
Grimsby DN34 152 A3
10 Thorne/Moorends DN8 93 A8
Durham Cl 18 YO8 49 F1
Durham Mews HU17 154 A1
Durham Rd
Cleethorpes DN35 153 C1
Hatfield DN7 92 D4
Durham St HU8 141 C1
Durlston Dr YO32 14 A7
Dursley Ave 1 DN36 113 F7
Dyer La HU17 154 A3
Dyke Cl 2 HU13 69 F4
Dyke Rd DN36 115 C5
Dykelands Cl YO19 37 F7
Dykes La YO23 132 A1
Dymoke Dr DN37 102 B3
Dyon La YO8 50 B3
Dyon Rd YO8 50 D7

E

Eadon Pl DN14 78 B8
Eagle Bsns Ctr HU2 155 C4
Eagle Terr HU8 155 C4
Ealand Rd DN17 95 C6
Ealdane HU6 139 E8
Ealing Cl HU8 141 F5
Earfit La YO23 36 A8
Earl Ave DN36 114 A8
Earl St Grimsby DN31 152 C3
Scunthorpe DN16 151 B6
Earle St YO31 156 C4
Earle's Rd
Kingston upon Hull HU9 146 D7
North Coates DN36 115 C5
Earlescourt HU6 139 E7
Earls Wlk DN16 151 B6
Earlsborough Terr YO30 156 A3
Earlsgate Gdns DN15 82 F5
Earlsgate Rd DN15 83 A5
Earsham Cl HU8 142 C6
Earswick Chase YO32 127 F7
Earswick Village YO32 127 F7
Easby Ct HU5 139 C2
Easedale Ave HU9 142 D3
Easenby Ave HU10 143 C6
Easenby Cl 3 HU14 69 C7
Easington CE VC Prim Sch HU12 90 F5
Easington Rd
Easington HU12 91 B2
Skeffling HU12 90 E6
Eason Rd
8 Grimsby DN33 102 D1
York YO24 132 E8
Eason View YO24 132 E8
East Acridge 7 DN18 84 F8
East Back Side YO25 10 C3
East Bank DN7 92 C7
East Boundary Rd DN16 151 F6
East Carr Rd
Keyingham HU12 73 D5
Kingston upon Hull HU8 141 F7
East Cl HU17 136 D6
East Comm La
Scunthorpe DN16 151 B4
Selby YO8 148 F4
East Cross St 15 DN21 108 B1
East Dale Dr DN21 108 B2
East Dale Rd HU14 68 E5
East Dock Rd DN40 87 E2
East Ella Dr HU4 144 C6
East End
Humberside Airport DN39 100 A6
Walkington HU17 55 C8
East End Cl DN33 102 E1
East End Rd HU12 58 D1
East Ferry Rd
Laughton DN21 106 D1
Wildsworth DN21 117 A8
East Field Rd DN7 92 C8
East Gate Rudston YO25 9 F6
Thorne/Moorends DN8 79 B2
East Gate N YO25 124 E5
East Gate S YO25 124 F4
East Gn DN17 107 D7
East Gr
Barton-upon-Humber DN18 69 F1
Kingston upon Hull HU4 144 D4
East Halton Prim Sch DN40 86 D6
East Halton Rd DN40 86 E3
East Hann La DN19 70 E1
East Hull Pools HU9 146 C8
East La Beverley HU17 136 D5
Corringham DN21 118 B2
Sigglesthorne HU11 45 F8
Stainforth DN7 92 C6
East Lambwath Rd HU11 46 D3
East Lound Rd
Haxey DN9 105 D2
East Lound Rd *continued*
Owston Ferry DN9 106 A3
East Marsh Rd DN19 71 C3
East Mid Mere Rd DN40 86 F4
East Moor Gdns YO19 133 F5
East Mount 8 HU14 69 A4
East Mount Ave HU8 142 B5
East Mount Rd YO24 156 A1
East Newton Rd HU11 47 D1
East Parade Brigg DN20 98 C2
Goole DN14 149 D3
York YO31 130 F6
East Pk HU17 45 B8
East Pk Ave HU8 141 E3
East Ravendale CE Prim Sch DN37 113 B2
East Rd
Bridlington YO15 122 D1
Keadby with Althorpe DN17 95 C6
East Riding Bsns Pk HU17 137 C3
East Riding Coll Beverley Campus HU17 136 C5
East Riding Coll Bridlington Campus YO16 122 D4
East Riverside DN40 87 E3
East Scar YO15 5 A3
East St
Dalton Holme HU17 31 E1
Grimsby DN32 152 E3
Hibaldstow DN20 108 F5
Kilham YO25 9 C3
5 Kingston upon Hull HU9 146 B7
Leven HU17 45 A8
Roxby cum Risby DN15 83 A4
East St Mary's Gate 3 DN31 152 D3
East View
7 Campsall DN6 76 E1
10 Knottingley WF11 61 A2
East Way YO31 127 E2
East Wlk DN15 151 B7
East Yorkshire Coll YO16 122 D4
East Yorkshire Hospl (Artificial Limb Unit) HU2 155 B3
Eastbourne Gr YO31 130 F5
Eastbourne Rd HU18 134 D4
Eastbourne St HU3 145 A5
Eastbourne Way 12 DN33 113 E8
Easterfield Ct 10 YO25 124 F4
Eastern Ave DN21 117 C1
Eastern Inway DN34 152 A1
Eastern Terr YO31 130 E6
Eastfield
5 Humberston DN36 114 D8
Hunmanby YO14 2 F8
Eastfield Ave
Grimsby DN33 113 E8
Haxby YO32 127 C7
Eastfield Cl
3 Beverley HU17 137 A6
North Frodingham YO25 34 A8
Eastfield Cres YO10 131 C2
Eastfield Ct YO10 131 C2
Eastfield Est HU12 60 B1
Eastfield Inf & Jun Schools DN40 87 C1
Eastfield La
Dunnington YO19 26 F8
Kellington DN14 61 F4
Rise HU11 45 F6
Eastfield Prim Sch HU4 144 D6
Eastfield Rd
Barton-upon-Humber DN18 84 F7
Brandesburton YO25 34 C2
Bridlington YO16 122 E5
Brigg DN20 98 C2
Easington HU12 91 A5
Epworth DN9 105 E6
Fangfoss YO41 28 D7
Great Driffield YO25 124 E5
1 Keelby DN41 101 A5
Keyingham HU12 73 D4
Kingston upon Hull HU4 144 D6
Market Weighton YO43 135 E3
Messingham DN17 107 D7
North Killingholme DN40 86 F4
Scunthorpe DN16 151 C1
Eastfield Rise 4 DN36 114 A5
Eastgate Beverley HU17 154 B2
2 Goole DN14 149 D4
Grimsby DN32 152 E4
4 Hornsea HU18 134 B4
Kingston upon Hull HU13 143 E2
Lund YO25 31 F2
Nafferton YO25 125 F7
North Newbald YO43 53 F7
Patrington HU12 74 D1
Scotton DN21 107 C2
Eastgate Ct HU18 134 C5
Eastgate View HU18 134 B4
Easthall Rd LN7 110 B4
Eastholme Cl YO25 124 F5
Eastholme Dr YO30 126 E1
Eastholme Gdns 9 DN15 82 B4
Eastholme La HU12 73 C7
Easthorpe Dr YO26 126 A1
Eastland Ave YO24 129 E2
Eastlands YO25 125 F7
Eastlands Rd YO25 19 E2
Eastmount Recn Ctr HU8 142 B6
Eastoft CE Prim Sch DN17 81 A3
Eastoft Rd Crowle DN17 94 D8
Luddington & Haldenby DN17 81 C3
Easton Ave HU8 141 A2
Easton Rd YO16 122 A4
Easton Wlk YO16 122 B4
Eastrington Ponds Nature Reserve★ DN14 65 E8
Eastrington Prim Sch DN14 51 F1
Eastrington Sta DN14 66 A8
Eastside Rd
Grimsby DN31 152 F5
Scunthorpe DN16 151 F6
Eastville Rd 10 DN33 102 D2
Eastward Ave YO10 133 E7
Eastwold 2 YO43 53 F7
Eastwood Ave DN32 102 E2
Eastwood Ct DN15 150 B6
Eastwood Dr 8 DN20 97 E4
Eaton Ct Grimsby DN34 152 C2
7 York YO24 132 B8
Eaton Rd 13 DN40 87 C1
Ebberston Gr 5 HU5 139 E3
Ebor Ave HU18 134 D2
Ebor Cl HU8 142 B6
Ebor Ct 7 YO8 148 C6
Ebor Ind Est YO31 156 C3
Ebor Manor 1 HU12 73 C4
Ebor Prep Sch YO30 130 A7
Ebor St Selby YO8 148 C5
York YO23 156 B1
Ebor View YO43 135 E4
Ebor Way YO26 126 A2
Ebsay Dr YO30 127 A1
Eccles Cl YO30 126 D2
Eccles Ct DN20 98 D4
Ecclesfield Ave HU9 142 D1
Eccleston Rd DN3 92 A3
Eddlemere La YO25 32 E7
Eden Ave YO8 148 D3
Eden Cl Beverley HU17 136 D5
York YO24 132 C7
Eden Dene DN16 151 D1
Eden Dr HU8 141 C3
Eden Field Rd 12 DN3 92 A2
Eden Gdns YO15 4 D2
Eden Gr Rd 1 DN3 92 A1
Eden Rd HU17 136 D5
Eden Rise HU10 138 C2
Edencroft Dr 14 DN3 92 A2
Edendale HU7 140 F6
Edenfield Ave HU18 134 C2
Edenthorpe Hall Prim Sch DN3 92 A1
Edgar Cl DN21 107 C4
Edgar St HU3 145 D5
Edgbaston Ave 27 DN17 96 C2
Edge Ave DN33 102 E1
Edgecliffe Villas 4 YO15 122 F4
Edgecumbe St HU5 140 C2
Edgemere DN15 150 B7
Edgeware Ave 1 HU9 141 F1
Edgware Rd YO10 130 E2
Edinburgh Dr 4 DN36 114 A6
Edinburgh Rd 3 DN17 95 D6
Edinburgh St
Goole DN14 149 C4
Kingston upon Hull HU3 145 A5
Edison Gr HU9 141 E2
Edith Cavell Ct 4 HU5 139 F4
Edmonds Way DN31 152 D4
Edmund Cl DN21 118 A1
Edmund Wilson Swimming Baths YO24 129 D1
Edward Collins Sq 2 HU9 146 C7
Edward Ct 6 DN8 79 B1
Edward Heneage Prim Sch DN32 152 F3
Edward Rd 11 DN21 117 B1
Edward St
Beverley HU17 154 B3
Cleethorpes DN35 153 E1
Grimsby DN32 152 F3
Kingston upon Hull HU13 143 F1
1 Pocklington YO42 29 A4
6 Withernsea HU19 74 F7
Edwardian Dr YO15 122 C1
Edwards Rd DN15 150 F8
Edwins Garth YO43 135 F6
Eelmere La HU11 47 A5
Egginton Cl HU10 143 C7
Egginton St HU2 155 B3
Eglins Rd DN8 79 C1
Eglinton Ave HU8 141 F3
Egremont Cl 11 YO41 15 D2
Egrom's La HU19 75 A5
Egton Ave DN17 107 D7
Egton St HU8 155 C4
Egypt St HU9 147 B7
Eighth Ave
Bridlington YO15 122 F4
Fixborough Stather DN15 82 A1
York YO31 130 F5
Eildon Hills Cl HU7 57 B5
Elba St HU9 147 C7
Elderberry Dr HU4 144 D4
Elderberry Way 4 DN35 103 B1
Elderwood Ct 6 HU3 145 D5
Eldon Dr 11 HU12 58 C1
Eldon Gr
Kingston upon Hull HU5 140 D2
Thorne/Moorends DN8 79 C2
Eldon St YO31 156 C4
Eldon Terr YO31 156 C4
Eldwick Cl YO30 126 F2
Eleanor Ct HU9 142 B2
Eleanor St DN32 152 F4
Elgar Cl YO31 127 E1
Elgar Rd HU4 144 B4
Elizabeth Ave 6 DN3 92 A2
Elizabeth Cl
Bridlington YO15 122 C1
4 Gainsborough DN21 117 B2
14 Grimsby DN33 113 D8
Scotter DN21 107 C4
Elizabeth Ct 7 YO8 148 B6
Elizabeth Dr YO25 124 D3
Elizabeth St DN15 151 A8
Ella Ct HU10 143 C8
Ella Pk HU10 143 D7
Ella St HU5 140 B2
Ellen Way 9 DN36 113 F8
Ellerbeck Ct HU7 141 D7
Ellerburn Ave HU6 140 A7
Ellerburn Dr 3 YO16 122 C5
Ellerby Gatehouse★ HU11 46 A1
Ellerby Gr HU9 141 F2
Ellerby Rd HU11 45 F2
Ellerington La HU17 42 F6
Ellerker La HU15 53 F1
Ellerker Rd HU17 154 A2
Ellerker Rise HU10 138 D2
Ellerker Wold La HU15 54 B1
Ellesmere Ave HU8 142 A4
Ellesmere Gr DN7 92 D6
Ellesmere Rise DN34 102 B2
Ellifoot La HU12 73 B7
Ellingham Cl HU8 142 B6
Elliot Ct YO10 133 D7
Elliot Way YO43 135 D3
Ellis Cl 4 HU12 58 D1
Ellis St HU9 146 C8
Ellis Way DN31 152 E4
Ellison Ave DN16 96 D1
Ellison St DN8 93 A7
Elliston Inf Sch DN35 153 D4
Elliston Jun Sch DN35 153 C4
Elliston St DN35 153 C3
Ellmore La LN7 110 B4
Elloughton Dale HU15 68 D8
Elloughton Gr 4 HU16 138 E6
Elloughton Prim Sch HU15 68 C7
Elloughton Rd HU15 68 C5
Ellwood Ct YO10 130 D2
Elm Ave 15 Brough HU15 68 C6
Burstwick HU12 73 A6
Cleethorpes DN35 153 E2
Goole DN14 149 B4
Grimsby DN34 152 A2
Kingston upon Hull HU8 141 C2
Elm Cl HU17 136 D5
Elm Dr HU17 43 A5
Elm End 9 YO32 13 E5
Elm Garth HU12 60 B1
Elm Gdns DN35 153 E2
Elm Gr 1 Aldbrough HU11 47 C1
Healing DN41 102 A5
Scunthorpe DN16 151 B4
York YO31 127 F2
Elm La Goxhill DN19 71 A1
Laceby DN37 101 E1
Elm Rd
Cleethorpes DN35 153 E2
Great Driffield YO25 124 F2
Waltham DN37 113 E6
Elm St
Kingston upon Hull HU5 140 D2
Selby YO8 148 D6
Elm Terr HU5 140 D2
Elm Tree Ave
9 Poppleton YO26 12 F1
5 Thorngumbald HU12 72 E5
Elm Tree Cl
Keyingham HU12 73 C4
6 Thorngumbald HU12 72 E5
Elm Tree Ct
Cottingham HU16 139 B6
Kingston upon Hull HU9 142 C1
Elm Tree Farm Rd 1 HU12 73 A6
Elm Tree Gr 4 DN8 93 B7
Elm Way Brigg DN20 98 B2
Messingham DN17 107 C7
Elma Ave YO16 122 D2
Elma Gr 3 YO30 126 E2
Elma Villas 5 YO16 122 D2
Elmbridge Par 3 HU9 142 E1
Elmdale 16 DN18 84 E8
Elmfield HU6 140 B6
Elmfield Ave YO31 130 F8
Elmfield Dr
16 Brandesburton YO25 34 B2
Kingston upon Hull HU16 139 A6
Elmfield Terr YO31 130 F7
Elmhirst Rd DN8 93 B8
Elmlands Gr YO31 130 F8
Elmpark Vale YO31 131 A8
Elmpark View YO31 131 A8
Elmpark Way YO31 131 A8
Elms Cl 2 YO19 36 F1

Elms Dr HU10 ....143 C8
Elms The
 4 Gilberdyke HU15 ....66 D7
Stockton on the Forest
 YO32 ....14 D2
Elmsall Dr HU17 .....136 C6
Elmswell Spellowgate
 YO25 ....20 B6
Elmswood HU13 ......143 C2
Elmtree Ave 9 HU14 ..69 A4
Elmtree Gdns 3 YO26 .129 C3
Elsenham Rd DN31 ...162 E3
Elsham Gr 21 DN33 ...102 D2
Elsham Dr DN37 ......113 D6
Elsham Hall Ctry & Wildlife
 Pk★ DN20 ....98 F6
Elsham Rd DN20 ......98 D7
Elsham Rise HU13 ....143 D1
Elsham Wold Ind Est
 DN20 ....99 A8
Elsie St DN14 ....149 C5
Elsiemere Wlk 6 HU4 .144 B6
Elsternwick Ave HU8 .141 B2
Elston Cl
 Kingston upon Hull HU6 .140 D6
 York YO30 ....130 A8
Elston Pl YO8 ....148 C6
Elvaston Ave HU18 ...134 C5
Elvaston Pk 10 HU7 ...56 E5
Eveley Dr HU13 ......143 A7
Elvington CE Prim Sch
 YO41 ....27 B3
Elvington Cl HU4 .....140 A6
Elvington Cres HU17 ..43 D5
Elvington Ind Est YO41 .27 A3
Elvington La YO19 ....26 E5
Elvington Pk YO41 ....27 A3
Elvington Terr YO10 ..130 E4
Elwell Ave HU17 .....154 A2
Elwes St 9 DN20 .....98 C2
Elwick Gr YO10 ......131 C4
Elwyn Pl 2 DN35 .....103 B1
Elwyn Way 40 HU12 ...72 D7
Embankment The
 YO25 ....124 B3
Emberton Pk 12 HU7 ..56 F6
Embleton Dr 1 YO30 ..126 F1
Emerald Gr 8 HU3 ....145 A4
Emerald St YO31 .....156 C4
Emerson Ave DN7 ....92 C5
Emfield Gr DN33 .....113 E7
Emfield Rd DN33 .....113 D8
Emily Mews YO10 ....130 E4
Emily St 8 HU9 ......146 C7
Eminson Cl DN21 ....107 C4
Emmanuel Rd DN16 ..151 F2
Emmanuel Ct
 Grimsby DN34 ....152 A2
 Scunthorpe DN16 ....151 B2
Emmanuel Dr 18 DN16 .96 D2
Emmerson St 2 YO31 .130 E5
Emmery Cl DN20 .....97 D4
Emmott Rd HU6 ......140 C7
Empringham St 5 HU9 146 D7
Empson Ave DN14 ...149 B6
Empson Terr HU17 ...154 A2
Emsdale Wlk YO16 ...122 B4
Ena St HU3 ....145 B6
Enclosure Gdns 1
 YO10 ....131 B1
Endcliffe Ave DN17 ..96 C1
Endeavour Cres 3 HU9 142 B1
Endeavour High Sch
 HU3 ....140 E1
Enderby Rd DN17 ....150 D1
Enderby Rd Inf Sch
 DN17 ....96 C2
Endfields Rd 1 YO10 .133 E8
Endike La HU6 ....140 A6
Endike Prim Sch HU6 .140 C6
Endsleigh Holly Child RC VA
 Prim Sch HU6 ....140 C4
Endsleigh St HU3 ....145 A4
Endyke La HU6 ......139 D6
Endymion St HU8 ....141 B1
Enfield (New Waltham) Prim
 Sch DN36 ....114 A7
Enfield Ave DN36 ....114 A7
Enfield Cres 1 YO24 .130 A3
Enfield Mews HU17 ..154 B3
Engine La HU11 .....58 D7
Engine St 19 DN20 ...98 B2
England Rd HU11 ....142 F7
English Cl HU3 ......145 E4
English Martyrs' RC Prim Sch
 YO24 ....129 F3
English St HU1 ......155 A1
Ennerdale HU1 ......140 E7
Ennerdale Ave YO31 .131 B5
Ennerdale Cl 13 DN36 103 C1
Ennerdale Leisure Ctr
 HU7 ....140 E6
Enstone Garth 20 HU7 .57 A5
Enterprise Pk HU7 ...137 B3
Enterprise Rd LN7 ...111 A4
Enterprise Way
 Bridlington YO16 ....122 C2
 Grimsby DN32 ....153 A2
 Winterton DN15 .....82 F5
Ephams La DN41 ....101 E7
Epping Cl HU8 ....141 E6
Eppleworth Rd HU10 .105 D6
Epworth L Ctr DN9 ..105 D6
Epworth Prim Sch
 DN9 ....105 D6

Epworth Rd Hatfield DN7 .92 F4
 Haxey DN9 ....105 D3
 Owston Ferry DN9 ...106 A4
Epworth Rd W 9 DN7 .92 E4
Epworth St HU5 .....140 D1
Epworth Turbary Nature
 Reserve★ DN9 .....105 B6
Eric Bielby Cl HU17 ..154 B3
Ermine St Appleby DN15 .97 D8
 Winteringham DN15 ..83 B8
Ernest Hill Ct 1 HU5 .140 A2
Ernest Kirkwood Cl 4
 HU5 ....139 D1
Eryholme Cres DN15 .150 F7
Escart Ave DN32 ....153 B2
Escrick CE VC Prim Sch
 YO19 ....37 A5
Escrick Ct YO19 .....37 A5
Escrick Pk Gdns YO19 .37 B5
Escrick St YO10 .....156 C1
Escrick Terr YO10 ...156 C1
Esk Dr YO26 ....129 B8
Eskdale Ave
 2 Kingston upon Hull
 HU9 ....141 E1
 York YO10 ....131 C3
Eskdale Dr YO16 ....122 F8
Eske Cl HU17 ....44 C5
Eske La HU17 ......44 C5
Eskham Cl 19 DN35 ..103 C2
Eskholme La DN14 ..78 B4
Eskwood Wlk DN14 ..149 F6
Esmond St HU6 .....140 D5
Esplanade
 Bridlington YO15 ....122 F2
 Hornsea HU18 ......134 D5
 York YO30 ....156 A2
Esplanade Ct YO30 ..156 A3
Essex Dr 7 DN15 ....82 B4
Essex St HU4 ......144 E3
Estate Ave DN20 ....97 D3
Estate Rd No 1 DN31 .152 A6
Estate Rd No 2 DN31 .152 A5
Estate Rd No 3 DN31 .102 C5
Estate Rd No 4 DN31 .102 C5
Estate Rd No 5 DN31 .152 A6
Estate Rd No 6 DN37 .102 C5
Estate Rd No 7 DN37 .102 C5
Estate Rd No 8 DN37 .102 C5
Estcourt Prim Sch
 HU9 ....146 D8
Estcourt St
 Goole DN14 ....149 D4
 Kingston upon Hull HU9 .146 D8
Estcourt Terr DN14 ..149 D4
Estuary Way DN31 ..152 B6
Ethel Ct 5 DN15 ....151 B7
Ethelstone Rd DN34 .152 A3
Etherington Cl 6 HU12 .73 C4
Etherington Ct HU7 ..137 B3
Etherington Dr HU6 ..140 D5
Etherington La YO25 .124 E4
Etherington Rd HU6 ..140 C5
Etive Pl YO24 ......132 B7
Eton Dr 7 Haxby YO32 .13 D5
 Scunthorpe DN17 ....96 C2
Eton Rd DN14 ......149 B5
Eton St HU3 ....145 C4
Etton Cl HU16 ......138 E5
Etton Dikes HU17 ...43 A6
Etton Gr HU6 ....139 F5
Etton Rd HU17 .....43 A5
Etty Ave YO10 .....131 A4
Etty Cl 24 HU5 .....15 D2
Europa Bsns Pk DN31 .152 A6
Europa Way Brigg DN20 .98 B2
 Immingham DN41 ....87 E1
Europarc Innovation Ctr
 DN37 ....102 B6
Eva Ave YO30 ......126 D2
Evelyn Cres YO30 ...130 B7
Evelyn Gr N DN32 ...153 B2
Evelyn Gr S DN32 ...153 B2
Evendine Ct 2 DN36 .114 B5
Ever Thorpe Cl 5 HU3 .145 C5
Everest Rd DN16 ....151 C1
Evergreen Dr HU6 ...56 D5
Evergreen Way 1 HU7 .48 D1
Everingham La YO42 .40 A4
Everingham Wlk HU5 .139 C2
Eversfield Cl 21 HU7 ..57 A5
Everthorpe Rd HU15 .53 D3
Evesham Ave DN14 ..102 C3
Evesham Croft 1 YO16 .122 C6
Exchange Pl 6 DN20 .98 B2
Exchange St
 Great Driffield YO25 .124 E4
 Kingston upon Hull HU5 .140 C2
Exeter Ct 11 DN34 ...102 B2
Exeter Gr HU9 ......142 A2
Exeter Rd DN15 ....150 F7
Exeter St HU16 .....139 C7
Exhibition Sq YO1 ..156 B3
Exmoor Ave DN15 ..96 B8
Exmoor Rd DN7 ....150 C4
Exmouth St HU5 ....140 C3
Exton Cl HU7 ......56 F5
Eyre Ave DN16 .....151 B1
Eyre Cl YO8 ....148 B4

F

Faber Cl YO23 ......132 B3
Faber St YO31 ......130 E5
Faceby Wlk HU5 ....139 E3
Fair Pl HU18 ....134 B4

Fair View Ave DN35 ..153 E2
Fairbourne Cl 1 HU7 .57 A7
Faircourt HU6 ......139 E7
Fairfax 15 YO41 ....15 D2
Fairfax Ave
 Kingston upon Hull HU5 .139 F3
 Selby YO8 ....148 B4
Fairfax Croft YO23 ..132 B2
Fairfax Dr HU12 ....72 C8
Fairfax House★ YO1 .156 C2
Fairfax Rd DN34 ....152 B3
Fairfax St YO1 ......156 B1
Fairfield Goole DN14 .149 F6
 North Cave HU15 ....53 D2
 Rawcliffe DN14 ......79 B8
Fairfield Ave
 Grimsby DN33 ......113 E8
 Kingston upon Hull
 HU10 ....138 C1
Fairfield Cl
 5 Broughton DN20 ..97 E3
 Nafferton YO25 .....125 F7
Fairfield Croft 8 DN9 .105 E6
Fairfield Ct 4 DN35 .103 D1
Fairfield Dr
 25 Barton-upon-Humber
 DN18 ....84 F8
 Messingham DN17 ...107 D7
Fairfield La LS25 ....61 A6
Fairfield Pit Nature
 Reserve★ DN19 .....70 D3
Fairfield Prim Sch
 DN33 ....113 E8
Fairfield Rd
 Bridlington YO15 ....122 D1
 Grimsby DN33 ......113 E8
 Kingston upon Hull HU5 .139 F3
 Scunthorpe DN15 ....150 C8
Fairfield View 5 HU15 .68 D5
Fairfields 21 DN21 ...108 B1
Fairfields Dr YO30 ..126 B5
Fairholme La HU7 ...56 F7
Fairisle Rise 5 DN40 .101 C8
Fairlawn HU17 .....136 C6
Fairmont Cres DN16 .151 B6
Fairmont Rd DN32 ..153 A3
Fairtree Wlk 21 DN8 .93 A8
Fairway Selby YO8 ...148 A4
 Waltham DN37 ......113 E7
 York YO30 ....130 A8
Fairway Ave DN21 ..117 B2
Fairway Ct DN35 ....103 E1
Fairway Dr 18 YO26 ..12 F1
Fairway The
 Kingston upon Hull
 HU10 ....143 A8
 Thorne/Moorends DN8 .79 B2
Fairways The
 Kingston upon Hull HU8 .142 A6
 Scunthorpe DN15 ....150 B6
Falcon Cl YO32 ....13 F5
Falcon Ct HU4 .....144 D2
Falconer St 1 YO24 .129 F3
Falconers The DN21 .108 F2
Falkirk Cl 7 HU7 ....57 A7
Falkland Rd HU9 ....142 D1
Falkland St YO1 ....156 B1
Falkland Way HU12 ..69 F1
Fallowfield Rd DN33 .113 D6
Falmouth St HU5 ...140 C3
Falsgrave Cres YO30 .130 B7
Falsgrave Gr HU4 ...144 D7
Fangfoss Pottery★
 YO41 ....28 C8
Fannystone Rd DN34 .152 B3
Far Bank La DN7 ....92 C3
Far Comm Rd DN7 ..93 A4
Far Field Cl 15 DN3 ..92 A2
Far Field Rd DN3 ....92 A2
Far Ings La DN15 ...69 C1
Far Ings National Nature
 Reserve★ DN18 ....69 D2
Far Ings Rd DN18 ...69 D1
Far La YO25 ....35 A5
Faraday St HU9 .....141 E2
Farbridge La HU12 ..72 C6
Fardell Rd DN16 ....151 D3
Farebrother St DN32 .152 E1
Farfield YO26 ......129 C6
Farfield La YO19 ...26 E8
Farfield lane YO19 ..14 E1
Faringdon Rd DN31 .153 A6
Farlington Cl HU9 ..142 C5
Farm Cl
 4 Edenthorpe DN3 ..92 A1
 Gunness DN15 ......95 E6
Farm Ct YO43 ......135 C5
Farm La 2 DN17 ....106 D8
Farm Way YO8 .....148 B2
Farmers Way YO23 ..132 B3
Farmhouse Mews 11
 DN36 ....114 A7
Farmlands Rd 1 YO24 .132 D8
Farms La DN14 .....66 A8
Farmstead Rise YO32 .127 D7
Farndale Ave
 Kingston upon Hull HU9 .141 E1
 York YO10 ....131 D4
Farndale Cl 1 YO32 ..13 F5
Farndale Rd 1 YO16 .122 E7
Farndale St YO10 ...130 D2
Farndale Way
 2 Grimsby DN31 ....152 D4
 1 Winterton DN15 ..83 A5
Farnella Cl HU3 ....145 A5
Faroes Cl 1 HU9 ...142 A1
Farrand Rd HU12 ...72 C7
Farrar St YO10 .....130 E3

Farriers Croft 2 YO23 .132 B3
Farriers Fold 13 DN9 .105 D2
Farriers Wlk HU17 ...45 A8
Farrières La DN18 ...84 A8
Farrishes La DN18 ...84 A8
Farrows Pond DN19 .71 A1
Farthing Ave DN15 ..150 E8
Farthing Ct 2 HU7 ..56 E5
Farthing La YO25 ...125 C4
Fauconberg Ave 6
 DN33 ....102 E1
Faulding La DN40 ...40 C4
Faulding Way DN37 .102 B4
Faversham Ave HU4 .144 B6
Fawcett Cl HU4 ....144 D1
Fawcett Gdns 9 YO25 .124 F4
Fawcett St
 26 Gainsborough DN21 .117 B1
 York YO10 ....156 C1
Fawkes Dr YO26 ....129 C4
Fawley Cl HU5 .....140 E3
Faxfleet La DN14 ...67 A3
Feasegate YO1 .....156 B2
Feather La 5 DN19 ..85 C7
Featherbed La YO42 .29 C4
Felbridge Cl 1 HU9 .142 E2
Feldane HU6 ....139 E8
Fellbrook Ave YO26 .129 B4
Felstead Rd DN34 ..102 C3
Fen La DN36 ....114 D1
Fen Wlk DN36 .....115 C5
Fenby Cl 3 DN37 ...102 B3
Fenchurch St 1 HU5 .140 E1
Fenland Rd 12 DN8 .93 B7
Fenners Ave 29 DN17 .96 C2
Fenton St 1 DN15 ..151 B7
Fenwick Comm La DN6 .77 D2
Fenwick Ct DN36 ...114 A5
Fenwick La DN6 ....77 B1
Fenwick Rd 10 DN33 .102 D1
Fenwick St YO23 ...130 C2
Fenwick's La YO10 ..133 D7
Feoffee La YO42 ....28 C5
Ferens Art Gall★ HU1 .155 B2
Ferens Ave HU6 ....140 B4
Ferens Ct 2 HU9 ...141 D1
Ferens Gdns HU16 ..138 F8
Ferensway HU2 ....155 A3
Ferguson Rd 2 HU17 .55 B7
Ferguson Way YO32 .127 F1
Fern Cl Driffield YO25 .124 D2
 Kingston upon Hull HU2 .155 A4
 York YO32 ....128 A4
Fern Croft 18 DN9 ..105 E6
Fern Ct HU13 ......144 A1
Fern St YO31 ......156 C4
Fernbank 1 DN9 ...105 D7
Ferndale Ave HU10 .138 D1
Ferndale Dr DN8 ...79 B1
Ferndale Gr DN14 ..149 C6
Ferndale Terr 11 YO15 .122 E2
Ferndown DN37 ....102 B5
Fernhall Cl 17 DN3 ..92 A2
Fernhill 5 DN37 ....102 B4
Fernhill Rd HU5 ....139 D3
Fernholme Cl 15 HU15 .68 C5
Fernlea Cl YO8 .....148 D4
Fernley Gn Cl 6 WF11 .61 A2
Fernway YO10 .....131 C3
Ferriby Gr HU6 .....139 F5
Ferriby High Rd HU14 .69 B5
Ferriby La DN33 ....102 E1
Ferriby Rd
 Barton-upon-Humber
 DN18 ....84 E8
 Hessle HU13 ....143 B1
 Scunthorpe DN17 ...150 E1
Ferriby Sta HU14 ...69 A4
Ferries St HU9 .....146 D7
Ferry Cl 11 HU8 ....49 F1
Ferry Farm Cl 2 YO19 .36 D3
Ferry La Airmyn DN14 .149 A8
 Bishopthorpe YO23 ..133 B4
 Bubwith YO8 ....50 C5
 Goole DN14 ....65 B5
 Snaith & Cowick DN14 .63 C1
 Thorganby YO19 ....38 B5
 Winteringham DN15 ..68 B1
 Woodmansey HU17 ..56 C7
Ferry Mdw Pk 24 HU7 .56 F5
Ferry Rd
 Barrow upon Humber
 DN19 ....70 C1
 Fishlake DN8 ....78 F1
 Goxhill DN19 ....85 F8
 Haxey DN9 ....105 D1
 Keadby with Althorpe
 DN17 ....95 D4
 Kilpin DN14 ....65 B5
 Kingston upon Hull
 HU13 ....143 E1
 Scunthorpe DN17 ...150 D8
 South Cave HU15 ...53 E1
 Wawne HU17 ....56 D8
 Wold Haven YO42 ...29 A3
Ferry Rd E DN19 ...85 C8
Ferry Rd W DN15 ..96 A7
Ferry View
 Keyingham HU12 ...73 C4
 Thorngumbald HU12 .72 E5
Ferryman Pk HU12 ..72 D7
Fetherston Ct 19 YO42 .29 A3
Fetter La YO1 ......156 B2
Feversham Cres 4
 YO31 ....130 C7
Fewson Garth 28 HU12 .72 D7

Fewster Way YO10 ..156 C1
Fewston Dr 9 YO30 .126 F1
Field Ave YO8 ......48 B1
Field Cl 10 Laceby DN37 .101 F1
 Snaith DN14 ....78 C8
Field Head
 Laceby DN37 ....101 E1
 Wilberfoss YO41 ....27 F6
Field La Eastoft DN17 .81 A4
 Gowdall DN14 ......77 F8
 Hambleton YO8 .....48 B1
 Hensall DN14 ......62 D2
 Heslington YO10 ....131 C2
 Morton DN21 ......116 F3
 Rawcliffe DN14 .....64 A1
 Thornton YO42 .....39 A8
 Wistow YO8 ....48 C7
 Wroot DN9 ....104 D5
Field La Sports Ctr YO8 .48 B1
Field Rd
 Bridlington YO16 ....122 C4
 Crowle DN17 ....94 D7
 Stainforth DN7 .....92 C6
 Thorne/Moorends DN8 .93 A8
 West Haddlesey YO8 .62 A5
Field Side DN8 .....93 A8
Field St HU9 ....146 B7
Field The DN32 ....153 C2
Field View YO31 ....130 C7
Fieldend La HU12 ...59 B2
Fieldfare YO25 .....125 B5
Fieldhouse Rd 7 DN36 .103 D1
Fielding Way 19 DN21 .117 C1
Fields Cl 2 DN9 ....105 D7
Fields Cl Rd HU12 ..73 E4
Fields Rd DN9 .....105 E2
Fieldside Blyton DN21 .117 F5
 Crowle DN17 ....94 D7
 Epworth DN9 ....105 D6
Fieldside Garth HU6 .56 D5
Fifth Ave
 Bridlington YO15 ....123 A4
 Fixborough Stather DN15 .82 A1
 Goole DN14 ....149 C5
 Scunthorpe DN17 ...150 B2
 York YO31 ....130 F4
Fifth Ave Prim Sch
 HU6 ....140 A6
Fiftyeights Rd DN10 .104 B2
Figham Rd HU17 ...137 B3
Figham Springs Way
 HU17 ....154 B1
Fildes St DN31 .....152 D3
Filey Rd Grimsby DN32 .153 A1
 Hunmanby YO14 ...3 A8
Filey Terr YO30 ....130 C7
Fillingham Cres
 Cleethorpes DN35 ..103 C2
 Gunness DN15 .....150 B7
Fimber Ave HU16 ..139 A5
Finch Croft 5 HU7 ..141 D7
Finch Pk HU17 .....136 D5
Finchcroft La HU17 ..43 B2
Finchley Cl HU8 ....141 F5
Finchley Ct DN31 ..152 A4
Findlay Cres DN36 .114 A7
Findon Cl 28 HU7 ..56 F6
Fingall Mews 1 HU5 .139 D3
Finkle La DN18 ....69 F1
Finkle St
 2 Bishop Burton HU17 .43 A2
 Hensall DN14 ......62 D2
 Kingston upon Hull HU2 .155 B1
 Kingston upon Hull
 HU16 ....139 A6
 Market Weighton YO43 .135 D4
 2 North Cave HU15 ..53 D3
 Selby YO8 ....148 C5
 Stainforth DN7 .....92 C7
Finningley Garth 14 HU7 .57 A5
Finnley's La DN14 ..78 C7
Finsbury Ave YO23 ..130 C1
Finsbury Dr 7 DN33 .102 D1
Finsbury St YO23 ...130 C1
Fir Cl 11 Brough HU15 .68 D5
 Scunthorpe DN16 ...96 D2
Fir Heath Cl 6 YO24 .129 C1
Fir Tree Cl YO8 ....48 B2
Fir Tree Dr 11 DN6 .76 E2
Fir Tree La YO8 ....48 B2
Fir Tree Way YO8 ..48 B2
Fir Trees HU10 ....143 D6
Fir Trees The YO8 ..48 B2
Firbank Cl 9 YO32 ..14 A7
Fircroft Way DN34 ..152 A3
Firethorn Cl 3 HU3 .145 D5
Firsby Cres DN33 ..102 D1
First Ave
 Bridlington YO15 ....122 F4
 Flixborough DN15 ..82 A1
 3 Goole DN14 ......149 C4
 Grimsby DN33 ......102 E2
 Scunthorpe DN17 ...150 C2
 York YO31 ....130 F6
First Comm La YO8 .48 D4
First La
 Kingston upon Hull
 HU10 ....144 A5
 South Cave HU15 ...54 A2
Firth Field Rd DN7 .92 F4
Firth La DN9 ....104 D5
Firtholme Rd HU12 ..91 A4
Firtree Cl
 4 Earswick YO32 ...127 F7
 York YO24 ....129 E3
Firtree Dr DN20 ....98 F7
Firwood Whin 5 YO32 .127 F3
Fish Dock Rd DN31 .152 F6

Fish La HU15 .....52 D2
Fish St HU1 .....155 B1
Fishemore Ave HU13 .143 F2
Fisher Cl HU10 .....138 D2
Fisher La YO25 .....22 E5
Fisher Pl DN35 .....153 D3
Fisher Sq HU17 .....154 A2
Fishergate YO10 .....156 C1
Fishergate Prim Sch
YO10 .....156 C1
Fisherman's Wharf
DN31 .....152 D4
Fishermans Wlk 2 HU3 145 C4
Fishlake Nab DN7 .....92 C7
Fishpond Hill YO42 .....29 C4
Fishwick Ave 5 HU13 .143 E1
Fiskerton Cl 20 DN34 ..102 C2
Fiskerton Way DN31 ...102 C6
Fitling Rd HU11 .....59 B5
Fitties La DN36 .....115 C5
Fitzroy St HU5 .....140 D2
Fitzwilliam Mews 2
DN35 .....103 C1
Five Rivers DN14 .....149 C5
Flaen Cl YO15 .....5 A2
Flaen Rd YO15 .....5 A2
Flag Wlk 1 HU6 .....140 C8
Flag Yd YO16 .....122 C4
Flamborough CE VC Prim
Sch YO15 .....5 A2
Flamborough Cliff Nature
Reserve* YO15 .....5 C4
Flamborough Head Nature
Reserve* YO15 .....5 D2
Flamborough Outer
Headland Nature Reserve*
YO15 .....5 D2
Flamborough Rd
Bempton YO15 .....4 E1
Bridlington YO15 .....122 F4
Flarepath The DN20 ...99 A8
Flashley Carr La DN6 ...77 F1
Flat La YO42 .....28 D4
Flatgate DN14 .....65 B7
Flavian Gr YO30 .....129 F8
Flaxdale Ct HU5 .....139 E1
Flaxley Ct YO8 .....148 B5
Flaxley Rd YO8 .....148 A7
Flaxman Ave YO10 .....131 A4
Flaxman Croft YO23 ...132 B3
Flaxmill Wlk 2 HU15 ....66 D7
Flaxton Rd
Kingston upon Hull HU5 ..139 D1
Strensall YO32 .....14 B7
Fleet Garth 11 HU12 .....72 D7
Fleet La DN14 .....64 A7
Fleetgate 11 DN18 .....69 E1
Fleets Cl DN7 .....92 C7
Fleetway DN36 .....115 A3
Fleetwood Cl 4 DN33 ..113 E8
Fleming Ave 3 YO31 ...130 E5
Fleming Wlk
Cottingham HU16 .....139 A4
Gipsyville HU4 .....144 D2
Flemingate HU17 .....154 C2
Flemingdale HU7 .....140 F7
Fletcher Cl
Kingston upon Hull
HU13 .....143 E2
6 Scunthorpe DN15 .....96 B7
Fletcher Ct 14 YO32 .....13 E5
Fletcher Gate HU12 .....72 C7
Fletcher Rd DN34 .....102 C4
Fletcher's Croft YO23 ..132 C3
Flinton Gr HU9 .....142 A1
Flinton Rd
Aldbrough HU11 .....58 F8
Humbleton HU11 .....59 A7
Flinton St HU3 .....145 B3
Flixborough Rd DN15 ...82 A4
Floral Hall HU18 .....134 D5
Florence Ave HU13 .....143 F1
Florence Gr YO30 .....126 D2
Florence Nightingale 3
HU5 .....139 F4
Florence St DN32 .....152 E1
Florin Dr 3 HU7 .....56 E5
Flottergate Mall 8
DN31 .....152 D3
Flour Sq DN31 .....152 E5
Fog La YO42 .....38 E4
Folk Mus* HU18 .....134 C4
Folkestone St HU5 .....140 D2
Folks Cl 13 YO32 .....13 F5
Folkton Ave HU16 .....139 A4
Follies The DN15 .....97 E7
Folly La LN7 .....110 C5
Football Gn HU18 .....134 C3
Forber Ave HU9 .....142 C2
Forbes Ave HU6 .....140 C8
Ford Cl HU17 .....136 F4
Ford La DN20 .....108 F5
Ford's Ave 9 DN41 .....101 F5
Fordlands YO8 .....48 B2
Fordlands Cres YO19 .....133 E5
Fordlands Rd YO19 .....133 E6
Fordon La Willerby YO12 ..1 E7
Wold Newton YO25 .....2 A6
Foredyke Ave HU7 .....141 A4
Foredyke Prim Sch
HU9 .....142 A1
Forest Cl 27 YO32 .....13 E5
Forest Dr DN36 .....103 D1
Forest Gr YO31 .....130 F6
Forest La Fulford YO19 ...26 A2
Strensall YO32 .....14 A8
Forest of Galtres Prim Sch
YO30 .....12 F5
Forest Way
24 Humberston DN36 .....103 D1
York YO31 .....130 F6
Forester Way HU4 .....144 D3
Forester's Wlk YO24 ...129 B1
Foresters Way YO16 .....123 A7
Foresters Wlk YO41 .....15 C1
Forestgate YO32 .....127 C7
Forge Cl
Huntington YO32 .....128 A2
Melbourne YO42 .....39 B6
South Kelsey LN7 .....110 A1
8 Thorngumbald HU12 .....72 E5
Wheldrake YO19 .....38 A7
Forge Cres 3 DN39 .....86 A1
Forge La YO19 .....37 A7
Forge Pl HU16 .....138 B7
Forge The YO25 .....124 E3
Forge Way 3 DN36 .....114 A6
Forkedale DN18 .....84 E8
Formby Cl HU6 .....139 E5
Forrester St 20 DN20 .....98 B2
Forrester's Cl 3 DN6 .....76 E2
Forster St 25 DN21 .....117 B1
Forsythia Ave 14 DN41 ..101 F5
Forsythia Dr DN33 .....102 E1
Fort Paull Battery*
HU12 .....72 B4
Fort Terr 6 YO15 .....122 F2
Forth St YO26 .....129 F6
Fortuna Way 2 DN37 ...102 B4
Fortune Cl HU8 .....141 F4
Forty Acre HU10 .....143 F7
Forty Foot La DN39 .....99 F6
Forty Stps HU10 .....143 F7
Fortyfoot YO16 .....122 F4
Fortyfoot Ct YO16 .....122 E4
Fortyfoot Gr 1 YO16 ...122 F4
Forum Ctr* YO15 .....122 F2
Fosham Rd HU11 .....46 D2
Foss Bank YO31 .....156 C3
Foss Ct YO31 .....127 E1
Foss Field La YO23 .....36 B8
Foss Garth YO41 .....27 F5
Foss Gr HU8 .....142 B6
Foss Islands Rd YO31 ..156 C3
Foss Wlk YO26 .....129 B8
Fossdale Cl HU8 .....141 E6
Fosse Hill Jet Ski Ctr*
YO25 .....34 C1
Fossgate YO1 .....156 C2
Fossland View 4 YO32 ..14 A7
Fossway
Stamford Bridge YO41 .....15 D1
York YO31 .....130 D7
Foster Gate YO8 .....148 D4
Foster Rd 9 DN8 .....93 A8
Foster St HU8 .....141 A2
Fostergate YO8 .....48 A8
Foston Gr
Kingston upon Hull HU9 ..142 A1
4 York YO31 .....130 F8
Foston La Beeford YO25 ...22 B1
North Frodingham YO25 ...21 F1
Fotherbie Garth 11 HU12 72 C7
Fotherby Rd 4 DN17 .....96 C2
Fotherby St DN31 .....152 E5
Fotherby Wlk HU17 .....154 C4
Fothergill Dr 16 DN3 .....92 A2
Foundry Garth HU12 .....59 D1
Foundry La 5 WF11 .....61 A2
Foundry Sh Ctr The
DN15 .....151 B7
Fountain Cl
Kingston upon Hull HU2 ..155 A4
Northfield HU13 .....143 C3
6 Waltham DN37 .....113 D7
Fountain Ct DN40 .....87 D1
Fountain Hill DN10 .....116 B3
Fountain Hill Rd DN10 .116 B4
Fountain Rd HU2 .....140 E1
Fountain Rd Ind Est
HU2 .....155 C4
Fountain St
16 Caistor LN7 .....111 B4
Kingston upon Hull HU3 ..145 D6
Fountains Ave YO16 .....122 D7
Fountains Way HU15 .....53 D3
Fountayne Rd 13 YO14 .....2 F8
Fountayne St
Goole DN14 .....149 E5
York YO31 .....130 C7
Four Acre Cl HU10 .....143 C6
Fourth Ave
Bridlington YO15 .....123 A4
Fixborough Stather DN15 ..82 A1
Goole DN14 .....149 C4
Scunthorpe DN17 .....150 C2
York YO31 .....130 E5
Fourways 9 DN36 .....114 D4
Fowler Ct 3 DN15 .....83 A5
Fowler Rd DN16 .....151 C3
Fox Covert
Hibaldstow DN20 .....108 F5
York YO31 .....127 F2
Fox Covert La DN10 ...116 D4
Fox Covert Rd WF8 .....76 C1
Fox Ct DN17 .....94 D8
Fox Garth YO26 .....126 A3
Fox Glade YO41 .....15 C2
Fox Hill (Tumulus)*
YO25 .....21 D8
Fox Hill La YO8 .....148 A3
Fox La
Chapel Haddlesey YO8 ...62 C5
Hambleton LS25 .....61 D8
Laxton DN14 .....65 E3
Thorpe Willoughby YO8 ...48 B1
Fox St DN15 .....150 F7
Foxcroft 3 YO32 .....127 C7
Foxdale Ave YO8 .....48 B1
Foxglove Cl
22 Brigg DN20 .....98 B2
16 Kingston upon Hull HU7 .56 F5
Foxglove Gdns 5 DN34 102 C3
Foxhill DN37 .....102 B4
Foxhill Cl HU9 .....142 E2
Foxhill La YO8 .....148 A3
Foxhill Rd DN8 .....93 B7
Foxhills Ind Pk DN15 ...96 C8
Foxhills Rd DN15 .....96 C7
Foxhills Tech Coll
DN15 .....96 C7
Foxholme Rd HU7 .....141 D7
Foxthorn Paddock
YO10 .....131 D3
Foxton Cl YO24 .....132 C8
Foxwood La 3 YO24 ...129 C1
Foynes Gn 6 HU8 .....142 C5
Frampton Cl HU7 .....141 B6
Frances Ct 8 DN37 .....113 D7
Frances St
Scunthorpe DN15 .....151 A7
York YO10 .....130 D1
Francis Askew Prim Sch
HU4 .....144 E4
Francis Ave 10 HU19 .....75 A6
Francis Ct 7 YO8 .....48 B2
Francis St HU2 .....155 B3
Francis Terr YO25 .....124 E5
Francis Way 3 HU12 .....74 D1
Frank Walsham Ct
DN32 .....153 A4
Frankland Cl DN20 .....98 E3
Frankland Pl DN35 .....153 D3
Franklin Cres DN16 .....151 E2
Franklin Rd DN21 .....107 C4
Franklin Sixth Form Coll
DN34 .....152 B1
Franklin St HU9 .....146 C8
Franklin Way DN38 .....99 F5
Fraser St DN32 .....152 F3
Frazer Ct YO30 .....129 E8
Frederic St YO30 .....156 A3
Frederick Gough Sch
DN16 .....96 E2
Frederick Holmes Specl Sch
HU6 .....140 A5
Frederick St
Cleethorpes DN35 .....153 E2
Goole DN14 .....149 E5
Grimsby DN31 .....152 D4
Frederick Ward Way
DN31 .....152 D3
Freehold St HU3 .....145 D7
Freeman Ave 4 HU15 .....68 C5
Freeman Ct DN36 .....114 B5
Freeman St DN32 .....152 F4
Freeman Way 1 DN32 ...152 F5
Freemans La DN20 .....84 C2
Freeport Hornsea Outlet
Village HU18 .....134 C1
Freeport Wharf DN31 ...152 E4
Freeschool La or Gr
DN14 .....52 A2
Freeston St DN35 .....153 B4
Freetown Ct HU6 .....140 B5
Freetown Way HU2 .....155 A3
Freightliner Rd HU3 .....144 F2
Fremantle Ave HU9 .....142 D2
Frensham Cl 9 HU7 .....56 F6
Fresh Fields 12 HU15 .....68 C5
Freshney Bog Nature
Reserve* DN34 .....102 B3
Freshney Dr DN31 .....152 C4
Freshney Pl 9 DN31 .....152 D3
Freshney Places Sh Ctr
DN31 .....152 D3
Friar's Wlk YO31 .....130 E8
Friargate YO1 .....156 B2
Friargate Theatre
YO1 .....156 B2
Friars Cl YO19 .....26 D7
Friars La HU17 .....154 B2
Friars Mdw YO8 .....148 C8
Friars Rd DN17 .....150 E2
Friary Ct 5 HU3 .....140 D1
Friendship Ct 2 YO8 .....148 C6
Frith Mews 4 YO8 .....148 C6
Frobisher Ave DN32 .....153 B2
Frodingham Footpath 2
DN15 .....151 B7
Frodingham Inf Sch
DN15 .....151 B6
Frodingham La HU12 ...74 D4
Frodingham Rd
Brandesburton YO25 .....34 B4
Scunthorpe DN15 .....151 A8
Frodingham S Rd
DN16 .....151 E5
Frodsham St HU9 .....147 B7
Froebel House Sch
HU17 .....136 C6
Frome Rd HU8 .....142 C7
Front La HU12 .....59 A3
Front St
Alkborough DN15 .....82 C8
Burton Fleming YO25 .....2 E3
East Stockwith DN21 .....116 E5
Elsham DN20 .....98 F7
Gainsborough DN21 .....117 A2
Grasby DN38 .....110 E7
Langtoft YO25 .....8 C5
Laxton DN14 .....65 E4
Lockington YO25 .....32 B2
Middleton YO25 .....31 C4
Front St continued
Naburn YO19 .....36 D8
Ulceby DN39 .....86 A1
Wold Newton YO25 .....2 A4
York YO24 .....129 C3
Froscoles Cl 6 HU15 ....53 D3
Frusher Ave 7 DN33 .....102 E2
Fryston 11 HU15 .....68 C6
Fryston Comm La LS25 .61 A8
Fuchsia Croft DN15 .....150 F6
Fuchsia Dr HU4 .....144 B2
Fulbeck Rd DN16 .....151 C2
Fulford Cres
Kingston upon Hull
HU10 .....144 A8
3 New Holland DN19 .....70 E2
Fulford Cross YO10 .....130 D1
Fulford Gr HU9 .....142 E2
Fulford Mews YO10 .....133 E6
Fulford Pk YO10 .....133 D7
Fulford Rd YO10 .....133 D8
Fulford Sch YO10 .....133 E7
Fulfordgate YO10 .....133 E7
Fulham La DN14 .....76 E7
Fulham Pk 2 DN33 .....102 D1
Fuller St DN35 .....153 D4
Fulmar Cl HU7 .....141 D8
Fulstow Cty Prim Sch
LN11 .....121 E8
Fulstow Gr 22 DN33 .....102 D2
Furlong Rd 23 YO41 .....15 D2
Furness Cl 8 HU7 .....57 A7
Furness Dr YO30 .....126 E1
Furniss Ct 25 DN18 .....84 E8
Furnwood 2 YO32 .....127 D7
Furze Rd HU12 .....60 B2
Fussey Gdns DN20 .....84 C1
Fylingdales Ave 6
YO30 .....126 E1

G

Gable Pk YO23 .....24 C6
Gables Cl 8 DN14 .....61 D4
Gadwall Cl 2 HU15 .....52 F1
Gain Hills Balk YO16 ...10 D4
Gainas Ave DN21 .....117 B1
Gainford Gr HU9 .....142 E2
Gainford Rd DN8 .....79 B2
Gainford Sq 18 DN8 .....79 B2
Gainsborough Cl YO32 ..14 B8
Gainsborough La
DN20 .....108 F8
Gainsborough Rd
Blyton DN21 .....117 E4
20 Kirton in Lindsey DN21 108 B1
Scotter DN21 .....107 B3
Gainsthorpe Rd E
DN21 .....108 D4
Gainsthorpe Rd W
DN21 .....108 C4
Gale Farm Ct 6 YO24 ..129 C3
Gale La Thorganby YO19 ..37 F4
York YO24 .....129 C2
Gale The YO19 .....36 D4
Galecarr La YO42 .....39 E6
Galegate YO43 .....53 E7
Galfrid Rd HU11 .....142 F7
Gallagher Ret Pk
DN15 .....150 A7
Gallands Cl HU14 .....69 A7
Galleon Ct HU9 .....145 C6
Galley Ct HU9 .....146 C6
Galliard Cl 11 HU3 .....145 A4
Galligap La YO10 .....131 C4
Gallops The YO24 .....132 B8
Galloway Ct 4 YO25 .....124 F4
Galloway La 3 YO25 .....124 F4
Gallows Bridge Rd
HU11 .....59 A7
Gallows Hill* YO25 .....9 A2
Gallows La HU17 .....136 D5
Galmanhoe La YO30 .....156 A3
Galtres Ave YO31 .....131 B7
Galtres Gr YO30 .....129 F7
Galtres Rd YO31 .....131 B7
Gandhi Wy HU1 .....155 C2
Ganstead Gr HU9 .....142 A2
Ganstead La HU11 .....142 D6
Gant Wlk 7 YO8 .....148 D5
Ganton Ave HU16 .....139 A5
Ganton Ct 3 HU8 .....142 B5
Ganton Hill YO12 .....1 B7
Ganton Pl YO24 .....132 E7
Ganton Rd YO25 .....1 C4
Ganton Specl Sch
HU10 .....144 A7
Ganton Way HU10 .....143 F8
Gap Cres YO14 .....3 D7
Gap Rd YO14 .....3 D8
Garbett Way 1 YO23 ..133 B3
Garburn Gr 3 YO30 .....126 E1
Garbutt Cl 2 HU12 .....58 D1
Garbutt Gr YO26 .....129 D5
Garbutt Pl 3 DN35 .....103 D2
Garden Dr DN36 .....114 A8
Garden Flats La YO19 ...26 E7
Garden La 11 WF11 .....61 A3
Garden Pl YO1 .....156 C2
Garden St 14 Brigg DN20 .98 C2
Grimsby DN32 .....152 D3
York YO31 .....156 B4
Garden Wlk 12 YO15 .....122 E2
Gardeners Cl 8 YO23 .....132 B3
Gardeners Row YO25 .....7 B3
Gardenia Dr 21 DN17 .....96 D1
Gardens The HU3 .....145 C5
Gardham La YO25 .....35 A6
Gardham Rd HU17 .....42 E5
Gare La DN14 .....66 A6
Garends Rd 4 YO15 .....5 A2
Garfield Cl HU9 .....142 D1
Garfield St 21 DN21 .....117 B1
Garfield Terr YO26 .....129 F5
Garibaldi St DN32 .....152 F5
Garland Cl HU9 .....142 C4
Garland St 2 YO26 .....129 E4
Garlands The YO30 .....130 A8
Garman Carr La YO8 ...48 D6
Garner St DN32 .....152 E2
Garnet Gr 6 HU3 .....145 A4
Garnet Terr YO26 .....129 E5
Garnett St DN35 .....153 D4
Garrick Cl Brayton YO8 ..148 B1
Kingston upon Hull HU8 ..141 F4
15 Pocklington YO42 .....29 A3
Garrick La 21 DN36 .....114 A8
Garrison Rd HU9 .....155 C1
Garrison St YO15 .....122 F2
Garrow Hill YO10 .....130 F2
Garrow Hill Ave YO10 ..131 A3
Garroway Way YO10 .....26 A4
Garrowby Hill YO41 .....16 F3
Garrowby Rd YO42 .....16 F2
Garrowby St YO41 .....16 E3
Garrowby View 5 YO41 ..15 D2
Garrowby Wlk HU5 .....139 C2
Garth Ave
Kingston upon Hull HU11 ..58 A3
4 North Duffield YO8 .....50 A7
Garth Cl 6 YO8 .....48 D6
Garth Ct YO32 .....128 A4
Garth End YO32 .....127 F4
Garth Ends Rd HU17 .....43 A2
Garth Glebe 8 YO8 .....49 B5
Garth La Goole DN14 .....65 C4
Grimsby DN31 .....152 D4
Garth Mill 1 DN14 .....61 D4
Garth Morrell YO8 .....148 C2
Garth Rd YO32 .....127 F4
Garth Terr YO30 .....130 B7
Garth The HU16 .....139 A5
Garth's End YO10 .....133 E8
Garthends La
3 Hemingbrough YO8 .....49 F1
Mappleton HU11 .....47 B5
Garthorpe Rd
Luddington & Haldenby
DN17 .....81 C4
Twin Rivers DN14 .....81 E7
Garths End 20 Haxby YO32 13 F5
Pocklington YO42 .....29 A4
Garths End La YO42 .....29 A8
Garthway
18 Holton le Clay DN36 ..114 A5
4 York YO32 .....127 D3
Garton Balk YO25 .....20 D8
Garton Gr
Grimsby DN32 .....153 A1
3 Kingston upon Hull
HU4 .....144 C7
Garton Hill YO25 .....19 E7
Garton Rd HU11 .....47 C1
Garton Slack YO25 .....19 D6
Garton-on-the-Wolds CE VC
Prim Sch YO25 .....20 A6
Garvey Way 34 HU12 .....72 D7
Gas House La 13 DN14 ..65 B7
Gascoigne Wlk YO23 .....156 B1
Gashouse La DN9 .....106 B3
Gate La 11 DN33 .....102 E1
Gate Way DN31 .....152 C6
Gateforth New Rd YO8 ..62 A8
Gatehead La YO42 .....38 D7
Gatehouse* DN39 .....86 B5
Gatehouse Rd DN19 .....85 F7
Gatehowe Rd YO17 .....17 A7
Gateland Cl YO32 .....127 C7
Gateland Field La DN14 .64 B6
Gatesby Rd DN14 .....149 C6
Gatewood La DN7 .....92 E1
Gatherums The DN35 ..153 E1
Gatwick Garth 15 HU7 ...57 A5
Gaufer Hill YO43 .....41 D3
Gautry La DN9 .....106 B4
Gay Mdws YO32 .....14 D2
Gayles Mews 3 HU5 ....139 D3
Gayton Rd DN35 .....103 D2
Gedney Cl 8 DN37 .....102 B4
Gee St HU3 .....145 C5
Geeseness La DN14 .....78 D2
Geldof Rd YO32 .....127 F1
Gembling La YO25 .....22 A4
Gembling Prim Sch
YO25 .....22 A3
Gemel Rd HU12 .....59 C2
Gemsbok Way 3 HU4 ..144 D2
General La YO42 .....38 E6
Genesis Way DN31 .....102 B6
Geneva Sq DN8 .....79 C2
Geneva Way HU7 .....141 B5
George Ave DN17 .....95 D5
George Butler Cl 16
DN37 .....101 F1
George Cayley Dr
YO30 .....127 A3
George Ct YO31 .....156 C3
George Hudson St
YO1 .....156 B2
George Janney Ct
DN32 .....153 A5
George La HU17 .....55 D8

George Mews **8** LN7 ....**111** B4
George Odey Ct HU17 ..**154** B2
George St
2 Barton-upon-Humber
  DN18 ....**84** F8
Beverley HU17 .....**154** B3
Bridlington YO15 ....**122** C1
Broughton DN20 ....**97** D3
Cleethorpes DN35 ...**153** E1
Cottingham HU16 ...**139** A7
Gainsborough DN21 ..**117** A1
Great Driffield YO25 .**124** C4
Grimsby DN31 ......**152** D3
28 Hedon HU12 ....**72** C7
Keadby DN17 ....**95** D5
Kingston upon Hull HU1 ..**155** B2
11 Kirton in Lindsey DN21 **108** B1
Pocklington YO42 ....**29** A4
Scunthorpe DN15 ...**151** A8
4 Selby YO8 ....**148** D6
Snaith DN14 ....**63** C1
7 Wistow YO8 ......**48** D6
3 Withernsea HU19 ...**74** F7
York YO1 ....**156** C1
George Terr **1** YO8 ...**49** B4
Georgian Mews
  Bridlington YO15 ....**122** C1
4 Great Driffield YO25 .**124** F3
Georgian Way YO15 ...**122** C1
Georgina Ct **8** DN18 ..**84** E8
Gerard Ave YO31 .....**131** A5
Germain Rd YO8 .....**148** E4
German Nook La HU17 ..**56** D8
Gershwin Ave HU4 ....**144** B4
Gertrude St DN32 ....**152** E1
Gervase St DN15 .....**151** A7
Giant Hill★ HU11 ....**57** D6
Gibraltar La DN37 ....**101** F1
Gibraltar Way HU7 ....**56** E5
Gibson La **36** Hedon HU12 **72** D7
  Welton HU14 ....**68** E4
Gibson Rd **4** DN7 ...**104** A8
Gibson St YO25 ......**124** E5
Gifford Cl HU7 ....**57** A6
Gilberdyke Prim Sch
  HU15 ....**66** D8
Gilberdyke Sta HU15 ..**66** D7
Gilbert St YO16 ......**122** D3
Gilbey Rd DN31 ......**152** B5
Gilcross Rd HU12 .....**90** C6
Gildane HU6 ....**139** E8
Giles Ave YO31 ......**131** A5
Giles St DN35 ....**153** E2
Gillamoor Ave YO31 ..**131** B5
Gillamoor Cl **16** HU8 ..**141** E7
Gillann St **15** WF11 ...**61** A2
Gillatts Cl DN20 .....**98** D4
Gillett St HU3 ....**145** B4
Gilliatt St HU3 ....**151** A7
Gilling Mews **4** HU5 ..**139** D3
Gillingwood Rd YO30 ..**126** F3
Gillshill Prim Sch
  HU8 ....**141** D5
Gillshill Rd HU8 ......**141** D4
Gillus La **5** YO15 ....**4** D3
Gillyon Cl **3** HU17 ...**137** B3
Gipsey Cnr YO19 .....**26** E3
Gipsy La
  Holton le Moor LN7 ..**110** C1
  Owston Ferry DN9 ...**116** F8
Girton Cl **5** DN16 ...**96** D2
Girvan Cl YO24 ......**132** B7
Gisburn Rd HU13 .....**143** F2
Givendale Gr **3** YO10 .**131** C4
Givendale Hill YO42 ..**29** C6
Givendale La YO42 ...**29** A8
Glade Rd YO19 ......**37** B2
Glade The
  Beverley HU17 .....**137** B3
  Escrick YO19 ......**37** A6
  York YO31 ....**131** B7
Gladstone Dr DN16 ..**151** C5
Gladstone St
  Hessle HU13 ....**143** E1
  Kingston upon Hull HU3 .**145** C6
  York YO24 ....**129** D3
  York YO31 ....**156** C4
Gladstone Terr **6** YO15 **122** F3
Glaisby Ct YO31 .....**131** A6
Glaisdale YO24 ......**132** D7
Glaisdale Cl YO16 ...**122** F7
Glaisdale Gr HU9 ....**146** F8
Glaisdale Rd DN16 ..**151** E1
Glamis Rd HU13 .....**143** F2
Glanford Gr **6** DN19 ..**85** D8
Glanford Rd
  28 Brigg DN20 .....**98** C2
  Scunthorpe DN17 ...**96** C2
Glanford Way DN15 ...**150** B7
Glanville Ave DN17 ..**150** F4
Glanville Cres DN17 ..**150** F4
Glasgow St HU3 .....**145** A5
Glass House Row HU8 .**141** A1
Glebe Ave
  Full Sutton YO41 ....**16** A2
  York YO26 ....**129** D5
Glebe Cl
  Burton upon Stather
  DN15 ....**82** A5
5 Holton le Clay DN36 .**114** A6
3 Strensall YO32 .....**14** B7
2 Wawne HU7 ....**56** E7
Glebe Farm HU7 .....**56** E7
Glebe Gdns YO25 ....**22** D1

Glebe Lands The **4**
  YO43 ....**135** E4
Glebe Rd **3** Brigg DN20 .**98** C2
  Campsall DN6 ......**76** E1
  Cleethorpes DN35 ...**153** E2
  Grimsby DN33 .....**102** F1
  Humberston DN36 ...**114** C8
  Kingston upon Hull HU7 **141** A4
  Scunthorpe DN15 ...**151** B8
  Thorne/Moorends DN8 ..**93** B8
  Wawne HU7 ....**56** E7
Glebe Way
  Barton-upon-Humber
  DN18 ....**85** A8
26 Haxby YO32 ....**13** E5
Glebelands HU12 .....**59** D2
Glen Almond HU11 ...**142** D6
Glen Ave YO31 ......**130** E5
Glen Cl YO10 ....**133** E6
Glen Cres YO42 .....**39** A7
Glen Hall Rise **11** DN19 .**85** C8
Glen Rd YO31 ......**130** E5
Glen The
  Beverley HU17 .....**137** B2
  Kingston upon Hull
  HU10 ....**138** B1
Glencoe Cl **22** DN7 ...**92** D4
Glencoe St
  Kingston upon Hull HU3 .**144** F6
1 York YO30 ....**130** B7
Glencourt HU6 ......**139** E6
Glendale Cl HU10 ...**138** C1
Gleneagles **15** DN37 ..**113** D7
Gleneagles Cres **4** DN19 **70** E2
Gleneagles Pk HU8 ..**141** F6
Glenfell Cl HU8 ......**141** D5
Glenfield Ave YO43 ..**135** D4
Glenfield Dr HU4 ....**138** B1
Glenfield Rd DN37 ...**102** B4
Glenham Dr HU10 ...**143** E7
Glenholme Ct YO25 ..**32** E7
Glenridding YO24 ...**132** D7
Glenrock Pk HU15 ...**68** B6
Glenville Cl YO25 ....**33** F8
Glenwood Cl HU8 ....**141** C3
Glenwood Dr **2** HU4 ..**144** B6
Glews Hollow Bsns
  Enterprise Pk DN14 .**149** B2
Glimpse The YO16 ...**123** A7
Globe Mews HU17 ...**154** A3
Gloria Way **3** DN37 ..**102** B4
Glossop Rd DN15 ....**150** B6
Gloucester Ave
  Grimsby DN34 .....**102** C2
  Scunthorpe DN16 ...**151** B3
Gloucester Rd HU10 ..**138** C2
Gloucester St HU4 ...**144** E3
Glover Rd DN17 .....**150** A4
Glovers Ave DN17 ...**95** D4
Goathead La DN14 ...**78** E8
Goathland Cl HU3 ...**145** A6
Goble Cl DN18 ......**85** A8
Godbold Cl HU17 ....**154** C3
Goddard Ave HU5 ...**140** D2
Goddard Cl **9** DN18 ..**84** E8
Godfrey Rd **11** DN8 ..**93** A8
Godman's La HU10 ...**143** B8
Godnow Rd DN17 ...**94** C6
Godwinsway **18** YO41 .**15** C2
Gold Thread La **5** YO8 .**48** B8
Goldcrest Cl
1 Kingston upon Hull
  HU7 ....**141** D8
  Scunthorpe DN15 ...**96** F1
Golden Ct **10** HU9 ...**142** A3
Golden Gr HU11 .....**142** D6
Goldgarth DN32 .....**153** A1
Goldings The DN9 ...**105** D2
Goodfell Rd HU17 ....**137** A6
Goodhand Cl DN18 ..**85** A8
Goodhart Rd HU7 ...**141** B8
Goodmanham Rd
  Market Weighton YO43 .**135** D5
  Middleton YO25 ....**31** C3
Goodmanham Way **6**
  HU16 ....**138** C6
Goodramgate YO1 ..**156** B2
Goodrich Cl HU17 ...**140** E1
Goods Yd The YO8 ..**148** D5
Goodwin Par **1** HU3 ..**145** D5
Goodwood DN17 ....**96** B2
Goodwood Cl HU17 ..**136** E6
Goodwood Gr YO24 ..**129** F1
Goole & District Hospl
  DN14 ....**149** C6
Goole Coll DN14 ....**149** B4
Goole L Ctr DN14 ...**149** D3
Goole Musuem★
  DN14 ....**149** D4
Goole Rd Goole DN14 ..**65** C3
  Swinefleet DN14 ....**80** C4
Goole Sta DN14 .....**149** C4
Gooseacre DN17 ....**107** D7
Goosenook La HU17 ..**45** A8
Gordan Pk HU16 ....**139** C6
Gordon Rd YO16 ....**122** C4
Gordon St Goole DN14 .**149** C4
4 Kingston upon Hull
  HU3 ....**145** B5
  York YO10 ....**130** E3
Gordons Terr YO25 ..**124** E4
Gore La DN14 ......**77** B5
Goring Pl DN35 .....**153** D3
Gormire Ave **2** YO31 ..**127** E2

Gorse Cl Hatfield DN7 ..**92** C3
  Selby YO8 ....**148** C2
Gorse Hill **1** YO19 ...**26** F7
Gorse Paddock YO32 .**127** F2
Gorsedale HU7 .....**140** E7
Gorton Rd DN10 ....**143** F7
Gorton St DN31 .....**152** F6
Gosport Rd DN34 ...**152** A2
Gosport Wlk HU4 ...**144** A4
Gossips Wood Rd DN14 .**79** B8
Gothenburg Way HU7 .**140** E6
Goths La HU17 ......**154** B4
Gott Cl YO25 ....**124** C2
Gouldesborough Ct **2**
  HU5 ....**140** C3
Goulding Ct HU17 ...**154** A3
Goulton St **4** HU3 ..**145** B3
Gouthwaite Cl YO30 ..**126** F2
Government House Rd
  YO30 ....**130** A6
Government St **1** DN14 **149** D4
Gowdall Broach DN14 ..**77** E8
Gowdall La
  Pollington DN14 ....**77** F7
  Snaith & Cowick DN14 ..**63** B1
Gowdall Rd DN14 ...**62** C2
Gowdall Way **1** DN14 ..**65** A7
Gower Rd
  Kingston upon Hull HU4 ..**144** B3
  York YO24 ....**132** E8
Gowthorpe YO8 .....**148** C5
Gowthorpe La DN14 ..**66** E4
Goxhill Airport DN19 ..**86** B8
Goxhill Gdns **17** DN34 .**102** C2
Goxhill Prim Sch DN19 .**86** A8
Goxhill Rd DN19 ....**85** E8
Goxhill Sta DN19 ....**85** F8
Grafton St
  Grimsby DN32 .....**153** A5
  Kingston upon Hull HU5 .**140** C2
Gragdale Cl HU8 ....**141** E7
Graham Ave HU4 ...**144** C2
Graingers Rd HU18 ..**134** D3
Grains Gate LN11 ...**115** E1
Grainsby Ave
  Cleethorpes DN35 ...**103** B2
  Holton le Clay DN36 ..**114** B5
Grainsby Healing★
  DN36 ....**113** F3
Grainsby La
  Grainsby DN36 .....**113** E1
  Tetney DN36 ......**114** D3
Graizelound Fields Rd
  DN9 ....**105** D1
Grammar Sch La DN20 .**98** C3
Grammar Sch Rd
  Brigg DN20 ....**98** C2
  Kingston upon Hull HU5 .**139** E2
Grammar Sch Rd S **7**
  DN20 ....**98** C2
Grammar Sch Wlk
  DN16 ....**96** E2
Grammar Sch Yd HU1 .**155** B1
Grampian Cl **4** YO32 .**127** F5
Grampian Way
23 Grimsby DN33 .....**113** E8
  Kingston upon Hull HU7 ..**57** A4
  Thorne/Moorends DN8 ..**93** A7
Granary Cl DN21 ....**117** A3
Granary Croft **7** DN9 ..**105** D2
Granary Ct YO25 ....**156** B3
Grandale HU7 ......**140** E7
Grange Ave
12 Barton-upon-Humber
  DN18 ....**84** E8
  Hatfield DN7 ......**92** D4
14 Laceby DN37 .....**101** F1
  Misterton DN10 ....**116** D5
Grange Cl
2 Buckton/Bempton YO15 ..**4** C3
  Full Sutton YO41 ...**16** A2
5 Hatfield DN7 ......**92** D4
  Kingston upon Hull HU2 .**155** B4
  Misterton DN10 ....**116** D4
  Skelton YO30 ......**126** B5
Grange Cres
  Kingston upon Hull
  HU10 ....**143** E6
  Tickton HU17 ......**137** F8
Grange Dr
  Kingston upon Hull
  HU16 ....**139** A7
  Misterton DN10 ....**116** D4
Grange Farm Cl YO8 ..**49** B5
Grange Farm La **20**
  DN36 ....**114** A7
Grange Field DN20 ..**98** D4
Grange Garth YO10 ..**130** D2
Grange Gr **3** DN8 ...**79** B2
Grange Ind Est DN15 .**151** D4
Grange Ind Est The
  DN14 ....**149** B4
Grange Jun & Inf Sch
  DN34 ....**102** C3
Grange La
  Covenham St Bartholomew
  LN11 ....**121** F6
  Molescroft HU17 ....**137** A7
  North Kelsey LN7 ...**110** A3
  Rufforth YO26 .....**24** A4
  Utterby LN11 ......**121** C4
Grange La Inf Sch
  DN16 ....**151** D1
Grange La Jun Sch
  DN16 ....**151** D1
Grange La N DN16 ..**151** D1
Grange La S DN16 ..**151** D1

Grange Pk
1 Brough HU15 .....**68** C5
  Gainsborough DN21 ..**117** A3
2 Kirk Sandall DN3 ..**92** A3
  Swanland HU14 ....**69** B6
Grange Pk La HU10 ..**138** B2
Grange Rd
3 Bridlington YO16 ..**122** D5
8 Campsall DN6 ....**76** E1
  Garthorpe & Fockerby
  DN14 ....**81** E8
  Goole DN14 ....**149** B4
7 Leconfield HU17 ...**43** D6
  North Frodingham YO25 .**34** B6
  Snaith DN14 ......**78** C8
  Thorne/Moorends DN8 ..**79** B2
  Thorngumbald HU12 ..**72** F5
Grange St YO10 ....**130** D2
Grange Way HU17 ..**136** E7
Grange Wlk
  Grimsby DN34 .....**152** A2
  Misterton DN10 ....**116** D5
Grangeland Wlk YO42 .**28** E3
Granger Ave YO26 ..**129** C4
Granger's Yd **8** HU18 .**134** C4
Grangeside Ave HU6 ..**139** F5
Gransmoor La YO25 ..**22** A5
Gransmoor Rd YO25 ..**22** D5
Grant St
  Cleethorpes DN35 ...**153** E3
  Grimsby DN31 .....**153** B5
Grantchester Cl HU5 ..**139** C1
Grantham Ave
  Grimsby DN33 .....**102** E1
11 Kingston upon Hull HU7 .**56** F6
Grantham Dr YO26 ..**129** E4
Grantley Gr HU9 ....**142** C2
Grants Ave YO10 ...**133** E8
Granville St
  Grimsby DN32 .....**152** F2
1 Kingston upon Hull
  HU3 ....**145** A6
Granville Terr **4** YO10 .**130** E3
Grape La YO1 ......**156** B3
Grasby All Saints CE Prim
  Sch DN38 ....**110** E8
Grasby Cres DN37 ...**102** B4
Grasby Rd
  Great Limber DN37 ..**100** C3
  Kingston upon Hull HU8 .**142** A4
  North Kelsey LN7 ...**110** D5
  Scunthorpe DN17 ...**150** E1
Grasby Wold La DN38 .**110** F8
Grasmere Cl
  Gainsborough DN21 ..**117** C1
  Goole DN14 ....**149** D5
Grasmere Dr YO10 ..**131** B4
Grasmere Gr
  Bridlington YO16 ...**122** E7
11 Humberston DN36 ..**103** C1
5 York YO30 ....**126** F1
Grassam Cl **3** HU12 ..**58** D1
Grassdale Pk **3** HU15 .**68** B5
Grassholme YO24 ...**132** C7
Grassington Cl **11** HU7 ..**57** A4
Grassmoor Ct **2** DN15 .**150** B6
Gravel Pit Hill DN10 ..**109** D6
Gravel Pit La DN39 ..**100** A6
Gravel Pit Rd
  Barton-upon-Humber
  DN18 ....**84** D7
  Scotter DN21 ......**107** C4
Gravelhill La DN14 ..**76** F7
Gravelholes La DN10 ..**116** C4
Gravelpit La
  Kirkburn YO25 .....**19** F1
  Sancton YO43 .....**41** E2
Graves La YO42 ....**39** B6
Gray Friars DN37 ...**102** B4
Gray Rd DN17 .....**150** D2
Gray St Goole DN14 ..**149** C5
  York YO23 ....**156** A1
Grayburn Ct HU17 ..**154** A3
Grayburn La HU17 ..**154** A2
Grayham Rd **19**
  DN21 ....**108** B1
Grayling Cl **15** DN37 ..**102** B4
Grays Croft HU12 ...**59** C2
Grayshon Dr YO26 ..**129** B5
Greame Rd YO16 ...**123** A5
Great Barn St **4** YO16 .**122** D5
Great Cl YO8 ......**48** B8
Great Coates Prim Sch
  DN37 ....**102** B5
Great Coates Rd
  Grimsby DN37 .....**102** B4
  Healing DN41 .....**101** F3
Great Coates Sta
  DN37 ....**102** B5
Great Field La HU9 ..**147** C6
Great Gutter La HU10 .**55** C1
Great Gutter La E
  HU10 ....**138** C2
Great Gutter La W
  HU10 ....**138** A2
Great Hatfield Rd HU11 .**46** D4
Great Mdw Rd YO16 ..**122** E5
Great N Way YO26 ..**129** B8
Great Pas St **1** HU1 ..**155** A1
Great Thornton St
  HU3 ....**145** D6
Great Union St HU9 ..**155** C3
Grebe Rd HU15 ....**52** F1
Greek St HU3 ......**144** F5
Green Acres HU10 ..**143** C6
Green Balk YO42 ...**17** D1
Green Bank DN8 ...**93** D6

Green Cl
  Kingston upon Hull HU6 ..**139** F6
  York YO31 ....**130** A8
Green Dike YO32 ...**127** C8
Green Dikes La YO25 ..**8** F1
Green Dykes La YO10 .**130** F3
Green Hill **10** DN35 ..**103** B2
Green Hills YO60 ...**15** B7
Green Island HU9 ...**142** E5
Green La Acomb YO24 .**129** D2
  Appleton Roebuck YO23 ..**36** B6
  Barmby on the Marsh
  DN14 ....**64** A6
  Barrow upon Humber
  DN19 ....**85** D8
  Barton-upon-Humber
  DN18 ....**84** F8
  Belton DN9 ....**94** D2
  Bishopthorpe YO24 ..**133** A6
  Brigsley DN37 ....**113** D4
  Broughton DN20 ...**97** E3
  Buckton/Bempton YO15 ..**4** D3
  Cottingham HU16 ...**138** E6
  Cottingwith YO42 ..**38** C5
  Fimber YO25 ......**18** F6
  Hatfield DN7 ......**92** E1
  Heck DN14 ....**77** D8
  Kingston upon Hull HU2 .**155** B4
  Langtoft YO25 .....**8** D5
  Moor Monkton YO26 ..**24** A8
  Nafferton YO25 ....**125** D7
  North Duffield YO8 ..**49** F8
  North Kelsey LN7 ...**110** A4
  Pilham DN21 ......**118** A4
  Rawcliffe YO30 ....**127** A1
  Selby YO8 ....**148** A3
  Skidby HU10 ......**138** B4
  South Cave HU15 ...**53** D1
  Sutton Ings HU13 ..**144** A1
  Swine HU11 ....**57** E2
  Tibthorpe YO25 ....**19** D2
  Tickton HU17 .....**137** F8
  Weaverthorpe YO25 ..**8** A8
  Wetwang YO25 ....**18** D5
  Wigginton YO32 ...**13** D5
  Wressle DN14 .....**64** D8
Green Marsh Rd HU12 .**72** E4
Green Mdws YO31 ...**131** A7
Green Rd
  Gringley on the Hill
  DN10 ....**116** A1
15 Hedon HU12 .....**72** C7
Green Sward YO31 ..**131** A8
Green The
  Barmby Moor YO42 ..**28** D3
5 Brough HU15 .....**68** D6
20 Dunnington YO19 ..**26** F7
  Great Driffield YO25 .**125** A4
  Lund YO25 ....**31** F3
7 Market Weighton
  YO43 ....**135** D4
  Rawcliffe DN14 ....**64** A1
20 Scotter DN21 .....**107** C3
1 Skelton YO30 .....**126** B5
  Sproatley HU11 ....**58** D5
1 Swanland HU14 ...**69** B7
20 Thorne/Moorends DN8 ..**93** A8
  Wistow YO8 ......**48** D6
  York YO26 ....**129** C3
Green Top Fst Sch DN8 .**93** A7
Green Way YO32 ...**127** F4
Green Ways **2** YO8 ...**48** D6
Greenacre Cl
  Dunsville DN7 .....**92** D2
  Pocklington YO42 ..**29** B3
Greenacre Pk
  Gilberdyke HU15 ...**66** D8
  Hornsea HU18 ....**134** C1
Greenacres
4 Swanland HU14 ...**69** C7
  York YO32 ....**127** F4
Greenacres Cl **8** YO8 ..**48** D1
Greenacres Cres **7** YO8 .**48** D1
Greenacres Dr **4** YO8 ..**48** D1
Greenacres Gr **3** YO8 ..**48** D1
Green's Rd DN7 ....**92** C3
Greencliffe Dr YO30 ..**130** A6
Greencroft Ct **14** YO19 .**26** F7
Greencroft La **17** YO19 .**26** F7
Greendale Ct HU16 ..**138** E5
Greenfield Cl **6** DN3 ..**92** A3
Greenfield Dr
6 Brayton YO8 ......**48** D1
  Hibaldstow DN20 ..**109** A5
Greenfield Garth HU6 ..**56** D5
Greenfield La YO25 ..**31** C4
Greenfield Pk Dr
  YO31 ....**131** A7
Greenfield Rd
  Bridlington YO16 ....**122** B2
  Middleton-on-the-Wolds
  YO25 ....**31** C4
Greenfields DN14 ...**77** F6
Greenfinch Dr **8** DN35 .**103** C1
Greengales Ct YO19 ..**38** A8
Greengales La YO19 ..**38** A8
Greengarth DN17 ...**96** C1
Greengate DN9 ....**105** E6
Greengate La Cliffe YO8 .**49** F6
2 Goxhill DN19 .....**86** A8
Greengate Rd WF8 ..**76** C1
Greenhill **3** DN20 ...**97** D3
Greenhill Rd DN9 ...**105** C2
Greenhoe Rd DN17 ..**96** B2
Greenhow Cl HU8 ...**141** E7
Greenland La DN14 ..**78** C4
Greenlands YO25 ...**124** F5

Greenlands Ave 13
DN36 114 A7
Greenlands La YO8 48 C3
Greenoak La DN14 66 B7
Greens Cl 11 DN15 151 B7
Greens La
Burstwick HU12 73 B8
Burton Pidsea HU12 59 C1
Wawne HU7 56 E7
Greensborough Ave 3
YO26 129 B5
Greenshaw Dr YO32 127 C8
Greenshaw La HU12 74 D1
Greenside
18 Dunnington YO19 26 F7
8 Flamborough YO15 5 A2
Greenside Cl 24 YO19 26 F7
Greenside Wlk 23 YO19 26 F7
Greenstiles La HU14 69 C7
Greenway
8 Barton-upon-Humber
DN18 69 F1
10 Waltham DN37 113 E6
Greenway The
2 Haxby YO32 127 C7
Hornsea HU18 134 C2
1 Kingston upon Hull
HU4 144 C6
Greenways
Great Driffield YO25 124 F5
2 North Ferriby HU14 69 A5
Greenways Cl YO16 122 F6
Greenways Dr 1 YO8 48 D6
Greenways Wlk YO16 122 F6
Greenwich Ave HU9 142 C4
Greenwood Ave
Beverley HU17 154 C3
Kingston upon Hull HU6 139 E5
Greenwood Gdns
HU17 136 F7
Greenwood Gr YO24 132 C8
Greetham's La DN32 153 B1
Greet's Hill YO17 16 E7
Gregory Cl YO30 126 C5
Grenley St 8 WF11 61 A2
Grenville Bay HU11 142 D6
Grenwich Cl 5 YO30 126 E3
Gresley Ct 3 YO26 129 B4
Gresley Way DN40 87 D2
Greville Rd HU12 72 D7
Grey St
Gainsborough DN21 117 A1
Kingston upon Hull HU2 145 D7
Greyfriars Cres HU17 154 A1
Greyfriars Rd DN20 97 E3
Greygarth Cl 14 HU7 56 F6
Greystoke Rd YO30 126 E1
Greystone Ave HU4 144 E7
Greystone Ct YO32 127 C7
Greystones Rd DN21 117 A2
Griffin Prim Sch HU9 142 C3
Griffin Rd HU9 142 C3
Griffiths Way 18 HU12 73 C4
Grime St DN31 152 E4
Grimsby Coll DN34 152 C1
Grimsby Docks DN32 152 F5
Grimsby L Ctr DN34 152 A4
Grimsby Maternity Hospl
DN33 102 E2
Grimsby Rd
Caistor LN7 111 C4
Cleethorpes DN35 153 D4
Fotherby LN11 121 D1
Humberston DN36 103 B1
Laceby DN37 101 F1
Swallow LN7 112 B6
Waltham DN37 113 E7
Grimsby Town Football Club
DN35 153 C5
Grimsby Town Sta
DN32 152 D3
Grimscott Cl 2 HU7 56 F5
Grimston Bar YO19 131 F4
Grimston Rd
12 Hunmanby YO14 3 A8
5 Kingston upon Hull
HU10 143 F6
Grimston St HU1 155 B3
Grimthorpe Hill YO42 29 B7
Grimwith Garth YO30 126 F2
Grindale La YO16 122 A7
Grindale Rd
Bempton YO16 4 A3
Grindale YO16 3 F2
Grindell St HU9 146 D8
Gringley Rd DN10 116 B4
Grinsdale Rise YO25 125 F7
Grizedale HU7 140 F7
Grosmont Cl HU8 141 E7
Grosvenor Ave DN14 149 A5
Grosvenor Cres 1
DN32 152 D3
Grosvenor Ct DN7 92 D8
Grosvenor House
YO30 156 A4
Grosvenor Pk YO30 156 A4
Grosvenor Pl HU17 136 D2
Grosvenor Rd
Hornsea HU18 134 D4
York YO30 156 A4
Grosvenor St
Grimsby DN32 152 D2
Kingston upon Hull HU3 145 D8
Grosvenor St N DN15 151 A8
Grosvenor St S DN15 151 A8
Grosvenor Terr YO30 156 A4
Grove Cl HU17 154 B4
Grove Cres DN32 153 C3
Grove Ct YO25 124 F3
Grove Gdns 12 YO26 12 F1
Grove Hill HU13 143 E1
Grove Hill Ind Est
HU17 137 C4
Grove House View
HU5 140 D3
Grove La DN37 113 E6
Grove Pk 7 Barlby YO8 49 B5
Beverley HU17 154 A4
Misterton DN10 116 C5
Grove Rd DN7 92 D8
Grove St
Kingston upon Hull HU5 140 D1
Kirton in Lindsey DN21 108 A1
Grove Terr La YO31 156 C4
Grove The
Barrow upon Humber
DN19 85 D8
Beckingham DN10 116 D1
Kellington DN14 62 A3
York YO24 132 E6
Grove View YO30 130 A6
Grove Wharf* DN15 95 E7
Grove Wood Rd DN10 116 C5
Grove Wood Terr
DN10 116 C5
Grovehill HU17 137 C4
Grovehill Rd HU17 154 C3
Grovenor Ct 11 DN35 103 D1
Groves Ct YO31 156 C3
Groves La YO31 156 C3
Groves The
Great Driffield YO25 125 A3
Kingston upon Hull HU4 144 B2
Grundale HU10 143 C6
Grundell's Yd 4 YO16 122 D4
Grundill La
Hatfield HU11 46 A8
Seaton HU11 35 A1
Guardians Rd 2 HU12 74 D1
Guernsey Gr 1 DN40 101 C8
Guest Field HU11 47 B1
Guildford Ave HU8 141 D4
Guildford Cl HU17 136 E1
Guildford St 20 DN32 153 A5
Guildhall Rd HU1 155 B2
Guilicarr La LN7 109 E4
Guisefield Rd 5 DN9 105 D6
Gull Nook YO15 5 A2
Gullane Dr HU6 56 D5
Gunby Pl 9 DN35 103 C2
Gunby Rd Bubwith YO8 50 D5
Scunthorpe DN17 150 E1
Gunbywood Rd YO8 50 D6
Gunness & Burringham CE
Prim Sch DN17 95 E5
Gunness La DN15 95 F8
Gunthorpe Rd DN9 116 F8
Gurnell St DN15 151 A8
Gurth Ave DN3 92 A1
Gus Walker Dr YO42 29 B4
Guy Garth 8 HU12 72 D7
Guy's Cres 8 HU9 142 A5
Gypsey Rd YO16 122 B4

H

Habrough La DN39 100 C6
Habrough Rd
Immingham DN40 87 A1
South Killingholme DN40 86 E2
Habrough Sta DN40 100 E8
Hackforth Wlk HU5 139 D4
Hackness Gr 2 HU5 144 D8
Haddlesey Rd WF11 61 D5
Haddon Cl YO24 129 C2
Haddon Rd YO16 122 D7
Haddon St HU3 144 F4
Hadds La DN8 78 F3
Hadds Nook Rd DN8 78 F2
Hadleigh Cl 4 HU3 140 E1
Hadleigh Ct DN15 151 A8
Hadleigh Gn 4 DN17 95 D4
Hadleigh Rd DN40 87 C1
Hadrian Ave YO10 131 B3
Hag La YO42 38 C4
Hagg La Belton DN17 94 E3
Cottingwith YO42 38 E8
Dunnington YO19 26 F6
Hemingbrough YO8 49 F3
Haggs La Fenwick DN6 77 D2
Kingston upon Hull
HU10 138 E3
Hague Pk La 12 YO25 124 F4
Haig Ave DN16 151 B5
Haig Rd DN8 79 B2
Haig St YO8 148 B6
Haigh Ct DN32 102 F2
Haigh La DN14 77 A6
Haigh St DN35 103 D3
Haile Rd DN36 103 D1
Hailgate DN14 65 A7
Hailgate Cl 8 DN14 65 B7
Hainton Ave DN32 152 F2
Haith's La DN36 114 B1
Haldane Ct HU4 144 D2
Haldane St DN21 117 A1
Hale Hill La DN7 92 E3
Hales Cl 3 DN16 96 D1
Hales Cres 12 HU12 72 C7
Hales Entry HU9 146 C6
Hales La YO8 63 E5
Haley's Terr YO31 130 D8
Half Acre Wood 1 DN17 95 D4
Halfacres La YO42 40 A6
Halifax App DN20 99 A8
Halifax Ave DN14 149 C6
Halifax Cl
Full Sutton YO41 16 A2
8 Pocklington YO42 28 F4
Halifax Ct 7 YO30 127 A1
Halifax Way
Elvington YO41 27 A3
Pocklington YO42 28 E3
Halkon Cl DN17 81 D3
Hall Cl 5 Airmyn DN14 64 E4
Cawood YO8 36 D1
Nafferton YO25 125 E7
7 Snaith DN14 78 C8
Hall Ct DN17 81 A3
Hall Farm Cl 4 YO19 48 F8
Hall Farm Ct YO42 16 F2
Hall Gdns
Rawcliffe DN14 64 B2
Winterton DN15 83 B5
Hall La Elsham DN20 98 F7
Stainforth DN7 92 A6
Hall Mdw DN20 84 C2
Hall Pk Swanland HU14 69 C6
Wistow YO8 49 A5
York YO10 131 B1
Hall Pk Rd YO14 2 F8
Hall Rd Goole DN14 149 D1
Hornsea HU18 134 D5
Kingston upon Hull HU6 139 E5
Market Weighton YO43 135 D4
Sproatley HU11 58 D5
Hall Rd Prim Sch HU6 139 F4
Hall Rise 12 Haxby YO32 13 F5
Messingham DN17 107 D7
Hall Spinney The 5
DN14 65 B7
Hall St HU2 145 D7
Hall View DN17 107 D7
Hall Way DN38 99 F5
Hall Wlk 1 Brough HU15 68 D6
Kingston upon Hull
HU16 139 B6
Walkington HU17 55 B8
Halladale Cl 1 YO24 132 B7
Hallard Way 7 YO32 14 B7
Hall's Rd DN10 116 A2
Hallbrook Ct 4 DN16 96 D1
Hallcroft 1 DN39 86 A1
Hallcroft La YO23 132 A3
Hallcroft Rd 1 DN9 105 D2
Haller St HU9 146 E8
Hallfield Rd YO31 130 E5
Hallgarth DN36 115 B2
Hallgarth Ave DN16 151 B6
Hallgarth Way HU17 154 B2
Hallgate
Kingston upon Hull
HU16 139 A6
10 Pocklington YO42 29 A4
Hallgate Jun & Inf Sch
HU16 139 B7
Halliwell Cl HU9 147 E8
Halls La 13 Keelby DN41 101 A4
North Kelsey LN7 110 A4
Hallytreeholme Rd
YO25 33 E3
Haltemprice L Ctr
HU10 143 E7
Haltemprice St HU3 144 F5
Halton Cl 5 DN21 119 C8
Halton Pl DN35 103 B2
Halton Way DN34 102 D2
Halyard Croft HU1 155 B1
Halycon Ave 1 HU13 143 E2
Hambledon Cl HU7 141 B6
Hambleton Ave YO10 131 C4
Hambleton Terr YO31 130 C7
Hambleton View 10
YO32 13 D5
Hambleton Way YO32 127 F3
Hambling Dr HU17 136 E7
Hamburg Rd HU7 141 A5
Hamden Rd YO42 28 E3
Hamerton Cl 11 YO14 3 A8
Hamerton Rd 10 YO14 3 A8
Hamilton Cl 7 DN34 102 B2
Hamilton Dr
Kingston upon Hull HU8 141 F6
York YO24 129 E2
Hamilton Dr E YO24 129 F2
Hamilton Dr W YO24 129 D2
Hamilton Hill Rd YO25 23 A6
Hamilton Rd
Bridlington YO15 122 D2
Scunthorpe DN17 150 F4
Hamilton St DN32 153 B5
Hamilton Way YO24 129 E2
Hamish Wlk 27 DN40 87 B1
Hamlet The 8 DN14 61 F2
Hamling Way HU4 144 D2
Hamlyn Ave HU4 144 E7
Hamlyn Dr HU4 144 E6
Hammersike Rd YO8 48 A4
Hammersmith Rd 1
HU8 141 F5
Hammerton Cl 3 YO26 129 B3
Hammerton Rd 25 DN17 96 C2
Hammond Rd HU17 154 C4
Hamont Rd DN32 153 B3
Hampden Cres 1 DN7 104 A8
Hampden St YO1 156 B1
Hampshire St HU4 144 E3
Hampson Gdns
19 Kirk Sandall DN3 92 A2
York YO30 130 B8
Hampstead Ct 6 HU3 140 D1
Hampstead Pk 6 DN33 102 D1
Hampston Cl HU6 140 A7
Hampton Cl 18 DN35 103 C1
Hampton Gdns YO30 130 C8
Hampton Rd
Hatfield DN7 92 C4
Scunthorpe DN16 151 B4
Hancock La HU15 52 F3
Handel House Prep Sch
DN21 117 B1
Handley Cl YO30 127 A2
Hands on History Mus*
HU1 155 B2
Hanger La DN14 63 B3
Hankins La YO42 38 D1
Hanley Rd HU5 139 D3
Hanover Ct
Beverley HU17 154 C3
Kingston upon Hull HU1 155 A2
Hanover Gdns DN16 151 C2
Hanover Grange YO16 122 D4
Hanover Sq HU1 155 B2
Hanover St E 5 YO26 129 F5
Hanover St W 7 YO26 129 F5
Hansard Cres
6 Caistor LN7 111 B4
5 Gilberdyke HU15 66 D8
Hansard Dr 6 HU15 66 D8
Hanson Pl YO31 130 C7
Hanson Cl YO43 135 D3
Hanson Way DN32 153 B4
Ha'penny Bridge Way
HU9 146 B5
Harborough Cl 20 YO14 2 F8
Harbour Rd YO15 122 F2
Harbour Way HU9 146 C6
Harcourt Cl
Bishopthorpe YO23 133 A4
Wheldrake YO19 37 F7
Harcourt Dr HU9 146 C8
Harcourt St YO31 130 E5
Hardane HU6 139 E8
Harden Cl YO30 126 F2
Hardenshaw La YO8 63 B4
Hardington Cl HU8 142 B7
Hardisty Mews YO26 130 A4
Hardmoor La YO43 53 C5
Hardrada Way 3 YO41 15 D1
Hardwick St HU5 145 B8
Hardy Rd DN17 150 D2
Hardy St
Kingston upon Hull HU5 140 C3
Selby YO8 148 E4
Hardy's Rd DN35 103 C2
Hardys Rd 4 HU12 72 C7
Hare St DN32 152 F2
Harewood HU17 136 B6
Harewood Ave
Bridlington YO16 122 D6
Kingston upon Hull HU9 142 A3
4 Kirk Sandall DN3 92 A2
Harewood Cl
Rawcliffe YO30 126 D2
5 Wigginton YO32 13 D5
Harewood Gr 17 DN35 103 C1
Harewood Way YO10 131 A2
Harfry Wlk DN14 149 F6
Hargrave St DN31 152 B5
Hargreave Cl HU17 136 E6
Hargreaves Way DN15 96 D7
Hariff La HU12 73 B4
Harington Ave YO10 130 F4
Harker St 12 WF11 61 A2
Harland La YO25 124 E4
Harland Rd
Bridlington YO16 122 F5
6 Brough HU15 68 C6
Harland Way HU16 138 E8
Harlech Cl 1 HU7 57 A6
Harlech Way DN32 152 F4
Harleigh Ave HU7 141 A5
Harlequin Dr 15 HU7 56 F5
Harleston Cl 5 HU8 142 B5
Harlestone Ct 8 DN34 102 B3
Harley St HU2 155 A4
Harlow Cl
2 Kingston upon Hull
HU8 142 C6
1 York YO24 129 F2
Harlow Rd YO24 129 F2
Harlow St DN31 152 B5
Harlthorpe Gn YO8 51 A8
Harneis Cres DN37 101 F1
Harold Ct YO24 129 D3
Harold St
Grimsby DN32 153 A4
Selby YO8 148 F4
Harolds Way 1 YO41 15 D1
Harome Gr HU4 144 C7
Harpenden Cl 12 DN7 92 D3
Harpendon Dr 6 DN7 92 D3
Harper Cl YO42 29 A3
Harper St
8 Great Driffield YO25 124 F4
2 Selby YO8 148 C5
Harpham Gr HU9 142 A1
Harpham La YO25 9 D2
Harpham Rd DN36 115 B2
Harpings Rd HU5 139 F1
Harpswell Hill DN21 119 B1
Harpswell La DN21 118 F1
Harrier Rd 2 DN18 69 F1
Harrington Cl 33 HU12 72 D7
Harrington Pl DN16 151 A1
Harrington Rd YO16 122 B2
Harrington St DN35 153 B5
Harris St HU3 144 F5
Harrison Cl
Sproatley HU11 58 D5
Winteringham DN15 83 B8
Harrison St
Grimsby DN31 152 C3
York YO31 130 F6
Harrow Cl 12 DN21 117 C1
Harrow Gdns 12 DN17 96 C2
Harrow Glade 5 YO30 127 A1
Harrow St HU3 145 B4
Harrowdyke 10 DN18 84 E8
Harry Moor La YO8 48 B2
Harry's Ave HU8 141 B3
Harrybeck La YO43 53 D4
Harrys Dream 3 DN20 97 E3
Harsell La HU11 34 F2
Harswell La
Everingham YO43 40 D5
Holme-on-Spalding-Moor
YO42 40 C2
Hart Dr 26 YO42 29 A3
Hart Hill Cres YO41 16 A2
Hart La DN15 83 B5
Hart St DN35 153 C4
Hartendale Cl 22 YO15 5 A2
Hartford Wlk HU8 142 C7
Harthill Ave HU17 43 D6
Harthill Dr HU3 145 C5
Hartland Cl HU7 140 F8
Hartley Bridge HU9 146 C6
Hartley Ct YO15 122 D1
Hartley St HU18 134 D5
Hartoft Rd HU5 139 E2
Hartoft St YO10 130 D2
Harts Cl HU18 134 B4
Hartshead Ave DN15 150 C7
Hartshead Wlk YO16 122 B4
Hartsholme Pk 27 HU7 56 F5
Harvest Ave 19 DN18 84 E8
Harvest Cl 13 DN3 92 A2
Harvest Cres 4 DN37 113 D6
Harvest Rise 1 DN19 85 C8
Harvester Cl DN9 105 F6
Harwood Dr 1 HU4 144 B6
Hase Wlk HU13 143 E1
Haslemere Ave YO15 122 E3
Hassacarr La YO19 26 F6
Hastings Ave 1 HU5 140 E2
Hastings Cl 4 YO30 127 A1
Hastings Gr HU4 144 E7
Hastings Wlk YO16 122 C2
Hatcliffe Cl 20 DN33 102 D2
Hatfield & Stainforth Sta
DN7 92 C5
Hatfield Cl 3 YO30 126 E3
Hatfield Crookesbroom Prim
Sch DN3 92 A1
Hatfield La
Barnby Dun DN3 92 A4
Edenthorpe DN3 92 A1
Hatfield Manor CE VA Jun
Sch DN7 92 E4
Hatfield Pl DN14 149 C1
Hatfield Rd DN7 93 A6
Hatfield Sheep Dip La Prim
Sch DN7 92 D4
Hatfield Travis CE Inf Sch
DN7 92 E4
Hatfield Visual Arts Coll
DN7 92 D4
Hatfield Wlk
Kingston upon Hull HU8 141 C1
York YO24 132 B8
Hatfield Woodhouse Prim
Sch DN7 93 A3
Hatfield Wr Pk* DN7 92 E5
Hathersage Ct DN15 150 B6
Hathersage Rd HU7 141 C4
Hatkill La YO41 16 B1
Hatters Cl YO23 132 B3
Hatton Gr 32 DN33 102 D2
Haugh La YO8 61 F8
Haughton Rd YO30 130 C7
Hauling La YO23 36 C8
Hauxwell Gr 6 HU8 142 A5
Havelock Cres YO16 122 D3
Havelock Mews DN32 153 C2
Havelock Pl YO16 122 D3
Havelock Sch DN32 153 C2
Havelock St
Bridlington YO16 122 D3
Kingston upon Hull HU3 145 A4
Haven Ave
2 Brough HU15 68 B5
Grimsby DN31 152 C4
Haven Basin Rd HU12 72 C6
Haven Cl DN21 117 F5
Haven Garth
1 Brough HU15 68 B5
2 Hedon HU12 72 D7
Haven Gdns DN31 152 A5
Haven Rd
Barton-upon-Humber
DN18 69 E1
North Killingholme DN40 87 A6
Patrington HU12 89 C8
Haven Staithes 24 HU12 72 C7
Haven Terr DN31 152 C4
Haven The
Kingston upon Hull HU9 146 B6
Selby YO8 148 D5
2 Walkington HU17 55 D8
Haverah Ct YO30 126 F1
Havercroft Rd 15 YO14 3 A8
Haverflats Cl 3 HU5 139 F1
Haverstoe Pl 7 DN35 103 B2
Hawdon Ave YO8 148 D5
Hawerby Rd DN37 101 F1

Hawes Wlk HU5 . . . . .139 D3
Hawke Garth **5** YO14 . . . . . . .3 A8
Hawkesbury St HU8 . . . . . .141 E3
Hawkins Gr DN32 . . . . . . .153 B2
Hawkins Way **3** DN40 . . . . . .86 E3
Hawkshead Cl **3** YO24 . . .132 B8
Hawling Rd YO43 . . . . . . .135 C2
Haworth Cl DN15 . . . . . . .150 D8
Haworth St HU6 . . . . .140 C4
Haworth Wlk YO16 . . . . . .122 B4
Hawse Rd YO8 . . . . .63 E8
Hawthorn Ave
  2 Brigg DN20 . . . . .98 C2
  Gainsborough DN21 . . . . . .117 B1
  1 Immingham DN40 . . . . . .87 D4
  Kingston upon Hull HU3 . . .144 F5
Hawthorn Cl
  Healing DN41 . . . . .101 F6
  5 Newport HU15 . . . . . . .52 F1
  Wootton DN39 . . . . .85 E2
Hawthorn Ct **1** HU3 . . . .144 F6
Hawthorn Dr
  Wilberfoss YO41 . . . . .27 E5
  Wistow YO8 . . . . .49 A5
Hawthorn Garth 61 F4
Hawthorn Gate **17** DN18 . .84 F8
Hawthorn Gr
  Gainsborough DN21 . . . . . .117 B1
  York YO31 . . . . .130 E5
Hawthorn Pl YO32 . . . . . .127 E4
Hawthorn Rise **6** DN19 . .85 C8
Hawthorn Spinney
  YO32 . . . . .127 E3
Hawthorn St **1** YO31 . . .130 E5
Hawthorn Terr
  Goole DN14 . . . . .149 B5
  York YO32 . . . . .127 D4
Hawthorn Terr Cent **2**
  YO32 . . . . .127 D3
Hawthorn Terr N
  YO32 . . . . .127 D4
Hawthorn Terr S
  YO32 . . . . .127 D3
Hawthorn Way **9** HU15 . .66 D7
Hawthorne Ave
  Cleethorpes DN35 . . . . . .153 D4
  23 Grimsby DN33 . . . . . .113 E8
  Hatfield DN7 . . . . .92 C2
  12 Haxby YO32 . . . . .13 E5
  Kingston upon Hull
   HU10 . . . . .138 D1
  5 New Waltham DN36 . . .113 F7
  Scunthorpe DN17 . . . . . .150 F4
  4 Thorne/Moorends DN8 . .79 A1
Hawthorne Cl
  10 Thorpe Willoughby YO8 . .48 B2
  12 Winterton DN15 . . . . . .83 A5
Hawthorne Cres DN17 . . .150 F4
Hawthorne Dr YO43 . . . . . .40 A1
Hawthorne Garth
  HU17 . . . . .136 F7
Hawthorne Gdns DN19 . . .86 A8
Hawthorne Gr
  5 Thorne/Moorends DN8 . .79 A1
  York YO31 . . . . .130 E5
Hawthorne Mews YO32 . . .14 A8
Hawthorne Rd DN8 . . . . . .79 A1
Hawthorne Rise HU13 . . .143 B3
Hawthorns **3** Riccall YO19 48 F8
  2 Riccall YO19 . . . . .48 F8
Hawthorns The
  12 Kingston upon Hull
   HU8 . . . . .141 F7
  5 Long Riston/Arnold
   HU11 . . . . .45 C5
Hawton Cl **1** DN21 . . . .117 C1
Haxby Moor Rd
  Haxby YO32 . . . . .13 F7
  Towthorpe YO32 . . . . .14 A7
Haxby Rd Clifton YO31 . . .127 D1
  New Earswick YO32 . . . . .127 D6
  York YO31 . . . . .156 B4
Haxby Rd Prim Sch
  YO31 . . . . .130 D7
Haxey CE Prim Sch
  DN9 . . . . .105 C3
Haxey Gate Rd DN10 . . . .116 C7
Haxey Grange **8** DN9 . .105 D2
Haxey La DN9 . . . . .105 D2
Haxey Rd DN10 . . . . .116 C6
Hayburn Ave HU5 . . . . . .139 F2
Haycroft Ave DN31 . . . . .152 C3
Haycroft St DN31 . . . . . .152 C3
Haydock Garth **6** HU7 . .57 A5
Haydon Cl HU10 . . . . . . .143 D8
Hayes La DN7 . . . . .78 D1
Hayfield Cl
  Barnby Dun DN3 . . . . .92 A4
  9 Haxey DN9 . . . . .105 A4
Hayforth Cl YO30 . . . . . .127 A2
Hayling Mere **29** DN35 . .103 C1
Haymarket Cl HU8 . . . . . .141 F4
Haymer Dr HU12 . . . . .72 D7
Haynes Cl **2** DN8 . . . . . .93 B7
Haynes Gdns **15** DN8 . . . .93 B7
Haynes Gn **9** DN8 . . . . . .93 B8
Haynes Gr **1** DN8 . . . . . .93 B7
Haynes Gr DN8 . . . . .93 B8
Hays Cl **3** DN36 . . . . . .114 A5
Hayton Cl DN15 . . . . .83 A5
Hayton Dr HU4 . . . . .144 D4
Hayton's La HU15 . . . . . . .83 D2
Hayward Cl **3** HU17 . . . .55 D8
Hazel Ave HU19 . . . . .75 A5

Hazel Cl
  Great Driffield YO25 . . . . .124 E3
  Messingham DN17 . . . . . .107 C7
  York YO32 . . . . .127 D2
Hazel Cres **12** HU15 . . . . .66 D7
Hazel Croft **5** DN40 . . . .87 B1
Hazel Ct YO31 . . . . .130 E4
Hazel Garth YO31 . . . . . .131 B2
Hazel Gr Goole DN14 . . . .149 D1
  2 Kingston upon Hull
   HU3 . . . . .145 D5
  20 Yaddlethorpe DN17 . . . .96 D1
Hazel Old La DN14 . . . . . .62 C2
Hazel Rd DN7 . . . . .92 C5
Hazelbarrow Dr HU10 . . .143 D4
Hazelmere Ct YO32 . . . . .127 E3
Hazelnut Gr YO30 . . . . . .127 B2
Hazelwood Ave YO10 . . . .131 D4
Hazing La DN14 . . . . .77 B6
Headingley Ave **20** DN17 . .96 C2
Headingley Rd **7** DN6 . . .76 E2
Headland Cl **30** YO32 . . . .13 C5
Headland View HU18 . . . .134 D5
Headlands Cl YO16 . . . . . .122 F6
Headlands Dr
  Aldbrough HU11 . . . . .47 C1
  Bridlington YO16 . . . . . . .122 F6
  Kingston upon Hull
   HU13 . . . . .143 C2
Headlands Lower Sch
  YO16 . . . . .122 E4
Headlands Prim Sch
  YO32 . . . . .127 D8
Headlands Rd HU11 . . . . .47 C1
Headlands Sch & Com
  Science Coll YO16 . . . . .122 F5
Headlands Wlk YO16 . . . .122 E6
Headley Cl **2** YO30 . . . . .127 B1
Heads La HU13 . . . . .143 C1
Healey Gr YO31 . . . . .130 F8
Healey Rd DN16 . . . . .151 C2
Healing Prim Sch
  DN41 . . . . .101 F5
Healing Rd DN41 . . . . . . .101 D6
Healing Sch DN41 . . . . . .101 F5
Healing Sta DN41 . . . . . .101 F6
Heanor Ct DN15 . . . . . . .150 B7
Heapham Rd DN21 . . . . . .117 C1
Hearfield Terr HU13 . . . .143 E1
Heater Cnr HU17 . . . . . . .31 F1
Heath Cl **2** YO24 . . . . . .129 F2
Heath Croft YO10 . . . . . .133 F7
Heath Moor Dr YO10 . . . .133 F8
Heath Ride YO32 . . . . . . .14 B8
Heathcote St HU6 . . . . . .140 D4
Heather Bank
  13 Stamford Bridge YO41 . .15 C3
  York YO10 . . . . .131 C4
Heather Cl
  7 Kingston upon Hull
   HU5 . . . . .139 D1
  Selby YO8 . . . . .148 A3
  York YO32 . . . . .128 A4
Heather Croft **4** YO31 . .127 E2
Heather Garth YO25 . . . . .124 E2
Heather Gr **1** DN16 . . . . .96 F2
Heatherdale Cl **9** DN33 .113 E8
Heathfield Cl **8** DN3 . . . .92 A3
Heathfield Ct DN34 . . . . .152 B1
Heathfield Rd **1** YO10 . .131 A3
Hebden Ave HU8 . . . . . . .142 C5
Hebden Rd DN15 . . . . . . .150 C8
Hebdon Rise **2** YO26 . . .129 D4
Heber St DN14 . . . . .149 C2
Hebrides Cl HU9 . . . . . . .142 A3
Heck & Pollington Lake
  DN14 . . . . .77 E2
Heck La DN14 . . . . .77 C7
Heckdyke La DN10 . . . . . .116 F7
Hedgerow Cl **4** DN7 . . . .85 C8
Hedgerow La **24** DN20 . . .98 C2
Hedley Cl **7** HU15 . . . . . .53 F1
Hedon Mus★ HU12 . . . . . .72 C7
Hedon Prim Sch HU12 . . .72 C7
Hedon Rd HU9 . . . . .146 B6
Heigholm La HU25 . . . . . . .34 A1
Heigholme La HU17 . . . . . .44 F8
Heimdal Rd DN33 . . . . . .102 E1
Helen Cres **9** DN40 . . . . .87 B1
Helene Gr DN32 . . . . .153 B3
Heliport HU15 . . . . .68 C4
Hellyer Cl HU14 . . . . .69 A5
Hellyers Ct HU14 . . . . . . .144 D2
Helm Dr HU9 . . . . .146 C6
Helms Ave **6** HU12 . . . . .58 C1
Helmsdale YO24 . . . . .132 C6
Helmsley Gr
  16 Haxby YO32 . . . . .13 D5
  Kingston upon Hull HU5 . .144 C7
Helperby Wlk HU5 . . . . . .139 E3
Helperby Wlk HU5 . . . . . .139 E3
Helsinki Rd HU7 . . . . . . .140 F5
Helston Wlk DN17 . . . . . .150 C4
Helvellyn Cl **10** HU7 . . . .57 A6
Hemble Way HU7 . . . . . . .56 F5
Hemingbrough CP Sch
  YO8 . . . . .49 F1
Hemlock Ave YO31 . . . . .127 C1
Hemmingway Wlk
  HU13 . . . . .143 E3
Hempbridge Cl YO8 . . . . .148 A5
Hempbridge Rd YO8 . . . .148 A5
Hempdyke Rd DN15 . . . . .150 E8
Hempland Ave YO31 . . . .130 F6
Hempland Dr YO31 . . . . .131 A7
Hempland Jun Sch
  YO31 . . . . .131 B6
Hempland La YO31 . . . . .131 A7

Hempland Prim Sch
  YO31 . . . . .131 A6
Hemsell Ave HU9 . . . . . . .147 D8
Hemswell Dr **6** DN37 . . .102 C4
Hemswell La DN21 . . . . . .119 A1
Henderson Ave DN15 . . . .150 F8
Henderson Ave Prim Sch
  DN15 . . . . .150 F8
Henderson Cres DN15 . . .150 F8
Henderson St DN31 . . . . .153 A6
Henderson Way DN15 . . . .83 A5
Hendon Garth YO30 . . . . .127 A1
Heneage Rd DN32 . . . . . .152 F2
Hengate HU17 . . . . .154 A3
Henley Ct **6** DN21 . . . . .117 B1
Henley Dr HU9 . . . . .141 E1
Henlow Ave **1** YO32 . . . .119 C8
Henry Boot way HU4 . . . .144 B1
Henry St **8** DN8 . . . . . . .79 B1
Henry St Goole DN14 . . . .149 B4
  Grimsby DN31 . . . . .152 C4
  Scunthorpe DN15 . . . . . .150 F7
Henry Verone Ct HU2 . . .155 B1
Henwick Hall La HU8 . . . .148 C1
Hepscott Wlk HU8 . . . . . .142 D6
Hepworth's La DN14 . . . . .63 C2
Herbert St **6** YO10 . . . .130 E3
Herberts Way YO31 . . . . .130 F7
Herdsman Dr YO32 . . . . .132 C3
Herdsman Rd **3** YO24 . .132 D8
Herdwick Cl **1** YO30 . . .127 B1
Hereford Ave DN34 . . . . .152 C1
Hereford Cl **4** HU17 . . . .136 E1
Hereford Rd YO42 . . . . . . .28 E3
Hereford St HU4 . . . . . . .144 E3
Hereford Tech Sch The
  DN34 . . . . .152 B1
Hereward Pl DN16 . . . . . .151 E3
Herman Wlk YO24 . . . . . .132 C8
Hermes Cl HU9 . . . . .142 C4
Hermitage Rd YO16 . . . . .122 C4
Hermitage The **5** DN8 . . .79 B2
Heron Ave YO24 . . . . . . .132 C8
Heron Cl Grimsby DN32 . .103 A2
  16 Hedon HU12 . . . . . . .72 C7
  10 Scunthorpe DN15 . . . .96 B7
Heron Holt **1** DN40 . . . .97 D4
Heron Mews YO15 . . . . . . .11 B4
Heron Rise YO32 . . . . . . .127 F5
Heron St HU3 . . . . .145 B5
Heron Way **6** DN36 . . . .114 A6
Herrick Rd DN17 . . . . . . .150 D3
Herriot Way DN15 . . . . . .150 C7
Hersey Rd **24** LN7 . . . . . .111 B4
Hertfordshire Cl **2**
  HU5 . . . . .139 D1
Hesketh Bank HU10 . . . . .131 D3
Hesketh Dr DN3 . . . . .92 A2
Heslerton Ave HU16 . . . . .139 A4
Heslin Cl **8** YO32 . . . . . .127 C8
Heslington Croft YO10 . . .133 F7
Heslington Ct **2** YO10 . .131 B1
Heslington La
  Heslington YO10 . . . . . . .131 A1
  York YO10 . . . . .130 F3
Heslington Rd YO10 . . . . .130 E3
Hessay Pl **2** YO26 . . . . .129 A3
Hessle High Sch
  HU13 . . . . .143 C2
Hessle Lower Sch
  HU13 . . . . .143 E3
Hessle Mount Sch
  HU13 . . . . .143 C3
Hessle Penshurst Prim Sch
  HU13 . . . . .143 F3
Hessle Rd HU1 . . . . .155 A1
Hessle View **22** DN18 . . .84 E8
Hesslewoude La YO43 . . . .42 A4
Hetherton St YO30 . . . . . .156 A3
Hewde La DN15 . . . . .83 A8
Hewitt's Ave DN36 . . . . . .114 A8
Hewitt's Cir DN36 . . . . . .103 B1
Hewitts Manor **3** DN35 .103 B1
Hewley Ave HU10 . . . . . .131 A4
Heworth YO31 . . . . .131 A6
Heworth CE Prim Sch
  YO31 . . . . .130 F6
Heworth Gn YO31 . . . . . .156 C4
Heworth Hall Dr YO31 . . .130 F6
Heworth Mews YO31 . . . .130 E6
Heworth Pl YO31 . . . . . . .130 F6
Heworth Rd YO31 . . . . . .130 F6
Heworth Village YO31 . . .131 A6
Hewson Rd DN36 . . . . . . .114 D8
Hewson St DN17 . . . . . . .107 D7
Hey St DN35 . . . . .153 F1
Heythrop Rd DN35 . . . . . .103 C2
Hibaldstow Cl **21** DN34 .102 C2
Hibaldstow Prim Sch
  DN20 . . . . .109 A5
Hickleton Cl HU8 . . . . . . .141 C1
Hickman Cres DN21 . . . . .117 B2
Hickman Gr DN21 . . . . . .117 B2
High Bridge Rd DN8 . . . . .93 C7
High Brighton St **18**
  HU19 . . . . .75 A6
High Burgage **2** DN15 . . .68 B1
High Catton Rd YO41 . . . . .27 D8
High Croft **7** YO14 . . . . . .2 F8
High Eggborough La
  DN14 . . . . .62 A1
High Farm Cl HU11 . . . . .142 F7
High Field YO10 . . . . . . .131 D4
High Field Rd DN20 . . . . . .98 D3
High Garth YO17 . . . . .96 C1
High Gn YO16 . . . . .122 D5

High Hazel Rd DN8 . . . . . .79 B2
High La Carnaby YO25 . . . .10 C3
  Sutton upon Derwent
   YO41 . . . . .27 D3
High Levels Bank
  Belton DN8 . . . . .94 A4
  Hatfield DN8 . . . . .93 A6
High Leys Rd DN17 . . . . . .96 C2
High Mdw Gowdall DN14 . .63 A1
  Selby YO8 . . . . .148 B6
High Mdws HU10 . . . . . . .143 C8
High Moor La YO30 . . . . . .12 C8
High Newbiggin St
  YO31 . . . . .156 B3
High Oaks YO31 . . . . .131 B7
High Ousegate YO1 . . . . .156 B2
High Peter La YO25 . . . . . .20 D7
High Petergate YO1 . . . . .156 B3
High Rd
  Elloughton-cum-Brough
   HU15 . . . . .68 C8
  North Cave HU15 . . . . . . .53 E3
High Ridge Sch Specialist
  Sports Coll DN14 . . . . .150 E7
High Risby Medieval
  Village★ DN15 . . . . .83 A1
High Row YO41 . . . . .16 D4
High Sewerby Rd
  YO15 . . . . .123 C7
High Side YO25 . . . . .34 A8
High St Airmyn DN14 . . . . .64 E3
  Aldbrough HU11 . . . . .47 C1
  Barmby on the Marsh
   DN14 . . . . .64 A7
  Barrow upon Humber
   DN19 . . . . .85 D8
  Barton-upon-Humber
   DN18 . . . . .69 E1
  Beckingham DN10 . . . . . .116 D1
  Belton DN9 . . . . .94 E1
  Blyton DN21 . . . . .117 F5
  Boynton YO16 . . . . .10 D7
  Bridlington YO16 . . . . . . .122 C4
  Broughton DN20 . . . . .97 D3
  Buckton/Bempton YO15 . . . .4 C3
  Burringham DN17 . . . . . . .95 D4
  Burton upon Stather
   DN15 . . . . .82 B4
  Caistor LN7 . . . . .111 A4
  Carlton DN14 . . . . .63 C2
  Cawood YO8 . . . . .48 B8
  Cleethorpes DN35 . . . . . .153 E2
  Corringham DN21 . . . . . .118 A1
  Cottam YO25 . . . . .7 E5
  4 Crowle DN17 . . . . . . .94 D7
  Easington HU12 . . . . .90 F6
  East Butterwick DN17 . . . .106 D8
  East Ferry DN21 . . . . . . .106 B2
  Eastoft DN17 . . . . .81 A3
  Eastrington DN14 . . . . . . .65 F8
  Epworth DN9 . . . . .105 E6
  7 Flamborough YO15 . . . .5 A2
  Flixborough DN15 . . . . . . .82 B1
  Garthorpe & Fockerby
   DN17 . . . . .81 E5
  Goole DN14 . . . . .65 C4
  Great Limber DN37 . . . . .100 D3
  Gringley on the Hill
   DN10 . . . . .116 A1
  Hatfield DN7 . . . . .92 C2
  Haxey DN9 . . . . .105 D2
  Holme-on-Spalding-Moor
   YO43 . . . . .40 A1
  Humberside Airport
   DN39 . . . . .100 A6
  Kilham YO25 . . . . .9 A8
  Kingston upon Hull HU1 . .155 C1
  Kirby Grindalythe YO17 . . . .6 D8
  Kirton in Lindsey DN21 . . .108 B1
  Laceby DN37 . . . . .101 F1
  Langtoft YO25 . . . . .8 C8
  Luddington & Haldenby
   DN17 . . . . .81 C4
  Market Weighton YO43 . . .135 D4
  Messingham DN17 . . . . . .107 C7
  Misterton DN10 . . . . .116 C5
  Nafferton YO25 . . . . .125 E7
  Nettleton LN7 . . . . .111 C2
  North Ferriby HU14 . . . . . .69 A5
  North Kelsey LN7 . . . . . .110 A4
  North Thoresby DN36 . . . .114 A1
  14 Norton DN6 . . . . . . .76 E1
  Owston Ferry DN9 . . . . . .106 B3
  Rawcliffe DN14 . . . . .64 A1
  Redbourne DN21 . . . . . . .108 F2
  Roxby cum Risby DN15 . . .82 E1
  Sancton YO43 . . . . .41 D2
  Scotter DN21 . . . . .107 C3
  Scotton DN21 . . . . .107 C1
  Scunthorpe DN15 . . . . . .151 A7
  Snaith DN14 . . . . .63 B1
  South Ferriby DN18 . . . . . .84 A7
  Swinefleet DN14 . . . . .65 D1
  Ulceby DN39 . . . . .86 A1
  Walkeringham DN10 . . . . .116 C3
  Waltham DN37 . . . . .113 E6
  West/East Butterwick
   DN17 . . . . .95 D1
  Wharram YO17 . . . . .6 A6
  Winterton DN15 . . . . .83 A5
  Withernwick HU11 . . . . . .46 D3
  Wootton DN39 . . . . .85 E2
  Wroot DN9 . . . . .104 D6
High St E DN15 . . . . .151 C7
High St W DN21 . . . . . . .107 C4
High Stile HU17 . . . . .45 B8
High Thorpe Cres
  DN35 . . . . .103 B2

High Trees Mount
  HU7 . . . . .141 E6
Higham Cl HU8 . . . . .141 E7
Higham Way HU15 . . . . . .68 D5
Highcliff Gdns DN15 . . . .150 E7
Highcliffe Ct YO30 . . . . . .130 A6
Highcourt HU6 . . . . .139 E7
Highcroft HU17 . . . . .43 C5
Highdales HU10 . . . . .143 C8
Highfield
  Kingston upon Hull HU7 . .141 D6
  Pollington DN14 . . . . .77 F7
  Withernsea HU19 . . . . . . .75 A6
Highfield Ave
  Great Driffield YO25 . . . . .124 E6
  Grimsby DN32 . . . . .152 E1
  22 Immingham DN40 . . . .87 B1
  Scunthorpe DN15 . . . . . .150 E7
Highfield Cl
  Barnby Dun DN3 . . . . .92 A4
  Fangfoss YO41 . . . . .28 C8
  Gainsborough DN21 . . . . . .117 C1
  Kingston upon Hull HU7 . .141 D6
  5 North Thoresby DN36 . .114 B1
  Wold Newton YO25 . . . . . .2 A4
Highfield Cres
  Barlby with Osgodby YO8 . .49 B5
  15 Barton-upon-Humber
   DN18 . . . . .84 F8
  Kingston upon Hull
   HU11 . . . . .142 F7
  9 Thorne/Moorends DN8 . .79 A1
  2 Westwoodside DN9 . . .105 B2
Highfield Ct YO8 . . . . . . .148 B1
Highfield Dr **1** DN21 . . .108 B1
Highfield Gr **4** DN20 . . . .98 C3
Highfield La
  Fangfoss YO41 . . . . .16 B1
  Womersley DN6 . . . . .76 D5
Highfield Rd
  Beverley HU17 . . . . .136 F6
  North Thoresby DN36 . . . .114 B1
Highfield Rise **1** HU12 . . .58 D1
Highfield View **3** YO8 . . .49 B4
Highfield Way HU14 . . . . .69 A4
Highfields
  10 Barrow upon Humber
   DN19 . . . . .85 C8
  Crowle DN17 . . . . .94 D8
  South Cave HU15 . . . . . . .54 A2
Highgate Balne DN14 . . . . .77 D6
  Beverley HU17 . . . . .154 B2
  Cherry Burton HU17 . . . . . .42 E4
  Cleethorpes DN35 . . . . . .153 E1
Highgate Cl HU8 . . . . . . .142 A5
Highgrove DN17 . . . . .107 D7
Highgrove Cl **7** YO30 . . .126 E3
Highgrove Way HU7 . . . . .56 F6
Highland Tarn **31** DN40 . .87 B1
Highlands Ave **5** YO32 . .14 B7
Highlands Prim Sch
  HU7 . . . . .57 A6
Highmoor Cl YO24 . . . . . .132 D8
Highmoor Rd YO24 . . . . . .132 D8
Highthorn Rd YO31 . . . . .127 E2
Highwood YO25 . . . . .124 E6
Higrove Way **32** HU7 . . . .56 F6
Hilary Gr HU4 . . . . .144 B2
Hilary Rd **11** DN33 . . . . .113 E4
Hilbeck Gr YO31 . . . . . . .131 B6
Hilbra Ave YO32 . . . . . . .127 C6
Hilda St Goole DN14 . . . .149 C5
  Grimsby DN32 . . . . .153 A4
  6 Selby YO8 . . . . .148 C5
  York YO31 . . . . .130 E3
Hildenthorpe Inf Sch
  YO15 . . . . .122 C1
Hildenthorpe Jun Sch
  YO15 . . . . .122 C1
Hildenthorpe Rd YO15 . . .122 D2
Hildyard Cl
  19 Hedon HU12 . . . . . . .72 D7
  1 Kingston upon Hull
   HU10 . . . . .143 F6
Hildyard St DN32 . . . . . . .153 A4
Hiles Ave DN15 . . . . .83 A5
Hill Brow HU10 . . . . .143 B6
Hill Crest YO19 . . . . .14 F1
Hill Crest Gdns YO24 . . . .129 F1
Hill Field 148 B8
Hill Rd DN21 . . . . .118 B1
Hill Rise Brough HU15 . . . .68 C6
  Market Weighton YO43 . . .135 E4
Hill Rise Dr YO43 . . . . . .135 E4
Hill St Bridlington YO16 . .122 D3
  Kingston upon Hull HU8 . .141 D4
  York YO24 . . . . .129 E3
Hill The DN20 . . . . .98 C3
Hill Top La DN21 . . . . . . .117 E5
Hill Top Pl DN34 . . . . . . .102 B2
Hill Top Rd **4** YO8 . . . . .48 D6
Hill Top View HU11 . . . . . .57 F6
Hill View YO31 . . . . .131 C7
Hillam Comm La LS25 . . . .61 B7
Hillam H Cl **5** LS25 . . . . .61 A7
Hillam Hall La **1** LS25 . .61 A7
Hillam Hall View **3** LS25 .61 A7
Hillam La LS25 . . . . .61 A7
Hillary Garth **9** YO26 . . .129 E4
Hillary Rd DN16 . . . . .151 B1
Hillary Way DN37 . . . . . .102 C4
Hillcrest Beverley HU17 . .136 C6
  8 Monk Fryston LS25 . . . .61 A8
Hillcrest Ave
  Kingston upon Hull
   HU13 . . . . .143 C2

Hillcrest Ave *continued*
Poppleton YO26 ....126 A2
Hillcrest Dr
Beverley HU17 ....136 D6
Burton upon Stather
DN15 ....82 A4
Hillerby La HU18 ...134 B4
Hillfield Dr HU11 ....45 D2
Hillgarth Ct 4 YO41 ...27 B2
Hillman Rd HU13 ...143 F3
Hills Dr 6 DN36 .....114 D4
Hillsborough Terr 5
YO30 ....130 C7
Hillside Cl
Bootham Stray YO30 .....127 B2
9 Monk Fryston LS25 .....61 A4
Hillside Cres DN38 .....99 B5
Hillside Dr DN18 ......84 E8
Hillside Gdns YO25 ......8 D5
Hillside Rd DN20 ......97 E4
Hillside Way YO17 ......7 B8
Hillsmere Gr 5 DN15 ...83 A5
Hillstead Cl 5 DN36 ...114 D4
Hillsway Cl HU8 ....141 D4
Hillsyde Ave HU10 ...116 C5
Hilltop Ave DN15 .....150 E8
Hilston Gr HU9 ......142 B1
Hilton Ave DN15 .....150 B7
Hilton Cl DN9 ....94 E2
Hilton Ct DN35 ....103 D1
Hinch Garth HU12 ......60 B1
Hinderwell St HU5 ....140 C1
Hindon Wlk DN17 .....150 C4
Hinkler St DN35 ......153 E1
Hinkley Dr 2 DN40 ....87 B2
Hinman Wlk DN15 ....151 B7
Hinsley La DN14 ....63 C2
Hinton Ave 1 YO24 ...132 C8
Hirncroft Cl 10 HU8 ...141 E7
Hirst Courtney & Temple
Hirst CP Sch YO8 ......62 E3
Hirst Rd YO8 ....63 A3
Hive La DN14 ....52 B1
Hob Moor Com Prim Sch
YO24 ....129 D2
Hob Moor Dr YO24 ....129 E2
Hob Moor Jun Sch
YO24 ....129 E2
Hob Moor Oaks Sch
YO26 ....129 C6
Hobb La 14 DN21 .....107 C3
Hobgate YO24 ....129 D3
Hobman La YO25 ......32 E7
Hobmoor Terr YO24 ...129 F1
Hobson Cl YO23 ......132 B1
Hobson Ct HU17 .....154 B4
Hobson Rd 5 HU15 ....68 C6
Hobson Way DN41 ...101 F8
Hodder Gr HU8 ......142 C6
Hoddesdon Cres 18 DN7 .92 D3
Hoddy Cows La YO15 ...4 C3
Hodge Ct 3 HU9 .....146 C7
Hodge La WF8 ....76 B3
Hodgson Ave HU17 ...154 B4
Hodgson La Roos HU12 ..60 A1
Upper Poppleton YO26 ...24 F8
Hodgson St HU8 .....155 C3
Hodgson's Fields Nature
Reserve ★ HU12 ....90 D7
Hodsow Fields YO42 ....28 E4
Hodsow La YO42 ......28 F3
Hogg La HU10 ....143 B8
Hogsea La YO25 ....60 B4
Holbeck Pl 17 DN40 ....87 B1
Holborn St HU8 ......146 B7
Holbrook Cl 2 HU7 ...141 B4
Holburns Croft 3 YO10 ..131 B1
Holcombe Cl HU8 ....142 B7
Holcroft Garth 10 HU12 ..72 D7
Holden Gdns YO8 .....48 D2
Holderness Com Coll
HU18 ....134 C4
Holderness Cres
HU17 ....154 B3
Holderness Rd HU9 ...146 C8
Holgate Bridge Gdn 7
YO24 ....130 A3
Holgate Cl 2 HU17 ...137 B3
Holgate Lodge Dr
YO26 ....129 E4
Holgate Pl 12 HU14 ....69 B7
Holgate Rd
Scunthorpe DN16 .....151 D4
York YO24 ....156 A1
Holland Ave
Crowle DN17 ....94 D8
Scunthorpe DN15 .....150 E8
Holland St HU9 ......146 C8
Holles St DN32 ......152 E3
Hollicarrs Cl YO19 .....37 A2
Hollies The
Barlby with Osgodby YO8 ..49 C4
Beverley HU17 ....137 A4
Hornsea HU18 ....134 D2
Kingston upon Hull
HU10 ....138 E2
Snaith & Cowick DN14 ...78 C8
Hollin Bridge La DN7 ...93 A3
Hollingsworth Ave 12
DN40 ....87 B2
Hollingsworth Cl 14
DN35 ....103 B1
Hollingsworth La 22
DN9 ....105 E6
Hollis Cres YO32 ......14 B6
Hollowgate Hill DN21 ..119 A3

Hollows The 9 YO16 ...122 C5
Holly Bank Gr 3 YO24 ..129 F2
Holly Bank Rd YO24 ...129 F2
Holly Cl
Acaster Malbis YO23 ......36 C8
Full Sutton YO41 ....16 A1
13 Scunthorpe DN16 .....96 E2
Stallingborough DN41 ...101 D6
Holly Dr HU16 ....138 E5
Holly Gr
11 Gilberdyke HU15 ......66 D7
Selby YO8 ....148 B3
8 Thorpe Willoughby YO8 ..48 B2
Holly Hill HU15 ....68 C6
Holly Rd 11 DN8 ....79 B1
Holly Terr YO10 ......130 D1
Holly Tree Croft 7 YO19 .26 F7
Holly Tree Garth YO32 ...14 C4
Holly Tree La
Dunnington YO19 ....26 F7
Haxby YO32 ....127 D8
Holly Wlk 10 DN8 ......79 B1
Hollybush Way HU17 ..136 D4
Hollycroft YO25 ....23 A6
Hollygarth La DN14 ....61 D4
Hollym Rd
Patrington HU19 ....74 D1
Withernsea HU19 ....75 A5
Hollyrood Rd YO30 ...126 C3
Hollytree Ave 2 HU4 ..144 B7
Hollywood YO8 ......148 B7
Holm Garth Dr HU8 ...142 B4
Holm Rd DN9 ....105 B2
Holme Ave DN36 .....114 A7
Holme Church La
HU17 ....154 C1
Holme Cl 19 Brigg DN20 ..98 C2
Holme-on-Spalding-Moor
YO43 ....40 A1
Paull HU12 ....72 A5
Holme Cres HU16 ....138 E6
Holme Ct YO43 ......135 D4
Holme Dene DN9 .....105 C2
Holme Dr DN15 ......82 B5
Holme Farm Cl DN37 ..102 B5
Holme Gdns 11 DN7 ....92 C6
Holme Hall Ave DN16 ...96 D2
Holme Hill La YO10 ....26 C4
Holme La YO43 ....52 C6
Holme La Holme DN16 ...96 E2
Messingham DN17 .....107 D8
Scunthorpe DN16 ....96 D2
Selby YO8 ....148 D6
Holme on Spalding Moor
Prim Sch YO43 ....40 A1
Holme Rd YO43 ......135 B3
Holme St DN32 ......152 E3
Holmefield Cl 3 YO8 ..148 A1
Holmefield Cl 2 YO8 ..148 A1
Holmefield La YO10 ...131 A1
Holmes Dr 2 YO19 .....37 A1
Holmes House ★ YO8 ...50 B3
Holmes Ind Est YO8 ...148 D6
Holmes La Bilton HU11 ...58 A4
Roxby cum Risby DN15 ....83 D5
Holmes Pk DN14 ......51 F1
Holmes The YO8 .....148 C6
Holmfirth Rd DN15 ...150 C8
Holmpton Gr HU9 ....142 B1
Holmpton Rd
Patrington HU12 ....74 E1
Withernsea HU19 ....75 A5
Holms La YO43 ....53 E7
Holmshaw Cl 18 DN3 ...92 A2
Holray Pk DN14 ....63 C2
Holroyd Ave YO31 ....131 A5
Holstein Dr 2 DN16 ....96 D1
Holt The DN21 ....117 C1
Holtby Cl HU9 ....142 C5
Holtby Gdns HU16 ...134 C6
Holtby La Holtby YO19 ...14 D1
Stockton-on-the-Forest
YO32 ....128 F2
Holtby's Yd YO16 .....122 C4
Holton Cl 3 DN36 ....114 A5
Holton le Clay Jun Sch
DN36 ....114 B5
Holton Mount 7 DN36 .114 A5
Holton Rd
Holton le Moor LN7 .....110 F1
Tetney DN36 ....114 C5
Holwell Rd HU7 ......141 A5
Holwick Mews HU5 ...139 D4
Holy Family CP Sch
DN7 ....92 D6
Holy Family RC High Sch
DN14 ....63 C3
Holy Name RC Prim Sch
HU6 ....139 E7
Holy Well ★ DN15 .....83 C4
Holy Well La LN11 ....121 D4
Holydyke DN18 ....84 E8
Holyoake Rd DN32 ...153 C2
Holyroad Dr DN15 .....96 B7
Holyrood Ave YO15 ...122 F3
Home Beat Dr DN20 .....97 C3
Home Cl HU4 ....144 C5
Home Gn HU16 ......138 D4
Home Paddock 5 DN37 .113 E6
Home St DN15 ......151 B8
Homefield Ave 8 DN33 .102 C4
Homefield Cl YO23 ....132 A4
Homestead Cl
Eggborough DN14 ....62 A2
2 York YO32 ....127 F1

Homestead Garth 3
DN7 ....92 D4
Homestead Rd HU12 ....72 F5
Homethorpe HU6 .....140 A8
Honey Pot 5 YO8 ......50 D7
Honeypots La HU12 ....59 A2
Honeysuckle Cl
20 Brough HU15 ....68 C5
Selby YO8 ....148 C2
Honeysuckle Ct
24 Bottesford DN16 ......96 E2
Humberston DN35 .....103 C1
Honeysuckle Farm ★
HU18 ....35 C3
Honeysuckle Pl 15 HU15 .68 D5
Honiton Rd HU7 ......141 A8
Hood Gr DN14 ......149 B6
Hood Rd DN17 ......150 D2
Hood St HU8 ....155 C4
Hook CE VC Prim Sch
DN14 ....65 B4
Hook La DN14 ......149 C6
Hook Pasture La
DN14 ....149 C1
Hook Rd DN14 ......149 E4
Hooks La Holmpton HU19 .75 B2
Thorngumbald HU12 .....72 E4
Hoop End DN36 .....114 D4
Hop Hills La DN7 ......92 D5
Hope St
Cleethorpes DN35 .....103 D3
Grimsby DN32 ....152 F4
York YO10 ....156 C1
Hopewell Rd HU9 ....142 C1
Hopfield DN20 ......109 A5
Hopgarth DN9 ......105 D2
Hopgrove La N YO32 ..128 C3
Hopgrove La S YO32 ..128 C3
Hopkins Ave DN17 ...151 A3
Hopkins St HU9 .....142 A3
Hopwood Cl HU3 ....145 D8
Hopwood La HU15 .....52 F1
Horbury Ave HU9 ....142 B2
Horbury Cl DN15 ....150 D8
Hords La YO25 ....21 D4
Horkstow Rd DN18 .....84 A6
Hornbeam Cl DN16 ...151 A1
Hornbeam Dr HU16 ...139 C5
Hornbeam Wlk HU16 ..139 B5
Hornby Gr HU30 ......142 C3
Horner St YO30 ......130 B7
Hornsby Cres DN15 .....96 C7
Hornsea & District War Meml
Hosp HU18 ....134 C5
Hornsea Bridge Ind Est
HU18 ....134 C2
Hornsea Burton Prim Sch
HU18 ....134 C4
Hornsea Burton Rd
HU18 ....134 D3
Hornsea Leisure Ctr
HU18 ....134 D4
Hornsea Par 5 HU9 ...146 C8
Hornsea Rd
Aldbrough HU11 ....47 B2
Atwick HU18 ....134 A8
Hatfield HU11 ....46 D6
Leven HU17 ....45 B8
Seaton HU11 ....35 B1
Skipsea YO25 ....23 B1
Hornsea Sch & Language Coll
HU18 ....134 C4
Hornsey Garth 25 YO32 ..13 E5
Hornsey Hill Rd DN21 ..106 D1
Horse Carr La YO25 ....10 B1
Horse Fair Gn 21 DN8 ...93 A8
Horse Mkt 17 LN7 .....111 B4
Horsefair La YO25 ....124 B5
Horsefair The YO25 ...124 C5
Horsegate Field Rd
DN19 ....86 A8
Horseman Ave YO23 ..132 A3
Horseman Cl 2 YO23 ..132 A3
Horseman Dr YO23 ...132 A3
Horseman La YO23 ...132 A3
Horseshoe Cres YO43 ...40 A1
Horseshoe Dr YO15 ..123 C6
Horseshoe The
Great Driffield YO25 ....124 E3
York YO24 ....132 E7
Horsfield Way YO19 ....26 F7
Horsforth Ave YO15 ..122 D1
Horsman Ave YO10 ...156 C2
Horstead Ave DN20 ....98 C3
Hospital Fields Rd
YO10 ....130 D1
Hospital La YO8 ....48 B4
Hospitium The ★ YO1 ..156 A3
Hotham Ave YO26 ....129 B2
Hotham Dr HU5 ......144 B8
Hotham Rd N HU5 ....139 E3
Hotham Rd S HU5 ....144 B8
Hotham Sq HU17 ....137 B4
Hotham St HU9 ......146 D7
Hothams Ct YO1 .....156 C2
Hotspur Rd 1 DN21 ...117 B1
Hotton Cl HU11 ......142 C1
Houghton La HU17 .....41 C1
Houghton Wlk HU5 ...139 C2
Houndale La YO25 ....125 E8
Houndsway 6 YO24 ...132 B8
Houps Rd 10 DN8 ......93 B8

Hourne Ct HU13 .....143 E2
Hourne The HU13 ....143 E2
House Ct HU16 ....96 E2
Housemartin Dr 4 HU8 141 D8
Houston Dr HU5 .....140 D3
Hove Rd HU5 ....139 D1
Hovedene Dr DN14 ....65 A6
Hovingham Cl 17 HU8 .141 E7
Howard Dr YO30 .....126 C2
Howard Gr DN32 ....153 B2
Howard Link YO30 ...126 C2
Howard Rd YO32 .....14 B6
Howard St YO10 .....130 D2
Howdale Rd HU8 .....141 B7
Howden CE Jun & Inf Sch
DN14 ....65 B7
Howden Croft Hill
HU15 ....68 A8
Howden La YO19 ....133 E1
Howden Marsh Nature
Reserve ★ DN14 ....65 A7
Howden Rd 4 Barlby YO8 49 A4
Eastrington DN14 ....65 F8
Holme-on-Spalding-Moor
YO43 ....51 F6
Howden St DN14 ....65 B7
Howdens Hill DN15 ...151 A6
Howdenshire Way
DN14 ....64 F6
Howe Hill ★ DN39 .....85 D2
Howe Hill Cl YO26 ...129 E4
Howe Hill Rd YO26 ...129 E4
Howe La Goxhill DN19 ...85 F8
Kirby Underdale YO41 ....17 A5
Nafferton YO25 ....125 F7
Howe St YO24 ......129 D3
Howes La YO25 ....33 E8
Howes Rd 8 YO14 ......3 A8
Howgate La YO43 ......41 A8
Howl Gate YO41 ....27 E8
Howl La YO25 ....32 E8
Howlett Rd 4 DN35 ...103 D2
Howsham Cl HU9 ....142 D5
Howsham La DN38 ...110 C8
Howville Ave DN7 .....92 F3
Howville Rd DN7 .....92 F3
Hoylake Cl HU6 .....139 E5
Hoylake Dr 6 DN40 ....87 C2
Hoylake Rd DN17 .....96 B2
Hubert St
1 Withernsea HU19 ....74 F7
2 York YO23 ....130 B1
Huby Ct YO10 ......130 B3
Hucknall Garth 16 HU7 .57 A5
Huddleston Rd DN32 ..153 B3
Hudson Ave DN15 .....96 C7
Hudson Cl YO41 ......15 D2
Hudson Cres 2 YO30 ..130 A7
Hudson Ct
Kingston upon Hull
HU13 ....143 D1
Market Weighton YO43 ..135 D4
Hudson Gdns 2 HU5 ..140 D1
Hudson St
Kingston upon Hull HU3 .145 D8
6 York YO30 ....130 C7
Hudson's La YO25 ......31 B3
Huggate Dikes ★ YO42 ..17 F2
Huggate Hill YO17 .....17 E7
Huggate La YO25 ....18 B5
Huggin Carr Rd DN7 ....92 F1
Hugh Field La YO8 .....50 A8
Hugh Field N La YO8 ...38 A1
Hugh Hill La DN7 ......92 D6
Hulberry Cl HU4 .....144 A1
Hull & E Riding Hospl
HU10 ....143 E5
Hull & E Riding Mus ★
HU1 ....155 C2
Hull Arena HU1 ......145 E4
Hull Bridge Rd
Beverley HU17 ....154 B4
Tickton HU17 ....137 C7
Hull City AFC HU4 .....144 F7
Hull Coll (Local History Unit)
HU9 ....146 B8
Hull Coll East Ella HU3 .144 F7
Kingston upon Hull HU1 .155 C3
Hull Coll of F Ed HU1 ..155 C3
Hull Coll Pk St Ctr
HU2 ....155 B3
Hull Coll Sch of Art & Design
HU2 ....155 C3
Hull Gram Sch HU5 ...140 C3
Hull High Sch HU10 ...143 C5
Hull Maritime Mus ★
HU1 ....155 B2
Hull Maternity Hospl
HU9 ....147 A4
Hull New Theatre
HU2 ....155 B3
Hull Nuffield Hospl
HU5 ....140 B1
Hull Rd Aldbrough HU11 .59 B7
Beverley HU17 ....137 B3
Cliffe YO8 ....49 E2
Coniston HU11 ....57 F5
Easington HU12 ....90 C6
Hatfield HU11 ....46 C5
Hemingbrough YO8 .....50 B1
Hornsea HU18 ....134 B1
Howden DN14 ....65 B7
Keyingham HU12 ....73 C4
Marfleet HU12 ....147 F6
Northfield HU13 ....143 F1
Osbaldwick YO10 .....131 D3
Preston HU12 ....72 A7
Rimswell HU12 ....74 E6

Hull Rd *continued*
Woodmansey HU17 .....137 D2
York HU17 ....131 B3
Hull Rd Ave 4 DN14 ....65 B7
Hull Royal Infmy HU3 .145 C6
Hull Sta HU1 ....155 A2
Hull Trinity Ho Sch
HU1 ....155 B2
Hull Truck Theatre ★
HU2 ....145 D7
Humber Bank S DN31 .153 A6
Humber Bridge Ctry Pk ★
HU13 ....69 D4
Humber Bridge Ind Est
DN18 ....70 A1
Humber Bridge Rd
DN31 ....153 A5
Humber Cres
5 Brough HU15 ....68 C5
Scunthorpe DN17 .....150 F2
Humber Dock St HU1 .155 B1
Humber Dr 5 HU12 ....14 B6
Humber La
Patrington HU12 ....74 D1
Skeffling HU12 ....90 D5
Welwick HU12 ....90 A7
Humber Pl HU1 ......155 B1
Humber Rd
Barton-upon-Humber
DN18 ....69 E1
North Ferriby HU14 .....69 A4
South Killingholme DN40 .86 F3
Humber Side La
Easington HU12 ....90 F4
Welwick HU12 ....89 F6
Humber Side Rd HU12 .90 B6
Humber St
Cleethorpes DN35 .....153 F1
Goole DN14 ....149 D1
Grimsby DN31 ....153 A5
Kingston upon Hull HU9 .155 C1
Market Weighton YO43 ..135 F4
Humber Terr DN31 ....152 C4
Humber View
Barton-upon-Humber
DN18 ....84 E8
Kingston upon Hull
HU13 ....143 C2
5 Swanland HU14 ....69 B6
Humberdale Cl 4 HU14 .69 B6
Humberdale Dr HU14 ...69 C5
Humberside Int Airport
DN38 ....99 F5
Humberston Ave 13
DN36 ....114 D8
Humberston CE Prim Sch
DN36 ....114 D8
Humberston Cloverfields
Prim Sch DN36 ....114 C8
Humberston Rd DN36 .103 B1
Humberston Sch The
DN36 ....114 C8
Humberstone Rd
DN32 ....153 A2
Humberville Rd DN40 ...87 C1
Humbleton Rd
East Garton HU12 ....59 C6
Elstronwick HU12 ....58 E3
Hume Brae DN40 ......87 B1
Hume St DN31 ......152 C3
Hund Oak Dr DN7 .....92 C3
Hungate
13 Barton-upon-Humber
DN18 ....69 E1
York YO1 ....156 C2
Hungate Ct
11 Hunmanby YO14 ......2 F8
Market Weighton YO43 ..135 D5
Hungate La YO14 ......2 F8
Hunger Hills Balk YO25 .10 C4
Hungerhills Dr HU11 ...58 A4
Hunmanby Prim Sch
YO14 ....2 F8
Hunmanby Rd
Burton Fleming YO25 ....2 E3
Reighton YO14 ....3 C6
Hunmanby Sta YO14 ....3 A7
Hunsley Ave 3 HU5 ...139 B1
Hunsley Cres DN32 ...103 B2
Hunsley Dr DN41 ....101 E6
Hunsley Rd HU17 ......55 A7
Hunt Ct YO31 ......156 C3
Hunt Rd DN16 ......151 C1
Huntcliffe Sch DN21 ...108 C3
Hunter Cl
1 Patrington HU12 ....74 D1
5 Preston HU12 ....58 D1
Hunter Gr HU3 ......145 A4
Hunter Rd HU15 ......68 C6
Hunter's Croft DN9 ...105 D3
Hunters Cl
Dunnington YO19 ....26 E7
10 Haxby YO32 ....127 C8
Hunters Gate DN37 ...102 B5
Hunters Way
Selby YO8 ....148 B4
York YO24 ....132 F7
Hunters Wlk YO8 ......63 D7
Hunters Wood Way 21
YO19 ....26 F7
Huntingdon Cres 5
DN15 ....82 B4
Huntingdon St HU4 ...144 E3
Huntington Mews
YO31 ....130 D7

Huntington Prim Sch
YO32 . . . .**127** F4
Huntington Rd YO31 . . . .**156** C4
Huntington Sec Sch
YO32 . . . .**127** E3
Huntington Sports Club
YO32 . . . .**128** A5
Huntley Dr HU5 . . . .**140** A1
Hunts Cl 7 DN20 . . . .**97** E4
Hunts La DN20 . . . .**108** F5
Huntsman's Wlk YO24 .**129** B1
Huntsmans Chase 8
DN36 . . . .**113** F8
Huntsmans La YO41 . . .**15** C2
Hurford Pl DN37 . . . . .**113** E7
Hurley Cl HU8 . . . .**141** F3
Hurlstone Cl 20 DN3 . . .**92** A2
Hurn Cl HU8 . . . .**141** E6
Hurns La YO30 . . . .**126** A4
Hurricane Way YO30 . .**126** E3
Hurst La DN17 . . . .**96** C2
Hurst's Yd YO1 . . . .**156** C2
Hurstlea Dr 19 DN36 . . .**103** D1
Hurton's La LN11 . . . . .**121** F6
Hushells La DN14 . . . . .**78** C2
Hustler Rd YO16 . . . . . .**122** F5
Hutch La DN14 . . . .**66** C3
Hutchinson Rd DN35 . .**153** D3
Hutchinson St 1 YO8 .**148** B6
Huteson La DN15 . . . . .**82** C8
Hutt St HU3 . . . .**145** D7
Hutton Balk YO25 . . . . .**32** D8
Hutton Cl
Kingston upon Hull HU5 .**139** E2
Poppleton YO26 . . . .**126** A2
Hutton Cranswick Com Prim
Sch YO25 . . . .**32** E7
Hutton Rd
Grimsby DN31 . . . .**153** A6
Hutton Cranswick YO25 . .**32** A5
Hutton St YO26 . . . .**24** A5
Huzzard Cl 5 HU17 . . . .**55** D8
Hyde Pk Cl 15 DN33 . . .**102** D1
Hykeham Cl 17 HU7 . . . .**56** F6
Hymers Ave HU3 . . . . . .**145** B7
Hymers Cl 11 YO25 . . . .**34** B2
Hymers Coll HU3 . . . . . .**145** B7
Hyperion St HU9 . . . . . .**155** C3
Hyrst Gr YO31 . . . .**130** E6
Hytec Way 7 HU15 . . . .**68** B5

I

Icehouse Rd HU3 . . . . .**145** D6
Icelandic Cl HU3 . . . . .**145** C5
Idas Cl HU9 . . . .**155** C1
Idle Bank Epworth DN9 . .**94** A2
Haxey DN9 . . . .**104** F4
Ikin Way YO32 . . . .**127** F6
Ilchester Cl HU7 . . . . . .**141** B5
Ilford Rd HU5 . . . .**139** C1
Ilkeston Ave DN14 . . . .**149** B5
Ilkeston Ct DN15 . . . . .**150** B7
Ilthorpe HU6 . . . .**140** A8
Ilton Garth YO30 . . . . .**127** A2
Immingham Dock
DN40 . . . .**87** D3
Immingham Medieval
Village DN40 . . . .**87** B2
Immingham Mus
DN40 . . . .**87** C1
Immingham Sch The
DN40 . . . .**87** C1
Immingham Sports Ctr
DN40 . . . .**87** C1
Immingham Swimming Pool
DN40 . . . .**87** C1
Impala Way HU4 . . . . . .**144** D2
Imperial Ave DN35 . . . .**153** C4
Imperial Ct 12 HU9 . . . .**142** A3
Ing Nook Rd HU15 . . . . .**52** C2
Inghams La 12 DN36 . . .**114** D4
Inghams Rd DN36 . . . . .**114** D4
Ingland Ct HU9 . . . .**142** B1
Ingleborough Ave
YO10 . . . .**131** B4
Ingleby Cl HU8 . . . .**141** F7
Ingleby Rd DN17 . . . . . .**107** D7
Inglefield Cl 7 HU17 . . .**55** E8
Inglemire Ave HU6 . . . .**140** C4
Inglemire La HU6 . . . . .**139** E5
Inglenook Dr 1 DN8 . . .**93** B8
Ingleton Ave HU4 . . . . .**144** C6
Ingleton Wlk 3 YO31 . .**131** A5
Inglewood Dr 4 HU4 . . .**144** B5
Ingmires 3 HU15 . . . . . .**68** D6
Ingram Ave HU11 . . . . .**142** F6
Ingram Cres DN7 . . . . .**92** C4
Ingram Gdns DN20 . . . .**108** E8
Ingram Gr DN7 . . . .**92** C4
Ingram Pl DN35 . . . . . .**103** B2
Ingram Rd DN7 . . . .**92** C3
Ingrish La YO23 . . . . . .**24** C1
Ings Ct DN14 . . . .**61** F4
Ings Dr YO43 . . . .**53** F7
Ings La Beal DN14 . . . . .**61** D4
Bishop Wilton YO42 . . . . .**16** D2
Brough HU15 . . . .**68** C5
Carlton DN14 . . . .**63** E2
Cawood YO8 . . . .**48** D8
Cottingwith YO42 . . . .**38** C5
Dunswell HU6 . . . .**56** D2
Ellerker HU15 . . . .**67** F8
Hensall DN14 . . . .**62** D2

Ings La continued
Hibaldstow DN20 . . . . . .**109** A5
Immingham DN40 . . . . . .**87** D1
Kellington DN14 . . . .**61** F4
Keyingham HU12 . . . .**73** C4
Kirk Bramwith DN7 . . . . .**92** C7
Nether Poppleton YO26 . .**126** B1
North Coates DN36 . . . . .**115** A3
North Ferriby HU14 . . . . .**69** A4
Patrington HU12 . . . .**74** C1
Riccall YO19 . . . .**48** E8
Riston HU11 . . . .**45** C2
South Cave HU15 . . . . . .**67** E7
Spaldington DN14 . . . . . .**51** C4
Thorganby YO19 . . . .**38** B5
Utterby LN11 . . . .**121** E4
Walkerith DN21 . . . .**116** F3
Waltham DN37 . . . .**113** E6
West Stockwith DN10 . . .**116** F6
Wheldrake YO19 . . . .**38** B7
Whitton DN15 . . . .**67** E3
Winterton DN15 . . . .**83** D7
Wistow YO8 . . . .**49** A6
York YO10 . . . .**131** A1
Ings Prim Sch HU8 . . . .**141** F4
Ings Rd Cliffe YO8 . . . . .**49** D2
Kingston upon Hull HU7 . .**141** D5
Kirton in Lindsey DN21 . .**107** F1
Molescroft HU17 . . . .**136** D2
Snaith DN14 . . . .**63** C1
Thorganby YO19 . . . .**38** B4
Wilberfoss YO41 . . . .**27** E6
Ings View YO30 . . . . . .**126** D2
Inmans Prim Sch HU12 .**72** D7
Inmans Rd HU12 . . . . . .**72** D7
Innescourt HU6 . . . . . .**139** E7
Innovation Cl YO10 . . .**131** B2
Innovation Way
Great Coates DN31 . . . . .**102** B6
York YO10 . . . .**131** B2
Innsworth Garth 17 HU7 .**57** A5
Inrea Hill YO42 . . . .**29** F5
Intake Ave YO30 . . . . .**130** C8
Intake Hill YO43 . . . . .**135** C8
Intake La
Acaster Malbis YO23 . . . .**36** C7
Beal WF11 . . . .**61** D5
Dunnington YO19 . . . .**26** F7
Heck DN14 . . . .**77** C8
West Haddlesey YO8 . . . .**61** F6
Intakefield Rd YO8 . . . . .**50** D7
Intakes La YO42 . . . .**39** A6
Intax Farm Mews
DN32 . . . .**152** F2
Inverewe Way 2 HU16 .**138** F5
Inverness Rd 24 DN7 . . .**92** D4
Invicta Ct YO24 . . . . . .**132** B8
Iona Cl
8 Gainsborough DN21 . .**117** C1
Kingston upon Hull HU8 .**141** E2
Iona Dr DN36 . . . .**114** D8
Iona Rd YO16 . . . .**122** F4
Irby Ct 8 DN35 . . . .**103** B2
Irby Rd DN17 . . . .**150** E1
Ireland Wlk HU4 . . . . . .**144** B4
Irvine Rd DN16 . . . .**151** C1
Irvine Way YO24 . . . . . .**132** B7
Irwin Ave YO31 . . . .**130** E6
Isaac Newton Sch
HU9 . . . .**142** D1
Isaac's Hill DN35 . . . . .**153** E2
Isis Ct HU9 . . . .**146** B5
Island Carr Rd DN20 . . .**98** B2
Island Rd DN17 . . . .**81** E6
Isle Cl DN17 . . . .**94** D8
Isledane HU6 . . . .**139** E8
Itlings La HU13 . . . .**143** F1
Itterby Cres DN35 . . . . .**103** B2
Ivanhoe Rd DN16 . . . . .**151** C5
Iver Cl YO26 . . . .**129** C5
Iveson Ct 27 HU12 . . . . .**72** C7
Ivy Cl DN7 . . . .**92** E4
Ivy Farm Ct 6 DN41 . . .**101** F5
Ivy La Grainthorpe LN11 .**115** E1
Hedon HU12 . . . .**72** C7
Snaith & Cowick DN14 . . .**78** D8
Ivy Mdw HU12 . . . .**59** C2
Ivy Pk Rd DN14 . . . . . .**149** E6
Ivy Pl YO32 . . . .**127** D3
Ivy Rd DN8 . . . .**79** A1
Ivybridge Wlk 5 HU9 . .**142** E1

J

Jack Rd YO43 . . . .**53** C8
Jack Row La DN7 . . . . . .**92** B8
Jack Taylor La HU17 . . .**137** B4
Jackey La HU11 . . . .**58** B8
Jacklin La DN17 . . . .**81** C3
Jacklins App DN16 . . . . .**96** D2
Jackson La YO41 . . . . . .**27** E4
Jackson Mews 7 DN40 . .**87** B1
Jackson Rd DN15 . . . . .**150** E7
Jackson St Goole DN14 .**149** C4
Grimsby DN31 . . . .**152** C4
Kingston upon Hull HU3 . .**145** D4
York YO31 . . . .**156** C4
Jackson's Pl DN36 . . . .**103** B1
Jackson's Wlk YO23 . . .**24** D3
Jacksonville DN14 . . . .**149** C5
Jacobi Cl YO30 . . . .**130** A7
Jacques' La YO8 . . . . . .**49** E4
Jade Gr 1 HU3 . . . .**145** A4
Jalland St HU8 . . . .**141** C1
James Backhouse Pl
YO24 . . . .**129** E3

James Cl 1 HU19 . . . . . .**75** A6
James Ct 5 DN8 . . . .**79** B1
James Nicholson Way
YO30 . . . .**127** A2
James Nicolson Link
YO30 . . . .**127** A2
James Niven Ct 1 HU9 .**141** D1
James Pl DN39 . . . .**86** B1
James Reckitt Ave
HU8 . . . .**141** D1
James St 21 Brigg DN20 . .**98** B2
Goole DN14 . . . .**149** D2
Grimsby DN31 . . . .**152** C4
Selby YO8 . . . .**148** C5
York YO10 . . . .**130** E4
James Way 29 DN40 . . . .**87** B1
Jameson Rd YO16 . . . . .**122** C4
Jameson St HU1 . . . . . .**155** A2
Jamieson Terr YO23 . . .**130** B1
Janton Ct 23 DN36 . . . .**114** A8
Japan Rd DN21 . . . .**117** A1
Japonica Hill 8 DN40 . . .**87** C1
Jaque's Bank DN8 . . . . .**94** A5
Jarratt Hill La HU15 . . . .**67** C8
Jarratt St HU1 . . . .**155** B3
Jasmine Cl
10 Snaith DN14 . . . .**63** C1
York YO32 . . . .**127** D2
Jasmine Ct 8 DN19 . . . . .**86** A8
Jasmine Gr 17 HU7 . . . . .**56** F5
Jasmine Way DN40 . . . . .**87** C1
Jason Cl YO16 . . . .**122** E6
Jason Garth 1 HU7 . . . . .**57** B5
Jaywick Cl YO32 . . . .**14** B8
Jedwell Cl YO32 . . . . . .**127** D5
Jefferson Cl Goole DN14 .**65** C4
Molescroft HU17 . . . .**136** E6
Jefferson Dr HU15 . . . . .**68** C5
Jefferson St DN14 . . . . .**149** C4
Jeffrey La DN9 . . . .**94** E1
Jellicoe Ct DN16 . . . . . .**151** C5
Jendale HU7 . . . .**140** F8
Jenkins Cl 30 YO42 . . . .**29** A3
Jenkinson La YO25 . . . . .**32** D8
Jenner Ct DN35 . . . .**153** B4
Jenner Pl DN35 . . . .**153** B4
Jennifer Gr 4 YO24 . . . .**129** F2
Jenning St HU8 . . . .**155** C4
Jenny Brough La
HU13 . . . .**143** B3
Jenny Brough Mdws
HU13 . . . .**143** B3
Jenny Cl HU13 . . . .**143** B3
Jenny La DN14 . . . .**77** B5
Jenthorpe HU6 . . . .**140** A8
Jericho La DN40 . . . .**86** D7
Jervis Ct YO41 . . . .**27** C1
Jervis Rd
Kingston upon Hull HU9 .**142** D5
York YO24 . . . .**132** E8
Jesmond Ave 28 DN17 . .**96** C2
Jesmond Gdns HU9 . . .**141** D1
Jesmond Rd HU16 . . . . .**139** C6
Jetcourt HU6 . . . .**139** E7
Jevans Ct 2 YO25 . . . . .**124** F4
Jewbury YO31 . . . .**156** C3
Jewison La
Bempton YO16 . . . .**4** D1
Flamborough Maltings
YO15 . . . .**123** B8
Jill Gr HU13 . . . .**143** F1
Jipdane HU6 . . . .**139** F8
Jobsons Cl 11 HU15 . . . .**53** F1
Joby La HU17 . . . .**43** A2
Jockey La HU17 . . . .**137** F2
John Bull World of Rock
YO15 . . . .**10** F3
John Coupland Hospl
DN21 . . . .**117** A2
John Gray Ct HU10 . . . .**138** D1
John Harrison CE Prim Sch
DN19 . . . .**85** C8
John Harrison's Cl 1
DN19 . . . .**85** D8
John Leggott Coll
DN17 . . . .**150** E4
John Newton Way HU7 .**56** F5
John St
Kingston upon Hull HU2 .**155** B3
Scunthorpe DN15 . . . . . .**151** B7
Selby YO8 . . . .**148** D6
York YO31 . . . .**130** E4
Johnny Moor Long La
DN14 . . . .**79** B6
Johnson Cl DN9 . . . .**94** E2
Johnson Dr
21 Bottesford DN16 . . . .**96** E2
Scotter DN21 . . . .**107** C4
Johnson St
Cleethorpes DN35 . . . . .**153** B4
Selby YO8 . . . .**148** B4
Johnson's Ct DN17 . . . . .**94** C7
Johnston Ct HU17 . . . . .**136** D7
Johnston's Rd DN7 . . . . .**92** E7
Joiners La YO25 . . . .**19** B6
Jonquil Ave 16 DN16 . . .**96** E2
JORVIK YO1 . . . .**156** C2
Jorvik Cl DN15 . . . .**129** C5
Joscelyn Ave HU7 . . . . .**141** B5
Joseph Ogle Cl 8 DN36 .**113** F8
Joseph Rowntree Sec Sch
YO32 . . . .**127** E5
Joseph St DN31 . . . . . .**152** C4
Jowland Winn La YO8 . . .**63** A4
Jubbergate YO1 . . . . . .**156** B2
Jubilee Ave YO16 . . . . .**122** D4
Jubilee Cres 34 DN21 . .**117** B1
Jubilee Ct YO32 . . . . . .**127** D8

Jubilee Gr 8 YO16 . . . .**122** D5
Jubilee La HU12 . . . .**59** C2
Jubilee Rd YO8 . . . .**48** D6
Jubilee Sq HU2 . . . .**155** B3
Jubilee Terr YO26 . . . . .**129** F5
Jubilee Way 8 DN15 . . .**151** B7
Jubilee Wlk YO16 . . . . .**122** D5
Julia Way YO32 . . . .**128** B2
Julian Cl HU4 . . . .**144** A7
Julian St DN32 . . . .**153** A3
Julian's Bower (Maze) ★
DN15 . . . .**82** C8
Julian's Wlk 8 HU10 . . .**143** F6
Junction Rd DN7 . . . . . .**92** C6
Junella Cl HU3 . . . .**145** A4
Jungle The ★ DN35 . . . .**103** D2
Juniper Chase HU17 . . .**136** D4
Juniper Cl Crosby DN15 . .**96** B7
York YO32 . . . .**127** D3
Juniper Way DN33 . . . .**102** E1
Justice Hall La 3 DN17 .**94** D8
Justice La DN14 . . . .**81** B8
Jute Rd YO26 . . . .**129** B5
Jutland Ct 13 DN36 . . . .**114** A8

K

Karelia Ct HU4 . . . .**144** B5
Karen Ave 2 DN41 . . . .**101** A4
Kathleen Ave
Cleethorpes DN35 . . . . .**153** D4
Scunthorpe DN16 . . . . . .**151** B1
Kathleen Gr DN32 . . . . .**153** C3
Kathleen Rd HU8 . . . . .**141** B2
Kathleen Rice Cl
DN32 . . . .**153** A4
Kathryn Ave YO32 . . . .**128** A2
Katrine Cl HU7 . . . .**141** D5
Kay Kendall Ct 16 HU19 .**75** A6
Kaye Dr YO8 . . . .**49** B4
Kaymile Cl DN36 . . . . . .**114** A7
Kealholme Rd DN17 . . .**107** D7
Keats Ave DN17 . . . . . .**150** D3
Keats Cl YO30 . . . .**129** F8
Keb La DN15 . . . .**83** D2
Keble Cl YO23 . . . .**133** B3
Keble Dr YO23 . . . .**133** B3
Keble Gdns YO23 . . . . .**133** B2
Keble Pk Cres YO23 . . .**133** A2
Keble Pk N YO23 . . . . . .**133** A3
Keble Pk S YO23 . . . . . .**133** A2
Keddington Rd 13 DN17 .**96** C2
Kedrum Rd HU9 . . . . . .**141** F1
Keel Ct HU17 . . . .**137** B3
Keel Rd HU6 . . . .**140** A3
Keelby CP Sch
Scunthorpe DN17 . . . . . .**150** F1
Stallingborough DN41 . . .**101** C6
Keeper's Hill YO25 . . . . .**7** A1
Keeper's Way 2 DN9 . . .**94** E1
Keepers Way 11 YO19 . . .**26** F7
Keir Hardie Wlk 13
DN32 . . . .**152** D3
Keirhardie Wlk 4 DN32 **152** E1
Keith Ave YO32 . . . .**128** A4
Keith Cres DN37 . . . . . .**101** E1
Kelberdale Cl 30 HU7 . . .**56** F6
Keldale 4 YO32 . . . .**13** F5
Keldgarth YO25 . . . .**32** F6
Keldgate HU17 . . . .**154** A2
Keldgate Cl HU17 . . . . .**154** A2
Keldgate Rd
Beverley HU17 . . . .**136** C2
Cottingham HU16 . . . . . .**138** D7
Keldmarsh Nature Reserve ★
HU17 . . . .**154** B1
Keldspring La 2 HU17 . . .**28** E4
Kelfield Rd 9 YO19 . . . . .**48** F8
Kelgate Cl 11 HU8 . . . . .**141** E7
Kelham Rd DN32 . . . . . .**153** D2
Kelk La YO25 . . . .**22** B6
Kelleythorpe Ind Est
YO25 . . . .**124** B3
Kellington La DN14 . . . . .**61** F2
Kellington Prim Sch
DN14 . . . .**61** F3
Kelsey Ave DN15 . . . . .**150** B7
Kelsey Cl YO43 . . . .**135** D2
Kelsey Dr 3 HU12 . . . . . .**73** C4
Kelsey La DN17 . . . .**95** D4
Kelstern Ct DN34 . . . . .**152** A1
Kelston Dr 2 HU13 . . . .**144** A3
Kelvin Hall Sch HU5 . . .**139** E3
Kelvin St HU9 . . . .**141** E2
Kemp Rd
Grimsby DN31 . . . .**153** A7
North Ferriby HU14 . . . . .**69** B6
Kempton Cl
Beverley HU17 . . . .**136** E6
2 York HU24 . . . .**129** C1
Kempton Dr DN7 . . . . . .**92** C2
Kempton Rd HU3 . . . . .**144** E6
Kendal Cl 6 YO19 . . . . . .**26** F7
Kendal Dr DN16 . . . . . .**151** C2
Kendal Rd DN40 . . . .**87** D1
Kendal Way HU4 . . . . . .**144** C7
Kendale Rd DN16 . . . . .**151** E4
Kendale View YO25 . . .**124** E6
Kendon Gdns DN8 . . . . .**93** B8
Kendrew Cl 3 YO32 . . .**127** F3
Kenerdales La YO43 . . . .**53** E8
Kenford Cl 1 DN36 . . . .**114** A8
Kenilworth Ave HU5 . . .**139** F3
Kenilworth Rd
6 Cleethorpes DN35 . . .**103** B2

Kenilworth Rd continued
Scunthorpe DN16 . . . . . .**151** C5
Kenlay Cl YO32 . . . .**127** D4
Kenmar Rd DN37 . . . . .**101** F1
Kenmore Dr HU6 . . . . . .**56** D5
Kennedy Cl DN20 . . . . . .**98** D2
Kennedy Dr
Goole DN14 . . . .**149** D5
32 Haxby YO32 . . . .**13** E5
Kennedy Way Sh Ctr
DN40 . . . .**87** C1
Kennet Rd HU8 . . . .**142** C6
Kenneth Ave 5 DN7 . . . .**92** C6
Kennington Wlk HU16 . .**139** D6
Kenrick Pl 5 YO26 . . . . .**129** B5
Kensal Rise YO16 . . . . .**130** D2
Kensington Ct 1 YO24 . .**132** F8
Kensington Gdns 14
DN14 . . . .**65** A7
Kensington Pl 3 DN33 . .**113** F8
Kensington Rd
Rawcliffe YO30 . . . .**126** D2
Scunthorpe DN15 . . . . . .**150** B7
Kensington St YO23 . . .**130** B1
Kent Cl HU9 . . . .**146** C7
Kent Dr DN20 . . . .**109** A5
Kent Rd
Bridlington YO16 . . . . . .**122** A2
Goole DN14 . . . .**149** B4
Kingston upon Hull
HU16 . . . .**139** A5
Selby YO8 . . . .**148** A6
Kent Sq YO16 . . . .**122** A2
Kent St Grimsby DN32 . .**152** F5
York YO10 . . . .**156** C1
Kentmere Cl 2 HU7 . . . .**57** A7
Kentmere Dr YO30 . . . .**126** F1
Kents Gdns 14 DN8 . . . .**79** B2
Kenwardly Rd HU10 . . .**143** E8
Kenwood HU9 . . . .**145** A5
Kenya Dr 3 DN17 . . . . . .**96** C1
Kenyon Cl 28 DN8 . . . . .**93** A8
Keppel Dr YO16 . . . . . .**123** A8
Kerdane HU6 . . . .**139** F8
Kerries Wlk DN17 . . . . .**150** C2
Kerrside YO30 . . . .**129** C6
Kerry Dr HU10 . . . .**143** C6
Kerry Pit Way HU10 . . .**143** C6
Kerver La YO19 . . . .**26** F7
Kesgrave St DN31 . . . .**153** A5
Kesteven Ct 6 DN40 . . .**100** E8
Kesteven Gr 9 DN17 . . .**94** D8
Kesteven Way HU7 . . . .**56** F5
Kestrel Ave HU7 . . . . . .**141** D8
Kestrel Cl YO25 . . . . . .**125** A5
Kestrel Dr YO15 . . . . . .**123** B7
Kestrel Rd DN17 . . . . . .**150** E2
Kestrel Wood Way
YO31 . . . .**127** F2
Keswick Gdns HU6 . . . .**139** E6
Keswick Way 5 YO32 . .**127** F5
Kettering Rd DN16 . . . .**151** C6
Kettlebridge La DN40 . .**86** D6
Kettleby La DN20 . . . . . .**98** E3
Kettleby View DN20 . . . .**98** D2
Kettlestring La YO30 . .**127** A3
Kettlethorpe Hill HU15 . .**53** F4
Kettlewell Cl 2 HU7 . . . .**56** F6
Kettlewell St DN32 . . . .**152** E1
Ketwell La 19 HU12 . . . .**72** C7
Kew Rd DN35 . . . .**153** E2
Kexby Ave YO10 . . . . . .**130** F3
Kexby Bridge ★ YO41 . . .**27** C6
Kexby Stray YO41 . . . . .**27** A5
Key Way YO19 . . . .**133** F5
Keyholme La DN36 . . . .**115** D2
Keyingham Inf Sch
HU12 . . . .**73** D4
Keyingham Jun Sch
HU12 . . . .**73** C3
Keyingham Rd HU12 . . .**73** D3
Keynes Pk 22 HU7 . . . . .**56** F5
Keyworth Dr 5 LN7 . . .**111** B4
Kidd La Brough HU15 . . . .**68** D6
Melbourne YO42 . . . .**39** A6
Kiddier Ave 12 DN33 . . .**113** D8
Kidhill La HU11 . . . .**45** B2
Kilburn Ave HU2 . . . . . .**155** A4
Kilburn Rd YO10 . . . . . .**130** D2
Kildale Cl HU8 . . . .**141** E6
Kilham CE VC Prim Sch
YO25 . . . .**9** C3
Kilham La Kilham YO25 . . .**9** A5
Thwing YO25 . . . .**9** B8
Kilham Rd YO25 . . . .**8** D5
Kilkoy Dr 4 HU7 . . . .**57** F6
Killingholme CE Prim Sch
DN40 . . . .**86** E3
Killingholme Haven Pits
Nature Reserve ★
DN40 . . . .**87** A6
Killingholme Rd DN40 . .**86** F1
Killingwoldgraves La
HU17 . . . .**43** C2
Kiln Beck Bsns Pk
HU17 . . . .**137** C3
Kiln La 17 Brigg DN20 . . .**98** B2
Patrington HU12 . . . .**74** D1
Stallingborough DN41 . . .**101** D8
Kiln La Ind Est DN40 . . .**101** E8
Kiln La Trading Est
DN40 . . . .**87** F1
Kilnhouse La HU12 . . . .**60** C2
Kilnsea Gr HU9 . . . .**141** F2
Kilnwick Ave HU5 . . . . .**139** C2
Kilnwick Garth 2 YO42 . .**29** A3
Kilnwick La YO25 . . . . . .**32** B2

Kilnwick Percy Hill
YO42 . . . . .29 D4
Kilnwick Rd YO42 . . . . .29 D4
Kilpin Broad La DN14 . . . .65 E6
Kilton Ct 12 HU8 . . . . . .141 D7
Kilvin Dr HU17 . . . . .137 A6
Kimberley St HU3 . . . . .145 C7
Kimberlows Wood Hill 3
YO10 . . . . .131 C3
Kimmeridge Cl HU7 . . . .141 B6
Kinbrace Dr YO24 . . . . . .132 B7
Kinderscout Cl 15 HU7 . . .56 F6
King Charles Cl HU10 . . .143 E7
King Edward Cres 9
DN8 . . . . .79 B1
King Edward Fst Sch
DN8 . . . . .93 B8
King Edward Rd DN8 . . . .93 A8
King Edward St
Belton DN9 . . . . .94 E2
Grimsby DN31 . . . . .152 E5
Kingston upon Hull HU1 . .155 A3
12 Kirton in Lindsey DN21 .108 B1
Scunthorpe DN16 . . . . . . .151 A5
King Edwards Terr 4
HU15 . . . . .68 B5
King George V Athletic
Stadium DN32 . . . . .153 B1
King Georges Ct DN7 . . . .92 C5
King Rudding Cl 6 YO19 49 A8
King Rudding La YO19 . . .49 B8
King St
1 Barton-upon-Humber
DN18 . . . . .84 F8
Bridlington YO15 . . . . . . .122 E2
6 Cawood YO8 . . . . .48 B8
Cottingham HU16 . . . . . . .139 B6
East Halton DN40 . . . . . . .86 D7
Goxhill DN19 . . . . .86 A8
Great Driffield YO25 . . . . .124 F4
1 Hornsea HU18 . . . . . . .134 C3
19 Keelby DN41 . . . . . . .101 A4
Kingston upon Hull HU1 . .155 B2
Sancton YO43 . . . . .41 E2
Scunthorpe DN15 . . . . . . .151 B8
Thorne/Moorends DN8 . . . .93 A8
Winterton DN15 . . . . .83 A5
17 Withernsea HU19 . . . . .75 A6
Woodmansey HU17 . . . . . .137 D1
York YO1 . . . . .156 B2
King's Ave DN20 . . . . . . .98 C2
King's Bench St HU3 . . . .145 B5
King's Cl 7 DN7 . . . . .92 D4
King's Cross Cl 2 HU3 . .145 C6
King's Cswy
Reedness DN14 . . . . .80 E8
Swinefleet DN14 . . . . .65 D1
King's Mill Rd YO25 . . . .124 D3
King's Pl 29 HU12 . . . . . .72 C7
King's Rd
Barnetby le Wold DN38 . . . .99 B5
Cleethorpes DN35 . . . . . .103 D2
King's Sq
Beverley HU17 . . . . .154 B3
York YO1 . . . . .156 C2
King's Staith YO1 . . . . . .156 B1
Kingerby Rd DN17 . . . . .150 E1
Kingfisher HU7 . . . . . . .141 D6
Kingfisher Cl
Kingston upon Hull HU7 . .141 D8
1 Leven HU17 . . . . .45 A8
Scunthorpe DN15 . . . . .96 B7
Kingfisher Dr YO15 . . . . .11 B4
Kingfisher Rise HU7 . . . .141 E6
Kings Acre YO31 . . . . . .131 B6
Kings Cl 5 Barlby YO8 . . .49 B5
24 Pocklington YO42 . . . . .29 A3
Kings Croft 3 DN17 . . . . .94 E6
Kings Ct Scawby DN20 . .108 F8
Scunthorpe DN15 . . . . . . .151 B8
York YO1 . . . . .156 B2
Kings Ct Rd 4 DN8 . . . . .79 B1
Kings Garth YO25 . . . . . .125 F7
Kings Lea YO8 . . . . .148 D3
Kings Leigh 1 HU3 . . . . .145 C6
Kings Mdw YO25 . . . . . .124 D4
Kings Mead
Great Driffield YO25 . . . . .124 D4
Woodmansey HU17 . . . . . .137 D1
Kings Mews DN35 . . . . .103 E1
Kings Mill Cl YO25 . . . . .124 D4
Kings Mill Pk YO25 . . . . .124 D4
Kings Mill Sch YO25 . . . .124 E4
Kings Moor Rd YO32 . . . . .14 D2
Kings Rd DN40 . . . . .87 D1
Kingsbury Way 7 HU7 . . .56 F6
Kingsclere YO32 . . . . . . .127 F6
Kingscott Cl 10 HU7 . . . .56 F5
Kingsdale DN17 . . . . .96 C1
Kingsgate
Bridlington YO15 . . . . . . .122 D1
Carnaby YO15 . . . . .10 F2
Cleethorpes DN32 . . . . . .153 A3
Kingsland Terr 11 YO26 .129 F5
Kingsley Ave HU9 . . . . . .141 E2
Kingsley Cl 6 HU15 . . . . .68 B5
Kingsley Dr HU10 . . . . . .138 D1
Kingsley Gr 4 DN33 . . . .102 E2
Kingsport Cl HU3 . . . . . .145 A7
Kingsthorpe YO24 . . . . . .129 D2
Kingston Ave
Grimsby DN34 . . . . .152 A2
Kingston upon Hull
HU13 . . . . .143 F1
Kingston Cl
Hilderthorpe YO15 . . . . . . .11 B4
8 Humberston DN35 . . . .103 D1
Kingston Cres YO15 . . . . .11 B4

Kingston Rd
Bridlington YO15 . . . . .11 B4
Kingston upon Hull
HU10 . . . . .138 D1
Scunthorpe DN16 . . . . . . .151 A3
Kingston Ret Pk HU1 . . . .155 A1
Kingston Rise HU10 . . . .138 C1
Kingston Sq HU2 . . . . . .155 B3
Kingston St
Goole DN14 . . . . .149 C2
Kingston upon Hull HU1 . .155 A1
Kingston View 27 DN18 . . .84 F8
Kingston Way HU7 . . . . .140 F5
Kingston Wharf HU1 . . . .155 A1
Kingsway 1 Brigg DN20 . .98 B2
Cleethorpes DN35 . . . . . .103 D3
Goole DN14 . . . . .149 C4
Kingston upon Hull
HU16 . . . . .139 B5
Scunthorpe DN15 . . . . . . .150 C7
14 Stainforth DN7 . . . . . . .92 C6
6 Stamford Bridge YO41 . .15 D2
Kingsway N YO30 . . . . . .130 B7
Kingsway Prim Sch
DN14 . . . . .149 E5
Kingsway Sta DN35 . . . .103 D2
Kingsway W YO24 . . . . .129 D1
Kingswood Gr YO23 . . . .129 D3
Kingswood High Sch
HU7 . . . . .57 A5
Kingswood Ret Pk HU7 . . .56 E5
Kingtree Ave HU16 . . . . .139 B6
Kinloch Way 28 DN40 . . . .87 B1
Kinloss Garth 2 HU7 . . . .57 B5
Kinloss Prim Sch HU7 . . .57 B5
Kinsbourne Gn 37 DN7 . . .92 C6
Kinsley Wlk 2 DN15 . . . .151 B7
Kinthorpe HU6 . . . . .140 A8
Kiplin Dr 14 DN6 . . . . . . .76 E2
Kipling Ave DN17 . . . . . .150 D3
Kipling Cl YO25 . . . . .31 C4
Kipling Cotes Medieval
Village ★ YO25 . . . . . . .30 D2
Kipling Wlk 1 HU4 . . . . .144 D2
Kiplingcotes La YO43 . . . .42 A5
Kiplingcotes Chalk Pit Nature
Reserve ★ YO43 . . . . . . .41 F6
Kiplingcotes Racecourse ★
YO25 . . . . .30 E1
Kiplington Cl HU3 . . . . . .145 A7
Kir Cres YO24 . . . . .129 C3
Kirby Cl YO43 . . . . .135 E2
Kirby Dr HU16 . . . . .139 B6
Kirby La YO25 . . . . .7 A4
Kirk Balk YO17 . . . . .16 E8
Kirk Balk La YO60 . . . . . .15 B7
Kirk Cl HU7 . . . . .141 D6
Kirk Croft HU16 . . . . .139 A6
Kirk Gate DN37 . . . . .113 E6
Kirk La Sykehouse DN14 . . .78 B4
Walkington HU17 . . . . .55 B7
Kirk Rd 2 HU12 . . . . .58 C1
Kirk Rise HU10 . . . . .143 C7
Kirk Smeaton CE VC Prim
Sch WF8 . . . . .76 B3
Kirk View 1 YO26 . . . . . .129 C3
Kirkby Ave YO8 . . . . .148 B7
Kirkby Cl DN14 . . . . .149 C5
Kirkby Rd
Scunthorpe DN17 . . . . .96 C2
Selby YO8 . . . . .148 B7
Kirkby St HU2 . . . . .155 B4
Kirkcroft YO32 . . . . .127 C8
Kirkdale Rd YO10 . . . . . .131 D4
Kirkden Paddocks DN9 . . .94 C2
Kirkfield Rd HU19 . . . . . . .75 A6
Kirkgate
Bridlington YO16 . . . . . . .122 D4
8 Pocklington YO42 . . . . .29 A4
Kirkgate Mews YO16 . . . .122 D5
Kirkham Ave 1 YO31 . . . .130 E8
Kirkham Cl HU13 . . . . . . .143 F2
Kirkham Ct DN14 . . . . . .149 E6
Kirkham Dr HU5 . . . . . . .140 B2
Kirkham Rd YO16 . . . . . .122 D7
Kirkholme Way HU17 . . . .137 B4
Kirkhouse Gn Rd DN7 . . . .92 A8
Kirkland Cl YO8 . . . . . . .148 D4
Kirkland St YO42 . . . . . . .29 A4
Kirklands YO32 . . . . .14 B6
Kirklands La YO41 . . . . . .16 C2
Kirklands Rd HU5 . . . . . .144 E8
Kirkside 2 DN37 . . . . . . .113 E6
Kirkstead Cres DN33 . . . .102 E2
Kirkstead St HU8 . . . . . . .141 A2
Kirkstone Dr YO31 . . . . .131 A6
Kirkstone Rd HU5 . . . . . .139 D2
Kirkway HU10 . . . . .143 B7
Kirkwell YO23 . . . . .133 A4
Kirman Cres 18 DN7 . . . . .96 C2
Kirmington CE Prim Sch
DN39 . . . . .100 A6
Kirmington Gdns
DN34 . . . . .152 A2
Kirncroft Cl 16 HU12 . . . . .73 C4
Kirton La DN7 . . . . .92 E6
Kirton La Prim Sch
DN7 . . . . .92 D7
Kirton Lindsey Prim Sch
DN21 . . . . .108 A1
Kirton Lindsey Sta
DN21 . . . . .108 B2
Kirton Rd Blyton DN21 . . .117 F6
Holme DN16 . . . . .97 B2
Kirton in Lindsey DN21 . . .108 A3
Messingham DN17 . . . . . .107 E6
Scawby DN20 . . . . .108 C8
Scotton DN21 . . . . .107 D2

Kishorn Ct 30 DN40 . . . . .87 B1
Kissing Gate HU12 . . . . . .59 D2
Kitchen Dr YO8 . . . . .148 D4
Kitchen La HU17 . . . . . . .154 A1
Kitchener Cl YO8 . . . . . .148 B5
Kitchener St Selby YO8 . .148 B6
York YO31 . . . . .130 D7
Kitemere Pl 2 YO24 . . . .132 B8
Kitty Garth YO19 . . . . . . .38 A7
Kitty Hill (Tumulus) ★
YO41 . . . . .16 E3
Knapton Ave 7 HU5 . . . .139 E3
Knapton Cl 1 YO32 . . . . .14 B6
Knapton Ct LN7 . . . . .111 C4
Knapton La YO26 . . . . . .129 B4
Knavesmire Cres
YO23 . . . . .130 B1
Knavesmire Prim Sch
YO23 . . . . .130 B1
Knavesmire Rd YO23 . .130 A1
Knedlington Rd DN14 . . . .65 A6
Knight St DN32 . . . . .153 B2
Knight's Ct 16 DN16 . . . . .96 D2
Knightly Way HU7 . . . . . .56 E5
Knights Cl Belton DN9 . . . .94 E2
8 Laceby DN37 . . . . .101 F1
Knights Ct HU17 . . . . . . .154 B2
Knights Way HU17 . . . . .154 B2
Knightsbridge 7 DN36 . .114 A8
Knightsbridge Ct 7
HU3 . . . . .140 D1
Knightsbridge Rd
DN17 . . . . .107 D7
Knightscourt HU6 . . . . . .139 E7
Knole Pk HU7 . . . . .56 F5
Knoll St DN35 . . . . .153 F2
Knoll The YO24 . . . . .129 B2
Knottingley High Sch
WF11 . . . . .61 A2
Knowle Rd YO7 . . . . .56 F5
Knowles Ave HU6 . . . . . .140 C8
Knowsley Ave HU16 . . . .139 A7
Kyffin Ave HU9 . . . . .142 D2
Kyle Cl HU8 . . . . .142 C6
Kyle Way YO26 . . . . .129 B2
Kyme St YO1 . . . . .156 B1

L

Labrador Dr 11 DN20 . . . .97 E4
Laburnham Ave 21
DN37 . . . . .113 D6
Laburnham Cl 22 DN37 .113 D6
Laburnum Ave
18 Gainsborough DN21 . . .117 B1
Gunness DN15 . . . . .95 C6
Hutton Cranswick YO25 . . . .32 E7
Kingston upon Hull HU8 . .141 D2
11 Thorne/Moorends DN8 . .79 B2
Laburnum Cl
Rufforth YO23 . . . . .24 D5
7 Snaith DN14 . . . . .63 C1
3 Thorpe Willoughby YO8 . .48 B1
Laburnum Ct
4 Bridlington YO16 . . . . .123 A6
Kingston upon Hull
HU13 . . . . .143 D1
Laburnum Dr
Beverley HU17 . . . . .137 A7
Grimsby DN34 . . . . .102 C4
3 Kingston upon Hull
HU4 . . . . .144 D1
Laburnum Garth 6
YO31 . . . . .130 F8
Laburnum Gr
Burton upon Stather
DN15 . . . . .82 B5
10 Crowle DN17 . . . . .94 D7
Scunthorpe DN16 . . . . . . .151 B3
Stillingfleet YO19 . . . . .36 D4
Laburnum Wlk 4 HU15 . . .66 D8
Laceby Acres Prim Sch
DN34 . . . . .102 B3
Laceby Rd
Grimsby DN34 . . . . .102 C2
Scunthorpe DN17 . . . . . . .150 E1
Lady Anne Ct YO1 . . . . .156 B1
Lady Frances Cres
DN35 . . . . .153 C1
Lady Hamilton Gdns
YO24 . . . . .129 C2
Lady Mill Garth YO30 . . .130 B8
Lady Peckitts Yd YO1 . . .156 B2
Lady Rd YO30 . . . . .130 B7
Lady Wortley Pl YO23 . . .133 B6
Ladybower Cl 4 HU7 . . . .141 E7
Ladygate HU17 . . . . .154 A3
Ladyside Cl 17 HU7 . . . . .57 A6
Ladysmith Ind Est
DN32 . . . . .153 A2
Ladysmith Mews 13
YO32 . . . . .14 A7
Ladysmith Rd
Grimsby DN32 . . . . .152 F3
Kingston upon Hull
HU10 . . . . .138 D1
Ladywell Gate 3 HU15 . .68 E6
Laforey Rd DN37 . . . . . .102 C6
Lagoon Dr HU7 . . . . .141 D8
Lagoon Rd DN17 . . . . . .150 B2
Lairgate HU17 . . . . .154 A2
Lairs La YO42 . . . . .30 A5
Lake Dr HU8 . . . . .141 E3
Lake View HU8 . . . . .141 E3
Lakeside
Acaster Malbis YO23 . . . . .36 C7

Lakeside continued
Great Coates DN31 . . . . . .102 B6
Lakeside Dr DN17 . . . . . .150 C6
Lakeside Gr
Kingston upon Hull HU4 . .144 D4
1 Strensall YO32 . . . . . . .14 B8
Lakeside Parkway
DN16 . . . . .151 F1
Lakeside Prim Sch
YO30 . . . . .126 F2
Lakeside Ret Pk DN16 . .151 F1
Lakeside Sta DN35 . . . . .103 E2
Laking La YO25 . . . . .2 A3
Lalrgate Pl 20 DN35 . . . .103 C1
Lamb Inn Rd 9 WF11 . . . .61 B1
Lamb La Newport HU15 . . .67 B8
Roos HU12 . . . . .60 A1
Lambert Ave 16 HU15 . . . .68 C6
Lambert Cl YO43 . . . . . . .135 E3
Lambert Ct YO1 . . . . .156 B1
Lambert Pk Rd 23 HU12 . .72 C7
Lambert Rd
Bridlington YO16 . . . . . . .122 F5
Grimsby DN32 . . . . .152 E5
Lambert St HU5 . . . . . . .140 D2
Lambourn Ct 25 DN35 . . .103 C1
Lambourne Rise 7 DN16 96 E2
Lambton St HU5 . . . . . . .140 C3
Lambwath La HU11 . . . . .46 A3
Lambwath Prim Sch
HU8 . . . . .141 F5
Lambwath Rd HU8 . . . . .141 C4
Lambwell Hill HU15 . . . . .54 E2
Lamel St YO10 . . . . .131 A3
Lamorna Ave HU8 . . . . . .141 B3
Lamplugh Cres YO23 . . .133 B3
Lamplugh La 7 YO15 . . . .122 F4
Lamplugh Rd YO15 . . . . .122 F4
Lamplugh Sq 6 YO15 . . .122 F4
Lampton Gr DN32 . . . . . .152 D2
Lanark St 3 HU5 . . . . . . .145 B8
Lancar Cl 18 YO32 . . . . . .13 D5
Lancaster App DN40 . . . . .86 D4
Lancaster Ave DN31 . . . .152 B3
Lancaster Ct 13 DN33 . . .102 D1
Lancaster Dr
Kingston upon Hull HU8 . .141 D4
2 Moorland Prison DN7 . .104 A8
Lancaster Gate DN36 . . .114 A4
Lancaster Rd
Carnaby YO15 . . . . .10 D2
Gringley on the Hill
DN10 . . . . .116 A1
Pocklington YO42 . . . . . . .28 E3
Scunthorpe DN16 . . . . . . .151 A5
Lancaster Way YO41 . . . .27 A1
Lancelot Ct HU9 . . . . . . .146 C6
Lancing Way 24 DN33 . . .113 E8
Land Dike LN11 . . . . .115 A1
Land Ends Rd DN8 . . . . . .78 F1
Land of Gn Ginger
HU1 . . . . .155 B2
Landalewood Rd YO30 . .126 F2
Landau Cl YO8 . . . . .129 F8
Landeck Ave DN34 . . . . .152 B2
Landing La
Asselby DN14 . . . . .64 D6
Barlby with Osgodby
YO8 . . . . .148 F8
Broomfleet HU15 . . . . . . .67 A7
Gilberdyke HU15 . . . . .52 D6
Haxby YO32 . . . . .127 E7
Hemingbrough YO8 . . . . . .63 F8
Newport HU15 . . . . .52 E1
Riccall YO19 . . . . .48 F8
York YO26 . . . . .129 E6
Landing Rd HU4 . . . . .62 A7
Landings The 21 YO32 . . . .13 F5
Landor Ave DN17 . . . . . .150 D3
Landress La HU17 . . . . . .154 A2
Lane The YO41 . . . . .15 B2
Laneham St HU5 . . . . . . .151 A7
Lanes The 7 DN36 . . . . .114 D4
Lang Ave YO10 . . . . .131 A4
Lang Rd
Bishopthorpe YO23 . . . . . .132 F4
York YO32 . . . . .127 F6
Langdale Ave
Beverley HU17 . . . . .154 B3
Grimsby DN33 . . . . .113 D8
Kingston upon Hull HU5 . .139 E2
York YO31 . . . . .131 B6
Langdale Cres HU16 . . . .139 A5
Langdale Dr 4 HU12 . . . . .73 C4
Langdale Gr YO8 . . . . . . .148 B3
Langdale Mews YO16 . . .122 E7
Langdale Rd YO43 . . . . . .135 E4
Langford Wlk 1 HU4 . . . .144 B7
Langham Rd 18 HU12 . . . .72 E5
Langholm Cl HU17 . . . . . .136 E7
Langholme Dr YO26 . . . .129 C6
Langholme La DN9 . . . . .116 B8
Langley Ct 1 YO32 . . . . . .13 E5
Langley Garth
11 Driffield YO25 . . . . . . .124 F4
Great Driffield YO25 . . . . .124 F4
Langley Pk 25 HU7 . . . . . .56 F5
Langley Pl 5 DN35 . . . . .103 C2
Langrick Ave 9 DN14 . . . .65 B7
Langrickgate La YO42 . . . .38 E3
Langsett Gr YO30 . . . . . .126 F3
Langsett Rd HU5 . . . . . . .141 D7
Langthorpe Rd HU11 . . . .45 D7
Langtoft Gr HU6 . . . . . . .139 F5
Langtoft Prim Sch YO25 . .8 C5
Langton Cl 16 DN33 . . . .102 D2

Langton Ct 1 YO32 . . . . .14 A6
Langton Dr DN33 . . . . . .102 D2
Langton Rd DN36 . . . . . .114 B5
Langtree Cl HU7 . . . . . . .140 F8
Langwith Stray YO10 . . . .26 C2
Lansdown Link 17 DN35 103 C2
Lansdown Rd
Goole DN14 . . . . .149 A5
13 Immingham DN40 . . . . .87 B1
Lansdown Way 7 YO32 . . .13 F5
Lansdowne Ave DN33 . . .102 E2
Lansdowne Cres 9
YO15 . . . . .122 F3
Lansdowne Rd YO15 . . . .122 F4
Lansdowne St HU3 . . . .145 C6
Lansdowne Terr 5
YO10 . . . . .130 E3
Lanshaw Croft YO30 . . . .126 F1
Lanyon Cl HU7 . . . . .141 C7
Laporte Rd DN40 . . . . . . .87 E2
Lapwing Cl HU7 . . . . . . .141 D8
Lapwing Rd YO25 . . . . . .125 B5
Larard Ave 2 HU6 . . . . . .140 C8
Larch Cl
2 Immingham DN40 . . . . . .87 B2
Kingston upon Hull HU5 . .140 D2
Larch Ct 11 DN21 . . . . . .117 C1
Larch Dr HU12 . . . . .72 C5
Larch Gr Scawby DN20 . .108 F8
Scunthorpe DN16 . . . . . . .151 B3
Larch Rd 6 DN16 . . . . . .103 B1
Larchfield YO31 . . . . .131 C7
Larchmont Cl 7 HU15 . . . .68 C6
Larden Ave 4 DN33 . . . . .113 E8
Larch Dr HU12 . . . . .72 C5
Lark Rise 2 DN21 . . . . . .107 B3
Larkfield Cl 1 YO23 . . . . .132 A3
Larkfield Rd YO8 . . . . . . .148 A4
Larkspur Ave DN41 . . . . .101 F5
Larmour Rd DN37 . . . . . .102 B4
Larne Rd HU9 . . . . .142 B4
Larsen Pk DN14 . . . . . . .149 A3
Larsen Rd DN14 . . . . . . .149 A3
Lascelles Ave HU19 . . . . .74 F6
Lasenby Cl YO32 . . . . . . .127 D5
Lashbrook Garth HU4 . . .144 B4
Lastingham 12 HU15 . . . . .68 C6
Lastingham Cl HU6 . . . . .139 F6
Lastingham Terr
YO10 . . . . .130 D2
Laughton Endowed CE Prim
Sch DN21 . . . . .117 E8
Laughton Rd
Beverley HU17 . . . . .154 B4
Blyton DN21 . . . . .117 B4
Laundry La YO25 . . . . . . .124 E5
Laura St DN14 . . . . .149 C5
Laurel Ave DN8 . . . . .79 B2
Laurel Cl
10 Gainsborough DN21 . . .117 C1
Gateforth YO8 . . . . .48 B1
3 Grimsby DN33 . . . . . . .102 E1
Kingston upon Hull HU4 . .144 B7
Laurel Way 19 DN16 . . . . .96 E2
Laurels Cl 1 DN40 . . . . .100 E8
Laurels The YO42 . . . . . . .28 D3
Laurence Gr YO8 . . . . . . .148 D3
Laurier St DN35 . . . . . . .153 D4
Laurold Ave DN7 . . . . . . .93 A3
Lauty La HU11 . . . . .45 C5
Lavender Cl 23 HU7 . . . . .56 F5
Lavender Gr
10 New Waltham DN36 . . .113 F8
York YO26 . . . . .129 E5
Lavender Way DN15 . . . .151 B6
Lavender Wlk
Beverley HU17 . . . . .154 A1
1 Kingston upon Hull
HU4 . . . . .144 C7
Lavenham Rd DN33 . . . .113 D8
Laveracks Ind Est YO41 . .27 B3
Lawn La DN6 . . . . .77 E3
Lawns The
Beverley HU17 . . . . .136 C6
Bridlington YO16 . . . . . . .122 E7
Grimsby DN34 . . . . .152 C2
Kirk Ella HU10 . . . . .143 D7
Sutton-on-Hull HU7 . . . . .141 D6
Lawnsgarth HU16 . . . . . .139 A7
Lawnswood HU13 . . . . . .143 D2
Lawnswood Cl HU7 . . . . .141 D5
Lawnswood Dr YO30 . . . .129 F8
Lawnway YO31 . . . . .131 A7
Lawrence Ave
Bewholme YO25 . . . . .34 E3
Kingston upon Hull HU8 . .141 F3
Lawrence St
Grimsby DN31 . . . . .152 C4
York YO10 . . . . .130 E3
Lawson Ave
Grimsby DN31 . . . . .152 B3
Kingston upon Hull
HU10 . . . . .139 D1
Lawson Cl
Kingston upon Hull HU6 . .140 B5
1 Walkington HU17 . . . . . .55 B7
Lawson Rd
Bridlington YO16 . . . . . . .122 D4
York YO24 . . . . .132 F7
Lawsons Cl YO14 . . . . .2 F7
Laxthorpe HU6 . . . . .140 A8
Laxton Garth HU10 . . . . .138 B1
Laxton Gr 5 DN16 . . . . . .96 D1
Layerthorpe YO31 . . . . . .156 C3
Lea Cres HU16 . . . . .139 A5
Lea Croft 2 YO43 . . . . . .135 E4

Lea Dr DN32 ....102 F2
Lea Field Rd YO25 .....31 E6
Lea Garth DN17 ......107 D7
Lea The HU15 ....54 A2
Lea Way YO32 ....128 A4
Leaburn Rd DN17 ....107 D7
Lead Mill La YO1 ....156 C1
Leadhills Way 6 HU7 ...57 B5
Leadley Croft YO23 ..132 A1
Leads Rd HU7 ....141 C6
Leake St YO10 ....130 E3
Lealholm Ct 11 HU8 ..141 D7
Leame Cl HU3 ....145 A7
Leamington Cl DN16 .151 C5
Leamington Ct DN16 .151 C5
Leander Rd HU7 ......142 B3
Learmans Way YO23 ..132 C3
Learning La DN14 .....61 F1
Leas Cl DN37 ....113 E7
Leas Jun & Inf Sch The
DN37 ....113 E7
Leas La HU11 ....34 F1
Lease La DN40 ....86 D6
Leases The HU17 ....154 A2
Leatherdog La HU15 ..52 E1
Leathley Cl 1 HU17 ..136 E1
Leavens La HU15 ......52 D2
Leconfield Cl HU9 ...142 D1
Leconfield Prim Sch
HU17 ....43 D6
Ledbury Dr 10 DN36 .114 A8
Ledbury Rd HU5 ......139 D2
Lee Ave HU19 ....75 A6
Lee Ct DN14 ....77 A7
Lee Fair Gdns DN17 ..96 C1
Lee Smith St HU9 ....146 E7
Lee St HU8 ....141 D3
Lee View DN14 ....77 A4
Leeds Rd YO8 ....148 A4
Leek Hill 9 DN15 .....83 A5
Leeman Rd YO26 .....156 A2
Leeming Garth 3 HU7 .57 B5
Lees Rest Houses
HU4 ....144 D6
Lees Wlk HU3 ....145 A7
Leeside YO24 ....132 E8
Legard Ave DN16 ....151 B2
Legard Dr HU10 .....143 F6
Legarde Ave HU4 .....144 C7
Leggott Way 1 DN41 .101 E6
Legion Cl 11 HU15 ....68 C5
Legsby Ave DN32 ....152 E2
Legsby Pl DN32 ......102 F2
Leicester St HU3 ....145 D8
Leicester Way YO1 ..156 C1
Leighton Croft 3 YO30 .126 F1
Leighton Gr 2 DN33 .102 C2
Leisure Pk YO32 .....128 A2
Leitholm Cl 2 HU7 ....57 A6
Lelley Rd
Humbleton HU11 .....58 F5
Preston HU12 ....58 D2
Lendal YO1 ....156 B2
Lenham La HU1 ......155 A2
Leningrad Rd HU7 ...140 F6
Lennox Cl 2 YO14 .....3 A8
Leonard Cl HU12 ......72 A5
Leonard Cres DN15 ..150 F7
Leonard St
4 Kingston upon Hull
HU3 ....145 D8
Kingston upon Hull HU2 .155 A4
Leopold Cl DN15 ....151 A2
Lerecroft Rd YO24 ..132 D8
Lesley Ave YO10 ....133 E8
Leslie Ct 6 DN15 ....151 B7
Lestrange St DN35 ..153 C3
Levels La DN9 ....104 A4
Levels The HU18 ....134 C4
Leven CE VC Prim Sch
HU17 ....45 B7
Leven Gr HU9 ....142 A2
Leven Rd
Scunthorpe DN16 ....151 D2
York YO24 ....132 D7
Leverstock Gn 35 DN7 .92 D4
Levington St DN32 ..153 A5
Levisham Cl HU6 ....139 F6
Levisham St YO10 ..130 F6
Levita Ave HU9 .....142 C2
Levitt Lanes YO25 ...31 F2
Lewis Rd DN35 ......153 D4
Lexington Dr HU4 ...144 C5
Leyburn Ave
Hornsea HU18 ......134 C2
Kingston upon Hull HU6 .139 E4
Leyden Cl 18 DN40 ...87 B1
Leyes The YO10 .....131 C4
Leyfield Cl 1 YO32 ...14 A7
Leyland Ave 6 DN7 ...92 E4
Leyland Rd YO31 ....131 A5
Leys Ct YO16 ....122 B4
Leys Farm Jun Sch
DN17 ....96 C2
Leys La Darrington WF11 .76 A8
Little Smeaton WF8 ..76 B4
Skipsea YO25 ....23 A1
Winterton DN15 ....83 B6
Leys Rd
Bridlington YO16 ....122 B4
Darrington WF11 .....76 A4
Leys The HU18 ......134 B4
Liberty La HU1 ......155 C2
Library Sq YO1 .....156 B3
Lichfield Ave DN17 ..150 C3

Lichfield Cl
Beverley HU17 ....136 E1
Kingston upon Hull HU2 .155 A4
Lichfield Ct
Cleethorpes DN32 ...153 B2
6 York YO23 ....130 B1
Lichfield Rd
Grimsby DN32 ......153 B2
40 Hatfield DN7 .....92 D4
Liddell St HU2 ......155 A3
Lidgard Rd DN36 ...103 D1
Lidgett Cl DN20 ....108 E8
Lidgett Gr YO26 ....129 B6
Lidgett Gr Sch YO26 .129 B6
Lidgett The 7 DN9 ..105 D6
Lidice Rd DN14 ......64 E2
Lighthouse Rd YO15 ..5 B2
Lilac Ave
Beverley HU17 ......136 F7
Scunthorpe DN16 ...151 C5
Summergangs HU8 .141 B2
Willerby HU10 ......138 D1
York YO10 ....131 B3
Lilac Cl YO25 ....124 D3
Lilac Gr YO32 ......127 D4
Lilac Rd 20 HU15 ....68 C5
Lilacs The 10 YO42 ..29 A3
Lilbourne Dr YO30 ..130 A8
Lilling Ave 3 YO31 .130 E8
Lily La YO15 ....5 A2
Lilywood Rd DN20 ..97 D3
Limber Ct DN34 ....152 A2
Limber Hill LN8 ....120 A4
Limber Rd
Humberside Airport
DN39 ....100 A6
Swallow LN7 ....112 A7
Limber Vale DN34 ..152 A2
Lime Ave Brough HU15 .68 C5
Kingston upon Hull
HU10 ....138 E1
Scunthorpe DN16 ....97 A3
York YO31 ....130 F7
Lime Cl YO25 ....124 F2
Lime Gr Goxhill DN19 .86 A8
Holton le Clay DN36 .114 A5
Humberston DN36 ..114 C7
Scunthorpe DN16 ...151 B3
Lime St Grimsby DN31 .152 C4
Kingston upon Hull HU8 .155 C4
Lime Tree 6 HU15 ...66 D7
Lime Tree Ave
Beverley HU17 ......137 A6
20 Gainsborough DN21 .117 B1
Goole DN14 ....149 D5
Northfield HU13 ....143 F2
Summergangs HU8 .141 C2
York YO32 ....127 D3
Lime Tree Gdns DN14 .149 D5
Lime Tree Gr
Selby YO8 ....148 A6
4 Thorne/Moorends DN8 .93 A8
Lime Tree La HU11 .142 F6
Lime Tree Mews 15 YO19 .26 F7
Lime Tree Villas HU7 .141 D6
Limedale View 3 DN3 ..92 A3
Limedane HU6 ......139 F8
Limegarth 10 YO26 ..12 F1
Limekiln Hill YO25 ...7 B3
Limekiln La YO16 ..123 A5
Limerick Cl HU8 ....142 B6
Limes Ct YO31 .....130 F6
Limes The
2 Beckingham DN10 .116 D1
3 South Cave HU15 ..53 F1
3 Stallingborough DN41 .101 D6
Stockton-on-the-Forest
YO32 ....14 D2
Limes Wlk YO25 ...124 F5
Limetree Ave
12 Grimsby DN33 ...102 E2
Kingston upon Hull HU7 .141 D6
Limetree Cl 2 YO8 ..48 B1
Lincoln Bvd DN31 ..152 B3
Lincoln Castle Way
DN19 ....70 D2
Lincoln Cl 18 DN7 ...94 D7
Lincoln Cres 2 DN21 .119 C8
Lincoln Ct DN16 ...151 B3
Lincoln Dr
24 Barton-upon-Humber
DN18 ....84 F8
Caistor LN7 ....111 B4
Winterton DN15 .....83 A5
Lincoln Gate DN36 .121 C6
Lincoln Gdns DN21 .151 A2
Lincoln Gdns Jun Sch
DN16 ....151 A2
Lincoln Gdns Prim Sch
DN16 ....151 B3
Lincoln Gn HU4 ....144 C7
Lincoln Rd
Cleethorpes DN35 ..153 C1
Moorland Prison DN7 .104 A4
Lincoln St
22 Gainsborough DN21 .117 B1
Kingston upon Hull HU2 .155 B4
York YO10 ....129 F5
Lincoln Way 9 HU17 .55 E8
Lincolnshire Wolds Rly*
LN11 ....121 C7
Lindale 2 YO24 .....132 C7
Lindale Ave HU18 ..134 B2
Lindale Gdns DN16 .151 C3
Linden Ave HU16 ..139 C7
Linden Cl 6 Hatfield DN7 .92 D4
York YO32 ....127 F5
Linden Gr 1 YO30 ..130 A8

Linden Way 9 YO8 ...48 B2
Lindengate Ave HU7 .141 B4
Lindengate Way HU7 .141 B5
Lindholme DN21 ....107 C3
Lindholme Bank Rd
DN7 ....93 B1
Lindisfarne Ave 4
DN36 ....113 F7
Lindley Rd YO30 ...126 F1
Lindley St
Scunthorpe DN16 ...151 A2
York YO31 ....129 F3
Lindley Wood Gr
YO30 ....126 E3
Lindrick Wlk 8 DN37 .113 D6
Lindsey DN36 ......114 A6
Lindsey Ave YO26 ..129 D4
Lindsey Ct 21 DN9 .105 E6
Healing DN41 ......102 A5
Holton le Clay DN36 .114 A6
Lindsey Lower Sch The
DN35 ....153 D2
Lindsey Pl HU4 ....144 D6
Lindsey Rd DN35 ..153 F1
Lindsey Rise 30 DN3 .113 C8
Lindsey Sch & Com Arts Coll
The DN35 ....103 C2
Lindsey St 2 DN16 .151 C6
Lindum Ave 23 DN40 .87 B1
Lindum Gr DN17 ....94 C7
Lindum Rd DN35 ...103 C2
Lindum St DN15 ....151 B7
Lindum Wlk LN7 ...110 A4
Linecroft La DN10 .116 E4
Linegate 4 YO43 ..135 D4
Ling House La DN7 ..92 A5
Linga La YO41 ......27 F6
Lingcourt HU6 .....139 F7
Lingcroft Cl YO8 ....63 D4
Lingcroft La YO19 .133 E3
Lingdale Rd HU9 ...142 E3
Lingfield Cres YO24 .129 F1
Lings La DN7 ....92 D3
Lings Rd HU17 .....42 E3
Link Ave YO30 .....130 C8
Link Rd
Huntington YO31 ...127 E2
Kingston upon Hull
HU16 ....139 B5
Link Rd Ct YO19 ..131 D4
Link The
Copmanthorpe YO23 .132 A3
Kingston upon Hull HU4 .144 C5
Selby YO8 ....148 A4
York YO10 ....133 E8
Linkfield Rd HU5 ..139 E4
Links Rd DN35 .....103 D2
Linkway Hatfield DN7 .92 F3
Norton DN6 ....76 E2
Linley HU17 ....45 A8
Linleyhill Rd HU17 ..33 C1
Linnaeus St HU3 ...145 C6
Linnet Cl DN15 .....96 B7
Linnet Dr HU7 .....141 D7
Linnet Way YO24 ..132 C8
Linthorpe Gr HU10 .143 E8
Linton 23 HU15 ....68 C6
Linton Cl HU17 ....154 A1
Linton on Ouse Prim Sch
YO30 ....12 A7
Linton Rd YO26 ...126 A1
Linton Rise DN15 ...82 A4
Linton St 5 YO26 ..129 E5
Linton Woods YO30 .12 A5
Linton Woods La YO30 .12 A8
Linwith La DN14 ....63 C3
Linwood Ave 17 DN33 .113 E8
Lisburn Gr DN33 ...102 E1
Lisle Ct HU2 ......155 B1
Lisle Marsden CE Aided Prim
Sch DN34 ....102 E2
Lismore Ave HU9 ..142 A3
Lissett Cl HU17 .....43 D6
Lissett Gr HU6 ....140 C7
Lissett La YO25 .....22 D4
Lister Rd DN15 ....150 C7
Lister St Grimsby DN31 .152 B4
Kingston upon Hull HU1 .155 A1
Lister Way YO30 ...130 A7
Little Ave YO30 ....130 B8
Little Beck Rd YO16 .122 B4
Little Belt The DN21 .117 B2
Little Burton 3 YO25 .34 B2
Little Clover HU17 ...12 F6
Little Coates Rd DN34 .102 C2
Little Comm La DN14 .77 C7
Little Dam La HU12 ..88 B8
Little Garth YO26 .126 A2
Little George St HU8 .155 C4
Little Grimsby La
LN11 ....121 D1
Little Hallfield Rd
YO31 ....130 E5
Little Heck Comm La
DN14 ....62 D1
Little John St DN34 .152 B3
Little La
Broomfleet HU15 ...67 C6
Ellerton YO42 ......38 C1
11 Haxby YO32 .....13 E5
Little Smeaton DN6 ..76 D4
Mappleton HU11 ...47 A5
Shipton Thorpe YO43 .40 E5
Watton YO25 ......32 E5
Wrawby DN20 ......98 D3
Little London DN14 .78 D8

Little Mason St HU2 .155 C3
Little Mdws YO32 ...127 D8
Little Michael St
DN34 ....152 B3
Little Moor La YO8 .148 A8
Little Queen St HU1 .155 A2
Little Reed St HU2 .155 A3
Little Shore HU11 ...45 E2
Little Stonegate YO1 .156 B3
Little Weighton Rd
Skidby HU16 ....138 A8
Walkington HU17 ...55 B7
Little Weighton Rowley CE
VC Prim Sch HU20 .55 A4
Little Westfield YO25 ..8 C3
Little Wlk DN21 ...116 E5
Little Wold La HU15 .54 A2
Littlebeck Cl HU3 .145 A7
Littlebeck Rd 4 DN36 .114 C8
Littlecoates Prim Sch
DN31 ....152 B5
Littlefair Rd HU9 ..147 A2
Littlefield Cl 5 YO26 .12 F1
Littlefield La
Grimsby DN34 .....152 B2
Marsh Chapel DN36 .115 B1
Littleham Cl HU7 ..141 B8
Littlemoor Cl HU15 ..53 D3
Littlethorpe Cl 7 YO32 .14 B8
Littlewood Rd
Rowley HU17 ......54 D7
11 Thorne/Moorends DN8 .93 B8
Littondale
Kingston upon Hull HU7 .140 F7
15 Welton HU15 ....68 D6
Liverpool St HU3 ..145 A3
Livesey Rd DN36 ..121 B6
Livingstone Rd HU13 .69 F4
Livingstone St YO26 .129 F5
Lloyd Cl YO10 .....131 B1
Lloyds Ave DN17 ..150 F4
Loatley Gn HU16 ..139 C5
Lob La YO41 ....15 D2
Lobelia Dr DN16 ....96 C1
Lochrin Pl 2 YO26 .129 B4
Lock Cl DN14 ......77 F6
Lock Hill DN8 ......93 A8
Lock Keepers Ct HU9 .146 B8
Lock La
Holme-on-Spalding-Moor
YO43 ....52 B8
Thorne/Moorends DN8 .93 A8
Lock Rd DN36 .....115 A4
Lockey Croft YO32 .127 C8
Lockgate Rd DN14 ..77 C4
Lockham Rd HU12 ..90 F4
Lockhill DN31 .....152 E6
Locking Garth LN11 .121 F5
Lockington CE VC Sch
YO25 ....32 B2
Lockington Rd YO25 .31 F3
Lockside Rd DN40 ..87 D3
Lockton Gr 1 HU5 .144 D8
Lockwood Bank DN9 .105 E6
Lockwood Cl 6 DN8 ..93 B8
Lockwood Ct DN15 .150 E8
Lockwood Dr HU17 .136 E7
Lockwood Rd HU17 .136 D7
Lockwood St
Great Driffield YO25 .124 E3
Kingston upon Hull HU2 .155 B4
York YO31 ....156 C3
Lockyer Cl 4 YO30 .130 A8
Lodge Ave DN18 ....84 F8
Lodge Cl
Elloughton HU15 ...68 C7
Kingston upon Hull
HU13 ....143 F1
Lodge Ct 35 DN7 ...92 D4
Lodge Farm Ct YO42 .39 B6
Lodge Gdns 5 DN14 .63 C1
Lodge La
Flixborough DN15 ...82 B2
Gowdall DN14 ......62 F1
Kirk Bramwith DN7 ..92 A8
Snaith DN14 ....78 D8
Lodge Rd DN15 ....150 C6
Lodge St HU9 ......141 E2
Lofthouse La YO41 ..27 D7
Loftsome Way 11 DN14 .65 B7
Loftus Gr HU9 .....142 E3
Logan Cl HU7 .....141 C7
Loganberry Dr HU4 .144 C4
Lombard St
Grimsby DN34 .....152 A3
Kingston upon Hull HU2 .155 A3
Lombardy Cl 8 HU4 .144 C7
Lomond Gr 1 DN36 .114 C8
Lomond Rd HU5 ...144 E8
Londesborough Ct
YO25 ....124 C4
Londesborough Gr 5
YO8 ....48 B2
Londesborough Hill
YO43 ....41 A8
Londesborough Rd
Hutton Cranswick YO25 .32 E7
Market Weighton YO43 .135 D6
Londesborough St
Kingston upon Hull HU3 .145 C7
5 Selby YO8 ....148 C5
London Ln DN6 .....77 D1
London St 15 YO42 ..29 A4
Long Barrow★
Beelsby DN37 ......112 D4
Thixendale YO17 ...17 A7
Willerby YO12 ......1 E7
Long Cl La YO10 ..156 C1

Long Field Dr DN3 ..92 A1
Long Field Rd DN3 ..92 A2
Long Furrow YO32 .127 C8
Long Hill YO42 .....29 D1
Long La Atwick YO25 ..35 D6
Beverley HU17 .....154 B3
Bridlington YO16 ...122 C5
Catton YO41 ....27 C8
Cawood YO8 ....48 A6
Driffield YO25 .....124 F7
Eastrington DN14 ...65 D8
Ellerby HU11 ....58 B8
Ellerton YO42 ......38 F1
Foston YO25 ....22 A3
Goole DN14 ....149 E7
Great Driffield YO25 .124 F6
Heck DN14 ....77 D8
Heslington YO10 ....26 C3
Humbleton HU11 ...58 F5
Kirk Smeaton WF8 ..76 B1
Market Weighton YO43 .41 B2
Nafferton YO25 ....20 E8
Pollington DN14 ....78 A7
Skeffling HU12 .....90 C5
Willoughton DN21 .119 B3
Woodmansey HU17 .154 B1
Long Mann Hills Rd
YO8 ....148 B4
Long Marston CE VC Prim
Sch YO42 ....24 A6
Long Rampart YO42 .38 D3
Long Rd DN15 .....150 E8
Long Ridge Dr YO26 .126 A1
Long Ridge La YO26 .126 A1
Long St YO25 ......9 F6
Long Toft Prim Sch
DN7 ....92 C6
Long Trods 5 YO8 .148 C6
Long Wood Rd DN21 .117 D1
Longbrough La HU12 .59 E4
Longcroft 2 YO32 ..13 E5
Longcroft Lower Sch
HU17 ....136 B5
Longcroft Pk HU17 .136 C5
Longcroft Sch & Performing
Arts Coll HU17 ....136 C5
Longdales La HU11 .142 F8
Longden St HU3 ...145 A7
Longfield Rd 4 DN34 .102 C2
Longfield Terr YO30 .156 A3
Longford Gr HU9 ..142 E2
Longhill Prim Sch
HU8 ....142 C6
Longhorn Cl 1 DN37 .113 C6
Longleat Ave YO16 .122 C7
Longmans Hill CP Sch
YO8 ....148 C3
Longmans La HU16 .139 B6
Longmeadow Rise 7
DN41 ....101 A4
Longmeadows Dr
DN37 ....101 F1
Longton Rd 13 DN3 ..92 A3
Longwood Link 8 YO30 .126 E3
Longwood Rd YO30 .126 F3
Lonsdale Cl DN36 ..114 D7
Lonsdale St 5 HU3 .145 A6
Lopham La DN37 ...112 F8
Lord Deramore's Prim Sch
YO10 ....131 C1
Lord Dr 27 YO42 ...29 A3
Lord Mayor's Wlk
YO31 ....156 B3
Lord Roberts Rd HU17 .154 B2
Lord St Grimsby DN31 .152 B4
Stainforth DN7 .....92 C6
Lords La
Barrow upon Humber
DN19 ....85 D8
Upper Poppleton YO26 .12 E2
Lords Moor La YO32 .14 C7
Lordship La 16 Barlby YO8 .49 A4
Wistow YO8 ....148 D8
Lorenzo Way HU9 ..141 F2
Loriners Dr 7 YO23 .132 B3
Lorne Cl HU2 ......155 B4
Lorne St YO23 .....130 B1
Lorraine Ave 3 YO41 .27 B2
Lorraine St HU8 ...141 A3
Loten Dr HU18 ....134 D6
Lothian Way HU7 ...57 A6
Lotting's La YO42 ..28 C4
Louis Dr HU5 ......144 B8
Louis St HU3 ......145 C8
Louth Rd
Fotherby LN11 .....121 D3
Grimsby DN33 ....102 C2
5 New Waltham DN36 .113 F7
Louville Ave HU19 ..75 A6
Lovat Cl HU3 ......145 C7
Love La
Gainsborough DN21 .117 B1
Hedon HU12 ....72 C7
Londesborough YO43 .41 A8
Nunthorpe YO10 ...133 C8
York YO24 ....130 A2
Loveden Ct 7 DN35 .103 D2
Lovell Rd 8 DN17 ..96 C2
Loveridge Ave HU5 .140 A2
Low Balk Rd HU17 ..42 F7
Low Burgage HU15 ..68 B1
Low Catton Rd YO41 .27 C8
Low Comm La HU15 ..68 D4
Low Croft 3 YO32 ...14 A7
Low Cross St 7 DN17 .94 D8
Low Deeps La DN10 .104 C1
Low Farm Rd HU11 ..57 E5

Low Field La
Carnaby YO25 . . . 10 C3
Welton HU14 . . . 68 E5
Low Fields Dr YO24 . . . 129 C3
Low Garth DN17 . . . 96 C1
Low Gate DN36 . . . 115 C1
Low Gn
Copmanthorpe YO23 . . . 132 B2
13 Knottingley WF11 . . . 61 A2
Low La
Heslington YO10 . . . 131 D1
Kirk Bramwith DN7 . . . 92 A6
Low Levels Bank DN8 . . . 93 E3
Low Leys Rd DN17 . . . 96 C1
Low Mdw YO8 . . . 148 C6
Low Mill Cl YO10 . . . 131 D3
Low Mill La HU15 . . . 53 C2
Low Moor Ave 3 YO10 . . . 133 F8
Low Moor La
Askham Richard YO23 . . . 24 D3
Hessay YO26 . . . 24 C8
Low Ousegate YO1 . . . 156 B2
Low Peter La YO25 . . . 124 C8
Low Petergate YO1 . . . 156 B3
Low Poppleton La
YO26 . . . 129 B7
Low Rd
Blyborough DN21 . . . 119 B6
Gowdall DN14 . . . 63 A1
Healing DN41 . . . 101 F5
Kellington DN14 . . . 61 F4
Kirby Grindalythe YO17 . . . 6 F7
Marsh Chapel DN36 . . . 115 A1
North Cave HU15 . . . 53 E2
Worlaby DN20 . . . 98 C8
Low St
Beckingham DN10 . . . 116 E1
Carlton DN14 . . . 63 C2
Haxey DN9 . . . 105 D2
North Ferriby HU14 . . . 69 A5
Sancton YO43 . . . 41 D2
South Ferriby DN18 . . . 84 A7
Winterton DN15 . . . 83 A5
Low Well Pk YO19 . . . 37 F7
Low Westfield Rd
YO23 . . . 132 A1
Lowcroft Ave 3 DN9 . . . 105 D2
Lowcroft Cl 4 DN9 . . . 105 D2
Lowcroft Mdw 10 DN9 . . . 105 D2
Lowdale Cl HU5 . . . 139 E1
Lower Bridge St DN14 . . . 149 C3
Lower Darnborough St
YO23 . . . 156 B1
Lower Derwent Valley Nat Nature Reserve★
YO42 . . . 50 C8
Lower Friargate YO1 . . . 156 B2
Lower Kenyon St 6 DN8 . . . 93 A8
Lower Mdws DN18 . . . 69 F1
Lower Priory St YO1 . . . 156 A1
Lower Spring St DN31 . . . 152 E5
Lowerdale 13 HU15 . . . 68 D6
Loweswater Rd 5 YO30 . . . 126 E1
Lowfield YO43 . . . 40 B1
Lowfield Cl
10 Barnby Dun DN3 . . . 92 A3
18 Kirton in Lindsey DN21 . . . 108 B1
Lowfield Dr YO32 . . . 13 E5
Lowfield House HU10 . . . 143 E6
Lowfield La
East Garton HU12 . . . 59 C5
Nunburnholme YO42 . . . 29 D3
Rufforth YO26 . . . 129 A4
Scrayingham YO41 . . . 16 A7
Lowfield Rd
Barlby with Osgodby YO8 . . . 49 B5
Beverley HU17 . . . 137 A7
Hillam LS25 . . . 61 C8
Kingston upon Hull
HU10 . . . 143 E5
Lowfield Sec Sch
YO24 . . . 129 D3
Lowgate Balne DN14 . . . 77 D5
Kingston upon Hull HU1 . . . 155 C2
Lowhill DN8 . . . 78 F1
Lowick YO24 . . . 132 C7
Lowland Cl 3 HU7 . . . 141 D8
Lowmoor Rd YO8 . . . 49 E6
Lown Hill YO24 . . . 129 C2
Lowndes Pk YO25 . . . 124 D5
Lowood Dr YO16 . . . 122 B4
Lowther Ct YO31 . . . 156 C4
Lowther Dr YO8 . . . 148 E3
Lowther St
Kingston upon Hull HU3 . . . 145 A7
York YO31 . . . 156 C4
Lowther Terr YO24 . . . 130 A3
Lowthorpe La YO25 . . . 125 F7
Loxley Cl YO30 . . . 126 F2
Loxley Gn HU4 . . . 144 B7
Loxley Way 7 HU15 . . . 68 D5
Loyd St HU10 . . . 143 F6
Loyds Cl 12 HU15 . . . 53 F1
Lucas Ave YO30 . . . 130 C8
Lucas Ct DN41 . . . 101 F5
Lucian Wlk HU4 . . . 144 A2
Luck La HU12 . . . 58 C1
Lucombe Way YO32 . . . 127 D4
Ludborough Pk DN36 . . . 121 B6
Ludborough Rd DN36 . . . 121 B8
Ludborough Way 21
DN35 . . . 103 C2
Luddington & Garthorpe Prim Sch DN17 . . . 81 C4
Luddington Rd DN17 . . . 81 E5
Ludford St DN32 . . . 152 E2
Ludgate Cl 4 DN37 . . . 113 D6
Ludlow Ave DN34 . . . 152 A3
Ludlow Pl DN35 . . . 153 E1
Lulworth Ave HU4 . . . 144 A3
Lulworth Ct DN17 . . . 150 D4
Lumby Hill LS25 . . . 61 A8
Lumby La LS25 . . . 61 A8
Lumley Rd YO30 . . . 130 B7
Lumsden Cl YO25 . . . 124 B2
Lund Ave HU16 . . . 138 E6
Lund Cl YO32 . . . 127 C8
Lund La Bubwith YO8 . . . 50 C4
Cliffe YO8 . . . 49 D4
Lund Rd YO25 . . . 32 A2
Lunds The HU10 . . . 143 C6
Lundy Cl 10 YO30 . . . 127 A1
Lundy Ct DN40 . . . 101 C8
Luneburg Pl 14 DN15 . . . 96 B7
Luneburg Way DN15 . . . 96 B7
Lunedale Cl HU8 . . . 141 E7
Lunedale Rd DN16 . . . 151 D1
Lunn La DN14 . . . 61 D3
Lunn's Cres DN18 . . . 84 E8
Luton Rd HU5 . . . 144 F8
Luttons CP Sch YO17 . . . 7 B8
Lycett Rd YO24 . . . 132 F6
Lych Gate DN20 . . . 97 D3
Lydbrook Rd DN16 . . . 151 A5
Lydford Rd DN40 . . . 87 C1
Lydham Ct 2 YO24 . . . 132 C8
Lydia Ct 6 DN40 . . . 87 B1
Lygon St DN16 . . . 151 B5
Lymington Garth HU4 . . . 144 A3
Lyndale Ave
8 Kirk Sandall DN3 . . . 92 A1
York YO10 . . . 131 C3
Lynden Way YO24 . . . 129 D3
Lyndhurst Ave
17 Grimsby DN33 . . . 102 E2
Kingston upon Hull
HU16 . . . 139 D6
Lyndhurst Cl
Beverley HU17 . . . 137 B4
2 Norton DN6 . . . 76 F2
Thorne/Moorends DN8 . . . 92 F8
Lyndhurst Dr 1 DN6 . . . 76 F2
Lyndhurst Rise 3 DN6 . . . 76 F2
Lynesykes Rd YO25 . . . 21 F5
Lynhams Rd
Bempton YO15 . . . 4 E1
Bridlington YO15 . . . 123 B8
Lynmouth Cl 9 HU7 . . . 57 A5
Lynmouth Dr DN17 . . . 150 C4
Lynngarth Ave HU16 . . . 139 C6
Lynton Ave HU4 . . . 144 B3
Lynton Cl Brayton YO8 . . . 148 B1
Scunthorpe DN15 . . . 150 D8
Lynton Gdns YO8 . . . 148 B1
Lynton Par DN31 . . . 152 B3
Lynton Rise 10 DN35 . . . 103 C2
Lynwith Cl DN14 . . . 63 C3
Lynwith Ct DN14 . . . 63 C3
Lynwith Dr DN14 . . . 63 C3
Lynwood Ave
3 Copmanthorpe YO23 . . . 132 A3
Kingston upon Hull
HU10 . . . 143 E6
Lynwood Cl YO32 . . . 14 A4
Lynwood View 4 YO23 . . . 132 A3
Lyric Cl 1 HU3 . . . 145 C5
Lysaghts Way DN15 . . . 82 C1
Lysander Cl YO30 . . . 127 A3
Lysander Dr YO43 . . . 135 E4
Lyth Cl 5 YO16 . . . 123 A7
Lytham Dr
Barnoldby le Beck DN37 . . . 113 D6
Kingston upon Hull
HU16 . . . 139 D6
Lythe Ave HU5 . . . 139 E4

M

M62 Trad Est DN14 . . . 149 A3
Mablethorpe Rd DN36 . . . 115 A3
MacAulay Jun & Inf Sch
DN31 . . . 152 B4
MacAulay St DN31 . . . 152 B4
MacAulay Way DN31 . . . 152 C4
MacDonald Ct 12 YO42 . . . 29 A3
Mace View HU17 . . . 154 B1
Machray Pl DN35 . . . 153 D3
MacKender Ct 3 DN16 . . . 151 B2
MacKenzie Pl 24 DN40 . . . 87 B1
MacLagan Rd YO23 . . . 132 F4
Maclure St DN31 . . . 152 F6
Madeira Ct HU5 . . . 140 A1
Madeley St HU3 . . . 145 C4
Madison Gdns 4 HU5 . . . 140 A1
Madron Cl HU7 . . . 141 B8
Maegan Way DN35 . . . 153 E2
Magazine La YO8 . . . 49 B3
Magazine Rd YO8 . . . 49 B4
Magdalen Cl 3 DN16 . . . 96 D2
Magdalen Ct 8 HU12 . . . 72 D7
Magdalen Gate HU12 . . . 72 D7
Magdalen La HU12 . . . 72 D7
Magdalene Rd 8 DN34 . . . 102 C3
Magnolia Cl YO25 . . . 124 D3
Magnolia Dr DN36 . . . 114 A5
Magnolia Gr YO32 . . . 127 D2
Magnolia Rise 9 DN40 . . . 87 C1
Magnolia Way DN16 . . . 151 A3
Magrath Ct 3 DN20 . . . 98 C2
Maida Gr YO10 . . . 130 D2
Maiden Cl 1 DN40 . . . 87 B1
Maiden Ct 8 HU7 . . . 57 B5
Maidensgrave Henge★
YO25 . . . 2 F1
Maidenwell La LN7 . . . 110 A4
Maidwell Way 1 DN34 . . . 102 B2
Main App Rd DN16 . . . 151 C7
Main Ave
Scunthorpe DN17 . . . 150 C2
York YO31 . . . 130 F5
Main Rd
Ashby cum Fenby DN37 . . . 113 D3
Burton Agnes YO25 . . . 10 C3
Burton Pidsea HU12 . . . 59 C2
Drax YO8 . . . 63 F5
Gilberdyke DN14 . . . 66 B7
Holmpton HU19 . . . 75 C2
Kilpin DN14 . . . 65 D7
Kingston upon Hull
HU11 . . . 142 E6
Mappleton HU11 . . . 47 A4
Newport HU15 . . . 53 A1
Skeffling HU12 . . . 90 D6
Thorngumbald HU12 . . . 72 F5
Ulrome YO25 . . . 22 E6
Utterby LN11 . . . 121 C4
Main St
Askham Bryan YO23 . . . 24 F3
Asselby DN14 . . . 64 D7
Bainton YO25 . . . 31 E7
Barmby Moor YO42 . . . 28 D3
3 Beal DN14 . . . 61 D4
Beeford YO25 . . . 22 C1
Beswick YO25 . . . 32 C4
Bilbrough YO23 . . . 24 C1
Bishopthorpe YO23 . . . 133 A4
Bonby DN20 . . . 84 C2
Boynton YO16 . . . 10 D6
Brandesburton YO25 . . . 34 B2
Bridlington YO16 . . . 122 A1
Broomfleet HU15 . . . 67 C6
Brough HU15 . . . 68 C6
Bubwith YO8 . . . 50 C7
Buckton/Bempton YO15 . . . 4 C3
Bugthorpe YO41 . . . 16 D4
Burstwick HU12 . . . 73 A6
Burton Agnes YO25 . . . 10 A1
Cadney DN20 . . . 109 D6
Carnaby YO16 . . . 10 E4
Catwick HU17 . . . 45 C8
Cherry Burton HU17 . . . 43 A5
Cliffe YO8 . . . 49 E2
Coniston HU11 . . . 57 F6
Copmanthorpe YO23 . . . 132 A2
Cottingwith YO42 . . . 38 C5
Crowle DN17 . . . 94 E6
Dalton Holme HU17 . . . 42 E8
Deighton YO19 . . . 37 A7
East/West Stockwith
DN10 . . . 116 F6
Ellerker HU15 . . . 68 A8
Ellerton YO42 . . . 38 C1
Elvington YO41 . . . 27 C2
Escrick YO19 . . . 37 B5
Etton HU17 . . . 42 F6
Fishlake DN7 . . . 92 D8
Foston YO25 . . . 22 A4
Fulstow LN11 . . . 121 F8
Ganton YO12 . . . 1 A8
Garton YO25 . . . 19 F6
Goodmanham YO43 . . . 41 D6
Gowdall DN14 . . . 63 A1
Graiselound DN9 . . . 105 D1
Grasby DN38 . . . 110 E7
Harpham YO25 . . . 21 F8
Hatfield HU11 . . . 46 C5
Hatfield DN7 . . . 92 F3
Heck DN14 . . . 77 C8
Hemingbrough YO8 . . . 49 F1
Hensall DN14 . . . 62 D2
Heslington YO10 . . . 131 B1
Hessay YO26 . . . 24 B8
Horkstow DN18 . . . 84 A5
Hotham YO43 . . . 53 D5
Humberside Airport
DN39 . . . 100 A6
Hutton Cranswick YO25 . . . 32 E7
Keadby with Althorpe
DN17 . . . 95 D4
Kelfield YO19 . . . 36 D1
Kelk YO25 . . . 21 F6
Kellington DN14 . . . 61 F3
Keyingham HU12 . . . 73 C4
Kirk Smeaton WF8 . . . 76 B3
Kirkburn YO25 . . . 19 F1
Knapton YO26 . . . 129 A5
Leconfield HU17 . . . 43 D6
Long Riston/Arnold HU11 . . . 45 C5
Monk Fryston LS25 . . . 61 A8
1 Naburn YO19 . . . 36 D8
North Duffield YO8 . . . 50 A8
North Frodingham YO25 . . . 33 F8
Nunthorpe YO10 . . . 133 D8
Ottringham HU12 . . . 73 E3
Patrington HU12 . . . 89 C8
Paull HU12 . . . 72 A5
Pollington DN14 . . . 77 F6
Poppleton YO26 . . . 12 F1
Preston HU12 . . . 58 C1
Reighton YO14 . . . 3 E5
Riccall YO19 . . . 49 A8
Roos HU12 . . . 60 A1
Scawby DN20 . . . 108 E7
Sculcoates HU2 . . . 140 F1
Searby cum Owmby
DN38 . . . 110 D8
Seaton HU11 . . . 35 A1
Shipton YO30 . . . 12 F5
Sigglesthorne HU11 . . . 45 F8
Skerne & Wansford YO25 . . . 21 A2
Skidby HU16 . . . 138 B8
Skipsea YO25 . . . 23 A1
Stamford Bridge YO41 . . . 15 D2
Main St *continued*
Swanland HU14 . . . 69 B7
Swine HU11 . . . 57 D6
Thornton Curtis DN39 . . . 85 E5
Thwing YO25 . . . 2 B1
Tibthorpe YO25 . . . 19 D2
Tickton HU17 . . . 137 E8
Ulrome YO25 . . . 22 E5
Watton YO25 . . . 32 D5
Wawne HU7 . . . 56 F7
Welwick HU12 . . . 90 A7
Wheldrake YO19 . . . 37 F7
Whitton DN15 . . . 67 E3
Wilberfoss YO41 . . . 27 E5
Willerby HU10 . . . 138 C2
Withernwick HU11 . . . 46 D3
Womersley DN6 . . . 76 C6
Worlaby DN20 . . . 98 D8
Maine Ave DN15 . . . 96 A7
Mains La YO42 . . . 39 E3
Maister Rd 12 HU12 . . . 73 C4
Majestic Ct 7 HU9 . . . 142 A3
Malbys Gr YO23 . . . 132 B2
Malcolm Rd DN34 . . . 102 C2
Maldon Dr HU9 . . . 146 C6
Malet Lambert Sch Lang Coll
HU8 . . . 141 E4
Malham Ave HU4 . . . 144 C6
Malham Gr YO31 . . . 131 B5
Malkinson Cl 11 DN15 . . . 83 A5
Mallalieu Ct DN15 . . . 150 E8
Mallard Ave
Barnby Dun DN3 . . . 92 A4
2 Leven HU17 . . . 45 A8
Mallard Cl
Beverley HU17 . . . 136 F6
Driffield YO25 . . . 125 A4
2 Healing DN41 . . . 101 F5
Ulrome YO25 . . . 23 A3
Mallard Dr LN7 . . . 111 A4
Mallard Mews DN32 . . . 152 E2
Mallard Rd
Kingston upon Hull HU9 . . . 142 B4
Scunthorpe DN17 . . . 150 E2
Mallard Way 11 YO32 . . . 13 F5
Mallards Reach HU16 . . . 139 C8
Malling Wlk 13 DN16 . . . 96 D1
Mallory Cl YO32 . . . 127 D4
Mallory Rd DN16 . . . 151 D1
Mallyan Cl 15 HU8 . . . 141 E7
Malm St HU3 . . . 145 B6
Malmesbury Dr DN34 . . . 152 C2
Malmo Rd HU7 . . . 140 E5
Malpas Cl 8 HU7 . . . 56 F5
Malt Kilns The DN14 . . . 149 D4
Malt Shoval Ct YO1 . . . 156 C2
Maltby Ave DN37 . . . 102 B2
Maltby La 12 DN18 . . . 69 E1
Maltby Rd DN17 . . . 150 E1
Malthouse La 5 YO16 . . . 122 D5
Malthouse Row DN14 . . . 149 C3
Maltings Ct 6 YO8 . . . 148 C6
Maltings The
Beverley HU17 . . . 154 C3
Kingston upon Hull HU2 . . . 155 B3
Nafferton YO25 . . . 125 F6
Maltings Way DN32 . . . 152 E4
Maltkiln La 4 DN20 . . . 98 F7
Maltkiln Rd DN18 . . . 69 F1
Maltlngs The 5 YO43 . . . 135 D4
Malton Ave YO31 . . . 130 E6
Malton La YO17 . . . 7 A8
Malton Mews HU17 . . . 137 B3
Malton Rd
Hunmanby YO14 . . . 2 F8
Huntington YO32 . . . 128 A1
Molescroft HU17 . . . 136 B6
York YO31 . . . 130 F7
Malton St HU9 . . . 155 C3
Malton Way YO30 . . . 129 F8
Malvern Ave
Grimsby DN33 . . . 102 D2
York YO26 . . . 129 D5
Malvern Cl
Huntington YO32 . . . 128 A5
4 Thorne/Moorends DN8 . . . 93 A7
Malvern Cres 9 HU5 . . . 139 D2
Malvern Rd
Goole DN14 . . . 149 D5
Kingston upon Hull HU5 . . . 139 D2
Scunthorpe DN17 . . . 150 F3
Manby Rd
Immingham DN40 . . . 87 B3
Scunthorpe DN17 . . . 96 C2
Manchester Rd YO42 . . . 28 E3
Manchester St
Cleethorpes DN35 . . . 153 D4
Kingston upon Hull HU3 . . . 145 A4
Mancklin Ave HU8 . . . 141 D5
Mancroft YO32 . . . 127 C8
Mandela Link DN31 . . . 152 C3
Manderville Cl 18 HU12 . . . 72 D7
Manet Rd HU8 . . . 141 C1
Manifold Rd DN16 . . . 151 E1
Manilla La DN18 . . . 69 F2
Manlake Ave DN15 . . . 83 A5
Manley Cl YO32 . . . 127 D4
Manley Ct 1 DN9 . . . 105 D6
Manley Gdns
Brigg DN20 . . . 98 B2
Cleethorpes DN35 . . . 103 C2
Manley St 12 DN15 . . . 151 B7
Mann La DN9 . . . 94 D2
Mannaberg Way DN15 . . . 96 D7
Manningtree Cl DN32 . . . 152 E2
Manor Ave DN32 . . . 152 D2
Manor Barns HU20 . . . 55 A4
Manor Beeches The 3
YO19 . . . 26 E7
Manor CE Sec Sch
YO26 . . . 129 C7
Manor Cl
Beverley HU17 . . . 154 A4
Great Driffield YO25 . . . 124 F4
5 Hemingbrough YO8 . . . 49 F1
4 Keelby DN41 . . . 101 A5
Kirk Smeaton WF8 . . . 76 B3
Nafferton YO25 . . . 125 F6
6 North Duffield YO8 . . . 50 A7
12 Norton DN6 . . . 76 E2
Skipsea YO25 . . . 23 A2
Sproatley HU11 . . . 58 D5
Upper Poppleton YO26 . . . 24 F8
Manor Croft YO42 . . . 16 F1
Manor Ct 6 Bubwith YO8 . . . 50 D7
Kingston upon Hull HU10 . . . 69 C8
Stallingborough DN41 . . . 101 E7
2 York YO32 . . . 127 F6
Manor Ct Rd 7 DN9 . . . 105 E6
Manor Dr Beeford YO25 . . . 22 C1
Bonby DN20 . . . 84 C2
Brough HU15 . . . 68 C6
Camblesforth YO8 . . . 63 C4
4 Dunnington YO19 . . . 26 E7
10 Gilberdyke HU15 . . . 66 D8
5 North Duffield YO8 . . . 50 A7
Scawby DN20 . . . 108 E8
Waltham DN37 . . . 113 E7
Manor Dr N YO26 . . . 129 D4
Manor Dr S YO26 . . . 129 D4
Manor Farm Cl
1 Brayton YO8 . . . 148 A1
Carlton DN14 . . . 63 C2
Copmanthorpe YO23 . . . 132 A2
Kellington DN14 . . . 61 F3
Messingham DN17 . . . 107 D6
Manor Farm Ct YO8 . . . 62 C4
Manor Farm La DN14 . . . 78 A3
Manor Farm Rd DN17 . . . 150 E2
Manor Fields
Kingston upon Hull HU10 . . . 69 C8
Market Weighton YO43 . . . 135 D4
Rawcliffe DN14 . . . 64 B2
14 Welton HU15 . . . 68 D6
Manor Garth
Barmby Moor YO42 . . . 28 D3
Haxby YO32 . . . 127 B8
Kellington DN14 . . . 61 F3
Keyingham HU12 . . . 73 C4
7 Norton DN6 . . . 76 F2
1 Riccall YO19 . . . 49 A8
Skidby HU16 . . . 55 C4
Manor Gdns
8 Hatfield DN7 . . . 92 E4
6 Hunmanby YO14 . . . 3 A8
Manor Gn Bolton YO41 . . . 28 D7
Church End YO25 . . . 33 F8
Manor Heath YO23 . . . 132 A3
Manor House St HU1 . . . 155 A1
Manor La
Barrow upon Humber
DN19 . . . 85 D8
Goxhill DN19 . . . 85 F8
Hollym HU19 . . . 75 A4
Rawcliffe YO30 . . . 126 D2
Manor Mid Sch DN7 . . . 92 E4
Manor Pk
Beverley HU17 . . . 154 A4
Preston HU12 . . . 58 D1
Seaton HU11 . . . 35 A1
Manor Pk Cl YO30 . . . 126 E2
Manor Pk Gr 2 YO30 . . . 126 E2
Manor Pk Rd YO30 . . . 126 E2
Manor Rd Beal DN14 . . . 61 C4
Beverley HU17 . . . 154 A3
Crowle DN17 . . . 94 C7
Goole DN14 . . . 149 C1
Hatfield DN7 . . . 92 E4
Kingston upon Hull HU5 . . . 144 B8
9 North Cave HU15 . . . 53 D3
Northorpe DN21 . . . 118 D8
Preston HU12 . . . 58 C1
Reedness DN14 . . . 65 F1
Scunthorpe DN16 . . . 96 D2
South Cliffe YO43 . . . 53 B7
Stainforth DN7 . . . 92 C7
Swanland HU14 . . . 69 B6
Thorngumbald HU12 . . . 72 F5
Twin Rivers DN14 . . . 81 E7
Manor St
6 Bridlington YO15 . . . 122 E2
6 Keelby DN41 . . . 101 A5
Kingston upon Hull HU1 . . . 155 B2
Manor Way
Kingston upon Hull
HU10 . . . 143 F6
York YO30 . . . 126 E2
Manorfield Ave YO25 . . . 124 F5
Manorfield Rd YO25 . . . 124 F4
Manorhouse La HU17 . . . 55 B8
Mansel St DN32 . . . 153 B4
Mansfield Ct 6 DN32 . . . 153 A5
Mansfield Pk HU5 . . . 140 B3
Mansfield Rd DN15 . . . 150 B6
Mansfield St YO31 . . . 156 C3
Mansgate Hill LN7 . . . 111 B3
Mansion Ct Gdns DN8 . . . 93 A8
Manson Cl 13 DN34 . . . 102 B2
Manston Garth 4 HU7 . . . 57 B5
Manton Ct DN20 . . . 108 F6
Manton La DN20 . . . 108 E6
Manton Rd DN21 . . . 108 A4

Manuel St DN14 ....**149** B4
Manvers St HU5 ......**140** C3
Maple Ave
  Bishopthorpe YO23 .....**133** A3
  Crowle DN17 ....**94** D7
  Flixborough DN15 ......**96** B7
  Grimsby DN34 ....**102** C4
  Keelby DN41 ....**101** A4
  Kingston upon Hull
  HU10 ....**143** F8
Maple CI
  2 Bridlington YO16 ....**123** A6
  Brigg DN20 ....**98** D2
  Gainsborough DN21 ....**117** A2
  Hambleton YO8 ....**48** B1
  12 Keelby DN41 ......**101** A4
  5 Kingston upon Hull
  HU4 ....**144** C7
  Messingham DN17 .....**107** D6
Maple Ct
  Wheldrake YO19 ....**37** D8
  York YO10 ....**133** E6
Maple Dr
  Beverley HU17 ....**136** F6
  Goole DN14 ....**149** F5
Maple Gr **12** Brayton YO8 .**48** D1
  8 Healing DN41 ....**101** F5
  1 Immingham DN40 .....**87** C2
  6 New Waltham DN36 ...**113** F7
  Northfield HU13 ....**143** B3
  Summergangs HU8 .....**141** C2
  York YO10 ....**130** D1
Maple Pk HU12 ....**72** D8
Maple Rd
  Bridlington YO16 ......**123** A6
  12 Thorne/Moorends DN8 ..**79** B1
Maple St HU5 ....**140** D2
Maple Tree Ave **10** YO8 ..**49** B4
Maple Tree CI E DN16 ..**151** A5
Maple Tree CI W
  DN16 ....**151** A5
Maple Tree Way DN16 ..**151** A5
Maple Wlk
  8 Brandesburton YO25 ...**34** B2
  Goole DN14 ....**149** F5
Maplehurst Ave YO31 ..**130** D7
Mapleleaf Ct **9** HU16 ..**138** F5
Maplewood Ave HU4 ....**144** B7
Maplewood Paddock **2**
  YO24 ....**129** C1
Mappleton Gr HU9 .....**142** A2
Mappleton Rd HU11 ....**46** D6
Marbury Pk
  29 Dunswell HU7 ....**56** F5
  3 Kingston upon Hull
  HU6 ....**140** A2
March St
  6 Kirton in Lindsey DN21 ..**108** B1
  York YO31 ....**156** C4
Marchant CI HU17 .....**136** D7
Marcus St Goole DN14 ..**149** B4
  Grimsby DN34 ....**152** A4
Marfleet Ave HU9 .....**147** B7
Marfleet Cnr DN36 .....**114** B1
Marfleet La HU9 ....**142** B3
Marfleet Prim Sch
  HU9 ....**147** C8
Margaret Ave DN17 ....**95** D5
Margaret Gr **1** HU13 ...**143** F1
Margaret Philipson Ct
  YO31 ....**156** C3
Margaret PI **18** DN36 ...**114** A7
Margaret St
  Grimsby DN32 ....**152** F3
  Immingham DN40 ......**101** C8
  York YO10 ....**156** C1
Margrave La
  Garthorpe & Fockerby
  DN17 ....**81** E5
  Reedness DN14 ....**80** E7
Marian Way DN37 .....**113** C6
Marigold CI YO8 ....**148** C2
Marigold Wlk **22** DN35 ..**103** C1
Marin Ct **7** HU17 ......**137** B3
Marina Ave **3** DN14 ....**63** B1
Marina Ct HU2 ....**155** B1
Marina View **6** DN8 ....**93** A7
Marine Ave HU14 ......**69** A4
Marine Dr HU18 ....**134** D5
Marine Valley **2** YO15 ...**5** B3
Marine Wharf HU1 .....**155** B1
Mariners Arms Flats
  DN17 ....**95** D6
Mariners CI HU9 ......**146** C6
Mariners Ct HU17 .....**154** C2
Mariners St **3** DN14 ...**149** C4
Marjorie Waite Ct
  YO30 ....**130** B7
Mark Rise DN21 ....**117** F5
Market Cross Sh Ctr **13**
  YO8 ....**148** C5
Market Ct **5** DN17 ....**94** D7
Market Gn HU16 ......**139** B6
Market Hall Sh Ctr
  DN31 ....**152** D3
Market Hill DN15 .....**151** B8
Market La
  12 Barton-upon-Humber
  DN18 ....**84** F8
  5 Brigg DN20 ....**98** B2
  14 Selby YO8 ....**148** C5
Market PI
  11 Barton-upon-Humber
  DN18 ....**84** F8
  Bridlington YO16 ......**122** C5

Market PI continued
  8 Brigg DN20 ....**98** B2
  11 Caistor LN7 ....**111** B4
  2 Cawood YO8 ....**48** B8
  5 Epworth DN9 ....**105** E6
  Great Driffield YO25 ...**124** E4
  31 Hedon HU12 ....**72** C7
  Hornsea HU18 ....**134** B4
  Kingston upon Hull HU1 ..**155** C1
  22 Kirton in Lindsey DN21 .**108** B1
  Market Weighton YO43 ..**135** D4
  Owston Ferry DN9 .....**106** B2
  Patrington HU12 ....**74** D1
  Pocklington YO42 ....**29** A3
  11 Selby YO8 ....**148** C5
  9 Snaith DN14 ....**63** C1
  South Cave HU15 ....**54** A2
Market St
  Cleethorpes DN35 .....**153** F2
  9 Pocklington YO42 ...**29** A4
  14 Winterton DN15 ....**83** A5
  York YO1 ....**156** B2
Market Weighton Inf Sch
  YO43 ....**135** D3
Market Weighton Rd
  Barlby with Osgodby YO8 .**49** B6
  Holme-on-Spalding-Moor
  YO43 ....**40** B2
  Market Weighton YO43 ..**135** A2
  Sancton YO43 ....**41** D3
Market Weighton Sch
  YO43 ....**135** F4
Market Wlk YO25 ......**124** E4
Marketbridge La YO42 ..**39** E7
Markham Cres YO31 ....**156** B4
Markham Mews DN37 ..**113** E6
Markham St YO31 .....**156** B4
Markham Way DN20 ...**98** E4
Markhams Orch DN33 ..**113** E8
Marklew Ave DN34 ....**152** B3
Markman La YO25 .....**125** D5
Marlborough Ave
  Goole DN14 ....**149** C5
  2 Haxey DN9 ....**105** C2
  Hornsea HU18 ....**134** C1
  Kingston upon Hull HU5 ..**145** A8
  Northfield HU13 ....**143** D2
Marlborough CI
  15 Cleethorpes DN32 ...**153** A5
  Rawcliffe YO30 ....**126** D3
Marlborough Dr DN16 ..**151** B4
Marlborough Gr YO10 ..**130** D2
Marlborough Rd **9** DN8 .**93** B7
Marlborough Terr
  8 Bridlington YO15 ....**122** F2
  Kingston upon Hull HU2 ..**155** A3
Marlborough Villas
  YO10 ....**130** D2
Marlborough Way
  DN35 ....**103** C1
Marlow Rd DN21 ......**117** C1
Marlowe Rd DN17 .....**150** D3
Marlowe St HU8 ......**141** C2
Marmaduke St **3** HU3 ..**145** C4
Marmiam Dr **2** YO32 ..**14** D2
Marmion Dr DN15 .....**83** A5
Marmion Rd DN16 .....**151** C3
Marne St HU5 ....**145** A8
Marples Mews DN35 ...**153** F1
Marquis Ave DN36 ....**114** A8
Marquis Ct YO26 ......**129** D5
Marr La HU15 ....**66** F7
Marris Dr DN15 ....**83** B5
Marritt Way **9** HU12 ...**73** C4
Marsdale HU7 ....**140** F7
Marsden Dr DN15 .....**150** D8
Marsden Gr **3** DN8 ....**93** A8
Marsden Landing
  HU6 ....**140** D8
Marsden Rd DN31 .....**153** A5
Marsh Dr HU17 ....**154** A1
Marsh End
  17 Howden DN14 ......**65** A4
  Knottingley WF11 ......**61** A3
Marsh Hill La DN14 ...**78** C4
Marsh La Asselby DN14 ..**64** D7
  Barlow YO8 ....**63** B8
  Barnetby le Wold DN38 ..**99** B4
  Barrow upon Humber
  DN19 ....**70** C2
  Barton-upon-Humber
  DN18 ....**69** F1
  2 Beal DN14 ....**61** D4
  Cawood YO8 ....**48** B8
  Keyingham HU12 ......**73** B3
  Knottingley WF11 ......**61** A2
  Misterton DN10 ....**116** D5
  New Holland DN19 .....**70** E2
  Ryehill HU12 ....**73** A4
  South Killingholme DN40 ..**87** B4
  Thorne DN8 ....**79** A2
  Thorngumbald HU12 ....**73** A4
  West Haddlesey YO8 ...**61** F5
  Winteringham DN15 ....**68** A1
Marsh La Gdns DN14 ...**61** F4
Marsh Rd Crowle DN17 ..**94** B7
  Easington HU12 ....**90** E5
  Keyingham HU12 ......**73** A2
  Ottringham HU12 ......**88** C8
  Walkingham DN10 .....**116** E3
Marsh Way DN36 .....**115** C5
Marshall Ave
  Bridlington YO15 ......**122** E2
  Grimsby DN34 ....**152** B3
  Kingston upon Hull
  HU10 ....**143** E8
  Preston HU12 ....**72** C8
Marshall Hill YO25 .....**19** D2

Marshall St HU5 ......**140** C2
Marshchapel CI **20**
  DN36 ....**103** C2
Marshchapel Prim Sch
  DN36 ....**115** B2
Marshfield Ave DN14 ..**149** E4
Marshfield Rd
  Goole DN14 ....**149** E4
  Scunthorpe DN16 .....**151** C1
Marshland Rd DN8 .....**79** B2
Marshlands Prim Sch
  DN14 ....**149** D1
Marske Wlk **1** HU5 ....**139** E3
Marston Ave YO26 .....**129** B3
Marston Cres YO26 ....**129** B3
Marston La
  Long Marston YO26 .....**24** A8
  Moor Monkton YO26 ....**12** A1
Marten CI **2** YO30 ....**130** A8
Martin Cheeseman Ct **3**
  YO24 ....**132** C8
Martin CI HU4 ....**142** B3
Martin La YO42 ....**29** C6
Martin St HU17 ....**137** D3
Martin Way **7** DN36 ...**113** F8
Martin's Alley HU2 .....**155** B1
Martin's CI YO26 ......**85** D8
Martins Ct YO26 ......**130** A5
Martins Rd DN39 ......**86** B1
Marton Ave YO16 .....**122** E5
Marton Ct **6** YO16 ....**123** A7
Marton Gr
  8 Grimsby DN33 ......**102** D2
  43 Hatfield DN7 ....**92** D4
  Kingston upon Hull HU6 ..**139** F5
Marton Rd
  Bridlington YO16 ......**122** D5
  Ellerby HU11 ....**46** B1
Marton View YO15 ....**123** B8
Martongate YO25 .....**123** A7
Martongate Prim Sch
  YO16 ....**122** F6
Martyn Rd DN32 ......**153** D2
Marvel St HU9 ....**146** B7
Marvelgarth La HU11 ...**35** A2
Mary St DN15 ....**151** A7
Mary Sumner Way
  DN15 ....**150** E8
Marydene Dr HU6 .....**140** C5
Marygate YO30 ....**156** A3
Marygate La YO30 ....**156** A3
Marylebone Wlk **3**
  DN33 ....**102** D1
Mascotte Gdns HU18 ..**134** D3
Mask La YO41 ....**27** D4
Mason Dr DN17 ....**96** C2
Mason St HU2 ....**155** B3
Masons Ct **6** DN18 ...**84** E8
Maspin CI **19** HU7 ....**56** F5
Maspin Moor Rd LS25 ..**61** C7
Massey Ct
  8 Epworth DN9 ....**105** D6
  Kingston upon Hull HU3 ..**145** A5
Massey St
  Kingston upon Hull HU3 ..**145** A4
  Selby YO8 ....**148** C5
Mast Dr HU9 ....**146** C6
Mathews St HU9 ......**153** C3
Matlock Ct DN15 .....**150** B6
Matlock Dr DN37 .....**102** C4
Matson CI YO16 ......**122** C2
Matson Rd YO16 ......**122** B1
Matthew Humberstone CE
  Sch DN35 ....**103** B2
Mattison Way YO24 ....**129** E2
Mattocks La HU12 ....**72** D8
Matty La HU12 ....**53** F7
Maude CI **10** HU12 ...**73** C4
Maulson Dr HU11 .....**58** A3
Maurice Ave HU8 .....**141** A2
Mavis Rd DN17 ....**150** E2
Mawson Gn La DN14 ..**78** C3
Maxwell Ct **9** DN34 ...**102** B3
Maxwell Rd YO42 .....**29** A4
Maxwell St HU8 ......**141** A4
May Ct **28** YO42 .....**29** A3
May Gdns HU7 ....**141** A4
May Gr HU13 ....**143** D2
May St
  Cleethorpes DN35 .....**153** D4
  Kingston upon Hull HU5 ..**140** C3
May Tree Ave HU8 ....**141** C2
Maybury Prim Sch
  HU9 ....**142** B3
Maybury Rd **1** HU9 ...**141** F3
Maye Gr
  Kingston upon Hull HU2 ..**155** C4
  Summergangs HU8 .....**141** B1
Mayfair Cres **18** DN37 ..**113** D6
Mayfair Ct
  3 Humberston DN35 ...**103** D1
  Kingston upon Hull HU3 ..**140** C2
Mayfair Dr W DN37 ...**102** B4
Mayfield & Broompark
  Nature Reserve*
  DN14 ....**149** E5
Mayfield DN14 ....**149** E6
Mayfield Ave
  2 Gainsborough DN21 ..**117** B2
  South Killingholme DN40 ..**86** F2
  Stainforth DN7 ....**92** D7
Mayfield CI DN33 .....**113** D8
Mayfield Dr **5** YO8 ...**148** A1
Mayfield Gr YO24 .....**132** E8
Mayfield Rd
  Brayton YO8 ....**148** A1
  Bridlington YO15 ......**122** D1

Mayfield St HU3 ......**145** C8
Mayflower Ave **6** DN40 ..**87** C1
Mayflower CI **2** DN40 ...**86** E3
Mayland Ave HU5 .....**144** A8
Mayland Dr HU16 .....**138** E6
Maypole Gdns YO8 ....**48** B8
Maypole Gr **3** YO19 ...**36** D8
Maypole St DN21 .....**119** A2
Maysfield Ct DN20 ....**109** A5
Maythorn Rd YO31 ....**127** E2
Maythorpe YO23 .....**24** C6
Maythorpe CI HU3 ....**145** A7
Mayville Ave HU8 .....**141** B3
Mcan CI YO10 ....**131** D4
McArthur Designer Outlet
  YO19 ....**133** D4
McGrath CI **25** YO42 ...**29** A3
McKintosh Dr YO25 ....**125** A3
McShane Ct **11** YO42 ...**29** A3
McVeigh Ct **10** DN41 ...**101** F5
Mead St HU8 ....**141** D5
Mead The **7** DN37 ....**101** F1
Mead Wlk HU4 ......**144** C6
Meadlands YO31 .....**131** B6
Meadley Ct HU17 .....**137** C4
Meadow Ave DN39 ....**86** A2
Meadow Bank **2** HU17 .**136** F7
Meadow CI
  5 Beeford YO25 ......**22** C1
  Thorpe Willoughby YO8 ..**48** C2
Meadow Croft
  Brayton YO8 ....**148** A3
  16 Kirk Sandall DN3 ....**92** A2
  Waltham DN37 ....**113** D7
Meadow Ct
  Grimsby DN37 ....**102** C4
  Hibaldstow DN20 .....**108** F5
  3 Kexby YO24 ....**132** E8
Meadow Ct Greyhound
  Stadium DN7 ....**92** C5
Meadow Dr
  Barton-upon-Humber
  DN18 ....**84** F8
  Burstwick HU12 ......**73** B6
  Grimsby DN33 ....**113** D8
  Healing DN41 ....**102** A5
  Market Weighton YO43 ..**135** E4
  Misterton DN10 ....**116** C5
  Thorpe Willoughby YO8 ..**48** B2
Meadow Field YO43 ...**40** A1
Meadow Garth
  Kingston upon Hull HU6 ..**56** D5
  Thorpe Willoughby YO8 ..**48** C2
Meadow La
  Driffield YO25 ....**125** B4
  1 Haxby YO32 ....**127** D8
  9 Newport HU15 ......**52** F1
Meadow PI **5** YO8 ....**148** B6
Meadow Rd
  Bridlington YO16 ......**122** B2
  Great Driffield YO25 ...**125** A4
  Scunthorpe DN16 .....**150** C2
Meadow Rise
  Barnby Dun DN3 ......**92** A3
  Blyton DN21 ....**117** F6
Meadow The LN7 .....**111** B3
Meadow Vale DN20 ...**108** F8
Meadow View
  Bainton YO25 ....**31** E7
  Bridlington YO16 ......**122** E7
  28 Humberston DN35 ...**103** C1
Meadow Way
  Heworth YO31 ....**130** F7
  Huntington YO32 .....**127** F4
  Kingston upon Hull
  HU16 ....**138** F5
  3 Walkington HU17 ....**55** C8
Meadow Wlk **6** HU14 ..**69** B7
Meadowbank
  4 Belton DN9 ....**94** E1
  Grimsby DN37 ....**102** B4
Meadowbank Rd HU3 ..**144** F2
Meadowbeck CI YO10 ..**131** B4
Meadowcroft Rd
  YO25 ....**125** A6
Meadowfield
  Barnby Dun DN3 ......**92** A3
  1 Bubwith YO8 ....**50** D7
Meadowfield CI **6** YO42 ..**28** E4
Meadowfield Rd YO15 ..**122** D1
Meadowfields Dr
  YO31 ....**127** D2
Meadows The
  Beverley HU17 ....**137** B2
  Brandesburton YO25 ...**34** B2
  Bransholme HU7 ......**140** E7
  4 Buckton/Bempton YO15 ..**4** C3
  Burringham DN17 .....**95** D4
  Carlton DN14 ....**63** C3
  Cherry Burton HU17 ...**43** A4
  Dunswell HU6 ....**56** D5
  Great Driffield YO25 ...**125** A4
  Howden DN14 ....**65** A6
  Leven HU17 ....**45** A8
  Messingham DN17 ....**107** D7
  7 Monk Fryston LS25 ..**61** A8
  Riccall YO19 ....**48** B8
  2 Skelton YO30 ......**126** B5
  13 South Cave HU15 ...**53** F1
  West Ella HU10 ......**69** C8
  5 Westwoodside DN9 ...**105** A2
Meadway YO8 ....**48** C2
Meadway Dr YO8 .....**48** D2
Meam CI YO10 ....**131** D4
Measham Dr DN7 ....**92** D4
Meaux Abbey (Site of)*
  HU17 ....**44** F2
Meaux La HU17 ......**44** F4

Meaux Rd HU7 ....**56** F8
Mechanic La **9** HU3 ...**145** D5
Meden Ave **8** HU15 ...**68** D5
Medforth Rd YO16 ....**122** C4
Medina Ave YO16 .....**122** D3
Medina Rd HU8 ......**142** C5
Medium Section Rd
  DN16 ....**97** A4
Medlar Dr **2** HU15 ....**68** D5
Medway PI DN34 .....**152** A1
Meggison's Turnpike
  YO25 ....**32** F7
Meggitt La DN15 ......**68** A1
Megson Way
  Thorngumbald HU12 ....**72** E5
  Walkington HU17 .....**55** D8
Melander CI YO16 ....**129** B4
Melander Gdns **5** YO32 .**127** D7
Melbourne Ave
  YO16 ....**122** D3
  18 Grimsby DN33 .....**102** E2
Melbourne CP Sch
  YO42 ....**39** A7
Melbourne Pk YO42 ...**39** A6
Melbourne Sq HU17 ...**43** D6
Melbourne St
  4 Kingston upon Hull
  HU5 ....**140** C3
  York YO10 ....**130** D2
Melbury Wlk DN17 ....**150** C4
Melcombe Ave **11** YO32 ..**14** A7
Melford Ct DN16 .....**151** E1
Mellood View DN9 ....**106** A3
Melrose CI **1** YO31 ...**131** A5
Melrose Pk HU17 .....**154** C4
Melrose Rd **5** DN21 ...**117** B1
Melrose St HU3 ......**144** F6
Melrosegate YO31 ....**130** F5
Melton Ave YO30 .....**129** F8
Melton Bottom HU14 ..**68** E5
Melton Dr
  Bishopthorpe YO23 ....**133** A3
  York YO30 ....**129** F8
Melton Fields HU14 ...**68** F5
Melton Gallows DN38 ..**99** A5
Melton Old Rd HU14 ..**68** E5
Melton Rd
  North Ferriby HU14 ....**69** A5
  Wrawby DN20 ....**98** F4
Meltonby Ave HU5 ....**139** C2
Meltonby La YO42 ....**28** E6
Melville CI **19** HU12 ...**73** C4
Melville St HU1 ......**155** A1
Melwood CI DN9 .....**105** F6
Melwood Gr
  Kingston upon Hull HU5 ..**140** D2
  York YO26 ....**129** B5
Melwood Hill DN9 ....**105** F6
Melwood View DN9 ...**105** F6
Memorial Ave **14** HU19 ..**75** A6
Menasha Way DN16 ..**151** E3
Mendip Ave
  Goole DN14 ....**149** D5
  Grimsby DN33 ....**113** D8
Mendip CI **2** YO32 ...**127** F5
Mendip Rd DN17 .....**150** D4
Menson Dr DN7 .....**92** D4
Mercer Rd **1** DN21 ...**117** A2
Merchant Adventurers Hall*
  YO1 ....**156** C2
Merchant Way YO23 ..**132** B3
Merchantgate YO1 ...**156** C2
Merchants Ct YO31 ...**130** E5
Mercia Way DN15 ....**96** C8
Mere Cres DN16 .....**151** D3
Mere Garth HU18 ....**134** B4
Mere La
  Dalton Holme HU17 ....**42** F4
  Edenthorpe DN3 ......**92** A1
  Winterton DN15 ......**83** A7
Mere View Ave HU18 ..**134** B2
Mere Way HU14 ......**69** B7
Mere Wlk **6** HU18 ...**134** C4
Meredith Ave DN17 ...**150** C4
Meredyke Rd DN17 ...**81** D3
Mereside **9** YO15 ....**5** A2
Mereside Terr HU18 ..**134** B4
Mereside View YO15 ..**5** A2
Meridian Point Ret Pk
  DN35 ....**103** D2
Merlin CI HU7 ....**141** D4
Merlin Covert **4** YO31 ..**127** F3
Merlin Dr DN20 ......**99** A8
Merlin Rd DN17 .....**150** E2
Merrick St HU9 ......**146** B7
Merryweather Garth HU12 .**72** C7
Merryweather Ct **14**
  DN16 ....**96** D1
Mersey Prim Sch HU8 .**141** C1
Mersey St HU8 ......**141** C1
Merton Gr **5** HU9 ...**141** F1
Merton Rd DN16 .....**96** C4
Messingham La DN20 ..**108** C7
Messingham Prim Sch
  DN17 ....**107** D7
Messingham Rd
  East Butterwick DN17 ..**106** D8
  Scotter DN17 ....**107** C4
  13 Scunthorpe DN17 ...**96** C2
  Scunthorpe DN16 .....**151** A1
Metcalfe La YO19 .....**131** C5
Metham La DN14 ....**65** F4
Mews The HU3 ......**145** C8
Meynell St DN21 .....**117** A8
Micklegate **1** Selby YO8 .**148** D5
  York YO1 ....**156** A2
Micklegate Bar Mus*
  YO24 ....**156** A1

Micklethwaite Gr 2 DN8 79 B2
Micklethwaite Rd 1 DN8 79 B2
Mickley Gr HU9 142 C2
Middle Banks 24 YO32 13 E5
Middle Barn Hill DN20 84 D1
Middle Ct DN31 152 E4
Middle Dike La HU16 139 D7
Middle Garth Dr HU15 54 A2
Middle La Amcotts DN17 95 E8
Brayton YO8 148 C1
14 Knottingley WF11 61 A2
Preston HU12 58 B1
5 Seaton HU11 35 A1
Middle St
Corringham DN21 118 B2
Foggathorpe YO42 39 A2
Kilham YO25 9 B3
Nafferton YO25 125 F7
North Kelsey LN7 110 A4
Rudston YO25 9 F6
Scotton DN21 107 C1
Wilberfoss YO41 27 F5
Willoughton DN21 119 B3
Middle St N YO25 124 E4
Middle St S YO25 124 F3
Middle Thorpe Rd
DN35 103 B2
Middlebrook Gdns
YO8 148 A2
Middlebrook La 23 DN8 93 A8
Middleburg St HU9 146 D8
Middlecroft Dr YO32 14 A7
Middlecroft Gr 2 YO32 14 B7
Middledyke La HU16 139 D6
Middlefield La WF8 76 A2
Middlegate Cl 9 DN19 85 C8
Middlegate La
Saxby All Saints DN20 84 B4
South Ferriby DN18 84 B7
Middleham Ave YO31 130 E8
Middleham Cl 3 HU9 146 E8
Middlehowe Gn 2 HU17 55 B8
Middlehowe Rd HU17 55 A8
Middlemarsh Cl 3 HU8 141 B4
Middleplatt Rd DN40 87 D2
Middlesex Rd HU8 141 F5
Middlethorpe Dr
YO24 132 E7
Middlethorpe Gr YO24 132 F7
Middlethorpe Prim Sch
DN35 103 B2
Middleton Cl
Beverley HU17 154 C4
Messingham DN17 107 D7
Middleton Ct
Bridlington YO16 122 D5
Kingston upon Hull HU5 145 B8
Middleton Hall* HU6 140 B4
Middleton Rd
Bainton YO25 31 D5
Scunthorpe DN16 96 D2
York YO24 129 C2
Middleton St HU3 145 C8
Middleton-on-the-Wolds CE VC Sch YO25 31 C4
Middlewood Cl YO23 24 C6
Midfield Pl DN36 114 D8
Midfield Rd DN36 114 D8
Midfield Way 1 DN41 101 A4
Midgley Cl
Kingston upon Hull HU3 145 C5
21 Stamford Bridge YO41 15 D2
Midland Ind Est DN15 151 D5
Midland Rd DN16 151 D5
Midland St HU1 155 A2
Midmere Ave HU7 141 B7
Midmere Prim Sch
HU7 141 C6
Midway Ave
Bridlington YO16 122 D2
Poppleton YO26 126 A1
Midway Gr HU4 144 E4
Milcroft Cres 13 DN7 92 D4
Mildred Gr 5 YO24 129 F2
Mile End Ave DN7 92 D3
Mile End Pk YO42 29 A4
Mile The YO42 29 A4
Miles La HU17 43 C6
Milestone Ave YO23 24 C6
Milford Ave YO16 122 C5
Milford Cres 4 YO16 122 C5
Milford Ct 19 DN32 153 A5
Milford Gr HU9 142 E1
Milford Mews 7 YO32 127 D7
Milford Way 8 YO32 127 D7
Mill Ave DN31 152 C4
Mill Balk DN14 77 C8
Mill Balk Pl DN14 78 B8
Mill Baulk Rd DN10 116 C3
Mill Beck La HU16 139 B8
Mill Cl Bridlington YO16 122 C5
15 Broughton DN20 98 B2
Great Driffield YO25 124 D4
Marshchapel DN36 115 C2
Monk Fryston LS25 61 A8
7 Waltham DN37 113 E6
Mill Cres 11 DN21 107 C3
Mill Croft Scawby DN20 108 F8
11 Scunthorpe DN16 96 E2
Scunthorpe DN16 151 D3
Mill Ct 10 YO16 122 C5
Mill Dr HU17 45 A8
Mill Falls YO25 124 D4
Mill Field Ct 5 DN3 92 A3
Mill Field Rd
Chapel Haddlesey YO8 62 B5
Fishlake DN7 92 C8
Scunthorpe DN16 151 E7
Mill Garth
12 Cleethorpes DN35 103 B2
14 Hemingbrough YO8 49 F1
Mill Gate YO16 122 C5
Mill Hill Ellerker HU15 68 A8
Escrick YO19 37 B5
Mill Hill Cres DN35 153 E1
Mill Hill Dr
6 Scunthorpe DN16 96 E2
York YO32 127 F4
Mill Hill Rd DN7 92 E3
Mill House La DN15 83 B5
Mill House Way HU11 45 D2
Mill La
Acaster Malbis YO23 36 C8
Askham Richard YO23 24 D2
Barlow YO8 63 B7
Barrow upon Humber DN19 85 C8
Beverley HU17 154 B4
Bielby YO42 39 E6
Bishop Burton HU17 43 B2
Brandesburton YO25 34 B2
Brayton YO8 62 C8
Bridlington YO16 122 C5
Brigg DN20 98 B1
Brough HU15 68 C6
Broughton DN20 97 E3
Caistor LN7 111 C4
Carlton DN14 63 D3
East Halton DN40 86 D6
Eastrington DN14 52 A1
Elstronwick HU12 58 F3
Foston YO25 21 F1
Gainsborough DN21 117 A2
Gilberdyke HU15 52 D1
Goxhill DN19 71 A1
Harpham YO25 21 E7
Haxby YO32 13 D5
Haxey DN9 105 B2
Hayton YO42 29 D1
2 Hemingbrough YO8 49 F1
Hessay YO23 24 B7
Holton le Clay DN36 114 B4
Hornsea HU18 134 B4
Huggate YO42 18 B1
Immingham DN40 87 A1
Inglemire HU16 138 E7
14 Keelby DN41 101 A4
Kilpin DN14 65 D5
Kirk Ella HU10 143 C6
Kirton in Lindsey DN21 108 C1
Langtoft YO25 8 C7
Laxton DN14 65 F3
Marshchapel DN36 115 C2
Newbald YO43 53 E6
Newland YO8 64 A3
Newport HU15 52 E1
3 North Cave HU15 53 D3
North Dalton YO25 31 C7
North Kelsey LN7 110 A4
Rawcliffe DN14 63 F1
1 Riccall YO19 37 A1
Rise HU11 45 E6
Scawby DN20 108 F8
Seaton HU11 35 A2
Seaton Ross YO42 39 D4
Skipsea YO25 23 B2
Sledmere YO25 6 F3
Snaith & Cowick DN14 78 C8
South Ferriby DN18 84 A7
Walkeringham DN10 116 C3
Warter YO42 30 A4
Watton YO25 32 D4
Welwick HU12 90 A7
Wilberfoss YO41 27 E6
Wrawby DN20 98 E3
York YO31 130 E6
Mill La Ct HU17 154 B3
Mill La W HU15 68 B6
Mill Mere Rd DN21 118 A2
Mill Mount YO24 130 A3
Mill Mount Ct YO24 130 A3
Mill Pl DN35 153 F2
Mill Race DN36 114 E4
Mill Rd Aldbrough HU11 47 C2
Burton Constable HU11 58 D7
Burton Fleming YO25 2 D4
Cleethorpes DN35 153 E1
Crowle DN17 94 D8
Hibaldstow DN20 108 E4
Keadby DN17 95 D5
Keyingham HU12 73 C4
Luddington & Haldenby DN17 81 C4
Skidby HU16 138 C7
Sproatley HU11 58 D5
Swanland HU14 69 A6
Mill Rise
Great Driffield YO25 124 D4
Skidby HU16 138 B8
Swanland HU14 69 A6
Mill Side YO25 9 C3
Mill Side Cl 6 YO25 9 C3
Mill St
Great Driffield YO25 124 E4
Hutton Cranswick YO25 32 E8
Kingston upon Hull HU1 155 A2
York YO1 156 C1
Mill View DN37 113 D6
Mill View Ct DN14 149 E4
Mill View Pl 5 HU17 137 B3
Mill View Rd HU17 154 C2
Mill Wlk HU16 139 C5
Millard Ave DN7 92 D4
Millard Nook 18 DN7 92 D4
Millbank 11 YO16 122 C5
Millbank St DN14 149 F5
Millbeck Bank HU15 67 E8
Millbeck Cl YO43 135 D5
Millbrook Way 23 DN18 84 F8
Milldane HU16 139 E8
Millennium Way DN14 149 F5
Miller Ave DN32 153 C2
Miller Cl
Barmby Moor YO42 28 F4
10 Thorne/Moorends DN8 93 B7
Miller La
Thorne/Moorends DN8 93 B7
Yapham YO42 29 A6
Miller Rd DN21 117 D1
Miller's Wlk HU5 139 F2
Millers Brook DN9 94 E1
Millers Croft 6 YO23 132 B3
Millers Quay 14 DN20 98 B2
Millfield Ave
16 Grimsby DN33 102 E2
York YO10 130 F3
Millfield Cl YO41 27 E5
Millfield Ct YO19 37 F7
Millfield Dr YO8 63 D4
Millfield Garth YO25 31 C4
Millfield Gdns YO26 126 A2
Millfield La
Nether Poppleton YO26 129 B8
Poppleton YO26 126 A2
York YO10 131 A3
Millfield Rd
4 Bridlington YO16 122 C5
17 Hemingbrough YO8 49 F1
Hemingbrough YO8 63 F8
Thorne/Moorends DN8 93 A8
York YO23 130 B2
Millfield The DN20 109 A6
Millfields
Barton-upon-Humber DN18 84 E8
23 Caistor LN7 111 B4
Millfields Way 7 DN19 85 C8
Millgate YO8 148 C6
Millgates YO26 129 C6
Millhill Rd DN14 149 E5
Millhouse La DN14 149 F5
Millhouse St Rise 3
DN40 87 B1
Millhouse Woods La
HU16 139 B8
Millington Woods Nature Reserve* YO42 29 D8
Millom Way DN32 152 F4
Millport Dr HU4 144 B2
Mills Dr DN7 104 A8
Mills Service Rd DN16 97 A4
Millthorpe Sec Sch
YO23 130 B2
Millview Gdns DN20 98 E3
Milne Rd HU9 142 C4
Milner Pl YO16 122 D4
Milner Rd YO16 122 D4
Milner St YO24 129 D3
Milson Cl
4 Barton-upon-Humber DN18 84 E8
Broughton DN20 97 D4
Milson Gr YO10 131 A3
Milson Rd 8 DN41 101 A4
Milton Carr 8 YO30 126 F1
Milton Cl
5 Gainsborough DN21 117 C1
12 Howden DN14 65 A7
Milton Rd
3 Gainsborough DN21 117 C1
Grimsby DN33 102 D2
Scunthorpe DN16 151 B1
Milton St Goole DN14 149 C4
York YO10 130 F3
Minchin Cl 3 YO30 127 B1
Minehead Rd HU7 57 A5
Mineral Quay Rd DN40 87 C3
Minerva Terr HU1 155 B1
Minnow Cl 14 DN37 102 B4
Minshull Rd 12 DN35 103 C2
Minster Ave
Beverley HU17 154 B2
York YO31 127 F2
Minster Cl
3 Haxby YO32 127 C8
Kingston upon Hull HU8 141 D5
York YO1 156 B3
Minster Ct
Beverley HU17 154 A2
11 Howden DN14 65 A7
York YO31 156 B3
Minster Moorgate
HU17 154 A2
Minster Moorgate W
HU17 154 A2
Minster Rd
Misterton DN10 116 C5
Scunthorpe DN15 150 B6
Minster Sch The YO1 156 B3
Minster View YO32 127 C8
Minster Yd YO1 156 B3
Minster Yd N HU17 154 B2
Minster Yd S HU17 154 B2
Mint Wlk HU17 154 B1
Minter Cl 2 YO24 129 B1
Mintfields Rd HU17 154 C3
Minton St HU5 140 D3
Mires La HU15 53 D2
Mires The YO43 53 F7
Mirfield Gr HU9 142 C1
Mirfield Rd
Grimsby DN32 102 F2
Scunthorpe DN15 150 C8
Mirkhill Rd YO8 148 B6
Misson Bank DN9 104 C3
Misterton Prim Sch
DN10 116 C4
Mistral Ct YO31 130 E8
Mitcham Rd HU8 142 A5
Mitchell Cl DN7 92 D5
Mitchell La YO41 27 D8
Mitchell Way YO30 126 E3
Mitchel's La YO10 133 F8
Miterdale 4 YO24 132 C7
Mitford Cl 3 YO14 2 F8
Mitford Rd 2 YO14 2 F8
Mitten Ave 10 DN14 78 C8
Mizzen Rd HU6 140 B8
MLS Bsns Centres
YO30 127 A2
Moat Field YO10 131 C4
Moat House Rd DN21 108 A1
Moat La 4 DN40 86 E3
Moat Rd DN15 82 C1
Moat Way YO8 48 D1
Moatside Ct YO31 156 B3
Modder St DN16 151 B2
Model Farm La DN39 86 B1
Moffat Cl HU8 141 C4
Moins Ct YO10 131 D4
Moira Cl DN7 92 D7
Moiser Cl YO32 127 D4
Molescroft Ave 3
HU17 136 D6
Molescroft Dr HU17 136 D6
Molescroft Mews
HU17 136 C6
Molescroft Pk 4 HU17 136 D6
Molescroft Prim Sch
HU17 136 D6
Molescroft Rd HU17 136 C6
Molescroft W Cl 2
HU17 136 D6
Mollison Ave DN35 153 F1
Mollison Rd HU4 144 A3
Monarch Way YO26 129 D6
Mond Ave DN14 149 D5
Money Hill (Tumulus)*
YO43 42 A8
Monic Ave HU13 143 F2
Monk Ave YO31 130 F7
Monk Bar & Richard III Mus*
YO31 156 C3
Monk Bar Ct YO31 156 B3
Monk Fryston CE VC Prim Sch LS25 61 A8
Monk Fryston Prim Sch
LS25 61 A8
Monk La YO8 148 C7
Monkbridge Ct YO31 156 C4
Monkgate YO31 156 C3
Monkgate Cloisters
YO31 156 C3
Monks Cl DN7 92 D5
Monks Cross Dr YO32 128 A3
Monks Cross Link
YO32 128 B4
Monks Cross Sh Pk
YO32 128 B3
Monks Rd DN17 150 F2
Monks Wlk The HU17 154 B2
Monkton 11 HU15 68 D6
Monkton Cl 10 HU16 138 F5
Monkton Rd 5 YO31 127 F1
Monkton Wlk 8 HU8 142 C6
Monmouth St HU4 144 E3
Mons St HU5 145 A8
Monson Rd DN21 118 D8
Montague Rd YO23 133 A3
Montague St
Cleethorpes DN35 153 B5
Goole DN14 149 C4
York YO23 130 C1
Montague Wlk 6 YO26 12 F1
Montbretia Dr 25 DN16 96 D1
Montcalm Wlk 8 HU16 138 F5
Montgomery Rd DN35 153 D1
Montgomery Sq YO25 124 C2
Montreal Cres 4 HU16 138 F5
Montrose Ave YO31 130 D8
Montrose Ct DN14 149 F5
Montrose Dr DN14 149 F5
Montrose St
Kingston upon Hull HU8 141 B1
Scunthorpe DN16 151 B6
Moody La DN31 152 A7
Mook St YO60 16 B8
Moor Carr La YO8 49 B5
Moor Cl YO19 37 F8
Moor Cottage Rd YO25 34 D5
Moor Dike Rd DN7 104 A8
Moor Edges Rd DN8 93 B8
Moor End YO43 52 B8
Moor Gn HU4 144 B7
Moor Gr YO24 132 E8
Moor La 6 Barlby YO8 49 B5
Bilbrough LS24 24 B1
Bishopthorpe YO23 132 E2
Burton Agnes YO25 10 C2
Caistor LN7 111 A4
Carnaby YO16 10 E4
Cliffe YO8 49 F4
Copmanthorpe YO23 132 A1
Earswick YO32 128 C8
Full Sutton YO41 15 F1
Harpham YO25 22 A8
Hatfield DN8 93 D3
Haxby YO32 13 D7
Humbleton HU11 58 E6
Kelfield YO19 36 E2
Murton YO19 131 F8
Naburn YO19 36 D8
Moor La *continued*
Newton-on-Ouse YO30 12 C7
Rufforth YO23 24 E6
Skelton YO30 126 D6
Strensall YO32 14 B7
Sykehouse DN14 78 A4
Thorne DN8 79 B1
Wroot DN9 104 C6
York YO24 132 C6
Moor Lee La
Eggborough DN14 77 B8
Heck DN14 62 B1
Moor Owners Rd DN8 93 D8
Moor Rd
Bottesford DN17 96 B1
Bridlington YO15 123 D7
Crowle DN17 94 C8
Hunmanby YO14 3 B7
Rawcliffe DN14 79 B7
Sancton YO43 53 C8
Stamford Bridge YO41 15 D2
Thorne DN8 93 C7
Moor Way YO32 128 A4
Moorbeck Cl HU6 139 F4
Moorcroft Rd YO24 132 D7
Moore Ave YO10 131 B4
Moorends Rd DN8 79 A4
Moorfield Dr YO41 27 E6
Moorfield Rd YO16 122 D3
Moorfield Way YO41 27 E6
Moorfields 3 YO8 48 D6
Moorfields La
Kilpin DN14 65 D3
Reedness DN14 80 F7
Moorfoot Cl 8 HU7 57 A6
Moorgarth Ave 10 YO24 129 F2
Moorgate YO24 129 D3
Moorhouse Rd 1 HU5 139 B1
Moorings Ct DN14 65 C4
Moorings The DN20 98 A2
Moorland Ave 3 DN10 116 C3
Moorland Cl 4 DN10 116 C3
Moorland Dr 16 DN36 114 A8
Moorland Garth 2 YO32 14 A7
Moorland Gdns YO23 132 A1
Moorland Rd
Goole DN14 149 D1
York YO10 133 D8
Moorland Way 12 DN9 105 E6
Moorlands Skelton YO32 13 B5
6 Westwoodside DN9 105 A2
Moorlands Cl YO10 131 C4
Moorlands Fields
YO10 133 E8
Moorlands La YO30 126 C6
Moorlands Nature Reserve*
YO32 13 B5
Moorlands The HU15 53 E1
Moors La HU15 53 E2
Moors Rd DN15 150 C7
Moortown Rd
Brandesburton YO25 34 B4
Nettleton LN7 111 A3
Moorwell Rd DN17 96 C1
Moot Hill* YO25 124 E5
Morcar Rd YO41 15 D1
Mordacks Dr YO16 123 B8
Mordacks Rd YO16 123 A7
Mordaunt Ave DN33 113 D8
More Hall Dr HU7 141 D7
Morecambe Ave DN16 151 A1
Morehall Cl YO30 126 F2
Moreton Bay HU11 142 E5
Morfield Gr 3 DN9 105 D6
Morgan Cl 32 YO42 29 A3
Morgan Way DN19 70 D2
Morley Rd DN17 150 F1
Morley St Goole DN14 149 D1
Kingston upon Hull HU8 141 A2
Morley's Yd HU17 154 A3
Morpeth St HU3 145 D7
Morpeth Wlk DN34 152 A3
Morrell Ct YO24 132 B8
Morrell Way YO10 131 A2
Morrets La YO8 48 A1
Morrill St HU9 141 D1
Morris Rd HU3 144 E7
Morritt Cl 3 YO31 130 F8
Morrow Ave HU18 134 D5
Mortal Ash Hill DN16 97 C2
Mortimer Dr HU10 143 F6
Mortimer Wlk YO25 125 A3
Mortlake Cl HU8 141 E5
Morton Cl
4 Gainsborough DN21 117 A2
Immingham DN40 87 B2
Morton La
Beverley HU17 154 B3
Hambleton YO8 62 A8
Morton Rd
Gainsborough DN21 117 B2
Grimsby DN34 152 B3
Laughton DN21 117 E8
Morton St HU3 145 C8
Morton Terr DN21 117 B1
Morton Trentside Prim Sch
DN21 117 A2
Moseley Hill HU11 142 E6
Moss Gn La
Brayton YO8 148 A2
Hirst Courtney YO8 62 F3
Moss Haven DN6 77 D1
Moss Rd Grimsby DN32 152 E3
Kirk Bramwith DN7 92 A8
Moss DN6 77 B1

Moss St YO24 ....156 A1
Mosscroft La DN7 ......92 E2
Motherwell Cl HU7 ....141 C4
Moulton Cl 6 DN34 ...102 B2
Mount Ave
　13 Barton-upon-Humber
　　DN18 ....84 E8
　Bridlington YO16 ......122 E6
　Kingston upon Hull
　　HU13 ....143 D2
　Selby YO8 ....148 B3
　Winterton DN15 ......83 B5
Mount Cres YO16 ....122 E6
Mount Dr YO16 ......122 E6
Mount Ephraim 6
　YO24 ....130 A3
Mount Gr YO8 ......148 B3
Mount Par YO24 ....130 A3
Mount Pk YO19 ......49 A8
Mount Pleasant
　Aldbrough HU11 ....47 D2
　Harpham YO25 ....9 D3
　9 Holton le Clay DN36 ..114 A5
　1 Hornsea HU18 ......134 B4
　Kingston upon Hull HU8 ..141 A1
　New Holland DN19 .....70 E2
　Waltham DN37 ....113 C4
Mount Pleasant CE Jun Sch
　YO43 ....135 D3
Mount Pleasant Rd
　Goole DN14 ....149 D5
　North Frodingham YO25 ..34 A7
　Thorne DN8 ....79 A2
Mount Pleasant Windmill ★
　DN21 ....108 B2
Mount Royale Cl 4
　DN39 ....86 A1
Mount Sch The YO24 ..130 A3
Mount Terr YO24 ....130 A3
Mount The
　Great Driffield YO25 ...124 F5
　7 Kirk Sandall DN3 ....92 A1
　Selby YO8 ....148 B3
　York YO24 ....156 A1
Mount Vale YO24 ....130 A2
Mount Vale Dr YO24 ..130 A2
Mount Vernon HU11 ..142 E6
Mount View HU14 .....69 A5
Mountbatten Cl 7 DN16 .96 D2
Mountbatten Mews
　DN14 ....149 C5
Mountbatten Prim Sch
　HU9 ....142 E3
Mowbray Cl DN9 .....105 D3
Mowbray Ct 20 DN9 ..105 E6
Mowbray Dr YO26 ....129 C4
Mowbray Rd 18 DN8 ..93 B7
Mowbray St
　Epworth DN9 ....105 E4
　3 Gainsborough DN21 ..117 B1
Mowthorpe Medieval
　Village ★ YO17 ....6 C6
Moy Ct HU6 ....140 A6
Mucky La HU12 ....59 C6
Muirfield 16 DN7 .....113 D6
Muirfield Croft 4 DN40 ..87 C1
Muirfield Way 6 YO26 ..129 B5
Mulberry Ave 12 DN8 ..79 B2
Mulberry Cl
　Great Driffield YO25 ...124 D3
　North Thoresby DN36 ..114 B1
Mulberry Ct YO32 ....127 F6
Mulberry Dr
　11 Crowle DN17 ......94 D7
　7 Haxby YO32 ....13 E5
Mulberry La HU11 .....45 E4
Mulcourt HU6 ....139 F7
Mulgrave St HU8 .....155 C4
Mulgrave St S DN15 ..151 A8
Mull Way DN40 ......101 C8
Mullion Cl HU7 ....141 C7
Mulwith Cl YO31 .....131 A6
Mumby Cl 7 DN36 ...114 B1
Muncastergate YO31 ..130 E7
Munroe Cl HU8 ......141 C4
Munster St 5 DN32 ...153 A5
Murham Ave DN14 ....149 C6
Murray Cl 3 YO42 ....29 A4
Murray Cres HU16 ....138 F5
Murray St
　Grimsby DN31 ....152 F6
　York YO24 ....129 F3
Murrayfield Rd HU5 ..139 F1
Murrough Wilson Pl 3
　YO31 ....130 C7
Murton Garth YO19 ..131 F6
Murton La YO19 ......26 D7
Murton Way YO19 ....131 E5
Museum St YO1 ......156 B2
Muston Ave HU16 ....139 A5
Muston Rd YO14 ......2 F4
Muswell Ct HU8 .....142 A5
Mutton La DN10 .....116 C1
Mylor Cl 18 HU7 .....57 A5
Myrtle Ave
　Bishopthorpe YO23 ....133 B3
　Selby YO8 ....148 B3
Myrtle Rd DN7 ....92 C4
Myrtle Way 14 HU15 ..68 D5
Myton St HU1 ....155 A2
Mytongate HU1 ......155 A1

N

Nab Dr DN14 ....149 C6
Nab La DN7 ....92 C8
Naburn CE Prim Sch
　YO19 ....36 D8
Naburn La
　Deighton YO19 ....37 A7
　Fulford YO19 ....133 D4
Naburn Pk Mews YO19 .36 E8
Naburn St HU3 ......145 A4
Nacton St DN31 .....152 F5
Nafferton Prim Sch
　YO25 ....125 E6
Nafferton Sta YO25 ..125 F6
Nairn Cl YO24 ......132 C6
Nalton Cl YO23 .....132 A1
Nalton Ct HU16 .....139 A5
Nalton St YO8 ......148 C5
Nan Sampson Bank
　DN9 ....104 B4
Nandike Cl 4 HU10 ..143 F6
Napier Cl HU7 ......154 A4
Narrow Boats The 13
　DN20 ....98 B2
Narrow La
　Cottingham YO42 ......38 D7
　Eastrington DN14 ......52 A2
　Kilpin DN14 ....65 D6
　Twin Rivers DN14 .....81 C8
Narvick Rd HU7 .....140 E5
Naseby Cl 14 DN7 ....92 D3
Naseby Dr DN31 .....152 B3
Naseby Gr DN31 .....152 B4
Nashcourt HU6 ......139 F7
National Ave HU5 ....144 F8
National Ctr for Early
　Music ★ YO1 ....156 C2
National Fishing Heritage
　Ctr ★ DN31 ....152 D4
National Rly Mus ★
　YO26 ....130 A4
Navensby Cl DN31 ...102 C5
Navigation La LN7 ...111 A4
Navigation Rd YO1 ..156 C2
Navigation Way HU9 ..146 C6
Nayfield Cl 7 YO25 ..124 F4
Naylor's Row 3 HU9 ..146 B7
Neap House Rd DN15 ..95 E6
Neasden Cl HU8 .....141 E5
Neasden Prim Sch
　HU8 ....141 E5
Neat Marsh Rd HU12 ..58 B1
Neatgangs La DN19 ...71 A3
Neath Rd DN16 ......151 A5
Neatshead Garth 9 HU7 .57 B5
Needham Cl HU17 ....137 B4
Nelson Cl HU1 ......155 B1
Nelson Rd HU5 ......144 B7
Nelson St
　Bridlington YO15 .....122 E2
　Gainsborough DN21 ...117 B1
　Kingston upon Hull HU1 .155 C1
　York YO31 ....156 C4
Nelson Way DN34 ....102 B3
Nelson's La YO24 ....129 F1
Nelthorpe Cl 6 DN39 .86 A1
Neptune St
　Bridlington YO15 .....122 E1
　Cleethorpes DN35 ....153 E3
　Kingston upon Hull HU1 .145 D4
Ness La
　Garthorpe & Fockerby
　　DN17 ....81 E6
　1 Preston HU12 ......58 C1
Ness Rd 5 YO8 ......148 D6
Nessgate YO1 ....156 B2
Nestlings The HU8 ...141 D4
Nestor Gr HU9 ......142 C5
Neswick La YO25 .....31 F7
Nether Way 20 YO26 ..12 F1
Nethergate
　Nafferton YO25 ......125 F7
　Westwoodside DN9 ...105 B2
Netherlands Way DN41 .87 E1
Netherton Rd HU4 ...144 B4
Netherwindings 18 YO32 .13 F5
Netherwoods 6 YO32 ..14 B8
Nettle Hill 12 HU15 ...52 F1
Nettleholme 2 DN7 ...92 D4
Nettleton Garth 3 HU12 .73 A6
Nettleton Prim Sch
　LN7 ....111 A3
Nettleton Rd LN7 ....111 B3
Neville Ave HU17 ....154 C3
Neville Cl
　2 Keadby with Althorpe
　　DN17 ....95 D4
　Kingston upon Hull HU13 .145 D5
Neville Cres DN15 ....83 A5
Neville Dr YO23 .....133 A3
Neville Garth 27 HU12 ..72 D7
Neville La DN7 ....92 A8
Neville Pits La DN14 ..77 B4
Neville Rd DN16 .....151 C6
Neville St
　Cleethorpes DN35 ....153 D4
　York YO31 ....156 C4
Neville Terr YO31 ...156 C4
Neville Turner Way 9
　DN37 ....113 D6
Nevinson Gr YO10 ...133 E8
Nevis Way YO24 .....132 B7
New Bridge La YO25 ..125 F5
New Bridge Rd HU9 ..146 C8

New Burlington Rd 2
　YO15 ....122 D2
New Carr La DN14 ....52 A3
New Cartergate 5
　DN31 ....152 D3
New Chapel La 6 DN37 101 F1
New Church Terr 12
　YO25 ....148 C5
New Cl 1 DN33 ......102 E2
New Clee Sta DN31 ..153 B5
New Cleveland St
　HU8 ....155 C4
New Cross St HU2 ...155 B3
New Cut YO25 ....22 E5
New Delights DN36 ..114 F3
New Earswick Prim Sch
　YO32 ....127 D4
New Earswick Sports Club
　YO32 ....127 D3
New Fen La YO8 ......48 F6
New Finkle Ct HU16 ..139 A6
New Forge Ct 15 YO32 ..13 F5
New Gdn St HU1 .....155 B3
New George St HU2 ..155 B3
New Gn 2 DN7 ....92 C8
New Haven Terr DN31 .152 B5
New Holland CE & Methodist
　Prim Sch DN19 ......70 E2
New Holland Rd DN19 .85 D8
New Holland Sta DN19 .70 E3
New Inn La DN7 ....92 C7
New La Beal DN14 .....61 D3
　Bishopthorpe YO23 ....133 A4
　Holgate YO24 ....129 C3
　Holme-on-Spalding-Moor
　　YO43 ....52 C4
　Humbleton HU11 ......59 A5
　Huntington YO32 .....127 F1
　Huntington YO32 .....128 A1
　Laxton DN14 ....65 E4
　Long Marston YO23 ....24 B3
　Newland YO8 ....64 A3
　Rawcliffe DN14 ....79 A8
　Reedness DN14 ....80 E8
　Selby YO8 ....148 C5
　Strensall YO32 ....14 B8
New Laids La HU12 ...73 B7
New Michael St HU1 ..155 A1
New Mill Field Rd DN7 ..92 E3
New Millgate YO8 ....148 C6
New Pasture Cl 6
　YO16 ....122 C5
New Pasture La YO16 ..122 B5
New Pasture La Prim Sch
　YO16 ....122 B5
New Pasture Prim Sch
　YO16 ....122 B5
New Pasture Wlk
　YO16 ....122 B5
New Pk Est DN7 ......92 D7
New Potter Grange Rd
　DN14 ....64 E2
New Rd
　Beningbrough YO30 ...12 C6
　Brandesburton YO25 ...33 E3
　Brantingham HU15 .....68 C8
　Burton Pidsea HU12 ...59 C2
　Cleethorpes DN35 ....153 F2
　Etton HU17 ....43 A6
　Foggathorpe YO42 ....39 A2
　Great Driffield YO25 ..124 F4
　Harpham YO25 ....21 C8
　Heck DN14 ....62 D1
　Hedon HU12 ....72 C7
　Hessay YO23 ....24 C8
　Holme-on-Spalding-Moor
　　YO43 ....40 B1
　Hornsea HU18 ....134 D4
　Hunmanby YO14 ......2 F7
　Keyingham HU12 ......73 D5
　Kirby Grindalythe YO17 ..6 B6
　Laceby DN37 ....113 A8
　Long Drax YO8 ....63 E6
　Nafferton YO25 ......125 D7
　Norton DN6 ....76 F2
　Ottringham HU12 .....73 E3
　Reighton YO14 ....3 E5
　Roos HU12 ....59 F3
　Scunthorpe DN17 .....150 B2
　Stapleton WF8 ....76 B5
　Swinefleet DN14 ......80 C4
　Waltham DN37 ....113 E6
　Wheldrake YO19 ......37 C7
　Worlaby DN20 ....98 D8
New Row DN17 ......107 D7
New St 18 Brigg DN20 ..98 C2
　Gainsborough DN21 ...117 B1
　Grimsby DN31 ....152 E3
　Pocklington YO42 .....29 A3
　York YO1 ....156 B2
New Trent St DN17 ...94 E6
New Village Rd
　Kingston upon Hull
　　HU16 ....139 C7
　Little Weighton HU20 ..55 A4
New Walkergate
　HU17 ....154 A3
New Waltham Prim Sch
　DN36 ....114 A8
New Wlk
　Beverley HU17 ....136 D5
　Great Driffield YO25 ..124 F4
　North Ferriby HU14 ...69 A4
New Wlk Cl YO25 ....124 F4
New Wlk Terr YO10 ..130 D2
New Wlk YO25 ......124 F4
Newbald Gr HU6 .....139 F6
Newbald Prim Sch
　YO43 ....53 F8

Newbald Rd HU17 ....136 A2
Newbald Way 1 HU16 .138 E6
Newbegin
　Beverley HU17 ....154 A3
　Hornsea HU18 ....134 C4
Newbigg Crowle DN17 ..94 C8
　Westwoodside DN9 ...105 B2
Newbolt Ave DN15 ..150 F8
Newbolt Cl LN7 ......111 A3
Newborn Ave DN15 ..150 F8
Newborough St YO30 .156 A4
Newbridge La YO41 ...28 A7
Newbridge Rd HU2 ...73 B6
Newbury Ave
　Grimsby DN37 ....102 C5
　York YO24 ....129 D1
Newbury Gr 2 DN34 ..102 C2
Newby La DN14 ....77 F8
Newby Rd DN31 .....152 C3
Newby Terr YO31 ....130 C7
Newclose La DN14 ...149 D6
Newcomen St HU9 ...141 D1
Newcroft YO8 ....148 B4
Newdale 3 YO32 .....13 F5
Newdown Rd DN17 ...96 B2
Newfield Cl DN3 .....92 A3
Newfield La
　Burstwick HU12 ....58 F2
　South Cave HU15 ......53 E1
Newfields Ave DN8 ...79 B1
Newfields Cl DN8 .....79 B1
Newfields Dr DN8 ....79 B1
Newgate YO1 ....156 B2
Newgate Ct YO1 .....156 B2
Newgate St YO16 ....139 B6
Newhall Rd 8 DN3 ...92 A2
Newhay La YO8 ....49 E1
Newholme Cl HU6 ...139 F6
Newholme Dr 8 DN8 ..79 B2
Newington Ave HU4 ..144 E5
Newington Prim Sch
　HU3 ....145 A4
Newington St HU3 ...144 F4
Newland Ave
　Great Driffield YO25 ..124 D4
　Kingston upon Hull HU5 .140 C2
　Scunthorpe DN15 ....150 E6
Newland Ave Prim Sch
　HU5 ....140 C2
Newland Dr DN15 ....150 D7
Newland Gr 1 HU5 ...140 C3
Newland Pk HU5 .....140 A3
Newland Pk Ave HU6 ..140 B4
Newland Pk Cl YO10 ..131 A3
Newland Pk Dr YO10 ..130 F3
Newland Rd DN14 ....149 C5
Newland Sch for Girls
　HU6 ....140 A4
Newland St John CE VA Prim
　Sch HU6 ....140 A4
Newland View 11 DN9 ..105 E6
Newland Wlk DN15 ..150 D7
Newlands 17 DN21 ...117 C1
Newlands Dr YO26 ...129 C4
Newlands La Paull HU12 .72 D3
　Upper Poppleton YO26 ..24 E8
Newlands Pk 28 DN36 .103 D1
Newlands Rd
　Bishopthorpe YO23 ....132 F4
　Sunk Island HU12 .....89 D6
Newlands The HU6 ...140 C4
Newlyn Cl
　4 Kingston upon Hull
　　HU13 ....144 A2
　New Waltham DN36 ...114 A8
　Sutton-on-Hull HU7 ...141 C7
Newmarket St DN32 ..152 F4
Newnham Cres 12 DN16 .96 D2
Newport Ave YO8 ....148 B4
Newport Cl 4 HU4 ...145 D5
Newport Dr DN15 ....83 A6
Newport Prim Sch
　HU15 ....52 F1
Newport Rd HU15 ....53 C2
Newport St
　Barton-upon-Humber
　　DN18 ....69 E1
　Goole DN14 ....149 B4
Newroad End WF8 ...76 A6
Newsam Cl 4 YO25 ..22 D1
Newsam Abbey (Site of) ★
　DN39 ....100 C3
Newsham Dr DN34 ...152 A3
Newsham Garth HU4 ..144 B5
Newsham Gdns HU19 .75 A5
Newsham Hill La YO16 ..4 C2
Newsham La DN39 ...100 D8
Newstead Ave DN36 ..114 B5
Newstead Cres YO16 ..122 D6
Newstead Rd DN35 ..103 C2
Newstead St HU5 ....145 A8
Newthorpe Rd 2 DN6 ..76 E2
Newton Dr HU17 ....154 A1
Newton La LN8 ......120 A5
Newton Marsh La
　DN36 ....114 F6
Newton Pk YO30 .....12 B7
Newton Rd DN16 ....151 E2
Newton St 3 HU3 ...145 B4
Newton Terr YO1 ....156 B1
Newtondale HU7 .....140 F7
Newtondale Garth
　YO16 ....122 F7
Newtown Ct HU9 ....146 E7
Newtown Sq HU9 ....146 E7
Nicholas Ct 7 DN18 ..84 E8
Nicholas Gdns YO10 ..130 F3
Nicholas St YO10 ....130 F3

Nicholson Cl HU17 ...137 B4
Nicholson Ct YO42 ...29 A3
Nicholson La 2 HU11 ..35 A1
Nicholson Rd
　Healing DN41 ....102 A3
　Immingham DN40 .....86 E4
Nicholson St
　Cleethorpes DN35 ....153 F1
　5 Kingston upon Hull
　　HU5 ....140 E2
Nicholson Way 6 DN9 .105 D7
Nicholson's La HU12 ..74 B3
Nicholsons Ct HU16 ..139 A6
Nickey Nackey La YO8 ..48 B8
Nicolgate La 27 DN20 ..98 C2
Nicolson Dr 16 DN18 ..84 F8
Nidd Cl YO26 ....129 B8
Nidd Gr YO24 ....132 E8
Nidd St DN14 ....149 D1
Nidderdale HU7 .....140 F6
Nidderdale Cl 1 YO16 .123 A7
Nigel Gr 7 YO24 ....129 F2
Nightingale Cl
　Scunthorpe DN15 .....96 B7
　4 Walkington HU17 ...55 D8
　York YO32 ....127 E1
Nightingale Dr YO16 .122 F5
Nightingale Rd YO16 .122 F5
Nine Dikes Rd YO25 ...9 D8
Ninescores La DN9 ..104 B4
Ninth Ave
　Fixborough Stather DN15 .82 A1
　York YO31 ....130 F5
Nith Gr HU8 ....142 C6
Nithdale Gdns HU5 ..140 E2
Noddle Hill Way HU7 .141 D8
Noel St 2 DN21 .....117 B1
Nolloth Cres HU7 ....154 B4
Noodle Hill Way HU7 ..57 B5
Nook The YO8 ......148 D6
Nooking La DN37 ....101 D2
Nooking The DN9 ...105 D3
Nookings Dr DN20 ..109 A5
Nordale Cl 9 HU8 ...141 E7
Nordham HU15 ....53 D3
Norfolk Ave DN15 ....82 B4
Norfolk Bank La HU15 .24 F8
Norfolk Ct 11 DN32 ..153 A5
Norfolk La DN35 ....153 E3
Norfolk St
　Beverley HU17 ....136 D5
　Kingston upon Hull HU2 .155 A3
　York YO23 ....130 C2
Norland Ave HU4 ....144 C6
Norlands La YO16 .....4 A1
Norman Cl
　Barton-upon-Humber
　　DN18 ....84 F8
　7 Thorpe Willoughby YO8 .48 B1
Norman Cres DN17 ..150 F4
Norman Dr
　3 Hatfield DN7 ....92 D3
　York YO26 ....129 B6
Norman Rd
　Grimsby DN34 ....152 B3
　Hatfield DN7 ....92 D3
Norman St 5 YO10 ...131 A3
Normanby Ent Pk
　DN15 ....151 B8
Normanby Hall Ctry Pk ★
　DN15 ....82 C3
Normanby Rd
　Burton upon Stather
　　DN15 ....82 B4
　Nettleton LN7 ....111 B2
　Scunthorpe DN15 ....151 A8
Normandy Ave HU17 ..55 E8
Normandy Cl 4 YO8 ..148 B6
Normandy Rd DN35 ..153 D1
Normandy Way DN14 .149 A3
Normanton Rise HU4 .144 C7
Nornabell Dr HU17 ..136 E7
Nornabell St 1 HU8 ..146 C8
Norrison Ave HU6 ...140 C8
Norsefield Ave 1 DN37 .113 E7
Norseman Cl 7 YO19 ..48 F8
Norseway 2 YO41 ....15 D1
North Axholme Comp Sch
　DN17 ....94 D6
North Back La
　2 Bridlington YO16 ..122 D4
　Kilham YO25 ....9 B3
North Bar Within
　HU17 ....154 A3
North Bar Without
　HU17 ....136 D4
North Bridge St DN32 .152 F5
North Burton La YO14 ..3 B4
North Carr Dales Rd
　HU9 ....74 F4
North Carr La
　Saxby All Saints DN20 ..83 F3
　Tickton HU17 ....44 F4
North Carr Rd
　Scotter DN17 ....106 C5
　West Stockwith DN10 ..116 E5
North Cave CE VC Prim Sch
　HU15 ....53 D3
North Cave Rd YO43 ..53 D4
North Cave Wetland Nature
　Reserve ★ HU15 .....53 C3
North Church Side
　1 Easington HU12 .....90 F6
　Kingston upon Hull HU1 .155 B2
North Cliff Rd DN21 ..108 C2
North Cliffe Wood Nature
　Reserve ★ YO43 .....53 A8

North Coates Rd
DN36 . . . . .115 A4
North Comm Rd DN8 . .78 F2
North Cotes CE Sch
DN36 . . . . .115 B3
North Cotes Rd
Hunmanby YO25 . . . . .2 C5
Wold Newton YO25 . . . . .1 E5
North Ctry Ct 2 HU9 . .141 F1
North Cty Prim Sch The
DN21 . . . . .117 A1
North Dr
Kingston upon Hull
HU10 . . . . .143 E6
Swanland HU14 . . . . .69 B7
North Duffield CP Sch
YO8 . . . . .50 A8
North Eastern Rd DN8 . .93 A8
North Eastern Terr
YO24 . . . . .132 E8
North Elkington La
LN11 . . . . .121 B1
North End
5 Flamborough YO15 . . . .5 A2
Goxhill DN19 . . . . .86 A8
Seaton Ross YO42 . . . . . . .39 D4
South Ferriby DN18 . . . . . .84 A8
North End Cres 13
DN36 . . . . .114 D4
North End La LN7 . . . . .110 A2
North End Rd
Halsham HU12 . . . . .73 F5
Roos HU12 . . . . .60 A2
1 Tetney DN36 . . . . .114 D4
North Farm Rd DN17 . .96 B2
North Ferriby CE VC Prim
Sch HU14 . . . . .69 A5
North Field La
Askham Bryan YO23 . . . . . .24 F3
Upper Poppleton YO26 . . . . .24 F7
North Frodingham Prim Sch
YO25 . . . . .33 F8
North Frodingham Rd
YO25 . . . . .34 B8
North Grange Ct YO30 .156 A4
North Holme 8 DN36 .114 D4
North Ings Rd DN7 . . . .92 E5
North Intake La DN9 . .116 F8
North Kelsey Prim Sch
LN7 . . . . .110 A4
North Kelsey Rd LN7 .110 F4
North La
Dringhouses YO24 . . . . . .132 E8
Huntington YO32 . . . . . . .127 F5
Marsh Chapel DN36 . . . . .115 C2
Sykehouse DN14 . . . . .78 B4
Wheldrake YO19 . . . . .37 F7
North Leas Ave YO16 .122 E7
North Leas Dr YO16 . .122 E7
North Leas Wlk YO16 .122 E7
North Leys Rd HU19 . . .75 B4
North Lincoln Rd
DN16 . . . . .151 D6
North Lindsey Coll
DN17 . . . . .150 E4
North Marine Dr
YO15 . . . . .123 A4
North Marine Rd 1 YO15 .5 B3
North Marsh Rd HU11 . .91 B3
North Moor 7 YO32 . .127 F5
North Moor Dr 1 DN10 116 C3
North Moor Gdns
YO32 . . . . .127 F5
North Moor La
Bottesford DN17 . . . . .96 B1
Cottingham HU16 . . . . . . .139 D8
Messingham DN17 . . . . . .107 B8
North Moor Rd
3 Flamborough YO15 . . . .5 B3
Messingham DN17 . . . . . .107 C6
Walkeringham DN10 . . . . .116 C3
York YO32 . . . . .127 F5
North Moss La DN41 . .101 C4
North Newbald Becksies
Nature Reserve*
YO43 . . . . .53 F8
North Ormsby Medieval
Village* LN11 . . . . .121 A3
North Parade
Scunthorpe DN16 . . . . . .151 D2
York YO30 . . . . .156 A3
North Pinfold Way 2
YO16 . . . . .122 D6
North Pk HU12 . . . . . . .58 F2
North Promenade
Cleethorpes DN35 . . . . . .153 E3
Withernsea HU19 . . . . .75 A7
North Quay DN31 . . . .153 A7
North Rd Atwick YO25 . .35 C6
Bewholme YO25 . . . . .35 A5
Halsham HU12 . . . . .73 F6
Hatfield HU11 . . . . .46 C5
Keadby with Althorpe
DN17 . . . . .95 C6
Kingston upon Hull HU4 . .144 E4
Lund YO25 . . . . .31 F3
Ulrome YO25 . . . . .23 A4
Withernsea HU19 . . . . .74 F7
North Rise 2 HU12 . . . .73 A6
North Sea La DN36 . . .103 D1
North St Aldbrough HU11 .47 C1
Barmby on the Marsh
DN14 . . . . .64 A7
Barrow upon Humber
DN19 . . . . .85 D8
Bridlington YO15 . . . . . .122 E2
Caistor LN7 . . . . .111 B4
Cleethorpes DN35 . . . . . .153 F2

North St continued
Crowle DN17 . . . . .94 D8
6 Gainsborough DN21 . .117 A2
Goole DN14 . . . . .149 D4
Great Driffield YO25 . . . .124 E5
Kingston upon Hull HU2 . .155 A3
Kirk Ella HU10 . . . . .143 E6
Leven HU17 . . . . .45 A8
Nafferton YO25 . . . . .125 E8
Owston Ferry DN9 . . . . . .106 B3
1 Scunthorpe DN15 . . . .151 B8
West Butterwick DN17 . . . .95 D1
West/East Butterwick
DN17 . . . . .106 D8
York YO1 . . . . .156 B2
North Thoresby Prim Sch
DN36 . . . . .114 A1
North Townside Rd
YO25 . . . . .33 F8
North Turnpike YO25 . .23 A4
North View
Beverley HU17 . . . . .137 C4
Skidby HU20 . . . . .55 B4
North View Terr YO15 .122 F3
North Walls HU1 . . . . .155 C2
North Warren Rd
DN21 . . . . .117 A1
North Way DN36 . . . . .115 B2
Northampton Rd
DN16 . . . . .151 C5
North's La DN37 . . . . .112 D8
Northcote Ave YO24 . .129 E3
Northcott Specl Sch
HU7 . . . . .56 F5
Northcroft 5 YO32 . . . .13 F5
Northcroft 13 HU8 . . .141 E7
North-dale Ct 2 DN21 .108 B2
Northdale Pk 3 HU14 . .69 B7
Northern Acad of Performing
Arts HU1 . . . . .155 A2
Northern Ave 3 DN8 . .98 C3
Northern Backlight Theatre
YO31 . . . . .156 C4
Northern Gateway
HU9 . . . . .147 A7
Northern Gateway Rd
HU9 . . . . .147 A7
Northferry La DN9 . . . .94 C1
Northfield 3 Barlby YO8 .49 B5
Rimswell HU19 . . . . .74 F7
Swanland HU14 . . . . .69 B7
Northfield Ave
Great Driffield YO25 . . . .124 F6
Kingston upon Hull
HU13 . . . . .143 E3
Northfield Cl
Driffield YO25 . . . . .124 F6
2 Pocklington YO42 . . . . .28 C1
1 Scunthorpe DN16 . . . .151 C2
5 South Cave HU15 . . . . .53 F1
2 Tetney DN36 . . . . .114 D4
West Butterwick DN17 . . . .95 D1
Womersley DN6 . . . . .76 C6
Northfield Cotts DN6 . .96 D1
Northfield Cres YO25 .124 F5
Northfield Inf Sch
YO25 . . . . .124 F6
Northfield La
Amcotts DN17 . . . . .81 F2
Kirton in Lindsey DN21 . . .119 B8
3 Riccall YO19 . . . . .36 F1
Thornton Curtis DN39 . . . .85 D5
Welwick HU12 . . . . .90 A8
Willoughton DN21 . . . . . . .119 A4
Womersley DN6 . . . . .76 C7
Northfield Rd
Beverley HU17 . . . . .136 C6
Bubwith YO8 . . . . .50 E8
Coniston HU11 . . . . .57 F7
Great Driffield YO25 . . . .124 E6
Kingston upon Hull HU3 . .144 F6
Market Weighton YO43 . . .135 E4
Messingham DN17 . . . . . .107 D8
Pocklington YO42 . . . . . . .28 F4
Wetwang YO25 . . . . .19 A6
Northfield Rise 7 YO42 .28 F4
Northfield Sch YO26 . .129 B5
Northfield Terr YO24 . .132 E8
Northfield Wlk YO25 . .124 F6
Northfields
Barmby Moor YO42 . . . . . .28 D4
5 Strensall YO32 . . . . . . .14 B8
Northgate
Cottingham HU16 . . . . . . .139 A7
Hornsea HU18 . . . . .134 C5
Hunmanby YO14 . . . . .2 F8
Northfield HU13 . . . . .143 E2
Thorne/Moorends DN8 . . . .79 B2
Walkington HU17 . . . . .55 B8
Northgate Gr YO43 . . .135 C4
Northgate La YO41 . . . .15 A3
Northgate Vale YO43 . .135 C4
Northlands Ave
1 Earswick YO32 . . . . . .127 F7
2 Winterton DN15 . . . . . .83 A5
Northlands Rd DN15 . . .83 A6
Northlands Rd S DN15 .83 A5
Northminster Bsns Pk
YO26 . . . . .24 F7
Northmoor Rd DN17 . . .80 C1
Northolmby St 20 DN14 .65 A7
Northolme DN21 . . . . .117 B1
Northolme Circ 2
HU13 . . . . .143 E2
Northolme Cres
Kingston upon Hull
HU13 . . . . .143 E2

Northolme Cres continued
Scunthorpe DN15 . . . . . . .150 F7
Northolme Dr YO30 . . .126 E1
Northolme Rd HU13 . . .143 E2
Northolt Cl HU8 . . . . . .141 E6
Northorpe Cl HU9 . . . .142 C1
Northorpe Rd DN21 . . .107 D1
Northorpe Rise YO16 . .122 B5
Northorpe Wlk YO16 . .122 B5
Northside Haxey DN9 . .105 C2
Laxton DN14 . . . . .65 F4
Patrington HU12 . . . . .74 D1
Northside Ct 6 HU12 . . .74 D1
Northside Rd HU19 . . . .75 A4
Northstead Cl HU10 . . .138 E1
Northumberland Ave
Hornsea HU18 . . . . .134 B5
Kingston upon Hull HU2 . .155 B4
Northumberland Cl
DN34 . . . . .152 B2
Northway Fulstow LN11 .114 A1
Goole DN14 . . . . .149 B6
Northwood Cl HU8 . . . .142 C6
Northwood Dr HU13 . . .143 B3
Norton & Kirk Smeat
WF8 . . . . .76 C3
Norton Comm La DN6 . .76 F2
Norton Comm Rd DN6 . .77 A1
Norton Gr HU4 . . . . . . .144 D4
Norton La LN8 . . . . . . .119 F2
Norton Mill La DN6 . . . .76 E2
Norton Priory DN6 . . . .76 E2
Norton Rd DN16 . . . . . .151 B1
Norton St HU17 . . . . . .154 A1
Norway Dr YO10 . . . . . .133 D8
Norwich Ave 3 DN34 . .102 D2
Norwich Ct HU17 . . . . .136 E1
Norwood HU17 . . . . . . .154 B4
Norwood Ave DN15 . . .150 F6
Norwood Cl 3 HU10 . . .143 E7
Norwood Ct HU10 . . . . .154 B4
Norwood Dale HU17 . . .154 A3
Norwood Far Gr HU17 .154 B4
Norwood Gr HU17 . . . .154 B4
Norwood Rd DN7 . . . . . .92 C5
Norwood St HU3 . . . . . .145 C7
Noseley Way 31 HU7 . . .56 F6
Nostell Gr YO16 . . . . . .122 D7
Nostell Rd DN16 . . . . . .151 D5
Nostell Way YO16 . . . .122 D7
Nottingham Rd 6 HU11 .47 C1
Nouth-dale Cl 2 DN21 .108 B2
Nova Scotia Way 4
YO19 . . . . .49 A8
Novello Garth HU4 . . . .144 B4
Nuffield Cl 6 DN16 . . . .96 D2
Nun Monkton Foundation
Prim Sch YO26 . . . . .12 A5
Nunburnholme Ave
HU14 . . . . .69 A4
Nunburnholme Hill
YO42 . . . . .29 F3
Nunburnholme Pk
HU4 . . . . .144 B7
Nunmill St YO23 . . . . .130 C2
Nunnerley Pl DN17 . . . .113 E7
Nunnery Hill* YO25 . . . . .21 F6
Nunnery La 1 DN7 . . . .156 B1
Nunnery Wlk 4 HU15 . .53 F1
Nunnington Cl HU5 . . .140 B2
Nuns Rd DN17 . . . . .150 F2
Nunsthorpe Com Sch
DN33 . . . . .102 D2
Nunsthorpe Jun Sch
DN33 . . . . .102 D2
Nunthorpe Ave YO23 . .130 B2
Nunthorpe Cl 7 DN7 . . .92 D4
Nunthorpe Cres YO23 .130 B2
Nunthorpe Gr YO23 . . .130 B2
Nunthorpe Rd YO23 . . .156 A1
Nurseries The HU17 . . .136 D7
Nursery Cl
3 Barton-upon-Humber
DN18 . . . . .69 F1
19 Hemingbrough YO8 . . .49 F1
Kingston upon Hull HU4 . .144 B5
Scunthorpe DN17 . . . . . . .96 C2
Thorngumbald HU12 . . . . . .72 E5
Nursery Ct
14 Brough HU15 . . . . . . .68 C5
Nether Poppleton YO26 . . .126 A2
Nursery Dr YO24 . . . . .129 E3
Nursery Gdns
Beverley HU17 . . . . .154 A1
17 Holton le Clay DN36 . .114 A5
York YO10 . . . . .131 C3
Nursery Gr YO16 . . . . .122 B5
Nursery Rd YO26 . . . . .126 A2
Nursery Vale DN21 . . . .117 A3
Nursery Wlk HU16 . . . .139 D6
Nutana Ave HU16 . . . . .134 C7
Nutfields Gr 8 DN7 . . . .92 C6
Nuttles La HU12 . . . . . . .58 E2
Nutwood View 22 DN16 .96 E2

0

Oak Ave Brough HU15 . .68 C6
Goole DN14 . . . . .149 D1
Grimsby DN32 . . . . .102 F2
Kingston upon Hull
HU10 . . . . .138 D1
Scawby DN20 . . . . .108 F8
Withernsea HU19 . . . . .75 A5
Oak Cl Beverley HU17 . .137 A6

Oak Cl continued
Sproatley HU11 . . . . .58 C5
Oak Cres 7 DN8 . . . . . .79 A1
Oak Dene DN14 . . . . . .149 E6
Oak Dr
Kingston upon Hull HU4 . .144 B7
Newport HU15 . . . . .52 F1
5 Thorpe Willoughby YO8 .48 B1
Oak Field YO8 . . . . . . .148 A1
Oak Glade 6 YO31 . . . .127 F3
Oak Gr
9 Barnetby le Beck DN38 . .99 B4
Barrow upon Humber
DN19 . . . . .85 C7
9 Hedon HU12 . . . . .72 C7
Oak Hill HU10 . . . . .138 C2
Oak Rd Healing DN41 . .101 F5
Kingston upon Hull HU6 . .140 D5
2 North Duffield YO8 . . . .50 A7
Scunthorpe DN16 . . . . . .151 B3
Thorne/Moorends DN8 . . . .79 A1
Oak Rise 4 YO26 . . . . .129 C3
Oak Sq 3 HU17 . . . . . . .56 F7
Oak St 3 YO26 . . . . . . .129 C5
Oak Tree Ave 14 DN21 .117 C1
Oak Tree Cl
Beverley HU17 . . . . .136 D6
Strensall YO32 . . . . .14 B7
Oak Tree Ct
Bubwith YO8 . . . . .50 D7
4 Wigginton YO32 . . . . .127 C7
Oak Tree Dr HU17 . . . .136 D6
Oak Tree Est 10 HU12 . .58 C1
Oak Tree Gr YO32 . . . .127 D3
Oak Tree La YO32 . . . . .127 C7
Oak Tree Way 10 YO32 . .14 B7
Oak Way DN35 . . . . . . .103 B1
Oakdale Ave 3 HU10 . .143 E8
Oakdale Cl 6 DN14 . . . .78 C8
Oakdale Rd YO30 . . . . .126 F2
Oakdene HU16 . . . . . . .139 B6
Oakfield DN20 . . . . .98 D2
Oakfield Cl 1 HU6 . . . .139 F4
Oakfield Prim Sch
DN16 . . . . .151 A3
Oakford Cl DN17 . . . . .150 D4
Oakhill Cres 3 YO32 . . .14 A6
Oakington Garth HU7 . .141 C8
Oakland Ave
83 Hatfield DN7 . . . . .92 D4
York YO31 . . . . .131 A7
Oakland Dr YO31 . . . . .131 A7
Oaklands
Beckingham DN10 . . . . . .116 D1
Camblesforth YO8 . . . . . . .63 C5
Gilberdyke HU15 . . . . .66 D8
Hornsea HU18 . . . . .134 D2
Hutton Cranswick YO25 . . .32 E6
6 Strensall YO32 . . . . . . .14 B7
Oaklands Ave 3 DN14 . .65 B7
Oaklands Cres YO8 . . . .63 C5
Oaklands Dr
Northfield HU13 . . . . .143 D3
Willerby HU10 . . . . .138 C1
Oaklands Rd DN40 . . . . .87 C2
Oaklands Sec Sch
YO24 . . . . .129 C2
Oaklands Small Sch
DN14 . . . . .64 E4
Oaklands Sports Ctr
YO24 . . . . .129 C2
Oakleigh 9 DN16 . . . . . .96 E2
Oakmoor Gr DN8 . . . . . .79 B2
Oakmoor Rd DN8 . . . . . .79 B2
Oakney Wood Dr YO8 . .148 D1
Oaks La DN16 . . . . .116 C2
Oaktree Dr 4 HU7 . . . . .141 D7
Oakville St YO31 . . . . . .130 D7
Oakwell Ave YO16 . . . .123 A6
Oakwell Gr 2 HU8 . . . .141 B1
Oakwood Cl HU4 . . . . . .144 A4
Oakwood Dr DN37 . . . .102 B3
Oakwood Pk DN14 . . . . .77 F6
Oakwood Rise 1 DN16 . .96 D2
Oatlands Rd HU6 . . . . .123 A6
Oban Ave HU9 . . . . .142 A2
Oban Ct 32 DN40 . . . . . .87 B1
Occupation La
North Kelsey LN7 . . . . . . .110 A4
Swanland HU14 . . . . .69 B8
Ocean Bvd HU9 . . . . . .146 B6
Ocean Dr 7 HU15 . . . . .52 F1
Ochrepit Hill YO42 . . . . .17 A2
Octagon The HU10 . . . .138 D1
Octon Rd YO25 . . . . .9 A8
Odin Ct DN31 . . . . .102 D2
Ogilvy Dr DN17 . . . . . . .96 C2
Ogle Rd 11 YO15 . . . . . . .5 B2
Ogleforth YO31 . . . . . .156 B3
O'hanlon Ave DN20 . . . .98 C2
Old Annandale Rd
HU10 . . . . .143 C5
Old Boys Sch La 4 YO8 .48 B8
Old Bridge Rd HU18 . . .134 C4
Old Brumby St DN16 . . .151 A4
Old Carpenter's Yd
DN7 . . . . .92 B6
Old Chapel Cl 2 HU11 . .45 C1
Old Chapel La DN37 . . .101 F1
Old Clee Jun & Inf Sch
DN32 . . . . .153 B2
Old Coppice 14 YO32 . . .13 F5
Old Courts Rd DN20 . . . .98 C2
Old Crosby DN16 . . . . . .96 D7
Old Ct HU17 . . . . .136 D5
Old Dairy DN19 . . . . . . .85 D7
Old Dike Lands YO32 . .127 C8
Old Epworth Rd E DN7 . .92 F4

Old Farm Cl HU12 . . . . .73 E3
Old Farm Ct 5 DN37 . .113 D6
Old Farm Way YO8 . . . .148 B2
Old Field La DN7 . . . . . .92 A5
Old Fleet 2 DN37 . . . . .102 B3
Old Forge Rd 4 DN10 . .116 C5
Old Forge Way HU11 . . .45 D2
Old Gn La YO41 . . . . . . .28 A5
Old Hall La YO41 . . . . . .27 C5
Old Haxey Rd DN10 . . .116 C6
Old House Gdns YO8 . . .62 A5
Old Howe La YO25 . . . . .22 A3
Old Ironside Rd DN15 .151 D7
Old La Blacktoft DN14 . . .66 C4
Hirst Courtney YO8 . . . . . .62 F3
Long Marston YO26 . . . . . .24 A6
Reedness DN14 . . . . .80 E7
Sigglesthorne HU11 . . . . . .45 F8
Old Lea YO43 . . . . .40 B1
Old Leys La DN21 . . . . .119 C3
Old Main Rd
Barnetby le Beck DN37 . . .113 B6
Irby DN37 . . . . .112 D7
Old Manor Dr DN20 . . .108 E8
Old Manor Lawns
HU17 . . . . .154 B2
Old Mill Cl YO43 . . . . . .135 F3
Old Mill La
7 Broughton DN20 . . . . . .97 E3
Whitton DN15 . . . . .67 E3
Wrawby DN20 . . . . .98 D4
Old Mkt Pl 6 DN16 . . . .151 D3
Old Moor La YO24 . . . . .132 E7
Old Orchard YO32 . . . .127 D8
Old Orchard The
Fulford YO10 . . . . .133 E7
Shipton YO30 . . . . .12 F5
Old Penny Memories*
YO15 . . . . .122 F2
Old Plumtree La 2
DN36 . . . . .114 B1
Old Pond Pl 16 HU14 . . .69 A4
Old Post Office La
Barnetby le Wold DN38 . . .99 B4
5 South Ferriby DN18 . . . .84 A7
Old Rd Healing DN41 . .102 B5
Holme-on-Spalding-Moor
YO43 . . . . .40 B1
Leconfield HU17 . . . . .43 C6
Ottringham HU12 . . . . . . .73 E3
Old Rectory Gdns
DN16 . . . . .151 A1
Old Row The DN15 . . . .82 A4
Old Rugby Pk DN14 . . .149 C5
Old Sch Dr DN20 . . . . .108 F5
Old Sch La
Allerthorpe DN17 . . . . . . .95 D5
Barlby with Osgodby YO8 . .49 B5
Keadby DN17 . . . . .95 D5
North Kelsey LN7 . . . . . . .110 A4
20 Scunthorpe DN16 . . . .96 D2
Old Sch The
Kirk Bramwith DN7 . . . . . .92 A7
Roxby cum Risby DN15 . . .82 F4
Old Sch Yd 8 DN21 . . .108 B1
Old Showfields 8 DN21 .117 B1
Old Smithy & Heritage Ctr
The* DN9 . . . . .106 B3
Old Sunderlandwick La
YO25 . . . . .20 D1
Old Tatham YO43 . . . . . .40 B1
Old Thorne Rd DN7 . . . .92 E4
Old Trent Rd DN10 . . . .116 F1
Old Trough La HU15 . . . .52 C2
Old Vicarage La 5 LS25 .61 A8
Old Vicarage Pk DN20 .108 E8
Old Village Rd HU20 . . .55 A4
Old Village St DN15 . . . .95 E6
Old Village The YO32 . .127 E6
Old Warp La DN18 . . . . .84 A7
Old Waste HU17 . . . . . .154 A3
Oldbeck Rd HU17 . . . . .137 C4
Oldfield Ave HU6 . . . . .140 C6
Oldfield Cl
Barnby Dun DN3 . . . . .92 A4
Stainforth DN7 . . . . .92 B6
Oldfield Cres DN7 . . . . .92 C6
Oldfield La DN7 . . . . . . .92 B6
Oldfield Rd 11 DN8 . . . .93 B7
Oldfleet Prim Sch
HU9 . . . . .142 E2
Oldlane Gate DN14 . . . .80 D4
Oldman Ct YO24 . . . . . .132 C8
Oldstead Ave HU6 . . . .139 F5
Olinda Rd 2 YO15 . . . . .122 E2
Oliver Ct DN31 . . . . . . .152 D4
Oliver St DN35 . . . . . . .153 D4
Oliver's Cl 18 YO14 . . . . .2 F8
Olivers La YO16 . . . . . .122 E3
Olivier Ct HU4 . . . . . . .144 E3
Olympia Cres YO8 . . . .148 E6
Olympian Ct YO10 . . . .130 F4
Ombler Cl 11 HU12 . . . . .73 C4
Omega Bvd DN8 . . . . . . .92 F8
Omega Cl YO16 . . . . . . .123 A5
Omega Rd YO16 . . . . . .122 F5
On Hill HU14 . . . . .69 B6
Ontario Rd DN17 . . . . . .96 B2
Onyx Gr 2 HU3 . . . . . . .145 A4
Oole Rd DN35 . . . . .153 F2
Opsa Bsns Ctr YO1 . . .156 B2
Orb La DN15 . . . . .96 D8
Orby Gr 6 DN33 . . . . . .102 D2
Orchard Ave 8 DN21 . .107 C3

Orchard Cl
2 Barrow upon Humber DN19 85 C7
13 Barton-upon-Humber DN18 84 F8
Blyton DN21 117 F5
Bridlington YO16 122 E7
3 Burringham DN17 95 D4
Burton upon Stather DN15 82 B5
Driffield YO25 125 E7
Great Driffield YO25 124 D5
Hatfield DN7 92 C3
Kingston upon Hull HU10 143 F7
2 Kirton in Lindsey DN21 108 B1
Messingham DN17 107 D7
6 Monk Fryston LS25 61 A8
Morton DN21 117 A3
9 Norton DN6 76 E2
10 Pocklington YO42 28 F4
Roos HU12 74 A8
2 Scunthorpe DN16 151 B2
Selby YO8 148 A4
Wilberfoss YO41 27 E6
York YO24 129 E1
Orchard Cotts 4 YO19 26 F7
Orchard Croft
3 Epworth DN9 105 D7
10 Grimsby DN33 113 E8
Kingston upon Hull HU16 139 B8
Orchard Ct
3 Market Weighton YO43 135 E4
10 Waltham DN37 113 D6
Orchard Dr
Burton upon Stather DN15 82 B5
Goole DN14 65 C4
Gunness DN15 95 E6
Hatfield DN7 92 C3
Kingston upon Hull HU13 143 E1
Middleton-on-the-Wolds YO25 31 C4
1 Winteringham DN15 66 B1
Orchard End 20 YO8 49 F1
Orchard Garth
Beverley HU17 136 D6
Copmanthorpe YO23 132 B2
Orchard Gdns
4 Pocklington YO42 28 F4
York YO31 127 E2
Orchard Gr Hatfield DN7 92 D5
Misterton DN10 116 D4
Orchard La
Great Driffield YO25 124 E5
Hutton Cranswick YO25 32 E8
Thorne/Moorends DN8 79 B2
Orchard Paddock
34 Haxby YO32 13 E5
3 Haxby YO32 127 D8
Orchard Pk YO42 39 B6
Orchard Pk Rd HU6 139 F8
Orchard Rd
Kingston upon Hull HU4 144 B5
Selby YO8 148 A4
Skidby HU16 138 A8
Upper Poppleton YO26 126 A1
Orchard St DN8 93 A8
Orchard The
Beverley HU17 137 F8
Bishopthorpe YO25 133 A3
Fangfoss YO41 28 C8
Heslington YO10 131 A1
Kingston upon Hull HU9 142 B4
Leven HU17 45 A7
14 New Waltham DN36 114 A7
Orchard View 3 YO30 126 B5
Orchard Way
1 Gilberdyke HU15 66 D7
Hensall DN14 62 C2
Howden DN14 65 A6
9 Pocklington YO42 28 F4
Selby YO8 148 A4
Skirlaugh HU11 45 D2
1 Strensall YO32 14 B7
Thorpe Willoughby YO8 48 B2
York YO24 129 E1
Orchards The YO25 32 E8
Orchid Rise DN15 150 F6
Ordnance La YO10 130 D1
Ore Blending Rd DN16 97 A4
Oribi Cl HU4 144 C2
Oriel Cl 6 HU17 55 D8
Oriel Gr
Kingston upon Hull HU9 142 A1
York YO30 130 A8
Oriole Rd DN17 150 E2
Orion Cl 8 HU3 145 B5
Orion Way DN34 102 B2
Orkney Cl 7 HU8 141 E7
Orkney Pl 11 DN40 87 C1
Ormerod Cres 7 HU5 139 D2
Ormerod Rd HU5 139 D2
Ormesby Wlk 9 HU5 139 D3
Ormonde Ave HU6 140 D4
Ormsby Cl 9 DN35 103 B2
Ormsby Rd DN17 150 E1
Orniscourt HU6 139 F7
Orrin Cl YO24 132 C7
Orwell St DN31 152 F5
Osbaldwick La YO10 131 B4
Osbaldwick Link Rd YO19 131 D4
Osbaldwick Prim Sch YO10 131 C4
Osbaldwick Village YO10 131 C4
Osborne Dr DN36 114 A5
Osborne Rd DN41 101 E8
Osborne St
Cleethorpes DN35 153 F2
Grimsby DN31 152 D3
Kingston upon Hull HU1 155 A2
Osbourne Dr
Keyingham HU12 73 D4
4 York YO30 126 E3
Oshawa Dell YO42 29 A2
Oslear Cres DN35 153 E1
Oslo Rd HU7 140 F6
Osmington Gdns 10 YO32 14 A7
Osprey Cl
Kingston upon Hull HU6 140 B8
4 York YO24 132 B8
Ossett Cl HU8 141 C1
Ostler's Cl YO23 132 C3
Ostler's La DN18 84 A5
Ostman Rd YO26 129 C5
Oswald Rd DN15 151 A7
Otley Cl HU9 142 C2
Ottawa Cl 6 HU16 138 F5
Ottawa Rd 6 DN17 96 C2
Otterbirch Wharf HU17 137 B3
Otterburn St 6 HU3 145 A5
Otterwood Bank 6 YO24 129 B1
Otterwood La YO24 129 B1
Otterwood Paddock YO41 15 C2
Ottringham Rd HU12 73 D4
Oubrough La HU11 57 F8
Oundle Cl 5 DN16 96 E2
Our Ladys RC Prim Sch YO24 129 E1
Ouse Acres YO26 129 D6
Ouse Bank YO8 148 E5
Ouse Carr La DN14 65 A5
Ouse Lea YO30 130 A7
Ouseburn Ave YO26 129 C6
Ousecliffe Gdns YO30 130 A6
Ousegate YO8 148 D5
Out Gates Foston YO25 22 B3
Harpham YO25 21 E6
Out Holme La DN36 114 E3
Out Newton Rd
Holmpton HU19 75 C1
Skeffling HU12 90 D6
Outer Trinities HU17 154 B2
Outgaits Cl 4 YO14 2 F8
Outgaits La YO14 3 A8
Outgang La YO19 131 D6
Outgang The
Brantingham HU15 68 B7
South Cliffe YO43 53 B6
Outgate DN17 94 E6
Outlands Rd HU16 139 D5
Outram Cl HU2 155 A4
Outstray Rd HU12 89 C7
Oval The Brough HU15 68 C6
Grimsby DN33 102 E1
Hatfield DN7 92 C5
Kellingley DN14 61 C3
Kirk Ella HU10 143 E8
Pocklington YO42 29 A4
23 Scunthorpe DN17 96 C2
Summergangs HU8 141 C2
Overdale Cl YO24 132 D8
Overland Rd HU16 139 C5
Overstrand Dr HU7 141 D6
Overton Ave HU10 143 E8
Overton Ct 6 DN18 69 F1
Overton Rd YO30 12 F3
Ovington Terr YO23 130 B2
Owbridge Ct HU2 155 A2
Owen Ave HU13 144 A1
Owlwood Ct 7 YO19 26 E7
Owlwood La 6 YO19 26 E7
Owmby Hill DN38 110 D8
Owmby La LN7 110 C5
Owmby Mount DN38 110 D8
Owmby Rd DN38 110 D8
Owmby Wold La DN38 110 E8
Owst Rd HU12 73 C4
Owsthorpe La DN14 52 A1
Owston Ave 2 YO10 131 A3
Owston Ferry Rd DN9 116 E8
Owston Rd
1 Hunmanby YO14 2 F8
West Stockwith DN10 116 E6
Owthorne Cl YO16 122 B6
Owthorne Grange HU19 74 F6
Owthorne Wlk
Bridlington YO16 122 B5
Withernsea HU19 74 F7
Ox Calder Cl 16 YO19 26 F7
Ox Carr La YO32 14 B6
Ox Cl YO41 15 D2
Ox Pasture La DN17 81 C2
Oxcombe Cl DN37 113 D8
Oxen La YO8 49 E3
Oxenhope Rd HU6 140 D7
Oxford Cl 6 HU17 136 E1
Oxford Rd DN14 149 C5
Oxford St
Bridlington YO16 122 D3
Cleethorpes DN35 153 F1
Grimsby DN32 153 A4
Kingston upon Hull HU2 155 C4
Scunthorpe DN16 151 D2
5 York YO24 130 A3
Oxmardyke La HU15 66 E6
Oxmarsh La DN19 70 E2
Oyster Ct DN35 153 F1

P

Packman La HU10 143 B8
Paddock Cl
Askham Richard YO23 24 D3
Copmanthorpe YO23 132 A2
Paddock Ct
Bridlington YO16 122 E7
Great Driffield YO25 124 F5
33 Immingham DN40 87 B1
Paddock La
Blyton DN21 117 F5
West Butterwick DN17 95 C1
Paddock La E DN21 117 F5
Paddock Rise 8 DN19 85 C8
Paddock The
14 Airmyn DN14 64 E4
Beverley HU17 136 D6
1 Buckton/Bempton YO15 4 D3
3 Burton upon Stather DN15 82 B4
Cottingham HU16 139 C6
East Ella HU4 144 B5
13 Gilberdyke HU15 66 D8
1 North Ferriby HU14 69 A5
8 Selby YO8 148 C6
2 Swanland HU14 69 C7
Wilberfoss YO41 27 E5
York YO26 129 C6
Paddock Way YO26 129 C6
Paddocks The
Barnoldby le Beck DN37 113 B6
Beckingham DN10 116 D1
6 Crowle DN17 94 D7
Great Driffield YO25 124 D3
Hutton Cranswick YO25 32 E7
Kingston upon Hull HU10 143 B7
Middleton YO25 31 C4
Pademoor Terr DN17 81 A2
Padstow Cl 7 HU7 56 F5
Padstow Wlk DN17 150 C4
Pagehall Cl DN33 102 E1
Paghill Est HU12 72 A5
Pagnell Ave YO8 148 E4
Paignton Ct DN33 113 E7
Painsthorpe La YO41 17 B5
Paisley Prim Sch HU3 145 A6
Paisley St HU3 145 A7
Palace Ave YO15 122 E2
Palanza Terr 8 YO15 122 E2
Pale La YO8 61 F7
Palmcourt HU6 139 F7
Palmer Ave HU10 143 D8
Palmer Gr YO8 148 A3
Palmer La
Barrow upon Humber DN19 85 D8
York YO1 156 C2
Palmes Cl YO19 36 E8
Pam Cl 19 DN40 87 C1
Pamela Rd DN40 87 C1
Panama Dr HU11 45 D2
Panman La YO19 26 F8
Paper Mill Rd DN14 79 B8
Parade Ct YO31 130 F6
Parade The HU5 140 D1
Paradise Cotts YO17 17 F8
Paradise Pl 9 Brigg DN20 98 B2
3 Goole DN14 149 D4
Paradise Sq HU17 154 B2
Paragon Sq HU1 155 A2
Paragon St
Kingston upon Hull HU1 155 A2
York YO10 156 C1
Parcevall Dr 32 HU7 56 F5
Parish Church Prim Sch DN21 117 B1
Parishes Sh Ctr The DN15 151 B7
Park Ave Barlow YO8 63 C7
Barton-upon-Humber DN18 84 E8
Beverley HU17 154 A4
1 Brandesburton YO25 34 B2
Bridlington YO15 122 F3
Cottingham HU16 139 A7
Crowle DN17 94 D7
Goole DN14 149 B5
Great Driffield YO25 124 E6
Grimsby DN32 152 D1
Misterton DN10 116 C6
New Earswick YO32 127 D5
Northfield HU13 143 E3
Scunthorpe DN17 96 C2
Snaith DN14 78 D8
Withernsea HU19 75 A6
Park Ave W HU5 140 A1
Park Cl 6 Airmyn DN14 64 E4
Great Driffield YO25 124 E5
Immingham DN40 87 C1
Melbourne YO42 39 A7
Skelton YO30 126 B4
Westwoodside DN9 105 A2
Park Cres
11 Thorne/Moorends DN8 93 A7
York YO31 156 C4
Park Ct DN15 151 B8
Park Dr Campsall DN6 76 E1
Grimsby DN32 152 E1
4 Westwoodside DN9 105 A2
Park Est YO32 127 D8
Park Farm Rd DN15 96 C8
Park Gate YO32 14 B8
Park Gdns 5 DN14 78 C8
Park Gr
Kingston upon Hull HU5 140 C1
Selby YO8 148 B3
York YO31 156 C4
Park Gr Sch YO31 156 C4
Park Hill DN21 108 B1
Park La Balne DN14 77 C5
Barlow YO8 63 C7
Bishop Wilton YO42 16 F1
Burn YO8 62 D7
Humberston DN35 103 C1
Luttons YO17 7 C8
Redbourne DN21 108 F3
Rowley HU17 55 B6
Saxby All Saints DN20 84 A3
Scawby DN20 108 F8
Snaith & Cowick DN14 78 C6
Tickton HU17 44 D2
Westwoodside DN9 105 A2
Wilberfoss YO41 27 E5
Womersley DN6 76 D6
York YO24 129 F3
Park La Cl
Bishop Wilton YO42 16 F1
Hatfield DN7 92 C2
Park La E HU4 144 C6
Park La Rd DN7 92 C2
Park La W HU4 144 C5
Park Lodge YO32 127 D4
Park Pl YO31 156 C4
Park Rd Airmyn DN14 64 E4
Barlow YO8 63 C7
Brough HU15 68 E5
Dalton Holme HU17 42 C8
Kingston upon Hull HU3 140 D1
Sproatley HU11 58 C5
Thorne/Moorends DN8 79 B2
Park Rise 17 YO14 2 F8
Park Rose E Coast Leisure & Ret Park★ YO15 10 F3
Park Row
Hornsea HU18 134 D4
Kingston upon Hull HU3 145 D7
Northfield HU13 143 E2
Selby YO8 148 D5
Sproatley HU11 58 C5
Park Sq DN15 151 A6
Park St
Cleethorpes DN35 153 B4
Hotham YO43 53 D5
Kingston upon Hull HU3 145 D6
Messingham DN17 107 D7
Selby YO8 148 D5
Swinefleet DN14 80 D8
Winterton DN15 83 B5
York YO24 156 A1
Park Terr YO32 127 D5
Park View
Barton-upon-Humber DN18 84 F8
2 Bridlington YO16 122 F4
Cleethorpes DN35 153 C3
Crowle DN17 94 D6
Kingston upon Hull HU4 144 E4
Messingham DN17 107 D7
10 Thorne/Moorends DN8 93 A7
Park View Cl DN19 85 C7
Park View Terr DN17 106 C8
Park Wlk HU4 144 B5
Parkdale 15 DN18 84 E8
Parker Ave YO26 129 B2
Parker Rd DN36 114 D8
Parker St DN35 153 F1
Parker's La DN16 151 C2
Parkfield Ave HU14 69 A4
Parkfield Dr
Bridlington YO16 122 B5
Kingston upon Hull HU3 144 F6
Parkhill Cres DN3 92 A4
Parkhill Rd DN3 92 A4
Parkhill Rise DN15 83 B5
Parkhurst Cl 4 HU8 142 C6
Parkin Ave YO8 148 E4
Parkin Rd DN17 96 C2
Parkinson Ave DN15 151 A7
Parkland Way YO32 127 D8
Parklands Beeford YO25 34 C8
Goole DN14 149 B5
3 West/East Butterwick DN17 106 D8
Parklands Cres 10 HU14 69 A5
Parklands Dr 9 HU14 69 A5
Parklands The 2 HU15 54 A2
Parks Cl 8 DN39 86 A1
Parks Prim Sch The HU6 139 E7
Parks Rd DN7 92 C4
Parkside YO43 135 D4
Parkside Cl
Cottingham HU16 138 F6
Newland HU5 140 B1
York YO24 129 E3
Parkside Commercial Ctr YO23 156 C1
Parkside Prim Sch DN14 149 B6
Parkstone Gr 8 DN7 92 D4
Parkstone Prim Sch HU6 140 D7
Parkstone Rd HU6 140 C7
Parkway The
Cottingham HU16 139 A5
Kirk Ella HU10 143 E8
9 Snaith DN14 78 C8
Parkways 12 Hatfield DN7 92 D4
Selby YO8 148 B3
Parkwood Jun & Inf Sch DN17 150 C4
Parkwood Rise DN3 92 A3
Parliament St
8 Brough HU15 68 D6
Goole DN14 149 C4
Kingston upon Hull HU1 155 B2
York YO1 156 B2
Parris Pl DN35 153 D3
Parsonage Cl YO25 125 E7
Parson's La DN14 65 A7
Parson's Wlk 11 DN14 64 E4
Parsons Cl 10 DN14 64 E4
Parsons La YO26 12 E1
Parthian Rd HU9 142 C3
Parthridge Cl YO15 11 B4
Partridge Cl
Caistor LN7 111 B4
Scunthorpe DN17 150 E2
Partridge Dr LN7 111 F2
Parva Rd HU18 134 D4
Pashley Rd 20 DN8 93 B7
Paston Wlk YO23 156 B1
Pasture Ave
5 Burringham DN17 95 D4
Goole DN14 149 D5
Pasture Cl Kilham YO25 9 B3
2 Leconfield HU17 43 D6
Market Weighton YO43 135 E4
Skelton YO30 126 B5
2 Strensall YO32 14 B6
Wistow YO8 48 D6
Pasture Farm Cl YO10 133 D6
Pasture Hill YO17 16 E8
Pasture House Mews HU17 136 D4
Pasture La
Amcotts DN17 81 D1
Beverley HU17 136 D4
23 Brough HU15 68 C5
Ellerton YO42 38 C1
Garthorpe & Fockerby DN17 81 D6
Heworth YO31 131 B8
Sproatley HU11 58 D6
Pasture Prim Sch DN14 149 C5
Pasture Rd
Barton-upon-Humber DN18 69 F1
Goole DN14 149 C4
Hornsea HU18 134 D4
Pasture Rd N DN18 69 F1
Pasture Rd S DN18 69 F1
Pasture Rise YO16 122 B5
Pasture St DN32 152 E3
Pasture Terr HU17 136 D4
Pasture Way YO8 48 D6
Pasture Wharf Nature Reserve★ DN18 70 A1
Pastures Ct DN17 107 D7
Pastures La HU12 60 B4
Pastures The
Carlton DN14 63 C3
Hutton Cranswick YO25 32 F7
4 York YO24 132 E8
Pately Pl 1 YO26 129 D4
Patrick Pool YO1 156 B2
Patrick St DN32 152 E1
Patricks Cl LN7 110 A4
Patrington CE VC Prim Sch HU12 74 D1
Patrington Garth HU7 141 C8
Patrington Rd
Holmpton HU19 75 C2
Ottringham HU12 73 F3
Patterdale Dr YO30 126 E1
Patterdale Rd HU5 144 E8
Paul Cres 5 DN36 114 C8
Paul La DN15 83 D1
Paul's Wlk DN17 150 B3
Paull Lands Rd HU12 72 D5
Paull Prim Sch HU12 72 A5
Paull Rd HU12 72 B6
Pavement YO1 156 B2
Paver La YO1 156 C2
Pavilion Cl HU8 141 B2
Pavilion Gdns DN17 150 F6
Pavilion Leisure Ctr 20 HU19 75 A6
Pavilion Way 18 DN36 114 A5
Paxdale HU7 140 E8
Payton Cl 17 YO42 29 A4
Peace Haven 3 DN37 113 D7
Peace Wlk 6 HU12 58 D1
Peacehaven Cl 2 HU7 141 B7
Peach Tree Cl 3 DN16 96 E2
Peach Tree Ct 5 HU3 145 D5
Peacock St DN17 150 F1
Peaks Ave DN36 114 A8
Peaks La Grimsby DN32 152 F1
New Waltham DN36 114 A8
Peaks Parkway DN32 152 E2
Peaks Parkway Ret Park DN32 152 E3
Peaksfield Ave DN32 152 F1
Pear Tree Ave
Long Drax YO8 63 F7
8 Poppleton YO26 12 F1
Pear Tree Cl
Kingston upon Hull HU8 141 D4
11 Waltham DN37 113 D6
York YO32 127 F4
Pear Tree La
Covenham St Bartholomew LN11 121 E6
Kirk Bramwith DN7 92 A8
Utterby DN36 121 B5

Pearcy Lane (Smook Hills Rd) HU19 75 A4
Pearson Ave HU5 140 D1
Pearson Prim Sch HU3 145 D8
Pearson Rd DN35 103 C2
Pearson St HU2 155 A3
Peartree Ct YO1 156 C3
Peartree Pk 19 DN14 65 A7
Pease St HU3 155 A2
Peaseholme HU13 143 C1
Peasholme Gn YO1 156 C2
Peat Carr Bank DN9 104 C3
Peckham Cl HU8 141 E5
Peckitt St YO1 156 B1
Peel Castle Rd 8 DN8 93 B7
Peel Cl YO10 131 A1
Peel Hill Rd 5 DN8 93 B7
Peel Pl HU17 136 D4
Peel St
Kingston upon Hull HU3 145 D8
York YO1 156 C1
Pefham La YO17 17 F4
Pegasus Rd DN20 99 A8
Pegasus Way DN31 102 B6
Pelham Ave 8 DN33 102 E1
Pelham Cl
5 Barton-upon-Humber DN18 84 E8
5 Beverley HU17 55 F8
Pelham Cres 15 DN41 101 A4
Pelham Dr 1 HU9 146 C7
Pelham Ind Est DN40 87 C2
Pelham Pl
9 Grimsby DN33 102 E1
15 Strensall YO32 14 A7
Pelham Rd
Cleethorpes DN35 153 D3
Grimsby DN34 152 C2
1 Holton le Clay DN36 114 A5
Immingham DN40 87 C1
Pelham Sq DN35 153 E3
Pelham View DN20 108 F5
Pelham's Pillar* DN37 111 C6
Pem La 7 YO42 29 A4
Pemberton Dr 3 DN36 113 F7
Pemberton St 1 HU8 146 B7
Pembroke Ave
Grimsby DN34 152 A3
13 Scunthorpe DN16 96 D2
Pembroke Gr HU9 142 A1
Pembroke Rd DN34 152 A1
Pembroke St YO30 130 B7
Pembroke Terr YO15 122 E1
Pendeen Cl 7 DN21 117 C1
Pendeen Gr HU8 141 B3
Pendle Cl 18 HU7 57 A6
Pendreth Pl DN35 153 D3
Pendrill St HU3 140 E1
Penistone Ct 2 HU9 146 D7
Penley's Gr St YO31 156 C4
Pennine Cl
Immingham DN40 87 B2
York YO32 127 F4
Pennine Rd DN8 93 A7
Pennine Way HU7 57 A6
Pennington St HU8 146 B7
Penny La Ct YO1 156 C3
Pennyholme Cl 34 HU7 56 F6
Pennyman Rd HU17 154 C4
Penrose Cl 9 HU7 56 F5
Penshurst Ave HU13 143 F3
Penshurst Rd DN35 103 B2
Pentire Cl 11 YO30 127 A1
Pentland Ave DN14 149 D5
Pentland Cl HU8 141 F7
Pentland Dr YO32 127 E3
Penwith Dr HU10 143 F7
Penyghent Ave YO31 131 A5
Peploe Cres 6 DN19 70 E2
Peploe La DN19 70 E2
Peppercorn Cl 6 YO26 129 E4
Peppercorn Wlk
Grimsby DN32 152 E3
11 Holton le Clay DN36 114 A5
Peppercorns The 2 HU15 66 D8
Peppermint Way YO8 148 A5
Peppin La LN11 121 D2
Peppleton Cl HU8 141 C4
Percival St DN15 151 A8
Percy Cl HU17 43 C6
Percy Dr 4 DN14 64 E4
Percy Rd
14 Hunmanby YO14 3 A8
Pocklington YO42 29 A4
Percy St Goole DN14 149 C1
Kingston upon Hull HU2 155 A3
Scunthorpe DN16 151 B6
York YO31 156 B3
Percy's La YO1 156 C2
Peregrine Cl HU4 144 D2
Perivale Cl HU8 142 A5
Periwinkle Ct DN14 149 E6
Perkins Cl DN37 102 C4
Permain Cl DN33 102 F1
Perran Cl HU7 141 B7
Perry St HU3 145 A6
Pershore Ave DN34 102 B2
Perth St HU5 144 F8
Perth Way 3 DN40 101 B8
Petchell Way DN32 152 E4
Peter Hill Dr YO30 130 A8
Peter La YO1 156 B2
Peterborough Rd DN16 151 B3
Petercroft Cl 5 YO19 26 F7
Petercroft La YO19 26 F7
Peterhouse Rd DN34 152 A1
Petersfield Cl HU7 141 B6
Petersham Cl 1 HU8 142 A5
Petersway YO30 156 A4
Petre Ave YO8 148 E3
Petuaria Cl HU15 68 B6
Pevensey Cl 1 HU7 141 B7
Peveril Ave DN17 150 F4
Pew Tree Cl YO41 27 E6
Pexton Rd YO25 124 B3
Pheasant Cl DN17 150 E2
Pheasant Ct 1 LN7 111 B4
Pheasant Dr 5 YO24 132 B8
Phelps Pl DN32 153 C1
Phelps St DN35 153 B5
Philadelphia Terr 2 YO23 130 B2
Philip Ave
Cleethorpes DN35 103 B2
5 Waltham DN37 113 E7
Philip Gr DN35 103 B2
Philip Larkin Cl HU6 140 C4
Philips Cres DN15 150 F7
Phillips La 4 DN37 101 F1
Phoenix Bsns Ctr DN14 149 D2
Phoenix Bvd YO26 130 A4
Phoenix Cl HU8 141 F4
Phoenix House Sch DN32 153 B4
Phoenix Parkway DN15 96 B7
Phoenix St Goole DN14 149 D4
Grimsby DN32 152 E3
Phyllis Ave DN34 152 B3
Phyllis Taylor Gdns DN32 152 D3
Picadilly Ct YO1 156 C2
Piccadilly
8 New Waltham DN36 114 A7
York YO1 156 C2
Pick Haven Garth DN14 61 F3
Pickering Ave HU18 134 D2
Pickering Gr 9 DN8 93 A7
Pickering High Sch HU4 144 C4
Pickering Pk YO25 31 C4
Pickering Rd HU4 144 C3
Pickering View HU3 144 D3
Pickerings The 17 HU14 69 A4
Picksley Cres DN36 114 A5
Pidgeon Cote La 3 DN19 86 A8
Pier Rd HU19 75 A6
Pier St HU1 155 B1
Piggy La 4 HU19 75 A6
Pighill La HU17 136 D7
Pighill Nook Rd LS25 61 C7
Pike Hills Mount YO23 132 A3
Pilgrim Ave DN40 87 C1
Pilgrim St YO31 156 B4
Pilgrim's Cl 5 DN40 86 E3
Pilgrims Way DN40 87 B1
Pilham La DN21 117 E4
Pilmar La HU12 60 B1
Pilots Way HU9 155 C1
Pimpernel Way 15 DN16 96 E2
Pinchbeck Ave DN16 151 C6
Pincheon Gn La DN14 78 D4
Pindars Way YO8 49 B4
Pinderfield Cl 7 HU9 142 A5
Pine Cl DN37 102 B5
Pine Ct 8 DN35 103 B1
Pine Hall Rd DN3 92 A3
Pine Mdws HU10 143 B8
Pine Tree Cl YO8 48 B2
Pine Tree La 1 LS25 61 A7
Pine Wlk 4 Brough HU15 68 C6
Healing DN41 102 A5
Pinefield Ave 4 DN3 92 A3
Pinefield Pl 27 HU15 68 C6
Pinefield Rd DN3 92 A3
Pinelands 4 YO32 127 D7
Pinelands Way YO10 131 C3
Pinetree Ave 5 DN21 107 C3
Pinetree Cl 4 DN20 97 E4
Pinewood DN16 96 E2
Pinewood Cl 5 YO42 29 A3
Pinewood Cres DN33 102 C2
Pinewood Ct 4 YO42 29 A3
Pinewood Dr YO8 63 D4
Pinewood Gr
2 Kingston upon Hull HU4 144 C7
6 York YO31 127 E2
Pinewood Hill 4 YO10 131 C3
Pinewood Rd 3 YO42 29 A3
Pinfold 10 Epworth DN9 105 E6
South Cave HU15 53 F1
Pinfold Cl
4 Bridlington YO16 122 D6
Hutton YO25 32 E8
5 Riccall YO19 37 A1
Pinfold Ct
3 Bridlington YO16 122 D6
4 Preston HU12 58 C1
4 York YO30 130 A7
Pinfold Gdns
Bridlington YO16 122 D6
14 Holton le Clay DN36 114 B5
Pinfold Gr YO16 122 C6
Pinfold Hill YO8 48 D6
Pinfold Ind Est YO16 122 D6
Pinfold La Asselby DN14 64 F6
Bempton YO16 4 B1
Bridlington YO16 122 C7
Burstwick HU12 73 A6
Pinfold La *continued*
Fishlake DN7 92 D8
10 Grimsby DN33 102 E1
Holton le Clay DN36 114 A5
Kirk Smeaton WF8 76 B3
Misterton DN10 116 C5
Moss DN6 77 D1
Norton DN6 76 E2
Pollington DN14 77 F6
Roos HU12 60 A1
Stallingborough DN41 101 D6
25 Thorne/Moorends DN8 93 A8
Pinfold Mdws YO16 122 C6
Pinfold Mews HU17 154 B3
Pinfold St
Bridlington YO16 122 D5
Eastrington DN14 51 F1
Howden DN14 65 A6
Pinfold View DN14 77 F6
Pinfold Way N 2 YO16 122 D5
Pingley La DN20 98 C1
Pingley Mdw DN20 98 C1
Pinkney's La YO25 124 D4
Pinney's Ct 7 DN41 101 F5
Pinsent Ct YO31 130 E8
Piper Rd YO25 32 E8
Piper's La HU11 46 C2
Pippin Ct 11 DN15 96 B7
Pippin Dr 16 DN16 96 D1
Pit La HU12 73 A4
Pitbalk Hill YO43 53 E4
Pitman Ave DN18 84 E8
Pitmoor La 5 DN39 86 A1
Pitsfold Cl 11 HU7 57 A5
Pitt St HU3 144 F7
Plains La DN8 93 F3
Plane St HU3 145 A5
Plantain Cl 14 DN16 96 E2
Plantation Cl HU17 137 B4
Plantation Dr
Barlby with Osgodby YO8 49 B5
1 South Cave HU15 53 F1
Welton HU14 68 F5
York YO26 129 C6
Plantation Gr YO26 129 C6
Plantation Rd 22 DN8 93 A8
Plantation View YO16 123 A8
Plantation Way 23 YO32 13 E5
Plaxton Bridge Rd HU17 56 C7
Pleasure Island Theme Pk* DN35 103 E1
Plimsoll Way HU9 146 B6
Plough Garth The DN14 61 F3
Plough Hill 12 LN7 111 B4
Ploughlands 1 YO32 127 C7
Ploughman's Cl YO23 132 C3
Ploughmans' La YO32 127 C7
Plover Dr 9 HU15 68 C6
Plover Sq 2 LN7 111 B4
Plowden Rd HU3 144 F5
Plowright Theatre DN15 151 A6
Plum Tree Dr DN36 115 C2
Plum Tree Rd HU11 58 D5
Plum Tree Way DN16 151 A5
Plum Tree Wlk HU15 54 A2
Plume Cl YO43 135 D5
Plumer Ave YO31 131 A5
Plumtree Hill Rd DN7 92 C7
Plumtree La 1 DN36 114 B1
Plumtree Rd HU12 72 E4
Plym Gr HU8 142 C6
Plymouth Cl 8 DN15 83 A5
Plymouth Rd DN17 150 D4
Poacher's Croft 3 DN9 94 E1
Pochard Cl 3 HU15 52 F1
Pocklington CE VC Infants Sch YO42 29 A4
Pocklington Ind Est YO42 28 F3
Pocklington La
Bishop Wilton YO42 16 F2
Huggate YO42 18 A1
Pocklington Sch YO42 28 F3
Pockthorpe La YO25 8 F2
Poffinder Wood Rd DN7 92 E7
Poles Bank DN9 104 E6
Pollard Cl YO32 127 E3
Pollington Balne CE Prim Sch DN14 77 F6
Polton Cl DN7 92 D7
Polton Toft DN7 92 D7
Pomona Way YO25 124 D3
Pond Side DN39 85 E3
Pond St 3 YO8 148 D6
Ponds Way 6 DN18 69 E1
Pontefract Rd DN14 78 A8
Pool Ct 7 DN14 149 C4
Pool Dr DN17 96 C2
Poolbank La HU15 68 E5
Poorhouse La HU9 142 C1
Poplar Cl
Burstwick HU12 73 A6
Kingston upon Hull HU4 144 A5
Skirlaugh HU11 45 E2
Poplar Ct HU7 141 C6
Poplar Dr
Beverley HU17 136 F6
Bridlington YO16 123 A6
Brigg DN20 98 C3
3 Broughton DN20 97 D3
Goole DN14 65 C3
21 Humberston DN36 103 D1
Poplar Gdns Drax YO8 63 F5
Scunthorpe DN16 151 B3
Poplar Gr
Cleethorpes DN35 153 E3
10 Hedon HU12 72 C7
1 Scotter DN21 107 C3
York YO32 127 E3
Poplar La DN21 118 A2
Poplar Rd
Cleethorpes DN35 153 E3
Hatfield DN7 92 C4
Healing DN41 101 F5
Poplar St YO26 129 E5
Poplars The
15 Brandesburton YO25 34 B2
11 Brayton YO8 48 D1
Knottingley WF11 61 A1
5 Leconfield HU17 43 D6
Poplars Way HU17 136 D1
Popple St HU9 146 B6
Poppleton Hall Gdn YO26 126 A3
Poppleton Rd YO26 129 E4
Poppleton Rd Prim Sch YO26 129 E5
Poppleton Sta YO26 24 F8
Popplewell Cl DN9 94 E2
Popplewell Terr 14 DN9 105 E6
Poppy Cl
2 Scunthorpe DN15 96 B7
Selby YO8 148 C2
Poppyfield Way 23 DN20 98 B2
Porlock Dr HU7 57 A5
Port Ave HU6 140 C8
Portal Rd YO26 129 B6
Porter St
Kingston upon Hull HU3 155 A1
Scunthorpe DN15 151 A8
Portholme Cres 7 YO8 148 C5
Portholme Ct YO8 148 C4
Portholme Dr YO8 148 C4
Portholme Rd YO8 148 C5
Portington Rd DN14 51 F1
Portisham Pl 12 YO32 14 A7
Portland Ave DN32 152 E1
Portland Mews YO16 122 C3
Portland Pl
Bridlington YO16 122 C3
Grimsby DN32 102 F2
Kingston upon Hull HU2 155 A3
Portland St
Kingston upon Hull HU2 155 A3
Rawcliffe DN14 79 B8
York YO31 156 B4
Portmadoc Cl 5 HU7 56 F7
Portman Rd DN15 96 C7
Portobello St HU9 141 F3
Portsmouth Wlk HU4 144 B4
Post Office La
Ashby cum Fenby DN37 113 D3
Humberside Airport DN39 100 A6
Whitton DN15 67 E3
Post Office Row DN14 64 A1
Post Office St 12 YO15 5 A2
Postern Cl YO23 156 B1
Postern La YO42 38 D6
Posterngate HU1 155 B2
Postill Sq YO16 122 D4
Potter Cl YO43 135 D3
Potterdale Dr HU20 55 A4
Potterill La HU7 141 D6
Potters Dr 4 YO23 132 B3
Potters Way HU18 134 C1
Pottery La YO31 130 E7
Pottinger Gdns LN7 111 A2
Potts La DN17 94 D7
Poultney Garth 4 HU12 72 D7
Powell St YO8 148 B6
Powells Cres DN16 151 B2
Pratt's La HU11 46 D3
Prec The DN17 150 D3
Precentor's Ct YO31 156 B3
Prescott Ave 9 HU15 68 C5
Prescott Gr 23 DN7 92 D4
Preston Dr 1 DN20 98 C2
Preston La DN18 84 F8
Preston Prim Sch HU12 58 D1
Preston Rd Hedon HU12 72 C8
Kingston upon Hull HU9 141 F1
Prestongate HU13 143 E1
Prestwick Ct YO26 129 B5
Pretoria St HU3 144 F5
Pretymen Cres DN36 114 A7
Price's La YO23 156 B1
Prickett Rd YO16 122 C4
Priest Cl YO14 2 F8
Priest La YO19 26 F5
Priestgate
3 Barton-upon-Humber DN18 84 F8
Kingston upon Hull HU7 141 D6
Nafferton YO25 125 F6
Priestgate Cl YO25 125 F6
Primitive Chapel La DN40 86 F2
Primrose Cl 19 DN41 101 F5
Primrose Dr 1 HU5 144 C8
Primrose Gr YO8 148 A6
Primrose Hill 9 WF11 61 A3
Primrose Pk HU17 137 D1
Primrose Vale 1 WF11 61 A2
Primrose Way
Humberston DN35 103 C1
1 Scunthorpe DN15 96 B7
Prince Albert Gdns DN32 152 E5
Prince Charles Dr 20 DN18 84 F8
Prince Philip Dr 21 DN18 84 F8
Prince St
Bridlington YO15 122 F2
Kingston upon Hull HU1 155 B2
Prince's Ave HU19 75 A6
Prince's Dock St HU1 155 B2
Prince's Rd
Cleethorpes DN35 153 E2
Kingston upon Hull HU5 140 C2
Princes Ave
Grimsby DN31 152 C3
1 Hedon HU12 72 C7
Hessle HU13 143 E1
Kingston upon Hull HU5 145 C8
Princes Gdns HU17 154 A2
Princes St 17 DN20 98 C2
Princess Alexandra Ct 14 DN17 96 C2
Princess Ave DN7 92 C6
Princess Cl YO43 135 D3
Princess Dr
22 Barton-upon-Humber DN18 84 F8
West Haddlesey YO8 62 A5
York YO26 129 D6
Princess Par YO43 135 D3
Princess Quay Sh Ctr HU1 155 B2
Princess Rd
Market Weighton YO43 135 D3
Strensall YO32 14 B7
Princess Royal Hospl The HU8 142 A6
Princess St
4 Bridlington YO15 122 F2
Goole DN14 149 C2
Immingham DN40 87 C1
Kingston upon Hull HU2 155 B3
Princess Terr 5 YO15 122 F2
Princess Way
8 Beverley HU17 55 E8
Woodmansey HU17 136 D1
Printing Office La 6 DN17 94 D8
Prior's Wlk YO26 129 D6
Priors Cl DN36 114 A7
Priory Ave 13 HU14 69 A4
Priory Cell (Rems of)* DN37 113 A2
Priory Cl
Bridlington YO16 122 E5
10 Swanland HU14 69 B7
Wilberfoss YO41 27 F6
Priory Cres
Bridlington YO16 122 E4
Kingston upon Hull HU16 139 B5
Scunthorpe DN17 151 A3
Ulceby DN39 86 A2
Priory Dr HU5 139 D2
Priory Farm Dr 4 HU4 144 D2
Priory Gr HU4 144 D3
Priory La
Barrow upon Humber DN19 85 D8
Scunthorpe DN17 150 E2
1 Snaith DN14 63 C1
Priory La Inf Sch DN17 151 A3
Priory La Jun Sch DN17 150 F2
Priory Pk HU13 144 A1
Priory Pk Cl 3 LS25 61 A8
Priory Pk Gr 2 LS25 61 B8
Priory Prim Sch HU5 139 D1
Priory Rd
Beverley HU17 154 C2
Cottingham HU5 139 C3
Grimsby DN37 102 B3
Kingston upon Hull HU16 139 B5
Scunthorpe DN17 151 A2
Priory Rd or H DN6 76 E2
Priory Rise DN17 150 F2
Priory St YO1 156 A1
Priory Way
Kingston upon Hull HU4 144 A1
1 Snaith DN14 63 B1
Priory Wlk YO16 122 D4
Priory Wood Way YO31 127 F2
Proctor's Way DN20 109 A5
Promenade YO15 122 F2
Promenade The 15 HU19 75 A6
Promenades Sh Ctr The YO15 122 F2
Prospect Cl
Camblesforth YO8 63 D5
Pollington DN14 77 F6
Prospect Pl
Kingston upon Hull HU9 146 B7
Wistow YO8 48 D6
Prospect Rd DN14 79 B8
Prospect Sh Ctr HU2 155 A3
Prospect St
Bridlington YO15 122 E2
Kingston upon Hull HU2 155 A3
Prospect Terr
Fulford YO10 133 D6
York YO1 156 B1
Prospect Way YO8 148 D4
Prospect Way Ind Est YO8 148 D4
Providence Cres DN18 84 E8

Providence Pl
🔟 Bridlington YO15 ....**122** F3
1️⃣ Great Driffield YO25 ..**124** F4
Providence Row HU2 ..**155** A4
Prunus Ave HU10 ....**143** F8
Pryme Rd DN16 ....**151** C4
Pryme St Anlaby HU10 ..**143** F6
Kingston upon Hull HU2 ..**155** A3
Prystie Pl 1️⃣ DN35 ......**103** B1
Puddiners La DN14 ......**80** E7
Pudding Gate 8️⃣ HU17 ...**43** A2
Pudding La 48️⃣ DN7 ......**92** D4
Pulcroft Rd HU13 ......**143** F8
Pulfin Bog Nature Reserve★
HU17 ....**44** A7
Pulham La YO25 ....**19** B5
Pulleyn Cl 3️⃣ YO32 ....**14** C8
Pulleyn Dr YO24 ....**129** F1
Pulman St HU3 ....**145** A7
Pump Hill DN20 ....**109** D6
Pump La YO15 ....**150** C2
Punton Wlk DN14 ......**78** B8
Purbeck Rd
Grimsby DN33 ....**113** E8
Scunthorpe DN17 ....**150** C5
Purey Cust Nuffield Hospl
The YO31 ....**156** B3
Purton Gr HU7 ....**141** A7
Putney Cl HU8 ....**141** E5
Pyewipe Rd DN31 ....**152** C5
Pykestone Cl 15️⃣ HU7 ....**57** A6
Pyruss Dr HU4 ....**144** B2
Pytchley Wlk 1️⃣ DN35 ..**103** C1

Q

Quadrant The HU6 .....**139** F4
Quaker Gn 1️⃣ YO24 ....**132** C7
Quaker La HU17 ....**136** D4
Quaker Rd HU12 ....**59** F4
Quales Mews 2️⃣ HU18 ..**134** C4
Quant Mews YO10 ......**131** B3
Quantock Cl
7️⃣ Kingston upon Hull
HU3 ....**145** D5
Scunthorpe DN17 ....**150** D4
5️⃣ Thorne/Moorends DN8 ..**93** A7
Quantock Rd DN33 .....**113** E8
Quarrington Gr 19️⃣ HU7 ..**56** F6
Quarry Ave 20️⃣ WF11 ....**61** A2
Quarry Rd DN6 ....**76** F2
Quart La
Eastrington DN14 ....**65** F7
Reedness DN14 ....**80** D6
Quay La DN14 ....**80** C7
Quay Rd
Bridlington YO16 ....**122** D3
4️⃣ Thorne DN8 ....**78** F1
Quay St HU1 ....**155** B2
Quay The YO8 ....**148** D6
Quayside 1️⃣ DN8 ....**78** F1
Quebec Dr HU16 ....**138** E5
Quebec Rd DN17 ....**96** C2
Queen Annes Rd
YO30 ....**156** A3
Queen Dike★ YO17 ....**17** B8
Queen Elizabeth Ave 4️⃣
DN18 ....**84** A7
Queen Elizabeth High Sch
DN21 ....**117** B2
Queen Elizabeth Rd 6️⃣
DN36 ....**114** C8
Queen Elizabeth Way 19️⃣
DN18 ....**84** F8
Queen Margaret's Sch
YO19 ....**37** A5
Queen Mary Ave
DN35 ....**153** C3
Queen Mary Ave Inf Sch
DN35 ....**153** C3
Queen St
Barton-upon-Humber
DN18 ....**69** F1
Bridlington YO15 ....**122** E2
15️⃣ Brigg DN20 ....**98** C2
13️⃣ Epworth DN9 ....**105** E6
Great Driffield YO25 ...**124** F4
Grimsby DN32 ....**152** E3
Kingston upon Hull HU1 ..**155** C1
Kirton in Lindsey DN21 ..**108** B1
Scunthorpe DN16 ....**151** C6
16️⃣ Thorne/Moorends DN8 ..**93** A8
15️⃣ Winterton DN15 ....**83** A5
Withernsea HU19 ....**75** A6
York YO24 ....**156** A2
Queen St N HU17 ....**74** F7
Queen Victoria Sq
HU1 ....**155** B2
Queen Victoria St
YO23 ....**130** B1
Queen's Alley HU1 .....**155** C1
Queen's Ave 5️⃣ DN18 ...**69** F1
Queen's Cl Goole DN14 ..**149** C4
2️⃣ Kingston upon Hull
HU16 ....**139** B7
Queen's Cres DN7 ......**92** C6
Queen's Ct
17️⃣ Thorne/Moorends DN8 ..**93** A8
York YO1 ....**156** B2
Queen's Dr HU16 ....**139** A7
Queen's Gate HU16 .....**139** B7
Queen's Gate St HU3 ...**145** B5
Queen's Par DN35 ......**153** F1
Queen's Rd DN38 ....**99** B4

Queen's Staith Rd
YO1 ....**156** B2
Queen's View Cres
DN16 ....**151** D3
Queen's Way HU16 .....**139** B7
Queens Cres DN17 ......**95** D6
Queens Dock Ave
HU1 ....**155** B2
Queens Dr
7️⃣ Crowle DN17 ....**94** D7
Goole DN14 ....**149** D6
Queens Gdns HU18 .....**134** B3
Queens Par DN31 ....**152** C3
Queens Rd
Beverley HU17 ....**154** A1
Immingham DN40 ....**87** D1
Kingston upon Hull HU5 ..**140** C2
Queens Sq 13️⃣ YO16 ....**122** E2
Queens Staith Mews
YO1 ....**156** B1
Queensbury Way 2️⃣
HU14 ....**69** B6
Queensfield LN7 ....**110** A1
Queensgate
Beverley HU17 ....**154** A1
Bridlington YO16 ....**122** E4
Queensgate Sq YO16 ...**122** D3
Queensmead
Aldbrough HU11 ....**47** C1
Beverley HU17 ....**55** E8
Lund YO25 ....**31** F2
Queensway
Goole DN14 ....**149** D4
Grimsby DN37 ....**102** C4
Scunthorpe DN16 ....**151** A5
Woodmansey HU17 ......**56** B8
Queensway Ind Est
DN15 ....**151** E2
Queensway The HU6 ...**140** B8
Queenswood Gr YO24 ..**129** D2
Queenswood Rd 7️⃣ DN16 ..**96** E2
Quillcourt HU6 ....**139** E7
Quilter Ave HU4 ....**144** B5
Quilter Dr HU11 ....**142** F7
Quinton Rd DN32 ......**102** F2
Quorn Mews 26️⃣ DN35 ..**103** C2
Quorum The HU4 ....**144** D3

R

Racca Ave 11️⃣ WF11 .....**61** A2
Racca Gn WF11 ....**61** A2
Race La Carlton YO8 ....**63** B4
Wootton DN39 ....**85** C3
Racecourse Rd YO23 ...**133** B8
Rachel Cl 3️⃣ DN16 .....**117** B2
Radcliffe Cl DN16 ......**151** D4
Radcliffe Rd DN41 ......**101** F5
Radcroft La YO43 ....**53** D5
Radstock Wlk HU8 .....**142** C7
Raglan St HU5 ....**140** C3
Raich Carter Way HU4 ..**56** D5
Railway Cres 2️⃣ HU19 ..**75** A6
Railway Pl DN31 ....**152** F5
Railway St
Barnetby le Wold DN38 ..**99** B4
Beverley HU17 ....**154** B2
Grimsby DN32 ....**152** F4
Hornsea HU18 ....**134** D4
Kingston upon Hull HU1 ..**155** B3
Railway Terr
Grimsby DN32 ....**152** D3
York YO24 ....**130** A4
Railway View YO24 .....**132** E8
Raincliffe St 4️⃣ YO8 ....**148** C5
Raines Cl 5️⃣ HU12 ......**73** A6
Rainham Cl HU8 ....**141** E7
Rainhill Rd 2️⃣ HU5 .....**140** A2
Rainsborough Way 3️⃣
YO30 ....**130** A8
Rainsburgh La YO25 ....**2** A3
Rainsbutt Rd DN17 .....**94** C8
Rainswood Cl 8️⃣ HU7 ..**56** F6
Raithby Ave 3️⃣ DN41 ..**101** A4
Raithby Gr 12️⃣ DN33 ...**102** D2
Rake Bridge Bank DN7 ..**92** D1
Raker Cl YO19 ....**37** F7
Rakes Rd HU17 ....**42** E2
Raleigh Dr
Kingston upon Hull HU9 ..**146** D6
Sproatley HU11 ....**58** D5
Ralph Butterfield Prim Sch
YO32 ....**13** F5
Ram Bvd DN15 ....**96** C8
Ramsay Cl YO31 ....**156** C4
Ramsden Ave DN18 .....**84** E8
Ramsden Cl YO25 ......**124** A1
Ramsden Ct HU17 ......**154** C3
Ramsden Pl 11️⃣ HU16 ..**138** F5
Ramsey Ave YO23 ......**133** B3
Ramsey Cl YO16 ....**122** C2
Ramsey Rd YO16 ....**122** B2
Ramsgate Cl HU8 ....**141** E7
Ramskir La DN7 ....**92** C7
Ranby Cres HU18 ....**134** C2
Ranby Dr HU18 ....**134** C2
Ranby Rd DN17 ....**150** E1
Randall Garth YO25 ....**125** A3
Rands Est 7️⃣ HU12 .....**58** D1
Randsfield Ave 17️⃣ HU15 ..**68** C5
Rangely Cl 9️⃣ HU7 .....**57** A6
Rannoch Cl 6️⃣ HU7 ....**57** A6
Ransom Ct DN9 ....**100** A6
Ransome Way 14️⃣ HU15 ..**68** C6
Ratcliffe Ct YO30 ......**126** C5
Ratcliffe St YO30 ......**130** B7
Rattan Row YO25 ....**8** C6

Ratten Row
4️⃣ Bishop Burton HU17 ...**43** A2
5️⃣ North Newbald YO43 ..**53** F7
Rauceby Cl 10️⃣ HU7 ....**56** F6
Raven Cl DN20 ....**97** D4
Raven Gr YO26 ....**129** C4
Raven St HU9 ....**146** D7
Ravencroft La 1️⃣ DN10 ..**116** D1
Ravendale 18️⃣ DN18 ....**84** F8
Ravendale Cl 1️⃣ DN36 ..**114** B5
Ravendale Rd 10️⃣ DN35 ..**103** D2
Ravendale St N DN15 ...**151** B7
Ravendale St S DN15 ...**151** B7
Ravenhill Cl 14️⃣ DN35 ..**103** B2
Ravenscar Rd 9️⃣ DN37 ..**102** C5
Ravensfleet Rd DN21 ...**116** F6
Ravenspur Rd HU11 ....**58** A4
Ravenspurn YO16 ......**122** B6
Ravenspurn Gr 1️⃣ HU12 ..**142** A2
Ravenspurn Rd HU12 ...**89** C8
Ravenspurn St DN31 ...**152** D4
Ravenspurn Way 1️⃣
DN31 ....**152** D4
Raventhorpe Medieval
Village★ DN16 ....**97** B2
Rawcliffe Ave YO30 ....**129** F8
Rawcliffe Bridge Prim Sch
DN14 ....**79** B8
Rawcliffe Cl 5️⃣ YO30 ...**126** E2
Rawcliffe Croft YO30 ...**126** D2
Rawcliffe Dr YO30 .....**129** F8
Rawcliffe Gr HU4 .....**144** D5
Rawcliffe in Snaith Prim Sch
DN14 ....**64** A1
Rawcliffe Inf Sch
YO30 ....**126** E1
Rawcliffe La YO30 .....**126** F1
Rawcliffe Landing
YO30 ....**126** C3
Rawcliffe Rd DN14 .....**79** B8
Rawcliffe Sta DN14 ....**79** A8
Rawcliffe Village
YO30 ....**126** E3
Rawcliffe Way YO30 ...**126** E2
Rawdale HU15 ....**54** A2
Rawdon Ave YO10 .....**130** F4
Rawling Way HU3 ......**145** A5
Rawlinson Ave 22️⃣ LN7 ..**111** B4
Raymond Rd DN16 .....**151** C3
Raywell Cl HU10 ....**143** F7
Raywell St HU2 ....**155** A3
Read Cl YO8 ....**148** B5
Read Sch YO8 ....**63** F5
Reading Gate
Reedness DN17 ....**80** C3
Swinefleet DN14 ....**80** D7
Reading Rm Yd 4️⃣ HU14 ..**69** A4
Real Aeroplane Mus The★
YO8 ....**50** D3
Reangamoor La YO42 ...**39** D2
Reaper's Rise 15️⃣ DN9 ..**105** E6
Reaper's Way 8️⃣ DN9 ..**105** D2
Recreation Club La
HU17 ....**154** A4
Recreation Rd 2️⃣ YO8 ..**148** D6
Recto Ave DN32 ....**152** F1
Rectory Ave 33️⃣ DN21 ..**117** B1
Rectory Cl YO25 ....**125** F7
Rectory Gdns
3️⃣ Beckingham DN10 ....**116** D1
York YO23 ....**130** B1
Rectory La
Beeford YO25 ....**22** C1
Preston HU12 ....**58** C1
Roos HU12 ....**60** C3
Rectory Rd HU12 ....**74** A8
Rectory St DN9 ....**105** E6
Rectory View YO25 .....**32** C2
Rectory Way HU4 ......**144** A3
Rectory Wlk YO43 .....**40** B1
Rectory Wlk YO16 .....**122** B4
Red House La YO43 ....**135** A4
Red La
Market Weighton YO43 ..**135** E5
South Ferriby DN18 .....**83** F7
Red Lion St 2️⃣ DN14 ...**149** C4
Red Twr★ YO1 ....**130** E4
Redbarn Dr YO10 ......**131** D4
Redbourn Cl DN16 .....**151** B5
Redbourn E Rd DN16 ...**97** A6
Redbourn Way DN16 ...**151** B6
Redbourne Mere
DN21 ....**108** E2
Redbourne Rd
Grimsby DN33 ....**102** D2
Hibaldstow DN20 ....**108** F4
Waddingham DN21 .....**119** F8
Redbourne St
Kingston upon Hull HU3 ..**145** B5
3️⃣ Scunthorpe DN16 ....**151** C6
Redcap La YO42 ....**38** C5
Redcar Gr DN32 ....**153** A1
Redcar St HU8 ....**155** C4
Redcliff Dr 19️⃣ HU14 ...**69** A4
Redcliff Rd HU13 ......**69** E4
Redcoat Way 1️⃣ YO24 ..**132** B7
Redcombe La DN20 .....**98** B2
Redeness St YO31 ......**130** E5
Redfern Cl HU3 ....**145** D5
Redgates HU17 ....**55** B7
Redgrave Cl 4️⃣ YO31 ...**130** E8
Redhall Cl 7️⃣ DN3 .....**92** A2
Redhill Field La YO23 ..**24** F1
Redhouse La YO8 ......**63** F6
Redland Cres 2️⃣ DN8 ...**93** B8
Redland Dr HU10 ......**143** C6
Redman Cl
15️⃣ Gainsborough DN21 ..**117** C1
York YO10 ....**133** C8

Redmayne Sq YO32 ....**14** B8
Redmire Cl HU7 ....**57** A6
Redmires Cl YO30 ......**127** A2
Redruth Cl HU7 ....**141** C6
Redthorn Dr YO31 ......**127** F1
Redwing Dr YO25 ......**125** A5
Redwood Cl YO16 ......**122** E6
Redwood Ct DN16 ......**96** E2
Redwood Dr
7️⃣ Cleethorpes DN35 ....**103** B1
6️⃣ Haxby YO32 ....**13** E5
Redwood Gdns YO25 ...**124** F3
Redwood Way YO16 ....**122** D6
Redwoods The HU10 ...**138** C2
Reed St HU2 ....**155** A3
Reedham Garth HU4 ....**144** A3
Reedholme La DN8 .....**78** F4
Reedness Prim Sch
DN14 ....**66** A1
Reedsway 12️⃣ YO25 ....**34** B3
Rees Cl YO43 ....**135** D5
Reeth Wlk HU5 ....**139** D3
Reeves The YO24 ......**129** C5
Refinery Rd DN16 .....**151** F6
Reform St HU2 ....**155** B3
Regency Cl 8️⃣ DN16 ...**69** E1
Regency Mews 2️⃣ YO24 ..**132** F3
Regent Arc DN32 ......**152** D3
Regent Cl
Kingston upon Hull HU3 ..**145** C6
Willerby HU10 ....**138** E1
Regent Dr 18️⃣ DN17 ....**94** D7
Regent Gdns DN34 .....**152** C1
Regent St
Beverley HU17 ....**154** B2
York YO10 ....**130** E3
Regent St Pavement 8️⃣
YO42 ....**29** A3
Regent Terr 7️⃣ YO15 ...**122** F2
Regents Ct
Cottingham HU16 ....**139** A6
14️⃣ York YO26 ....**129** F5
Regimental Mus★
YO1 ....**156** B1
Regina Cres 2️⃣ HU5 ...**140** A1
Reginald Gr YO23 ......**130** C1
Reginald Rd DN15 .....**96** C7
Reginald Terr YO8 .....**148** B4
Regis Ct HU9 ....**142** B3
Register Sq HU17 ......**154** A2
Reigate Cl HU8 ....**142** A4
Reighton Ave YO30 ....**129** F8
Reighton Dr 10️⃣ YO30 ..**126** F1
Reina Dr YO25 ....**124** C4
Reldene Dr HU5 ....**144** B7
Remembrance Ct
YO16 ....**122** A2
Remillo Ave DN35 .....**152** F1
Remington Ave YO25 ...**34** E3
Remple Ave DN7 ....**93** A3
Remple Comm Rd DN7 ..**92** F2
Remple La DN7 ....**93** A3
Rendel St DN31 ....**152** D5
Rensburg St HU9 ......**141** D1
Renshaw Gdns 8️⃣ YO26 ..**129** E4
Renton Ct HU13 ....**143** F6
Reporto Ave DN32 .....**152** F1
Repton Dr
Kingston upon Hull HU7 ..**141** D5
21️⃣ Scunthorpe DN16 ....**96** D2
Reservoir Rd HU6 ......**140** F3
Responso Ave DN32 ....**152** F1
Reston Ct 8️⃣ DN35 .....**103** D2
Reston Gr 25️⃣ DN33 ....**102** D2
Retford Gr HU9 ....**142** E1
Retreat Hospl The
YO10 ....**130** F2
Revesby Ave
18️⃣ Grimsby DN34 ......**102** C2
Scunthorpe DN16 ....**151** A3
Revesby Ct DN16 ......**151** A4
Revigo Ave DN32 ......**152** F1
Revill Cl 17️⃣ DN21 .....**107** C3
Reygate Gr YO23 ......**132** B2
Reynolds Cl HU14 .....**68** E5
Reynolds Inf Sch
DN35 ....**153** D3
Reynolds Jun Sch
DN35 ....**153** D3
Reynolds St DN35 .....**153** D2
Reynoldson St HU5 ....**140** C2
Rhodena Ave YO16 ....**122** C2
Rhodes St HU3 ....**144** F5
Rhyl Cl 4️⃣ HU7 ....**56** F7
Rialto Ave DN32 ....**152** F1
Ribble St 4️⃣ HU3 ......**145** B4
Ribblesdale 3️⃣ HU7 ....**141** A4
Ribblesdale Cl YO16 ...**122** F7
Ribston Cl 9️⃣ DN16 ....**96** D1
Ribstone Gr YO31 .....**131** B6
Riby Ct DN36 ....**114** B5
Riby Rd Cabourne LN7 ..**111** D6
Keelby DN41 ....**101** A4
Scunthorpe DN17 ....**150** E1
Stallingborough DN41 ...**101** C4
Swallow LN7 ....**112** A7
Riby Sq DN32 ....**152** F5
Riby St DN31 ....**153** A5
Ribycourt HU6 ....**139** E7
Riccall Cl HU6 ....**140** A6
Riccall La YO19 ....**36** D1
Riccall CP Sch YO19 ...**36** F1
Richard Cooper St
DN14 ....**149** D4
Richard St
Grimsby DN31 ....**152** C4
Selby YO8 ....**148** B5
Richardson Cl DN36 ...**114** D8

Richardson St YO23 ...**130** C2
Richdale Ave DN21 ....**108** B1
Richmond Cl YO43 .....**135** F3
Richmond Dr
Goole DN14 ....**149** F5
10️⃣ Scunthorpe DN16 ....**96** E2
Richmond Gdns HU17 ..**136** D1
Richmond Rd
Cleethorpes DN35 ......**153** E1
Grimsby DN34 ....**152** A2
Kingston upon Hull
HU13 ....**143** F3
Thorne/Moorends DN8 ..**79** B2
Richmond St
Bridlington YO15 ....**122** D1
2️⃣ Kingston upon Hull
HU5 ....**145** B8
York YO31 ....**130** E5
Richmond Way 2️⃣ HU17 ..**55** E8
Richmond Wlk DN16 ...**136** D1
Rickaby Cl YO16 ....**122** D4
Ridding Cres DN14 .....**64** A1
Ridding La DN14 ....**64** A1
Riddings Infants Sch
DN17 ....**96** C2
Riddings Jun Sch DN17 ..**96** C2
Ridge View DN20 ......**98** C2
Ridge Way DN17 ....**150** E5
Ridgestone Ave HU11 ..**142** E7
Ridgeway YO26 ....**129** B3
Ridgeway Rd HU5 .....**144** B7
Ridgeway The DN34 ...**102** B3
Ridgewood Ave 6️⃣ DN3 ..**92** A1
Ridgewood Dr DN15 ...**82** A4
Riding Fields Sq
HU17 ....**154** C3
Riding Mews HU17 .....**154** B3
Ridings The
Beverley HU17 ....**136** C6
Cottingham HU16 ....**138** E6
East Ella HU5 ....**144** A8
Great Driffield YO25 ...**125** A6
15️⃣ North Ferriby HU14 ..**69** A4
Ridsdale HU7 ....**140** F7
Rifle Butts Quarry Nature
Reserve★ YO43 ....**41** D5
Rigby Cl HU7 ....**136** D7
Rileston Pl 12️⃣ DN16 ...**96** D1
Rillington Ave HU16 ...**139** A5
Rimswell Gr HU9 ......**142** A2
Ring Beck La HU15 .....**68** A8
Ringley Mdws 5️⃣ YO15 ..**4** C3
Ringrose St HU3 ....**144** F5
Ringstead Garth 4️⃣ HU7 ..**57** A5
Ringstone Rd
Bishopthorpe YO23 .....**133** B5
York YO30 ....**126** F3
Ringwood Cl DN16 .....**151** B1
Ripley Cl
Bridlington YO16 ....**122** D5
Kingston upon Hull HU6 ..**140** B7
Ripley Ct DN15 ....**150** B6
Ripley Gr 3️⃣ YO32 .....**13** E5
Ripley Pl YO43 ....**135** D4
Riplingham Rd
Kingston upon Hull
HU10 ....**143** A8
Skidby HU10 ....**138** A1
Ripon Ave HU17 ......**136** E1
Ripon Cl DN15 ....**150** C3
Ripon St DN31 ....**152** C3
Ripon Way HU9 ....**146** C8
Risby Garth HU16 .....**55** C4
Risby Gr HU6 ....**139** F5
Risby Hill HU17 ....**55** A4
Risby La HU17 ....**55** B7
Risby Medieval Village★
DN15 ....**83** A2
Risby Pl HU17 ....**154** A1
Risby Rd DN15 ....**82** C1
Rise Cl HU11 ....**45** C5
Rise La Catwick HU17 ..**45** D8
Rise HU11 ....**45** D5
Rise Rd HU11 ....**45** F7
Rise The
7️⃣ North Ferriby HU14 ...**69** A5
Scunthorpe DN17 ....**96** C6
South Ferriby DN18 .....**84** A4
Risedale 21️⃣ LN7 ......**111** B4
Riseway HU11 ....**45** C5
Risewood YO41 ....**15** B2
Rishworth Cl 5️⃣ HU7 ..**57** A6
Rishworth Gr YO30 ....**126** F2
Riston CE VC Prim Sch
HU11 ....**45** C5
Riston Rd HU17 ....**45** C7
Riston St HU3 ....**145** C5
Rivan Ave 5️⃣ DN33 ....**113** E8
Rivan Gr 6️⃣ DN33 .....**113** E8
Rivelin Cres DN16 .....**151** A4
Rivelin Pl DN16 ....**151** A4
Rivelin Rd DN16 ......**151** A3
Rivelin Way YO30 .....**126** F2
River Cl 1️⃣ Barlby YO8 ..**49** B5
Goole DN14 ....**149** F5
River Gr HU4 ....**144** E3
River Head YO25 ......**124** F3
River Head Dr 3️⃣ YO25 ..**124** F3
River La Fishlake DN7 ..**92** D8
Market Weighton YO43 ..**40** F2
West Haddlesey YO8 ...**62** A5
River Mdw DN20 ......**98** B1
River St 1️⃣ Selby YO8 ...**148** D6
York YO23 ....**156** B1
River View 1️⃣ Barlby YO8 ..**49** B5
28️⃣ Barton-upon-Humber
DN18 ....**84** F8
Goole DN14 ....**65** C3

River View *continued*
Kingston upon Hull HU13 ... 143 F1
River Wlk DN14 ... 65 C4
Riverbank Cl DN17 ... 95 D5
Riverbank Rise 24 DN18 ... 84 E8
Riverdale 4 DN14 ... 61 D4
Riverdale Rd
Kilpin DN14 ... 65 C1
Scunthorpe DN16 ... 151 A3
Riversdale 17 YO32 ... 13 F5
Riversdale Dr DN14 ... 149 F5
Riversdale Rd HU6 ... 140 D6
Riverside
11 Broughton DN20 ... 98 B2
Great Driffield YO25 ... 124 F3
Rawcliffe DN14 ... 64 A2
Scotter DN21 ... 107 C4
Riverside Cl
1 Elvington YO41 ... 27 C2
6 Great Driffield YO25 ... 124 F3
West Haddlesey YO8 ... 62 A5
Riverside Cres YO32 ... 127 F6
Riverside Ct
5 Hessle HU13 ... 69 E4
Rawcliffe DN14 ... 64 A2
Riverside Dr DN35 ... 103 D1
Riverside Gdns
2 Elvington YO41 ... 27 C2
2 Poppleton YO26 ... 12 F1
Riverside Mews 5 YO25 ... 124 F3
Riverside Specl Sch DN14 ... 149 E5
Riverside Wlk
1 Poppleton YO26 ... 12 F1
5 Strensall YO32 ... 14 A7
Riversvale Dr 21 YO26 ... 12 F1
Riverview Ave HU14 ... 69 A4
Riverview Gdns HU7 ... 140 E7
Riverview Rd HU17 ... 137 C4
Rivesby Ave DN16 ... 151 A3
Riviera Dr YO15 ... 123 B6
Rix Rd HU7 ... 141 A3
Roall La DN14 ... 61 F4
Robert Cl
Immingham DN40 ... 87 B1
3 Withernsea HU19 ... 75 A6
Robert St
Scunthorpe DN15 ... 151 B7
Selby YO8 ... 148 C5
Robert Wilkinson Prim Sch YO32 ... 14 A7
Robert Wood Ave HU17 ... 154 A2
Roberts St DN32 ... 153 A3
Robertson Cl YO42 ... 29 A3
Robin Gr 6 YO24 ... 129 F3
Robin Hood Cres 5 DN3 ... 92 A1
Robin Hood Rd 3 DN3 ... 92 A1
Robinia Dr HU4 ... 144 C2
Robinson Cl DN15 ... 150 E8
Robinson Ct YO1 ... 156 C2
Robinson Dr YO24 ... 129 B2
Robinson La DN31 ... 153 A6
Robinson Rd DN40 ... 87 E2
Robinson Row HU1 ... 155 B2
Robinson St E DN32 ... 152 E3
Robinson's Gr DN20 ... 109 A5
Robinson's La DN36 ... 114 B1
Roborough Cl HU7 ... 141 B8
Robson Ave HU6 ... 140 B8
Robson Rd DN35 ... 153 D3
Robson Way
Kingston upon Hull HU7 ... 141 D7
6 Preston HU12 ... 72 C7
Rochdale Rd DN16 ... 151 A1
Roche Ave YO31 ... 130 E8
Roche Dr DN14 ... 149 E6
Rochester Ave HU4 ... 144 A3
Rochester Cl DN17 ... 150 C3
Rochester Ct 2 DN35 ... 103 D1
Rockford Ave HU8 ... 141 B3
Rockford Gr HU8 ... 141 B3
Rockingham Ave YO31 ... 131 A5
Rockingham Ct 10 DN34 ... 102 B2
Rockley Ct HU10 ... 143 F6
Rod Mill Rd DN16 ... 151 E5
Rodney Cl HU2 ... 155 A4
Roe La LS25 ... 61 C7
Rogers Ct YO24 ... 132 C8
Rokeby Ave HU4 ... 144 B5
Rokeby Cl
Beverley HU17 ... 154 A4
Kingston upon Hull HU4 ... 144 B5
Rokeby Pk HU4 ... 144 B5
Rokeby Pk Prim Sch HU4 ... 144 B4
Roland Ct YO32 ... 127 E3
Roland Simpson Cl 1 DN14 ... 78 C8
Rolston Ave 3 YO31 ... 127 E2
Rolston Cl HU9 ... 142 C1
Rolston Rd HU18 ... 134 C2
Roman Ave N 17 YO41 ... 15 D2
Roman Ave S YO41 ... 15 D1
Roman Camps* YO30 ... 127 B2
Roman Rd DN20 ... 108 D8
Roman Rigg YO43 ... 53 D8
Roman Way DN17 ... 150 F2
Romans Cl YO19 ... 48 F8
Rombalds Croft 26 HU15 ... 68 C6
Romford Gr HU9 ... 142 E1
Romney Gdns 4 HU5 ... 140 E2
Romsey Ct 11 DN34 ... 102 B3
Romwood Cl 17 HU15 ... 68 D6
Romyn Cl YO16 ... 122 B2
Ronaldsway Cl 6 HU9 ... 142 A3
Ronson Cl HU9 ... 142 D3
Rook's La DN10 ... 116 C5
Rookery Ave 10 DN33 ... 102 E2
Rookery Croft 9 DN9 ... 105 E6
Rookery Rd 18 DN41 ... 101 F5
Rookery The
Scawby DN20 ... 108 F8
22 Scotter DN21 ... 107 C3
Rooklands 2 DN21 ... 107 C3
Rookley Cl 3 HU8 ... 142 C5
Roos CE VC Prim Sch HU12 ... 60 B1
Roos Cl HU17 ... 136 F7
Rootas La HU17 ... 43 A6
Rope Wlk
Bridlington YO15 ... 122 E2
Thorne/Moorends DN8 ... 93 A8
Roper St HU1 ... 155 A2
Ropers Ct YO23 ... 132 C3
Ropery Cl
Beverley HU17 ... 137 B4
Keyingham HU12 ... 73 D3
3 Kilham YO25 ... 9 C3
Thorngumbald HU12 ... 72 E5
Ropery La 1 DN18 ... 69 E1
Ropery Rd DN21 ... 117 A2
Ropery St
Grimsby DN32 ... 152 F3
Kingston upon Hull HU3 ... 145 D5
Ropewalk* DN18 ... 69 F1
Ropewalk The
9 Caistor LN7 ... 111 B4
York YO31 ... 130 E5
Rosaire Pl DN33 ... 113 E8
Rosalind Ave DN34 ... 152 B3
Rosamond St 7 HU3 ... 145 B4
Rose Carr Wlk HU18 ... 134 D6
Rose Gdns 4 DN40 ... 87 C2
Rose La HU17 ... 43 C5
Rose Lea Cl 2 LS25 ... 61 A7
Rose St YO31 ... 130 C7
Rose Tree Gr YO32 ... 127 D4
Rose Wlk DN15 ... 151 C7
Roseacres DN14 ... 65 C4
Roseberry Ave
Bridlington YO15 ... 122 C1
15 Hatfield DN7 ... 92 D4
Roseberry Gr YO30 ... 126 F3
Rosebery St YO26 ... 129 F6
Rosecomb Way 6 YO32 ... 127 D7
Rosecroft Way YO30 ... 129 E8
Rosedale Leven HU17 ... 45 B8
Scunthorpe DN17 ... 96 C1
Waltham DN37 ... 113 D7
Rosedale Ave
Kingston upon Hull HU9 ... 141 E1
York YO26 ... 129 C4
Rosedale Gr HU5 ... 144 D7
Rosedale St YO10 ... 130 E2
Rosedale Wlk
Beverley HU17 ... 136 E1
Bridlington YO16 ... 122 B4
Rosefields DN21 ... 117 C1
Rosemary Ave DN34 ... 102 C3
Rosemary Ct YO1 ... 156 C2
Rosemary Pl YO1 ... 156 C2
Rosemary Way
Beverley HU17 ... 154 C1
Humberston DN36 ... 103 C1
Rosemoor Cl 19 YO14 ... 2 F8
Rosemount Cl 3 HU6 ... 140 B8
Rosemount Dr DN16 ... 151 B2
Rosemount Grange HU13 ... 143 C3
Roseveare Ave DN34 ... 152 A3
Rosewood Cl
3 Bridlington YO16 ... 123 A6
4 Kingston upon Hull HU4 ... 144 B7
Rosewood Way 25 DN16 ... 96 D2
Rosewood Wlk YO16 ... 123 A6
Rosewoods DN14 ... 65 C8
Rosey Row 4 HU9 ... 146 C7
Rosina Gr N DN32 ... 153 B2
Rosina Gr S DN32 ... 153 B2
Roslyn Cres HU12 ... 72 C7
Roslyn Rd HU3 ... 144 E7
Rosmead St HU9 ... 146 D8
Rosper Rd DN40 ... 87 A4
Ross La Bainton YO25 ... 31 D7
Winterton DN15 ... 83 B5
Ross Rd DN31 ... 153 B5
Rossall Cl 4 DN16 ... 96 E2
Rosslyn St 1 YO30 ... 130 A6
Rostun Rd HU12 ... 60 B2
Roth Hill La YO19 ... 37 E3
Rothbury Rd DN17 ... 150 F3
Rothesay Cl 1 HU9 ... 141 E1
Rothwell Ave 15 DN33 ... 102 D2
Rothwell Rd
Cabourne LN7 ... 111 C3
Scunthorpe DN15 ... 150 D8
Rotsea La YO25 ... 33 B7
Rotterdam Rd HU7 ... 141 A5
Rotton Sykes La DN15 ... 67 F2
Rougier St YO1 ... 156 A2
Round Hill Link YO30 ... 126 F2
Roundhay Rd YO15 ... 122 D1
Roundway
Grimsby DN34 ... 152 C1
7 Immingham DN40 ... 87 C1
Roundway The HU4 ... 144 C5
Routh Ave HU17 ... 154 C3
Roval Dr DN40 ... 87 B1
Row La HU12 ... 90 A7
Rowan Ave
Beverley HU17 ... 136 F7
York YO32 ... 127 D4
Rowan Cl
3 Barrow upon Humber DN19 ... 85 C8
Gateforth YO8 ... 48 B1
2 Keelby DN41 ... 101 A4
10 Thorne/Moorends DN8 ... 79 B2
Rowan Cres 2 DN16 ... 96 E2
Rowan Ct 7 DN19 ... 86 A8
Rowan Dr
Healing DN41 ... 101 F5
6 Humberston DN36 ... 114 D8
Rowan Garth HU16 ... 55 C4
Rowan Pl YO32 ... 127 D4
Rowan Wlk HU18 ... 134 D2
Rowans The
23 Gainsborough DN21 ... 117 C1
Holme-on-Spalding-Moor YO42 ... 40 A1
1 Westwoodside DN9 ... 105 A2
Rowedale Cl 15 YO14 ... 2 F8
Rowland Rd DN16 ... 151 A6
Rowlandhall La DN14 ... 50 E1
Rowlandson St DN31 ... 152 F6
Rowley CE Sch HU20 ... 55 A4
Rowley Ct 2 YO32 ... 127 F7
Rowley Gr HU6 ... 139 F5
Rowley Rd HU20 ... 54 F3
Rowlston Gr HU9 ... 142 A2
Rowmans The YO30 ... 126 C4
Rowmills Rd DN16 ... 151 C4
Rowntree Ave YO30 ... 130 C8
Rowpit La HU17 ... 45 C8
Rowston Cl 7 DN21 ... 117 B1
Rowston St DN35 ... 103 D3
Rowton Dr HU11 ... 45 D2
Roxburgh St 1 HU5 ... 145 B8
Roxby Cswy DN15 ... 83 C4
Roxby Rd DN15 ... 82 F4
Roxton Ave DN41 ... 101 A5
Roxton Hall Dr 13 HU14 ... 69 A5
Roxton Medieval Village* DN40 ... 101 A7
Royal Chase YO24 ... 132 F8
Royal Cres YO15 ... 122 F2
Royal Ct 25 DN35 ... 103 D1
Royal Dr DN14 ... 79 A8
Royal Garth HU17 ... 154 A1
Royal Hull Hospitals NHS Trust HU3 ... 145 C6
Royal St DN31 ... 152 E6
Royal Wlk HU16 ... 139 D5
Royd's Rd YO8 ... 61 F6
Royston Gr HU8 ... 141 B1
Ruard Rd DN19 ... 86 B8
Ruards La DN19 ... 71 A1
Ruby St 3 YO23 ... 130 B1
Rudcarr La YO19 ... 14 E1
Rudding Dr YO16 ... 122 D7
Ruddings YO19 ... 38 A8
Ruddings Cl 9 YO32 ... 127 C8
Ruddings La YO42 ... 38 E2
Ruddings The YO8 ... 148 A4
Rudgate La DN14 ... 78 E4
Rudham Ave DN32 ... 102 F2
Rudston Beacon* YO25 ... 9 F4
Rudston Gr HU9 ... 142 A1
Rudston Monolith* YO25 ... 9 F6
Rudston Rd YO25 ... 9 F2
Rue De Nozay 2 DN20 ... 97 E4
Ruffhams Cl YO19 ... 37 F8
Rufford Rd 3 DN35 ... 103 C2
Rufforth Dr HU17 ... 43 D5
Rufforth Garth HU7 ... 141 C8
Rufforth Prim Sch YO23 ... 24 C6
Rugby Rd DN16 ... 151 A4
Rugby St 5 HU3 ... 145 B4
Ruislip Cl HU8 ... 142 A5
Runcorn Garth HU4 ... 144 B3
Rundle Ct 29 YO42 ... 29 A3
Runner End YO43 ... 40 A1
Runswick Ave YO26 ... 129 B4
Runswick Ct DN32 ... 153 A2
Runswick Rd DN32 ... 153 B2
Rupert Rd 9 DN33 ... 102 E2
Rushcarr La DN17 ... 95 C1
Rusholme La YO8 ... 64 A5
Rushtons Way DN20 ... 108 F5
Rushwood Cl 6 YO32 ... 13 F5
Ruskin St HU3 ... 145 B6
Ruskington Cl DN31 ... 102 C5
Russell Ct 13 DN35 ... 103 D1
Russell Dr
20 Keyingham HU12 ... 73 C4
York YO30 ... 129 E8
Russell Rd DN14 ... 149 B4
Russell St
Kingston upon Hull HU2 ... 155 A3
York YO23 ... 130 B2
Russell Wlk DN17 ... 107 D7
Russet Cl 12 DN15 ... 96 B7
Russet Dr YO31 ... 131 B5
Rustenburg St HU9 ... 141 D1
Rustic La DN21 ... 117 F6
Ruswarp Gr HU6 ... 139 E6
Rutherglen Dr HU9 ... 142 A3
Rutland Cl YO23 ... 132 A3
Rutland Dr 16 DN36 ... 114 A7
Rutland Rd
Goole DN14 ... 149 D6
Kingston upon Hull HU5 ... 144 E8
Scunthorpe DN16 ... 151 D3
Rutland St DN32 ... 153 A4
Ryburn Cl YO30 ... 126 F2
Rydal Ave
11 Grimsby DN33 ... 113 D8
York YO31 ... 131 A6
Rydal Gr HU16 ... 138 E6
Rydale Ct HU5 ... 140 E3
Rydales The HU5 ... 140 E3
Ryde Ave HU5 ... 140 D3
Ryde St HU5 ... 140 D2
Rye Cl YO32 ... 127 C8
Ryecroft 7 YO32 ... 14 A6
Ryecroft Ave
10 Norton DN6 ... 76 E2
York YO24 ... 132 C7
Ryecroft Cl YO31 ... 131 C8
Ryecroft Dr HU19 ... 75 A6
Ryecroft Gdns DN14 ... 62 A2
Ryecroft Rd DN6 ... 76 E1
Ryedale 12 HU15 ... 68 D6
Ryedale Ave DN15 ... 83 A6
Ryedale Way YO8 ... 148 C3
Ryehill Cl YO32 ... 127 D5
Ryehill Gr HU9 ... 141 F2
Ryehill La HU12 ... 73 A4
Ryelands Ave YO16 ... 123 A6
Ryemoor Rd YO32 ... 127 C8
Rylatt Pl YO26 ... 129 B3
Rymer Pl DN35 ... 103 D2
Rysome La HU19 ... 75 C1
Rysome Rd HU12 ... 90 B7

S

Sabina Ct HU8 ... 141 E7
Sable Cl HU4 ... 144 C2
Sackville Cl
5 Beverley HU17 ... 55 E8
14 Immingham DN40 ... 87 C1
Sackville Rd 15 DN40 ... 87 C1
Sackville St DN34 ... 152 C3
Sacred Gate HU12 ... 72 D6
Sadberge Ct YO10 ... 131 C3
Saddler's Way DN9 ... 105 D3
Saddlers Cl
1 Copmanthorpe YO23 ... 132 B3
Huntington YO32 ... 127 F2
Saddlers Way YO26 ... 24 A6
Saddleworth Cl 19 HU7 ... 57 A6
Saffron Dr 6 DN14 ... 63 C1
Saffron Garth 15 HU12 ... 74 D1
Saffrondale HU10 ... 143 E7
Sage Cl HU17 ... 154 B1
Sagefield Cl 6 DN33 ... 113 D8
Sailors Wharf HU9 ... 146 C6
Sails Dr YO10 ... 131 B3
Sainsbury Way HU4 ... 144 A1
St Abbs Cl HU9 ... 155 C1
St Aelreds Cl YO31 ... 130 F4
St Aelreds RC Prim Sch YO31 ... 131 B5
St Aidan Cres YO16 ... 122 E4
St Aidan Ct YO16 ... 122 E5
St Aidan Rd YO16 ... 122 E4
St Aiden Cl YO43 ... 135 E3
St Aiden Way HU9 ... 141 F2
St Alban Cl YO16 ... 122 E4
St Alban Rd YO16 ... 122 E4
St Alban's Cl HU11 ... 46 D3
St Albans Ave DN31 ... 152 A4
St Albans Cl
7 Beverley HU17 ... 136 E1
Hibaldstow DN20 ... 108 F5
Scunthorpe DN17 ... 150 C3
St Albans Mount HU6 ... 140 C4
St Andrew Pl YO1 ... 156 C2
St Andrew Rd YO16 ... 122 E4
St Andrew St HU17 ... 154 B2
St Andrew's CE VA Prim Sch HU7 ... 140 E8
St Andrew's Cl
Middleton-on-the-Wolds YO25 ... 31 C4
Paull HU12 ... 72 A5
Redbourne DN21 ... 108 E3
St Andrew's Dr DN15 ... 82 A4
St Andrew's Mount HU10 ... 143 C8
St Andrew's St DN21 ... 108 A1
St Andrew's Terr 6 DN14 ... 149 C4
St Andrew's Way
2 Barnby Dun DN3 ... 92 A3
Epworth DN9 ... 105 E7
St Andrewgate YO1 ... 156 B2
St Andrews Ave DN17 ... 96 C1
St Andrews Ct DN14 ... 149 C4
St Andrews Gr 10 DN7 ... 92 D4
St Andrews La 5 DN40 ... 87 B2
St Andrews Prim Sch HU10 ... 143 C7
St Andrews Way HU8 ... 141 C3
St Ann Ct YO10 ... 130 E2
St Ann's Ave DN34 ... 152 B2
St Ann's Ct YO10 ... 130 D2
St Anne's Cl HU17 ... 137 B5
St Anne's Com Specl Sch HU15 ... 68 E5
St Anne's Dr HU16 ... 139 D6
St Anne's Rd 6 DN41 ... 101 A5
St Anne's Wlk
9 Brough HU15 ... 68 D6
Driffield YO25 ... 125 A3
St Annes Rd YO15 ... 122 F3
St Anthony Rd YO16 ... 122 E4
St Anthony's Dr 24 HU12 ... 72 D7
St Anthony's Pk 25 HU12 ... 72 D7
St Athony's Cl HU6 ... 140 B4
St Aubyn's Pl YO24 ... 130 A2
St Augustine Ave DN32 ... 152 E1
St Augustine Cres DN16 ... 151 B1
St Augustine Dr HU11 ... 45 E2
St Augustine Webster RC Prim Sch DN15 ... 150 D8
St Augustine's Ct 2 HU5 ... 140 D3
St Augustine's Dr YO16 ... 122 E5
St Augustine's Gate 30 HU12 ... 72 C7
St Augustine's Gr YO16 ... 122 E5
St Austells Cl HU9 ... 141 F2
St Barbara's Cres 8 DN15 ... 82 B4
St Barnabas' CE Prim Sch
Barnetby le Wold DN38 ... 99 B4
Clifton Park YO26 ... 129 F5
St Barnabas Ct
4 Kingston upon Hull HU3 ... 145 C4
13 York YO26 ... 129 F5
St Barnabas Dr HU14 ... 69 C7
St Barnabas Rd DN38 ... 99 B4
St Bartholemew's Way HU8 ... 142 A5
St Bartholemew's Cl 17 DN41 ... 101 A4
St Bede Ct HU4 ... 144 E5
St Bede's RC Sch DN16 ... 151 B2
St Benedict Cl HU7 ... 57 B5
St Benedict Rd YO23 ... 156 A1
St Bernadette's RC Prim Sch DN16 ... 151 C2
St Bernard's Cl 9 DN20 ... 97 E4
St Boltophs Cl 4 WF11 ... 61 A2
St Botolph's Rd DN16 ... 151 C3
St Bridget's Ct YO23 ... 156 B1
St Catherine's Dr DN7 ... 92 C2
St Catherines YO30 ... 126 D6
St Catherines Cl YO30 ... 126 C5
St Catherines Cres 8 DN16 ... 96 D2
St Catherines Ct
6 Grimsby DN34 ... 102 C3
Kingston upon Hull HU5 ... 140 E2
Scunthorpe DN16 ... 151 D2
St Catherines Dr HU17 ... 43 C6
St Catherines Pl YO24 ... 130 A3
St Chad DN19 ... 85 D8
St Chad Cres YO16 ... 122 E4
St Chad Gr YO16 ... 122 E4
St Chad Rd YO16 ... 122 E4
St Chad's Rd DN16 ... 151 D3
St Chads Wharf YO23 ... 133 C8
St Charles' RC Prim Sch HU2 ... 155 A3
St Christopher Rd YO16 ... 122 E4
St Christopher's Rd DN36 ... 114 C8
St Clares Wlk 12 DN20 ... 98 C2
St Clement's Gr YO23 ... 130 C2
St Clements Pl HU2 ... 155 A4
St Clements Way
17 Holton le Clay DN36 ... 114 A5
Kingston upon Hull HU9 ... 141 F2
St Columba Rd YO16 ... 122 F5
St Crispins Cl DN40 ... 86 E4
St Cuthbert Rd YO16 ... 122 E4
St David Cl HU17 ... 154 B2
St David La YO15 ... 5 B3
St David's Cl HU16 ... 139 D6
St David's View 9 DN14 ... 64 E4
St Davids Cres DN17 ... 96 C2
St Deny's Cl 1 DN40 ... 86 E3
St Denys' Rd YO1 ... 156 C2
St Edmunds YO41 ... 15 D2
St Edmunds's Ct 4 HU5 ... 139 D2
St Edward's Cl YO24 ... 132 F8
St Edwins Cl 27 DN7 ... 92 D4
St Ellens Ct HU17 ... 154 B2
St Francis Ave DN31 ... 152 A4
St Francis Ct 1 HU5 ... 139 D2
St Francis Gr DN37 ... 101 E1
St Francis Prep Sch YO25 ... 125 E7
St George's Ave
Bridlington YO15 ... 122 E3
Hatfield DN7 ... 92 C3
St George's Ct DN21 ... 108 F3
St George's Pl YO24 ... 129 F2
St George's Prim Sch HU3 ... 145 A6
St George's RC Prim Sch YO10 ... 130 D2
St George's Rd HU3 ... 145 A5
St George's Wlk HU9 ... 142 B2
St Georges Cl 19 DN8 ... 93 B7
St Georges Gn DN14 ... 149 D6
St Georges Rd 16 DN8 ... 93 B7
St Giles' Ave DN33 ... 102 E1
St Giles Ct
Kingston upon Hull HU9 ... 142 C1
York YO31 ... 156 B3
St Giles Rd YO30 ... 126 B5
St Giles Way YO23 ... 132 A2
St Giles's Croft HU17 ... 154 A2
St Gregory's Mews YO1 ... 156 A2

St Hedda's Ct **6** HU5 ......139 D2
St Helena Gdns **3** HU5 .140 E2
St Helen's Ave YO42 ......29 B4
St Helen's Cl YO42 ......29 B4
St Helen's Cres 29 B4
St Helen's Dr **10** HU15 ....68 D6
St Helen's La YO14 ....3 C6
St Helen's Rd
   Brigg DN20 ....98 C2
   Pocklington YO42 ....29 B4
   5 York YO24 ....132 E8
St Helen's Rise YO19 .....38 A7
St Helen's Sq
   Barmby Moor YO42 ....28 D4
   3 Market Weighton
   YO43 ....135 D4
   York YO1 ....156 B2
St Helen's Well ★ YO43 ..41 D5
St Helens Ave DN33 .102 E2
St Helens Way DN21 ..119 E2
St Helier's Rd DN35 ....153 E3
St Hilda St
   3 Bridlington YO15 .....122 C2
   Kingston upon Hull HU3 ..140 E1
St Hilda's Ave DN34 ....152 B2
St Hildas Mews YO10 ..131 B4
St Hugh's Ave DN35 ....153 D2
St Hugh's Cres DN16 ...151 C4
St Hugh's Sec Specl Sch
   DN16 ....151 B5
St Hughs Hospl DN32 ..102 F1
St Hybald's Gr DN20 ...108 F7
St Ives Cl HU7 ....141 C7
St Ives Cres DN34 ......102 C3
St James Ave
   Grimsby DN34 ....152 A2
   Hatfield DN7 ....92 C3
St James' CE VC Prim Sch
   HU7 ....141 C6
St James Cl
   12 Crowle DN17 ....94 D7
   Kingston upon Hull HU7 ..141 D7
   York YO30 ....126 E3
St James' Ct DN34 .....152 C2
St James Ct
   Rawcliffe DN14 ....64 A1
   Scunthorpe DN15 ....151 A6
St James Mount YO24 .130 A2
St James Pl **5** YO42 ..129 D1
St James' Rd YO15 ....122 D1
St James Rd
   22 Brigg DN20 ....98 C2
   Welton HU14 ....68 F5
St James' Sch DN34 ....152 C2
St James St HU3 ....145 D5
St James Terr YO8 .....148 C5
St James's Rd DN20 ...108 E8
St Joan's Dr DN20 .....108 E8
St John Mews YO8 .....148 B7
St John of Beverley RC VA
   Prim Sch HU17 ....154 C4
St John St
   Beverley HU17 ....154 B2
   York YO31 ....156 B3
St John's Ave YO16 ....122 C2
St John's Ave W YO16 .122 C2
St John's Cl
   Bridlington YO16 ....122 C2
   11 Pocklington YO42 ....28 F4
St John's Cres YO31 ...154 B2
St John's Gdns YO25 ..124 E3
St John's Gr HU9 ......141 F1
St John's Pl **2** YO25 .124 F3
St John's Rd
   Great Driffield YO25 ....124 E3
   8 Humberston DN36 ....114 C8
   Scunthorpe DN16 ....151 C2
   9 Stamford Bridge YO41 ..15 D2
St John's St
   Bridlington YO16 ....122 D4
   15 Howden DN14 ....65 A7
St John's Well ★
   Harpham YO25 ....21 F8
   Scunthorpe DN16 ....96 D1
St John's Wlk
   Bridlington YO16 ....122 C3
   1 Great Driffield YO25 .124 F3
   Kingston upon Hull
   HU13 ....143 F2
St Johns Cl **1** HU17 ...55 F8
St Johns Ct
   Goole DN14 ....149 C4
   Grimsby DN34 ....152 A1
   Kingston upon Hull HU6 ..140 D4
St Joseph Dr HU4 .....144 C5
St Joseph's Cath Prim Sch
   DN14 ....149 D5
St Joseph's RC Prim Sch
   Cleethorpes DN35 ......103 B2
   Goole DN14 ....149 D5
St Jude Gr YO16 ......122 D4
St Jude Rd YO16 ......122 D4
St Jude's Ct **3** HU5 ..139 D2
St Julian's Wells
   HU10 ....143 D7
St Katherine's Rd **2**
   HU15 ....53 F1
St Lawrence Ave
   Kingston upon Hull
   HU16 ....138 F5
   Snaith DN14 ....78 B8
St Lawrence Rd DN7 ...92 C3
St Lawrence Sq HU11 ..45 F8
St Lawrence's Pl
   DN16 ....151 D3

St Lawrence's Rd
   DN16 ....151 D2
St Lawrences CE Prim Sch
   YO10 ....130 E3
St Leonard's Ave
   DN31 ....152 A4
St Leonard's Cl **2** YO25 ..22 D1
St Leonard's Pl YO30 ..156 B3
St Leonard's Rd
   Beverley HU17 ....136 C6
   Kingston upon Hull HU5 ..140 D2
St Leonards Ave **6** 49 B4
St Luke's Cl DN7 ......92 C2
St Luke's Cres **12** DN36 .114 C8
St Luke's Ct DN32 ....152 F4
St Luke's Gr YO30 ....130 B7
St Luke's Sch DN16 ...151 D3
St Luke's St HU3 .....155 A2
St Lukes Ct HU10 .....143 F8
St Margaret's Cl **9**
   DN37 ....101 F1
St Margaret's Cres **4**
   DN40 ....100 E8
St Margaret's Terr
   YO1 ....130 E4
St Margaret's Wlk
   DN16 ....151 C1
St Margarets Ave
   HU16 ....138 E6
St Margarets Cl
   Driffield YO25 ....124 E3
   Kingston upon Hull
   HU16 ....138 E6
St Margarets Ct **3** HU8 142 C6
St Margarets View **4**
   HU11 ....45 C5
St Mark St HU8 ....155 C4
St Mark's Gr YO30 ....126 E2
St Mark's Rd **13** DN36 .114 C8
St Mark's Sq HU3 .....145 D4
St Martin's Cl
   Blyton DN21 ....117 F5
   2 Burton Agnes YO25 ...10 A2
   Fangfoss YO41 ....28 C8
St Martin's Cres
   6 Grimsby DN33 ....102 E2
   Scawby DN20 ....108 E8
St Martin's Ct HU17 ...154 A4
St Martin's Dr **1** YO25 ..10 A2
St Martin's Gr YO16 ...122 C2
St Martin's La YO1 ....156 A2
St Martin's Pl **16** DN41 .101 A4
St Martin's Prep Sch
   DN32 ....152 D1
St Martin's Rd
   Scawby DN20 ....108 E8
   Thorngumbald HU12 ....72 E5
St Martins Ave **2** HU4 .144 E6
St Martins CE Prim Sch
   DN9 ....106 A3
St Martins CE VA Prim Sch
   YO41 ....28 C8
St Martins Dr YO16 ...122 C3
St Mary Queen of Martyrs RC
   Prim Sch HU7 ....140 F7
St Mary's YO30 ....156 A3
St Mary's Ave
   1 Barnetby le Wold DN38 .99 B4
   12 Hemingbrough YO8 ....49 F1
   Kingston upon Hull HU5 .139 D4
St Mary's CE Prim Sch
   HU17 ....136 D5
St Mary's CE VC Prim Sch
   HU17 ....136 D5
St Mary's Cl
   Beverley HU17 ....136 D5
   Brough HU15 ....68 C7
   Grimsby DN32 ....153 C2
   15 Haxby YO32 ....13 E5
   Strensall YO32 ....14 A7
   7 Thorngumbald HU12 ...72 E5
St Mary's Coll HU6 ....140 C5
St Mary's Cres YO16 ..122 D4
St Mary's Ct
   9 Scunthorpe DN15 ....96 B7
   York YO24 ....156 A1
St Mary's Dr
   Hatfield DN7 ....92 C2
   38 Hedon HU12 ....72 D7
St Mary's Gr YO10 ....131 C4
St Mary's La
   5 Barton-upon-Humber
   DN18 ....84 F8
   York YO30 ....156 A3
St Mary's Mkt Weighton RC
   Prim Sch YO43 ....135 E3
St Mary's Mus ★ YO1 ..156 B2
St Mary's RC Prim Sch
   Brigg DN20 ....98 C3
   Grimsby DN32 ....152 F4
   Selby YO8 ....148 B2
St Mary's RC Sch
   DN33 ....102 D2
St Mary's Rd DN7 .....92 C2
St Mary's Terr
   Beverley HU17 ....154 A4
   York YO30 ....156 A3
St Mary's Wlk
   Beverley HU17 ....154 A4
   Bridlington YO16 ....122 D4
St Marys CE Prim Sch
   YO23 ....24 D3
St Marys Cl
   Cottingwith YO42 ......38 C5
   6 South Field HU13 ....69 E5
St Marys La HU17 .....154 A3
St Marys Mount HU16 .139 C6

St Marys RC VA Prim Sch
   YO15 ....122 C2
St Marys Terr YO30 ...156 A3
St Matthew St HU3 ...145 B5
St Matthew's Cl **4** YO19 ..36 D8
St Matthew's Ct HU17 .154 B2
St Matthew's Rd **11**
   DN36 ....114 C8
St Matthews Ct HU17 .154 B2
St Maurice's Rd YO31 .156 C3
St Mawes Cres DN34 .152 A3
St Mews **34** HU12 .....72 C7
St Michael's Cl
   Kingston upon Hull HU8 .142 B5
   Skidby HU16 ....138 A8
   13 Thorne/Moorends DN8 .93 B7
St Michael's Cres
   DN16 ....151 C4
St Michael's Ct DN19 ..86 A8
St Michael's Dr
   39 Hedon HU12 ....72 D7
   Thorne DN8 ....93 B7
St Michael's Mount
   Kingston upon Hull HU6 .140 C5
   14 Swanland HU14 ......69 B7
St Michael's Rd DN34 .102 B2
St Michael's Wlk **3** YO15 .4 D3
St Monica's Ct **3** HU5 .140 C3
St Monicas Cl YO42 ....39 B6
St Nectan Cl **9** HU3 ...145 A4
St Nicholas Ave
   Kingston upon Hull HU4 .144 C2
   York YO19 ....133 D4
St Nicholas Cl
   Copmanthorpe YO23 ...132 A3
   8 Newbald YO43 ....53 F7
St Nicholas Cres
   YO23 ....132 A3
St Nicholas Croft YO23 ..24 E3
St Nicholas Dr
   Beverley HU17 ....154 C2
   Grimsby DN37 ....102 B3
   Hornsea HU18 ....134 C6
St Nicholas Fields Nature
   Reserve ★ YO10 ......130 F4
St Nicholas Gate HU12 ..72 D7
St Nicholas Gdns HU4 .144 C3
St Nicholas Pk **6** HU19 .75 A6
St Nicholas Pl **1** YO10 .130 F3
St Nicholas Rd
   Beverley HU17 ....154 C2
   Copmanthorpe YO23 ...132 A3
   Thorne/Moorends DN8 ..93 A8
St Nicholas' VA Prim Sch
   HU6 ....140 C4
St Nicholas Way **22** YO32 13 E5
St Norbert's RC Prim Sch
   DN17 ....94 D7
St Olaf's Dr DN32 .....152 D2
St Olave's Rd YO30 ...156 A4
St Olave's Sch YO30 ...156 A4
St Oswald Ct **5** HU5 ..139 D2
St Oswald Rd YO16 ...122 E4
St Oswald's CE Prim Sch
   YO10 ....133 E7
St Oswald's Cl YO41 ...27 F6
St Oswald's Rd YO10 ..133 D8
St Oswalds St YO10 ...133 E7
St Patrick's Gn **14** HU12 .74 D1
St Paul St HU2 ....155 A4
St Paul's CE Prim Sch
   YO24 ....130 A3
St Paul's Rd
   Gainsborough DN21 ....117 A2
   Scunthorpe DN16 ......151 B2
St Paul's Sq YO24 .....130 A3
St Paul's Terr YO24 ...130 A4
St Paulinus Cres **20**
   HU15 ....68 C6
St Pauls Dr HU17 .....137 E8
St Pauls Mews YO24 ..130 A3
St Pauls Way HU17 ...137 E8
St Peter St HU9 ....155 C2
St Peter's Ave
   Cleethorpes DN35 ......153 E2
   Kingston upon Hull
   HU10 ....143 E6
   Scunthorpe DN16 ......96 D2
St Peter's CE Prim Sch
   DN35 ....153 F2
St Peter's Cl
   10 Holton le Clay DN36 .114 A5
   16 Howden DN14 ....65 A7
St Peter's Cres **7** DN36 114 C8
St Peter's Gr
   2 Scotter DN21 ....107 C3
   York YO30 ....156 A4
St Peter's Rd Drax YO8 ..63 F5
   19 Scotter DN21 ....107 C3
St Peter's Sch YO30 ..156 A4
St Peter's Sq **14** YO42 ..29 A4
St Peters Cl
   East/West Stockwith
   DN21 ....116 E5
   Hutton Cranswick YO25 ..32 E8
   Rufforth YO26 ....129 A5
St Peters Ct YO30 ....156 A4
St Peters Gr DN37 ....101 E1
St Peters Orch DN18 ..69 F1
St Peters View HU11 ..42 F6
St Peters Wlk HU12 ...59 D2
St Philip's Gr YO30 ...130 A8
St Philips Rd HU12 ....73 C4
St Quintin Field YO25 .125 F7
St Quintin Pk **9** YO25 .125 F7
St Quintins Cl **6** HU9 .146 C8
St Richard's RC Prim Sch
   HU9 ....142 C1

St Sampsons Sq YO1 .156 B2
St Saviour's Pl YO1 ...156 C2
St Saviourgate YO1 ...156 C2
St Silas St HU2 ....155 B4
St Stephen Rd YO16 ..122 E4
St Stephen's Cl HU10 .138 C2
St Stephen's Cres **4**
   HU15 ....66 D8
St Stephen's Rd YO24 .129 C3
St Stephen's Sq YO24 .129 C3
St Stephens Cl YO25 ..124 E3
St Stephens Mews
   YO30 ....127 A2
St Stephens St HU2 ...145 D6
St Swithin's Wlk YO26 .129 E4
St Thomas Moore Rd
   HU4 ....144 A4
St Thomas More RC Prim Sch
   HU4 ....144 B4
St Thomas' Pl YO31 ...156 B4
St Thomas Rd YO16 ...122 E4
St Thomas' Rd **14** DN16 .151 B2
St Thomas's Cl **2** YO10 .131 C4
St Thomas's Grange **2**
   HU5 ....139 D2
St Vincent's Ave DN15 ..96 C7
St Vincent's RC Prim Sch
   HU5 ....140 D2
St Wilfred Rd YO16 ...122 E3
St Wilfred's RC Prim Sch
   YO31 ....156 C3
St Wilfrid's Cl **7** YO23 ..14 B6
St Wilfrid's Cres **9** YO8 .48 D1
St Wilfrid's Ct YO31 ...156 C3
St Wilfrid's Rd **8** YO32 ..14 B6
St Wilfrids Cl HU12 ....73 E3
St Williams Coll YO31 .156 B3
St Wulstan Cl YO31 ...130 E7
Saints Cl HU9 ....141 F2
Salacon Way **3** DN32 .153 A5
Saladine Ct **16** DN41 ..101 F5
Salamander Cl DN31 ..152 B4
Salcey Cl **23** HU7 .....56 F6
Salents La YO17 ....6 B6
Sales La DN14 ....78 B3
Salisbury Ave
   Beverley HU17 ....136 C1
   Goole DN14 ....149 E4
   Hornsea HU18 ....134 C2
   24 Waltham DN37 ......113 D6
Salisbury Cl
   Morton DN21 ....117 A3
   Scunthorpe DN17 ......150 C3
Salisbury Rd YO26 ....129 F5
Salisbury St
   6 Gainsborough DN21 ..117 B2
   Northfield HU13 ....143 D1
   Sculcoates HU5 ....140 B2
Salmon Gr HU6 ....140 B4
Salmonby Rd
   1 Scunthorpe DN17 ....96 C2
   Scunthorpe DN17 ......150 E1
Salmond Rd **5** YO24 .129 B1
Salsbury Ave DN34 ....152 B2
Salt End La HU12 ......72 A7
Saltash Rd HU4 ....144 A2
Saltaugh Rd HU12 .....88 B8
Saltburn Gr DN32 .....153 A1
Saltburn St HU3 ......145 A4
Saltergate Rd DN17 ..107 D7
Salters' La LN11 ......120 E4
Saltford Ave HU9 .....147 F8
Saltgrounds Rd HU15 ..68 B5
Salthouse La HU1 .....155 C2
Saltmarsh La HU12 ....89 D8
Saltmarshe Delph Nature
   Reserve ★ DN14 ......65 D1
Saltmarshe Sta DN14 ..65 E4
Salton Ave **4** HU5 ....139 E3
Saltshouse Rd HU8 ...141 E6
Saltwell Pk **29** HU7 ...56 F6
Salvesen Rd DN35 ....153 B5
Salvesen Way HU3 ....145 A3
Samman Cl HU10 .....143 D6
Samman Rd HU17 .....154 C4
Samphire Cl DN36 ....115 C4
Sample Ave HU17 .....154 B4
Sampson St DN17 .....81 A3
Samuel Ave DN32 .....153 B2
Sanbeds La DN9 ......105 B2
Sancton Cl HU16 .....138 E6
Sancton Rd YO43 .....135 E3
Sanctuary Way DN37 .102 B3
Sand Hutton CE VC Prim Sch
   YO41 ....15 B5
Sand Hutton Ct YO41 ..15 B5
Sand La
   Barlby with Osgodby YO8 ..49 B4
   Broughton DN20 ....97 D3
   Bubwith YO8 ....50 D5
   Caistor LN7 ....110 E4
   Manton DN21 ....108 A5
   Messingham DN17 .....107 A7
   Newton on Derwent YO41 ..28 B3
   North Cave HU15 ....53 D2
   Sancton YO43 ....53 D8
   South Cliffe YO43 ......52 B8
   Thornton YO42 ....39 D7
   Wistow YO8 ....48 E6
   Wroot DN9 ....104 C6
Sand Rd DN17 ....106 B8
Sandacre Ct YO26 ....129 D5
Sandale Ct HU5 ......139 E1
Sandbeck La DN21 ....117 C6
Sandcroft Cl **4** YO24 .132 D8
Sandcroft Rd YO24 ...132 D8
Sanderson Cl
   Driffield YO25 ....124 D2

Sanderson Cl *continued*
   Scunthorpe DN16 ......151 A5
Sanderson's Bank
   DN10 ....104 C2
Sandfield Cl
   Market Weighton YO43 ..135 B3
   Scunthorpe DN17 ......150 D1
Sandfield Dr **3** HU15 ..68 C5
Sandfield Gn YO43 ....135 B3
Sandford Cl HU7 ......56 F5
Sandford St DN31 ....152 B4
Sandgate Rd YO16 ...123 A6
Sandhall Dr DN14 ....149 F5
Sandhall Rd DN14 ....65 C3
Sandhill La Brayton YO8 .48 D2
   Sutton upon Derwent
   YO41 ....27 E2
Sandhill Rd DN14 .....81 B6
Sandholme
   2 Haxby YO32 ....13 F5
   Market Weighton YO43 .135 C3
Sandholme Cl **1** HU15 ..66 D8
Sandholme La HU17 ...44 F8
Sandholme Pk HU15 ..66 D8
Sandholme Rd HU15 ..66 C8
Sandholme Way **4** DN14 .65 A7
Sandhouse Cres DN16 .151 C5
Sandiacres **5** YO8 ....48 D1
Sandlemere Cl **3** HU3 .145 A5
Sandmartin Ct YO24 ..132 D8
Sandmoor Cl HU8 ....142 B6
Sandown Cl YO24 ....129 E2
Sandpiper Cl HU10 ...134 D6
Sandpiper Dr HU4 ....144 B1
Sandpits La HU11 ....47 C1
Sandringham Cl
   6 Bridlington YO16 ....122 D6
   Haxby YO32 ....127 C7
   Kingston upon Hull
   HU16 ....139 A7
Sandringham Cres **19**
   DN17 ....96 C2
Sandringham Dr
   DN14 ....149 B6
Sandringham Rd
   DN35 ....103 B2
Sandringham St
   2 Kingston upon Hull
   HU3 ....145 A6
   York YO10 ....130 D2
Sands Cl Keadby DN17 ..95 D6
   Reighton YO14 ....3 D7
Sands Ct **3** HU14 ....69 A4
Sands La Barmston YO25 ..22 F5
   Bridlington YO15 ......122 F3
   Brough HU15 ....68 C6
   Ellerker HU15 ....67 F6
   Holme-on-Spalding-Moor
   YO43 ....39 F1
   Hornsea HU18 ....134 D4
   Hunmanby YO14 ....3 A8
   Scotter DN21 ....107 C3
   South Ferriby DN18 ....84 A7
   Ulrome YO25 ....23 B3
Sands Rd Barmston YO15 .22 F7
   Hunmanby YO14 ....3 B7
Sands Top YO43 ......53 E7
Sandsacre Ave YO16 .123 A6
Sandsacre Dr **1** YO16 .123 A6
Sandsacre Rd YO16 ...123 A6
Sandsacre Way YO16 .122 F6
Sandsfield Ave YO43 ..40 E6
Sandstock Rd
   Pocklington YO42 ......29 A4
   York YO10 ....131 B7
Sandtoft Rd
   Epworth DN9 ....94 B3
   Hatfield DN7 ....93 A4
Sandwalk YO43 ....135 C3
Sandway Ave **12** YO8 .48 B1
Sandway Cl **11** YO8 ..48 B1
Sandway Dr
   Camblesforth YO8 ......63 D4
   1 Thorpe Willoughby YO8 .48 B1
Sandwith Ct HU17 ....154 B4
Sandwith La YO8 .....63 B4
Sandy Cl DN36 ....115 C5
Sandy Gap YO32 .....127 C7
Sandy La Harpham YO25 ..9 E2
   Harton YO60 ....15 B8
   16 Haxby YO32 ....13 E5
   North Duffield YO8 .....49 F8
   Stockton on the Forest
   YO32 ....14 E4
Sandy Point HU9 .....142 E5
Sandy Rise YO8 ......148 C3
Sandycroft Cl HU10 ..139 A1
Sandyland **29** YO32 ..13 E5
Sandyridge YO26 .....126 A1
Saner St HU3 ....145 B6
Saner's Cl HU16 ......139 B5
Santolina Way HU4 ...144 C2
Sapperton Cl **16** HU7 ..56 F6
Sapphire Gr **7** HU3 ..145 A4
Sarah Rhodes La DN14 .65 C3
Sarge Cl **18** DN36 ...114 A5
Sargent Ave YO23 ....132 F4
Sargent's Way **8** DN20 .108 F5
Sargon Way DN31 ....102 C6
Sassaby Cl HU4 ......144 C3
Saunby Gr DN35 .....153 C4
Saunders Cres **21** YO42 .29 A3
Saunders Croft **4** HU17 .55 B8
Saunders La HU17 ....55 B7
Saunders St DN31 ....152 C4
Savage Rd YO15 ......122 D2
Savery St HU9 ....141 D1
Savile Cl HU17 ....136 E6

Saville Gr YO30 . . . . .130 A8
Saville St HU1 . . . . .155 B2
Savoy Ct 12 DN36 . . . . . .114 A7
Savoy Rd HU8 . . . . .141 F4
Sawcliffe Medieval Village★
DN15 . . . . .82 F1
Sawley Cl HU18 . . . . . . .134 C5
Sawmill Yd 5 YO15 . . . . .122 E2
Sawston Ave HU5 . . . . . .139 C2
Sawyer's Cres YO23 . . . .132 C2
Sawyers Wlk 9 YO19 . . . .26 F7
Saxby Gr 17 DN33 . . . . .102 D2
Saxby Hill DN20 . . . . . . .84 B3
Saxby Rd Bonby DN20 . . .84 B2
Kingston upon Hull HU8 . .142 A5
Scunthorpe DN17 . . . . . .150 E1
Saxcourt HU6 . . . . .139 E7
Saxford Way 8 YO32 . . . .13 D5
Saxon Cl
Barton-upon-Humber
DN18 . . . . .84 F8
Shipton YO30 . . . . .12 F5
6 Thorpe Willoughby YO8 . .48 B1
Saxon Cres DN35 . . . . . .153 D2
Saxon Ct Blyton DN21 . . .117 F5
Scunthorpe DN16 . . . . . . .96 D2
Saxon Pl YO31 . . . . .130 E7
Saxon Rd YO41 . . . . .15 D2
Saxon Rise HU17 . . . . . .136 D7
Saxon Vale YO30 . . . . . . .12 F5
Saxon Villas 10 HU3 . . . .145 A4
Saxon Way
4 Caistor LN7 . . . . .111 B4
Kingston upon Hull
HU13 . . . . .143 F1
Saxondale HU4 . . . . .144 B7
Saxonfield LN7 . . . . .111 A4
Saxton Cl DN17 . . . . .150 E2
Scafell Cl 4 YO30 . . . . .126 E1
Scaife Cl HU17 . . . . .154 C2
Scaife Garth YO42 . . . . . .28 F3
Scaife Gdns YO31 . . . . . .130 C7
Scaife Mews HU17 . . . . .137 B3
Scaife St YO31 . . . . .130 C7
Scalby Gr HU5 . . . . .144 D8
Scalby La HU15 . . . . .66 D8
Scalby Pl HU18 . . . . .134 B4
Scale La HU1 . . . . .155 C2
Scale La Staith HU1 . . . .155 C2
Scallow La DN17 . . . . . . .107 D6
Scalm La YO8 . . . . .48 A4
Scampton Cl DN34 . . . . .152 A1
Scampton Garth HU7 . . . .141 C8
Scandinavian Way
DN41 . . . . .87 E1
Scarborough Cres 8
YO16 . . . . .122 C5
Scarborough Rd
Bempton YO16 . . . . .4 A1
Blyton DN21 . . . . .117 E5
7 Bridlington YO16 . . . . .122 C5
Great Driffield YO25 . . . .124 E6
Langtoft YO25 . . . . .8 C7
Scarborough St YO25 . . .145 A4
Scarborough Terr
YO30 . . . . .156 B4
Scarcroft Hill YO24 . . . . .130 B2
Scarcroft La YO23 . . . . . .156 A1
Scarcroft Prim Sch
YO23 . . . . .156 A1
Scarcroft Rd YO24 . . . . . .156 A1
Scarcroft View YO23 . . . .156 A1
Scardale Ct YO8 . . . . . . .148 A2
Scargate Cl YO16 . . . . . .123 A7
Scarrington Cres HU4 . . .144 B6
Scarrow Cl HU3 . . . . . . .145 C4
Scarsea Way YO15 . . . . . .4 C3
Scartho Jun & Inf Sch
DN33 . . . . .102 E1
Scartho Pk DN33 . . . . . . .102 D1
Scartho Rd DN33 . . . . . .102 E2
Scaudercroft 13 YO19 . . .26 F7
Scawby Hall★ DN20 . . . .108 F8
Scawby Prim Sch
DN20 . . . . .108 E8
Scawby Rd Brigg DN20 . . .98 A1
Broughton DN20 . . . . .97 E2
13 Grimsby DN33 . . . . . .102 D2
Scunthorpe DN17 . . . . . .150 E1
Scawton Ave 1 YO31 . . .127 E2
Schiphol Way DN8 . . . . . .99 E5
Schofield Ave HU17 . . . . .154 C3
Schofield Cl 5 DN19 . . . .85 C8
Scholefield Ave HU17 . . . .56 B8
School Cl Selby YO8 . . . .148 B3
16 Stamford Bridge YO41 . .15 D2
School Dr DN17 . . . . .107 D7
School Hill YO16 . . . . . . .10 E4
School House La 2
DN10 . . . . .116 C3
School Houses 6 DN20 . . .97 E4
School La Appleby DN15 . . .83 D1
Askham Richard YO23 . . . .24 D3
Beswick YO25 . . . . .32 B4
Beverley HU17 . . . . .154 B3
Bishopthorpe YO23 . . . . .133 A4
Bonby DN20 . . . . .84 C2
Buckton/Bempton YO15 . . . .2 C3
Burton Fleming YO25 . . . . .2 E3
Cabourne LN7 . . . . .111 D5
Copmanthorpe YO23 . . . .132 A2
10 Flamborough YO15 . . . .5 A4
Goxhill DN19 . . . . .86 A8
Grayingham DN21 . . . . . .119 B7
Heslington YO10 . . . . . . .131 B1
Holmpton HU19 . . . . .75 D2
Irby DN37 . . . . .112 D7
15 Keyingham HU12 . . . . .73 C4

School La continued
Kingston upon Hull
HU10 . . . . .143 C8
New Holland DN19 . . . . . .70 E2
5 North Ferriby HU14 . . . .69 A4
North Kelsey LN7 . . . . . . .110 A5
5 Pocklington YO42 . . . . .29 A4
23 Poppleton YO26 . . . . . .12 F1
Redbourne DN21 . . . . . . .108 F2
Rothwell LN7 . . . . .111 E2
South Ferriby DN18 . . . . . .84 A7
Tetney DN36 . . . . .114 C3
West/East Butterwick
DN17 . . . . .106 D8
York YO10 . . . . .133 E7
School La Mews HU17 . .154 B3
School Rd
Hemingbrough YO8 . . . . . .49 F1
7 Preston HU12 . . . . .58 C1
Scunthorpe DN16 . . . . . .151 B2
South Killingholme DN40 . .86 E3
Winteringham DN15 . . . . . .68 A1
School Rise YO43 . . . . . .53 F7
School St
Kingston upon Hull HU1 . .155 A2
York YO24 . . . . .129 D3
School Wlk DN35 . . . . . . .153 C1
Schooner Ct HU4 . . . . . .144 B3
Schubert Cl HU9 . . . . . . .142 A3
Scorborough La YO25 . . .43 D8
Scoreby La YO41 . . . . . . .15 B1
Scotney Ct 5 HU3 . . . . . .140 E1
Scott Ave DN17 . . . . .150 C2
Scott Cl 7 DN37 . . . . . . .102 C4
Scott Gdns 7 HU19 . . . . .75 A6
Scott Moncrieff Rd
YO32 . . . . .14 B6
Scott Rd YO8 . . . . .148 C6
Scott St
27 Gainsborough DN21 . . .117 B1
Kingston upon Hull HU2 . .155 B3
York YO23 . . . . .130 C2
Scotter Prim Sch
DN21 . . . . .107 C3
Scotter Rd
Laughton DN21 . . . . .117 F8
Messingham DN17 . . . . . .107 D5
Scotton DN21 . . . . .107 C2
Scunthorpe DN17 . . . . . .150 C3
Scotter Rd S
Bottesford DN17 . . . . .96 B1
Scunthorpe DN17 . . . . . .150 C1
Scotterthorpe Rd
DN21 . . . . .107 B4
Scotton Rd DN21 . . . . . .107 C3
Scotts Croft YO43 . . . . . .135 D3
Scotts Garth Cl HU17 . . .137 F8
Scotts Garth Dr HU17 . . . .44 C5
Scrap Bay Rd DN16 . . . . .97 A3
Scrivelsby Ct 9 DN35 . . .103 D2
Scriven Gr 8 YO32 . . . . .13 F5
Scrope Ave 4 YO31 . . . . .130 E5
Scrub La DN40 . . . . .86 E5
Scrubwood La HU17 . . . . .136 E6
Sculcoates La HU5 . . . . .140 E2
Scunthorpe CE Prim Sch
DN15 . . . . .151 A6
Scunthorpe General Hospl
DN15 . . . . .150 E6
Scunthorpe Leisure Ctr
DN15 . . . . .151 B7
Scunthorpe Mus & Art Gall★
DN15 . . . . .151 A6
Scunthorpe Sta DN16 . . .151 A6
Scunthorpe United Football
Club DN15 . . . . .150 A6
Sea La DN36 . . . . .115 B3
Sea Rd
Cleethorpes DN35 . . . . . .153 F2
Holmpton HU19 . . . . .75 D3
Sea View St DN35 . . . . . .153 F1
Seabrook Dr DN16 . . . . . .96 D1
Seacroft Rd
Cleethorpes DN35 . . . . . .103 D3
Withernsea HU19 . . . . . . .75 A6
Seafield Ave HU9 . . . . . .141 F3
Seafire Cl YO30 . . . . . . .127 A3
Seaford Rd DN35 . . . . . .103 D1
Seagate YO15 . . . . .123 C6
Seagate View YO15 . . . . .123 E6
Seagull Cl HU4 . . . . .144 E2
Seakel La YO23 . . . . .24 C1
Seamer Dr DN32 . . . . . . .153 A1
Sean La DN14 . . . . .65 F4
Searby Hill DN38 . . . . . .110 D8
Searby Rd DN17 . . . . .96 C2
Searby Wold La DN38 . . . .99 E1
Seascale Wlk DN32 . . . . .152 F4
Seaside La HU12 . . . . . . .60 C2
Seaside Rd
Aldbrough HU11 . . . . .47 C2
Easington HU12 . . . . .91 A5
Holmpton HU19 . . . . .75 C2
Withernsea HU19 . . . . . . .75 A7
Seathorne HU19 . . . . .74 F7
Seathorne Rd 1 YO16 . . .122 C5
Seathorne Wlk YO16 . . . .122 B5
Seaton Cl YO10 . . . . .131 C4
Seaton Gr
Grimsby DN32 . . . . .153 A1
Kingston upon Hull HU4 . .144 E5
Seaton Rd
Bewholme YO25 . . . . .35 A4
Hornsea HU18 . . . . .134 A4
Kingston upon Hull
HU13 . . . . .143 F2
Scunthorpe DN17 . . . . . .150 D4

Seavy Carr La HU15 . . . . .52 F2
Seavy Rd DN14 . . . . .149 B3
Seawall La DN36 . . . . . . .115 C5
Second Ave
Bridlington YO15 . . . . . . .123 A4
Fixborough Stather DN15 . .81 F1
4 Goole DN14 . . . . .149 C4
Grimsby DN33 . . . . .102 D2
Scunthorpe DN17 . . . . . .150 C2
York DN17 . . . . .148 B3
Second Comm La YO8 . . .48 C4
Sedbergh Ave HU5 . . . . .139 D3
Sedbury Cl 5 HU7 . . . . . .56 F6
Sedge Cl 2 DN18 . . . . . . .69 E1
Sedgebrook Gr 18 HU7 . . .56 F6
Sedgewood Way 13
DN15 . . . . .96 B7
Seed Cl La 3 DN37 . . . . .101 F1
Sefton Ave HU5 . . . . .130 F8
Sefton St 2 HU3 . . . . . . .145 B4
Seg La YO8 . . . . .63 F3
Segmere St DN35 . . . . . .103 D3
Segrave Gr HU5 . . . . . . .144 D8
Segrave Wlk 10 YO26 . . .129 E4
Selbourne Rd 5 DN34 . . .102 C2
Selby Abbey YO8 . . . . . . .148 D5
Selby Abbey CE Prim Sch
YO8 . . . . .148 C5
Selby Bsns Pk YO8 . . . . .148 D1
Selby Coll Selby YO8 . . . .148 F3
Selby CP Sch YO8 . . . . .148 B5
Selby Ct DN17 . . . . .150 D3
Selby High Sch YO8 . . . .148 B4
Selby Ironworks Bsns Ctr
YO8 . . . . .148 D1
Selby Rd
Eggborough DN14 . . . . . . .61 F1
Fulford YO19 . . . . .133 E6
Holme-on-Spalding-Moor
YO43 . . . . .39 F1
Howden DN14 . . . . .65 A7
Riccall YO19 . . . . .49 A8
Snaith DN14 . . . . .63 C1
Thorne DN8 . . . . .92 F8
Wistow YO8 . . . . .48 D6
Womersley DN14 . . . . . . .77 A4
Selby Rly Sports Club
YO8 . . . . .148 D5
Selby St HU3 . . . . .145 A5
Selby Sta YO8 . . . . .148 D5
Selby Town Football Club
YO8 . . . . .148 B5
Seldon Rd YO26 . . . . . . .129 C5
Selge Way DN33 . . . . . . .102 C1
Selkirk St HU5 . . . . .145 A8
Sellers Dr HU17 . . . . .43 D6
Selsey Cl 2 HU5 . . . . . . .140 D2
Selvage La DN14 . . . . . . .78 A6
Selwick Dr YO15 . . . . .5 D2
Selworthy Cl 3 HU7 . . . . .57 A5
Selwyn Ave 1 HU14 . . . . .69 A4
Sennefleet Rd DN21 . . . .107 B4
Sequana Ct HU9 . . . . . . .146 B6
Seraphim App Rd
DN16 . . . . .151 E5
Seraphim Rd DN16 . . . . .151 F4
Service Rd 1 12 DN37 . . .102 C4
Service Rd 2 15 DN37 . . .102 C4
Service Rd 3 17 DN37 . . .102 C4
Service Rd 4 3 DN37 . . . .102 C4
Service Rd 5 4 DN37 . . . .102 C4
Service Rd 6 8 DN37 . . . .102 C4
Service Rd 7 9 DN37 . . . .102 C4
Service Rd 8 1 DN37 . . . .102 C5
Service Rd 9 2 DN37 . . . .102 C5
Service Rd 10 3 DN37 . . .102 C5
Service Rd 11 4 DN37 . . .102 C5
Service Rd 12 5 DN37 . . .102 C5
Service Rd 13 6 DN37 . . .102 C5
Service Rd 14 7 DN37 . . .102 C4
Service Rd 15 19 DN37 . .102 C4
Service Rd 16 18 DN37 . .102 C4
Service Rd 17 10 DN37 . .102 C4
Service Rd 18 11 DN37 . .102 C4
Service Rd 19 13 DN37 . .102 C4
Service Rd 20 14 DN37 . .102 C4
Service Rd 21 13 DN37 . .102 B4
Service Rd 22 1 DN37 . . .102 C4
Service Rd 23 2 DN37 . . .102 C4
Service Rd 24 DN37 . . . . .102 C4
Service Rd 25 DN37 . . . . .102 C4
Service Rd 26 8 DN37 . . .102 C5
Service Rd No 1 DN32 . . .152 F5
Service Rd No 2 DN32 . . .152 F5
Services DN16 . . . . .151 E6
Setterwood Garth 2
HU10 . . . . .143 E8
Setting Cres 8 HU5 . . . . .139 D2
Setting Rd HU5 . . . . .139 D2
Seven Corners La
HU17 . . . . .136 D4
Seven Lakes L Pk★
DN17 . . . . .94 D6
Seven Quay Rd DN40 . . . .87 D3
Seventh Ave
3 Bridlington YO15 . . . . .122 F4
York YO31 . . . . .130 F5
Severn Gn YO26 . . . . . . .129 C8
Severn St HU8 . . . . .141 C1
Severus Ave YO26 . . . . . .129 D4
Severus St YO24 . . . . . . .129 D3
Sewer La HU1 . . . . .155 B1
Sewerby Ave YO16 . . . . .122 E5
Sewerby Cres YO16 . . . . .122 D5
Sewerby Ct 6 YO16 . . . . .122 D5
Sewerby Hall & Gdns★
YO15 . . . . .123 C7

Sewerby Headlands
YO16 . . . . .122 F5
Sewerby Heads YO16 . . .122 F5
Sewerby Pk Cl YO15 . . . .123 C5
Sewerby Rd YO16 . . . . . .122 D5
Sewerby Rise YO16 . . . . .122 D5
Sextant Rd HU6 . . . . .140 C8
Seymour Gr YO31 . . . . . .130 F6
Seymour Rd 6 HU12 . . . .73 C4
Seymour St HU3 . . . . . . .144 F5
Shadwell Rise 5 DN18 . . .69 E1
Shady La 3 YO25 . . . . . . .10 A2
Shaftesbury Ave
Goole DN14 . . . . .149 A5
Grimsby DN34 . . . . .152 B3
Hornsea HU18 . . . . .134 C5
Kellingley DN14 . . . . .61 C3
Kingston upon Hull HU8 . .141 F4
Shaftesbury Mews 1
DN36 . . . . .114 A7
Shaftesbury Rd YO15 . . .122 C1
Shakespeare Ave
2 Campsall DN6 . . . . . . .76 E1
Scunthorpe DN17 . . . . . .150 C2
Shakespeare Cl 6 HU3 . .145 D8
Shallowdale Gr 1 YO10 . .131 C3
Shambles YO1 . . . . .156 B2
Shannon Rd HU8 . . . . . . .142 C6
Shardeloes HU9 . . . . .142 E5
Shardlow Rd HU18 . . . . .134 C5
Sharp Ave HU12 . . . . .73 A6
Sharp Hill La YO8 . . . . . . .63 F6
Sharp St HU5 . . . . .140 B2
Sharpe Cl 20 DN18 . . . . .84 E8
Sharpe Howe★ YO11 . . . .2 A8
Sharps La HU17 . . . . .55 B7
Shaw Dr 1 DN33 . . . . . . .113 F8
Shaw La DN6 . . . . .77 D2
Shaw Rd DN10 . . . . .116 A2
Shaw St HU9 . . . . .146 B7
Shaw's Terr YO24 . . . . . .156 A1
Shawfield Cl 7 DN3 . . . . .92 A3
Shears Ct DN37 . . . . .113 E7
Sheep Cote La DN7 . . . . .92 D2
Sheep Dip La DN7 . . . . . .92 D2
Sheep Marsh La DN36 . .115 B3
Sheep Rake La YO25 . . . . .8 F4
Sheep Trod La HU12 . . . . .89 F6
Sheepdike La YO25 . . . . . .21 F2
Sheepdyke La
Bonby DN20 . . . . .84 C3
Hunmanby YO14 . . . . .3 A8
Sheepfold St DN32 . . . . .152 E3
Sheepman La YO25 . . . . . .32 F7
Sheeprake La YO15 . . . . .123 B8
Sheepswarth La HU17 . . . .54 F3
Sheepwalk La YO17 . . . . . .7 B7
Sheepwash La DN14 . . . . .77 A7
Sheffield Pk Ave DN15 . . .96 C7
Sheffield St DN15 . . . . . .151 A8
Sheffield St E DN15 . . . . .151 A8
Sheffield St W DN15 . . . .150 F8
Sheldon Cl HU7 . . . . .141 B8
Sheldrake Way HU17 . . . .136 F6
Shelford Ave DN14 . . . . . .65 A7
Shelford St DN15 . . . . . . .151 A7
Shelley Ave
Grimsby DN33 . . . . .102 D2
Kingston upon Hull HU9 . .142 C2
Shelley Gr YO30 . . . . . . .126 F1
Shelroy Cl DN15 . . . . .96 B7
Shenley Cl 11 DN7 . . . . . .92 D3
Shepherd La HU17 . . . . . .55 F8
Shepherd's Croft DN9 . . .105 D7
Shepherds Lea 6 HU17 . . .55 E8
Shepherdton Mere YO25 . .9 B1
Sheraton Dr 3 DN36 . . . .114 D8
Sherbrooke Ave HU5 . . . .139 E4
Sherburn Cres DN15 . . . .150 D8
Sherburn Rd YO8 . . . . . .148 A8
Sherburn St
1 Cawood YO8 . . . . .48 B8
Cleethorpes DN35 . . . . . .153 F1
Kingston upon Hull HU8 . .146 D8
Sherbuttgate Dr 13 YO42 .28 F4
Sherbuttgate Rd 14 YO42 .28 F4
Sheriff Highway HU12 . . . .72 C6
Sherringham Dr YO24 . . .132 D8
Sherwood Ave HU9 . . . . .141 E1
Sherwood Cl
13 Norton DN6 . . . . .76 E1
4 Walkington HU17 . . . . . .55 C8
Sherwood Ct HU9 . . . . . .142 D5
Sherwood Dr HU4 . . . . . .144 A7
Sherwood Gr
Huntington YO32 . . . . . . .127 F1
York YO26 . . . . .129 B6
Sherwood Rd DN34 . . . . .102 C2
Sherwood Vale DN15 . . . .150 D7
Shetland Cl 6 HU7 . . . . .141 E7
Shetland Way DN40 . . . . .101 C2
Shevington Wlk HU8 . . . .142 C6
Shields Rd 2 HU12 . . . . .72 C7
Shildon Gr DN8 . . . . .79 C2
Shilling Cl 26 DN37 . . . . .56 F5
Shilton Garth Cl 3
YO32 . . . . .127 F7
Shipcote Rd DN14 . . . . . .149 D1
Shipley Cl HU9 . . . . .142 D2
Shipman Rd YO43 . . . . . .135 D3
Shipton Cl HU9 . . . . .142 C5
Shipton Cres HU17 . . . . . .43 D6
Shipton La YO43 . . . . .40 E3
Shipton Low Rd YO30 . . .12 F5
Shipton Rd
Clifton YO30 . . . . .129 F8
Rawcliffe YO30 . . . . .126 D2
Scunthorpe DN16 . . . . . .151 C1

Shipton Rd continued
York YO30 . . . . .130 A7
Shipton St 3 YO30 . . . . .130 B7
Shipton St Inf Sch
YO30 . . . . .130 B7
Shipyard Ind Est YO8 . . .148 E5
Shipyard Rd YO8 . . . . . . .148 E5
Shirbutt La YO26 . . . . . . .24 C3
Shirley Ave YO26 . . . . . . .129 C6
Shirley Cres DN16 . . . . . .151 B4
Shoemaker's La DN21 . . .107 D5
Shopeth Way HU17 . . . . . .56 B8
Shore Rd DN17 . . . . .81 F5
Shoreditch Cl 2 HU8 . . . .141 F5
Short La Bempton YO16 . . . .4 C1
12 Bridlington YO16 . . . . .122 C5
Fotherby LN11 . . . . .121 C2
Market Weighton YO43 . . . .41 B2
West Haddlesey YO8 . . . . .61 F6
West Halton DN15 . . . . . . .82 E8
Short St
Cleethorpes DN35 . . . . . .153 E2
Kingston upon Hull HU1 . .155 A2
Shortacre La YO42 . . . . . .38 C2
Shorthill Croft HU17 . . . . .154 A1
Shorwell Cl 2 HU8 . . . . .142 C5
Shotel Cl YO30 . . . . .129 F8
Shropshire Cl HU5 . . . . . .139 C1
Shrubberies The YO8 . . . .49 E2
Shuttleworth Ct HU18 . . . .134 D4
Sibelius Rd HU4 . . . . . . .144 B4
Sicey La HU6 . . . . .56 D7
Side La DN33 . . . . .113 F8
Sidebottom St DN31 . . . .152 F6
Siding La YO8 . . . . .49 B5
Sidings Ct HU15 . . . . .68 B5
Sidmouth Prim Sch
HU5 . . . . .140 B3
Sidmouth St HU5 . . . . . . .140 C3
Sidney Ct DN35 . . . . .153 B4
Sidney Pl DN35 . . . . .153 B4
Sidney Rd
Grimsby DN34 . . . . .152 B3
Scunthorpe DN17 . . . . . .150 D2
Sidney St DN35 . . . . .153 B4
Sidney Way DN35 . . . . . .153 B4
Sidsaph Hill 2 DN10 . . . .116 D3
Sigglesthorne CE VC Prim
Sch HU11 . . . . .45 F8
Sigglesthorne Rd HU11 . .46 B6
Sigglesthorne Sta Nature
Reserve★ HU11 . . . . .46 B6
Signhills Ave 1 DN35 . . .103 D2
Signhills Jun & Inf Sch
DN35 . . . . .103 D2
Sigston Rd HU17 . . . . . . .154 C4
Silica Cres DN17 . . . . . . .150 D1
Silkstone Oval 15 DN8 . . .79 B2
Silkstone Wlk HU17 . . . . .141 C1
Sills La YO30 . . . . .12 B6
Silsden Ave 5 HU6 . . . . .140 C4
Silver Birch Rise 22
DN16 . . . . .96 D2
Silver St
Barnetby le Wold DN38 . . .99 B4
Barrow upon Humber
DN19 . . . . .85 C7
Holton le Clay DN36 . . . .114 A5
Huggate YO42 . . . . .18 C2
Kingston upon Hull HU1 . .155 B2
Owston Ferry DN9 . . . . . .106 B2
3 Riccall YO19 . . . . .49 A8
1 Stainforth DN7 . . . . . . .92 C6
24 Thorne/Moorends DN8 . .93 A8
Whitley DN14 . . . . .77 A4
Winteringham DN15 . . . . . .68 B1
York YO1 . . . . .156 B2
Silverdale Ct YO24 . . . . .132 C2
Silverdale Rd HU4 . . . . . .140 C6
Silvergarth DN32 . . . . . . .153 A1
Silversides La DN20 . . . . .98 A1
Silvertree Wlk DN14 . . . .149 D6
Sim Balk La YO24 . . . . . .132 E5
Simon Howe YO12 . . . . . .1 A5
Simons Pl DN35 . . . . . . .153 C3
Simpson Ave 6 YO14 . . . .2 F8
Simpson Cl DN19 . . . . . . .85 D8
Simpson's Yd 3 YO8 . . . .148 C6
Simson Ct HU8 . . . . .154 B4
Sinclair Cres HU8 . . . . . .141 F6
Sinderby Wlk HU5 . . . . . .139 C4
Sinderson Rd 18 DN36 . .103 D1
Sir Henry Cooper Sch
HU6 . . . . .56 D5
Sir James Reckitt Haven
HU8 . . . . .141 C1
Sir John Nelthorpe Lower
Sch DN20 . . . . .98 C2
Sir John Nelthorpe Sch
DN20 . . . . .98 C2
Sirius Cl 3 HU3 . . . . .145 B5
Sirocco Ct YO31 . . . . . . .130 D8
Siskin Cres DN16 . . . . . . .96 D1
Sissons La HU15 . . . . .53 B1
Sissons Way HU5 . . . . . .140 E3
Sittingbourne Cl HU8 . . . .141 E8
Sitwell Gr YO26 . . . . .129 C5
Sitwell St HU8 . . . . .155 C4
Siward St YO10 . . . . .131 A3
Siwards How★ YO10 . . . .131 B1
Siward's Way YO10 . . . . .131 A2
Sixhills St DN32 . . . . .152 F3
Sixth Ave
Bridlington YO15 . . . . . . .122 F4
Fixborough Stather DN15 . .82 A1

Sixth Ave continued
Scunthorpe DN17 ....150 B2
York YO31 ....130 E5
Skeckling Cl HU12 ....73 A6
Skeffling Rd HU12 ....90 B7
Skeldergate YO1 ....156 B2
Skelton Ave HU5 .....139 E2
Skelton Broad La DN14 .65 C4
Skelton Cres YO43 ....135 C4
Skelton Ct 8 YO30 ....130 A6
Skelton La YO32 .....126 D8
Skelton Prim Sch
YO30 ....126 C5
Skelton Rd DN17 .....150 C3
Skern Gr HU9 ....142 A2
Skerne Rd YO25 .....124 F2
Skewsby Gr YO31 ....127 F1
Skidby Carr La HU6 ....56 C6
Skidby CE VC Prim Sch
HU16 ....138 A7
Skidby Gr HU6 ......139 F5
Skidby Rd HU20 ......55 A4
Skidby Windmill & Mus of E
Riding Rural Life*
HU16 ....138 C7
Skiddaw YO24 ....132 C2
Skiff La Ind Est YO43 ..52 D6
Skilgate Rd 7 HU7 ....57 A5
Skillings La HU15 ....68 C5
Skinners La
8 South Ferriby DN18 ..84 A7
Waltham DN37 ....113 E6
Skipper La YO25 ......1 E3
Skippingdale Rd DN15 .96 C7
Skipsea Castle* YO25 .23 A1
Skipsea La YO25 .....23 A3
Skipsea Prim Sch YO25 .23 B1
Skipsea Rd Atwick YO25 .35 C7
Beeford YO25 ....22 D1
Bewholme YO25 ......35 A5
Skipwith Cl HU6 .....140 B6
Skipwith Comm Nature
Reserve* YO8 ....49 E8
Skipwith Rd YO19 ....37 B6
Skirbeck Rd HU8 .....141 D5
Skirlaugh CE VC Prim Sch
HU11 ....45 E2
Skirlaugh Rd
Ellerby HU11 ....45 F1
Swine HU11 ....57 E8
Skirlaw Cl 18 DN14 ...65 A7
Skitter Rd DN40 ......86 D8
Skylark Cl YO25 .....125 A5
Skylark Dr DN16 ......96 D1
Slack The DN17 ......94 D8
Slay Pit Cl DN7 ......92 F4
Slay Pit La DN7 ......92 F4
Sleaford Ave 3 HU9 ..142 E2
Sledmere CE VC Prim Sch
YO25 ....7 B3
Sledmere Gr HU4 ....144 E5
Sledmere House* YO25 .7 B3
Sledmere Rd YO25 .....8 B6
Sleightholme La 21 HU7 .56 F6
Sleights Cl HU3 .....145 A7
Sleights La Acklam YO17 .16 E7
Broomfleet HU15 .....67 B6
Eastrington DN14 .....51 E3
Slessor Rd YO24 .....129 B1
Slingsby Cl HU5 .....139 D2
Slingsby Gr YO24 ....132 E8
Sloe La HU17 ....136 D2
Sluice La DN18 ......83 D8
Sluice Rd DN18 ......83 F8
Smales' St YO1 .....156 B1
Smary La YO19 ......9 D7
Smeatley's La DN6 ...76 C4
Smeaton Gr YO26 ....129 C5
Smeaton Rd YO41 ....27 D7
Smedley Cl HU17 ....154 C2
Smith Cl YO10 ......133 F8
Smith Field 4 DN36 ..114 B1
Smith St Grimsby DN31 .152 F6
Scunthorpe DN15 .....150 F8
Smithall Rd HU17 ....136 E7
Smithfield Rd DN16 ..151 D2
Smithie Cl YO32 .....127 D5
Smithy La 7 DN38 ....99 B4
Smitton St DN31 ....153 A6
Smook Hills Rd (Pearcy
Lane) HU19 ....75 A4
Smythy La DN7 ......1 D4
Snainton Gr 4 HU5 ..144 D8
Snaith Rd
Pollington DN14 ......77 F7
Rawcliffe DN14 ......64 A1
Snaith DN14 ....78 D8
Snaith Sch The DN14 ..78 C8
Snaith Sec Sch DN14 ..78 B8
Snaith Sta DN14 .....63 C1
Snatchells La DN14 ...78 C2
Snowdon Cl YO23 ....24 D3
Snowdon Way HU7 ...57 A7
Snowdonia Ave YO25 ..96 B8
Snowdrop Garth YO42 .40 A1
Snowhill Cl 4 HU7 ....57 A6
Snuff Mill La HU16 ..139 B6
Sober Hill Dr YO43 ...40 A1
Soft La DN19 ....86 A6
Solomon Ct DN35 ....153 D1
Somerby Rd DN17 ....150 D8
Somerby Wold La
DN38 ....99 C1
Somerden Rd HU9 ...147 E7

Somersby St DN31 ....152 D4
Somerscales St HU2 ..155 A4
Somerset Cl 6 YO30 ..126 E3
Somerset Dr 6 DN15 ..82 B4
Somerset Rd YO31 ...130 D8
Somerset St HU3 ....145 A5
Somerton Dr DN7 ....92 F4
Somerton Rd DN40 ...87 C1
Somervell Rd DN16 ..151 C1
Sonia Crest DN40 ....87 B1
Sophia Ave 7 DN33 ..102 E1
Sophia Cl HU2 ......155 A4
Sorbus Ct 5 HU3 ....145 D6
Sorbus View 4 HU4 ..144 C7
Sorrel Cl HU7 ......136 E1
Sorrel Dr 5 HU5 ....144 D8
Sorrel Way DN15 .....96 B7
Sorrell La DN14 ......78 D1
Soss La DN10 ....116 D5
Sotheron St DN14 ...149 D4
Sour La DN8 ....92 E8
Soutergate 12 DN18 ..69 F1
South Ave YO25 ......31 F2
South Axholme Com Sch
DN9 ....105 D6
South Back La YO16 ..122 B4
South Bank DN17 ....95 D6
South Bank Ave YO23 .130 B1
South Bridge Rd HU9 .155 C1
South Carr Dales Rd
HU19 ....74 F3
South Carr La DN20 ..109 A4
South Carr Rd DN20 ..109 A4
South Carrs HU17 ....45 A8
South Cave CE VC Prim Sch
HU15 ....53 F1
South Church Side
2 Easington HU12 ....90 F6
Kingston upon Hull HU1 .155 B2
South Cl 7 Kilham YO25 .9 C3
Kingston upon Hull HU6 .140 C6
South Cliff Rd
4 Bridlington YO15 ...122 E2
Kirton in Lindsey DN21 .108 B1
South Dale LN7 ......111 B4
South Down Rd 3 YO32 .127 F5
South Dr YO25 ....31 C4
South Duffield Rd YO8 .49 C4
South Ella Dr HU10 ..143 D7
South Ella Way HU10 .143 D7
South End
Seaton Ross YO42 ....39 E3
Thorne/Moorends DN8 .93 A7
South End La DN14 ...77 B4
South End Rd
Ottringham HU12 .....73 E3
Roos HU12 ....60 B1
South Espl YO1 .....156 B1
South Ferriby Prim Sch
DN18 ....84 A7
South Field Ct 5 HU16 .138 F5
South Furlong Croft 17
DN9 ....105 E6
South Gate YO25 .....32 E6
South Glebe YO25 ...32 B1
South Gr 8 YO25 ....21 B2
South Holderness Tech Coll
HU12 ....72 D8
South Hunsley Sch
HU14 ....68 C5
South Ings La HU15 ..53 C2
South Intake La DN9 .116 F7
South La
Bishop Wilton YO42 ...16 F1
Cawood YO8 ....48 B7
Kingston upon Hull
HU13 ....143 E1
South Landing Nature
Reserve* YO15 ....5 A1
South Leys Comp Sch
DN17 ....96 C2
South Leys Rd HU19 ..75 A4
South Marine Dr
YO15 ....122 D1
South Marsh Rd DN41 .101 F7
South Moor Rd DN10 .116 C3
South Newbald Rd
YO43 ....53 F7
South Parade
Grimsby DN31 ....152 D4
Leven HU17 ....45 A7
8 Selby YO8 ....148 C5
Thorne DN8 ....93 A7
York YO24 ....156 A1
South Par Jun Sch
DN31 ....152 D4
South Parkway 4 DN14 .78 C8
South Pk HU12 ......60 B1
South Pk Rd DN17 ...96 B2
South Prom HU18 ....134 D4
South Rd
Keadby with Althorpe
DN17 ....95 C6
Thorne/Moorends DN8 .79 B2
South Rise HU16 ....138 B8
South Rise Cres 20 DN17 .96 C2
South Ruddings La
YO19 ....37 F7
South Sea Ave 28 YO15 .5 A2
South Sea La DN36 ..114 D7
South Sea Rd YO15 ...5 A2
South Side Kilham YO25 .9 B3
Winteringham DN15 ..68 A1
South Side La YO25 ...9 F6
South St
Barmby on the Marsh
DN14 ....64 A7
Barnetby le Wold DN38 .99 B4

South St continued
Bridlington YO15 ....122 E1
Burton Fleming YO25 ..2 E1
Cottingham HU16 ....139 A6
Goole DN14 ....149 C2
Keelby DN41 ....101 A5
Kingston upon Hull HU1 .155 A2
Leven HU17 ....45 A7
Middleton-on-the-Wolds
YO25 ....31 C4
North Kelsey LN7 ....110 A4
Owston Ferry DN9 ...106 B2
Roxby cum Risby DN15 .82 F3
West Butterwick DN17 .106 D8
Winterton DN15 .....83 A5
South St Mary's Gate 4
DN31 ....152 D3
South Townside Rd
YO25 ....34 A8
South View
Broughton DN20 .....97 D4
Grimsby DN34 ....152 A2
Healaugh LS24 ......24 A2
Holton le Clay DN36 ..114 B5
6 Humberston DN36 ..103 D1
Kingston upon Hull HU4 .144 B6
South View Ave
Brigg DN20 ....98 C2
Burringham DN17 ....95 D4
South Wold HU20 ....55 A4
South Wolds Sch HU17 .43 A4
South Wood Dr 12 DN8 .93 A7
Southburn Ave HU4 ..144 C4
Southburn Rd YO25 ..20 A1
Southcliff Rd HU19 ..75 A6
Southcliffe Rd 12 DN21 .107 E2
Southcoates Ave HU9 .141 E2
Southcoates La HU9 ..146 E8
Southcoates Prim Sch
HU9 ....141 F1
Southcote Cl 4 HU5 ..54 A2
Southcroft Dr 8 HU8 .141 E7
South-Dale Cl 1 DN21 .108 B2
Southern Dr HU4 ....144 C5
Southern Way DN40 ..87 C3
Southern Wlk DN33 ..113 E8
Southfield 1 Belton DN9 .94 E1
Kingston upon Hull HU13 .69 E4
Southfield Cl
Great Driffield YO25 ..124 F6
Rufforth YO23 ....24 D6
14 Thorne/Moorends DN8 .93 B7
Ulceby DN39 ....86 B1
Wetwang YO25 ......19 B5
Southfield Cres 2
YO24 ....132 E8
Southfield Dr
1 Beverley HU17 ....137 A6
4 Epworth DN9 .....105 D6
North Ferriby HU14 ..69 A4
Southfield La
Barmston YO25 ......23 A6
Elstronwick HU12 ....59 C3
Everingham YO42 ....40 B4
Kellington DN14 .....61 B2
Roos HU12 ....60 C1
Seaton Ross YO42 ...39 D1
Skipsea YO25 ....23 B2
Willoughton DN21 ...119 A3
Southfield Pk YO43 ..135 D3
Southfield Rd
1 Broughton DN20 ..97 D3
8 Crowle DN17 .....94 D7
Elstronwick HU12 ....59 A2
Great Driffield YO25 ..124 F6
Grimsby DN33 ......113 E8
15 Holton le Clay DN36 .114 A5
Kingston upon Hull HU5 .140 A2
North Kelsey LN7 ....109 E2
Pocklington YO42 ...28 F4
Scunthorpe DN16 ...151 C1
Thorne/Moorends DN8 .93 B7
Wetwang YO25 ......19 A5
Winterton DN15 .....82 F5
Southfield Well Balk
YO25 ....19 B5
Southfields HU15 ....52 E1
Southfields Rd YO32 .14 B7
Southgate
Hornsea HU18 ......134 C3
Kingston upon Hull
HU13 ....143 E1
Market Weighton YO43 .135 E3
4 Scunthorpe DN15 ..151 B7
Southgate Cl HU10 ..138 E2
Southgate Gdns 2
HU18 ....134 C3
Southlands
4 Haxby YO32 ......13 E5
16 Hemingbrough YO8 .49 F1
Southlands Ave 1
DN21 ....117 A2
Southlands Cl YO19 ..37 B6
Southlands Dr 3 DN21 .117 A2
Southlands Gdns 2
DN21 ....117 A2
Southlands Rd YO23 ..130 B2
Southmoor La WF11 ..61 B1
Southmoor Rd
Crowle DN17 ....94 C8
Thorganby YO19 .....37 F5
Southolme Dr 7 YO30 .126 F1
Southorpe Cl YO16 ..122 B5
Southorpe Cl DN21 ..118 D7
Southorpe Nature Reserve*
HU11 ....46 D8
Southorpe Rd HU11 ..134 A1

Southside HU12 ......74 D1
Southside Rd HU12 ...73 F5
Southwell Ave HU9 ..147 E8
Southwell Cl HU17 ..136 E1
Southwold Cres 25
DN33 ....113 E8
Southwood Ave HU16 .138 F6
Southwood Dr HU16 .139 A6
Southwood Gdns
HU16 ....138 F5
Southwood Rd
Kingston upon Hull
HU16 ....138 F5
Sutton upon Derwent
YO41 ....38 C8
Soutter Gate HU12 ...72 C7
Sovereign Cl 18 DN34 .102 B2
Sovereign Way 7 HU7 .56 E5
Sow Hill Rd HU17 ...154 A3
Sowerby Rd YO26 ...129 D4
Sowers La DN15 .....83 A5
Spa Hill DN21 ....108 B1
Spa Well La DN14 ...78 C8
Spalding Ave YO30 ..130 B7
Spalding Rd DN16 ...151 B4
Spark Mill La HU17 ..154 C1
Spark St DN34 ......152 A3
Sparkmill Terr HU17 .154 C2
Sparrowcroft La DN14 .66 E3
Speculation St YO1 ..130 E4
Speedwell Cres DN15 .96 B7
Speedwell La 1 HU15 .55 D8
Speeton Gate YO15 ...4 A4
Spellowgate YO25 ...20 C7
Spellowgate Cl YO25 .124 D5
Spen La
Holme-on-Spalding-Moor
YO43 ....39 C2
York YO1 ....156 C3
Spencer Ave DN15 ..150 F8
Spencer Cl
Beverley HU17 ......154 A3
Grimsby DN31 ......153 B5
Kingston upon Hull HU2 .155 A3
8 York YO23 ....156 B1
Spencer Way 1 HU16 .139 B7
Spencers Mead YO25 .124 E3
Spencers Way YO25 ..124 E4
Speng La YO26 ......24 B4
Spenser St DN40 ....87 C1
Sperrin Cl 2 HU9 ....142 A3
Spey Bank YO24 ....132 C6
Spicer's Rd HU12 ....72 C6
Spilsby Rd DN17 ....150 E1
Spindle Cl YO24 ....132 C8
Spindlewood 1 HU15 .68 C7
Spinnaker Cl HU3 ...145 D5
Spinney Cl 2 DN40 ..87 C1
Spinney Croft Cl 12 HU14 .69 A5
Spinney The
1 Barnby Dun DN3 ...92 A3
8 Barrow upon Humber
DN19 ....85 D8
Grimsby DN34 ......152 A3
Kingston upon Hull
HU16 ....139 A5
6 Newport HU15 ....52 F1
7 Swanland HU14 ...69 B7
York YO24 ....132 F7
Spire View 1 HU13 ..143 E1
Spital Hill DN21 ....117 B1
Spital Terr DN21 ....117 B1
Spittlerush La DN6 ...76 D2
Spout H YO42 ......28 D3
Spout Hill HU15 .....68 C8
Spratton Ct 2 DN37 ..102 B2
Spring Bank
Grimsby DN34 ......152 A3
Kingston upon Hull HU3 .145 A5
4 North Newbald YO43 .53 F7
Spring Bank W HU4 .144 D7
Spring Cl 7 DN15 ...124 D5
Spring Cottage Prim Sch
HU8 ....141 F6
Spring Field Cl HU11 .45 F8
Spring Gdns
Goole DN14 ....149 E4
Kingston upon Hull HU8 .141 D5
Spring Gdns E HU4 ..144 B6
Spring Gdns S HU4 ..144 B5
Spring Gdns W HU4 .144 B6
Spring Gr HU3 ......145 A7
Spring La
2 Buckton/Bempton YO15 .4 D3
11 Laceby DN37 .....101 F1
Long Marston YO26 ..24 A5
York YO10 ....131 A1
Spring Rd 1 YO43 ...135 E4
Spring St
Immingham DN40 ....87 C1
Kingston upon Hull HU2 .155 A3
Spring Vale HU9 ....142 D5
Spring Wlk DN14 ...148 A1
Springbank DN20 ...98 C2
Springbank Ave
Dunnington YO19 ...26 A7
Hornsea HU18 ......134 B4
Springbok Cl HU4 ..144 D2
Springburn St HU3 ..145 A5
Springdale Cl HU10 .143 F8
Springdale Rd YO43 .135 E5
Springdale Way HU17 .154 A1

Springfield
Holme-on-Spalding-Moor
YO43 ....40 A1
6 Howden DN14 ....65 B7
Springfield Ave
Bridlington YO15 ....122 E2
18 Brough HU15 ....68 C6
5 Hatfield DN7 .....92 E4
Springfield Cl
Barlby with Osgodby YO8 .49 B5
Heworth YO31 ......131 C7
2 Scunthorpe DN16 ..151 C2
Springfield Cres 3 WF8 .76 C3
Springfield Dr
9 Barlby YO8 ......49 B5
Beverley HU17 ......137 A6
Springfield Gdns YO43 .40 A1
Springfield Prim Sch
DN33 ....113 D8
Springfield Rd
26 Brigg DN20 ......98 C2
Grimsby DN33 ......113 D8
Kingston upon Hull HU3 .144 F6
Pocklington YO42 ...29 B3
4 Poppleton YO26 ...12 F1
Springfield Rise DN20 .98 C2
Springfield Way
Hook DN14 ....149 F6
Kingston upon Hull
HU10 ....143 E7
York YO31 ....131 B7
Springfields 18 WF11 ..61 A2
Springfields Ave 17
WF11 ....61 A2
Springhead Ave HU5 .144 A7
Springhead Cl 6 DN14 .65 A7
Springhead Ct HU10 .144 A6
Springhead Gdns
HU10 ....144 A7
Springhead La HU4 ..144 A7
Springhead Prim Sch
HU10 ....143 F7
Springs Rd DN10 ...104 C1
Springs Way DN20 ..98 B2
Springthorpe Rd
DN21 ....118 B1
Springville Ave HU13 .143 F2
Springway Cres DN34 .152 A3
Springwood YO32 ...127 D7
Springwood Cres 7
DN33 ....113 D8
Springwood Gr 16 HU16 .139 A6
Sproatley Endowed CE VC
Prim Sch HU11 ......58 D5
Sproatley Rd HU12 ..58 D3
Spruce Cl YO32 .....127 D2
Spruce La DN39 .....86 A1
Spruce Rd
Kingston upon Hull HU1 .155 A1
Leven HU17 ....45 B8
Spurn Ave 16 DN33 ..113 D8
Spurn Lightship*
YO23 ....155 B1
Spurn Rd HU12 .....91 B2
Spurr Ct YO24 .....132 C8
Spurriergate YO1 ...156 B2
Spyvee St HU8 .....155 C3
Square The
4 Easington HU12 ...90 F6
Goxhill DN19 ....86 A8
Kingston upon Hull
HU10 ....138 D1
Kingston upon Hull
HU13 ....143 E1
Skerne & Wansford YO25 .21 C3
Yapham YO42 ......28 E7
Squire La YO16 .....122 C4
Stable La 4 DN18 ...69 E1
Stable Rd YO8 ......63 D7
Stabler Cl 15 YO32 ..13 D5
Stablers Wlk YO32 ..127 F7
Staddlethorpe Broad La
HU15 ....66 D7
Stafford St
6 Kingston upon Hull
HU2 ....140 E1
Kingston upon Hull HU2 .155 A4
Staindale Cl YO30 ..126 E2
Staindale Rd DN16 ..151 E1
Staines Cl HU8 .....142 A4
Stainforth Moor Rd
DN7 ....93 C3
Stainforth Rd DN7 ...92 A5
Stainton Dr
Grimsby DN33 ......102 D2
15 Immingham DN40 ..87 B1
9 Scunthorpe DN17 ..96 C2
Staithe St 3 YO8 ....50 D7
Staithes Cl 4 YO26 ..129 B4
Staithes Rd HU12 ...72 B8
Stallingborough CE Prim Sch
DN41 ....101 E6
Stallingborough Rd
Healing DN41 ....101 E5
Immingham DN40 ....87 B1
Keelby DN41 ....101 A5
Stallingborough Sta
DN41 ....101 E6
Stalybridge Ave HU9 .142 E1
Stamford Bridge Inf Sch
YO41 ....15 D2
Stamford Bridge Rd
YO19 ....26 E7
Stamford Bridge W
YO41 ....15 C2
Stamford Gr HU9 ...142 E1
Stamford St E 10 YO26 .129 F5
Stamford St W 8 YO26 .129 F5

Stamford Wlk YO16 ...122 C2
Stan Valley 2 WF8 .....76 C3
Stanage Wlk DN32 ...152 F4
Stanbury Rd HU6 .....140 C7
Standage Rd 12 HU12 ..72 E5
Standidge Dr HU8 ....105 D6
Standish La 1 DN40 ....87 B2
Stanfield Rd 2 DN9 ..105 D6
Stanford Cl DN37 ....101 F1
Stanford Jun & Inf Sch
DN37 ....101 F1
Stanholme La DN36 ..114 A1
Stanhope Ave HU9 ...141 E2
Stanhope Pl DN35 ....153 C3
Stanhope St DN14 ....149 C4
Stanhurst La DN7 .....93 A5
Staniland Dr YO8 ....148 A5
Staniland Way 1 DN36 114 D8
Staniwell Rise DN17 .150 D3
Staniwells Dr 9 DN20 ..97 D3
Stanley Ave
Haxby YO32 ....127 D7
Hornsea HU18 ....134 C2
Stanley Gdns 15 DN7 ..92 C6
Stanley Rd
Scunthorpe DN15 ....150 C7
16 Stainforth DN7 ....92 C6
Stanley St Goole DN14 149 D4
Grimsby DN32 ....153 A4
Kingston upon Hull HU3 145 C4
York YO31 ....156 C4
Stannington Dr HU8 .142 D6
Stansfield Cl HU9 ....142 D1
Stansted St DN31 ....152 B5
Staple Rd DN40 ....86 F3
Stapleford Cl 4 HU9 .142 E2
Star Carr La DN20 ....98 C4
Star Hill Rd YO25 ....124 F5
Starboard Ave HU6 ..140 C8
Starcarr La DN20 .....34 A1
Starella Gr HU3 ......145 A4
Starham Rd LN7 .....109 C4
Starkbridge La DN14 ..78 A3
Starkey Cres YO31 ...131 A5
Startforth Wlk HU5 ..139 E3
Stather Rd
Burton upon Stather
DN15 ....82 A5
Flixborough DN15 .....82 A1
Stathers Wlk 3 HU10 143 F6
Station App
Bridlington YO16 ....122 E2
Cleethorpes DN35 ...153 F3
Station Ave
Bridlington YO16 ....122 D2
New Earswick YO32 .127 D3
New Waltham DN36 ..114 A7
York YO1 ....156 A1
Station Ct 47 Hatfield DN7 92 D4
Hornsea HU18 ....134 D4
Station Dr HU3 ....140 D1
Station Hill YO25 .....19 B6
Station La
Barmby on the Marsh
DN14 ....64 B7
Cliffe YO8 ....49 E3
Hedon HU12 ....72 C8
Holme-on-Spalding-Moor
YO43 ....39 F1
Searby cum Owmby
DN38 ....110 D7
Shipton YO30 ....12 E5
Station Mews DN14 ..134 D4
Station Rd Bainton YO25 31 E6
Blyton DN21 ....117 F6
Bridlington YO16 ....122 D2
Brough HU15 ....68 B5
Burringham DN17 ....95 D4
7 Burstwick HU12 ...73 A6
Burton Agnes YO25 ..10 A1
Carlton DN14 ....63 C3
Cleethorpes DN35 ...153 E3
Copmanthorpe YO23 .132 B2
Cottingham HU13 ....143 E1
East Halton DN40 ....86 D7
Eastrington DN14 ....65 F8
Epworth DN9 ....105 D7
Fulstow LN11 ....121 D7
Garthorpe & Fockerby
DN17 ....81 E6
Garton YO25 ....20 A5
Gilberdyke HU15 .....66 D8
Grasby DN38 ....110 E6
Grimsby DN37 ......102 B5
Gunness DN15 ....95 E5
Habrough DN40 .....100 E8
Harpham YO25 ......21 E8
Hatfield DN7 ....92 D4
Haxby YO32 ....13 F5
Haxey DN9 ....116 C7
Healing DN41 ....101 F5
Hensall DN14 ....62 C1
Holton le Clay DN36 .114 A4
Howden DN14 ....65 B8
Hutton Cranswick YO25 32 E7
Keadby with Althorpe
DN17 ....95 D6
Keyingham HU12 .....73 C7
Killingholme High DN40 87 B5
Kingston upon Hull
HU16 ....139 C7
Kirton in Lindsey DN21 108 B2
Lockington YO25 .....32 D1
Ludborough DN36 ...121 B6
Market Weighton YO43 135 D4
Middleton YO25 ......31 C5
Misterton DN10 .....116 D5
Nafferton YO25 .....125 F6

Station Rd continued
New Waltham DN36 ..114 A7
North Cave HU15 .....53 D3
North End DN19 ......71 A1
North Ferriby HU14 ...69 A4
North Kelsey LN7 ....110 A4
North Thoresby DN36 114 B1
Norton DN6 ....76 F2
Ottringham HU12 .....73 F4
Owston Ferry DN9 ...106 A2
Patrington HU12 .....74 C2
Pocklington YO42 ....29 A3
24 Poppleton YO26 ...12 F1
Preston HU12 ....72 C8
Rawcliffe DN14 ......64 A1
Riccall YO19 ....49 A8
Scawby DN20 ....108 F7
Scunthorpe DN15 ....151 B6
Selby YO8 ....148 D5
South Cave HU15 .....54 A2
South Kelsey LN7 ...110 D2
South Killingholme DN40 .87 A5
Stainforth DN7 ......92 C5
Stallingborough DN41 101 D6
Thorngumbald HU12 ..73 A5
Thornton Curtis DN39 .85 F5
Ulceby DN39 ....86 B1
Walkeringham DN10 .116 D3
Waltham DN37 ......113 E7
Whitton DN15 ....67 D3
Wistow YO8 ....48 C6
Womersley DN6 ......76 D5
York YO1 ....156 A2
Station Rise YO1 ....156 A2
Station Sq 4 YO32 ...14 B7
Station St YO10 .....156 C3
Station View Cliffe YO8 .49 E3
Little Weighton HU20 .55 A4
Staveley Rd HU9 ....142 C3
Staves Ct 10 DN36 ..114 D4
Staxton Ct HU9 .....146 D8
Staxton Hill YO12 .....1 C8
Staynor Ave YO8 ....148 E3
Steadings The DN15 .82 B1
Steele Cl YO43 .....135 D3
Steep Hill HU5 ......154 B2
Steeping Dr 11 DN40 .87 B1
Steeple Cl 4 YO32 ...13 D5
Steeton Ave 4 HU6 .140 C7
Stembridge Cl 2 HU9 142 E1
Stephen Cl 2 DN39 ..86 A1
Stephen Cres
14 Barton-upon-Humber
DN18 ....84 F8
Grimsby DN34 ......102 C2
10 Humberston DN36 114 C8
Stephen's Wlk YO8 .148 B1
Stephenson Cl
37 Hedon HU12 ......72 D7
Market Weighton YO43 135 D4
York YO31 ....127 E1
Stephenson St HU9 .141 E1
Stephenson Way
YO26 ....129 F5
Stephenson's Wlk
HU16 ....139 D6
Stephenwath La YO41 16 C5
Stepney Ave 13 YO16 122 C5
Stepney Gr YO16 ....122 C4
Stepney La HU5 .....140 E1
Stepney Prim Sch
HU5 ....140 E1
Sterling Cres DN37 .113 D6
Sterling Pk YO30 ...127 A3
Sterne Ave
7 Broughton DN20 ...97 D3
York YO31 ....131 A5
Stevenson Pl DN35 .153 D1
Stevenson's Way 18
DN18 ....84 E8
Steward Cl YO8 ......48 D1
Steward Garth HU16 138 E6
Stewart La YO19 .....36 C4
Steynburg St HU9 ..141 D1
Stirling Cl 2 DN21 ..117 C1
Stirling Gr YO10 ....133 F8
Stirling Rd
Barmby Moor YO42 ..28 E3
York YO30 ....126 F3
Stirling St
Grimsby DN31 ......153 B1
Kingston upon Hull HU3 144 F6
Stirrup Cl YO24 ....132 B8
Stockbridge La YO25 .32 F6
Stockbridge Pk 2 HU15 68 C7
Stockbridge Rd HU15 .68 B7
Stockhill Cl 1 YO19 ..26 E7
Stockholm Cl 1 YO10 133 D8
Stockholm Pk 28 HU12 72 D7
Stockholm Rd
Kingston upon Hull HU7 140 E5
16 Thorngumbald HU12 72 E5
Stocking La Hillam LS25 61 B7
Knottingley WF11 ....61 B2
Stockleigh Cl HU7 ..140 F8
Stocks Dr DN14 .....79 B8
Stocks Hill Belton DN9 94 E1
Huggate YO42 ....18 C1
Stockshill Rd DN16 .151 C2
Stockton Hall YO32 ..14 D3
Stockton La
Heworth YO32 ......128 D1
York YO31 ....131 A7
Stockton on the Forest Prim
Sch YO32 ....14 D3

Stockwell Gr HU9 ...147 E8
Stockwell La 13 YO25 .34 B2
Stockwell Prim Sch
HU9 ....147 E8
Stockwith Rd
Haxey DN9 ....105 E1
Owston Ferry DN9 ..116 E8
Walkeringham DN10 .116 D3
Walkerith DN21 .....116 E4
Stoke St HU2 ....155 A4
Stone Bridge Dr YO41 .27 F5
Stone Dale YO42 ....17 D3
Stone Hill DN7 ......93 A4
Stone Hill Rd DN7 ...93 A4
Stone La DN17 ......95 D4
Stone Riggs YO32 ...14 D2
Stonebow The YO1 ..156 C2
Stonebridge Ave HU9 142 D1
Stonecarr Ct HU7 ....56 F7
Stoneferry Prim Sch
HU8 ....141 A3
Stoneferry Rd HU8 .141 A2
Stonegate
Hunmanby YO14 ......2 F8
Thorne/Moorends DN8 93 A8
York YO1 ....156 B3
Stonegate Cl 3 HU7 .141 D7
Stoneknowle HU15 ...54 A8
Stonelands Ct 2 YO30 127 A1
Stonepit Balk YO17 ...6 C5
Stonepit Hill YO17 ....6 C4
Stonepit La YO15 .....4 E3
Ellerker HU15 ....54 A1
Welton HU15 ....68 E6
Stones Cl YO24 .....129 E2
Stones Mount HU16 139 A7
Stonesdale HU7 ....141 A6
Stonethwaite 5 YO24 132 C7
Stoney La HU15 ......53 A3
Stoney Way DN36 ..114 D4
Stony La HU15 ......53 A2
Stool Cl Rd DN9 .....94 E1
Stoop Cl YO27 ......127 C8
Storkhill Rd HU17 ..154 C4
Storking La YO41 ....27 F6
Stornaway Sq HU8 .141 F7
Stortford St DN31 ..152 B5
Story St HU1 ....155 A3
Stothards La 1 DN19 ..86 A8
Stottlebink 17 YO15 ...5 A2
Stovin Cres DN15 ....83 A5
Stow Cl 11 DN37 ...102 B4
Stow St YO32 ....127 E3
Stow Rd Atwick YO25 .35 D5
Scunthorpe DN16 ...151 B3
Stowe Garth YO16 ..122 F7
Straight La YO19 .....26 F8
Straits Rd HU11 ......46 D2
Strand Ave 4 DN33 ..102 D2
Strand Dr DN16 .....151 C5
Strand Way YO32 ...127 E3
Strand Wlk HU9 ....142 E1
Strand Inf Sch DN32 153 A5
Strand Jun Sch DN32 152 F5
Strand St DN32 .....152 F5
Stratford Ave 4 DN33 102 D2
Stratford Dr DN16 ..151 C5
Stratford Way YO32 127 E3
Stratford Wlk HU9 .142 E1
Strathcona Ave HU5 139 E4
Strathearn St 1 HU5 140 D3
Strathmore Ave
Burstwick HU12 ......73 A7
Kingston upon Hull HU6 140 C6
Stratton Cl HU8 ....142 B7
Stratton Pk 3 HU14 .69 B6
Strawberry Gdns
Hornsea HU18 ....134 C1
Kingston upon Hull HU9 145 B7
Strawberry Hill 2
DN7 ....113 C6
Strawberry St HU9 .146 B7
Stray Gdns YO31 ...130 F7
Stray Rd
Sunk Island HU12 ...89 B6
York YO31 ....131 B6
Stray The HU15 .....54 A2
Straylands Gr YO31 .130 F8
Street YO25 ....9 E1
Street La Bubwith YO8 50 F5
North Kelsey LN7 ...110 B4
Street Life Mus of
Transport* HU1 ...155 C2
Street The YO42 .....28 A2
Strensall Comm Nature
Reserve* YO60 ......14 D8
Strensall Pk YO32 ...14 A5
Strensall Rd
Earswick YO32 .....128 A7
Kingston upon Hull HU5 139 C1
York YO32 ....127 F6
Strickland Rd
Eastoft DN17 ....81 A2
13 Hunmanby YO14 ...3 A8
Strickland St HU3 ..145 C4
Strines Gr 9 HU7 ...141 D7
Stripe La YO30 .....126 B5
Stromness Way HU8 141 F7
Stroud Cres E HU7 .141 A7
Stroud Cres W HU7 141 A8
Strouther Cl YO42 ...29 A3
Stroykins Cl DN34 ..102 C5
Strubby Cl 6 DN35 .103 D2
Stuart Cl
Bridlington YO15 ...122 C1
Scunthorpe DN17 ....96 C1
4 Strensall YO32 .....14 C8
Stuart Gr
Eggborough DN14 ...62 A2

Stuart Gr continued
9 Thorpe Willoughby YO8 48 B1
Stuart Rd DN4 ......129 D1
Stuart Wortley St
DN31 ....152 F6
Stubbs La
Cridling Stubbs WF11 .76 A8
Norton DN6 ....76 F2
Stubbs Rd DN6 ......76 D3
Stubden Gr YO30 ...126 F2
Studcross DN9 .....105 D6
Studley Mdws YO16 122 D7
Studley St HU8 .....146 B8
Stump Cross* HU17 ..43 C2
Sturdee Gr YO31 ...130 D7
Sturmer Ct 15 DN16 ..96 D1
Sturton Gr 28 DN16 ..102 D2
Sturton La DN20 ....108 E7
Stygate La DN6 ......76 E1
Stylefield Rd 15 YO15 ..5 A2
Styles Croft HU14 ....69 C7
Subway St HU3 .....145 B3
Subway The DN16 ...97 A4
Suddaby Cl HU9 ....141 F2
Suddle Way 4 DN41 101 A4
Sudforth La DN14 ....61 C3
Suffolk Ct 13 DN32 .153 A5
Suffolk St HU5 .....140 D3
Sugar Mill Ponds Nature
Reserve* DN8 ......79 B8
Suggitt's Ct DN35 ..153 D4
Suggitt's La DN35 ..153 D4
Suggitt's Orch DN35 153 D4
Sullivan Rd HU4 ....144 B4
Summer Hill DN21 ..117 C1
Summerdale DN18 ...84 E8
Summerfield Ave 3
DN17 ....113 E7
Summerfield Cl
Great Driffield YO25 124 D5
4 Waltham DN37 ....113 E7
Summerfield Rd
Bridlington YO15 ...122 D1
York YO24 ....132 C7
Summergangs Dr 17
HU12 ....72 E5
Summergangs Rd
HU8 ....141 C3
Summergroves Way
HU4 ....144 B2
Summermeadows
HU11 ....142 D6
Summermeadows
HU20 ....98 C3
Sunbeam Rd HU4 ..144 D5
Sundrew Ave DN14 .149 D6
Sunk Island Rd HU12 88 E8
Sunningdale 12 DN37 113 D6
Sunningdale Ave 1
DN20 ....98 C3
Sunningdale Cl 1 YO26 129 B7
Sunningdale Dr 7 DN40 .87 C2
Sunningdale Rd
Gipseyville HU13 ...144 E4
Northfield HU13 ....143 F2
Scunthorpe DN17 ....96 B2
Sunny Bank
Kingston upon Hull HU3 145 B7
3 Knottingley WF11 ...61 A2
Sunny Cnr 13 DN33 ..102 E1
Sunny Hill 9 DN21 .108 B1
Sunnybank 1 DN18 ..84 E8
Sunnydale 3 YO32 ..127 D7
Sunway Gr DN16 ...151 A1
Surbiton Cl HU8 ....141 F5
Surrey Ct 12 DN32 .153 A5
Surrey Garth HU4 ..144 B4
Surrey Way YO30 ..129 F8
Surtees St
Grimsby DN31 ......152 F6
York YO30 ....130 B7
Sussex Cl
5 Kingston upon Hull
HU5 ....139 D1
York YO10 ....131 C2
Sussex Ct 14 DN32 .153 A5
Sussex Rd YO10 ....131 C2
Sussex St DN35 ....153 B4
Sussex Way 14 YO32 ..14 A7
Susworth Rd DN17 .106 D4
Sutcliffe Ave 18 DN33 102 E1
Sutherland Ave HU6 140 B6
Sutherland St YO23 130 B1
Sutor Cl YO23 ......132 B3
Sutton Bridge* YO41 27 C2
Sutton CE Sch HU7 .141 D7
Sutton Cl HU7 ......141 B8
Sutton Cl HU8 ......141 E6
Sutton Fields Ind Est
HU2 ....155 C4
Sutton Gdns HU7 ..141 B7
Sutton Ho Rd HU8 .141 D5
Sutton La
Barmby Moor YO42 ..28 B3
Byram cum Sutton WF11 61 A4
Sutton Pk Prim Sch
HU7 ....140 F7
Sutton Pl DN14 .....108 F7
Sutton Rd Howden DN14 65 A6
Kingston upon Hull HU6 140 D6
12 Kirk Sandall DN3 ...92 A3
Wawne HU7 ....56 F7
Sutton St DN14 .....149 D4
Sutton Upon Derwent CE VC
Prim Sch YO41 ......27 C2
Sutton Way
Kingston upon Hull HU9 142 B2
York YO30 ....130 B8
Swaby Dr DN35 ....103 B2
Swaby's Yd HU17 ..154 A3

Swaddale Ave HU10 138 F2
Swainby Cl HU7 ....141 D7
Swale Ave YO24 ....132 E3
Swaledale Ave HU9 141 E1
Swaledale Mews
YO16 ....122 F6
Swaledale Pl DN16 .151 D2
Swales Dr YO43 ....135 D3
Swales Rd DN36 ...114 D8
Swallow Ct 4 DN9 ..105 D7
Swallow Dr 3 DN41 101 F5
Swallow Grange 6
HU8 ....141 D7
Swallow La DN39 ....85 E2
Swallow Rd YO25 ...125 B5
Swallowfield Dr HU4 144 B2
Swallows The 3 YO32 14 B8
Swan Cl YO19 ....37 A7
Swan Farm Ct YO19 ..37 A7
Swan Hill* HU11 ...142 F6
Swan La DN14 ......149 D6
Swan Syke Dr 8 DN6 ..76 F2
Swanage Wlk HU4 ..144 B4
Swanella Gr HU3 ...145 A4
Swanfield Rd HU9 ..142 C2
Swanland Ave 3 YO15 122 F3
Swanland Butts Cl
HU10 ....143 C6
Swanland Cl 17 DN8 ..93 B7
Swanland Ct 28 DN8 ..93 B7
Swanland Dale HU14 69 B8
Swanland Garth 4 HU14 69 A5
Swanland Hill HU14 .69 A5
Swanland Prim Sch
HU14 ....69 B6
Swanland Rd HU13 143 C3
Swanland Way 3 HU16 138 E6
Swann St
Kingston upon Hull HU2 155 C4
York YO23 ....156 A1
Swannacks View
DN20 ....108 F7
Sweep Cl YO43 .....135 D3
Sweet Briar Cl 7 DN37 113 D7
Sweet Dews Gr HU9 146 D8
Sweyne Garth DN14 .65 D1
Swift Ave YO25 .....125 B5
Swift Dr DN20 ....98 B2
Swift Rd DN17 .....150 D2
Swiftsure Cres 16 DN34 102 B2
Swinburne La DN17 150 D3
Swinburne Rd DN17 150 D3
Swinburne St HU8 .141 D2
Swinderby Garth 19 HU7 57 A5
Swinderby Gdns DN34 152 A1
Swindon St YO16 ..122 D3
Swine Bank HU5 ...139 B2
Swine La HU11 ......57 E5
Swine Rd HU11 .....45 C1
Swinefleet Prim Sch
DN14 ....65 C1
Swinefleet Rd
Goole DN14 ....149 D2
Goole Fields DN14 ..80 C8
Swinegate
Kingston upon Hull
HU13 ....143 E1
York YO1 ....156 B2
Swinegate Ct E YO1 156 B3
Swinemoor Ind Est
HU17 ....137 B5
Swinemoor Inf Sch
HU17 ....154 C4
Swinemoor Jun Sch
HU17 ....154 C4
Swinemoor La HU17 137 B5
Swineridge Hill YO42 29 B6
Swineridge La YO42 29 C6
Swinescaif Hill Swine
HU15 ....54 A3
Swinescaif Rd HU15 54 A3
Swinster La DN40 ....86 C6
Swinsty Ct YO30 ...126 F1
Switchback LN8 ....120 A1
Swithin Cl HU13 ....144 A2
Sycamore Ave
15 Grimsby DN33 ...102 E2
York YO32 ....127 D4
Sycamore Cl
3 Barnetby le Wold DN38 99 B4
2 Broughton DN20 ...97 D3
Driffield YO25 ......124 D2
East Ella HU4 ......144 C7
14 Gilberdyke HU15 ..66 D8
Goole DN14 ....149 E6
1 Haxby YO32 ......127 D7
Hessle HU13 ....143 C3
Nafferton YO25 ....125 F7
8 Preston HU12 .....58 C1
Selby YO8 ....148 A4
Skelton YO30 ......126 C5
12 Snaith & Cowick DN14 78 C8
Sycamore Cres YO25 .32 F2
Sycamore Ct HU5 ..140 C5
Sycamore Dr
9 Gainsborough DN21 117 C1
3 Thorngumbald HU12 72 E5
Sycamore Pl
New Earswick YO32 127 D4
York YO30 ....156 A3
Sycamore Rd YO8 ...49 B5
Sycamore Terr YO30 156 A3
Sycamore View 17 YO26 12 F1
Sycamores The HU17 137 B3

Sydney Smith Sch HU10 144 A5
Sykehouse Rd DN14 78 C4
Sykes Balk YO25 21 E8
Sykes Cl
6 Kingston upon Hull HU10 143 F6
Swanland HU14 69 B7
Sykes La Garton YO25 124 A5
Goxhill DN19 71 A2
Sykes St HU2 155 B3
Sylvan Falls YO25 124 C4
Sylvan Lea YO25 124 C4
Sylvan Mead YO25 124 C4
Sylvester La HU17 154 A3
Sylvester Sq HU1 155 B3
Sylvester St 13 DN21 108 B1
Sylvia Cl HU6 139 F5
Symmons Cl 4 HU17 137 A6
Symons Cl HU2 155 A4
Symons Way 13 YO42 29 A3

T

Tabard Hamlet 5 DN14 61 F2
Tabard Rd 6 DN14 61 F2
Tabards The 7 DN14 61 F2
Tadcaster Rd YO24 129 F1
Tadcaster Rd Dringhouses YO23 132 E5
Tadman Cl HU17 136 E7
Tadman St HU3 145 D4
Talbot Circ DN3 92 A4
Talbot Rd DN40 87 C1
Talbot Wlk DN16 151 B6
Talisman Dr 6 DN16 96 D1
Tall Trees HU13 143 C3
Tallert Way 28 DN33 102 C2
Tamar Dr 14 DN36 114 A8
Tamar Gr HU8 142 C7
Tamar Wlk DN17 150 C4
Tamarisk Way 18 DN16 96 E2
Tamworth Rd 9 YO30 127 A1
Tan Dyke Way HU17 154 C2
Tanfield Gr HU9 142 C2
Tang Hall La YO31 131 A5
Tang Hall Prim Sch YO31 130 F5
Tanner Row YO1 156 A2
Tanner's Moat YO1 156 A2
Tanpit La DN6 76 E3
Tansley Ct DN15 150 B7
Tansley La HU18 134 D1
Tansterne La HU11 59 A7
Tarbert Cres 2 YO24 132 B7
Tardrew Cl HU17 136 E6
Target La 16 YO42 29 A4
Tarleton Cl 3 DN3 92 A2
Tarran Ave HU6 140 B8
Tasburgh St DN32 152 F2
Tate Cl YO8 48 D6
Tattersall Cl DN17 150 D1
Tattersall Dr 1 HU17 137 B3
Tattershall Ave 14 DN34 102 C2
Tattershall Cl HU2 140 E1
Tatton Cl YO30 127 A1
Taunton Rd HU4 144 A3
Taunton Way 19 DN33 113 E8
Taurus Ct YO23 156 A1
Tavella Ct 1 DN9 105 B2
Tavistock St HU5 140 C3
Taylor Ave HU9 142 C3
Taylor Cl DN9 94 E2
Taylor St DN35 153 B5
Taylor's Ave DN35 103 C2
Taylor's La HU19 75 C2
Taylors Cl 5 HU17 55 B7
Taylors Field YO25 124 E4
Teal Cl 12 Broughton DN20 98 B2
Walkington HU17 55 B7
Teal Dr
23 Barton-upon-Humber DN18 84 E8
York YO24 132 C8
Teal Garth YO15 11 B4
Teal Pl LN7 111 A4
Teal Rd 1 HU15 52 F1
Tealby Gr 19 DN33 102 D2
Tealby Rd DN17 150 D1
Teale St DN15 151 A8
Team Gate 1 DN37 102 B3
Teanby Dr DN15 83 A5
Tedder Rd YO24 129 B1
Teddington Cl HU8 141 E6
Tedworth Rd HU9 142 C5
Tee La DN15 82 B5
Tees Gr HU8 142 C7
Teesdale Ave HU9 146 E8
Teesdale Mews YO16 122 F7
Telford Pl DN34 152 A3
Telford St HU9 141 E2
Telford Terr 1 YO24 130 B2
Temper Rd DN16 151 F4
Temperance Ave DN17 107 D7
Temperton's La DN9 106 A2
Templar Cl DN14 61 F1
Templar Ct 17 DN16 96 D2
Templar Way YO8 148 C2
Templar's Bath* DN16 96 D1
Temple Ave YO10 131 B4
Temple Cl Belton DN9 94 E2
Welton HU15 68 E6
Temple Garth YO23 132 C1
Temple La
Aylesby DN37 101 E1
Carnaby YO16 10 E5
Copmanthorpe YO23 132 C1
Temple Manor* YO8 62 D4
Temple Rd YO23 132 F4
Temple St HU5 140 E1
Temple Wlk 2 HU15 68 E6
Templefield Rd DN21 119 A3
Templemans La DN36 114 A1
Templemead YO31 130 E8
Templewaters 31 HU7 56 F5
Temsdale 2 HU7 141 A6
Ten Thorn La YO26 129 A4
Tennant St YO8 148 B6
Tennent Rd YO24 129 B2
Tennison Ct HU16 139 A7
Tennyson Ave
Bridlington YO15 122 E3
1 Campsall DN6 76 E1
Kingston upon Hull HU5 140 A1
7 Thorne/Moorends DN8 93 B8
York YO30 130 C7
Tennyson Cl Brigg DN20 98 C1
Caistor LN7 111 A3
Tennyson Ct HU12 72 D7
Tennyson Mews 4 DN31 152 D4
Tennyson Rd
Cleethorpes DN35 153 E3
Scunthorpe DN16 151 D3
Tennyson St
32 Gainsborough DN21 117 B1
Goole DN14 149 C5
Grimsby DN31 152 D4
Tensing Rd DN16 151 C1
Tenterden Cl HU7 141 A6
Tern Gr HU8 142 C5
Terrington Cl YO32 14 B8
Terrington Pl 4 DN35 103 B2
Terry Ave YO1 156 B1
Terry St
Kingston upon Hull HU3 140 D1
York YO23 130 C1
Teskey King Specl Sch HU6 140 A5
Tetley Rd DN16 151 C3
Tetley View 2 DN17 94 E6
Tetney CP Sch DN36 114 D4
Tetney La DN36 114 B5
Tetney Lock Rd DN36 114 D4
Tetney Rd DN36 114 C8
Tewkesbury Dr DN34 152 C2
Thanet Prim Sch HU9 142 D6
Thanet Rd
Kingston upon Hull HU9 142 D5
York YO24 129 D1
Thatch Cl YO8 148 C4
Thatchers Croft YO23 132 C3
Thaxted Cl HU8 142 B6
Theaker Ave DN21 117 C1
Theakston Mews HU17 136 D1
Thealby La DN15 82 D5
Thearne Cl 7 HU5 140 C3
Thearne La HU17 56 D7
Theatre Mews HU2 155 B3
Theodore Rd DN15 150 E8
Theresa Cl 6 YO31 127 F1
Therm Rd HU8 155 C4
Thesiger St DN32 152 F5
Thesiger Wlk 2 DN32 152 F5
Thief La Barlow YO8 148 F1
York YO10 130 F3
Thimblehall La HU15 52 E2
Thinholme La DN9 105 A1
Third Ave
Bridlington YO15 123 A4
Fixborough Stather DN15 82 A1
Goole DN14 149 C4
Scunthorpe DN17 150 C2
York YO31 130 F5
Third La DN37 113 D3
Thirkleby Cres DN32 103 A2
Thirkleby Way YO10 131 C4
Thirlby Wlk HU5 139 D3
Thirlmere Ave DN33 113 E8
Thirlmere Dr YO31 131 A6
Thirlmere Wlk DN14 149 E6
Thirsk Mews HU5 139 D4
Thirtle Bridge La HU19 74 C8
Thirtleby La HU11 57 F6
Thirty Acre La 13 HU12 72 D7
Thiseldine Cl 6 YO43 53 F7
Thistle Cl YO8 148 C2
Thistleton Gdns 6 HU5 140 E2
Thixendale Rd
Bridlington YO16 122 F7
Fridaythorpe YO25 18 A7
Thomas Clarkson Way HU7 140 E8
Thomas Rd
Scunthorpe DN17 150 F4
17 Stainforth DN7 92 C5
Thomas St
Grimsby DN32 152 F3
Kingston upon Hull HU9 146 B7
6 Selby YO8 148 D6
2 York YO10 130 E3
Thomas Sumpter Comp Sch DN17 150 E3
Thompson Ave HU17 154 C3
Thompson Cl 9 YO8 49 B4
Thompson Dr
16 Hatfield DN7 92 D4
2 Strensall YO32 14 B8
Thompson Nook 14 DN7 92 D4
Thompson Pl 6 YO26 129 E5
Thompson Rd HU12 72 B7
Thompson St
Bridlington YO16 122 D3
Scunthorpe DN15 151 B7
Thonock Rd DN21 117 D4
Thoresby Ave YO16 122 D6
Thoresby Cl YO16 122 D6
Thoresby Mews 7 YO16 122 D6
Thoresby Pl 2 DN35 103 C2
Thoresby Prim Sch HU5 145 B8
Thoresby Rd
Fulstow LN11 121 D8
North Coates DN36 115 A2
Scunthorpe DN17 150 D1
Tetney DN36 114 D3
York YO24 129 B1
Thoresby St HU5 145 B8
Thoresway Gr 9 DN33 102 D2
Thorgam Ct DN31 152 C3
Thorganby Rd DN35 103 D2
Thorgill Gr HU5 139 E3
Thorn Bank DN9 104 E4
Thorn Barn Cl HU12 72 F5
Thorn Fields HU12 72 D5
Thorn La DN19 86 A8
Thorn Leigh 3 HU3 145 C6
Thorn Marsh Rd HU12 72 E2
Thorn Nook YO31 130 F8
Thorn Rd HU12 72 D7
Thornbridge Cl HU9 142 B3
Thornbury Rd DN40 87 C1
Thorncroft 8 YO19 26 F7
Thorndale HU7 140 E8
Thorndale Croft YO25 19 B5
Thorndale La YO25 19 A5
Thornden Bldgs YO8 148 D5
Thorndike Way DN21 117 D1
Thorne & Dikesmarsh DN8 79 A2
Thorne Brooke Prim Sch DN8 93 B7
Thorne Gram Sch DN8 93 B8
Thorne N Sta DN8 93 A8
Thorne Rd Hatfield DN7 92 F5
Kirk Sandall DN3 92 A1
3 Stainforth DN7 92 C6
Thorne S Sta DN8 93 B7
Thorne Swimming Baths DN8 93 B8
Thorne Waste Drain Rd DN8 79 D1
Thorneycroft Rd 14 HU12 72 E5
Thornfield Ave 5 YO31 130 F8
Thornfield Dr 7 YO31 127 E2
Thorngarth La DN19 85 C8
Thorngumbald Inf Sch HU12 72 D5
Thorngumbald Jun Sch HU12 72 F5
Thorngumbald Rd HU12 72 B4
Thornham Cl HU15 53 F1
Thornham's Way 6 HU15 68 C7
Thornhill Ave HU8 141 C4
Thornhill Cres 19 DN17 96 C2
Thornhill Gdns DN34 152 A3
Thornhills 19 YO32 13 F5
Thornholme Dr 14 DN16 96 D2
Thornleys HU17 43 A4
Thornton 10 HU15 68 C6
Thornton Abbey (Rems of)* DN39 86 B5
Thornton Abbey Sta DN39 86 A5
Thornton Ave DN16 151 A3
Thornton Cl HU13 143 D1
Thornton Cres DN35 103 C2
Thornton Ct 22 DN36 114 A8
Thornton Dam La HU15 66 D8
Thornton Gdns 5 DN41 101 A4
Thornton Gr
7 Grimsby DN34 102 C2
3 Preston HU12 58 C1
Thornton La YO25 20 A1
Thornton Moor Cl YO30 126 F2
Thornton Pl DN40 87 B1
Thornton Rd
Barrow upon Humber DN19 85 D6
Bridlington YO16 122 B2
Goxhill DN19 85 F6
South Kelsey LN7 110 A1
Thornton St DN19 85 C7
Thorntondale Dr YO16 122 F7
Thorntree Cl DN14 149 E6
Thorntree Gr YO30 127 B2
Thorntree La
Balne DN14 77 C6
Goole DN14 149 E6
Thornwick Ave HU10 143 E8
Thornwick Cl 2 HU3 145 C5
Thornwick Rd YO15 5 B3
Thornwood Covert 1 YO24 129 C1
Thorny La YO42 16 F2
Thorold Pl 11 DN3 92 A3
Thorold St DN31 153 A5
Thorpe YO25 32 B1
Thorpe La YO8 48 B8
Thorpe Leys YO25 32 B2
Thorpe Rd
6 Brough HU15 68 C5
Howden DN14 65 C8
Thorpe Rd Ave 2 DN14 65 B7
Thorpe St
9 Bridlington YO15 122 E2
York YO23 130 B2
Thorpe Willoughby CP Sch YO8 48 B2
Thorpehall Rd DN3 92 A2
Thorpepark Prim Sch HU6 140 A8
Thorpepark Rd HU6 139 F8
Three Lakes Ind Est YO8 148 D2
Three Lakes Ret Pk YO8 148 D3
Thrislington Sq 19 DN8 79 B2
Thronton Cl YO43 135 D5
Throughleys La YO42 39 A5
Thrunscoe Inf Sch DN35 153 F1
Thrunscoe Rd DN35 153 F1
Thrussendale Rd YO17 16 E8
Thurlow Ave
Beverley HU17 136 E6
22 Pocklington YO42 29 A3
Thurlow Garth YO25 125 F7
Thurlstone Cl 13 HU7 56 F6
Thurstan Cl
Beverley HU17 136 D2
Kingston upon Hull HU9 142 D2
Thurstan Rd HU17 154 A2
Thwaite St HU16 139 C6
Thwing Rd
Burton Fleming YO25 2 E2
Kilham YO25 9 B5
Thyme Way HU17 55 F8
Tibby La YO25 32 C4
Tichbourne Cl 6 HU3 145 C5
Tickton CE VC Prim Sch HU17 137 F8
Tickton Gr HU6 139 F4
Tickton Mdws HU17 137 F8
Tideswell Ct DN15 150 B6
Tideworth Hague La DN14 78 C3
Tiger La HU17 154 A3
Tilbury Prim Sch HU4 144 B3
Tilbury Rd HU4 144 B3
Tilia Cl
Kingston upon Hull HU4 144 B2
Scunthorpe DN16 96 E2
Tilmire Cl 2 YO10 133 F8
Tilworth Rd HU8 141 F4
Timberland DN16 96 E2
Timberley Dr 7 DN37 102 B4
Tindale Bank Rd DN10 116 C7
Tinker La YO23 24 D6
Tinkler's La WF11 61 D6
Tinley Cl HU16 139 B7
Tintagel Way DN36 114 A8
Tintern Ave YO16 122 E6
Tippaty La WF11 61 A4
Tippet La HU17 44 F2
Tison Garth HU10 143 F6
Tithe Barn Cl 9 HU12 74 D1
Tithe Barn La
8 Patrington HU12 74 D1
13 Thorne/Moorends DN8 93 B8
Tithe Barn Rd 2 WF11 61 A2
Tithe Barn Way DN14 61 F3
Tithe Cl YO24 129 B1
Tithe La YO25 22 E5
Tithe Rd HU12 58 A1
Tiverton Rd HU7 141 A8
Tiverton St DN35 153 C4
Tivoli Gdns DN32 152 F4
Toadham La DN14 77 C5
Toby Ct YO32 14 A7
Todd La DN21 117 F4
Todd's La HU15 68 A8
Todds Cl HU14 69 C6
Todds Ct DN17 107 D7
Todds La DN15 82 A4
Toft Gn YO1 156 A2
Tofts Rd 2 DN18 84 E8
Tokenspire Bsns Pk & Ret Outlet HU17 137 C2
Toll Bar Ave DN36 113 F7
Toll Gavel HU17 154 A3
Tollerton Rd YO30 12 B7
Tollesby La 9 DN7 92 D4
Tollymore Pk 28 HU7 56 F5
Tom Hammond Way DN32 153 A4
Tomline Rd 2 DN41 101 A5
Tomline St DN31 152 F5
Tomlinson Ave DN15 150 E7
Tonbridge 21 DN33 113 E8
Tonbridge Gr 2 HU9 142 E2
Tongue La HU15 66 E6
Tonnant Way 6 DN34 102 B3
Toogood St HU2 155 B4
Toothill Gdns 2 DN34 102 C3
Toothill Rd 1 DN34 102 C3
Top La
Copmanthorpe YO23 132 B3
Kirk Bramwith DN7 92 A7
Top Rd
South Killingholme DN40 86 E3
Winterton DN15 82 F6
Worlaby DN20 98 D8
Topaz Gr 3 HU3 145 A4
Topcliff Ct YO8 148 B7
Topcliffe Garth HU7 141 C8
Tophill Low Nature Reserve* YO25 33 D4
Torbay Dr DN33 113 E7
Torchil Cl HU10 143 C6
Toremill Cl YO32 127 D4
Torksey Dr DN33 102 D2
Torksey Pl 28 DN33 102 D2
Torksey St DN21 108 B2
Tornville Cres DN14 79 B8
Torridge Gr HU8 142 C6
Torridge Rd HU8 142 C6
Torridon Pl YO24 132 B7
Torrington Rd DN17 150 C4
Torrington St
Grimsby DN32 152 F1
5 Kingston upon Hull HU5 140 C3
Tostig Ave YO26 129 C5
Tostig Cl 14 YO41 15 D2
Totnes Rd DN33 113 E7
Tottenham Cl 3 HU8 141 F5
Tottering La DN14 51 B5
Tottermire La DN9 105 D7
Towan Cl 11 HU7 56 F5
Tower Hill
Kingston upon Hull HU13 143 E1
Westwoodside DN9 105 B2
Tower Hill Dr HU13 143 E1
Tower Hill Mews 2 HU13 143 E1
Tower House La HU12 147 F7
Tower Pl YO1 156 B1
Tower Rd
Rimswell HU12 74 C6
Roos HU11 60 A4
Tower St
Flamborough YO15 5 A2
31 Gainsborough DN21 117 B1
Kingston upon Hull HU9 155 C1
York YO1 156 B1
Tower View
Carlton DN14 63 C2
Kingston upon Hull HU10 143 C5
Town End Ave DN14 63 C3
Town End Gdns 3 YO32 13 D5
Town End La YO42 18 C2
Town End Rd HU12 72 A5
Town Farm Cl YO25 23 A2
Town Hall Sq DN31 152 E3
Town Hall St 1 DN31 152 E3
Town Hill DN20 97 E4
Town Hill Dr DN20 97 E4
Town Rd DN36 114 D4
Town St Hayton YO42 40 C8
Immingham DN40 86 E4
Nunburnholme YO42 29 F3
Shiptonthorpe YO43 40 F6
Townend Cswy DN14 66 D2
Townend La HU15 53 C3
Townend Rd
Ellerton YO42 38 D1
12 Newbald YO43 53 F7
Walkington HU17 55 B8
Townend St YO31 156 B4
Townsend Cl DN36 103 E1
Townshend Dr 1 HU16 138 F5
Townside DN36 86 D6
Townside Cl 1 YO43 53 F7
Townside Rd YO43 53 F7
Towthorpe YO43 135 D8
Towthorpe La YO43 135 B7
Towthorpe Medieval Village* YO43 135 B8
Towthorpe Moor La YO32 14 C5
Towthorpe Rd YO32 13 F5
Towton Ave 9 YO24 129 F2
Toynton Rd 27 DN33 102 D2
Trafalgar Ave 10 DN34 102 B3
Trafalgar Cres YO15 11 B4
Trafalgar Pk DN36 114 A8
Trafalgar St
5 Kingston upon Hull HU3 145 D7
Kingston upon Hull HU2 155 A4
York YO23 130 B1
Trafford Rd
Kingston upon Hull HU10 143 E8
4 Norton DN6 76 E2
Trafford St DN15 151 B8
Traffords Way DN20 108 F6
Train Ave HU6 140 C7
Train Gate DN21 108 B1
Tranby Ave
Kingston upon Hull HU13 143 D2
York YO10 131 D4
Tranby Croft HU10 143 C5
Tranby Dr DN32 103 A2
Tranby La Hessle HU10 143 B5
Swanland HU14 69 B6
Tranby Lodge Gdns HU13 143 C1
Tranby Mdws Pk HU13 143 C3
Tranby Ride HU10 143 C5
Trandy La DN14 65 D5
Tranmere Cl HU3 145 B5
Tranmere Pk HU18 134 D3
Tranmore La DN14 62 B3
Travis Ave 18 DN8 93 B8
Travis Cl 16 DN8 93 B8
Travis Cty Prim Sch DN7 92 E4
Travis Gr 17 DN8 93 B8
Travis Rd HU16 138 F5
Travis St YO15 122 E3
Traviss Cl DN16 151 B4
Trawden Cl HU7 56 F6

Treasurer's House★
 YO31 . . . . .156 B3
Tree Cl 9 DN9 . . . . .105 D6
Treece Gdns 10 DN18 . . . .69 F1
Trees The HU6 . . . . .140 C4
Treeton Rd DN14 . . . . . . .65 A6
Tremayne Ave 2 HU15 . . .68 C5
Trenchard Cl 3 DN40 . . . .87 D2
Trenchard Rd YO26 . . . . .129 B6
Trenfield Ct YO24 . . . . . .129 F3
Trent Ave 4 YO32 . . . . . .127 F6
Trent Pk 6 HU7 . . . . .56 F6
Trent Rd DN17 . . . . .95 D6
Trent Side
 4 Amcotts DN17 . . . . . . .81 F1
 Keadby with Althorpe
 DN17 . . . . .95 D6
Trent St DN16 . . . . .151 B6
Trent View DN17 . . . . . . .95 D6
Trent Way YO24 . . . . . . .132 D7
Trentham Cl YO16 . . . . .122 D6
Trentham Dr YO16 . . . . .122 D6
Trentham Mews 1
 YO16 . . . . .122 D6
Trentholme Dr
 Messingham DN17 . . . . .107 D7
 2 York YO24 . . . . .130 A2
Trenton Ave HU4 . . . . . .144 B6
Trentside
 Keadby with Althorpe
 DN17 . . . . .95 D6
 Morton DN21 . . . . .117 A2
Trentvale Prep Sch
 DN17 . . . . .95 D6
Trevor Cl 15 DN37 . . . . .101 F1
Trevor Gr 8 YO24 . . . . . .129 F2
Trevor St HU2 . . . . .155 B4
Triangle Dr HU14 . . . . . . .69 A4
Triangle The 11 HU14 . . . .69 A4
Tribune Way YO30 . . . . .127 B2
Trinity Ave YO15 . . . . . .122 F3
Trinity Cl
 Burstwick HU12 . . . . .73 A6
 Goxhill DN19 . . . . .86 A8
 Leven HU17 . . . . .45 B8
Trinity Ct
 5 Broughton DN20 . . . . .97 D4
 Kingston upon Hull HU2 . .155 B1
Trinity Garth HU16 . . . . .138 A8
Trinity Gr
 Beverley HU17 . . . . .154 B3
 1 Bridlington YO15 . . . .122 F3
 3 Kingston upon Hull
 HU9 . . . . .141 F1
 Kingston upon Hull
 HU13 . . . . .143 E2
Trinity House La HU1 . . .155 B2
Trinity La
 Beverley HU17 . . . . .154 B2
 York YO1 . . . . .156 A2
Trinity Mews 2 YO15 . . .122 F3
Trinity Rd
 Bridlington YO15 . . . . . .122 F3
 Cleethorpes DN35 . . . . .153 E1
 Hornsea HU18 . . . . .134 C2
 10 Scunthorpe DN16 . . . .96 D2
Trinity St
 Grimsby DN31 . . . . .153 A5
 Kingston upon Hull HU3 . .145 C7
Trinity Wlk 2 DN18 . . . . .69 E1
Trippett St HU2 . . . . . . .155 C3
Triton Rd HU9 . . . . .142 D3
Trolleybus Mus at Sandtoft
 The★ DN8 . . . . .94 A3
Trondheim Way DN41 . . .101 E8
Troon Cl 2 YO26 . . . . . .129 B5
Troon Ct HU8 . . . . .142 B6
Troon Rd DN7 . . . . .92 D4
Troutbeck 7 YO24 . . . . .132 C7
Troutsdale Ave YO30 . . .126 E2
Troutsdale Cl YO16 . . . .122 F7
Troutsdale Gr HU9 . . . . .146 F8
Trumfleet La DN6 . . . . . . .77 D1
Trumpett La DN6 . . . . . . .77 D1
Trundle Gate YO43 . . . . . .53 F6
Trundle La DN7 . . . . .92 C8
Trundles La 7 WF11 . . . . .61 A2
Trunkass La DN37 . . . . .112 D6
Trunscoe Jun Sch
 DN35 . . . . .153 E1
Truro Cl HU7 . . . . .141 C6
Tudor Cl
 Bridlington YO15 . . . . . .122 C1
 10 Thorpe Willoughby YO8 .48 B1
Tudor Ct HU10 . . . . .138 C1
Tudor Dr HU6 . . . . .140 B8
Tudor Rd YO24 . . . . .129 C2
Tudor Way YO32 . . . . . . .14 C8
Tudworth Field Rd DN7 . .93 B5
Tudworth Rd DN7 . . . . . .93 A5
Tuke Ave YO10 . . . . .131 B4
Tulip Rd DN17 . . . . .151 C7
Tummel Ct 4 DN40 . . . . .101 B8
Tune St YO8 . . . . .49 B4
Tunis St HU5 . . . . .140 E2
Tunnard St DN32 . . . . . .153 A4
Tunnel Rd DN20 . . . . .98 D4
Turbary La YO32 . . . . . .128 E6
Turbary Rd
 Epworth DN9 . . . . .105 B6
 Haxey DN9 . . . . .105 C3
Turf Moor Rd DN7 . . . . . .93 A3
Turkey La YO16 . . . . .10 E4
Turks Head Ct HU1 . . . . .156 C3
Turks Head Gdns 10
 HU15 . . . . .52 F1
Turmar View HU11 . . . . . .58 A4
Turmarr St HU12 . . . . . . .89 C8
Turmarr Villas 6 HU12 . .90 F6

Turner Ave YO15 . . . . . .122 F3
Turnberry App DN37 . . . .113 D6
Turnberry Dr YO26 . . . . .129 B4
Turnbull Dr 18 YO42 . . . . .29 A3
Turner Ave HU19 . . . . . . .75 A5
Turner Cl YO43 . . . . .135 D3
Turner Ct HU3 . . . . .155 A2
Turner Rd HU17 . . . . . . .154 B4
Turner St 5 DN21 . . . . . .108 B1
Turner's Croft YO10 . . . .131 A1
Turner's La 15 HU14 . . . . .69 A5
Turners Sq 9 YO8 . . . . . .148 C5
Turnham La YO8 . . . . .49 C2
Turnhead Cres YO8 . . . . .49 B5
Turnhead Ct YO8 . . . . . . .49 B6
Turnmire Rd 1 YO24 . . . .132 E8
Turpin Cl DN21 . . . . .117 C1
Turpin Ct YO1 . . . . .156 C1
Turpit La HU12 . . . . .72 A5
Turrets The 16 HU12 . . . .72 E5
Turver's La WF11 . . . . . . .61 C2
Tuxford Gr HU9 . . . . . . .142 E2
Tweed Gr HU8 . . . . .142 B5
Tween Dykes Rd HU7 . . .141 D6
Tweendykes Specl Sch
 HU7 . . . . .141 C6
Twickenham Cl 2 HU8 . .142 A5
Twin Pike Way 14 YO32 . .13 D5
Two Riggs HU17 . . . . .43 A4
Twyford Cl 7 HU9 . . . . . .142 E2
Twyning Pl DN35 . . . . . .153 D3
Tydeman Cl 2 DN16 . . . . .96 D1
Tyler Ave DN34 . . . . .152 A3
Tyn Garth YO19 . . . . .36 D8
Tyne St HU3 . . . . .145 B4
Tynedale 1 HU7 . . . . . . .141 A6
Tynedale Ct 1 DN3 . . . . .92 A2
Tysons Cl 7 DN18 . . . . . .69 F1
Tythe Garth 8 HU15 . . . . .53 D3

U

Ulceby Rd
 Scunthorpe DN17 . . . . . . .96 B2
 South Killingholme DN39 . .86 C2
 Wootton DN39 . . . . .85 F3
Ulceby St Nicholas' CE Prim
 Sch DN39 . . . . .86 A1
Ulceby Sta DN39 . . . . . . .86 C2
Ullswater YO24 . . . . .132 D7
Ullswater Cl HU8 . . . . . .141 D4
Ullswater Gr DN14 . . . . .149 E5
Ulrome Ct 1 HU9 . . . . . .142 B1
Ulster Ave 5 DN33 . . . . .102 E1
Ulster Rd DN21 . . . . . . .117 B1
Ulverston Rd HU4 . . . . . .144 A3
Ulyett La DN17 . . . . .106 C8
Undercroft 7 YO19 . . . . . .26 F7
Underground Bunker★
 HU19 . . . . .75 C1
Underwit Rd YO8 . . . . . . .63 C4
Unicorn Row 10 DN21 . . .108 B1
Union La YO8 . . . . .148 C4
Union Pl DN14 . . . . .149 D6
Union Rd DN8 . . . . .93 A8
Union St
 Great Driffield YO25 . . . .124 E4
 Kingston upon Hull HU2 . .155 B3
 20 Pocklington YO42 . . . .29 A4
Union Terr YO31 . . . . . . .156 B4
Unity Ave HU13 . . . . . . .143 F1
Unity Rd DN32 . . . . .153 C2
University of Hull
 Cottingham HU16 . . . . . .138 F8
 Kingston upon Hull
 HU16 . . . . .139 C5
 Kingston upon Hull HU6 . .140 B4
University of Humberside
 Kingston upon Hull HU6 . .140 C4
 Kingston upon Hull HU6 . .140 A4
University of Lincoln
 HU1 . . . . .155 B3
University of York
 Heslington YO10 . . . . . . .130 F1
 York YO10 . . . . .130 E3
 York YO10 . . . . .156 A3
University Rd YO10 . . . . .130 F2
Upavon Garth HU7 . . . . .141 C7
Upper Burgess St
 DN31 . . . . .152 D4
Upper Hanover St 6
 YO26 . . . . .129 F5
Upper Kenyon St 5 DN8 .93 A8
Upper Newborough St 1
 YO30 . . . . .130 C7
Upper Poppleton Jun Sch
 YO26 . . . . .12 F1
Upper Price St YO23 . . . .156 A1
Upper St Paul's Terr
 YO24 . . . . .130 A4
Upper Union St HU1 . . . .155 A2
Uppercommon La
 DN14 . . . . .61 D2
Uppercroft 4 YO32 . . . . .127 C8
Upperthorpe Hill DN9 . . .105 A2
Upton St HU8 . . . . .141 B1
Uredale Pl DN16 . . . . . . .151 E1
Usher La YO32 . . . . .13 F6
Utgard Way 4 DN33 . . . .102 D1
Utterby Dr DN34 . . . . . . .152 C1
Utterby Prim Sch
 DN36 . . . . .121 B5
Uxbridge Gr HU9 . . . . . .142 E1

V

Valda Vale 34 DN40 . . . . .87 B1
Vale Cres YO42 . . . . .16 F2
Vale of Anchholme Tech Coll
 DN20 . . . . .98 B2
Vale The
 Beverley HU17 . . . . .137 B2
 Kingston upon Hull
 HU10 . . . . .143 B7
 Skelton YO30 . . . . .126 B5
Valentine Cl
 1 Kingston upon Hull
 HU10 . . . . .144 A4
 6 Pocklington YO42 . . . .29 A3
Valiant Dr HU9 . . . . .142 D4
Valletta St HU9 . . . . .147 D7
Valley Dr HU10 . . . . .143 B7
Valley View 37 F7
Valley View Dr DN16 . . . . .96 B1
Vanburgh Dr YO10 . . . . .131 C3
Vanbrugh Way YO10 . . . .131 A2
Vancouver Dr 5 DN17 . . .96 C2
Vane St HU3 . . . . .145 D7
Vanessa Dr DN21 . . . . . .117 B2
Varah Cl DN18 . . . . .84 E8
Varlow Rd LN7 . . . . .111 B4
Varsity Cl 6 DN7 . . . . . .104 A8
Vaughan Ave DN36 . . . . .103 A2
Vaughan Rd
 10 Campsall DN6 . . . . . . .76 E1
 1 Kingston upon Hull HU13 .69 F4
Vavasour Ct YO23 . . . . . .132 B2
Veal St DN31 . . . . .152 C3
Ventnor St HU5 . . . . . . .140 C3
Venture Bsns Pk
 DN31 . . . . .152 B6
Vere Terr DN31 . . . . .152 C4
Verity Way YO25 . . . . . .125 A3
Vermont St HU5 . . . . . . .140 D3
Vermuyden Rd DN8 . . . . .79 C2
Vermuyden Sch DN14 . . .149 B5
Vermuyden Terr
 DN14 . . . . .149 D2
Vernon Cl YO23 . . . . . . .133 A3
Vernon Rd
 Bridlington YO15 . . . . . .122 F3
 York YO16 . . . . .126 E2
Vernon St HU1 . . . . .155 B2
Vesper Dr YO24 . . . . . . .129 B3
Vesper Wlk YO32 . . . . . .127 F6
Veterinary Cl YO25 . . . . . .9 A2
Vicar La Beverley HU17 . .154 A3
 Eastrington DN14 . . . . . . .51 F1
 Hollym HU19 . . . . .75 A4
 Kingston upon Hull HU1 . .155 B1
Vicarage Ave DN20 . . . . . .98 D3
Vicarage Cl
 2 Bubwith YO8 . . . . .50 D7
 12 Hunmanby YO14 . . . . . .2 F8
Vicarage Cres DN15 . . . . .82 B5
Vicarage Gdns
 2 Brough HU15 . . . . .68 C6
 Grimsby DN34 . . . . .152 C2
 Scunthorpe DN15 . . . . . .150 F6
 Wrawby DN20 . . . . .98 E4
 1 York YO10 . . . . .131 C4
Vicarage La
 Beckingham DN10 . . . . .116 D1
 Bishop Wilton YO42 . . . . .16 F2
 8 Buckton/Bempton YO15 . .4 D3
 Cadney DN20 . . . . .109 D6
 Elsham DN20 . . . . .98 F7
 Grasby DN38 . . . . .110 E7
 Immingham DN40 . . . . . . .86 E4
 3 Kingston upon Hull
 HU13 . . . . .143 E1
 Naburn YO19 . . . . .36 E8
 Redbourne DN21 . . . . . .108 F2
 Scawby DN20 . . . . .108 E8
 Skirlaugh HU11 . . . . .45 D2
 Wootton DN39 . . . . .85 F3
Vicarage Lawn DN34 . . . .152 C2
Vicarage Pk DN15 . . . . . .83 D1
Vicarage Rd
 Willoughton DN21 . . . . .119 B4
 Wrawby DN20 . . . . .98 D3
Vicar's La HU12 . . . . .91 A6
Vicar's Wlk 1 DN17 . . . . .94 D7
Vicars Cl YO23 . . . . .132 B2
Viceroy Cl HU12 . . . . .59 A3
Vickerman's La HU12 . . . .59 A3
Victor Charles Terr
 YO43 . . . . .135 D4
Victor St Grimsby DN32 . .153 A4
 2 Kingston upon Hull
 HU9 . . . . .146 C8
 York YO1 . . . . .156 B1
Victoria Ave
 Hatfield DN7 . . . . .92 D4
 Hornsea HU18 . . . . .134 D5
 Sculcoates HU5 . . . . . . .140 A1
 Willerby HU10 . . . . .138 C2
 12 Withernsea HU19 . . . . .75 A6
Victoria Ct
 Marshchapel DN36 . . . . .115 C2
 Stainforth DN7 . . . . .92 C5
 Wike Well End DN8 . . . . . .93 A7
Victoria Ct
 Burton upon Stather
 DN15 . . . . .82 B5
 15 Kingston upon Hull
 HU9 . . . . .129 F5
Victoria Dock Prim Sch
 HU9 . . . . .146 B6

Victoria Dr
 3 Barton-upon-Humber
 DN18 . . . . .69 E1
 3 Gilberdyke HU15 . . . . .66 D8
Victoria Farm Cl YO23 . . .24 C6
Victoria Gdns
 Hornsea HU18 . . . . .134 C6
 1 Kingston upon Hull
 HU5 . . . . .140 A1
Victoria Rd
 Barnetby le Wold DN38 . . .99 B4
 Beverley HU17 . . . . .154 A1
 Bridlington YO15 . . . . . .122 E3
 Great Driffield YO25 . . . .124 D5
 5 Keelby DN41 . . . . .101 A5
 2 Pocklington YO42 . . . . .29 A4
 Scunthorpe DN16 . . . . . .151 A1
 Woodmansey HU17 . . . . . .55 E8
Victoria Ret Pk DN31 . . . .152 E5
Victoria St Goole DN14 . .149 D4
 Kingston upon Hull
 HU13 . . . . .144 A1
 1 York YO23 . . . . .156 B1
Victoria St N DN31 . . . . .152 E4
Victoria St S 3 DN31 . . . .152 E4
Victoria St W 2 DN31 . . . .152 E4
Victoria Way 2 YO32 . . . .130 F8
Victoria's Way HU16 . . . .139 B6
Victory Way
 1 Barton-upon-Humber
 DN18 . . . . .69 E1
 9 Grimsby DN37 . . . . . .102 B2
Viking Cl
 2 Immingham DN40 . . . . .87 B1
 Kingston upon Hull
 HU10 . . . . .138 C2
 20 Stamford Bridge YO41 . .15 D2
Viking Dr 5 YO19 . . . . . . .48 F8
Viking Rd
 Bridlington YO16 . . . . . .123 B6
 Stamford Bridge YO41 . . .15 D2
 York YO26 . . . . .129 C5
Villa Cl YO8 . . . . .49 F1
Villa Ct YO8 . . . . .129 B7
Villa Fields 4 DN14 . . . . .63 C1
Villa Gr 2 YO31 . . . . . . .130 E6
Village Farm Cl 11 HU15 .52 F1
Village Farm Ct 7 DN14 . .61 D4
Village Farm Rd 5 HU12 .58 C1
Village Garth 1 YO32 . . . .13 E5
Village Rd
 Kingston upon Hull HU8 . .141 C1
 Sunk Island HU12 . . . . . . .88 C5
Village St YO30 . . . . . . .126 E3
Village The Haxby YO32 . .13 D3
 Skelton YO30 . . . . .126 B5
 Stockton on the Forest
 YO32 . . . . .14 D3
 Strensall YO32 . . . . .14 B7
 York YO10 . . . . .131 C4
Ville Rd DN16 . . . . .151 D2
Villiers Ct 7 HU12 . . . . . . .72 D7
Vincent Cl 3 HU4 . . . . . .144 A2
Vincent Way YO24 . . . . .132 C8
Vine Cl HU16 . . . . .139 A7
Vine Gdns YO8 . . . . .50 D7
Vine St YO23 . . . . .130 C2
Vinegarth 2 DN9 . . . . . .105 E6
Vinehall Rd DN9 . . . . . . .105 C2
Vinery The 18 DN14 . . . . .65 A7
Vineyards The 3 HU17 . . .45 A8
Violet Cl 16 DN35 . . . . . .103 C1
Viscount Way 2 DN36 . . .114 D8
Vivars Way YO8 . . . . . . .148 D5
Vivian Ave DN32 . . . . . . .153 B1
Voases Cl HU10 . . . . . . .143 E6
Voases La HU10 . . . . . . .143 E6
Volage Ct 3 YO42 . . . . . . .29 A4
Volta St YO8 . . . . .148 E4
Vulcan St HU6 . . . . .140 F4
Vulcan Way DN7 . . . . .93 A1
Vyner St YO31 . . . . .130 C7

W

Waby Cl DN37 . . . . .102 B4
Waddingham Pl
 3 Habrough DN40 . . . . .100 E8
 19 New Waltham DN36 . . .114 A7
Waddingham Rd LN7 . . . .109 F1
Waddington Ct HU5 . . . . .140 B3
Waddington Dr 24 DN17 . .96 C2
Waddington Pl DN34 . . . .152 A1
Wade Ave HU18 . . . . . . .134 C6
Wade House La YO8 . . . . .63 F4
Wadebridge Gr 4 HU9 . . .142 F1
Wadham Gr 4 HU9 . . . . .141 F1
Wadhurst Cl HU7 . . . . . .141 A6
Wadsworth Ave HU6 . . . .140 C8
Wadsworth Rd DN35 . . . .124 B3
Waggoners Dr 3 YO23 . . .132 B2
Wain's Gr YO24 . . . . .132 D7
Wain's Rd YO24 . . . . . . .132 D7
Waincroft 8 YO32 . . . . . . .14 A6
Wainers Cl 5 YO23 . . . . .132 B3
Wainfleet Ave HU16 . . . . .139 A6
Wainfleet Rd 33 DN33 . . .102 D2
Waite Cl 17 YO42 . . . . . . .29 A3
Waithe La DN37 . . . . . . .113 E4
Wake Ave HU16 . . . . . . .139 A5
Wakefield Ave
 Kingston upon Hull HU9 . .142 C2
 Scotter DN21 . . . . .107 D4
Wakefield La HU12 . . . . . .75 A2
Wakerley Rd 13 DN21 . . .107 C3
Walcot Rd DN15 . . . . .82 B8
Walcott St HU3 . . . . .145 C4

Tre - War 193

Waldby Garth Rd HU12 . .73 C4
Waldegrave Ave HU8 . . . .142 A4
Walden Stubbs Rd DN6 . .76 E2
Waldo Way DN15 . . . . . . .82 C1
Waldorf Rd DN35 . . . . . .103 C1
Walesby Cl 8 DN33 . . . . .113 D8
Walesby Rd DN17 . . . . . .150 E1
Walgrave St HU5 . . . . . . .140 C3
Walk La
 Humberston DN36 . . . . .114 C7
 Irby DN37 . . . . .112 D7
Walker Ave DN33 . . . . . .113 E8
Walker Cl DN15 . . . . .82 E7
Walker Dr
 Winterton DN15 . . . . .83 A5
 York YO24 . . . . .132 C8
Walker La YO19 . . . . .37 F7
Walker St HU3 . . . . .145 C5
Walker's Cl 2 DN38 . . . . .99 B4
Walkergate HU17 . . . . . .154 A3
Walkergate Prim Sch
 HU17 . . . . .154 A3
Walkeringham Cty Prim Sch
 DN10 . . . . .116 C3
Walkeringham Nature
 Reserve★ DN10 . . . . . .116 B3
Walkeringham Rd
 Beckingham DN10 . . . . .116 D2
 Gringley on the Hill
 DN10 . . . . .116 A2
Walkerith Rd 11 DN18 . . .117 A2
Walkers Cl 10 DN15 . . . .151 B7
Walkers Ct DN17 . . . . . .107 D7
Walkers Way DN39 . . . . . .86 B2
Walkington Dr YO43 . . . .135 C5
Walkington Heads
 HU17 . . . . .54 D8
Walkington La HU17 . . . . .12 B8
Walkington Prim Sch
 HU17 . . . . .55 C7
Walkington Rd
 Beverley HU17 . . . . .136 B1
 Rowley HU20 . . . . .55 A5
Wall St DN34 . . . . .152 A3
Waller St
 3 Hornsea HU18 . . . . . .134 C3
 Kingston upon Hull HU9 . .146 C8
Walliker St HU3 . . . . .145 A6
Wallingfen La HU15 . . . . .53 A1
Wallis Ct 9 DN33 . . . . . .102 F1
Walmgate YO1 . . . . .156 C2
Walmsgate DN33 . . . . . .102 D2
Walmsgate Pl 24 DN33 . .102 D2
Walmsley Cl 1 YO15 . . . . .4 C3
Walmsley St HU3 . . . . . .145 D7
Walney Rd YO31 . . . . . . .131 A5
Walnut Cl
 Kingston upon Hull
 HU16 . . . . .139 D5
 York YO10 . . . . .131 A1
Walnut Cres
 9 Cleethorpes DN35 . . . .103 B1
 11 Snaith & Cowick DN14 . .78 C8
Walnut Dr DN20 . . . . . . .108 F7
Walnut Gr YO25 . . . . . . .125 F8
Walnut Rd 1 DN17 . . . . . .79 A1
Walnut Way DN17 . . . . . .107 D7
Walpole St YO31 . . . . . . .130 D7
Walsall Garth HU4 . . . . .144 A4
Walter St 5 HU17 . . . . . . .74 F7
Walter's Terr 6 HU5 . . . .140 C3
Waltham Ct HU17 . . . . . .154 B4
Waltham Grange 24
 DN35 . . . . .103 C2
Waltham La HU17 . . . . . .154 A3
Waltham Rd
 Barnoldby le Beck DN37 . .113 C6
 Brigsley DN37 . . . . .113 E8
 Grimsby DN33 . . . . .113 E8
 Waltham DN37 . . . . .113 E8
 Waltham DN37 . . . . .155 B2
Waltham Tollbar Bsns & Ent
 Coll DN36 . . . . .113 F7
Waltham Windmill★
 DN37 . . . . .113 D6
Walton Gr 3 DN33 . . . . .102 E2
Walton La YO43 . . . . .53 E6
Walton Pl YO26 . . . . .129 B3
Walton St HU3 . . . . .145 A4
Walton St L Ctr HU3 . . . .145 A6
Walworth Cl HU8 . . . . . .141 E5
Walworth St N YO26 . . . .129 F5
Walworth St S 9 YO26 . .129 F5
Wand La DN14 . . . . .62 C3
Wandell's View HU15 . . . .68 C5
Wandhill 31 YO32 . . . . . .13 E5
Wandle The YO26 . . . . . .129 A2
Wanlass Dr HU16 . . . . . .139 C7
Wansbeck 3 YO24 . . . . .132 B7
Wansbeck Prim Sch
 HU8 . . . . .142 D7
Wansbeck Rd HU8 . . . . .142 C7
Wansford Gr HU9 . . . . . .142 A1
Wansford Rd
 Driffield YO25 . . . . .125 B3
 Nafferton YO25 . . . . . . .125 F5
Ward Ave HU11 . . . . .142 F7
Ward Ct YO23 . . . . .156 B1
Ward Lea YO25 . . . . .125 F7
Ward St DN35 . . . . .153 C4
Wardall St DN35 . . . . . . .153 F1
Waredale Cl YO16 . . . . . .122 F7
Wareham Cl HU7 . . . . . . .141 B6
Wares Way DN15 . . . . . .150 B7
Warfield Rd YO25 . . . . . .124 B2
Warley Ave DN16 . . . . . .151 C4

Warley Dr DN16 ....151 C4
Warley Rd DN16 ....151 C3
Warmer La HU12 ....90 E7
Warn Ave 18 HU12 ......72 C7
Warneford Gdns
　DN35 ....145 A8
Warneford Rd DN35 ....153 D4
Warping Way DN35 ....150 B7
Warren Cl DN21 ....117 A1
Warren Farm Cotts
　YO2 ....28 C1
Warren Rd DN15 ....96 D7
Warrendale DN18 ....84 E8
Warrenne Cl 31 DN7 ....92 D4
Warrenne Rd DN7 ......92 D4
Warter CE VC Prim Sch
　YO42 ....30 A5
Warter Rd Etton HU17 ...42 F6
　Middleton YO25 ....31 A4
Warthill CE VC Prim Sch
　YO19 ....14 F2
Warton Ave HU17 ......137 B4
Warton Dr HU17 ....56 B8
Warwick Ave 5 DN33 ..102 D2
Warwick Cl DN7 ....92 F4
Warwick Dr
　Barton-upon-Humber
　　DN18 ....84 E8
　Molescroft HU17 .....136 E6
Warwick Rd
　Cleethorpes DN35 ....153 D1
　Scunthorpe DN16 ....151 C5
Warwick St
　Kingston upon Hull HU9 .146 B7
　York YO31 ....130 D7
Warwickshire Cl 6
　HU5 ....139 D1
Wascana Cl HU4 ......144 B3
Wasdale Ave HU9 .....142 D4
Wasdale Cl 2 YO30 ...126 E1
Wasdale Gn 4 HU16 ..139 B7
Waseley Hill Way HU7 ..57 B5
Washdyke La
　Elsham DN20 ....98 E6
　Immingham DN40 .....87 B2
Washinghall La DN17 ..81 A2
Washington St
　Great Driffield YO25 ..124 E4
　Kingston upon Hull HU5 .140 D3
Wassand Balk HU11 ....46 A8
Wassand Hall & Gdns★
　HU11 ....35 B1
Wassand Rd HU11 .....35 B1
Wassand St HU3 ......145 C4
Water Bank DN9 ......104 E5
Water End YO26 ......129 E5
Water Garth DN14 .....61 F4
Water Hill La YO8 ....148 D6
Water La
　Bewholme YO25 ......35 A5
　Camblesforth YO8 ....63 D5
　8 Clifton YO30 .....127 A1
　Dunnington YO19 ....26 F7
　Eggborough DN14 ....62 A2
　20 Flamborough YO15 ..5 A2
　Goole DN14 ....65 C4
　Harpham YO25 ....21 E7
　Hemingbrough YO8 ...49 F1
　Kirby Grindalythe YO17 ...6 B6
　Kirk Bramwith DN7 ....92 C7
　Kirk Smeaton WF8 ....76 C3
　Selby YO8 ....148 C6
　South Cave HU15 .....53 F1
　West Halton DN15 ....82 E8
　York YO30 ....130 A7
Water Side DN15 ......68 A2
Water Way Garth DN14 .77 F6
Waterdale HU7 ....140 E8
Waterdale Pk YO31 ...127 E1
Waterhouse La HU1 ...155 A1
Wateringdike La YO43 .135 F7
Waterings 19 YO32 ....13 D5
Waterland Cl 15 HU12 ..72 D7
Waterloo Dr 14 DN33 ..102 D1
Waterloo St HU2 .....155 A4
Waterlow Dr 7 DN15 ...83 A5
Waterman Ct 3 YO24 ..129 B1
Waters Edge DN20 .....98 B2
Waters Edge Ctry Pk★
　DN18 ....69 F2
Watersedge YO25 ....124 F3
Waterside Goole DN14 ..65 C4
　3 Thorne DN8 ......78 F1
Waterside DN31 .....152 C4
Waterside Rd
　Barton-upon-Humber
　　DN18 ....69 E2
　Beverley HU17 ......137 B3
　2 Thorne DN8 ......78 F1
Waterton La DN7 ......92 D2
Waterways Mus & Adventure
　Ctr The★ DN14 ....149 B2
Waterworks La HU11 ..142 E6
Waterworks St DN40 ...87 C2
Watford Ave DN34 ....102 C2
Watford Wlk HU9 .....142 E1
Wath Gr HU8 ....141 C1
Wath La YO41 ....27 C8
Watkin St N DN31 ....152 C5
Watkin St S DN31 ....152 C5
Watkinson Cl 8 HU12 ..58 D1
Watson Ave HU19 .....142 C2
Watson Cl 9 YO14 .....3 A8
Watson Dr 30 HU12 ....72 D7

Watson St
　Kingston upon Hull HU7 .141 D6
　York YO24 ....130 A3
Watson Terr 2 YO24 ..130 A3
Watson's La YO14 ......3 D6
Watsons Ave YO16 ...122 D5
Watsons Croft DN7 ....92 D6
Watt St HU9 ....141 E1
Wattlers Cl YO23 ....132 C3
Watton Abbey★ YO25 ..32 E4
Watton Carr Nature
　Reserve★ YO25 .....33 C2
Watts Rd HU17 ......154 B4
Waudby Cl 2 HU17 ....55 C8
Wauldby Cl 4 HU10 ...143 E7
Wauldby View 11 HU14 .69 B7
Wavell St YO8 ......148 A6
Waveney Cl DN15 .....82 B5
Waveney Gr YO30 ....130 B8
Waveney Rd HU8 ....142 B6
Waverley Cl DN14 ....63 C2
Waverley St
　Kingston upon Hull HU1 .155 A1
　York YO31 ....156 C3
Wawne Lodge HU7 ....56 F6
Wawne Prim Sch HU7 ..56 F7
Wawne Rd HU7 ......141 C8
Waxholme Rd HU19 ....74 E8
Wayfbain La 20 HU12 ..72 C7
Waynefleet Gr 3 YO10 .131 A3
Wayside Cl
　Holton le Clay DN36 ..114 A5
　15 Scunthorpe DN16 ..96 D2
Wayside Cres YO16 ..122 B4
Wayside Dr DN36 ....114 A8
Wayside Rd YO16 ....122 B4
Weald Pk HU7 ....56 E6
Weardale HU7 ....140 F8
Weatherill St DN14 ...149 C4
Weaver Gr HU8 ......142 C7
Weavers Cl YO23 ....132 B3
Weavers Croft 8 DN9 .105 A2
Weavers Pk YO23 ....132 B3
Webb Cl DN18 ....84 E8
Webster Ave DN15 ...150 E7
Weddall Cl YO24 ....129 F1
Weekes Rd 16 DN35 ..103 C2
Weel Rd HU17 ......137 D8
Weeland Cl WF11 ....61 A2
Weeland Rd Beal DN14 .61 E3
　Hensall DN14 ....62 E2
Weelsby Ave DN32 ...152 E1
Weelsby Gr DN32 ...102 F2
Weelsby Prim Sch
　DN32 ....153 A4
Weelsby Rd DN32 ....152 E1
Weelsby St DN32 ....153 A4
Weelsby St S DN32 ...153 A3
Weelsby View DN36 ..114 A8
Weelsby Way HU13 ..143 C2
Weeping Elm Way
　DN16 ....96 E2
Weeton Cl HU11 ......58 A4
Weeton Dr YO25 ......19 B5
Weeton N La HU12 ....90 B8
Weeton Rd HU12 .....90 C7
Weeton Way 5 HU10 .143 E7
Weghill Rd HU12 ......58 D1
Weighton Ct 9 DN14 ..65 A7
Weighton Gr HU6 ...139 F5
Weighton Hill YO43 ..135 F4
Weir Cl YO8 ....105 A2
Weir Rd DN9 ....105 A2
Weir The HU13 ......143 E1
Welbeck Pl 9 DN35 ..102 C2
Welbeck Rd DN35 ....153 C1
Welbeck St HU5 .....145 B8
Welborn Cl YO10 ....131 A4
Welbourn Wlk HU4 ..144 B6
Welburn Gr 5 YO25 ...22 D1
Welburn Gr HU5 ....139 E2
Welbury Gr HU9 ....142 C2
Weldon Rd DN21 ....119 B1
Welgarth YO23 ....31 B7
Welham Ct 10 DN14 ..65 B7
Welholme Ave HU6 ..140 D4
Welholme Inf Sch
　DN32 ....152 F2
Welholme Jun Sch
　DN32 ....152 F2
Welholme Mus & Gall★
　DN32 ....152 F2
Welholme Rd DN32 ...152 E2
Well La Beverley HU17 .154 B2
　Bridlington YO16 ....122 B4
　Kingston upon Hull
　　HU10 ....138 E2
　Tibthorpe YO25 ......19 D2
Well St
　Messingham DN17 ...107 C7
　Tibthorpe YO25 ......19 D2
Well Vale DN33 ......113 D8
Welland Ave DN34 ...102 C2
Welland Dr DN15 .....82 B5
Welland Rd HU8 ....142 C7
Welland Rise YO26 ..129 D5
Wellbeck Cl 20 DN20 ..98 C2
Wellbeck Rd 8 DN34 .102 C2
Wellesley Ave HU6 ..140 D4
Wellesley Cl YO30 ..127 A2
Wellgarth DN32 .....153 B1
Wellington Ave HU18 .134 C2
Wellington Cl 5 YO42 ..28 D4
Wellington La HU3 ..145 D8
Wellington Rd
　Beverley HU17 ......154 B4

Wellington Rd continued
　Bridlington YO15 ....122 E2
　Pocklington YO42 ....28 E3
Wellington Row YO1 ..156 A2
Wellington St
　Grimsby DN32 ......152 F4
　Kingston upon Hull HU1 .155 B1
　York YO10 ....130 B3
Wellington St W HU1 .155 B1
Wellington Way DN20 ..99 A8
Wellingtonia Dr 5 DN6 .76 E1
Wellowgate DN32 ...152 D3
Wellowgate Mews
　DN32 ....152 D2
Wells Cl YO8 ....148 A5
Wells Cres 3 DN35 ..103 C1
Wells Gn DN14 .....149 B6
Wells La DN14 ....61 E3
Wells Rd DN37 .....101 D4
Wells St Grimsby DN34 .152 B3
　Kingston upon Hull HU3 .145 A4
　Scunthorpe DN15 ...151 B8
Wellsted St HU3 ....145 C5
Welshpool Cl 3 HU7 ..56 F7
Welton Ave
　2 Kingston upon Hull
　　HU16 ....138 E6
　York YO26 ....129 D5
Welton Cl
　17 Barton-upon-Humber
　　DN18 ....84 E8
　9 Beverley HU17 ...136 E1
Welton Gr HU6 .....139 F4
Welton Low Rd HU15 ..68 C6
Welton Old Rd HU15 ..68 E6
Welton Prim Sch HU15 .68 D5
Welton Rd HU15 .....68 C5
Welton Wold View
　HU14 ....69 B7
Welwick Rd HU12 .....74 D1
Welwick Saltmarsh Nature
　Reserve★ HU12 ....89 F6
Welwyn Dr YO10 ....133 E8
Welwyn Pk Ave HU6 .140 C7
Welwyn Pk Dr HU6 ..140 D7
Welwyn Pk Rd HU6 ..140 C7
Wembley Pk Ave HU8 .141 E5
Wembley Rd DN8 .....79 B2
Wenchirst La DN14 ...78 D2
Wendan Rd 7 DN8 ....93 A7
Wendover Cl
　Humberston DN36 ...114 D8
　Messingham DN17 ...107 D7
Wendover Rd DN17 ..107 D7
Wendover Rise DN35 .153 E1
Wendron Cl HU7 ....141 C6
Wenham Rd YO24 ...132 C8
Wenlock Dr YO19 .....37 B6
Wenlock St HU3 .....145 C7
Wenlock Terr
　Kingston upon Hull HU9 .141 E1
　York YO10 ....130 D1
Wenning Gr HU8 ....142 D7
Wensley Ave HU6 ...139 E4
Wensleydale HU7 ...140 F8
Wensleydale Cl YO16 .122 F6
Wensleydale Dr YO10 .131 D4
Wensleydale Rd DN16 .151 E2
Wentdale 1 WF8 ......76 C3
Wentworth Cl
　3 Beverley HU17 ....55 E8
　Camblesforth YO8 ....63 D4
　Kellington DN14 .....62 A2
　Kingston upon Hull
　　HU10 ....143 F8
Wentworth Cres 1 DN19 70 E2
Wentworth Dr
　Goole DN14 ....149 E5
　Messingham DN17 ...107 D7
Wentworth Gr 5 HU11 .47 C1
Wentworth Rd
　Bottesford DN17 .....96 B1
　Bridlington YO16 ....122 C4
　Grimsby DN34 ......152 B3
　York YO24 ....130 B2
Wentworth Way
　5 Hunmanby YO14 ....2 F8
　Kingston upon Hull HU9 .146 C1
　York YO10 ....130 D2
Werkdyke The YO1 ..156 C3
Werneth Rd DN32 ...152 F4
Wesley Cl
　3 Epworth DN9 .....105 E6
　South Cave HU15 ....54 A2
　Winterton DN15 ......83 A5
Wesley Cres 15 DN35 .103 C2
Wesley Ct
　10 Cleethorpes DN32 .153 A5
　7 Kingston upon Hull
　　HU3 ....145 C5
Wesley Pl 4 HU14 ....69 A7
Wesley Rd 5 Brigg DN20 .98 C2
　Scunthorpe DN16 ...151 E3
Wesley Sq 5 DN14 ..149 D4
Wesley St DN21 ....108 B1
West Acridge DN18 ...69 E1
West Ave
　Burton Fleming YO25 ..2 E3
　Stainforth DN7 ....92 C6
West Back Side YO25 .10 C4
West Bank
　Stainforth DN7 ....92 B7
　York YO24 ....129 E3
West Butterwick CE Prim Sch
　DN17 ....106 D8
West Carr La HU7 ...140 F6
West Cl Fangfoss YO41 .28 C8
　Nafferton YO25 .....125 E6

West Cl continued
　Newport HU15 ....52 E1
West Coates Rd DN31 .152 B6
West Comm Cres
　DN17 ....150 F4
West Comm Gdns
　DN17 ....150 F2
West Comm La DN17 .150 F3
West Comm N Rd
　DN17 ....107 A8
West Comm Rd DN17 .150 F2
West Crayke YO16 ...122 F6
West Cross St 16 DN31 .152 B6
West Ct 8 Riccall YO19 .48 F8
　8 Thorne/Moorends DN8 .93 A7
West Dale Cres DN21 .108 B2
West Dock Ave HU3 .145 B4
West Dock St HU3 ..145 B3
West Dr YO25 ......125 F6
West Edge Rd WF8 ...76 A3
West Ella Rd
　Kingston upon Hull
　　HU10 ....143 A7
　Swanland HU14 .....69 C7
West Ella Way HU10 .143 C7
West End Bainton YO25 .31 E7
　Dalton Holme HU17 ..42 E8
　Garthorpe & Fockerby
　　DN17 ....81 E6
　Kilham YO25 ....9 B3
　Lund YO25 ....31 E2
　Pollington DN14 .....77 F6
　Rawcliffe DN14 .....64 A2
　Seaton Ross YO42 ...39 D4
　South Cave HU15 ....53 F1
　Strensall YO32 ......14 A7
　Swanland HU14 .....69 B6
　Walkington HU17 ....55 B7
　Winteringham DN15 ..68 A1
West End Cl
　North Duffield YO8 ...50 A8
　9 Strensall YO32 ....14 B7
West End Farm Cl 6
　HU15 ....53 F1
West End Gdns
　Driffield YO25 ......125 F6
　Pollington DN14 .....77 F6
West End La DN36 ..115 B1
West End Rd
　Epworth DN9 ......105 C7
　2 Habrough DN40 ..100 E8
　Kingston upon Hull
　　HU16 ....138 F7
　Norton DN6 ....76 E2
　Ulceby DN39 ....85 F1
West Field La
　1 Swanland HU14 ...69 B6
　Upper Poppleton YO26 .12 C1
West Garth Kilham YO25 ..9 B3
　Rowley HU20 ....55 A4
West Gn
　Kingston upon Hull HU10 .69 C8
　Messingham DN17 ...107 D7
　Pocklington YO42 ....28 E3
West Gn Dr YO42 ....29 A3
West Gr
　Barton-upon-Humber
　　DN18 ....69 E1
　Kingston upon Hull HU4 .144 D4
West Hall Garth 10 HU15 .53 F1
West Halton La DN15 ..82 E8
West Hann La DN19 ...70 C1
West Haven Way DN40 .87 B3
West Hill 1 HU13 .....69 E4
West Ings Cl 4 WF11 ..61 A3
West Ings Cres 5 WF11 .61 A3
West Ings Ct 1 WF11 ..61 A3
West Ings La 2 WF11 ..61 A3
West Ings Mews 6
　WF11 ....61 A3
West Ings Way 3 WF11 .61 A3
West La Burton YO8 ..62 C6
　Burton Fleming YO25 ..2 C3
　Keelby DN41 ......101 A4
　Laxton DN14 ....65 D2
　Sykehouse DN14 .....77 F2
　Winterton DN15 ......83 B5
West Lambwath Rd
　HU11 ....46 D3
West Lea DN33 .....113 E8
West Leys Pk HU14 ...69 B6
West Leys Rd HU14 ...69 B6
West Marsh Ind Est
　DN31 ....152 D5
West Marsh La
　Barrow upon Humber
　　DN19 ....70 B1
　Goxhill DN19 ....71 A3
West Mid Mere Rd
　DN40 ....86 D3
West Mill Rise 4 HU17 ..55 B7
West Moor Rd DN10 .116 C3
West Newton Rd HU11 .58 D8
West Par Rd HU3 ...145 D6
West Parade
　Grimsby DN31 .....152 C3
　Kingston upon Hull HU3 .145 C7
West Parklands Dr 8
　HU14 ....69 A5
West Pk YO8 ....148 A4
West Point Trading Pk
　HU3 ....145 A3
West Promenade
　YO25 ....124 D4
West Rd
　Keadby with Althorpe
　　DN17 ....95 C6
　Sigglesthorne HU11 ..34 E1

West Rd continued
　Thorne/Moorends DN8 ...79 B2
West Rd Fst Sch DN8 ..79 B2
West Riverside DN40 ..87 C3
West St
　Barnetby le Wold DN38 ..99 B4
　Beverley HU17 .....137 C4
　Bridlington YO15 ...122 E1
　Cleethorpes DN35 ...153 F2
　21 Flamborough YO15 ..5 A2
　9 Gainsborough DN21 .117 A2
　Goole DN14 ....149 C5
　Hibaldstow DN20 ...108 F5
　Kingston upon Hull HU1 .155 A2
　Leven HU17 ....44 F8
　North Kelsey LN7 ...110 A4
　Roxby cum Risby DN15 .82 F3
　Scawby DN20 ......108 E8
　Scunthorpe DN15 ...151 A7
　Thorne/Moorends DN8 ..93 A7
　West Butterwick DN17 .106 C8
　West Halton DN15 ...82 E7
　Winterton DN15 .....83 A5
West St Mary's Gate
　DN31 ....152 D3
West Terr
　Beverley HU17 .....154 C2
　18 Brigg DN20 ......98 B2
West Terr St 3 DN17 ..94 D7
West Thorpe YO24 ..132 D8
West View
　Messingham DN17 ...107 C7
　12 North Ferriby HU14 .69 A4
　Scunthorpe DN17 ....96 C2
West View Cl 9 DN41 .101 A4
West Wood La YO23 ..24 E4
Westbeck Hill YO42 ...30 A5
Westbeck La DN21 ..118 C5
Westborough Way
　HU4 ....144 B6
Westbourne Ave
　Bridlington YO16 ...122 D3
　3 Hessle HU13 .....143 E2
　Kingston upon Hull HU5 .140 A1
Westbourne Ave W
　HU5 ....140 A1
Westbourne Dr DN17 ..94 D7
Westbourne Gdns
　YO8 ....148 C4
Westbourne Gr
　Goole DN14 ....149 D6
　15 Grimsby DN33 ...113 E8
　Kingston upon Hull
　　HU13 ....143 D2
　Selby YO8 ....148 C4
Westbourne Rd
　Hornsea HU18 .....134 D4
　Selby YO8 ....148 C4
Westbourne St 5 HU3 .145 A4
Westbourne Terr YO8 .148 C4
Westbrook Cres 3 HU6 66 D7
Westbrook Rd 12 HU15 .66 D8
Westbrooke Gr 18 LN7 .111 B4
Westburn Ave 2 DN19 .70 E2
Westbury Pk 10 DN35 .103 D1
Westbury Rd DN35 ..103 C1
Westcliff Gdns DN17 .150 F3
Westcliffe Prim Sch
　DN17 ....150 D2
Westcliffe Rd 16 DN21 .107 C3
Westcott Prim Sch
　HU8 ....141 C3
Westcott St HU8 ....141 C3
Westcroft 11 YO43 ....53 F7
Westend Falls YO25 ..125 E6
Westend La DN14 .....77 B6
Westenders Way HU1 .155 A1
Westerdale 4 HU14 ...69 B7
Westerdale Cl 8 HU12 .73 C2
Westerdale Ct 2 YO30 .130 A6
Westerdale Gr HU9 ..146 E4
Westerdale Rd DN16 .151 E2
Western Access Rd
　DN40 ....87 C3
Western Ave DN20 ...98 C3
Western Dr 7 DN18 ...69 E1
Western Gailes Way
　HU8 ....142 B5
Western Gn DN15 ....68 A1
Western Outway
　DN34 ....102 D2
Western Prim Sch
　DN34 ....102 B3
Western Rd DN14 ...149 C6
Western Tech Sch The
　DN34 ....102 C3
Western Terr YO32 ..127 D3
Westfield
　Patrington HU12 .....74 C1
　Selby YO8 ....148 B4
Westfield Ave
　Beverley HU17 .....136 D6
　3 Eggborough DN14 ..61 F2
　Goole DN14 ....149 D5
　11 Grimsby DN33 ..102 E2
　Rawcliffe DN14 .....64 A1
　Selby YO8 ....148 A4
Westfield Cl
　Easington YO19 .....90 F6
　2 Eggborough DN14 ..61 F2
　21 Haxby YO32 .....13 E5
　Kingston upon Hull
　　HU16 ....138 F6
　Nafferton YO25 ....125 E6
　3 Pocklington YO42 ..28 F4
Westfield Cres YO43 .135 C4
Westfield Ct YO23 ..132 A2

Westfield Dr
Messingham DN17 . . . .**107** D7
York YO10 . . . .**133** D8
Westfield Garth
 1 Crowle DN17 . . . .**94** E6
 1 Walkington HU17 . . . .**55** B8
Westfield Gr
 4 Eggborough DN14 . . . . . .**61** F2
Grimsby DN35 . . . .**153** D2
 12 Haxby YO32 . . . .**13** D5
Westfield La
East Garton HU12 . . . .**59** D5
Fishlake DN7 . . . .**92** B8
Hook DN14 . . . .**149** D8
Kirk Bramwith DN7 . . . . . .**78** B1
Norton WF8 . . . .**76** C2
Preston HU12 . . . .**58** B1
Thorganby YO19 . . . .**38** A5
Wigginton YO32 . . . .**13** D5
Westfield Pk HU15 . . . . . .**68** C6
Westfield Pl
 19 Haxby YO32 . . . .**13** E5
York YO24 . . . .**129** A1
Westfield Prim Com Sch
YO24 . . . .**129** B2
Westfield Prim Sch
HU16 . . . .**138** F6
Westfield Rd
Barton-upon-Humber
 DN18 . . . .**69** C1
Cottingham HU16 . . . .**138** F6
Easington HU12 . . . .**90** F5
East Ella HU4 . . . .**144** D5
 1 Eggborough DN14 . . . . .**61** F2
 4 Goxhill DN19 . . . .**86** A8
 4 Hatfield DN7 . . . .**92** A4
 20 Haxby YO32 . . . .**13** E5
Kirk Bramwith DN7 . . . . . .**92** A8
Market Weighton YO43 . . .**135** C4
 3 North Duffield YO8 . . . . .**50** A7
Pocklington YO42 . . . .**28** F4
Rawcliffe DN14 . . . .**64** A1
Scunthorpe DN17 . . . .**150** B2
Selby YO8 . . . .**148** B4
Skidby HU16 . . . .**138** A5
Waltham DN37 . . . .**113** D6
Westfield Rise
Beeford YO25 . . . .**34** B8
Kingston upon Hull
 HU13 . . . .**143** D2
 13 Withernsea HU19 . . . . . .**75** A6
Westfield Sq YO25 . . . . .**149** D6
Westfield Terr YO43 . . . .**135** C4
Westfield Villas **3** DN7 . .**92** E4
Westgarth Ave HU6 . . . . .**139** F5
West-Gate YO25 . . . .**124** E5
Westgate
Bridlington YO16 . . . .**122** B4
Grimsby DN31 . . . .**152** D5
Hornsea HU18 . . . .**134** B4
Nafferton YO25 . . . .**125** E6
North Cave HU15 . . . .**53** D3
North Newbald YO43 . . . . .**53** E7
Patrington HU12 . . . .**74** D1
Scotton DN21 . . . .**107** C1
Westgate Manor **4**
HU12 . . . .**74** D1
Westgate Mdws YO25 . . .**125** E6
Westgate Rd DN9 . . . .**94** D2
Westhill Rd DN34 . . . . . .**152** A1
Westholme Ave HU18 . . . .**134** C7
Westholme Cl **10** DN15 . . .**82** B4
Westholme Dr YO30 . . . . .**126** E1
Westholme La DN38 . . . . .**99** C5
Westkirke Ave **2** DN33 . .**113** F8
Westland Rd
Kingston upon Hull
 HU10 . . . .**143** B7
 3 Westwoodside DN9 . . . .**105** B2
Westlands Ave
Grimsby DN34 . . . .**152** C1
Tetney DN36 . . . .**114** D4
Westlands Cl **13** HU12 . . . .**72** C7
Westlands Dr HU12 . . . . . .**72** C7
Westlands Gr YO31 . . . . . .**130** F7
Westlands Mews
YO25 . . . .**124** D5
Westlands Rd
Hedon HU12 . . . .**72** C7
Kingston upon Hull HU5 . . .**144** B4
Sproatley HU11 . . . .**58** C5
Westlands Way HU17 . . . . .**45** C6
Westminster Ave HU8 . . .**141** E3
Westminster Bsns Ctr
YO26 . . . .**129** C8
Westminster Cl DN21 . . . .**117** A3
Westminster Ct DN14 . . .**149** E6
Westminster Dr
Grimsby DN34 . . . .**152** C2
Hatfield DN7 . . . .**92** C2
Westminster Pl YO26 . . . .**126** B1
Westminster Rd
 2 Broughton DN20 . . . . . .**97** D4
York YO30 . . . .**130** A6
Westmoreland Ave **3**
YO15 . . . .**122** F2
Westmoreland Cl DN9 . . .**105** A2
Westmoreland Gr **2**
YO15 . . . .**122** F2
Westmoreland St HU2 . . .**155** B4
Westoby La
Barrow upon Humber
 DN19 . . . .**85** C7
Rowley HU15 . . . .**54** E3
Weston Gr **3** DN40 . . . . . .**87** B2
Westover Dr DN15 . . . . . .**82** A4
Westparkside DN14 . . . . .**149** A6
Westpit La YO32 . . . .**14** A7

Westport Rd **27** DN35 . . .**103** C1
Westridge Rd YO15 . . . . .**122** C1
Westrum La DN20 . . . .**98** C1
Westside Rd DN31 . . . . . .**152** C6
Westview Cl YO26 . . . .**129** B7
Westward Cl DN34 . . . . . .**152** C1
Westward Ho DN34 . . . . .**152** B1
Westway Ave HU6 . . . .**139** F6
Westwick **25** HU12 . . . .**72** C7
Westwinds Gdns DN15 . . . .**83** A5
Westwinds Rd **10** DN15 . . .**83** A5
Westwold Rd **20** LN7 . . . . .**111** B4
Westwood
Beverley HU17 . . . .**136** D2
 4 Broughton DN20 . . . . . .**97** D4
Westwood Ave HU18 . . . . .**134** B4
Westwood Cl HU17 . . . . . .**141** C6
Westwood Dr **3** HU4 . . . .**144** B6
Westwood Gate HU17 . . . .**154** A1
Westwood Hospl
HU17 . . . .**136** D3
Westwood Mews **12**
YO19 . . . .**26** F7
Westwood Rd
Beverley HU17 . . . .**154** A3
 12 Healing DN41 . . . .**101** F5
Westwood Terr YO23 . . . .**130** B3
Westwood Way HU17 . . . .**136** D4
Westwoodside CE Prim Sch
DN9 . . . .**105** B2
Wetherby Cl HU6 . . . .**139** F7
Wetherby Rd YO26 . . . . . .**129** B3
Wetwang CE VC Prim Sch
YO25 . . . .**19** B5
Wexford Ave HU9 . . . .**142** E1
Weyford Rd **9** DN35 . . . . .**103** D1
Weymouth Cl HU7 . . . .**141** B6
Weymouth Cres DN17 . . .**150** C5
Whales La DN14 . . . .**61** E3
Wharf Rd Crowle DN17 . . .**94** D7
Misterton DN10 . . . .**116** C3
Wharf The DN36 . . . .**115** A5
Wharfdale Cl DN15 . . . . . .**95** E5
Wharfdale Ave HU9 . . . . .**141** E1
Wharfedale Dr YO16 . . . . .**122** F7
Wharfedale Pl DN15 . . . . .**151** D2
Wharfedale Way **3**
DN31 . . . .**152** D4
Wharncliffe Rd N
DN31 . . . .**153** A7
Wharncliffe Rd S HU5 . . .**145** A8
Wharnscliffe Dr YO30 . . .**126** F2
Wharram Field **3** YO25 . . .**22** D1
Wharram St HU2 . . . .**140** F1
Wharton Ave YO30 . . . . . .**130** B7
Wharton Rd
Blyton DN21 . . . .**117** D5
 8 Stamford Bridge YO41 . .**15** D2
Wharton St DN31 . . . .**152** B3
Wheatcroft **6** YO32 . . . . . .**14** A6
Wheatcroft Ave HU10 . . .**138** E2
Wheatfield Cl
 9 Barnby Dun DN3 . . . . . .**92** A3
Epworth DN9 . . . .**105** F6
 2 Kingston upon Hull
 HU4 . . . .**144** D2
Wheatfield Dr **2** DN7 . . .**113** D6
Wheatfield La YO32 . . . . .**127** C8
Wheatland Cl YO42 . . . . . .**29** B3
Wheatlands Dr HU17 . . . .**136** C6
Wheatlands Gr YO26 . . . .**129** C6
Wheatley Dr
Bridlington YO16 . . . .**123** A6
Haxby YO32 . . . .**127** C8
Wheatley Gdns HU8 . . . . .**141** D3
Wheeldale Cl **7** HU7 . . . .**141** D7
Wheeler Prim Sch
HU3 . . . .**144** F5
Wheeler St HU3 . . . .**144** F6
Wheelhouse The **4**
YO30 . . . .**126** B5
Wheels La YO8 . . . .**63** F3
Wheelwright Cl
Copmanthorpe YO23 . . . . .**132** B2
Sutton upon Derwent
YO41 . . . .**27** C1
Wheldrake CE Prim Sch
YO19 . . . .**38** A8
Wheldrake Ings Nature
Reserve* YO19 . . . .**38** C7
Wheldrake La
Deighton YO19 . . . .**26** B1
Escrick YO19 . . . .**37** B5
Whenby Gr YO31 . . . .**127** F1
Whernside Ave YO31 . . . .**131** A5
Whernside Cl **12** HU7 . . . . .**57** A6
Whimbrel Ave HU8 . . . . . .**134** C2
Whimbrel Way **12** DN36 . .**114** A8
Whin Cl **3** Stensall YO32 . . .**14** B6
York YO24 . . . .**132** F7
Whin Garth YO24 . . . .**132** F6
Whin La Burstwick HU12 . . .**73** C7
South Cave YO43 . . . .**54** B6
Whin Moor La HU15 . . . . . .**68** A7
Whin Rd YO24 . . . .**132** F6
Whincroft Ave DN14 . . . . .**149** C6
Whinhill La HU12 . . . .**73** F4
Whinns The HU17 . . . .**154** C1
Whinny Hagg La YO8 . . . . .**48** A2
Whinny La YO60 . . . .**15** A7
Whins Gate DN17 . . . .**81** A4
Whins La HU11 . . . .**45** D6
Whip-ma-whop-ma-gate
YO1 . . . .**156** C2
Whisby Ct DN36 . . . .**114** B5
Whistler Cl YO23 . . . .**132** C3
Whiston Way **9** DN18 . . . . .**69** F1

Whitby Ave YO31 . . . .**131** A7
Whitby Dr
Grimsby DN32 . . . .**153** A1
York YO31 . . . .**131** A7
Whitby St HU8 . . . .**146** B8
White Cross* HU11 . . . .**45** A6
White Cross Rd YO31 . . . .**130** D7
White Cross Way YO41 . . . .**16** A2
White Gap La HU20 . . . . . .**54** E5
White Gap Rd HU20 . . . . . .**54** F4
White Horse Cl **6** YO32 . . .**127** F5
White Horse La HU12 . . . . .**73** E3
White House Cl
 19 Hatfield DN7 . . . .**92** D4
Kingston upon Hull
 HU10 . . . .**138** C2
Kirk Bramwith DN7 . . . . . .**92** C7
White House Dale
YO24 . . . .**129** F1
White House Dr YO24 . . . .**129** F1
White House Garth **15**
HU14 . . . .**69** A5
White House Gdns **4**
YO24 . . . .**130** A2
White House Gr **1** YO41 . . .**27** B2
White House La DN15 . . . . .**82** E8
White House Mews **16**
HU14 . . . .**69** A5
White House Rise
YO24 . . . .**129** F1
White La YO24 . . . .**129** A2
White Ley Rd DN6 . . . .**76** C1
White Lodge YO8 . . . .**148** B4
White Rose Ave **3**
YO32 . . . .**127** D3
White Rose Cl YO26 . . . . .**126** C1
White Rose Gr **5** YO32 . . .**127** D3
White Rose Way YO26 . . .**129** C8
White Sprunt Hill YO17 . . . .**1** A1
White St
Kingston upon Hull HU3 . . .**144** F5
Selby YO8 . . . .**148** B6
White Wlk HU10 . . . .**143** C6
White's Cl La HU12 . . . .**59** A2
White's Rd DN35 . . . .**153** F1
Whitebeam Cl HU5 . . . . . .**145** D5
Whitecarr La YO42 . . . .**39** E8
Whitecross Gdns
YO31 . . . .**130** D7
Whitecross Rd HU11 . . . . . .**45** B6
Whitecross St DN18 . . . . . .**84** F8
Whitefield Bglws DN14 . . .**76** F8
Whitefield Cl DN14 . . . .**61** E1
Whitefields HU17 . . . .**136** C7
Whitefriargate HU1 . . . . .**155** B2
Whitegate Hill LN7 . . . . . .**111** C3
Whitehall Gdns **3** HU5 . . .**140** A1
Whitehall Rd **5** DN35 . . . .**103** D1
Whitehead Cl HU17 . . . . . .**154** B2
Whitehope Cl **18** HU7 . . . . .**57** A6
Whitehouse Wlk HU6 . . . . .**56** D5
Whitelands YO25 . . . .**124** D5
Whitemoor La YO8 . . . .**49** C6
Whiterose Dr YO41 . . . .**15** D7
Whitestone Dr YO31 . . . . .**127** E2
Whitestone Rd DN15 . . . . .**82** B4
Whitethorn Ave **11** HU19 . . .**75** A6
Whitethorn Cl YO31 . . . . .**127** E2
Whitethorn Way HU8 . . . .**141** D4
Whitewell Cl **3** DN21 . . . . .**108** F1
Whitfield Dr DN17 . . . .**150** D2
Whitgift Cl **13** DN37 . . . . . .**101** F1
Whitgift Sch DN14 . . . .**102** B4
Whiting Cl HU16 . . . .**139** A6
Whitley & Eggborough CP
Sch DN14 . . . .**61** F1
Whitley Bridge Sta
DN14 . . . .**61** F1
Whitley Cl YO30 . . . .**127** A1
Whitley Rd YO41 . . . .**27** A3
Whitley Thorpe La
DN14 . . . .**76** F7
Whitman Rd DN17 . . . . . .**150** C2
Whitstable Cl **3** HU8 . . . .**141** E7
Whitstone Cl HU7 . . . .**140** F8
Whitton Pl YO10 . . . .**131** C4
Whitton Rd DN15 . . . .**82** C8
Whitworth St HU9 . . . . . .**141** E2
Whoofer La DN21 . . . .**117** B7
Wickenby Cl **18** DN34 . . . .**102** C2
Wickenby Garth HU7 . . . .**141** C8
Wickham Rd DN31 . . . . . .**153** A6
Wickham Way YO25 . . . . .**124** D3
Wicklow Ave **22** DN33 . . . .**113** E8
Wickwane Rd HU17 . . . . . .**137** A6
Wicstun Way YO43 . . . . . .**135** C3
Wide La YO14 . . . .**3** E5
Widford Gn **7** DN7 . . . .**92** D3
Widop St DN14 . . . .**149** C5
Wigginton Prim Sch
YO32 . . . .**13** D5
Wigginton Rd YO31 . . . . .**156** B4
Wigginton Terr YO31 . . . .**130** C8
Wike Gate Cl **7** DN8 . . . . . .**93** B7
Wike Gate Gr **6** DN8 . . . . .**93** B7
Wike Gate Rd DN8 . . . .**93** B8
Wilbar Gr HU5 . . . .**140** B2
Wilberforce Ave DN8 . . . .**130** D7
Wilberforce Cres
HU17 . . . .**154** C4
Wilberforce Dr HU1 . . . . .**155** C3
Wilberforce House Mus*
HU1 . . . .**155** C2
Wilberforce Mon*
HU1 . . . .**155** C3
Wilberforce St HU3 . . . . . .**145** D6
Wilberforce VI Form Coll
HU8 . . . .**142** A5

Wilberfoss CE VC Prim Sch
YO41 . . . .**27** E6
Wilbert Cl HU17 . . . .**154** B3
Wilbert Gr HU17 . . . .**154** B3
Wiles Ct HU17 . . . .**154** C2
Wilfholme Rd YO25 . . . . . .**32** F3
Wilflete Ct HU9 . . . .**142** B3
Wilfreds Gr **8** YO8 . . . .**49** B4
Wilfreds Rd **5** YO8 . . . .**49** B4
Wilkie Cl HU17 . . . .**150** C7
Wilkinson Ave DN8 . . . .**79** B1
Wilkinson Way
 20 Bottesford DN16 . . . . . .**96** E2
 3 Strensall YO32 . . . .**14** A7
Willans Gr YO26 . . . .**129** E4
Willerby Carr Cl **2** HU5 **139** B1
Willerby Carr La Infants Sch
HU10 . . . .**138** C1
Willerby Carr La Jun Sch
HU10 . . . .**138** C1
Willerby Dr **2** DN14 . . . . . .**65** A7
Willerby Low Rd
HU10 . . . .**138** D3
Willerby Rd HU5 . . . .**144** C8
Willesden Cl **4** HU8 . . . . .**141** F5
William Barcroft Jun Sch
DN32 . . . .**153** C3
William Jacques Dr
YO8 . . . .**49** E2
William Plows Ave
YO10 . . . .**130** E2
William Rd YO8 . . . .**49** B4
William St
Cleethorpes DN35 . . . .**153** E1
Kingston upon Hull HU1 . . .**155** A1
Scunthorpe DN16 . . . .**151** B6
William Wright Dock
HU1 . . . .**145** B3
Williams Dr DN39 . . . .**86** B1
Williamson St HU9 . . . . . .**146** C7
Willing Way DN32 . . . .**152** F4
Willingham Garth **4**
HU12 . . . .**72** E5
Willingham St DN32 . . . . .**152** E2
Willingham Way HU10 . . .**138** B1
Willis St YO10 . . . .**130** E3
Willitoft Rd YO8 . . . .**50** F4
Willoughby Gr **12** DN34 . .**102** C2
Willoughby Rd
Hibaldstow DN20 . . . .**109** A5
Scunthorpe DN17 . . . .**150** E1
Willoughby Way YO24 . . .**132** B8
Willoughton CP Sch
DN21 . . . .**119** A4
Willow Ave
 2 Misterton DN10 . . . . . .**116** C5
Thorne/Moorends DN8 . . . .**79** A1
Willow Bank
 14 Brayton YO8 . . . .**48** D1
York YO32 . . . .**127** E4
Willow Cl
Barnetby le Beck DN38 . . . .**99** B4
 18 Gainsborough DN21 . . .**117** A2
Laceby DN37 . . . .**101** E1
Pollington DN14 . . . .**78** A6
Snaith DN14 . . . .**78** B8
Ulceby DN39 . . . .**86** B1
Willow Cres DN8 . . . .**79** A1
Willow Ct
Beverley HU17 . . . .**136** C6
Hutton Cranswick YO25 . . .**32** E6
Kexby YO41 . . . .**15** C2
Kingston upon Hull
 HU10 . . . .**138** D3
 9 Pocklington YO42 . . . . .**29** A3
Willow Dr
 11 Barton-upon-Humber
 DN18 . . . .**69** F1
Bridlington YO16 . . . .**123** A6
 12 Brough HU15 . . . .**68** D5
Goole DN14 . . . .**65** C3
Kingston upon Hull
 HU10 . . . .**143** D8
Messingham DN17 . . . .**107** D2
 1 North Duffield YO8 . . . . .**50** A7
 1 Thorngumbald HU12 . . . .**72** E5
Willow Garth
Eastrington DN14 . . . .**51** F1
Pollington DN14 . . . .**78** A6
Willow Garth La DN6 . . . . .**77** A1
Willow Gdns **2** DN19 . . . . .**85** D8
Willow Glade YO32 . . . . . .**127** F3
Willow Gn **7** HU15 . . . .**66** D8
Willow Gr
 3 Aldbrough HU11 . . . . . .**47** C1
Beverley HU17 . . . .**136** D4
Earswick YO32 . . . .**128** A7
Keadby DN17 . . . .**95** D6
Kingston upon Hull HU5 . . .**140** C2
Pollington DN14 . . . .**78** A6
Scawby DN20 . . . .**108** F8
Scunthorpe DN16 . . . .**151** B3
 3 Thorne/Moorends DN8 . .**79** B1
York YO31 . . . .**130** F7
Willow La Goxhill DN19 . . . .**86** A8
Pollington DN14 . . . .**78** A6
Woodmansey HU17 . . . . . .**154** B1
Willow Pk DN37 . . . .**113** C6
Willow Pk Rd YO41 . . . .**27** F5
Willow Rd
Burstwick HU12 . . . .**73** B6
 9 Campsall DN6 . . . .**76** E1
 10 Knottingley WF11 . . . . .**61** A3
 6 Thorne/Moorends DN8 . .**79** A1
Willow Tree Cl **9** DN40 . . .**87** C2
Willow Tree Garth **5**
HU17 . . . .**136** F2

Willow View YO8 . . . .**49** E3
Willowbridge Rd WF8 . . . .**76** C2
Willowbrook Dr DN20 . . . .**98** D2
Willowdale HU7 . . . .**140** F8
Willowdale Cl YO16 . . . . .**123** A7
Willowfield HU6 . . . .**140** A6
Willows Ave HU9 . . . .**141** F3
Willows Dr HU18 . . . .**134** C4
Willows Prim Sch
DN37 . . . .**102** C3
Willows The
Hornsea HU18 . . . .**134** C3
Howden DN14 . . . .**65** A6
Kingston upon Hull
 HU13 . . . .**143** E4
 3 Strensall YO32 . . . .**14** B7
Willy Howe* YO25 . . . .**2** C3
Wilmore La DN38 . . . .**110** E7
Wilson Cl
Market Weighton YO43 . . .**135** D3
 7 North Ferriby HU14 . . . . .**69** A4
Wilson St
Cleethorpes DN35 . . . .**153** D4
Gainsborough DN21 . . . . . .**117** A1
 5 Goole DN14 . . . .**149** C4
 4 Kingston upon Hull
 HU9 . . . .**146** B7
Kirk Ella HU10 . . . .**143** E6
Wilsons Cl **9** DN15 . . . . . .**151** B4
Wilsthorpe Gr **1** YO10 . . .**133** F8
Wilstrop Farm Rd
YO23 . . . .**132** A2
Wilton Rd
Hornsea HU18 . . . .**134** D3
Humberston DN36 . . . .**114** B8
Wilton Rd Ind Est
DN36 . . . .**114** B8
Wilton Rise YO24 . . . .**129** F3
Wilton St HU8 . . . .**146** B8
Wilton Terr HU17 . . . .**134** D4
Wiltshire Ave DN15 . . . . . .**82** B4
Wiltshire Rd HU4 . . . .**144** E2
Wimbledon Cl **4** HU8 . . . .**142** A5
Wimborn Ave DN34 . . . . .**152** B2
Wimbourne Cl HU7 . . . . . .**141** C6
Wimpole Cl **2** YO30 . . . . .**127** A1
Winceby Ave DN31 . . . . . .**152** A4
Winchcombe Ave **3**
DN34 . . . .**102** C2
Winchester Ave
 5 Beverley HU17 . . . .**136** F1
Grimsby DN33 . . . .**102** D2
Kingston upon Hull HU9 . . .**142** B4
 3 York YO26 . . . .**129** F4
Winchester Cl HU9 . . . . . .**142** B4
Winchester Dr DN16 . . . . . .**96** E2
Winchester Gr **1** YO26 . . .**129** E4
Winchester Rd **29** DN7 . . .**92** C4
Wincolmlee YO1 . . . .**155** C3
Windass Cl HU13 . . . .**143** E1
Windermere Cl YO23 . . . .**132** D7
Windermere Ave
DN33 . . . .**113** D8
Windermere Cres
 9 Humberston DN36 . . . .**103** C1
 10 Kirk Sandall DN3 . . . . . .**92** A2
Windermere Ct HU7 . . . . .**140** F7
Windermere Dr
Bridlington YO16 . . . .**122** E7
Goole DN14 . . . .**149** E5
Windgate Hill La YO8 . . . .**48** B6
Windham Cres **1** HU7 . . . .**56** F7
Windlass Cl **29** DN8 . . . . . .**93** A8
Windle Ave HU6 . . . .**140** C7
Windlesham Ave **10**
DN33 . . . .**113** D8
Windlestone Sq **17** DN8 . . .**79** B2
Windmill Gdns YO8 . . . . .**148** B2
Windmill Hill YO25 . . . . . .**124** E5
Windmill La Norton DN6 . . .**76** D1
York YO10 . . . .**131** B2
Windmill Mdw **13** DN6 . . . .**76** D2
Windmill Mdws YO41 . . . . .**27** E6
Windmill Rise YO26 . . . . .**129** E3
Windmill Way HU13 . . . . .**143** F1
Windsor Ave HU10 . . . . . .**143** E7
Windsor Cl
Beverley HU17 . . . .**137** B5
 3 Keelby DN41 . . . .**101** C4
Kingston upon Hull
 HU16 . . . .**139** B5
Windsor Cres
Bridlington YO15 . . . .**122** C2
Crowle DN17 . . . .**94** C7
Scunthorpe DN17 . . . .**96** C1
Windsor Ct
Cleethorpes DN32 . . . .**153** A5
 22 Grimsby DN35 . . . .**152** A5
Hatfield DN7 . . . .**92** C2
Windsor Dr
Caistor LN7 . . . .**111** B4
Goole DN14 . . . .**149** B5
 2 Haxby YO32 . . . .**13** D5
Windsor Garth YO24 . . . .**129** D1
Windsor Gr DN19 . . . .**71** A1
Windsor La DN17 . . . .**94** C7
Windsor Rd
Cleethorpes DN35 . . . .**153** C1
Crowle DN17 . . . .**94** C7
Kingston upon Hull HU5 . . .**139** F1
Windsor St **1** YO23 . . . . .**130** B1
Windsor Way
Barnetby le Wold DN38 . . . .**99** B5
Broughton DN20 . . . .**97** E4
Winestead Gr **3** HU9 . . . .**142** A2

Winestead Ings La
HU12 . . . . .74 A1
Winestead La HU12 . . . .74 B3
Wingate Rd DN37 . . . .102 B4
Wingfield Rd HU9 . . . .142 C2
Wingfield Way HU17 . . .55 E8
Winifred Holtby Tech Coll
HU7 . . . . .141 B7
Winn Ct DN35 . . . . . . .153 E1
Winn St 1 DN16 . . . . . .151 B6
Winscar Croft 8 HU7 . .141 D7
Winscar Gr 9 YO30 . . .126 E3
Winsetts Rd HU12 . . . . .90 D5
Winship Cl 4 HU4 . . . .145 C5
Winslow Dr DN40 . . . . .87 B1
Winslow Gr 15 DN34 . .102 C2
Winston Ave DN34 . . . .152 B2
Winston Cl HU12 . . . . . .73 A7
Winston Dr HU4 . . . . .138 F5
Winston Way DN20 . . . .98 D2
Winterdale YO25 . . . . .124 D5
Winteringham La DN15 . .82 E8
Winteringham Prim Sch
DN15 . . . . .68 A1
Winteringham Rd DN15 .83 B6
Winteringham Wlk
HU16 . . . . .139 A5
Winterscale Ct TO1 . . .130 D2
Winterscale St YO10 . .130 D2
Winterton CE Inf Sch
DN15 . . . . .83 B5
Winterton Comp Sch
DN15 . . . . .83 A6
Winterton Jun Sch
DN15 . . . . .83 B5
Winterton Rd
Roxby cum Risby DN15 . . .82 F2
Scunthorpe DN15 . . . . .151 B8
Winteringham DN15 . . . . .83 B8
Winthorpe Rd
Grimsby DN33 . . . . . . .102 D1
4 Kingston upon Hull
HU13 . . . . .144 A3
Wintringham 25 HU15 . .68 C6
Wintringham Rd DN32 .152 E2
Wintringham Sch
DN32 . . . . .102 F2
Wirral Ave 19 DN34 . . .102 C2
Wise Cl HU3 . . . . .136 F2
Wises Farm Rd 2 HU5 .139 F1
Wiske Ave 6 HU15 . . . .68 D5
Wisker La YO32 . . . . . .128 C2
Wisteria Dr DN41 . . . .101 E5
Wisteria Way DN16 . . .151 E1
Wistow Gr HU4 . . . . . .144 D5
Wistow Parochial CE VC Prim
Sch YO8 . . . . .48 D6
Wistow Rd YO8 . . . . . .148 A8
Wistowgate YO8 . . . . . .48 B8
Witch La YO25 . . . . .3 B2
Witham HU9 . . . . .155 C3
Witham Dr
Burton upon Stather DN15 .82 B5
York YO32 . . . . .128 A6
Withern Rd DN33 . . . . .102 D2
Withernsea High Sch & Tech
Coll HU19 . . . . .74 F7
Withernsea Hospl HU19 .75 A6
Withernsea Inf Sch
HU19 . . . . .74 F7
Withernsea Jun Sch
HU19 . . . . .74 F7
Withernsea Lighthouse
Mus HU19 . . . . .74 F6
Withernsea Rd
Hollym HU19 . . . . .75 A4
Holmpton HU19 . . . . . . .75 C3
Rimswell HU19 . . . . .74 D8
Roos HU19 . . . . .60 C1
Withernsea St HU8 . . .141 A1
Withernwick La HU11 . . .47 A4
Withernwick Prim Sch
HU11 . . . . .46 D3
Withernwick Rd
Aldbrough HU11 . . . . . . .47 A2
Hatfield HU11 . . . . .46 C5
Witty St HU3 . . . . .145 A3
Witty's Pass 7 HU18 . .134 C4
Wittys Paddock 4 HU11 .35 A1
Wivell Dr DN41 . . . . . .101 A5
Wivern Rd HU9 . . . . . .142 D3
Woad La DN37 . . . . . . .102 C5
Woburn Cl
Bridlington YO16 . . . . . .122 F6
Strensall YO33 . . . . .14 B8
Woburn Dr DN34 . . . . .149 E5
Woburn St HU3 . . . . . .144 F4
Wold Ave YO43 . . . . . .135 C3
Wold Garth YO42 . . . . .29 A3
Wold Hill HU15 . . . . . . .53 E4
Wold La YO12 . . . . .1 E8
Wold Newton Foundation
Sch YO25 . . . . .2 A1
Wold Newton Rd YO25 . .2 E3
Wold Prim Sch HU5 . . .139 B1
Wold Rd
Barrow upon Humber
DN19 . . . . .85 D7
Kingston upon Hull HU5 .139 B1
Kirby Grindalythe YO17 . . . .6 D1
Market Weighton YO43 . .135 F2
Nafferton YO25 . . . . .3 C6
Pocklington YO42 . . . . . .29 A4
Walkington HU17 . . . . . . .54 E7
Worlaby DN20 . . . . .84 E1

Wold Rise YO43 . . . . . .41 E2
Wold View Brigg DN20 . .98 C2
Caistor LN7 . . . . .111 B4
Elloughton-cum-Brough
HU15 . . . . .68 C6
Fotherby LN11 . . . . . . .121 D2
Fridaythorpe YO25 . . . . . .18 B5
6 Holton le Clay DN36 . .114 A5
Rothwell LN7 . . . . .111 F2
3 South Cave HU15 . . . .54 A2
Wold View Rd N YO25 . .124 E3
Wold View Rd S YO25 . .124 E3
Wold Wlk YO16 . . . . . .122 B4
Woldcarr Rd HU3 . . . . .144 F6
Woldcroft YO41 . . . . . . .27 C2
Woldgate
Bridlington YO16 . . . . . .122 A3
Carnaby YO16 . . . . .10 E6
Harpham YO25 . . . . .9 D3
5 North Newbald YO43 . .53 F7
Woldgate Coll YO42 . . .29 A4
Woldgate View 1 YO42 . .29 A3
Woldholme Ave YO25 . .124 D3
Wolds Cl 14 DN17 . . . . .94 D7
Wolds The Goole DN14 .149 D5
Kingston upon Hull
HU16 . . . . .138 E6
Wolds Village YO25 . . .31 E8
Woldview Rd YO41 . . . . .27 F5
Wolfe Ave YO31 . . . . . .130 F5
Wolfe Cl 7 HU16 . . . . .138 F5
Wolfreton Ct HU10 . . . .143 E6
Wolfreton Dr HU10 . . . .143 F6
Wolfreton Garth HU10 .143 D8
Wolfreton La HU10 . . . .143 F8
Wolfreton Mews HU10 .143 F7
Wolfreton Rd HU10 . . . .143 F7
Wolfreton Sch HU10 . . .138 D1
Wolfreton Villas HU10 .143 F7
Wollaston Rd DN35 . . . .153 E2
Wolsey Ave YO8 . . . . . .48 W8
Wolsey Dr
3 Barrow upon Humber
DN19 . . . . .85 C7
Bishopthorpe YO23 . . . . .133 A3
Wolsley St YO10 . . . . . .130 E3
Wolviston Ave YO10 . . .131 C3
Wombwell Gr 3 HU8 . . .141 B1
Womersley CE VC Jun & Inf
Sch DN6 . . . . .76 C4
Womersley Pk Gdns
DN6 . . . . .76 D5
Womersley Rd
Grimsby DN31 . . . . .153 A6
Knottingley WF11 . . . . . .61 A2
Wood Carr La DN9 . . . . .94 C2
Wood Cl
8 Grimsby DN33 . . . . .113 E8
7 Strensall YO23 . . . . . .14 A7
14 Thorpe Willoughby YO8 .48 B1
Wood Dr 1 HU14 . . . . . .69 A4
Wood Gate YO42 . . . . . .29 D7
Wood Hill Way HU16 . . .138 C8
Wood La
Acaster Selby YO23 . . . . .36 B2
Beverley HU17 . . . . .154 A3
Birkin WF11 . . . . .61 D6
Bubwith DN14 . . . . .51 A5
Cottingham HU16 . . . . . .139 B4
Fishlake DN7 . . . . .92 D8
18 Thorpe Willoughby YO8 .48 B1
Wressle DN14 . . . . .51 B2
Wood St Grimsby DN32 .152 F4
York YO31 . . . . .130 E6
Wood Vale DN16 . . . . . .96 E2
Wood View Airmyn DN14 .64 E3
Messingham DN17 . . . . .107 D8
Swanland HU14 . . . . .69 B7
Wood Way YO32 . . . . . .128 A4
Woodale Cl 3 DN15 . . . .96 B7
Woodall Ct 9 YO8 . . . . .48 D6
Woodapple Ct 2 DN41 .101 E6
Wood's La HU1 . . . . . . .155 A1
Woodbine Ave DN20 . . . .98 C2
Woodbine Cl HU2 . . . . .155 A4
Woodclose Rd DN17 . . .150 D2
Woodcoates Cl 1 HU17 .136 F7
Woodcock Cl 9 YO32 . . .13 F5
Woodcock Rd 1 YO15 . . .5 A2
Woodcock St HU3 . . . . .145 A4
Woodcroft Ave HU6 . . .139 F5
Wooden Beck Hill
DN10 . . . . .116 B2
Woodfield Cl 4 DN36 . .114 D8
Woodfield La HU13 . . . .143 C1
Woodfield Rd
Gainsborough DN21 . . . .117 C1
Goole DN14 . . . . .149 B6
Woodford L Ctr HU8 . . .141 E2
Woodford Pl 1 YO24 . . .129 D1
Woodgarr Ave 1 DN17 . .95 D6
Woodgate La HU5 . . . . .144 F8
Woodgate Rd
Kingston upon Hull HU5 .144 F7
Newbald YO43 . . . . .54 A8
Woodgates Cl 6 HU14 . .69 A5
Woodgates La HU14 . . . .69 A5
Woodgates Mount 3
HU14 . . . . .69 A5
Woodhall Dr
1 Beverley HU17 . . . . .136 D6
Waltham DN37 . . . . . . .113 D6
Woodhall La
Hemingbrough YO8 . . . . .50 B3
Womersley DN6 . . . . .76 D6
Woodhall Pk HU17 . . . .136 D7
Woodhall St HU8 . . . . .141 A2
Woodhall Way HU17 . . .154 A4

Woodhill Ave DN21 . . .117 C1
Woodhill Cl 2 HU10 . . .143 E7
Woodhill Rd DN21 . . . .107 A3
Woodhill Rise HU13 . . .143 C6
Woodhouse Gn Rd DN7 .92 B8
Woodhouse Gr 4 YO31 .131 A7
Woodhouse La
Beeford YO25 . . . . .22 C1
Belton DN9 . . . . .94 A3
Hatfield DN7 . . . . .92 D2
Pocklington YO42 . . . . . .29 A5
Riston DN14 . . . . .45 B3
Woodhouse Rd
Scunthorpe DN16 . . . . . .151 E4
Thorganby YO19 . . . . . . .38 A3
Woodhouse St HU9 . . . .146 D7
Woodings Ct 5 DN14 . . .65 A7
Woodland Ave
17 Brough HU15 . . . . . .68 C6
14 Gainsborough DN21 . .117 A2
Goole DN14 . . . . .149 C6
Woodland Chase YO30 .127 B1
Woodland Dr
Broughton DN20 . . . . . . .97 D4
1 Elsham DN20 . . . . . . .98 F7
Kingston upon Hull
HU10 . . . . .143 C6
Woodland End HU4 . . . .144 C5
Woodland Pl YO32 . . . .127 E4
Woodland Rise YO25 . .125 A6
Woodland View
Barnetby le Wold DN38 . . .99 B4
Scunthorpe DN15 . . . . . .150 C7
Woodland Way
8 Airmyn DN14 . . . . . .64 E4
19 Epworth DN9 . . . . . .105 E6
York YO32 . . . . .127 F4
Woodland Wlk 6 DN35 .103 C1
Woodlands
Beverley HU17 . . . . .136 D4
6 Driffield YO25 . . . . . .124 F3
Escrick YO19 . . . . .37 B5
Woodlands Ave
Haxby YO32 . . . . .127 C8
Immingham DN40 . . . . . .87 C2
Keelby DN41 . . . . .101 A4
Woodlands Cl
15 Barlby with Osgodby
YO8 . . . . .49 B4
4 Barrow upon Humber
DN19 . . . . .85 C7
Bridlington YO16 . . . . . .123 B7
Woodlands Ct 13 YO8 . .49 B4
Woodlands Dr
14 Barlby with Osgodby
YO8 . . . . .49 B4
Beverley HU17 . . . . .136 D4
Woodlands Gr YO31 . . .131 A7
Woodlands La
8 Brough HU15 . . . . . .68 C6
Hillam LS25 . . . . .61 B7
Woodlands Prim Sch
DN33 . . . . .102 D1
Woodlands Rd HU5 . . .144 B7
Woodlands Rise
5 North Ferriby HU14 . . .69 A5
Norton DN6 . . . . .76 E1
Woodlands Sports Ctr
DN40 . . . . .87 C2
Woodlands The
Kingston upon Hull HU5 .140 B2
Preston HU12 . . . . .72 B7
2 Stallingborough DN41 .101 D6
The Lawns HU16 . . . . . .138 F7
Woodlands View 11 YO8 .49 B4
Woodlea Ave YO26 . . . .129 C4
Woodlea Bank YO26 . . .129 D4
Woodlea Cres YO26 . . .129 D4
Woodlea Gr YO26 . . . . .129 D5
Woodleigh Cl 2 YO32 . . .14 A6
Woodleigh Dr HU7 . . . .141 D5
Woodman's Way HU17 .154 C1
Woodmansey CE VC Prim
Sch HU17 . . . . .56 C8
Woodmansey Mile
HU17 . . . . .154 A1
Woodmarketgate 26
HU12 . . . . .72 C7
Woodrow Pk DN33 . . . .102 E1
Woods La DN40 . . . . . . .86 F2
Woods Mdw DN20 . . . .108 F6
Woods Terr 7 DN21 . . .117 B2
Woodside
10 Gilberdyke HU15 . . . .66 D7
Kingston upon Hull HU13 .143 D1
Woodside Ave YO31 . . .131 A6
Woodside La DN9 . . . . .104 D6
Woodside Rd YO12 . . . . .1 A8
Woodsley Ave DN35 . . .153 E1
Woodsmill Quay YO1 . .156 B2
Woodstock Cl HU16 . . .138 F6
Woodstock Rd DN16 . . .151 D4
Woodthorpe Prim Sch
YO24 . . . . .132 C7
Woodview Cl DN14 . . . . .77 A7
Woodville Terr YO8 . . .148 E3
Woolam Hill HU12 . . . . .73 A6
Woollin Ave DN17 . . . . .151 A2
Woolnough Ave YO10 . .131 B3
Woolsheds Cl 11 HU15 .139 F1
Woolsthorpe Gr 20 HU7 .56 F6
Woolwich Dr 2 HU4 . . .144 B2
Wootton Cl DN17 . . . . .150 C4
Wootton Rd
Grimsby DN33 . . . . .102 D2
Wootton DN39 . . . . .85 F2
Wootton St Andrew's CE Prim
Sch DN39 . . . . .85 E3

Worcester Ave DN34 . . .152 A1
Worcester Cl 11 DN16 . .96 D1
Worcester Dr YO31 . . . .131 B5
Worcester Rd HU5 . . . .139 C1
Worcestershire Cl 1
HU5 . . . . .139 D1
Wordsworth Ave 4 DN6 .76 E1
Wordsworth Cres
YO24 . . . . .132 D7
Wordsworth Ct
Cleethorpes DN32 . . . . .153 A5
21 Grimsby DN35 . . . . .153 A5
Wordsworth Rd DN17 . .150 D2
Wordsworth St HU8 . . .155 A3
Workington Ave 8 HU4 .144 B6
Worlaby Prim Sch DN20 .98 D8
Worlaby Rd 1 DN33 . . .113 D8
Worldwide Way
Immingham DN41 . . . . . .101 F8
Stallingborough DN41 . . . .87 F1
Wormley Hill La DN14 . .78 E2
Worsborough Cl 10
HU7 . . . . .141 D7
Worsendale Rd YO42 . . .16 F2
Worship St HU2 . . . . . .155 B3
Worsley Cl
7 Holton le Clay DN36 . .114 A5
Immingham DN40 . . . . . .87 C1
Worsley Rd DN40 . . . . . .87 C1
Worthing St HU5 . . . . .140 D3
Wortley St DN16 . . . . . .151 A6
Wragby Dr DN17 . . . . .150 D1
Wragby St DN32 . . . . . .152 F3
Wrangbrook Cl 3 DN14 . .65 A7
Wrangham Dr 1 YO14 . . .3 A8
Wrangman Dale Rd
YO43 . . . . .54 A8
Wrawby La HU12 . . . . . .58 D2
Wrawby Postmill
DN20 . . . . .98 E3
Wrawby Rd Brigg DN20 . .98 C2
Scunthorpe DN17 . . . . . .150 E1
Wrawby St 8 DN20 . . . . .98 C2
Wrawby St Mary's CE Prim
Sch DN20 . . . . .98 E3
9 Waltham DN37 . . . . .113 D7
Wray St 14 DN21 . . . . .108 B3
Wray's Ave YO31 . . . . . .127 E1
Wren Cl 4 Healing DN41 .101 F5
17 Scunthorpe DN16 . . . .96 D1
Wren Cres DN33 . . . . . .102 D1
Wren Hall La YO8 . . . . . .63 E6
Wren La 2 YO8 . . . . . . .148 D5
Wressle Rd DN20 . . . . . .97 E4
Wressle Sta YO8 . . . . . .50 D2
Wright Cl YO16 . . . . . . .122 B2
Wright Cres YO16 . . . . .122 B2
Wrights Gdns 1 DN10 .116 D3
Wrights La WF11 . . . . . .76 B8
Wroot Rd DN9 . . . . . . .104 A2
Wroot Travis Charity Prim
Sch DN9 . . . . .104 D5
Wroots Ave DN14 . . . . .149 D1
Wroxham Ave DN34 . . .102 C3
Wrygarth Ave 7 HU15 . .68 C5
Wyatt Ave DN20 . . . . . .97 D3
Wybeck Rd DN15 . . . . . .96 D7
Wybers Way DN37 . . . .102 B4
Wybers Wood Jun & Inf Sch
DN37 . . . . .102 B4
Wycliffe Ave YO10 . . . .131 B3
Wycliffe La YO15 . . . . .122 E2
Wydale Rd YO10 . . . . . .131 B3
Wyke St HU9 . . . . .146 D7
Wyke VI Prim Coll
HU5 . . . . .139 E2
Wykeham Cl
2 Bridlington YO16 . . . .122 C5
1 Kingston upon Hull
HU7 . . . . .141 D7
Wykehan Cl YO25 . . . . .124 D3
Wylies Rd HU17 . . . . . .154 A3
Wymark View 26 DN33 .102 C2
Wymersley Rd HU5 . . . .144 A8
Wynam La YO41 . . . . . . .27 C1
Wynburg St HU9 . . . . . .141 D1
Wyndham Cl 4 HU17 . . .43 D6
Wyndham Rd 10 DN36 .114 A7
Wyndham St HU3 . . . . .145 C7
Wynmoor Rd DN17 . . . .150 F3
Wyntryngham Cl 14
HU17 . . . . .72 D7
Wyredale Rd DN16 . . . .151 D1
Wysteria Way HU8 . . . .141 E7
Wytherstone Cl 3 HU7 . .56 F6
Wyton Gr HU9 . . . . . . .142 A2
Wyton Rd HU12 . . . . . . .58 B2
Wyvern Cl DN17 . . . . . .94 D8

Y

Yapham Rd YO42 . . . . . .28 F5
Yarborough Camp
DN39 . . . . .99 E7
Yarborough Cl 2 DN36 .114 A5
Yarborough Cres 6
DN20 . . . . .97 D4
Yarborough Ct 4 DN15 .150 B6
Yarborough Dr DN31 . . .152 C4
Yarborough Jun Sch
DN34 . . . . .152 A3
Yarborough Prim Sch
DN34 . . . . .102 C4

Yarborough Rd
25 Brigg DN20 . . . . . . .98 C2
Grimsby DN34 . . . . .152 A3
Keelby DN41 . . . . .101 A5
Scunthorpe DN16 . . . . . . .97 A4
Yarburgh Cl 4 DN14 . . . .63 B1
Yarburgh Gr 2 YO26 . . .129 E5
Yarburgh Way YO10 . . .131 C3
Yardley Way 3 DN34 . . .102 B2
Yarmouth Ave 3 HU4 . .144 A3
Yarra Rd DN35 . . . . . . .153 F2
Yarrow Rd DN34 . . . . . .102 C4
Yatesbury Garth 18 HU7 .57 A5
Yeadon Garth HU7 . . . .141 C8
Yearsley Cres YO31 . . .130 D7
Yearsley Gr YO31 . . . . .127 E1
Yearsley Gr Prim Sch
YO32 . . . . .127 F1
Yearsley Swimming Pool
YO31 . . . . .130 D8
Yedingham Wlk HU16 . .139 A5
Yeoman Dr 1 HU17 . . . .136 D1
Yew Dr DN16 . . . . .96 D1
Yew Tree Cl
Acaster Malbis YO23 . . . .36 C8
Rufforth YO23 . . . . .24 C6
Selby YO8 . . . . .148 C6
Yew Tree Mews YO19 . .131 C5
Yew Tree Pk DN14 . . . . .77 A7
Yews La DN37 . . . . .101 E1
Yewtree Dr HU4 . . . . . .144 B7
Yiewsley Cl HU8 . . . . . .141 E6
Yokegate DN14 . . . . . . .51 E3
Yordas Ct 3 YO16 . . . . .123 A7
York Abbey YO30 . . . . .156 A3
York Art Gall YO30 . . . .156 B3
York Ave DN16 . . . . .96 D2
York Barbican Leisure Ctr
YO10 . . . . .156 C1
York Castle Mus
YO1 . . . . .156 C1
York City Football Club
YO30 . . . . .156 A4
York Cl YO43 . . . . .135 D4
York Coll YO24 . . . . . . .132 E6
York District Hospl
YO30 . . . . .156 A4
York Dungeon YO1 . . .156 B2
York La Flaxton YO60 . . .14 E8
Huggate YO42 . . . . .18 A2
York Minst YO1 . . . . .156 B3
York Model Rly
YO24 . . . . .156 A2
York Pl DN35 . . . . .103 B2
York Racecourse (The
Knavesmire) YO24 . .130 A1
York Rd Barlby YO8 . . . . .49 B5
Beverley HU17 . . . . .136 D4
Bilbrough YO23 . . . . .24 B2
Bishop Burton HU17 . . . . .42 F3
Bridlington YO15 . . . . . .122 F3
Brigg DN20 . . . . .98 C2
Cliffe YO8 . . . . .49 E3
Cottam YO25 . . . . .8 D2
Driffield YO25 . . . . .124 B5
Dunnington YO19 . . . . . . .26 D6
Fridaythorpe YO25 . . . . . .18 B5
Garton YO25 . . . . .19 D8
Great Driffield YO25 . . . .124 D5
28 Hatfield DN7 . . . . . . .92 D4
Haxby YO32 . . . . .127 D7
Kilham YO25 . . . . .8 B3
Kingston upon Hull HU6 .139 F7
1 Kirton in Lindsey DN21 .119 C8
Long Marston YO26 . . . . .24 A6
Market Weighton YO43 . .135 A5
Naburn YO19 . . . . .36 D8
North Duffield YO8 . . . . . .50 A8
Riccall YO19 . . . . .37 A1
Shipton Thorpe YO43 . . . .40 E6
Sledmere YO25 . . . . .7 E1
Stillingfleet YO19 . . . . . . .36 D4
Strensall YO32 . . . . .14 A6
Sutton-on-the-Forest
YO61 . . . . .13 C8
York YO26 . . . . .129 C3
York Rd Gallows Hill
YO43 . . . . .135 A6
York St
5 Dunnington YO19 . . . .26 E7
Grimsby DN31 . . . . .152 C4
Kingston upon Hull HU2 .155 C4
1 Selby YO8 . . . . .148 C5
York St John Coll
YO31 . . . . .156 B3
York St John Coll of the Univ
of Leeds YO10 . . . . . .131 B3
York Sta YO24 . . . . . . .156 A2
York Steiner Sch
YO10 . . . . .130 D1
York Terr DN10 . . . . . . .116 D6
Yorklands YO25 . . . . . .124 D5
Yorkshire Air Mus
YO41 . . . . .26 F3
Yorkshire Cl 3 HU5 . . .139 D1
Yorkshire Mus YO30 . .156 A3
Yorkshire Mus of Farming
YO19 . . . . .26 D7
Yorkshireside DN17 . . . .81 A3
Young Pl DN35 . . . . . . .153 B3
Young St HU19 . . . . .75 A7
Youth Ctr YO25 . . . . . .125 A5

Z

Zeigfield Ct 11 HU9 . . .142 A3
Zetland St HU3 . . . . . .145 A5

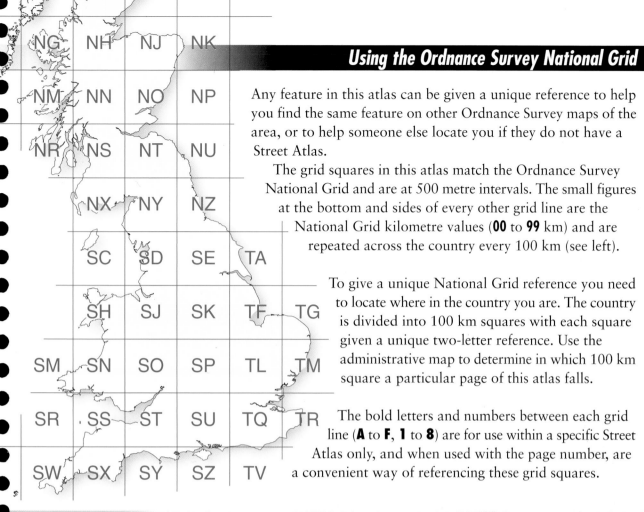

Any feature in this atlas can be given a unique reference to help you find the same feature on other Ordnance Survey maps of the area, or to help someone else locate you if they do not have a Street Atlas.

The grid squares in this atlas match the Ordnance Survey National Grid and are at 500 metre intervals. The small figures at the bottom and sides of every other grid line are the National Grid kilometre values (**00** to **99** km) and are repeated across the country every 100 km (see left).

To give a unique National Grid reference you need to locate where in the country you are. The country is divided into 100 km squares with each square given a unique two-letter reference. Use the administrative map to determine in which 100 km square a particular page of this atlas falls.

The bold letters and numbers between each grid line (**A** to **F**, **1** to **8**) are for use within a specific Street Atlas only, and when used with the page number, are a convenient way of referencing these grid squares.

Example *The railway bridge over DARLEY GREEN RD in grid square B1*

Step 1: Identify the two-letter reference, in this example the page is in **SP**

Step 2: Identify the 1 km square in which the railway bridge falls. Use the figures in the southwest corner of this square: Eastings **17**, Northings **74**. This gives a unique reference: **SP 17 74**, accurate to 1 km.

Step 3: To give a more precise reference accurate to 100 m you need to estimate how many tenths along and how many tenths up this 1 km square the feature is (to help with this the 1 km square is divided into four 500 m squares). This makes the bridge about **8** tenths along and about **1** tenth up from the southwest corner.

This gives a unique reference: **SP 178 741**, accurate to 100 m.

Eastings (read from left to right along the bottom) come before Northings (read from bottom to top). If you have trouble remembering say to yourself "Along the hall, THEN up the stairs"!

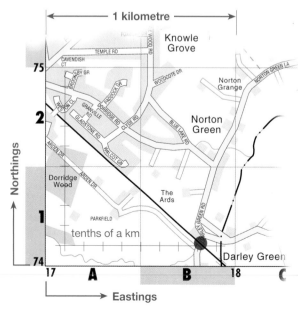

PHILIP'S MAPS

the Gold Standard for drivers

◆ **Philip's street atlases cover every county in England, Wales, Northern Ireland and much of Scotland**

◆ Every named street is shown, including alleys, lanes and walkways

◆ Thousands of additional features marked: stations, public buildings, car parks, places of interest

◆ Route-planning maps to get you close to your destination

◆ Postcodes on the maps and in the index

◆ Widely used by the emergency services, transport companies and local authorities

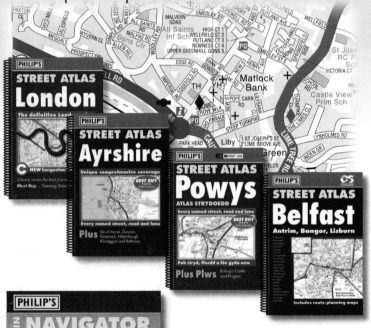

For national mapping, choose **Philip's Navigator Britain** the most detailed road atlas available of England, Wales and Scotland. Hailed by Auto Express as 'the ultimate road atlas', the atlas shows every road and lane in Britain.

'The ultimate in UK mapping'
The Sunday Times

Street atlases currently available

England
Bedfordshire and Luton	Surrey
Berkshire	East Sussex
Birmingham and West Midlands	West Sussex
Bristol and Bath	Tyne and Wear
Buckinghamshire and Milton Keynes	Warwickshire and Coventry
Cambridgeshire and Peterborough	Wiltshire and Swindon
Cheshire	Worcestershire
Cornwall	East Yorkshire Northern Lincolnshire
Cumbria	North Yorkshire
Derbyshire	South Yorkshire
Devon	West Yorkshire
Dorset	
County Durham and Teesside	**Wales**
Essex	Anglesey, Conwy and Gwynedd
North Essex	Cardiff, Swansea and The Valleys
South Essex	Carmarthenshire, Pembrokeshire and Swansea
Gloucestershire and Bristol	
Hampshire	Ceredigion and South Gwynedd
North Hampshire	Denbighshire, Flintshire, Wrexham
South Hampshire	
Herefordshire Monmouthshire	Herefordshire Monmouthshire
Hertfordshire	Powys
Isle of Wight	
Kent	**Scotland**
East Kent	Aberdeenshire
West Kent	Ayrshire
Lancashire	Dumfries and Galloway
Leicestershire and Rutland	Edinburgh and East Central Scotland
Lincolnshire	Fife and Tayside
Liverpool and Merseyside	Glasgow and West Central Scotland
London	Inverness and Moray
Greater Manchester	Lanarkshire
Norfolk	Scottish Borders
Northamptonshire	
Northumberland	**Northern Ireland**
Nottinghamshire	County Antrim and County Londonderry
Oxfordshire	County Armagh and County Down
Shropshire	
Somerset	Belfast
Staffordshire	County Tyrone and County Fermanagh
Suffolk	

How to order
Philip's maps and atlases are available from bookshops, motorway services and petrol stations. You can order direct from the publisher by phoning **0207 531 8473** or online at **www.philips-maps.co.uk**
For bulk orders only, e-mail philips@philips-maps.co.uk